John Willis
Theatre World
1984-1985 SEASON

VOLUME 41

CROWN PUBLISHERS, INC.

225 PARK AVENUE SOUTH • NEW YORK, NEW YORK 10003

T O
IRVING BERLIN

composer-lyricist, with gratitude for your genius and your many contributions to the musical theatre, including the theme song for those involved in the performing arts: "There's No Business Like Show Business"; also, with gratitude for the myriad of other popular songs you have written that help keep the world singing, including "God Bless America." Thank you, and God bless you, Mr. Berlin.

CONTENTS

EDITOR: JOHN WILLIS

Assistants: Herbert Hayward, Jr., Stanley Reeves, John Sala, Tiko Vargas
Staff Photographers: Bert Andrews, Evan Romero, J. M. Viade, Van Williams
Designer: Peggy Goddard

(front row) Brian Tarantina, Alan Ruck, Matt Mulhern, (middle row) Penelope Ann Miller, Matthew Broderick, Randall Edwards, (top row) Geoffrey Sharp, Bill Sadler, Barry Miller in Neil Simon's "Biloxi Blues"—winner of 1985 "Tony" Award for Best Play and Best Director (*Jay Thompson Photo*)

THE SEASON IN REVIEW
(June 1, 1984–May 31, 1985)

Although this season saw the smallest number of productions of any season this century, it was not a complete disaster. Grosses were the third highest on record, but lower than last season. The boxoffice intake, however, was not indicative of an increase in number of productions, nor of an increase in quality of those presented. It resulted from an increase in the price of admissions for Broadway, Off Broadway, and touring companies. The absence of any musical hits accounted for the decrease in income. The revival of "The King and I" with Yul Brynner in his farewell performance was the only new musical to sell out. Other hits were holdovers from past seasons. The winner of the Pulitzer Prize for 1985 was the Stephen Sondheim musical "Sunday in the Park with George." "Big River" opened near the end of this season and received the "Tony" Award for Best Musical, and gave every indication of becoming a hit. Ron Richardson of that production received a "Tony" as Outstanding Featured Actor. The "Tony" nominating committee declined to name candidates for outstanding actor and actress in a musical. At the end of the season, only three of the new musicals were still playing, and two of them closed shortly thereafter.

Of Broadway's 31 productions, 12 were revivals, 5 were imports, 3 came from Off Broadway, 8 from regional theatres, 2 were solo performances (Alec McCowen as Kipling, and Whoopi Goldberg's characterizations made her a star immediately), and 1 was Doug Henning's Magic Show. "Tony" Awards went to "Biloxi Blues" and to Barry Miller in that play for Outstanding Featured Actor, Derek Jacobi for Outstanding Actor in "Much Ado about Nothing," Stockard Channing for Outstanding Actress in a Play ("Joe Egg" that won a "Tony" for Outstanding Reproduction), and Judith Ivey for Outstanding Featured Actress in a Play ("Hurlyburly"). The New York Drama Critics Circle cited "Ma Rainey's Black Bottom" as Best Play, but failed to name a musical or an imported production. Other memorable productions were "Death of a Salesman" with Dustin Hoffman and John Malkovich, "Cyrano de Bergerac" (the Royal Shakespeare Company's other offering in repertory with Derek Jacobi giving an exemplary performance in the title role), "Strange Interlude" with Glenda Jackson, "A Pack of Lies" with Rosemary Harris and Patrick McGoohan, "Aren't We All?" with a stellar cast including Claudette Colbert and Rex Harrison, and "Doubles." Other congratulatory performances were given by Evalyn Baron, Matthew Broderick, Susan Browning, Pat Carroll, Peggy Cass, Patti Cohenour, John Cullum, Sinead Cusack, Jim Dale, Christine Ebersole, Randall Edwards, Brenda Forbes, Beth Fowler, Joanna Gleason, Harry Groener, Bob Gunton, Mark Hamill, Glenne Headly, Jonathan Hogan, William Hurt, Bill Irwin, Dana Ivey, Betty Johnson, Robert Judd, Stubby Kaye, Ken Kliban, Kevin Kline, Kurt Knudsen, Ron Leibman, Lou Liberatore, George N. Martin, Armelia McQueen, Theresa Merritt, Matt Mulhern, Cynthia Nixon, Timothy Nolen, Carroll O'Connor, Mary Beth Peil, Edward Petherbridge, Anne Pitoniak, David Proval, Jonathan Pryce, Lynn Redgrave, Tony Roberts, George Rose, Bill Sadler, Matt Salinger, Joe Seneca, John Short, Frances Sternhagen, Brian Tarantina, Marianne Tatum, Maria Tucci, Lee Wallace, Sigourney Weaver, Gary Landon Wright. Once again, Alexander H. Cohen produced the Tony-Award presentations (this year in the Shubert Theatre), and, as with previous ceremonies, it was unanimously acclaimed as the best of television's awards specials.

Off Broadway, once primarily experimental theatre, is becoming more commercial every year with the use of Broadway actors, directors and designers partially responsible for soaring production costs. The price of tickets escalated to Broadway scale at several theatres, reaching an unprecedented $35 top, and resulting in a decreasing attendance. The nonprofit theatres were also effected by having many of their grants reduced or canceled, and corporate donations withdrawn. Productions worthy of mention are "The Accrington Pals," "After the Fall," "As Is," "Avner the Eccentric," "The Ballad of Soapy Smith," "Balm in Gilead," "Blue Window," "Coming of Age in SoHo," "Danny and the Deep Blue Sea," "Diamonds," "Endgame," "The Foreigner," "The Golden Land," "Gifts of the Magi," "Hang on to the Good Times," "Hannah Senesh," "Hurlyburly" that was moved to Broadway, "The Incredibly Famous Willy Rivers," "Kuni-Leml," "A Kurt Weill Cabaret," "Madwoman of Chaillot," "The Marriage of Bette and Boo," "The Miss Firecracker Contest," "Music Moves Me," "The Mystery of Irma Vep," "Once on a Summer's Day," "Pacific Overtures," "Quilters," "Rap Master Ronnie," "The Return of Herbert Bracewell," "Rockaby," "Romance Language," "Salonika," "Shades of Harlem," "Short Eyes," "Sullivan and Gilbert," "Three Guys Naked from the Waist Down," "Through the Leaves" and "What's a Nice Country Like You Still Doing in a State Like This?" Once more, Off Broadway presented a greater number of quality productions than "the Great White Way."

Noteworthy performances Off Broadway include, Ernest Abuba, Denis Arndt, Elizabeth Berridge, Philip Bosco, John Bowman, Kate Burton, Vincent Caristi, David Carroll, Maxwell Caulfield, Richard Chaves, Patti Cohenour, Jane Connell, Brian Cox, John Danelle, Laura Dean, Avner Eisenberg, Patricia Elliott, Tovah Feldshuh, Vittorio Gassman, Kevin Gray, Jeffrey Hayenga, Katharine Houghton, Anthony Heald, Holly Hunter, Ernestine Jackson, John Kassir, Christine Lahti, Kym LeMon, Charles Ludlum, Mary Elizabeth Mastrantonio, Howard McGillin, Elizabeth McGovern, Laurie Metcalf, Michael O'Keefe, Lenka Peterson, Lonny Price, Gordana Rashovich, Jay O. Sanders, Camille Saviola, Ward Saxton, Sheila Smith, Frances Sternhagen, Jessica Tandy, Lara Teeter, John Turturro, Diane Venora, Christopher Walken, James Ray Weeks, Amelia White, Dianne Wiest, Lori Wilner, Elizabeth Wilson, Charlaine Woodard.

For the first time in 50 years, a new theatre (seating 420) was built Off Broadway. It was christened the Minetta Lane Theatre after the street on which it is located. It opened on Sept. 6, 1984 with "Balm in Gilead" that was transferred from the Circle Repertory Theatre. The Lion Theatre was re-named the Judith Anderson to honor one of our great actresses. One of the two auditoriums in the 48th Street Theatre became the Audrey Wood (for the literary agent), and the other was named the Tennessee Williams Theatre. However, the name had to be removed from the marquee when Mr. Williams' estate refused permission for the use of his name. It subsequently became the Jack Lawrence Theatre for its owner. Manhattan Theatre Club moved into renovated space downstairs at City Center, and opened there with its production of "In Celebration." Roundabout Theatre also moved to a new location in the renovated auditorium of the old Tammany Hall Building. Richard Crinkley resigned as executive director of the Lincoln Center theatre complex (Vivian Beaumont and Mitzi Newhouse theatres) and Bernard Gersten was chosen executive producer with Gregory Mosher as artistic director. After eight years of inactivity, it is hoped the lights will burn brightly again on both stages and that responsive audiences will fill the seats.

Actors Equity Association and the League of Resident Theatres (LORT) reached an agreement averting a strike against 77 houses. According to *Theatre Facts,* published by Theatre Communications Group, "Higher attendance and increased box office revenues for non-profit professional theatres throughout the U.S. do not outweigh the impact of rising costs, federal government cuts, and declining support from foundations. The widening gap between income and expenses threatens the growth, planning, and survival of these institutions. Some 30 theatres have ceased operation since 1980." After many years of bargaining, producers and playwrights reached an agreement on playwrights royalties and rights of actors. Hopefully this will bring more new works for production in the near future. Colleen Dewhurst became president of Actors Equity Association, succeeding its first woman president, Ellen Burstyn. Both were active in organizing Save the Theatres Inc. to secure landmark designation for historic, irreplaceable theatres in the Broadway district, New York City's most priceless asset and world-wide identity. Since 1942, 21 theatres have been demolished to make way for commercial projects. May there be no more theatre obituaries added to this number in the coming years.

BROADWAY PRODUCTIONS
(June 1, 1984 through May 31, 1985)

GOTTA GETAWAY!

Conceived and Created by Stephen Nisbet, James Lecesne; Writer, James Lecesne; Director-Choreographer, Larry Fuller; Co-choreographer, Marianne Selbert; Producer-Artistic Director, Patricia Morinelli; Associate Producer, Stephen Nisbet; Title Song, Glen Roven; Original Music, Marc Elliot, Chip Orton, Gene Palumbo, Marc Shaiman, Eric Watson; Musical Director, Gene Palumbo; Orchestrators, Michael Gibson, Bill Brohn; Conductor, Robert Billig; Vocal Arrangements, Gene Palumbo, Robert Billig; Dance Arrangements, Michael Rice; Scenery, Eduardo Sicangco; Costumes, Michael Casey; Lighting, Clarke W. Thornton; Music Video, Neil Wagman; Production Manager, Steven Rivellino; Props, Joseph Bivone, Sr.; Wardrobe, Barbara Van Zandt; Hairstylist, Gloria Rivera; Assistant Conductor, Michael Battistelli; Production Assistant, John Henry Lipscomb; Production Associate, Roberta Haze; Stage Managers, Raymond Chandler, Howard Kolins, Nelson Wilson, Laurie Clark; Press, Neil S. Friedman, Ellen M. Schiebelhuth; Presented by Radio City Music Hall Productions. Opened at Radio City Music Hall, Friday, June 8, 1984 and closed September 3, 1984 after 149 performances.

CAST

Liliane Montevecchi, Tony Azito, Loretta Devine, Alyson Reed, Ron and Joy Holiday, and The Rockettes
CRUISETTES: Arminae Azarian, Ellia English, Connie Kunkle, Jacqueline Reilly, Bonnie Schon, Freida Williams
STEWARDS: Ciscoe Bruton, John Clonts, Joe DeGunther, Brian Feehan, Darrell Greene, Marc Hunter, David Michael Johnson, Robert Kellett, Lacy Darryl Phillips, Jeff Shade, Paul Solen, Alan Stuart, John M. Wiltberger
MUSICAL NUMBERS: Gotta Getaway, I'm Throwing a Ball Tonight, Use Your Imagination, Too Marvelous for Words, This Heart of Mine, Bubble Bubble, La Cumparcita, Here in Minipoora, Hot VooDoo, Hello Beautiful, Le Denier Pierrot, Folies Bergeres, Stairway to Paradise, Higher and Higher, Come to the Super Market in Old Peking, Peking Ballet, Once You've Seen a Rainbow, Manhattan, Take Good Care of That Lady

Kenn Duncan Photos

Loretta Devine

**Liliane Montevecchi, and above with
Tony Azito, Loretta Devine, Alyson Reed**

DESIGN FOR LIVING

By Noel Coward; Director, George C. Scott; Scenery, Thomas Lynch; Costumes, Ann Roth; Lighting, Marc B. Weiss; Wigs, Paul Huntley; Hughes Moss Casting; Presented by Circle in the Square Theatre (Theodore Mann, Artistic Director; Paul Libin, Managing Director); Hairstylist, David Lawrence; Wardrobe, Claire Libin; Company Manager, William Conn; Stage Managers, Michael F. Ritchie, Ted William Sowa; Press, Merle Debuskey, David Roggensack, William Schelble. Opened at Circle in the Square Theatre on Thursday, June 21, 1984.*

CAST

Gilda	Jill Clayburgh[†1]
Ernest Friedman	Richard Woods
Otto	Frank Langella[†2]
Leo	Raul Julia[†3]
Miss Hodge	Helena Carroll
Grace Torrence	Lisa Kirk[†4]
Henry Carver	Robertson Carricart
Helen Carver	Anne Swift[†5]
Matthew	Arthur French

STANDBYS & UNDERSTUDIES: Mart Hulswit (Leo/Otto), Donald Buka (Ernest), Anne Swift (Gilda)

A comedy in 3 acts and 6 scenes. The action takes place during 1932 in Otto's studio in Paris, Leo's flat in London, and Ernest's apartment in New York City in 1934.

*Closed Jan. 20, 1985 after 245 performances and 19 previews. Original production opened Jan. 24, 1933 with Alfred Lunt, Lynn Fontanne and Noel Coward and played 135 performances.
†Succeeded by: 1. Anne Swift, 2. Frank Converse, Jim Piddock, 3. John Glover, 4. Louise Troy, 5. Cecilia Hart, Holly Barron

Martha Swope Photos

Top Right: Lisa Kirk, Jill Clayburgh, Anne Swift, Robertson Carricart

Raul Julia, Jill Clayburgh,
Frank Langella

Anne Swift, John Glover (center),
Frank Converse

HURLYBURLY

By David Rabe; Director, Mike Nichols; Setting, Tony Walton; Costumes, Ann Roth; Lighting, Jennifer Tipton; Sound, Otts Munderloh; Presented by Icarus Productions and Frederick M. Zollo with Ivan Bloch and ERB Productions; Associate Producer, William P. Suter; Production Associate, Georgianne Walken; General Management, Gatchell & Neufeld; Props, George Green, Jr, Robert Bostwick; Wardrobe, Chip Mulberger; Makeup and Hairstylist, J. Roy Helland; Company Managers, Roger Gindi, Tony Magner; Stage Managers, Peter Lawrence, Jim Woolley; Production Assistants, Alexander Cary, John Swanbeck; Press, Bill Evans, Sandra Manley, Jim Baldassare. Opened at the Ethel Barrymore Theatre on Tuesday, August 7, 1984.*

CAST

Phil	Harvey Keitel†1
Eddie	William Hurt†2
Mickey	Ron Silver
Artie	Jerry Stiller†3
Donna	Cynthia Nixon†4
Darlene	Sigourney Weaver†5
Bonnie	Judith Ivey†6

STANDBYS: Alison Bartlett (Donna), John Christopher Jones (Eddie/Mickey), Harris Laskawy (Artie/Phil), Natalia Nogulich (Bonnie/Darlene)

A play in three acts. The action takes place "a little while ago" in a house in the Hollywood Hills.

*Closed June 2, 1985 after 343 performances and 18 previews. It had previously played 18 previews and 45 performances (June 5,–July 29, 1984) in the Off-Broadway Promenade Theatre. Judith Ivey received a "Tony" and a Drama Desk Award for Outstanding Featured Actress in a Play.
†Succeeded by: 1. Harris Laskawy, Danny Aiello, 2. John Rubinstein, John Christopher Jones, Frank Langella, 3. Harris Laskawy, Kevin Spacey, 4. Alison Bartlett, Lauren Tom, 5. Natalia Nogulich, Candice Bergen, Susan Anton, 6. Christine Baranski

Martha Swope Photos

Left: (L to R seated) Ron Silver, John Rubinstein, Susan Anton, Alison Bartlett, Christine Baranski, (standing) Harris Laskawy, Jerry Stiller
Top: (seated) Ron Silver, William Hurt, Sigourney Weaver, Cynthia Nixon, Judith Ivey, (standing) Harvey Keitel, Jerry Stiller

Cynthia Nixon, William Hurt

William Hurt, Sigourney Weaver

DEATH OF A SALESMAN

By Arthur Miller; Director, Michael Rudman; Scenery, Ben Edwards; Costumes, Ruth Morley; Music, Alex North; Lighting, Thomas Skelton; Makeup, Ann Belsky; Hairstylist, Hiram Ortiz, Alan D'Angerio; Costumer, Franke Piazza; Wardrobe, James McGaha; Presented by Punch Productions and Marvin A. Krauss; General Management, Marvin A. Krauss Associates; Wigs, Paul Huntley; Casting, Terry Fay; Company Manager, Allan Williams; Stage Managers, Thomas A. Kelly, Charles Kindl, Kenneth Cox; Press, Patricia Krawitz, Keith Aaron. Opened at the Broadhurst Theatre on Friday, September 14, 1984.*

CAST

Willy Loman	Dustin Hoffman
Linda	Kate Reid
Happy	Stephen Lang†1
Biff	John Malkovich†2
Bernard	David Chandler
Woman from Boston	Kathy Rossetter
Charley	David Huddleston†3
Uncle Ben	Louis Zorich†4
Howard Wagner	Jon Polito
Jenny	Patricia Fay†5
Stanley	Tom Signorelli
Miss Forsythe	Linda Kozlowski
Letta	Karen Needle
Waiter	Michael Quinlan

UNDERSTUDIES & STANDBYS: John Turturro (Biff/Happy/Stanley), Clifford A. Pellow (Charley/Uncle Ben/Stanley; Anne McIntosh (Miss Forsythe/Letta), Michael Quinlan (Bernard/Howard)

A drama in two acts. The action takes place in a 24-hour period in Willy Loman's house and yard, and in various places he visits in New York and Boston.

*Closed Nov. 18, 1984 after limited engagement of 158 performances and 9 previews. The same company had appeared last season from March 29, through July 1, 1984 for 97 performances, and received a "Tony" for outstanding reproduction of a play. Original production with Lee J. Cobb, Mildred Dunnock, Cameron Mitchell and Arthur Kennedy opened at the Morosco Theatre Feb. 10, 1949 and played 742 performances. The 1975 revival with George C. Scott, Teresa Wright, Harvey Keitel, James Farentino played 71 performances at the Circle in the Square Theatre.
†Succeeded by: 1. Andrew Bloch, 2. Stephen Lang, 3. Louis Zorich, 4. Bruce Kirby, 5. Anne McIntosh

Inge Morath Photos

Top: Kate Reid, Dustin Hoffman Right: Hoffman, David Chandler Below: Chandler, Stephen Lang, Reid, Hoffman, John Malkovich, David Huddleston

David Chandler, John Malkovich, Kate Reid, David Huddleston, Stephen Lang

KIPLING

By Brian Clark; Based on the works of Rudyard Kipling with the permission of the National Trust; Director, Patrick Garland; Design, Pamela Howard; Lighting, Neil Peter Jampolis; Produced by arrangement with Astramead Ltd. and Freeshooter Productions Ltd.; Presented by Roy A. Somlyo; Wardrobe, Clarence Sims; Company Manager, Jodi Moss; Stage Managers, Thomas A. Kelly, Keith Waggoner; Press, Michael Alpert, Ruth Jaffe. Opened at the Royale Theatre on Wednesday, October 10, 1984.*

CAST

ALEC McCOWEN
as
Kipling

A solo performance in two acts.

*Closed Oct. 21, 1984 after limited engagement of 12 performances.

Alec McCowen

MA RAINEY'S BLACK BOTTOM

By August Wilson; Director, Lloyd Richards; Costumes, Daphne Pascucci; Setting, Charles Henry McClennahan; Lighting, Peter Maradudin; Musical Direction, Dwight Andrews; Sound, Jan Nebozenko; Casting, Meg Simon/Fran Kumin; Presented by Ivan Bloch, Robert Cole, Frederick M. Zollo; The Yale Repertory Theatre production; Associate Producers, Bart Berman, Hart Productions, William P. Suter; Production Associates, Deborah D. Mathews, Georgianne Walken; Props, Val Medina; Wardrobe, Darthula McQueen; Stage Managers, Mortimer Halpern, K. White; Press, Jeffrey Richards, C. George Willard, Robert Ganshaw, Eileen McMahon, Ben Morse, Toby Mailman, Bill Shuttleworth, Naomi Grabel. Opened at the Cort Theatre on Thursday, October 11, 1984.*

CAST

Sturdyvant, studio owner ....John Carpenter
Irvin, Ma's manager ....Lou Criscuolo
Cutler, trombonist ....Joe Seneca[1]
Toledo, pianist .... Robert Judd
Slow Drag, bassist ....Leonard Jackson[2]
Levee, trumpeter ....Charles S. Dutton
Ma Rainey ....Theresa Merritt[3]
Dussie Mae ....Aleta Mitchell
Sylvester, Ma's nephew ....Scott Davenport-Richards
Policeman ....Christopher Loomis[4]

UNDERSTUDIES: Peter Boyden (Sturdyvant/Irvin/Policeman), Bill Cobbs (Cutler), Arthur French (Slow Drag/Toledo), Ebony Jo-Ann (Ma Rainey/Dussie Mae), Victor Raider-Wexler (Sturdyvant/Irvin/Policeman), Thomas Martell Brimm (Cutler), Lou Myers (Slow Drag/Toledo), Damien Leake (Levee/Sylvester).

A play with music in two acts. The action takes place during early March of 1927 in the bandroom and recording studio of a record company in Chicago.

*Closed June 9, 1985 after 267 performances and 4 previews. It received a NY Drama Critics Circle Award as Best Play of the season. Charles S. Dutton received a Theatre World Award, and a Drama Desk citation as Outstanding Featured Actor in a Play. †Succeeded by: 1. Bill Cobbs, 2. Arthur French, 3. Ebony Jo-Ann during illness, 4. John Randolph Jones

Bert Andrews Photos

Right: Scott Davenport-Richards, Charles S. Dutton, Leonard Jackson, Theresa Merritt, Robert Judd, Joe Seneca, (above) Lou Criscuolo, John Carpenter
Top: Dutton, Jackson, Merritt, Judd

Charles S. Dutton, Aleta Mitchell

Leonard Jackson, Joe Seneca

THE ROYAL SHAKESPEARE COMPANY

Directed by Terry Hands; Settings, Ralph Koltai; Costumes, Alexander Reid; Music, Nigel Hess; Lighting, Terry Hands; American Production Designed in association with John Kasarda (Settings), Jeffrey Beecroft (Lighting); Musical Director, Donald Johnston; Sound Supervision, T. Richard Fitzgerald; Assistant Director, Brigid Larmour; Choreography, Doreen Hermitage; Fencing Consultant, Ian McKay; Presented by James M. Nederlander, Elizabeth I. McCann, Nelle Nugent, Cynthia Wood, Dale Duffy, Allan Carr; Artistic Directors, Terry Hands, Trevor Nunn; Production Manager, Simon Opie; Wardrobe, Susan Honey; Company Manager, Susan Gustafson; Production Assistant, Beth Pollack; Stage Managers, Jane Tamlyn, Alan Hall, Vikki Heywood, Jill MacFarlane, Stephen Dobbin, Michael Dembowicz, Hilary Groves; Press, Solters/Roskin/Friedman, Joshua Ellis, Adrian Bryan-Brown, Keith Sherman, Cindy Valk, Jackie Green. Opened at the Gershwin Theatre on Sunday, October 14, 1984.*

MUCH ADO ABOUT NOTHING by William Shakespeare

CAST

Leonato	Edward Jewesbury
Antonio	Jeffery Dench
Hero	Clare Byam Shaw
Margaret	Alexandra Brook
Ursula	Cathy Finlay
Josetta	Jane Tottman
Beatrice	Sinead Cusack
Friar Francis	George Parsons
Boy	Amy Chang or Samuel Schieffelin Nordberg
Don Pedro	Ken Bones
Don John	John Carlisle
Count Claudio of Florence	Christopher Bowen
Signior Benedick of Padua	Derek Jacobi†
Borachio	Geoffrey Freshwater
Conrade	John Bowe
Lord	Richard Clifford
Balthasar	Philip Dennis
Dogberry	Christopher Benjamin
Verges	Jimmy Gardner
Sexton	Ray Llewellyn
George Seacoal	David Shaw-Parker
Hugh Oatcake	Dennis Clinton
Third Watch	Tom Mannion
Fourth Watch	Simon Clark

UNDERSTUDIES: Alexandra Brook (Beatrice), Cathy Finlay (Hero/Margaret), Jane Tottman (Ursula), John Bowe (Benedick), Simon Clark (Balthasar/Borachio), Richard Clifford (Don Pedro/Conrade), Dennis Clinton (Antonio/Friar), Philip Dennis (Sexton/Messenger), Ray Llewellyn (Leonato), Tom Mannion (Claudio/Messenger), George Parsons (Don John), David Shaw-Parker (Dogberry/Verges), Robert Craig (Balthasar).

Left: Derek Jacobi
Top: Sinead Cusack, Derek Jacobi

Derek Jacobi, Sinead Cusack

Christopher Bowen, Clare Byam Shaw, Derek Jacobi, Sinead Cusack

CYRANO DE BERGERAC by Edmond Rostand

Translated and adapted by Anthony Burgess

CAST

Doorkeeper/Capuchin	Jimmy Gardner
Bellerose/Cadet	David Shaw-Parker
Jodelet/Theophraste Renaudot	Raymond Bowers
Cavalryman/Cadet	Richard Clifford
D'Artagnan/Cadet	Robert Clare
Flunkey/Cadet	Philip Dennis
Flunkey/Cadet	John Tramper
Musketeer	Geoffrey Freshwater
Flower Girl/Sister Claire	Alexandra Brook
Eater/Cadet	Niall Padden
Drinker/Cadet	Phillip Walsh
Citizen	Simon Clark
His Son	Jayne Tottman
Food Seller/Sister Marthe	Cathy Finlay
Pages	Alex Flagg, Amy Chang, Samuel Schieffelin Nordberg
Pickpocket	Ray Llewellyn
Cuigy	Dennis Clinton
Brisaille	Edward Jewesbury
Marquises	Jeffery Dench, David Glover
Ligniere the Poet	George Parsons
Baron Christian de Neuvillette	Tom Mannion
Precieuses	Penelope Beaumont, Clare Byam Shaw
Ragueneau	Pete Postlethwaite
Le Bret	John Bowe
Roxane	Sinead Cusack
Her Duenna	Brenda Peters
Le Comte de Guiche	John Carlisle
Le Vicomte de Valvert	Christopher Bowen
Montfleury	Christopher Benjamin
Cyrano de Bergerac	Derek Jacobi†
Lise/Mother Marguerite	Penelope Beaumont
Captain Carbon de Castel Jaloux	Ken Bones

UNDERSTUDIES: Penelope Beaumont (Duenna), Alexandra Brook (Lise), Clare Byam Shaw (Roxane), Brenda Peters (Mother Marguerite), Jayne Tottman (Sisters), Ken Bones (Cyrano), Christopher Bowen (Christian), Raymond Bowers (Ragueneau), Robert Clare (Le Bret/Valvert), Simon Clark (Carbon/Montfleury), Richard Clifford (DeGuiche), Ray Llewellyn (Citizen/Capuchin), Niall Padden (Musketeer), David Shaw-Parker (Doorkeeper/Renaudot), John Tramper (D'Artagnan/Jodelet/Bellerose), Phillip Walsh (Ligniere/Pickpocket/Cavalier)

*Closed January 19, 1985 after 53 performances and 4 previews of "Much Ado about Nothing," and 59 performances and 5 previews of "Cyrano." Derek Jacobi received a "Tony" for his performance in "Much Ado about Nothing."
†Played by Ken Bones during Mr. Jacobi's illness.

Chris Davies, John Brown Photos

Right: Derek Jacobi as Cyrano

Sinead Cusack, Tom Mannion, Derek Jacobi

John Bowe, Pete Postlethwaite, Geoffrey Freshwater, Derek Jacobi

13

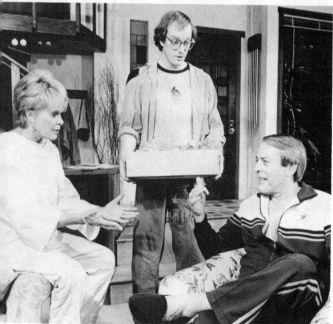

Janis Paige, Don Howard, Kevin McCarthy

ALONE TOGETHER

By Lawrence Roman; Director, Arnold Mittelman; Scenery, Karl Eigsti; Costumes, Jane Greenwood; Lighting, Arden Fingerhut; General Management, Theatre Now, Inc.; Casting, Stuart Howard Associates; Presented by Arnold Mittelman and Lynne Peyser; Technical Supervisor, Jeremiah J. Harris; Props, Peter Gardner; Wardrobe, Peter Fitzgerald; Stage Managers, Larry Forde, Mark Rubinsky; Press, Mark Goldstaub, Kevin P. McAnarney, Philip Butler, Daniel Kellachan. Opened at the Music Box on Sunday, October 21, 1984.*

CAST

George Butler	Kevin McCarthy
Helene Butler	Janis Paige
Keith Butler	Dennis Drake
Michael Butler	Don Howard
Elliott Butler	Kevin O'Rourke
Janie Johnson	Alexandra Gersten

STANDBYS & UNDERSTUDIES: Tudi Wiggins (Helene), George Guidall (George), William Fichtner (Michael/Elliott/Keith), Mary Ellen Stuart (Janie)

A comedy in 2 acts and 6 scenes. The action takes place in the Butler home in Los Angeles at the present time during September.

*Closed Jan. 12, 1985 after 97 performances and 15 previews.

Martha Swope Photos

Top: Don Howard, Janis Paige, Alexandra Gersten, Kevin McCarthy, Kevin O'Rourke

14

WHOOPI GOLDBERG

Written by Whoopi Goldberg; Production supervised by Mike Nichols; Visual Consultant, Tony Walton; Lighting, Jennifer Tipton; Sound, Otts Munderloh; An Icarus Production presented by Mike Nichols, Emanuel Azenberg, and the Shubert Organization (Gerald Schoenfeld, Chairman; Bernard B. Jacobs, President); General Manager, Robert Kamlot; Company Manager, Max Allentuck; Assistant Company Manager, Brian Dunbar; Stage Managers, Martin Herzer, Lisa Hogarty; Press, Bill Evans, Sandra Manley, Jim Baldassare, Lilli Afan. Opened in the Lyceum Theatre on Wednesday, October 24, 1984.*

CAST

WHOOPI GOLDBERG

A solo performance of characters created by Miss Goldberg, and performed with one intermission.

*Closed March 10, 1985 after 150 performances and 18 previews. Miss Goldberg received a Theatre World Award and a Drama Desk citation for her outstanding talent.

Martha Swope Photos

Whoopi Goldberg (also at top)

15

THE THREE MUSKETEERS

Music, Rudolf Friml; Lyrics, P. G. Wodehouse, Clifford Grey; Book, William Anthony McGuire; In a New Version by Mark Bramble; Based on novel by Alexandre Dumas; Director, Tom O'Horgan; Choreography, Lester Wilson; Fight Choreography, Steve Dunnington; Presented by Irvin Feld, Kenneth Feld, Ina Lea Meibach, Jerome Minskoff; General Management, Joseph Harris, Steven E. Goldstein, Peter T. Kulok, Nancy Simmons; Company Managers, Steven H. David, Ken Shelley; Assistant Choreographer, Dwight Baxter; Scenery, Nancy Winters; Costumes, Freddy Wittop; Sound, Jan Nebozenko; Music adapted, arranged and supervised by Kirk Nurock; Conductor, Gordon Lowry Harrell; Orchestrations, Larry Wilcox; Vocal and Fight Arrangements, Kirk Nurock; Dance Arrangements, Wally Harper, Mark Hummel; Casting, Slater-Wilson; Stage Managers, Steven Zweigbaum, Arturo E. Porazzi, Amy Pell, Todd Lester; Technical Supervisor, Jeremiah Harris; Props, Paul Biega, Joseph Harris, Jr.; Wardrobe, Nancy Schaefer, Daniel P. Lomax; Hairstylists, Angela Gari, Dale Brownell; Associate Conductor, Peter Philips; Production Assistant, Jonathan Cerullo; Press, Judy Jacksina, Glenna Freedman, Marcy Granata, Susan Chicoine, Marc Thibodeau, Kevin Boyle, Jane Steinberg. Opened Sunday, November 4, 1984.*

CAST

Queen Anne of France	Darlene Anders
Lady Constance Bonacieux	Liz Callaway
Cardinal Richelieu	Ed Dixon
Sergeant Jussac	Raymond Patterson
Innkeeper/Selenus/Major Domo	J. P. Dougherty
Duke of Buckingham	Joseph Kolinski
Compte de la Rochefort	Michael Dantuono
Milady de Winter	Marianne Tatum
D'Artagnan	Michael Praed
Athos	Chuck Wagner
Aramis	Brent Spiner
Porthos	Ron Taylor
Laundress/Lady	Susan Goodman
de Beauverais	Steve Dunnington
Captain Treville	Peter Samuel
King Louis XIII	Roy Brocksmith
Patrick	Perry Arthur

CARDINAL'S GUARDS: Bill Badolato, Steve Dunnington, Craig Heath Nim, Steve Marder, Mark McGrath, Sal Viviano, Faruma Williams
CHARACTERS TOO NUMEROUS TO MENTION: Janet Aldrich, Perry Arthur, Bill Badolato, Tina Belis, Steven Blanchard, Steve Dunnington, Elisa Fiorillo, Terri Garcia, Susan Goodman, Patty Holley, Jeff Johnson, Steve Marder, Mark McGrath, Craig Heath Nim, Suzan Postel, Wynonna Smith, Sal Viviano, Faruma Williams, Sandra Zigars.

UNDERSTUDIES: Jeff Johnson (D'Artagnan), Mark McGrath (Athos/Innkeeper), Peter Samuel (Porthos/Cardinal), Steven Blanchard (Aramis), Elisa Fiorillo/Janet Aldrich (Constance), Suzan Postel (Queen), Craig Heath Nim (Rochefort/Treville), Sal Viviano (Buckingham), Faruma Williams (Jussac), J. P. Dougherty (King), Patty Holley (Laundress), Janet Aldrich (Milady), Perry Arthur (Planchet), Swings: De Dwight Baxter, Kirsti Carnahan, Craig Frawley, Todd Lester, Jacqueline Smith-Lee
MUSICAL NUMBERS: Prologue, Gascony Bred, All for One, Only a Rose, My Sword and I, Carnival of Fools, L'Amour Toujours L'Amour, Come to Us, March of the Musketeers, Bless My Soul, Vive La France, The Actor's Life, My Belle, The Chase, Dreams, Gossip, Finale

A musical in 2 acts and 17 scenes. The action takes place in 1626 in France and England.

*Closed Nov. 18, 1984 after 9 performances and 14 previews.

Martha Swope Photos

Top Left: Chuck Wagner, Michael Praed, Ron Taylor, Brent Spiner Below: Michael Praed, Darlene Anders

Marianne Tatum, Michael Praed

ACCIDENTAL DEATH OF AN ANARCHIST

By Dario Fo; Adapted by Richard Nelson; Based on translation by Suzanne Cowan; Director, Douglas C. Wager; Casting, Meg Simon/Fran Kumin; Set, Karl Eigsti; Lighting, Allen Lee Hughes; Costumes, Patricia Zipprodt; Hairstylist, Joseph Dal Corso; Presented by Alexander H. Cohen and Hildy Parks; Co-Producer, Bernard Gersten; General Manager, Martha Mason; Company Manager, G. Warren McClane; Technical Supervisor, Arthur Siccardi; Props, George Green; Wardrobe, Elonzo Dann; Production Associate, Seymour Herscher; Stage Managers, Robert L. Borod, Marc Schlackman; Press, Merle Debuskey, William Schelble, Rebecca Robbins. Opened at the Belasco Theatre on Thursday, November 15, 1984.*

CAST

The Fool	Jonathan Pryce
The Sergeant	Bill Irwin
Inspector Bertozzo	Gerry Bamman
Captain Pisani	Joe Grifasi
Chief Bellati	Raymond Serra
The Reporter	Patti LuPone

STANDBYS & UNDERSTUDIES: Seth Allen (The Fool), Robert Fitch (Sergeant/Inspector), Frank Biancamano (Chief/Captain), Maia Danziger (Reporter)

A farce in two acts and three scenes. The action takes place in Central Police Headquarters in Rome, Italy, in the second and fourth floor offices.

*Closed Dec. 1, 1984 after 20 performances and 15 previews.

Martha Swope Photos

Jonathan Pryce, Bill Irwin

Top: Patti LuPone, Jonathan Pryce, Joe Grifasi, Gerry Bamman, Raymond Serra, Bill Irwin

HAARLEM NOCTURNE

Conceived by Andre De Shields; Written and Directed by Andre De Shields, Murray Horwitz; Musical Direction, Orchestrations, Vocal Arrangements, Marc Shaiman; Presented by Barry and Fran Weissler; Set, David Chapman; Costumes, Jean-Claude Robin; Lighting, Marc B. Weiss; Sound, Bill Dreisbach; Hairstylist, Bruce C. Edwards; Assistant to Directors, Gary Sullivan; Associate Producer, Alecia Parker; General Management, National Artists Management Co./Barbara Darwall; Assistant Company Manager, Karen B. Hermelin; Technical Supervisor, Val Medina; Wardrobe, Suzanne Gallo; Stage Managers, Bruce H. Lumpkin, Meryl Vladimer; Press, Jacqueline Burnham, Edward Callasghan, Merle Frimark, Jeanne Browne, Fran Colgan, Ina Goldberg, Jill Larkin, David Lotz, Gary Murphy. Opened at the Latin Quarter on Sunday, November 18, 1984.*

CAST

Andre De Shields

Debra Byrd   Marc Shaiman
Ellia English   Freida Williams

MUSICAL NUMBERS: Love in the Morning, Wishful Thinking, New York Is a Party, Jungle Hip Hop, Sweet Dreams Are Made of This, What Becomes of the Broken Hearted, Love's Sad Glance, Secret Love, Say It Again, Heads or Tails, Hit the Road Jack, Waterfaucet Blues, Streetcorner Symphony, Release Yourself, Bad Boy, Symphony Rap, Mary Mack, Pastiche, Sermon, Harlem Nocturne, Louie, B.Y.O.B., Now Is the Time

A musical in two acts.

*Closed Dec. 30, 1984 after 49 performances and 15 previews.

Kenn Duncan Photos

Marc Shaiman, Freida Williams, Andre De Shields, Debra Byrd, Ella English Top: Andre De Shields

DOUG HENNING AND HIS WORLD OF MAGIC

Conceived and Directed by Doug Henning; Staged and Choreographed by Charlene Painter; Music Composed and Directed by Peter Matz; Costumes, Jef Billings; Set, Bill Bohnert; Lighting Design and Stage Manager, Michael McGiveney; Music Designer and Coordinator, Jim Steinmeyer; Head Illusion Engineer and Additional Illusions, William Kennedy; Illusions Design and Construction, John Gaughan; Magical Consultant, Charles Reynolds; Animal Trainer, Rick Glassey; Illusion Engineers, Jon Sipos, Wayne Saks, Frank Carra; Sound Engineer, Bud Beauchamp; Wardrobe, Nancy Nedell; Assistant Choreographer, Victor Heineman; Additional Costumes, Bill Hargate; Photography, Allan S. Adler, Peter Cunningham, Jim Ward, John Zimmerman, Zox, ITC Entertainment, NBC Photo Department; Presented by James M. Nederlander and Arthur Rubin; General Managers, Steve Kirsner, Camille Ranson; Company Manager, Gino Giglio; Press, Michael Alpert, Ruth Jaffe. Opened at the Lunt-Fontanne Theatre on Tuesday, December 11, 1984*

CAST

Doug Henning
Debby Henning

Victor Heineman   D. J. Mergenthaler
Gina Rose   Kathleen White

*Closed January 27, 1985 after 60 performances.

Right: Doug Henning

Doug Henning, Debby Henning

HOME FRONT

By James Duff; Director, Michael Attenborough; Original Set, Sue Plummer; Adapted for Broadway by Frank J. Boros; Costumes, John Falabella; Lighting, Ken Billington; Presented by Richard Barr, Charles Woodward, David Bixler; Associate Producer, Peter Jedlin; General Manager, Michael Kasdan; Associate Manager, David Jannone; Production Associate, S. Clark Bason; Props, Michael Durnin, Jim Gallagher; Wardrobe, Patricia Britton; Stage Managers, Donald Walters, Charles Kindl; Press, Shirley Herz, Sam Rudy, Peter Cromarty. Opened at the Royale Theatre on Wednesday, January 2, 1985.*

CAST

Bob .... Carroll O'Connor
Maurine .... Frances Sternhagen
Jeremy .... Christopher Fields
Karen .... Linda Cook

STANDBYS & UNDERSTUDIES: David Leary (Bob), Estelle Kemler (Maurine), Debbie Silver (Karen), Steven Weber (Jeremy)

A play in 2 acts and 4 scenes. The action takes place in suburban Dallas-Fort Worth, Texas, on Thanksgiving Day of 1973.

*Closed Jan. 12, 1985 after 13 performances and 11 previews.

Martha Swope Photos

Frances Sternhagen, Carroll O'Connor

Top: Linda Cook, Carroll O'Connor, Frances Sternhagen

DANCING IN THE END ZONE

By Bill C. Davis; Director, Melvin Bernhardt; Set, Douglas W. Schmidt; Costumes, Patricia McGourty; Lighting, Dennis Parichy; Presented by Morton Gottlieb in association with Sally Sears; Associate Producers, Richard Seader, Ben Rosenberg, Milly Schoenbaum; General Manager, Sylrich Management; Production Assistant, Patrick Herold; Wardrobe, Claudia Kraneb; Production Associate, Dennis Aspland; Stage Managers, Duane Mazey, Warren Crane; Press, Milly Schoenbaum, Leo Stern, Marc Routh. Opened Thursday, January 3, 1985.*

CAST

James Bernard ....Matt Salinger
Madeleine Bernard ....Pat Carroll
Dick Biehn ....Laurence Luckinbill
Jan Morrison ....Dorothy Lyman

Understudies: Brian Evers, Gavin Troster

A play in two acts. The action takes place at the present time in a mid-western university town.

*Closed Jan. 26, 1985 after 28 performances and 14 previews

Martha Swope Photos

Right: Laurence Luckinbill, Pat Carroll

Pat Carroll, Dorothy Lyman, Matt Salinger

THE KING AND I

Music by Richard Rodgers; Book and Lyrics, Oscar Hammerstein 2nd; Based on book "Anna and the King of Siam" by Margaret Landon; Producer-Director, Mitch Leigh; Original Choreography, Jerome Robbins; Reproduced by Rebecca West; Settings, Peter Wolf; Costumes, Stanley Simmons based on original costumes by Irene Sharaff; Lighting, Ruth Roberts; Sound, Scott Marcellus; Musical Director, Richard Parrinello; Production Supervisor, Conwell Worthington II; Casting, Mark Reiner; Executive Producer, Milton Herson; Associate Producer, Manny Kladitis; Company Manager, Abbie M. Strassler; Props, Sam Bagarella, John Godsey; Wardrobe, Rebecca Denson, Gigi Nelson; Hairstylist, Michael Gouty; Stage Managers, Kenneth L. Peck, John M. Galo, Charles Reif; Musical Coordinator, Martin Grupp; Associate Conductor, Al Cavaliere; Press, Solters/Roskin/Friedman, Joshua Ellis, Keith Sherman, Adrian Bryan-Brown, Cindy Valk, Jackie Green. Opened at the Broadway Theatre on Monday, January 7, 1985.*

CAST

Louis Leonowens	Jeffrey Bryan Davis
Captain Orton	Burt Edwards
Anna Leonowens	Mary Beth Peil
The Interpreter	Jae Woo Lee
Kralahome	Jonathan Farwell
The King	Yul Brynner
Lead Royal Dancer/Eliza	Kathy Lee Brynner
Lun Tha	Sal Provenza
Tuptim	Patricia Welch
Lady Thiang	Irma-Estel LaGuerre
Prince Chulalongkorn	Araby Abaya
Princess Ying Yaowalak	Yvette Laura Martin
Fan Dancer/Angel	Patricia Weber
Sir Edward Ramsey	Edward Crotty
Uncle Thomas	Hope Sogawa
Little Eva	Evelina Deocares
Topsy	Deborah Harada
Simon	Rebecca West

ROYAL DANCERS & WIVES: Marla F. Bingham, Young-Hee Cho, Carolyn DeLany, Evelina Deocares, Deborah Harada, Valerie Lau-Kee, Suzen Murakoshi, Hope Sogawa, Sylvia Yamada.

PRINCES & PRINCESSES: Max Barabas, Michael Bulos, Amy Chin, Lisa Chui, Mark Damrongsri, Kate Gwon, Tracie Mon-Ting Lee, Michelle Nigalan, Steven Tom, Luke Trainer, Annie Woo.

NURSES & AMAZONS: Alis-Elaine Anderson, Joyce Campana, Mariann Cook, Janet Jordan.

PRIESTS & SLAVES: Cornel Chan, Kaipo Daniels, Gary Bain Domasin, Stanley Earl Harrison, Thomas Heath, Andre Lengyel, Ron Stefan.

STANDBYS & UNDERSTUDIES: Jonathan Farwell (King), Mariann Cook (Anna), Edward Crotty (Orton), Luke Trainer (Louis), Kaipo Daniels (Interpreter), Jae Woo Lee (Kralahome), Carolyn DeLany (Tuptim), Joyce Campana (Lady Thiang), Michael Bulos (Chulalongkorn), Tracie Mon-Ting Lee (Princess Ying), Thomas Heath (Lun Tha), Burt Edwards (Ramsey), Deborah Harada (Angel/Fan Dancer), Evelina Deocares (Lead Royal Dancer), Sylvia Yamada (Eliza), Thom Cordeiro Kam (Simon), Sandy Sueoka (Topsy), Maria F. Bingham (Uncle Thomas), Young-Hee Cho (Eva), Swings: Sandy Sueoka, Thom Cordeiro Kam.

MUSICAL NUMBERS: Overture, I Whistle a Happy Tune, My Lord and Master, Hello Young Lovers, March of the Siamese Children, A Puzzlement, The Royal Bangkok Academy, Getting to Know You, We Kiss in a Shadow, Shall I Tell You What I Think of You?, Something Wonderful, Western People Funny, I Have Dreamed, The Small House of Uncle Thomas, Song of King, Shall We Dance, Finale.

A musical in two acts. The action takes place in and around the King's Palace in Bangkok, Siam, in the 1860's.

*Closed June 30, 1985 after 191 performances. Mr. Brynner received a Special "Tony" Award.

Henry Grossman Photos

Top Left: Mary Beth Peil, Yul Brynner

Yul Brynner
(Ernst Haas Photo)

Yvette Martin, Yul Brynner, Tracie Mon-Ting Lee
Top: Mary Beth Peil with royal wives and children

Yul Brynner, Mary Beth Peil

HARRIGAN 'N HART

Book, Michael Stewart; Music, Max Showalter; Lyrics, Peter Walker; Songs of the Period, Edward Harrigan, David Braham; Based on material compiled by Nedda Harrigan Logan and "The Merry Partners" by E. J. Kahn, Jr.; Director, Joe Layton; Choreography, D. J. Giagni; Scenery, David Mitchell; Costumes, Ann Hould-Ward; Lighting, Richard Nelson; Music Supervision, Orchestrations and Arrangements, John McKinney; Musical Director, Peter Howard; Sound, Otts Munderloh; Casting, Warren Pincus, Marjorie Martin; Presented by Elliot Martin, Arnold Bernhard, The Shubert Organization (Gerald Schoenfeld, Chairman; Bernard B. Jacobs, President); General Management, Joseph Harris, Peter T. Kulok, Steven E. Goldstein, Nancy Simmons; Company Manager, Mitzi Harder; Stage Managers, Mary Porter Hall, Marc Schlackman, Rita Calabro; Dance Captain, Michael Gorman; Assistant Manager, Russ Rosensweig; Technical Supervisor, Jeremiah J. Harris; Props, Paul Biega, Joseph Harris, Jr.; Wardrobe, Nancy Schaefer; Hairstylists, Jerry Masarone, Hector Garcia, Vincent Tucker; Associate Conductor, Michael Skloff; Production Assistant, Jeffrey Markowitz; Press, Fred Nathan, Bert Fink, Anne Abrams, Leslie Anderson, Ted Kilmer. Opened at the Longacre Theatre on Thursday, January 31, 1985.*

CAST

Stetson/Andrew LeCouvrier/Judge/	
Johnny Wild/Captain/William Gill	Mark Fotopoulos
Edward Harrigan	Harry Groener
Tony Hart	Mark Hamill
Archie White/Sam Nichols/Felix Barker/Uncle Albert	Clent Bowers
Old Colonel/Billy Gross/Nat Goodwin	Cleve Asbury
Colonel's Wife/Elsie Fay/Belle	Barbara Moroz
Eleanor/Ada Lewis	Roxie Lucas
Martin Hanley	Oliver Woodall
Alfrd J. Dugan/Harry Mack/Judge Hilton/Doctor	Christopher Wells
Annie Braham Harrigan	Tudi Roche
Chester Fox/Photographer/Newsboy	Kenston Ames
Lily Fay/Adelaide Harrigan/Nurse	Merilee Magnuson
Mrs. Annie Yeamons	Armelia McQueen
Jennie Yeamons/Newsgirl	Amelia Marshall
Gerta Granville	Christine Ebersole

STANDBYS & UNDERSTUDIES: Christopher Wells (Harrigan/Hart), Merilee Magnuson (Gerta), Barbara Moroz (Annie), Roxie Lucas (Mrs. Yeamons), Michael Gorman (Martin/Archie/Felix/Sam/Uncle Albert), Swings: Michael Gorman, Alison Mann

MUSICAL NUMBERS: Put Me in My Little Bed, Wonderful Me, Mulligan Guard, I Love to Follow a Band, Such an Education Has My Mary Ann, Maggie Murphy's Home, McNally's Row of Flats, Something New Something Different, That's My Partner, She's Our Gretel, What You Need Is a Woman, Knights of the Mystic Star, Skidmore Fancy Ball, Sweetest Love, The Old Barn Floor, Silly Boy, We'll Be There, Ada with the Golden Hair, That Old Featherbed, Sam Johnson's Colored Cakewalk, Dip Me in the Golden Sea, I've Come to Stay, If I Could Trust Me, I Need This One Chance

A musical in 2 acts and 16 scenes. The action takes place from 1871 to 1888.

*Closed Feb. 3, 1985 after 5 performances and 24 previews.

Martha Swope Photos

Harry Groener, Mark Hamill (also top right)
Below: Mark Hamill (center)

Harry Groener, Armelia McQueen
Above: Christine Ebersole, Mark Hamill

PACK OF LIES

By Hugh Whitemore; Director, Clifford Williams; Set and Costumes, Ralph Koltai; Lighting, Natasha Katz; Presented by Arthur Cantor and Bonnie Nelson Schwartz by arrangement with Michael Redington in association with Bernard Sandler and Eddie Kulukundis; Production Manager, Mitchell Erickson; Associate Producer, Harvey Elliott; General/Company Manager, Harvey Elliott; Wardrobe, Warren Morrill; Props, Val Medina; Production Assistant, Nancy Rosenberg; Stage Manager, John Handy; Press, Arthur Cantor Associates, Tom Siracusa. Opened Monday, February 11, 1985 at the Royale Theatre.*

CAST

Bob Jackson ....George N. Martin
Barbara Jackson ....Rosemary Harris
Julie Jackson ....Tracy Pollan
Helen Kroger ....Dana Ivey
Peter Kroger ....Colin Fox
Stewart ....Patrick McGoohan
Thelma ....Kaiulani Lee
Sally ....June Ballinger

STANDBYS & UNDERSTUDIES: Elizabeth Sheherd (Barbara), Richard Neilson (Bob/Stewart/Peter), June Ballinger (Helen/Thelma), Juli Cooper (Julie/Sally)

A drama in two acts. The action takes place in Ruislip, a London suburb, during the autumn and winter of 1960–1961. The main events of the story are true.

*Closed May 25, 1985 after 120 performances and 5 previews. Rosemary Harris received a Drama Desk Award for Outstanding Performance by an Actress.

Martha Swope Photos

Right: Rosemary Harris, Dana Ivey

Patrick McGoohan, George N. Martin, Tracy Pollan, Rosemary Harris Above: Colin Fox, Dana Ivey, Pollan, Martin, Harris

Patrick McGoohan, Rosemary Harris, George N. Martin

NIGHT OF 100 STARS II

Written and Produced by Hildy Parks; Director, Clark Jones; Presented by Alexander H. Cohen and Bentwood Television Productions (Bernard Gersten, President); Musical Direction, Elliot Lawrence; Staging, Albert Stephenson; Settings, Robert Randolph; Costumes, Alvin Colt; Lighting, Ralph Holmes; Co-Producer, Martha Mason; Production Supervisor, Robert L. Borod; Produced to benefit The Actors' Fund of America; Film Segments Created and Produced by John Springer; Television Segment: Special Music & Lyrics, Buz Kohan; Sport Segment Produced by Joe Goldstein, David Herscher; Dance and Vocal Arrangements, Glen Roven; Talent Consultant, Gus Schirmer; "A New Pair of Shoes" by John Kander, Fred Ebb; "This Is a Star" by Richard Mullins, Jim Morgan and Mary Jo Kaplan, adapted by Mr. Mullins from "Sing Your Praise to the Lord"; Additional Orchestrations, Michael Gibson, Tommy Newsom, Lanny Meyers, Torrie Zito; Hair Designs, Joe Tubens; Make-up, Joe Cranzano; Associate Director, Enid Roth; Assistant Choreographer, Ed Nolfi; Production Coordinator, Vern T. Calhoun; Film Segment Coordinator, Lori Golden; Production Supervisor, Susan Kerber; Production Associate, Gary Natoli; Assistant Production Manager, Glen Gardali; Stage Manager, James Woolley; Press, Merle Debuskey, Solters/Roskin/Friedman, Rebecca B. Robbins. Presented Sunday evening, February 17, 1985 and televised on Sunday, March 10, 1985.

PARTICIPATING ARTISTS

Ann-Margret, Hank Aaron, Edwin E. "Buzz" Aldrin, Muhammad Ali, Debbie Allen, Peter Allen, Harry Anderson, Eddie Arcaro, Lucie Arnaz, Ashford & Simpson, Ed Asner, Tracy Austin, Scott Baio, Lucille Ball, Dr. Christiaan Barnard, Doug Barr, Drew Barrymore, Hinton Battle, Anne Baxter, Warren Beatty, Geoffrey Beene, Shari Belafonte-Harper, Patty Berg, Valerie Bertinelli, Leonard Bernstein, David Birney, Meredith Baxter Birney, Jacqueline Bisset, Tempest Bledsoe, Bob & Ray, Lisa Bonet, Laura Branigan, David Brenner, Lloyd Bridges, Valerie Brisco-Hooks, Morgan Brittany, Charles Bronson, Pierce Brosnan, Georg Stanford Brown, Jim Brown, Yul Brynner, Don Budge, Gregg Burge, Carol Burnett, George Burns, Ellen Burstyn, Dick Button, Red Buttons, Sid Caesar, Michael Caine, Dr. Helen Caldicott, Zoe Caldwell, Cab Calloway, Dyan Cannon, Albert Capraro, Diahann Carroll, Lynda Carter, Nell Carter, Oleg Cassini, Marge Champion, Carol Channing, Cesar E. Chavez, Tiffany Chin, Dick Clark, Kenneth B. Clark, Petula Clark, Gary Coleman, Charles "Honi" Coles, Joan Collins, Don Correia, Howard Cosell, Candy Costie, Walter Cronkite, Cathy Lee Crosby, Glenn Cunningham, Tim Daggett, Tyne Daly, William Daniels, Tony Danza, Michael Davis, Olivia DeHavilland, Jacqueline de Ribes, Colleen Dewhurst, Angie Dickinson, Joe DiMaggio, Placido Domingo, Michael Douglas, Billie Dove, Richard Dreyfuss, Sandy Duncan, Nancy Dussault, David Emanuel, Elizabeth Emanuel, Georgia Engel, Linda Evans, Nanette Fabray, Fabrice, Morgan Fairchild, Cristina Ferrare, Bob Fitch, Peggy Fleming, Alan Flusser, Doug Flutie, John Forsythe, Bob Fosse, Michael J. Fox, Tony Franciosa, Bonnie Franklin, David Frost, Soleil Moon Frye, Vincent Gardenia, Teri Garr, Mark Gastineau, Gatlin Brothers, Mitch Gaylord, Ben Gazzara, Theodor S. Geisel, Marla Gibbs, Lillian Gish, Sharon Gless, Alexander Godunuv, Whoopi Goldberg, Martha Graham, Linda Gray, Joe Greene, Cynthia Gregory, Victor Griffin, Gene Hackman, Deidre Hall, Halston, Mark Hamill, Scott Hamilton, Marvin Hamlisch, Julie Harris, Gregory Harrison, Kitty Carlisle Hart, Lisa Hartman, Jim Hartung, David Hasselhoff, Goldie Hawn, Florence Henderson, Doug Henning, Jim Henson and the Muppets, Woody Herman, Carolina Herrera, Edward Herrmann, Gregory Hines, Maurice Hines, Dustin Hoffman, Geoffrey Holder, Jennifer Holliday, Lee Horsley, Lena Horne, Beth Howland, Rock Hudson, Daniel Hugh-Kelley, Jeremy Irons, Michael Ives, Kate Jackson, Malcolm Jamal Warner, Scott Johnson, Van Johnson, James Earl Jones, Leatrice Joy, Elaine Joyce, Danny Kaye, Billie Jean King, Perry King, Robert Klein, Mayor Edward I. Koch, Laura LaPlante, Lorenzo Lamas, Linda Lavin, Michele Lee, Janet Leigh, Gloria Loring, Ronn Lucas, Susan Lucci, Patti LuPone, Ali MacGraw, Bob Mackie, Gavin MacLeod, Manhattan Transfer, Dan Marino, Wynton Marsalis, Vera Maxwell, Willie Mays, Mary McFadden, McGuire Sisters, Rod McKuen, Julianne McNamara, Donna Mills, Tracy Mills, Yvette Mimieux, Dick Moore, Mary Tyler Moore, Melba Moore, Anne Murray, Stan Musial, Jim Nabors, Joe Namath, Bob Newhart, James Noble, Donald O'Connor, Jennifer O'Neill, Laurence Olivier, Jerry Orbach, Bobby Orr, Donny Osmond, Jack Palance, Jameson Parker, Bert Parks, Rosa Parks, Dr. Linus Pauling, The Parkettes, Pointer Sisters, Sidney Poitier, Jane Powell, Priscilla Presley, Robert Preston, Vincent Price, Juliet Prowse, Keshia Knight Pulliam, Charlotte Rae, Tony Randall, Lee Roy Reams, Christopher Reeve, Alfonso Ribeiro, Chita Rivera, Pernell Roberts, Tony Roberts, The Rockettes, Ginger Rogers, Kenny Rogers, Wilma Rudolph, Tracy Ruiz, Fernando Sanchez, Jane Seymour, Roby Gasser's Sea Lions, William Shatner, Brooke Shields, Dinah Shore, Cynthia Sikes, Neil Simon, Jaclyn Smith, Rex Smith, Jill St. John, Gloria Steinem, James Stewart, Dan Sullivan, Lynn Swann, Inga Swenson, Heather Thomas, Richard Thomas, Y. A. Tittle, Mel Torme, Daniel J. Travanti, Pauline Trigere, Lana Turner, Leslie Uggams, John Updike, Joan Van Ark, Dick Van Dyke, Gwen Verdon, Peter Vidmar, Michaele Vollbracht, Robert Wagner, Christopher Walken, Barbara Walters, Raquel Welch, Billy Dee Williams, Esther Williams, Treat Williams, Lee Wright, Henny Youngman, Stephanie Zimbalist, Claudia Cardinale, Kitty & Peter Carruthers, Dabney Coleman, Henry Steele Commager, Angel Cordero, Vic Damone, Matt Dillon, Al Jarreau, Patti LaBelle, Carl Lewis, Anita Morris, Al Unser, Robert Urich, Sarah Vaughan, Joe Williams, and Dancers: Tina Belis, Mamie Duncan, Lisa Guignard, Nancy Keller, Jane Lanier, Peggy Parten, David Askler, Paul Charles, Michael Dalton, Dennis Edenfield, Michael Ragan, Jeff Shade

James Stewart and Robert Wagner with Rockettes
Above: Geoffrey Holder, Burgess Meredith

STRANGE INTERLUDE

By Eugene O'Neill; Director, Keith Hack; Sets, Voytek with Michael Levine; Costumes, Deirdre Clancy; Lighting, Allen Lee Hughes; Music, Benedict Mason; Sound, Valerie Spradling; Casting, Hughes/Moss; Presented by Robert Michael Geisler, John Roberdeau, Douglas Urbanski, James M. Nederlander in association with Duncan C. Weldon with Paul Gregg, Lionel Becker and Jerome Minskoff; General Management, Kingwill & Goossen; Company Manager, Leonard Mulhern; Assistant, Paul Matwiow; Production Assistant, Richard Delehanty; Props, Val Medina; Wardrobe, Tina Ryan; Stage Managers, Jane E. Neufeld, William Hare; Press, Marilynn LeVine/P.R. Partners, Merle Frimark, Meg Gordean, Fran Colgan, Bruce Allardice. Opened at the Nederlander Theatre on Thursday, February 21, 1985.*

CAST

Mary, the maid	Jane Fleiss
Charles Marsden	Edward Petherbridge
Professor Henry Leeds	Tom Aldredge
Nina Leeds, his daughter	Glenda Jackson
Edmund Darrell	Brian Cox
Sam Evans	James Hazeldine
Mrs. Amos Evans, Sam's mother	Elizabeth Lawrence
Gordon, Nina's son	Patrick Wilcox
Madeline Arnold	Caitlin Clarke
Gordon Evans as a young man	Charley Lang

STANDBYS: Neil Vipond (Marsden/Prof. Leeds), Tim Choate (Gordon), Ken Ryan (Darrell), Jane Fleiss (Madeline), Jordan Marder (Young Gordon)

A drama in 9 acts performed with two intermissions. The action takes place from 1919 to 1921 in the Leeds home and the Evans home.

*Closed May 5, 1985 after a limited engagement of 63 performances and 7 previews.

Zoe Dominic, Peter Cunningham Photos

James Hazeldine, Glenda Jackson, Edward Petherbridge, Brian Cox
Top Left: Glenda Jackson

THE OCTETTE BRIDGE CLUB

By P. J. Barry; Director, Tom Moore; Scenery, John Lee Beatty; Costumes, Carrie Robbins; Lighting, Roger Morgan; Presented by Kenneth Waissman, Lou Kramer in association with M.T.M. Enterprises, Inc.; General Management, Theatre Now, Inc.; Casting, Johnson/Liff Associates; General Manager, Edward H. Davis; Company Manager, Hans Hortig; Props, Michael Fedigan; Sound, Bruce Cameron; Wardrobe, Peter J. FitzGerald; Hairstylists, Paul Huntley, Tiv Davenport, Ken Davis; Production Assistant, Allison Sommers; Stage Managers, Steve Beckler, Lynne Guerra; Press, Betty Lee Hunt, Maria Cristina Pucci, James Sapp. Opened at The Music Box on Tuesday, March 5, 1985.*

CAST

(in order of character's birth)

Martha (Mrs. Michael McDermitt) ....Anne Pitoniak
Mary (Margaret Donavan) ....Bette Henritze
Connie (Mrs. David Emerson) ....Nancy Marchand
Nora (Mrs. Lawrence Hiller) ....Elizabeth Franz
Alice (Mrs. Walter Monahan) ....Lois de Banzie
Ann (Mrs. John Conroy) ....Elizabeth Huddle
Lil (Mrs. Peter Carmody) ....Peggy Cass
Betsy (Mrs. Daniel Bailey) ....Gisela Caldwell
and
Robert Foster, a photographer ....Nicholas Kaledin

UNDERSTUDIES: Jen Jones (Connie/Lil/Martha/Mary), Ruth Livingston (Nora/Alice/Mary/Ann), William Fichtner (Foster)

A play in two acts. The action takes place in the living room of Ann (Mrs. John Conroy) in a Rhode Island town on a Friday night in late October of 1934, and on the night before Halloween in 1944.

*Closed March 23, 1985 after 24 performances and 9 previews.

Gerry Goodstein Photos

Right: Gisela Caldwell, Peggy Cass, Elizabeth Huddle, Nancy Marchand, Elizabeth Franz, Anne Pitoniak, Lois de Banzie, Bette Henritze Top: Henritze, Caldwell, de Banzie, Marchand, Cass, Franz, Pitoniak, Huddle

Gisela Caldwell, Elizabeth Franz, Bette Henritze, Nancy Marchand, Nicholas Kaledin, Elizabeth Huddle, Peggy Cass, Anne Pitoniak, Lois de Banzie

THE LOVES OF ANATOL

By Arthur Schnitzler; Adapted by Ellis Rabb and Nicholas Martin; Director, Ellis Rabb; Presented by Circle in the Square (Theodore Mann, Artistic Director; Paul Libin, Managing Director); Musical Staging, Donald Saddler; Scenery, Lawrence Miller; Costumes, Robert Morgan; Lighting, Richard Winkler, James Hilton; Music Design, Catherine MacDonald; Improvisation on Solo Piano, John Bayless; Hairstylist, Paul Huntley; Solo Vocalist, Patricia Brooks; Props, Frank Hauser; Wardrobe, Claire Libin; Casting, Hughes/Moss; Company Manager, William Conn; Stage Managers, Michael F. Ritchie, Ted William Sowa; Press, Merle Debuskey; William Schelble. Opened in the Circle in the Square Theatre on Wednesday, March 6, 1985.*

CAST

Max	Philip Bosco
Anatol	Stephen Collins
Cora	Mary-Joan Negro
Johann, Maitre D'	Louis Turenne
Annie	Valerie Mahaffey
Gabrielle	Michael Learned
Emilie	Mary-Joan Negro
Franz	Reed Jones
Ilona	Michael Learned
Bianca	Pamela Sousa
Baron Diebl	Kurt Johnson†
Annette	Valerie Mahaffey
Flieder	Daniel Southern
Dancing Lady in Black	Pamela Sousa
Young Gentleman Dancer	Reed Jones
Gentlemen	Louis Turenne, Kurt Johnson, Daniel Southern

UNDERSTUDIES: Kurt Johnson (Anatol), Louis Turenne (Max), Wendy Radford (Gabrielle/Ilona/Emilie/Bianca), Cora-Leah Doyle (Annie/Annette), Mark Fotopoulos (Franz/Flieder/Diebl/Johann)

A play in two acts. The action takes place before and after the turn of the century in Max's study in Vienna, in Anatol's memory, then twenty years later on the terrace of an inn some distance from Vienna.

*Closed April 14, 1985 after 46 performances and 15 previews.
†Succeeded by Mark Fotopoulos

Martha Swope Photos

Pamela Sousa, Valerie Mahaffey, Stephen Collins, Michael Learned, Mary-Joan Negro
Top Right: Philip Bosco, Stephen Collins, Michael Learned

29

REQUIEM FOR A HEAVYWEIGHT

By Rod Serling; Director, Arvin Brown; Presented by Zev Bufman, Ken Butler, Walter Barnett and Ivan Bloch; Scenery, Marjorie Bradley Kellogg; Costumes, Bill Walker; Lighting, Ron Wallace; Casting, Deborah Brown; General Management, Theatre Now, Inc.; Fight Direction, B. H. Barry; The Long Wharf Theatre production produced in association with Jujamcyn Theatres (Richard G. Wolff, President); Associate Producer, Jay M. Coggan; Company Manager, Rob Wallner; Production Supervisor, Jeremiah J. Harris; Props, Chet Perry II; Wardrobe, Sydney Smith; Stage Managers, James Harker, Tracy B. Cohen; Press, Susan L. Schulman, Ted Killmer. Opened Thursday, March 7, 1985 at the Martin Beck Theatre.*

CAST

Photographer/Packy the Counterman	John C. McGinley
Policeman/The Kid	Kevin Carrigan
Army Hakes	David Proval
Leo "The Lion Hearted" Loomis	Eugene Troobnick
Maish Resnick	George Segal
Harlan "Mountain" McClintock	John Lithgow
Max Greeny	Dominic Chianese
Doctor	Daniel F. Keyes
Perelli	Cosmo F. Allegretti
Golda	Joyce Ebert
Charlie	John C. Moskoff
Morrell	Mike Starr
Grace Miller	Maria Tucci
Fan	Kit Flanagan
Fighters	Ellis "Skeeter" Williams, Herbert Rubens, John Capodice

UNDERSTUDIES: Lanny Flaherty (Harlan), John C. Moskoff (Maish), Kit Flanagan (Grace/Golda), Ellis "Skeeter" Williams (Army), Herbert Rubens (Leo/Perelli/Max), Steven J. Parris (Doctor/Packy/Photographer/Fighters), John Capodice (Charlie), John C. McGinley (Morrell/The Kid)

A drama in 2 acts and 14 scenes. The action takes place during 1956 in New York City.

*Closed March 9, 1985 after 4 performances and 8 previews. John Lithgow received a Drama Desk Award for Outstanding Actor.

Ray Fisher Photos

Top: Maria Tucci, John Lithgow

George Segal, John Lithgow (also top)

JOE EGG

By Peter Nichols; Original title was "A Day in the Death of Joe Egg"; Director, Arvin Brown; The Roundabout Theatre production is presented by The Shubert Organization, Emanuel Azenberg, Roger Berlind, Ivan Bloch and MTM Enterprises; Scenery, Marjorie Bradley Kellogg; Costumes, Bill Walker; Lighting, Ronald Wallace; Casting, David Tochterman; General Managers, Richard Berg, Bruce Birkenhead; Company Manager, Max Allentuck; Props, Jan Marasek; Technical Supervisor, Theatrical Services; Wigs, Charles LoPresto; Wardrobe, Barbara Hladsky, Alan Collins, Miriam Nieves-Adger; Stage Managers, Franklin Keysar, Kathy J. Faul; Press, Bill Evans, Sandra Manley, Jim Baldassare, Leslie Anderson. Opened at the Longacre Theatre on Wednesday, March 27, 1985.*

CAST

Bri	Jim Dale
Sheila	Stockard Channing
Joe	Tenney Walsh
Pam	Joanna Gleason
Freddie	John Tillinger
Grace	Margaret Hilton

UNDERSTUDIES: Larry Pine (Bri/Freddie), Barbara eda-Young (Sheila/Pam), Karyn Lynn Dale (Joe), Paddy Croft (Grace)

A play in two acts. The action takes place on a winter evening during the late 1960's in the living room of Bri and Sheila's home.

*Closed June 22, 1985 after 101 performances and 7 previews. Prior to Broadway, this production played 53 performances in the Haft Theatre Off Broadway. It was the recipient of a 1985 "Tony" and Drama Desk Awards for Outstanding Revival. Stockard Channing received a "Tony" for Outstanding Actress in a Play. Original production opened Feb. 1, 1968 and played 154 performances at the Brooks Atkinson Theatre with Albert Finney and Zena Walker in the leads.

Martha Swope Photos

Stockard Channing, Jim Dale
Above: Jim Dale, Tenney Walsh

Joanna Gleason, John Tillinger
Top: Jim Dale

31

BILOXI BLUES

By Neil Simon; Director, Gene Saks; Presented by Emanuel Azenberg in association with Center Theatre Group/Ahmanson Theatre of Los Angeles; Setting, David Mitchell; Costumes, Ann Roth; Lighting, Tharon Musser; Sound, Tom Morse; Casting, Meg Simon/Fran Kumin; General Manager, Robert Kamlot; Technical Supervision, Arthur Siccardi, Pete Feller; Props, John Wright, Jan Marasek; Manager, Leslie Butler; Wardrobe, John Guiteras; Stage Managers, Charles Blackwell, Henry Velez, Joyce O'Brien; Press, Bill Evans, Sandra Manley, Jim Baldassare, Leslie Anderson. Opened at the Neil Simon Theatre on Thursday, March 28, 1985.*

CAST

Roy Selridge	Brian Tarantina
Joseph Wykowski	Matt Mulhern
Don Carney	Alan Ruck
Eugene Morris Jerome	Matthew Broderick†
Arnold Epstein	Barry Miller
Sgt. Merwin J. Toomey	Bill Sadler
James Hennesey	Geoffrey Sharp
Rowena	Randall Edwards
Daisy Hannigan	Penelope Ann Miller

STANDBYS: Geoffrey Sharp, Greg Germann (Eugene), Woody Harrelson (Selridge/Wykowski), Jim Fyfe (Carney/Hennesey), Greg Germann (Epstein), Jamey Sheridan (Sgt. Toomey), Joan Goodfellow (Rowena), Joyce O'Brien (Daisy)

A play in 2 acts and 14 scenes. The action takes place during 1943 in Biloxi and Gulfport, Mississippi.

*Still playing May 31, 1985. Recipient of 1985 "Tonys" for Best Play and Best Director. Barry Miller received Tony, Drama Desk, and Theatre World Awards.
†Played by Geoffrey Sharp during Mr. Broderick's absence.

Martha Swope Photos

Left: Bill Sadler, Matthew Broderick, Matt Mulhern, Barry Miller, Brian Tarantina, Geoffrey Sharp, Alan Ruck

Matthew Broderick, Brian Tarantina, Matt Mulhern, Alan Ruck, Barry Miller
Top Left: Broderick, Ruck, Geoffrey Sharp, Tarantina, Miller (top)

Barry Miller, Bill Sadler
Top: Matthew Broderick, Randall Edwards

Matthew Broderick, Penelope Ann Miller
Top: Bill Sadler, Matthew Broderick

LEADER OF THE PACK

Music and Lyrics by Ellie Greenwich & Friends; Liner Notes, Anne Beatts; Additional Material, Jack Heifner; Based on original concept by Melanie Mintz; Directed and Choreographed by Michael Peters; Presented by The Pack (Elizabeth I. McCann, Nelle Nugent, Francine LeFrak, Clive Davis, John Hart Associates, Rodger H. Hess, Richard Kagan); Settings, Tony Walton; Costumes, Robert de Mora; Lighting, Pamela Cooper; Musical Director-Adapter, Jimmy Vivino; Vocal Arrangements, Marc Shaiman; Dance Arrangements, Timothy Graphenreed; Sound Abe Jacob; Assistant to Mr. Peters, Geneva Burke; Hairstylists, Phyllis Della, Angeli Gari, Hector Garcia, Sonia Rivera; General Management, McCann & Nugent; Production Coordinator, Mary T. Nealon; Business Manager, Daniel Kearns; Company Manager, Susan Gustafson; Dance Captain, Keith McDaniel; Props, Timothy Abel; Wardrobe, Rosalie Lahm; Musical Coordinator, Mel Rodnon; Production Assistant, Gerald Taylor; Casting, Hughes/Moss; Production Associate, Alan Palmer; Stage Managers, William Dodds, Kenneth Hanson, Christopher Gregory; Press, Solters/Roskin/Friedman, Joshua Ellis, Cindy Valk, Adrian Bryan-Brown, Keith Sherman, Jackie Green. Opened at the Ambassador Theatre on Monday, April 8, 1985.*

CAST

Darlene Love	Darlene Love
Annie Golden	Annie Golden
Young Ellie Greenwich (1960's)	Dinah Manoff
Rosie, Ellie's mother	Zora Rasmussen
Shelley	Barbara Yeager
Mickey	Jasmine Guy
Jeff Barry	Patrick Cassidy
Gus Sharkey	Dennis Bailey
D. J. Voice	Peter Neptune
Waitress	Jasmine Guy
Lounge Singer	Pattie Darcy
Dance Couple	Shirley Black-Brown, Keith McDaniel
Gina	Gina Taylor
Ellie Greenwich (1980's)	Ellie Greenwich

GIRLS & GUYS: Shirley Black-Brown, Pattie Darcy, Christopher Gregory, Jasmine Guy, Danny Herman, Lon Hoyt, Keith McDaniel, Jodi Moccia, Peter Neptune, Zora Rasmussen, Joey Sheck, Gina Taylor, Barbara Yeager.

UNDERSTUDIES: Pattie Darcy (Young Ellie), Peter Neptune (Jeff), Zora Rasmussen (Ellie Greenwich), Joey Sheck (Gus), Jasmine Guy (Annie), Gina Taylor (Darlene), Swings: Lisa Grant, Kevyn Morrow

MUSICAL NUMBERS: Be My Baby, Wait Till My Bobby Gets Home, A . . . My Name Is Ellie, Jivette Boogie Beat, Why Do Lovers Break Each Others Hearts, Today I Met the Boy I'm Gonna Marry, I Want to Love Him So Bad, Do Wah Diddy, And Then He Kissed Me, Hanky Panky, Not Too Young to Get Married, Chapel of Love, Baby I Love You, Leader of the Pack, Look of Love, Christmas Baby Please Come Home, I Can Hear Music, Rock of Rages, Keep It Confidential, Da Doo Ron Ron, What a Guy, Maybe I Know, River Deep Mountain High, We're Gonna Make It after All

A musical performed without intermission. The action takes place here and now. . . . and in the days of beehives and 45's.

*Closed July 21, 1985 after 120 performances and 52 previews. Original cast album available on Elektra Music Records.

Martha Swope Photos

Jasmine Guy, Dinah Manoff, Pattie Darcy
Top Right: Dinah Manoff, Patrick Cassidy

Darlene Love
Above: Ellie Greenwich

TAKE ME ALONG

Music and Lyrics, Bob Merrill; Book, Joseph Stein, Robert Russell; Based on play "Ah, Wilderness!" by Eugene O'Neill; Director, Thomas Gruenewald; Musical Direction, Lynn Crigler; Choreography and Musical Staging, Dan Siretta; The Goodspeed Opera House Production presented by the John F. Kennedy Center for the Performing Arts; Scenery, James Leonard Joy; Lighting, Craig Miller; Costumes, David Toser; Orchestrations, Philip J. Lang; Dance Arrangements, Allen Cohen; Additional Orchestrations, Lynn Crigler, Allen Cohen; Casting, Warren Pincus; Associate Conductor, Patrick Vacciarello; Sound, Jan Nebozenko; Hairstylist, Stephen LoVullo; General Management, Alan C. Wasser; Props, Larry Palazzo; Wardrobe, Sherri Barron; Stage Managers, John J. Bonanni, Bryan Harris, Andy Hostettler; Press, David Powers. Opened at the Martin Beck Theatre on Sunday, April 14, 1985.*

CAST

Nat Miller (Editor of the Globe)	Robert Nichols
Essie Miller (His wife)	Betty Johnson
Arthur Miller (Older son)	Stephen McDonough
Mildred Miller (His daughter)	Alyson Kirk
Lily Miller (Nat's sister)	Beth Fowler
Muriel Macomber (David's daughter)	Taryn Grimes
Richard Miller (Younger son)	Gary Landon Wright
David Macomber (store owner)	Richard Korthaze
Sid Davis (Essie's brother)	Kurt Knudson
Belle (artiste for hire)	Nikki Sahagen
Wint (Arthur's friend)	Joel Whittaker
Bartender	David Vosburgh
Salesman	John Witham

TOWNSFOLK: Kathy Andrini, Blake Atherton, Michael Kelly Boone, Ed Brazo, Richard Dodd, Andy Hostettler, Richard Korthaze, Patrick S. Murphy, Mercedes Perez, Keith Savage, David Vosburgh, Joel Whittaker, Betty Winsett, John Witham

UNDERSTUDIES: David Vosburgh (Nat), Betty Winsett (Essie/Lily), Joel Whittaker (Arthur), Kathy Andrini (Mildred/Muriel), Michael Kelly Boone (Richard/Wint), Patrick S. Murphy (Richard), Keith Savage (David/Bartender/Salesman), John Witham (Sid), Mercedes Perez (Belle), Swings: Kimberly Campbell, Erik Geier

MUSICAL NUMBERS: Marvelous Fire Machine, Oh Please, I Would Die, Sid Ole Kid, Staying Young, I Get Embarrassed, We're Home, Take Me Along, The Only Pair I've Got, In the Company of Men, Knights on White Horses, That's How It Starts, If Jesus Don't Love Ya, Promise Me a Rose, Green Snake, Nine O'Clock, But Yours, Finale.

A musical in 2 acts and 15 scenes. The action takes place in 1906 in Centerville, Connecticut.

*Closed April 14, 1985 after 1 performance and 7 previews. Original production opened Oct. 22, 1959 in the Shubert Theatre and ran for 448 performances. Among the cast were Jackie Gleason, Walter Pidgeon, Eileen Herlie, Una Merkel and Robert Morse.

Wilson H. Brownell Photos

Robert Nichols, Betty Johnson
Top Right: Kurt Knudson, Beth Fowler

Kurt Knudson, Robert Nichols
Above: Gary Landon Wright, Taryn Grimes

GRIND

Music by Larry Grossman; Lyrics, Ellen Fitzhugh; Book, Fay Kanin; Director, Harold Prince; Choreographer, Lester Wilson; Presented by Kenneth D. Greenblatt, John J. Pomerantz, Mary Lea Johnson, Martin Richards, James M. Nederlander, Harold Prince, Michael Frazier in association with Susan Madden Samson and Jonathan Farkas; Scenery, Clarke Dunham; Costumes, Florence Klotz; Lighting, Ken Billington; Musical Director, Paul Gemignani; Orchestration, Bill Byers; Dance Music Arrangements, Tom Fay; Executive Producers, Ruth Mitchell, Sam Crothers; Assistant Choreographer, Larry Vickers; Hair and Make-up, Richard Allen; Sound, Otts Munderloh; General Manager, Theatre Now, Ralph Roseman; Company Manager, Sally Campbell; Dance Captain, Dwight Baxter; Assistant Conductor, Tom Fay; Props, George Green, Abe Einhorn; Wardrobe, Stephanie Edwards, Bud Coleman; Hairstylist, Charles LoPresto; Stage Managers, Beverley Randolph, Richard Evans, William Kirk; Press, Mary Bryant, Becky Flora, Glen Gary. Opened in the Mark Hellinger Theatre on Tuesday, April 16, 1985.*

CAST

Leroy	Ben Vereen†
Harry	Lee Wallace
Gus	Stubby Kaye
Solly	Joey Faye
Vernelle	Marion Ramsey
Ruby	Hope Clarke
Fleta	Valarie Pettiford
Kitty	Candy Brown
Linette	Wynonna Smith
Maybelle	Carol Woods
Romaine	Sharon Murray
Satin	Leilani Jones
Louis, the stage manager	Brian McKay
Mike, the doorman	Oscar Stokes
Stooge	Leonard John Crofoot
Doyle	Timothy Nolen
Grover	Donald Acree
Mrs. Faye	Ruth Brisbane

KNOCKABOUTS, BUMS, TOUGHS: Leonard John Crofoot, Ray Roderick, Kelly Walters, Steve Owsley, Malcolm Perry
STANDBYS & UNDERSTUDIES: Candy Brown (Satin), Obba Babatunde (Leroy), Brian McKay (Doyle/Doorman), Joey Faye (Gus), Oscar Stokes (Harry/Solly), Dana Lorge (Romaine), Gayle Samuels (Ruby/Kitty/Vernelle/Fleta/Linette), Ruth Brisbane (Maybelle), Carol Woods (Mrs. Faye), Raymond Rickman (Grover), David Reitman (Stage Manager/Swing)

MUSICAL NUMBERS: This Must Be the Place, Cadava, A Sweet Thing Like Me, I Get Myself Out, My Daddy Always Taught Me to Share, All Things to One Man, The Line, Katie My Love, The Grind, Yes Ma'am, Why Mama Why, This Crazy Place, From the Ankles Down, Who Is He?, Never Put It in Writing, I Talk You Talk, Timing, These Eyes of Mine, New Man, Down, A Century of Progress, Finale

A musical in two acts. The action takes place in and around Harry Earle's Burlesque Theatre in Chicago, Illinois, during 1933.

*Closed June 22, 1985 after 79 performances and 25 previews. Leilani Jones received "Tony", Drama Desk, and Theatre World Awards for her performance.
†Succeeded by Obba Babatunde

Martha Swope Photos

Stubby Kaye, Timothy Nolen, Leilani Jones
Above: Timothy Nolen, Leilani Jones, Ben Vereen

Leilani Jones
Top Left: Opening number
Ben Vereen (center)

AREN'T WE ALL?

By Frederick Lonsdale; Director, Clifford Williams; Presented by Douglas Urbanski, Karl Allison, Bryan Bantry, James M. Nederlander in association with Duncan C. Weldon with Paul Gregg, Lionel Becker and Jerome Minskoff; Sets, Finaly James; Costumes, Judith Bland; Lighting, Natasha Katz; Sound, Jan Nebozenko; Casting, Hughes/Moss; General Management, Jay Kingwill, Larry Goossen; Associate Producers, Robert Michael Geisler, John Roberdeau; Assistant Company Manager, Susan Sampliner; Production Assistant, Lisa Contadino; Props, Liam Herbert; Wardrobe, James M. Kabel; Hairstylist, David H. Lawrence; Wigs, Paul Huntley; Original Music, David Filman; Stage Managers, Warren Crane, William Weaver, David Silber; Press, Solters/Roskin/Friedman, Joshua Ellis, Cindy Valk, Adrian Bryan-Brown, Keith Sherman. Opened at the Brooks Atkinson Theatre on Monday, April 29, 1985.*

CAST

Morton	Peter Pagan
Hon. William Tatham	Jeremy Brett
Lady Frinton	Claudette Colbert
Arthur Wells	Steven Sutherland
Martin Steele	John Patrick Hurley
Kitty Lake	Leslie O'Hara
Lord Grenham	Rex Harrison
Hon. Mrs. William Tatham	Lynn Redgrave
Roberts	George Ede
Angela Lynton	Brenda Forbes
Rev. Ernest Lynton	George Rose
John Willocks	Ned Schmidtke

STANDBYS & UNDERSTUDIES: Peter Pagan (Lord Grenham), Sybil Lines (Mrs. Tatham/Kitty), George Ede (Rev. Lynton), John Patrick Hurley (Willocks), Steven Sutherland (Tatham), David Silber (Morton/Roberts/Arthur/Martin), Betty Low (Lady Frinton/Mrs. Lynton)

A comedy in 2 acts and 4 scenes. The action takes place in William Tatham's house in Mayfair, and in Grenham Court sometime in the past.

*Closed July 21, 1985 after 96 performances and 16 previews. Rex Harrison and Claudette Colbert received a Special Drama Desk Award "for the continuing pleasure of their company." The original New York production opened at the Gaiety Theatre May 21, 1923 and played 284 performances. The cast included Leslie Howard, Mabel Terry-Lewis, Cyril Maude and Alma Tell.

Left: (front) Rex Harrison, Claudette Colbert,
(back) Jeremy Brett, Lynn Redgrave, George Rose
Martha Swope, Zoe Dominic Photos

Brenda Forbes, George Rose

Rex Harrison, Claudette Colbert

BIG RIVER

Music & Lyrics, Roger Miller; Book, William Hauptman; Adapted from the novel "The Adventures of Huckleberry Finn" by Mark Twain; Staged by Des McAnuff; Presented by Rocco Landesman, Heidi Landesman, Rick Steiner, M. Anthony Fisher and Dodger Productions; Scenery, Heidi Landesman; Costumes, Patricia McGourty; Lighting, Richard Riddell; Sound, Otts Munderloh; Musical Supervision, Danny Troob; Orchestrations, Steven Margoshes & Danny Troob; Dance & Incidental Music, John Richard Lewis; Musical Direction & Vocal Arrangements, Linda Twine; Choreography, Janet Watson; Stage Movement & Fights, B. H. Barry; Casting, Stanley Sable, Jason LaPadura; General Management, David Strong Warner Inc.; Associate Scenic Designer, Robert Shaw; Sound Effects, John Kilgore; Hairstylist, Angela Gari; Associate Producers, Arthur Katz, Emily Landau, Fred Mayerson, TM Productions; Company Manager, Sandra Carlson; Assistant Conductor, Kenneth Kosek; Makeup, Ann Belsky; Props, Andrew Acabbo, Nicholas Laudano; Wardrobe, Joseph Busheme; Production Assistant, Chris Fielder; Associate Scenic Designer, Bob Shaw; Stage Managers, Frank Hartenstein, Steven Adler, Marianne Cane; Press, Solters/Rosklin/Friedman, Joshua Ellis, Keith Sherman, Adrian Bryan-Brown, Cindy Valk. Opened at the Eugene O'Neill Theatre on Thursday, April 25, 1985.*

CAST

Mark Twain	Gordon Connell
Huckleberry Finn	Daniel H. Jenkins
Widow Douglas/Sally Phelps	Susan Browning
Miss Watson/Harmonia Player	Evalyn Baron
Jim	Ron Richardson
Tom Sawyer	John Short
Ben Rogers/Hank/Young Fool	William Youmans
Jo Harper/Joanna Wilkes	Andi Henig
Simon	Aramis Estevez
Dick/Andy/Man in crowd/Hiredhand	Michael Brian
Pap Finn/Sheriff Bell	John Goodman
Judge Thatcher/Harvey Wilkes/Silas Phelps	Ralph Byers
The King	Bob Gunton
The Duke	Rene Auberjonois
Lafe/Counselor Robinson/Hired Hand	Reathel Bean
Mary Jane Wilkes	Patti Cohenour
Susan Wilkes	Peggy Harmon
Bill, a servant	Franz Jones
Alice, a slave	Carol Dennis
Alice's daughter	Jennifer Leigh Warren

UNDERSTUDIES: Peggy Harmon (Ensemble), Elmore James (Jim), George Merritt (Ensemble), Andrew Hill Newman (Huck/Ensemble)

MUSICAL NUMBERS: Do You Want to Go to Heaven?, The Boys, Waiting for the Light to Shine, Guv'ment, Hand for the Hog, I Huckleberry Me, Muddy Water, Crossing Over, River in the Rain, When the Sun Goes Down in the South, The Royal Nonesuch, Worlds Apart, Arkansas, How Blest We Are, You Ought to Be Here with Me, Leaving's Not the Only Way to Go, Free at Last

A musical in two acts. The action takes place along the Mississippi River Valley, sometime in the 1840's.

*Still playing May 31, 1985. "Tony" Awards were given for Best Musical, Book, Score, Director, Scenic Design, Lighting Design, and Featured Actor (Ron Richardson). Patti Cohenour received a Theatre World Award for her Broadway debut. Drama Desk Awards were given to Ron Richardson, Rene Auberjonois as Outstanding Actor and Featured Actor respectively, Scenery, Lighting, and to Steven Margoshes and Danny Troob for Orchestrations, Roger Miller for Score and Lyrics.

Top Left: entire cast
Below: Evalyn Baron, Daniel Jenkins,
Ron Richardson, Susan Browning
Martha Swope Photos

Bob Gunton, Daniel H. Jenkins, Rene Auberjonois

Ron Richardson, Daniel H. Jenkins, Patti Cohenour
Top: Bob Gunton, Rene Auberjonois

Daniel H. Jenkins, John Short
Top: Ron Richardson, Daniel H. Jenkins

AS IS

By William M. Hoffman; Director, Marshall W. Mason; Presented by John Glines/ Lawrence Lane, Lucille Lortel, The Shubert Organization (Gerald Schoenfeld, Chairman; Bernard B. Jacobs, President); Setting, David Potts; Lighting, Dennis Parichy; Costumes, Michael Warren Powell; Sound, Chuck London Media/Stewart Werner; Associate Producer, Paul A. Kaplan; A Circle Repertory Company and The Glines Production; General Manager, Albert Poland; Company Manager, Claire Abel; Wardrobe, Joan E. Weiss; Hairstylist, Patrik D. Moreton; Casting, Eve Battaglia; Stage Manager, Denise Yaney; Press, Betty Lee Hunt/Maria Cristina Pucci. Opened at the Lyceum Theatre on Wednesday, May 1, 1985.*

CAST

Hospice Worker	Claris Erickson
Rich	Jonathan Hogan
Saul	Jonathan Hadary
Chet	Steven Gregan
Lily	Lily Knight
Business Partner	Claris Erickson
Brother	Ken Kliban
Clones	Mark Myers, Lou Liberatore
Pat	Lou Liberatore
Barney	Ken Kliban
Nurse	Claris Erickson
Orderly	Lou Liberatore

STANDBYS: Patricia Fletcher (Hospice Worker/Lily/Nurse), Reed Jones (Saul/ Chet), Bruce McCarty (Rich/Brother/Barney/Pat/Orderly)

A drama performed without intermission. The action takes place at the present time in New York City.

*Still playing May 31, 1985. This production was moved from the Circle Repertory Theatre where it opened on March 10, 1985 and played for 62 performances. It received a Drama Desk Award as Outstanding Play of the season.

Lou Liberatore, Jonathan Hogan, Lily Knight, Ken Kliban, Mark Myers
Top Right: Jonathan Hogan, Jonathan Hadary, Lily Knight

DOUBLES

By David Wiltse; Director, Morton Da Costa; Presented by Multi Production Partnership, Richard Horner, Lynne Stuart, Hinks Shimberg, Gold 'n Gay Productions; Set and Costumes, Robert Fletcher; Lighting, Craig Miller; Sound, Robert Kerzman; Produced in association with Jujamcyn Theaters-Richard G. Wolff; General Management, Richard Horner Associates; Production Assistant, Scott Perrin; Wardrobe, Arlene Konowitz; Stage Managers, Elliott Woodruff, Amy L. Richards; Press, Richard P. Pheneger. Opened at the Ritz Theatre on Wednesday, May 8, 1985.*

CAST

Guy .... John Cullum †1
Lennie .... Ron Leibman †2
Arnie .... Austin Pendleton †3
George .... Tony Roberts †4
Heather .... Kate Collins
Chuck .... Nicholas Wyman
Tennis Players .... Sarah Daly, Peter Flint

UNDERSTUDIES: Peter Flint (Guy/Chuck), David Rogers (Lennie/Arnie/George), Sarah Daly (Heather)

A comedy in two acts. The action takes place at the present time in the men's locker room of the Norwalk, Connecticut, Racquet Club.

*Still playing May 31, 1985.
†Succeeded by: 1. Keir Dullea, 2. Cliff Gorman, 3. Charles Repole, 4. Robert Reed

James J. Kriegsmann Photos

**John Cullum, Ron Leibman,
Austin Pendleton, Tony Roberts**

Charles Repole, Cliff Gorman, Kate Collins, Keir Dullea, Robert Reed

41

ARMS AND THE MAN

By George Bernard Shaw; Director, John Malkovich; Presented by Circle in the Square (Theodore Mann, Artistic Director; Paul Libin, Managing Director); Scenery, Thomas Lynch; Costumes, Ann Roth; Lighting, Richard Nelson; Hairstylist, Paul Huntley; Music, Louis Rosen; Company Manager, William Conn; Casting, Hughes/Moss; Props, Frank Hauser; Wardrobe, Claire Libin; Stage Managers, Michael F. Ritchie, Ted William Sowa; Press, Merle Debuskey, William Schelble. Opened in the Circle in the Square Theatre on Thursday, May 30, 1985.*

CAST

Catherine Petkoff	Dimitra Arliss
Raina Petkoff	Glenne Headly
Captain Bluntschli	Kevin Kline†
Louka	Caitlin Clarke
Russian Officer	Guy Paul
Nicola	George Morfogen
Major Paul Petkoff	Louis Zorich
Major Sergius Saranoff	Raul Julia

UNDERSTUDIES: Guy Paul (Capt. Bluntschli/Major Saranoff), Debra Engle (Raina/Louka), Joanne Dorian (Catherine), Tom Brennan (Nicola/Major Petkoff)

A comedy in three acts. The action takes place in a lady's bedchamber in a small town in Bulgaria near the Dragoman Pass in late November of 1885, and in Major Petkoff's garden and library in March of 1886.

†Succeeded by John Malkovich.

John Malkovich

Caitlin Clarke, George Morfogen Top Left: Glenne Headly, Raul Julia, Dimitra Arliss, Kevin Kline, Louis Zorich *(Martha Swope Photos)*

BROADWAY PRODUCTIONS FROM PAST SEASONS
THAT PLAYED THROUGH THIS SEASON

A CHORUS LINE

Conceived, Choreographed and Directed by Michael Bennett; Book, James Kirkwood, Nicholas Dante; Music, Marvin Hamlisch; Lyrics, Edward Kleban; A New York Shakespeare Festival Production presented by Joseph Papp in association with Plum Productions; Co-Choreographer, Bob Avian; Musical Direction/Vocal Arrangements, Don Pippin; Associate Producer, Bernard Gersten; Set, Robin Wagner; Costumes, Theoni V. Aldredge; Lighting, Tharon Musser; Sound, Abe Jacobs; Music Coordinator, Robert Thomas; Orchestrations, Bill Byers, Hershy Kay, Jonathan Tunick; Assistant to Choreographers, Baayork Lee; Musical Director, Robert Rogers; Wardrobe, Alyce Gilbert; Production Supervisor, Jason Steven Cohen; Original Cast Album by Columbia Records; General Managers, Robert Kamlot, Laurel Ann Wilson; Company Manager, Bob MacDonald; Stage Managers, Tom Porter, Wendy Mansfield, Morris Freed, Bradley Jones, Ronald Stafford; Press, Merle Debuskey, William Schelble, Richard Kornberg. Opened at the Shubert Theatre on Friday, July 25, 1975.*

CAST

Roy	Evan Pappas
Kristine	Christine Barker†1
Sheila	Kathryn Ann Wright†2
Mike	Don Correia†3
Val	Mitzi Hamilton
Butch	Roscoe Gilliam
Larry	J. Richard Hart†4
Maggie	Pam Klinger†5
Richie	Reggie Phoenix†6
Tricia	Robin Lyon
Tom	Frank Kliegel
Zach	Eivind Harum
Mark	Chris Marshall
Cassie	Wanda Richert
Judy	Melissa Randel
Lois	Laurie Gamache
Don	Michael Danek
Bebe	Pamela Ann Wilson
Connie	Sachi Shimizu
Diana	Loida Santos
Al	Buddy Balou'
Frank	Fraser Ellis
Greg	Justin Ross†7
Bobby	Matt West†8
Paul	Sammy Williams†9
Vicki	Ann Louise Schaut†10
Ed	Morris Freed
Jarad	Troy Garza
Linda	Catherine Cooper†11
Douglas (formerly Sam)	Sam Piperato†12
Ralph	Bradley Jones
Hilary	Roxann Cabalero†13

UNDERSTUDIES: Roxann Cabalero (Diana/Maggie/Connie/Bebe), Michael Danek (Zach), Fraser Ellis (Mark/Bobby/Don), Cynthia Fleming (Cassie/Sheila/Kristine/Judy), Morris Freed (Mark), Laurie Gamache (Kristine/Bebe/Judy/Cassie), Troy Garza (Mike/Greg/Paul/Larry), J. Richard Hart (Zach), Bradley Jones (Bobby/Greg), Frank Kliegel (Don/Zach/Bobby), Jim Litten (Mike), Robin Lyon (Bebe/Diana/Val/Maggie), Evan Pappas (Mark/Al/Paul/Larry), Laureen Valuch Piper (Sheila/Val), Tommy Re (Greg/Al/Larry/Mike), Pamela Ann Wilson (Val/Judy)
MUSICAL NUMBERS: I Hope I Get It, I Can Do That, and. . ., At the Ballet, Sing!, Hello 12 Hello 13 Hello Love, Nothing, Dance 10 Looks 3, Music and the Mirror, One, Tap Combination, What I Did for Love, Finale

A musical performed without intermission. The action takes place in 1975 during an audition in the theatre.

*Still playing May 31, 1985. Cited as Best Musical by NY Drama Critics Circle, winner of 1976 Pulitzer Prize, 1976 "Tonys" for Best Musical, Best Book, Best Score, Best Direction, Best Lighting, Best Choreography, Best Musical Actress (Donna McKechnie), Best Featured Actor and Actress in a Musical (Sammy Williams, Kelly Bishop), and a Special Theatre World Award was presented to each member of the creative staff and original cast. SEE THEATRE WORLD, Vol. 31. On Thursday, Sept. 29, 1983 it became the longest running show in Broadway history.
†Succeeded by: 1. Kerry Casserly, 2. Susan Danielle, 3. J. Richard Hart, 4. Jim Litten, 5. Ann Heinricher, Pam Klinger, 6. Eugene Fleming, Gordon Owens, 7. Danny Weathers, 8. Ron Kurowski, 9. Wayne Meledandri, 10. Cynthia Fleming, 11. Laureen Valuch Piper, 12. Tommy Re, 13. Cynthia Onrubia, Roxann Cabalero

Michael Danek, Susan Danielle, Eivind Harum, Wanda Richert (also above), Ron Kurowski

Martha Swope Photos

43

BRIGHTON BEACH MEMOIRS

By Neil Simon; Director, Gene Saks; Presented by Emanuel Azenberg, Wayne M. Rogers, Radio City Music Hall Productions in association with Center Theatre Group/Ahmanson Theatre; Set, David Mitchell; Costumes, Patricia Zipprodt; Lighting, Tharon Musser; Casting, Marilyn Szatmary, Jane E. Cooper, Hank McCann; Technical Supervisors, Arthur Siccardi, Pete Feller; Props, Jan Marasek, Arthur Hoaglund; Wardrobe, Nancy Schaefer, Mary Eno; Assistant to Producers, Leslie Butler; Assistant to Director, Jane E. Cooper; General Managers, Jose Vega, Robert Kamlot; Company Managers, Maria Anderson, Jane Robinson, Bruce Birkenhead; Stage Managers, Martin Herzer, Barbara-Mae Phillips, Lani Ball; Press, Bill Evans, Sandra Manley. Opened in the Alvin Theatre (re-named Neil Simon Theatre) on Sunday, March 27, 1983.*

CAST

Eugene	Matthew Broderick†1
Blanche	Joyce Van Patten†2
Kate	Elizabeth Franz†3
Laurie	Mandy Ingber†4
Nora	Jodi Thelen†5
Stanley	Zeljko Ivanek†6
Jack	Peter Michael Goetz†7

STANDBYS: Donna Haley (Blanche/Kate), Louise Roberts (Nora), Sarah Rose (Laurie), Robert Levine (Jack), Peter Birkenhead (Stanley), Marc Riffon (Eugene) A comedy in two acts. The action takes place during September 1937 in the home of Jack and Kate Jerome in Brighton Beach, Brooklyn, N.Y.

*Still playing May 31, 1985. Selected by NY Drama Critics Circle as Best Play of the season. Mr. Broderick received a "Tony" Award as Best Supporting Actor in a Play, and a Theatre World Award for his Broadway debut. Mr. Saks received a "Tony" for Best Director of a Play. For original production, see THEATRE WORLD, Vol. 39.
†Succeeded by: 1. Doug McKeon, Fisher Stevens, Roger Raines, Jon Cryer, Matthew Broderick, Nicholas Strouse, Jonathan Silverman, 2. Kathleen Widdoes, Anita Gillette, Verna Bloom, 3. Marilyn Chris, Barbara Tarbuck, Dorothy Holland, 4. Theresa Diane, Elizabeth Ward, Royana Black, Olivia Laurel Mates, Jennifer Blanc, 5. Marissa Chibas, Wendy Gazelle, 6. J. Patrick Breen, Mark Nelson, 7, Dick Latessa

Right: Nicholas Strouse, Jonathan Silverman
Top: Roger Raines, Jon Cryer

Marilyn Chris, Marissa Chibas, Fisher Stevens, Royana Black, J. Patrick Breen, Kathleen Widdoes, Peter Michael Goetz
Martha Swope Photo

CATS

Based on "Old Possum's Book of Practical Cats" by T. S. Eliot; Additional Lyrics, Trevor Nunn, Richard Stilgoe; Music, Andrew Lloyd Webber; Director, Trevor Nunn; Associate Director/Choreographer, Gillian Lynne; Presented by Cameron Mackintosh, The Really Useful Company, David Geffen, The Shubert Organization; Executive Producers, R. Tyler Gatchell, Jr., Peter Neufeld; Design, John Napier; Lighting, David Hersey; Sound, Martin Levan; Musical Director, Rene Wiegert; Production Musical Director, Stanley Lebowsky; Casting, Johnson Liff; Orchestrations, David Cullen, Andrew Lloyd Webber; Original Cast Album on Geffen Records; Company Manager, James G. Mennen; General Management, Gatchell & Neufeld; Associate Musical Directors, Keith Herrmann, Kevin Farrell; Production Assistant, Nancy Hall Bell; Wardrobe, Adelaide Laurino; Makeup, Candace Carell; Hairstylists, Leon Gagliardi, Ann Miles, Charles McMahon, Richard Orton, Fred Patton, Thelma Pollard, Frank Paul; Assistant Choreographer, Jo-Anne Robinson; Stage Managers, David Taylor, Lani Sundsten, Sally J. Greenhut, Jeff Lee, Donald Walters, Sherry Cohen; Technical Supervisors, Theatre Services, Inc.; Wigs, Paul Huntley; Production Dance Supervisor, T. Michael Reed; Props, George Green, Jr., Merlyn Davis, George Green III; Company Manager, James G. Mennen; Press, Fred Nathan, Eileen McMahon, Anne S. Abrams, Leslie Anderson, Ted Killmer, Bert Fink. Opened in the Winter Garden Theatre on Thursday, October 7, 1982.*

CAST

Alonzo	Hector Jaime Mercado[1]
Bustopher Jones/Asparagus/Growltiger	Steven Hanan[2]
Bombalurina	Donna King[3]
Carbucketty	Stephen Gelfer
Cassandra	Rene Ceballos[4]
Coricopat/Mungojerrie	Rene Clemente[5]
Demeter	Wendy Edmead[6]
Etcetera/Rumpleteazer	Christine Langner[7]
Grizabella	Betty Buckley[8]
Jellylorum/Griddlebone	Bonnie Simmons
Jennyanydots	Anna McNeely
Mistoffolees	Timothy Scott[9]
Munkustrap	Harry Groener[10]
Old Deuteronomy	Ken Page[11]
Plato/Macavity/Rumpus Cat	Kenneth Ard[12]
Pouncival	Herman W. Sebek[13]
Rum Tum Tugger	Terrence V. Mann[14]
Sillabub	Whitney Kershaw[15]
Skimbleshanks	Reed Jones[16]
Tantomile	Janet L. Hubert[17]
Tumblebrutus	Robert Hoshour[18]
Victoria	Cynthia Onrubia[19]
Cats Chorus	Susan Powers, Joel Robertson, Walter Charles [20], Carol Richards [21]

STANDBYS & UNDERSTUDIES: Scott Wise, Rene Clemente, Mark Frawley, Jack Magradey (Alonzo), Steven Gelfer, Joel Robertson (Bustopher/Asparagus/Growltiger), Nora Brennan, Deborah Henry (Bombalurina), Scott Wise, Steven Hack, Jack Magradey (Carbucketty), Nora Brennan, Deborah Henry, Lily-Lee Wong (Cassandra), Rene Clemente, Mark Frawley, Steven Hack, Jack Magradey (Coricopat/Mungojerrie), Denise DiRenzo, Deborah Henry (Demeter), Jane Bodle, Denise DiRenzo, Dodie Pettit, Lily-Lee Wong (Etcetera/Rumpleteazer), Denise DiRenzo, Deborah Henry, Janene Lovullo (Grizabella), Dodie Pettit, Susan Powers (Jellylorum/Griddlebone), Jane Bodle, Dodie Pettit, Susan Powers (Jennyanydots), Joe Anthony Cavise, Rene Clemente, Michael Scott Gregory (Mistoffolees), Robert Hoshour, Jack Magradey, Brian Sutherland (Munkustrap), Erick Devine (Old Deuteronomy), Scott Wise, Brian Sutherland (Plato/Macavity/Rumpus Cat), Brian Andrews, Steven Hack (Pouncival), Mark Frawley, Jack Magradey, Claude R. Tessier (Rum Tum Tugger), Jane Bodle, Dodie Pettit (Sillabub), Mark Frawley, Jack Magradey (Skimbleshanks), Jane Bodle, Denise DiRenzo, Nora Brennan, Lily-Lee Wong (Tantomile), Brian Andrews, Steven Hack, Scott Wise (Tumblebrutus), Paige Dana, Sundy Leight Leake, Dodie Pettit, Lily-Lee Wong (Victoria)
MUSICAL NUMBERS: Jellicle Songs for Jellicle Cats, The Naming of Cats, Invitation to the Jellicle Ball, Old Gumbie Cat, Rum Tum Tugger, Grizabella the Glamour Cat, Bustopher Jones, Mungojerrie and Rumpleteazer, Old Deuteronomy, The Awefull Battle of the Pekes and Pollicles, Marching Songs of the Pollicle Dogs, The Jellicle Ball, Memory, Moments of Happiness, Gus the Theatre Cat, Growltiger's Last Stand, Skimbleshanks, Macavity, Mr. Mistoffelees, Journey of the Heaviside Layer, The Ad-Dressing of Cats.
A musical in 2 acts and 21 scenes.
*Still playing May 31, 1985. Winner of 1983 "Tonys" for Best Musical, Best Musical Book, Best Musical Score, Best Musical Director, Best Supporting Musical Actress (Betty Buckley), Best Costume Design, Best Lighting Design. For original production see THEATRE WORLD Vol. 39.
†Succeeded by: 1. Brian Sutherland, 2. Timothy Jerome, 3. Marlene Danielle, 4. Christina Kumi Kimball, Nora Brennan, Charlotte d'Amboise, 5. Guillermo Gonzalez, Joe Antony Cavise, 6. Jane Bodle, 7. Paige Dana, 8. Laurie Beechman, 9. Herman W. Sebek, 10. Claude R. Tessier, 11. Kevin Marcum, 12. Scott Wise, Brian Andrews, 13. Ramon Galindo, 14. Jamie Rocco, Terrence V. Mann, 15. Denise DiRenzo, 16. Michael Scott Gregory, 17. Sundy Leigh Leake, 18. Jay Poindexter, 19. Valerie C. Wright, 20. Erick Devine, 21. Colleen Fitzpatrick, Janene Lovullo

Laurie Beechman

DREAMGIRLS

Book and Lyrics, Tom Eyen; Music, Henry Krieger; Presented by Michael Bennett, Bob Avian, Geffen Records, The Shubert Organization; Direction/Choreography, Michael Bennett; Co-Choreographer, Michael Peters; Sets, Robin Wagner; Costumes, Theoni V. Aldredge; Lighting, Tharon Musser; Sound, Otts Munderloh; Musical Supervision/Orchestrations, Harold Wheeler; Musical Director, Yolanda Segovia, Paul Gemignani; Vocal Arrangements, Cleavant Derricks; Hairstylist, Ted Azar; Production Supervisor, Jeff Hamlin; Technical Coordinator, Arthur Siccardi; Props, Michael Smanko; Wardrobe, Alyce Gilbert, Stephanie Edwards; Assistant to Choreographers, Geneva Burke; Production Assistant, Charles Suisman; Assistant Conductor, Nick Cerrato; Casting, Olaiya, Johnson/Liff; Original Cast Album, Geffen Records; General Management, Marvin A. Krauss, Eric L. Angelson, Gary Gunas, Steven C. Callahan, Joey Parnes; Assistant Company Manager, Nina Skriloff; Dance Captain, Brenda Braxton; Stage Managers, Jeff Hamlin, Zane Weiner, Frank DiFilia, Jake Bell; Press, Merle Debuskey, Diane Judge. Opened in the Imperial Theatre on Sunday, December 20, 1981.*

CAST

The Stepp Sisters .... Deborah Burrell[1], Vanessa Bell[2], Tenita Jordan[3], Brenda Pressley[4]
Charlene .... Cheryl Alexander[5]
Joanne .... Linda Lloyd[6]
Marty .... Vondie Curtis-Hall
Curtis Taylor, Jr. .... Ben Harney[7]
Deena Jones .... Sheryl Lee Ralph[8]
M.C. .... Larry Stewart[9]
Tiny Joe Dixon/Nightclub Owner .... Joe Lynn
Lorrell Robinson .... Loretta Devine[10]
C. C. White .... Obba Babatunde[11]
James Thuder Early .... Cleavant Derricks[12]
Effie Melody White .... Jennifer Holliday[13]
Edna Burke .... Sheila Ellis[14]
Wayne .... Tony Franklin[15]
Dave & The Sweethearts .... Paul Binotto[16], Candy Darling, Carol Logen[17]
Press Agent Frank .... David Thome[18]
Michelle Morris .... Deborah Burrell[19]
Morgan .... Larry Stewart[20]
Film Executives .... Paul Binotto[21], Scott Plank[22], Weyman Thompson[23]
The Five Tuxedos .... Charles Bernard, Jamie Patterson, Charles Randolph-Wright, Eric Riley, Larry Stewart
Les Style .... Cheryl Alexander, Ethel Beatty, Mary Denise Bentley, Brenda Pressley
Little Albert & the Tru-Tones/James Early Band .... Barry Bruce, Abe Clark, Thomas Scott Gordon, Gordon Owens, Eric Riley, Christopher Gregory

GUESTS, FANS, STAGEHANDS, ETC.: Mary Denise Bentley, Barry Bruce, Abe Clark, Candy Darling, Ronald Dunham, Thomas Scott Gordon, Christopher Gregory, Nina Hennessey, Adriane Lenox, Gordon Owens, Kecia Lewis, Hal Miller, Brenda Pressley, Eric Riley, Johnnie Teamer, Graciela Simpson, Leon Summers, Jr., Gina Taylor, Johnnie Teamer, Buddy Vest.
UNDERSTUDIES: Brenda Pressley, Johnnie Teamer (Deena), Brenda Pressley, Kecia Lewis (Effie), Teresa Burrell, Adriane Lenox (Lorrell), Vondie Curtis-Hall, Larry Stewart (Curtis), Larry Stewart, Phillip Gilmore (James Thunder Early), Wellington Perkins, Gordon Owens (C.C.), Brenda Pressley, Johnnie Teamer (Michelle), Leon Summers, Jr., Larry Stewart (Marty), Hal Miller (Jerry/Dave), Charles Bernard, Gordon Owens, Eric Riley (Wayne), Hal Miller, Frank DiFilia (Frank), Abe Clark (M.C./Morgan), Charles Bernard (Tiny Joe Dixon), Swings: Charles Bernard, Brenda Braxton, Phillip Gilmore, Allison Williams.
MUSICAL NUMBERS: I'm Looking for Something, Goin' Downtown, Takin' the Long Way Home, Move, Fake Your Way to the Top, Cadillac Car, Steppin' to the Bad Side, Party Party, I Want You Baby, Family, Only the Beginning, Heavy, It's All Over, And I Am Telling You I Am Not Going, Love You Baby, I Am Changing, One More Picture Please, When I First Saw You, Got to Be Good Times, Ain't No Party, Quintette, The Rap, I Meant You No Harm, I Miss You Old Friend, One Night Only, I'm Somebody, Faith in Myself, Hard to Say Goodbye My Love
A musical in 2 acts and 20 scenes. The action takes place in the early 1960's and 1970's.

Top Right: Loretta Devine, Sheryl Lee Ralph, Teresa Burrell Below: Deborah Burrell (L), Roz Ryan (R)

*Closed Aug. 4, 1985 after 1522 performances. Winner of 1982 "Tonys" for Best Book, Lighting, Choreography, Supporting Actor (Cleavant Derricks), Best Actor and Actress in a Musical (Ben Harney, Jennifer Holliday)
†Succeeded by: 1. Teresa Burrell, 2. Brenda Pressley, 3. Graciela Simpson, 4. Gina Taylor, 5. Khandi Alexander, Adriane Lenox, 6. Ethel Beatty, Johnnie Teamer, 7. Vondie Curtis-Hall during vacation, Weyman Thompson, 8. Linda Leilani Brown during vacation, Deborah Burrell, 9. Leon Summers, Jr. 10. Cheryl Alexander, Adriane Lenox, Loretta Devine, 11. Tony Franklin, Wellington Perkins, Lawrence Clayton, 12. Hinton Battle, David Alan Grier, Cleavant Derricks, 13. Vanessa Townsell, Julia McGirt, Roz Ryan, 14. Julia McGirt, Allison Williams, 15. Wellington Perkins, Eric Riley, 16. Richard Poole, Ray Benson, 17. Nina Hennessey, 18. Buddy Vest, 19. Teresa Burrell, 20. Leon Summers, Jr., 21. Ray Benson, 22. Hal Miller, 23. Eric Riley

Martha Swope Photos

42ND STREET

Music, Harry Warren; Lyrics, Al Dubin; Book Michael Stewart, Mark Bramble from novel by Bradford Ropes; Direction/Choreography, Gower Champion; Scenery, Robin Wagner; Costumes, Theoni V. Aldredge; Lighting, Tharon Musser; Presented by David Merrick; Musical Direction, Philip Fradkin; Orchestrations, Philip J. Lang; Dance Arrangements, Donald Johnston; Vocal Arrangements, John Lesko; Sound, Richard Fitzgerald; Hairstylist, Ted Azar; Casting, Feur & Ritzer; Wardrobe, Gene Wilson, Kathleen Foster; Assistant Musical Director, Bernie Leighton; General Manager, Leo K. Cohen; Assistant Company Manager, Marcia Goldberg; Dance Captain, Debra Ann Draper; Props, Leo Herbert, Kim Herbert; Assistant Musical Director, Bernie Leighton; Stage Managers, Barry Kearsley, Jack Timmers, Janet Friedman, Dennis Angulo; Press, Solters/Roskin/Friedman, Joshua Ellis, Cindy Valk, Adrian Bryan-Brown, Keith Sherman, Jackie Green. Opened in the Winter Garden Theatre on Monday, August 25, 1980.*

CAST

Andy Lee	Danny Carroll
Oscar	Robert Colston
Mac/Thug/Doctor	Stan Page
Annie	Clare Leach[†1]
Maggie Jones	Jessica James[†2]
Bert Barry	Joseph Bova
Billy Lawlor	Lee Roy Reams[†3]
Peggy Sawyer	Lisa Brown[†4]
Lorraine	Ginny King[†5]
Phyllis	Jeri Kansas[†6]
Julian Marsh	Jerry Orbach[†7]
Dorothy Brock	Elizabeth Allen[†8]
Abner Dillon	Don Crabtree[†9]
Pat Denning	Steve Elmore
Thugs	Stan Page, Ron Schwinn
Doctor	Stan Page[†10]

ENSEMBLE: Diane Abrams, Dennis Angulo, Carole Banninger, Dennis Batutis, Paula Joy Belis, Jeffrey Cornell, Ronny De Vito, Rob Draper, Brandt Edwards, Judy Ehrlich, Cathy Greco, Jennifer Hammond, Elisa Heinsohn, Jeri Kansas, Jack Karcher, Billye Kersey, Karen Klump, Terri Ann Kundrat, Neva Leigh, Maureen Mellon, Gwendolyn Miller, Ken Mitchell, Bill Nabel, Sheila O'Connor, Tony Parise, Don Percassi, Rosemary Rado, Michael Ricardo, Lars Rosager, Linda Sabatelli, Ron Schwinn, Pamela S. Scott, Yveline Semeria, Marla Singer, J. Thomas Smith, Michael Steuber, Susanne Leslie Sullivan, Vickie Taylor.

STANDBYS & UNDERSTUDIES: Connie Day (Dorothy/Maggie), Steve Elmore/Stan Page (Julian), Vickie Taylor (Peggy), Rob Draper/Dennis Angelo (Billy), Don Percassi (Andy), Stan Page (Abner/Pat), Billye Kersey/Linda Sabatelli (Annie), Bill Nabel/Ron Schwinn (Bert/Mac), Bernie Leighton (Oscar), Lizzie Moran/Debra Ann Draper (Phyllis/Lorraine), Ensemble: Debra Ann Draper, Ida Henry, Patice McConachie, Lizzie Moran, Dennis Angulo, Rick Conant.

MUSICAL NUMBERS: Audition, Young and Healthy, Shadow Waltz, Go into Your Dance, You're Getting to Be a Habit with Me, Getting Out of Town, Dames, I Know Now, Sunny Side to Every Situation, Lullaby of Broadway, About a Quarter to Nine, Shuffle Off to Buffalo, 42nd Street

A musical in 2 acts and 16 scenes. The action takes place during 1933 in New York City and Philadelphia.

*Still playing May 31, 1985. Recipient of 1981 "Tonys" for Best Musical and for Outstanding Choreography. For original production, see THEATRE WORLD Vol. 37.

†Succeeded by: 1. Billye Kersey, Dorothy Stanley, Beth Leavel, 2. Peggy Cass, 3. James Brennan, Lee Roy Reams, 4. Karen Ziemba, Gail Benedict, Lisa Brown, Clare Leach, 5. Gail Lohla, Marla Singer, 6. Gail Pennington, Jeri Kansas, 7. Stephen G. Arlen, Don Chastain, 8. Millicent Martin, Anne Rogers, Millicent Martin, 9. Stan Page, 10. Bill Nabel

Martha Swope Photos

Top Right: Lee Roy Reams, Lisa Brown
Below: Peggy Cass (L)

Millicent Martin, Lee Roy Reams

LA CAGE AUX FOLLES

Music and Lyrics, Jerry Herman; Book, Harvey Fierstein; Based on play of same title by Jean Poiret; Director, Arthur Laurents; Choreography, Scott Salmon; Presented by Allan Carr, Kenneth D. Greenblatt, Marvin A. Krauss, Stewart F. Lane, James M. Nederlander, Martin Richards; Settings, David Mitchell; Costumes, Theoni V. Aldredge; Lighting, Jules Fisher; Sound, Peter J. Fitzgerald; Hairstylist, Ted Azar; Musical Direction/Vocal Arrangements, Donald Pippin; Orchestrations, Jim Tyler; Dance Music Arrangements, G. Harrell; Assistant Choreographer, Richard Balestrino; Casting, Pulvino & Howard; Produced in association with Jonathan Farkas, John Pomerantz, Martin Heinfling; Executive Producers, Barry Brown, Fritz Holt; Original Cast Album, RCA Records; General Management, Marvin A. Krauss, Gary Gunas, Steven C. Callahan; Company Manager, Allan Williams; Dance Captain, Linda Haberman; Props, Charles Zuckerman, Jack Cennamo, Alan Steiner; Wardrobe, Gayle Patton, Irene Bunis; Music Coordinator, John Monaco; Assistant Conductor, Rudolph Bennett; Production Assistant, Trey Hunt; Makeup, Max Factor; Stage Managers, James Pentecost, David Caine, Robert Schear; Press, Shirley Herz, Sam Rudy, Peter Cromarty, Pete Sanders. Opened in the Palace Theatre on Sunday, August 21, 1983.*

CAST

Georges	Gene Barry†1
Les Cagelles:	
Chantal	David Cahn†2
Monique	Dennis Callahan
Dermah	Frank DiPasquale†3
Nicole	John Dolf†4
Hanna	David Engel
Mercedes	David Evans†5
Bitelle	Linda Haberman
Lo Singh	Eric Lamp†6
Odette	Dan O'Grady
Angelique	Deborah Phelan
Phaedra	David Scala
Clo-Clo	Sam Singhaus
Francis	Brian Kelly
Jacob	William Thomas, Jr.†7
Albin	George Hearn†8
Jean-Michel	John Weiner
Anne	Leslie Stevens†9
Jacqueline	Elizabeth Parrish
Renaud	Walter Charles†10
Mme. Renaud	Sydney Anderson
Paulette	Betsy Craig
Hercule	Jack Neubeck
Etienne	Jay Pierce
Babette	Marie Santell
Colette	Jennifer Smith†11
Tabarro	Mark Waldrop
Pepe	Ken Ward†12
Edouard Dindon	Jay Garner
Marie Dindon	Merle Louise

STANDBYS & UNDERSTUDIES: Jack Davison (Albin/Dindon), Thom Sesma (Jacob), Drew Geraci (Jean-Michel/Hercule/Tabarro/Chantal/Hanna/Mercedes/Dermah), Jan Leigh Herndon (Anne/Mme. Renaud/Paulette/Babette/Colette/Angelique), Betsy Craig (Mme. Dindon), Sydney Anderson (Jacqueline), Frank DiPasquale (Francis), David Klatt (Etienne/Photographer/Pepe/Phaedra), Jack Neubeck (M. Renaud), Jamie Ross (Georges)

MUSICAL NUMBERS: We Are What We Are, A Little More Mascara, With Anne on My Arm, The Promenade, Song on the Sand, La Cage aux Folles, I Am What I Am, Masculinity, Look Over There, Cocktail Counterpoint, The Best of Times, Finale

A musical in two acts. The action takes place during summer in St. Tropez, France, at the present time.

*Still playing May 31, 1985. Winner of 1984 "Tonys" for Best Musical, Musical Book, Musical Score, Outstanding Actor in a Musical (George Hearn), Outstanding Direction of a Musical, Outstanding Costumes.

†Succeeded by: 1. Jamie Ross, Keith Michell, Van Johnson, 2. Frank DiPasquale, 3. K. Craig Innes, 4. Eric Underwood, 5. Drew Geraci, 6. David Klatt, 7. Pi Douglass during vacation, 8. Keene Curtis during vacation, Walter Charles, 9. Jennifer Smith, 10. Jack Davison, 11. Pamela Cecil, 12. Thom Sesma

Martha Swope Photos

Top Left: Van Johnson, William Thomas, Jr.,
George Hearn Below: Les Cagelles

Frank DiPasquale, David Scala, George Hearn, Dan O'Grady, Sam Singhaus

48

NOISES OFF

By Michael Frayn; Director, Michael Blakemore; Presented by James Nederlander, Robert Fryer, Jerome Minskoff, The Kennedy Center, Michael Codron, in association with Jonathan Farkas, MTM Enterprises; Settings and Costumes, Michael Annals; Lighting, Martin Aronstein; Casting, Howard Feuer/Jeremy Ritzer; General Management, Joseph P. Harris, Peter T. Kulok, Steven E. Goldstein; Assistant Manager, Tom Santopietro; Technical Supervisor, Jeremiah Harris; Production Assistants, Russ Rosensweig, Lauren Schneider; Props, Paul Biega, Tommy Ciaccio; Wardrobe, Karen Lloyd; Stunt Coordinator, B. H. Barry; Hairstylist, Patrik D. Moreton; Stage Managers, Susie Cordon, Laura deBuys, David Bulasky; Press, Fred Nathan, Anne Abrams, Leslie Anderson, Ted Killmer, Bert Fink. Opened at the Brooks Atkinson Theatre on Sunday, December 11, 1983.*

CAST

Dotty Otley ....Dorothy Loudon†1
Lloyd Dallas ....Brian Murray†2
Garry Lejeune ....Victor Garber†3
Brooke Ashton ....Deborah Rush†4
Poppy Norton-Taylor ....Amy Wright†5
Frederick Fellowes ....Paxton Whitehead†6
Belinda Blair ....Linda Thorson†7
Tim Allgood ....Jim Piddock†8
Selsdon Mowbray ....Douglas Seale†9
STANDBYS: Patricia Kilgarriff (Dotty/Belinda), Emily Heebner (Brooke/Poppy), Herb Foster (Selsdon), Rudolph Willrich (Lloyd/Frederick), David Bulasky (Garry/Tim)

A comedy in three acts. The action takes place at the present time on stage in the Grand Theatre, Weston-Super-Mare, Monday, January 14; Theatre Royal, Goole, Wednesday matinee, February 13; Municipal Theatre, Stockton-on-Tees, Saturday, March 8th.

*Closed Apr. 6, 1985 after 553 performances and 12 previews.
†Succeeded by: 1. Carole Shelley, 2. Paul Hecht, 3. Patrick Clear, Randle Mell, 4. Diane Stilwell, 5. Julie Boyd, 6. Patrick Horgan, 7. Concetta Tomei, 8. Alexander Spencer, 9. George Hall

Martha Swope Photos

Paul Hecht, Diane Stilwell, George Hall, Concetta Tomei, Patrick Horgan, Carole Shelley, Randle Mell Top: Hecht, Horgan, Shelley, Mell, Tomei (above)

OH! CALCUTTA!

Devised by Kenneth Tynan; Conceived and Directed by Jacques Levy; Producer, Norman Kean; Presented by Hillard Elkins, Norman Kean, Robert S. Fishko; Production Supervisor, Ron Nash; Authors and Composers, Robert Benton, David Newman, Jules Feiffer, Dan Greenburg, Lenore Kandel, John Lennon, Jacques Levy, Leonard Melfi, Sam Shepard, Clovis Trouille, Kenneth Tynan, Sherman Yellen; Music and Lyrics, Robert Dennis, Peter Schickele, Stanley Walden, Jacques Levy; Choreography, Margo Sappington; Musical Director, Stanley Walden; Music Conductor, Tim Weil; Scenery and Lighting, Harry Silverglat Darrow; Costumes, Kenneth M. Yount; Sound, Sander Hacker; Assistant to Director, Nancy Tribush; Projected Media Design, Gardner Compton; Live Action Film, Ron Merk; Company Manager, Doris J. Buberl; Assistant, Tobias Beckwith; Production Associate, Kimberly Walton; Dance Captain, Ron Nash; Casting, Feuer & Ritzer; Assistant Conductor, Dan Carter; Wardrobe, Mark Bridges; Stage Managers, Maria Di Dia, Ron Nash; Press, Les Schector. Opened at the Eden Theatre on Friday, June 17, 1969, and at the Edison Theatre on Friday, Sept. 24, 1976.*

CAST

Deborah Robertson	Cheryl Hartley
Nannette Bevelander	David Heisey
Michael A. Clarke	Mary Kilpatrick
Terry Hamilton	James E. Mosiej
Charles E. Gerber	Jodi Johnson

MUSICAL NUMBERS & SKITS: Taking Off the Robe, Will Answer All Sincere Replies, Playin', Jack and Jill, The Paintings of Clovis Trouille, Much Too Soon, Dance for George, Delicious Indignities, Was It Good for You Too?, Suite for Five Letters, One on One, Clarence, Rock Garden, Spread Your Love Around, Love Lust Poem, Four in Hand, Coming Together Going Together
An "erotic musical" in two acts.
*Still playing May 31, 1985. For original production, see *Theatre World,* Vol. 33.

Martha Swope/Carol Rosegg Photos

Deborah Robertson, Michael A. Clarke, James E. Josiej, Cheryl Hartley, Charles E. Gerber,
Nannette Bevelander, Jodi Johnson, David Heisey
Top: Bevelander, Gerber

THE REAL THING

By Tom Stoppard; Director, Mike Nichols; Presented by Emanuel Azenberg, The Shubert Organization (Gerald Schoenfeld, Chairman; Bernard B. Jacobs, President), Icarus Productions, Byron Goldman, Ivan Bloch, Roger Berlind and Michael Codron; Scenery, Tony Walton; Costumes, Anthea Sylbert; Lighting, Tharon Musser; Sound, Otts Munderloh; Production Supervisor, Martin Herzer; General Managers, Jose Vega, Robert Kamlot; Technical Supervisor, Theatre Services Inc.; Props, Jan Marasek, Michael Durnin; Wardrobe, Penny Davis; Hair and Makeup Supervisor, Kelvin Trahan; Makeup, J. Roy Helland; Hairstylist, Richard Stein; Casting, Mary Goldberg/David Rubin; Wigs, Paul Huntley; Assistant Company Manager, Leslie Butler; Stage Managers, Alan Hall, Jane E. Cooper, Thomas P. Carr; Press, Bill Evans, Sandra Manley, Jim Baldassare. Opened in the Plymouth Theatre on Thursday, January 5, 1984.*

CAST

Max	Kenneth Welsh[†1]
Charlotte	Christine Baranski[†2]
Henry	Jeremy Irons[†3]
Annie	Glenn Close[†4]
Billy	Peter Gallagher[†5]
Debbie	Cynthia Nixon[†6]
Brodie	Vyto Ruginis[†7]

STANDBYS: Lewis Arlt (Henry/Max), Mary Denham, Joanna Gleason (Annie/Charlotte), Mary O'Sullivan (Debbie), Steven Weber (Billy/Brodie)

A comedy in two acts. The action takes place at the present time. Two years elapse between acts one and two.

*Closed May 12, 1985 after 566 performances and 16 previews. Recipient of 1984 "Tonys" for Best Play, Outstanding Actor in a Play (Jeremy Irons), Outstanding Actress in a Play (Glenn Close), Outstanding Featured Actress in a Play (Christine Baranski), Outstanding Director of a Play. The NY Drama Critics Circle also cited this as the Best New Play of the season, as did the Drama Desk.

†Succeeded by: 1. Simon Jones, 2. Sara Botsford, Leslie Lyles, 3. John Vickery, Jeremy Irons, Nicol Williamson, 4. Caroline Lagerfelt, Laila Robins, 5. Todd Waring, Anthony Fusco, Peter Gallagher, D. W. Moffett, 6. Yeardley Smith, Cynthia Nixon, Anne Marie Bobby, 7. Todd Waring, Campbell Scott

Martha Swope Photos

John Vickery, Sara Botsford, Caroline Lagerfelt, Simon Jones
Top: Nicol Williamson, Laila Robins

Harry Groener, Maryann Plunkett

SUNDAY IN THE PARK WITH GEORGE

Music and Lyrics, Stephen Sondheim; Book, James Lapine; Director, Mr. Lapine; Presented by The Shubert Organization and Emanuel Azenberg by arrangement with Playwrights Horizons; Scenery, Tony Straiges; Costumes, Patricia Zipprodt, Ann Hould-Ward; Lighting, Richard Nelson; Special Effects, Bran Ferren; Sound, Tom Morse; Hair and Makeup, LoPresto/Allen; Movement, Randolyn Zinn; Musical Direction, Paul Gemignani; Orchestrations, Michael Starobin; Set and Costume Designs adapted from the Georges Seurat painting entitled "Sunday Afternoon on the Island of the Grand Jatte"; Chromolum Music programmed by Michael Starobin; Casting, John S. Lyons; General Manager, Robert Kamlot; Company Manager, Richard Berg; Technical Supervision, Arthur Siccardi, Pete Feller; Props, Jan Marasek, Timothy Abel; Wardrobe, Barbara Hladsky, Nancy Schaefer; Stage Managers, Fredric H. Orner, Loretta Robertson, Steven Shaw; Press, Fred Nathan, Leslie Anderson, Anne Abrams, Ted Killmer, Bert Fink. Opened in the Booth Theatre on Wednesday, May 2, 1984.*

CAST

Act I:

George, an artist	Mandy Patinkin†1
Dot, his mistress	Bernadette Peters†2
Old Lady	Barbara Bryne
Her Nurse	Judith Moore
Franz, a servant	Brent Spiner†
Boy bathing in the river	Danielle Ferland†
Young Man Sitting on the bank	Nancy Opel
Man lying on the bank	Cris Groenendaal†
Jules, another artist	Charles Kimbrough
Yvonne, his wife	Dana Ivey†
Boatman	William Parry
Celeste 1	Melanie Vaughan
Celeste 2	Mary D'Arcy†
Louise, daughter of Jules and Yvonne	Danielle Ferland†
Frieda, a cook	Nancy Opel
Louis, a baker	Cris Groenendaal†
Soldier	Robert Westenberg†
Man with bicycle	John Jellison
Mr.	Kurt Knudson†
Mrs.	Judith Moore

Act II:

George, an artist	Mandy Patinkin†1
Marie, his grandmother	Bernadette Peters†2
Dennis, a technician	Brent Spiner†
Bob Greenberg, museum director	Charles Kimbrough
Naomi Eisen, composer	Dana Ivey†
Harriet Pawling, patron of the arts	Judith Moore
Billy Webster, her friend	Cris Groenendaal†
Photographer	Sue Anne Gershenson
Museum Assistant	John Jellison
Charles Redmond, visiting curator	William Parry
Alex, an artist	Robert Westenberg†
Betty, an artist	Nancy Opel
Lee Randolph, publicist	Kurt Knudson†
Blair Daniels, art critic	Barbara Bryne
Waitress	Melanie Vaughan/Joanna Glushak
Elaine	Mary D'Arcy†

UNDERSTUDIES: Joanna Glushak (Dot/Marie/Celeste 1 and 2/Waitress/Elaine), Sara Woods (Old Lady/Blair Daniels/Nurse/Mrs./Harriet Pawling/Yvonne/Naomi Eisen), Cris Groendaal (George/Franz/Dennis/Soldier/Alex), Michele Rigan (Boy/Louise), Sue Anne Gershenson (Young Man/Frieda/Betty/Celeste 1 & 2/Waitress/Elaine), T. J. Meyers (Man/Louis/Billy/Boatman/Charles Redmond/Museum Assistant/Mr./Lee Randolph), John Jellison (Boatman/Charles Redmond/Jules/Greenberg)

MUSICAL NUMBERS: Sunday in the Park with George, No Life, Color and Light, Gossip, The Day Off, Everybody Loves Louis, Finishing the Hat, We Do Not Belong Together, Beautiful, Sunday, It's Hot Up Here, Chromolume 7, Putting It Together, Children and Art, Lesson 8, Move On.

A musical in two acts. Act I takes place on a series of Sundays from 1884 to 1886 and alternates between a park on an island in the Seine just outside Paris, and George's studio. Act II takes place in 1984 at an American art museum, and on the island in the Seine. Although suggested by the life of Georges Seurat and by his painting, all characters are products of the author's imagination.

*Closed October 13, 1985 after 604 performances and 35 previews. Recipient of NY Drama Critics Circle as well as Drama Desk citation for Best Musical, and 1984 "Tonys" for Outstanding Scenic Design, and Outstanding Lighting Design. It received the 1985 Pulitzer Prize.

Martha Swope Photos

Top Left: Robert Westenberg, Bernadette Peters
Below: Pamela Burrell, Charles Kimbrough

THE TAP DANCE KID

Book, Charles Blackwell; Music, Henry Krieger; Lyrics, Robert Lorick; Based on novel "Nobody's Family Is Going to Change" by Louise Fitzhugh; Director, Vivian Matalon; Presented by Stanley White, Evelyn Barron, Harvey J. Klaris, Michel Stuart; Associate Producers, Mark Beigelman, Richard Chwatt; Produced in association with Michel Kleinman Productions; General Management, Theatre Now, Inc.; Dances and Musical Staging, Danny Daniels; Musical Supervision/Orchestra and Vocal Arrangements, Harold Wheeler; Scenery, Michael Hotopp, Paul dePass; Costumes, William Ivey Long; Lighting, Richard Nelson; Musical and Vocal Direction, Don Jones; Dance Music Arrangements, Peter Howard; Sound, Jack Mann; Assistant Choreographer, D. J. Giagni; Scenic Photography, Mark Feldstein; Wigs, Paul Huntley; Company Manager, Mark A. Schweppe; Props, Liam Herbert, Walter Wood; Wardrobe, Kathleen Gallagher, Randy Beth; Hairstylists, Andrew Reese, James Jeppi; Assistant Conductor, Jerry Sternbach; Production Associates, Roberta Haze, Sally Fisher; Stage Managers, Joe Lorden, Jack Gianino, Ed Fitzgerald; Press, Judy Jacksina, Glenna Freedman, Susan Chicoine, Marcy Granata, Marc P. Thibodeau, Kevin Boyle. Opened Wednesday, December 21, 1983 in the Broadhurst Theatre, and moved to the Minskoff Theatre on March 27, 1984.*

CAST

Willie	Alfonso Ribeiro†1
Ginnie	Hattie Winston†2
Dulcie	Barbara Montgomery
Emma	Martine Allard
William	Samuel E. Wright†3
Dipsey	Hinton Battle†4
Mona	Karen Paskow
Carole	Jackie Lowe
Daddy Bates	Alan Weeks
Winslow	Michael Blevins†5
Joe	Byron Easley
Offstage Voice	Lloyd Culbreath

LITTLE RIO DANCERS & NEW YORKERS: Leah Bass, Kevin Berdini, Karen Curlee, Lloyd Culbreath, Rick Emery, Karen E. Fraction, Tony Jaeger, J. J. Jepson, Rodney Alan McGuire, Kimberly Meyers, Karen Paskow, Jamie M. Pisano, Ken Prescott, James Young

STANDBYS & UNDERSTUDIES: Lloyd Culbreath (Dipsey/Daddy Bates), Michelle Weeks (Emma), Hassoun Tatum (Willie), Leah Bass (Carole/Dulcie), Kevin Berdini (Winslow), Jamie M. Pisano (Mona), Donny Burks (William), Vanessa Shaw (Ginnie)

MUSICAL NUMBERS: Another Day, Four Strikes Against Me, Class Act, They Never Hear What I Say, Dancing Is Everything, Crosstown, Fabulous Feet, I Could Get Used to Him, Man in the Moon, Like Him, Someday, My Luck Is Changing, I Remember How It Was, Lullabye, Tap Tap, Dance If It Makes You Happy, William's Song, Finale

A musical in 2 acts and 15 scenes. The action takes place at the present time in NYC's Manhattan and Roosevelt Island.

*Closed March 11, 1985 after 669 performances and 38 previews. Winner of 1984 "Tonys" for Outstanding Featured Actor in a Musical (Hinton Battle), and Outstanding Choreography

†Succeeded by: 1. Jimmy Tate, Savion Glover, 2. Gail Nelson, 3. Ira Hawkins, 4. Eugene Fleming, 5. Tony Jaeger

Martha Swope, Kenn Duncan, Marc Raboy Photos

Alfonso Ribeiro, Hinton Battle
Above: Ribeiro, Martine Allard

Alan Weeks, Hinton Battle
Top Left: Hinton Battle

P. J. Benjamin, Bruce Toms

TORCH SONG TRILOGY

By Harvey Fierstein; Director, Peter Pope; Presented by Kenneth Waissman, Martin Markinson, John Glines, Lawrence Lane with BetMar and Donald Tick; Associate Producer, Howard Perloff; Sets, Bill Stabile; Costumes, Mardi Philips; Lighting, Scott Pinkney; Musical Direction/Arrangements, Ned Levy; Original Music, Ada Janik; Assistant Director, Judy Thomas; Technical Supervisor, Jeremiah Harris; Sound, Richard Fitzgerald, John Sullivan; Wardrobe, Kathy Powers, Larry Tarzy; Hairstylist, Andre Tavernise; Production Assistant, George Phelps; General Assistants, David Kratz, Barbara Hodgen; Casting, Hughes/Moss; General Management, Theatre Now, Inc.; General Manager, Edward H. Davis; Props, Ronnie Lynch, Sr., Stage Managers, Herb Vogler, Billie McBride; Press, Betty Lee Hunt, Maria Cristina Pucci, James Sapp. Opened in The Little Theatre (changed to Helen Hayes Theatre) on Thursday, June 10, 1982.*

CAST

Lady Blues	Susan Edwards
Arnold Beckoff	Harvey Fierstein[1]
Ed	Court Miller[2]
Laurel	Diane Tarleton
Alan	Paul Joynt[3]
David	Fisher Stevens[4]
Mrs. Beckoff	Estelle Getty[5]

STANDBYS AND UNDERSTUDIES: Susan Edwards (Laurel), Diane Tarleton (Lady Blues), Jeffrey Rogers (Alan/David), Sylvia Kauders (Mrs. Beckoff), Roger Leonard (Keyboard), Charles Adler (Arnold), Peter Ratray (Ed)

A play in 3 acts and 10 scenes. Part 1: "The International Stud" takes place backstage, in a bar, Ed's apartment, Arnold's apartment, at the present time from January to November; Part 2: "Fugue in a Nursery" a year later in Arnold's apartment, and in various rooms of Ed's farmhouse; Part 3: "Widows and Children First" five years later in Arnold's apartment, and on a bench in the park.

*Closed May 18, 1985 after 1222 performances and 8 previews. Recipient of 1983 "Tonys" for Best Play, and Best Actor in a Play (Harvey Fierstein).

†Succeeded by: 1. Richard DeFabees, Donald Corren, Jonathan Hadary, David Garrison, Max Cantor, Philip Astor, Harvey Fierstein, P. J. Benjamin, 2. Robert Sevra, Peter Ratray, David Orange, Court Miller, Jared Martin, Court Miller, Raymond Baker, Sam Freed, Tom Stechschulte, 3. Christopher Stryker, Craig Sheffer, Jeffrey Rogers, 4. Jon Cryer, Christopher Collett, Mathew Vipond, Christopher Gartin, 5. Chevi Colton

Gerry Goodstein Photos
Top: Jonathan Hadary, Chevi Colton
Left: Harvey Fierstein, Diane Tarleton

THE FANTASTICKS

Book and Lyrics, Tom Jones; Music, Harvey Schmidt; Suggested by Edmund Rostand's play "Les Romanesques"; Presented by Lore Noto; Director, Word Baker; Original Musical Direction/Arrangements, Julian Stein; Designed by Ed Wittstein; Associate Producers, Sheldon Baron, Dorothy Olim, Robert Alan Gold; Assistant Producers, Bill Mills, Thad Noto; Original Cast Album by MGM Records; Production Assistant, John Krug; Stage Managers, Geoffrey Brown, James Cook, Jim Charles; Press, David Powers, Bill Shuttleworth. Opened in the Sullivan Street Playhouse on Tuesday, May 3, 1960.*

CAST

The Narrator .... Sal Provenza†1
The Girl .... Virginia Gregory†2
The Boy .... Howard Paul Lawrence†3
The Boy's Father .... Lore Noto
The Girl's Father .... William Tost
The Old Actor .... Bryan Hull
The Man Who Dies/Indian .... Robert R. Oliver
The Mute .... Jim Charles†4
At the piano .... Jeffrey Saver†5
At the harp .... Winifred W. Starks†6
UNDERSTUDIES: Kim Moore (Narrator/Boy), Susan Dow (Girl), William Tost (Boy's Father)
MUSICAL NUMBERS: Try to Remember, Much More, Metaphor, Never Say No, It Depends on What You Pay, Soon It's Gonna Rain, Rape Ballet, Happy Ending, This Plum Is Too Ripe, I Can See It, Plant a Radish, Round and Round, They Were You
A musical in two acts.
*The world's longest running musical was still playing May 31, 1985.
†Succeeded by: 1. Dennis Parlato, 2. Karen Culliver, 3. Bill Perlach, 4. Kim Moore, 5. Dorothy Martin, 6. Elizabeth Etters

Martha Swope Photos

Top Right: Tom Jones (book and lyrics), Harvey Schmidt (music), with cast: (back) Jim Charles, Sal Provenza, (center) Robert R. Oliver, William Tost, Howard Paul Lawrence, Virginia Gregory, Lore Noto, Bryan Hull

FORBIDDEN BROADWAY

Concept and Lyrics, Gerard Alessandrini; Director, Mr. Alessandrini; Presented by Playkill Productions (Sella Palsson, Executive Producer); Costumes, Chet Ferris; Press, Becky Flora, Opened at Palsson's on Friday, Jan. 15, 1982 and still playing May 31, 1985.

CAST†

Gerard Alessandrini
Bill Carmichael
Nora Mae Lyng
Fred Barton
Chloe Webb

A musical satire in two acts.
†Succeeded by: Fred Barton, Davis Gaines, Herndon Lackey, Nora Mae Lyng, Jan Neuberger

Henry Grossman Photos

Herndon Lackey, Jan Neuberger, Davis Gaines, Nora Mae Lyng

FOOL FOR LOVE

By Sam Shepard; Director, Mr. Shepard; Presented by Circle Repertory Company (Marshall W. Mason, Artistic Director); Set, Andy Stacklin; Costumes, Ardyss L. Golden; Lighting, Kurt Landisman; Sound, J. A. Deane; Associate Director, Julie Herbert; Company Manager, Lynn Landis; Production Managers, Kate Stewart, Alex Baker; Stage Managers, Suzanne Fry, Jody Boese, Ginny Martino, Red Reinglas; Producer, Eric Krebs; General Manager, Whitbell Productions; Press, Reva Cooper, Gail Bell. Opened at the Circle Repertory Theatre on Wednesday, May 18, 1983, and moved to the Douglas Fairbanks Theatre on Wednesday, November 30, 1983.*

CAST

May .... Kathy Whitton Baker†1
Eddie .... Ed Harris†2
Martin .... Dennis Ludlow†3
Old Man .... Will Marchetti†4
A drama performed without intermission. The action takes place at the present time in a motel room on the edge of the Mojave Desert.
*Still playing May 31, 1985.
†Succeeded by: 1. Ann Gentry, Moira McCanna Harris, Frances Fisher, Katherine Cortez, Deborah Strang, Suzanna Hay, 2. Will Patton, Bruce Willis, Aidan Quinn, David Andrews, George Gerdes, Matthew Locricchio, Justin Deas, 3. Stephen Mendillo, 4. John Nesci, Tom Aldredge, J. D. Swain, Richard Hamilton, John Seitz, Page Johnson

Gerry Goodstein Photos

(standing) Page Johnson, Stephen Mendillo,
(seated) George Gerdes, Katherine Cortez

ISN'T IT ROMANTIC

By Wendy Wasserstein; Director, Gerald Gutierrez; Presented by Playwrights Horizons (Andre Bishop, Artistic Director; Paul S. Daniels, Managing Director) by arrangement with Lucille Lortel; Set, Andrew Jackness; Costumes, Ann Emonts; Lighting, James F. Ingalls; Sound, Scott Lehrer; Music Coordinator, Jack Feldman; Dance Sequences, Susan Rosenstock; Wardrobe, Maggie Taylor, Janet Anderson; Props, Virginia Addison, Kim Hanson; Production Manager, Carl Mulert; Company Manager, Berenice Weiler; Manager, Bruce Klinger; Stage Managers, John Vivian, Corbey Rene Low; Press, Bob Ullman. Opened in the Playwrights Horizons Theatre on Thursday, December 15, 1983; moved to the Lucille Lortel Theatre on Wednesday, June 20, 1984.*

CAST

Janie Blumberg	Cristine Rose†1
Harriet Cornwall	Lisa Banes†2
Marty Sterling	Chip Zien†3
Tasha Blumberg	Betty Comden†4
Simon Blumberg	Stephen Blumberg†5
Lillian Cornwall	Jo Henderson†6
Paul Stuart	Jerry Lanning†7
Vladimir	Tom Robbins†8
Stagehands	Peter Becker, Ralph Marrero, Robert Verlacque, David Boor

TELEPHONE MESSAGES by Timmy Geisler (Schlomo), Kevin Kline (Hart Farrell), Swoosie Kurtz (Julie Stern), Patti LuPone (Tajlei Kaplan Singleberry), Ellis Rabb (Operator), Meryl Streep (Cynthia Peterson), Jerry Zaks (Milty Sterling)
UNDERSTUDIES: Becky London (Harriet/Janie), Stephen Berger (Marty), Sally-Jane Heit (Tasha/Lillian), Richard Council (Simon/Paul/Vladimir)
A comedy in two acts. The action takes place at the present time in New York City.
*Closed September 1, 1985 after 233 performances.
†Succeeded by: 1. Sally Faye Reit, Robin Bartlett, 2. Alma Cuervo, Christine Healy, 3. Mitchell Greenberg, Tom Robbins, Gerald Gutierrez, Alan Rosenberg, David Wohl, 4. Marge Kotlisky, Barbara Barrie, Lynn Cohen, Joan Copeland, Elizabeth Perry, 5. Steven Gilborn, James Harder, 6. Peg Murray, Scotty Bloch, Pippa Scott, Julia Meade, 7. Nicholas Hormann, James Redhorn, 8. Stephen Berger.

Peter Cunningham, Martha Swope Photos

David Wohl, Robin Bartlett
Top: Elizabeth Perry, Julia Meade

LITTLE SHOP OF HORRORS

Book and Lyrics, Howard Ashman; Based on film by Roger Corman; Music, Alan Menken; Director, Howard Ashman; Set, Edward T. Gianfrancesco; Lighting, Craig Evans; Costumes, Sally Lesser; Sound, Otts Munderloh; Puppets, Martin P. Robinson; Vocal Arrangements/Musical Supervision, Robert Billig; Orchestrations/Musical Direction, Robby Merkin; Musical Staging, Edie Cowan; Presented by WPA Theatre (Kyle Renick, Artistic Director), David Geffen, Cameron Mackintosh and the Shubert Organization; Original Cast Album on Geffen Records & Tapes; General Manager, Albert Poland; Company Manager, Peter Schneider; Assistant to Director, Constance Grappo; Makeup and Wigs, Lenora Brown; Props, Donna Drake; Wardrobe, Craig Aspen, Dan Paul; Puppeteers, Donna Drake, Craig Aspen, Dan Paul; Casting, Albert Tavares; Stage Managers, Peter B. Mumford, Donna Fletcher; Press, Milly Schoenbaum, Kevin Patterson, Marc Routh. Opened at the Orpheum Theatre, Tuesday, July 27, 1982.*

CAST

Chiffon	Leilani Jones†1
Crystal	Jennifer Leigh Warren†2
Ronnette	Sheila Kay Davis†3
Mushnik	Fyvush Finkel
Audrey	Marsha Skaggs†4
Seymour	Brad Moranz†5
Derelict	Anthony B. Asbury†6
Orin/Bernstein/Snip/Luce	Robert Frisch†7
Audrey II: Manipulation	Anthony B. Asbury†6
Voice	Ron Taylor

STANDBYS: Katherine Meloche (Audrey), Michael Pace (Seymour/Orin/Bernstein/Snip/Luce/Everyone Else/Audrey II Voice), Arn Weiner (Mushnik), William Szymanski (Derelict/Audrey II Manipulation & Voice), Nicky Rene (Chiffon/Crystal/Ronnette)
MUSICAL NUMBERS: Prologue (Little Shop of Horrors), Skid Row (Downtown), Da-Doo, Grow for Me, Don't It Go To Show Ya Never Know, Somewhere That's Green, Closed for Renovations, Dentist!, Mushnik and Son, Feed Me (Git It), Now (It's Just the Gas), Call Back in the Morning, Suddenly Seymour, Suppertime, The Meek Shall Inherit, Finale (Don't Feed the Plants)
A musical in two acts.
*Still playing May 31, 1985 (1189 performances). Recipient of 1983 citation from NY Drama Critics Circle as Best Musical.
†Succeeded by: 1. Suzzanne Douglas, 2. Tena Wilson, 3. Louise Robinson, 4. Eydie Alyson, 5. Andrew Hill Newman, 6. Lynn Hippen, 7. Ken Land

Peter Cunningham Photos

Right: Fyvush Finkel, Eydie Alyson, Andrew Hill Newman Top: Suzzanne Douglas, Tena Wilson, Louise Robinson

Audrey II

Ken Land (Top), Andrew Hill Newmann

OFF-BROADWAY PRODUCTIONS

(South Street Theatre) Sunday, June 3, 1984–
American Grass Roots Opera & Theatre Co. (David Arrow, Associate Producer) presents:
ROBERT FROST: FIRE AND ICE by June August and Arthur Peterson; Based on the life and works of Robert Frost; Director, Ellen Bailey; Scenery, Douglas E. Powell; Lighting, David Arrow; Costumes, Norma Lorraine; Original Music composed and performed by Glenn Smith; Production Assistants, Larry Dorrell, Debbie Martin; Stage Managers, Janet Herzenberg, Regina Paleski, Jill Larmett; Press, Jeffrey Richards, Robert Ganshaw, C. George Willard, Ben Morse, Richard Dahl. CAST: Arthur Peterson

(Central Park Bandshell) Tuesday, June 5,–July 1, 1984 (20 performances in NYC parks) Joseph Papp presents the Riverside Shakespeare Co. (W. Stuart McDowell, Artistic Director; Gloria Skurski, Executive Director) performing:
ROMEO AND JULIET by William Shakespeare; Director, John Clingerman; Associate Director, Mary Lowry; Scenery, Kevin Lee Allen; Costumes, Cecilia A. Friederichs; Music, Philip Rosenberg; Fight Choreographer, Robert Walsh; Production Manager, H. Bradford Johnson; Stage Manager, Susan Feltman. CAST: Jennifer Campbell (Ensemble Woman), Ensemble: Richard Raether, David Longworth, Andrew McCutcheon, Jim Acheson, Bernadette Anderson, Grace Miglio, Kevin McGuire (Benvolio), Todd Jamieson (Tybalt), Herbert Mark Parker (Chorus/Prince), William Pollock, Jeff Shoemaker (Officers to the Prince), Ronald Durling (Capulet), Martitia Palmer (Lady Capulet), Stockman Barner (Montague/Apothecary), Marian Baer (Lady Montague/Nurse), Michael Golding (Romeo), Albert Owens (Paris), Andrew McCutcheon (Peter), Constance Boardman (Juliet), Richard Raether (Servant/Follower/Friar John/Watchman), Saul Stein (Mercutio), Jeff Shoemaker (Friar Lawrence), David Longworth (Balthasar), Jim Acheson (Watchman). Performed without intermission.

(Circle in the Square Downtown) Wednesday, June 6,–Sept. 16, 1984 (117 performances and 18 previews). Circle in the Square Theatre (Theodore Mann, Artistic Director; Paul Libin, Managing Director) and Robert Pesola, Ann Schindler, Stuart Bader in association with Circle Repertory Company present:
DANNY AND THE DEEP BLUE SEA by John Patrick Shanley; Director, Barnet Kellman; Scenery, David Gropman; Lighting, Richard Nelson; Costumes, Marcia Dixcy; Company Manager, Gail Bell; Stage Manager, Karen Armstrong; Production Assistants, Martin Shelby, Laura Isko; Press, Merle Debuskey, David Roggensack. CAST: June Stein (Roberta), John Turturro (Danny). Standbys: Deborah Offner, John C. McGinley. A drama performed in three scenes without intermission. The action takes place in the Bronx at the present time.

(Theatre of the Riverside Church) Monday, June 7–24, 1984 (12 performances). Theatre of the Riverside Church (David K. Manion, Artistic Director) presents:
THE EMPEROR OF MY BABY'S HEART with Book by Lawrence DuKore; Music, Mark Barkan; Lyrics, Mr. DuKore, Mr. Barkan; Director, David Gold; Musical Director, James Mironchik; Choreography, Ricky Schussel; Costumes, Natalie Garfinkle; Lighting, Chenault Spence; Scenic Paintings, George Pissaro; Technical Director, David Seavey; Stage Managers, Laura Kravets, Paul A. Kochman. CAST: Robert Grossman (Clarence), Alan Ellington (Johnny), Mary C. Robare (Daisy), David Nighbert (Gaylord), Adam Heller (Buster), Louis Vuolo (Demetrios), Judith Keithley (Clarissa), John Corbo (Domingo), Christopher Wilde (Irwin), Lauri Taradash (Madrugada), Chorus: Andrea Calarco, Christina Ljungman, Stephanie Lewis, Robin Blackburn (Standby). A musical in 2 acts and 9 scenes. The action takes place in New York City and Baja, California during the winter of 1941. Musical Numbers: Your Time Is My Time, Time Is Money, Sweet Nightingale, The Star That Never Got to Shine, Baja Californi-ah, Lady Picasso, Humanity, Keep You Company, No Yesterdays, Welcome to the Big C Ranch, In the Beginning, Boogie Woogie Boy from Brooklyn, Last Day at Coney Island, You Could Be the One, I'm Not the Man I Used to Be, Nice, Emperor of My Baby's Heart

(Actors Repertory Theatre) Thursday, June 7,–July 2, 1984 (22 performances) Actors Repertory Theatre (Warren Robertson, Artistic Director) with Tombigbee Productions (George Culver, Executive Producer) presents:
I DON'T WANT TO BE ZELDA ANYMORE by Marty Martin; Director, Jason Buzas; Set, Bobby Berg; Lighting, William Armstrong; Sound, Tom Gould; Costumes, Robert Wojewodski; Original Music, Bruce Coughlin; Production Manager, Bonnie Arquilla; Stage Manager, Jeffrey Markowitz; Art Producer, Janet Doeden; Associate Producer, Pam Mobilia; Press, Kevin Patterson. CAST: Margie Bolding (Zelda Sayre Fitzgerald)

(New Federal Theatre) Thursday, June 7,–24, 1984 (15 performances). Henry Street Settlement's New Federal Theatre (Woodie King, Jr., Producer) presents:
OH! OH! OBESITY with Lyrics, Music and Story by Gerald W. Deas; Script Collaboration and Direction by Bette Howard; Executive Director, Michael Frey; Set, May Callas; Costumes, Vicki Jones; Sound, Bernard Hall; Lighting, Zebedee Collins; Musical Director, John McCallum; Choreography, Ronn Pratt; Production Manager, Llewellyn Harrison; Company Manager, Linda Herring; Production Coordinator, Bill Harris; Production Assistant, Garland Thompson, Jr.; Technical Director, Yvonne Cumberbatch; Wardrobe, Yvonne Cumberbatch; Stage Manager, Malik; Press, Max Eisen, Madelon Rosen
CAST: Sandra Reaves-Phillips (Fat Momma), Karen Langerstrom (Ms. Knosh), Reginald Veljohnson (Fat Daddy), Stuart D. Goldenberg (Blimpie), Mennie F. Nelson (Fatsie), Jacquelyn Bird (Nurse/3 Pretty Girls), Regina Reynolds Hood/Erica Ariis Smith (Church Sisters/Chorus), Kent C. Jackman (Dr. Do-Nothin')
MUSICAL NUMBERS: Oh! Oh! Obesity, I Don't Eat a Thing, You've Got to Stay Real Cool, Han-Some, You're Gonna Need Somebody, If De Boot Don't Fit You Can't Wear It, Jellybread Falls on Jellyside Down, I'm Fat, Everybody Wants to Be a Star, Gym Jam Boogie, I Fried All Night Long, Finale
A musical in 2 acts and 13 scenes. The action takes place at the present time.

(Wonderhorse Theatre) Friday, June 8–28, 1984 (16 performances) Cherubs Guild (Carol Avila, Executive Director; Hillary Wyler, Artistic Director) in association with the North Carolina School of the Arts (Malcolm Morrison, Dean) presents:
OREGON by Peter Hedges; Director, Paul Stephen Myers; Set, David Lane; Lighting, John Todd; Sound, Dan Van Pelt; Stage Manager, Sandy Adams. CAST: Scott Cunningham, William Muto, Mary Kay Wildenhain. **TINY DEMONS** by Angus MacLachlan; Director, Jared Sakren; Set, Peter Rogness; Lighting, John Todd; Stage Manager, Sandy Adams. CAST: Florence Barrett, Steve Coulter, Veronique Gusdon, DeAnn Simmons, Timothy Wagner

(Actors Outlet) Monday, June 11,–July 29, 1984 (40 performances) Artists Unlimited (David Charles Keeton, Producer) presents:
BUT MOSTLY BECAUSE IT'S RAINING by David Mauriello; Director, Jordan Fletcher; Set, Leon Munier; Lighting, Randall Whitescarver; Costumes, Ellen Seeling; Technical Director, Michael Kondrat; General Manager, Karen Lesley-Lloyd; Stage Manager, Elizabeth Katherine Carr; Press, Francine L. Trevens
CAST: Linden Ashby (Tom), Wesley Stevens (Michael) A play in 2 acts and 5 scenes. The action takes place in Boston earlier this year.

(Theatre Guinevere) Tuesday, June 12,–December 9, 1984 (207 performances). The Gero Organization (Frank Gero, President; Woji Gero, Vice President) and Force 10 Productions (John Roach, Producer) present the Production Company (Norman Rene, Artistic Director; Abigail Franklin, Managing Director) production of:
BLUE WINDOW by Craig Lucas; Director, Norman Rene; Set, Loy Arcenas; Costumes, Walker Hicklin; Lighting, Debra J. Kletter; General Management, Gero Communications (Erik Murkoff, Amy Miller); Props/Sound, Bob Morrissey; Stage Manager, M. A. Howard; Press, Jeffrey Richards Associates
CAST: Maureen Silliman (Emily), Lawrence Joshua (Tom), Randy Danson (Libby), Matt Craven (Norbert), Jane Galloway (Boo), Brad O'Hare (Griever), Margo Skinner (Alice), Understudies: Susan Blommert, Dan Butler

June Stein, John Turturro in "Danny and the Deep Blue Sea" (Martha Swope Photo)

59

(Trinity Church Theatre) Thursday, June 14,–29, 1984 (13 performances). Trinity Theatre presents:
TALKING DIRTY by Sherman Snukal; Director, Anthony Giaimo; Assistant Director, John Kennedy; Set, Randy Benjamin; Set Decoration, Robert Thompson; Costumes, Gordon Ball; Stage Manager, Kara Sheridan
CAST: Susan Cella, Brian Connors, Dara Norman, Lloyd Pace, Cheryl Lesley Royce

(47th Street Theatre) Thursday, June 14,–30, 1984 (20 performances and 7 previews) Multi Production Partnership (Lynne Stuart, Hinks Shimberg, Gold 'n Gay Productions, Richard Horner) and Terry Hodge Taylor present:
KENNEDY AT COLONUS by Laurence Carr; Director, Stephen Zuckerman; Conceived and commissioned by Terry Hodge Taylor; Associate Producer, Ted Tobias; Set & Costumes, Philipp Jung; Lighting, Betsy Adams; Sound, Robert Kerzman; General Management, Richard Horner Associates; Company Managers, Matthew Bernstein, Marc Routh; Hairstylist, Antonio; Technical Director, Bill Lehne; Stage Managers, David Wahl, Mimi Bensinger; Press, Henry Luhrman Associates
CAST: Christopher Curry (Robert F. Kennedy), Will Jeffries, Nicholas Wyman, Beth McDonald, Daniel Whitner, Understudies: Elton Cormier, Mimi Bensinger, Tommy Hicks
A drama in two acts. The play begins in June of 1968 in Malibu, California, the day of the California Primary Election, then moves to various times and locations between 1936 and 1968.

(Boat Basin Rotunda) Friday, June 15–July 8, 1984 (24 performances). The Pelican Theater in association with the People's Playhouse presents:
ROMEO AND JULIET by William Shakespeare; Directors, Katharine Fehl, Jeff Glickman; Fight Director, Nels Hennum; Choreographer, Shela Xoregos; Lighting, Bruce Bowen; Sets/Costumes/Masks, Elissa Bromberg; Managing Director, John C. Forman; Stage Managers, Dennis Cameron, Mark Sorre; Press, Shirley Herz, Peter Cromarty
CAST: Matthew Allen (Abram/Friar John/Watchman), Bruce Altman (Gregory), Doug Anderson (Lord Capulet), Seva Anthony (Dancer/Citizen), Henrietta Bagley (Nurse), Richard Bassett (Citizen), Diane Behrens (Citizen), Kathleen Blake (Dancer/Citizen), Kate Burton (Juliet), Michael Butler (Tybalt), Mary Ann Chance (Lady Montague), Paula Clare (Dancer/Assistant Choreographer), Dan Cleary (Sampson/Watchman), Tom Constantin (Old Capulet/Action Coordinator), Leslie Cove (Citizen), Kathleen Cullen (Rosaline), Jacki Del Val (Dancer/Citizen), Jack Di Monte (Pepe), Ellen Duerden (Citizen), Richard Duggan (Balthasar), Derek Evans (Prince), Scott Franklin (Dancer/Citizen), Thomas Freeman (Citizen/Paris' Page), Janna Gjesdal (Lady Capulet), Harry Isaacs (Merchant/Old Capulet's Page), Maureen Grady (Citizen), Randy Kovitz (Friar Lawrence), Paul Lauren (Dancer/Citizen), Mark Metcalf (Romeo), Clark Middleton (Peter), Nancy Nemechek (Citizen), Michael Quill (Apothecary), Alan Ravage (Lord Montague), John Rensenhouse (Paris), Tait Ruppert (Mercutio), Tony Spiridakis (Benvolio), Devin Ward (Prince's Son), Jeanine Ward (Dancer/Prince's Wife)

(INTAR Theatre) Friday, June 15,–July 15, 1984 (32 performances). Bear Market Productions in association with Ernest M. Back and Clayton Phillips presents:
EVEN IN LAUGHTER by Lee and Marilyn Nestor; Director, J. Barry Lewis; Set, Robert Alan Harper; Lighting, Eric Cornwell; General Manager, Kate Harper; Associate Managing Producer, Alvin Railey; Technical Director, David Porter; Props, Doug Fogel; Costumes, Pegeen Shean; Stage Manager, Nancy Young; Press, FLT/Francine L. Trevens, Andrew Shearer, Melissa Thea
CAST: Vincent Carroll (Matthew Gattens), Frederick Walters (Harry Donahue), Rebecca Nestor (Jennifer Gattens), Von Rae Wood (Crystal Gattens Townsend), Amy Beth Williams (Sheila Gattens Hammond), David Schall (George Hammond)
A drama in 2 acts and 4 scenes. The action takes place at the present time in Matthew Gattens' house in Bucks County, Pennsylvania.

(Samuel Beckett Theatre) Friday, June 15,–October 21, 1984 (130 performances). Moved Tuesday, September 4, 1984 to Cherry Lane Theatre. The Harold Clurman Theatre (Jack Garfien, Artistic Director) and Byron Lasky present:
ENDGAME by Samuel Beckett; Director, Alvin Epstein; Setting and Costumes, Avigdor Arikha; Lighting, Jennifer Tipton; General Manager, Andrew Cohn; Company Manager, Craig S. Dorfman; Technical Director, Gordon Juel; Production Assistant, Glen Hauser; Casting, Lynn Kressel; Stage Manager, Jody Boese; Press, Jeffrey Richards Associates
CAST: Alvin Epstein (Hamm), Peter Evans succeeded by Joe Grifasi (Clov), James Greene succeeded by King Donovan (Nagg), Alice Drummond (Nell). Performed without intermission.

**Kate Burton, Mark Metcalf
in "Romeo and Juliet"
(Carol Rosegg Photo)**

(Actors Outlet) Monday, June 18–July 14, 1984 (24 performances). Artists Unlimited (David Charles Keeton, Producer) presents:
BRUT FORCE by Arch Brown; Director, Francine L. Trevens; Set, Leon Munier; Lighting, Randall Whitescarver; Costumes, Ellen Seeling; Technical Director, Michael Kondrat; General Manager, Karen Lesley-Lloyd; Stage Managers, Jerry Thomas, Jeremiah Lemons; Press, FLT Associates
CAST: James Valis (Dale), Bob J. Mitchell (Merrill), Ed Bergman (Rod), Clarence McFeeley (Arthur), Robert Rowley (Sam), Louis P. Miles (Brad). A play in 2 acts and 5 scenes. The action takes place in Merrill's West Village apartment in New York City in June 1973.

(Westbeth Theatre Center) Monday, June 18–30, 1984 (12 performances) Friends Theatre Company in association with The Actors Space presents:
THE UNDERLINGS by Tom Fontana; Director, Byam Stevens; Set & Costumes, Cam Lorendo
CAST: Deborah Allison, Ben Gotleib, Bram Lewis, Jim Oyster, George Spelvin, Robin Tilghman
A drama in two acts. The action takes place in a large city and in the state park 200 miles away.

(Actors Outlet) Thursday, June 21,–July 22, 1984 (25 performances). Artists Unlimited (David Charles Keeton, Producer) presents:
ERNIE AND ARNIE by Roger Rochowiak; Director, Arnold Willens; Set, Leon Munier; Lighting, Randall Whitescarver; Costumes, Ellen Seeling; Technical Director, Michael Kondrat; Stage Manager, Janine Trevens; Press, Francine Trevens/FLT
CAST: Sally Ruth Philbin (Arnie Summers), Rick Tolliver (Ernie Summers), Bill Corsair (Dave Freeman), Carol Siskind (Shirley Freeman), William Snovell (Rev. Dennis Coleman), Irma Larrison (Mrs. Helen Daniels)
A comedy in two acts. The action takes place at the present time in the apartment of Ernie and Arnie on a Friday evening in June.

**Alice Drummond, James Greene, Peter Evans,
Alvin Epstein in "Endgame"
(Martha Swope Photo)**

(Promenade Theatre) Thursday, June 21,–July 29, 1984 (45 performances and 18 previews). Moved to Broadway August 7, 1984 (see Broadway Calendar). Icarus Productions, Frederick M. Zollo with Ivan Bloch, ERB Productions present:
HURLYBURLY by David Rabe; Director, Mike Nichols; Set, Tony Walton; Costumes, Ann Roth; Lighting, Jennifer Tipton; Associate Producer, William P. Suter; General Management, Gatchell & Neufeld; Associate to Production, Georgianne Walken; Company Manager, Roger Gindi; Props, Jay Klein; Wardrobe, Terry LaVada; Stage Managers, Peter Lawrence, Jim Woolley; Press, Bill Evans, Sandra Manley, Jim Baldassare
CAST: Harvey Keitel (Phil), William Hurt (Eddie), Christopher Walken (Mickey), Jerry Stiller (Artie), Cynthia Nixon (Donna), Sigourney Weaver (Darlene), Judith Ivey (Bonnie), Understudies: Harris Laskawy, Natalia Nogulich
   A play in three acts. The action takes place a little while ago in a house in the Hollywood Hills.

William Hurt, Christopher Walken in "Hurlyburly"
(Martha Swope Photo)

(Terrace Theatre) Thursday, June 21, 1984– The American Stage (Anita Khanzadian, Artistic Director) presents:
A COUNTRY FOR OLD MEN by Anthony F. Doyle; Director, Jerry Heymann; Sets, David Raphel; Lighting, Greg MacPherson; Sound, Gary Harris; Costumes, Gary Jennings; Stage Manager, Carol Boland
CAST: Edward Seamon (Jimmy Thorne), Dan Lounsbery (Timothy Slaughter), George Gerdes (Rafton Pounder), Joseph Daly (MacParland)

(The Real Stage) Thursday, June 28,–July 21, 1984 (15 performances). The Bandit Company presents:
ACTION/KILLER'S HEAD by Sam Shepard; Lighting, Alan Hostetter; Sound, Doug Dowling; Set and Costumes, The Bandit Company; Stage Manager, Lenore Wolf; Press, Burnham-Callaghan, Gary Murphy
CAST: "Killer's Head" directed by Robert Clem: Frank Licato (Mazon). "Action" directed by Frank Licato: Paul D'Amato (Jeep), Joanne Hoersch (Shooter), Nancy Rothman (Liza), Larry Banner (Lupe)

(Riverwest Theatre) Monday, July 2–22, 1984 (20 performances). CHS Productions and J. C. Bua in association with Riverwest Theatre present:
LAUTREC by Brent Collins; Director, Jon-Christopher Bua; Sets, Rachel Keebler; Lighting, Leslie Ann Kilian; Costumes, Michele Reisch; Sound, Scott Johnson; Composer/Musical Director, Scott Johnson; Choreographer, Dafna Soltes; Press, FLT/Francine Trevens
CAST: Jennie Ventriss (Leontine), Wayne Rodda (Valentin), Robert Coles (Vincent Van Gogh), Edward Baran (Count Alphonse), Brent Collins (Lautrec), Pamela Davis (La Goulone), Cly Fowkes, Alice Barrett, Jane Popelas, Dru-Ann Chuchran, Dafna Soltes

(TOMI Theatre) Monday, July 9–14, 1984 (10 performances and 4 previews). Quantum Leap and John Van Ness Philip present:
CRIME AND PUNISHMENT by Fyodor Dostoyevsky; New adaptation by L. A. Sheldon adapted from the translation by David Magarshack; Directors, Virginia Castillo, Maria Mazer; Sets and Lights, John Sowle; Costumes, Jan Finnell; Sound, John Sowle, Virginia Castillo; Special Staging, John Sowle; Stage Managers, Tracy Crum, Susan Selig; Press, Hunt/Pucci Associates
CAST: Caroline Arnold (Sonia), Terence Burk (Chief Clerk/Caretaker/Driver), Sully Boyar (Porfiry), Cassie Ehrenberg (Polya), David Ehrenberg (Kolya), Julie Follansbee (Lisaveta/Mrs. Marmeladov), Wendy Fulton (Whore/Dunya), Geena Goodwin (Pawnbroker/Matron/Mrs. Raskolnikov), Bruce Harpster (Dr. Zossimov/Nikolay), Alan Reed Jacobs (Priest), David Kimball (Razumikhin), Evelyn Solann (Landlady), Shan Sullivan (Raskolnikov), Stan Weston (Marmeladov/Svidrigaylov), Mark Zeisler (Police Messenger/Bank Clerk/Lebezyatnikov). A drama in three acts. The action takes place in St. Petersburg, Russia, in the summer of 1866.

(Lincoln Center Reflecting Pool) Tuesday, July 10–18, 1984 (9 performances). The Japan Society of Boston in association with New York Japan Society presents:
KYOGEN the Nomura Kyogen Theater/Classic Comedies of Japan (Mansaku Nomura, Artistic Director); Stage Director, Hitoshi Hamatani; Sets, Hitoshi Hamatani, Jun Maeda; Lighting, Alan Blacher, Richard Gonchi; Production Management, The Maverick Group, Dale Ward; Production Manager, Peter Weicker. Productions: Fukuro Yamabushi (The Owl Priest), Futari-Bakama (Two Men in a Single Suit of Pants), and Bo-Shibari (Tied to a Pole)

(Musical Theatre Works) Monday, July 16–25, 1984 (8 performances). Staret . . . The Directors Company (Artistic Directors, Michael Parva, Victoria Lanman) presents:
HOLDING PATTERNS with Scenes and Songs by Jeffrey Sweet; Director, John Monteith; Musical Director, Scott Berry; Lighting, William J. Plachy; Costume Coordinator, Neal Bishop; Stage Manager, Dara Hershman
CAST: Fran Brill, Colleen Dodson, Bob Higgins, Lee Wilkof

(Vivian Beaumont Theater) Tuesday, July 17–22, 1984 (8 performances). The American Hellenic Alliance, Mel Howard/World Festivals, Inc. present the Greek National Theatre production of:
OEDIPUS REX by Sophocles; Director, Minos Volanakis; Setting, Robert Mitchell; Music, Theodore Antoniou; Costumes, Dionysis Fotopoulos; Assistant Directors, Vassilis Kyritsis, George Vouros; Company Manager, Thomas Shovestull; Press, Susan Bloch Company, Bob Larkin, Walter Vatter, Ellen Zeisler
CAST: Nikos Kourkoulos/Alexis Mingas (Oedipus), Stathis Samartzis (Priest), Nikos Kavvadas/Kostas Tsapekos (Kreon), G. Danis/Stelios Kappatos/Alex Mylonas (Tiresias), Katerina Helmi/Lambrini Liva (Jocaste), Theodore Moridis/Kostas Tsapekos (Men from Corinth), Andreas Lazaris/Alex Mylonas (Shepherd of Laios), Spyros Mavidis/Andreas Vaios (Messenger), Paya Veaki/Lambrini Liva (Daughters of Oedipus), Christos Biros/Christos Demertzis/Yannis Siopis (Chorus Leaders) Performed without intermission.

(West End Theatre) Wednesday, July 18–August 12, 1984 (16 performances) Herman D. Farrell, Jr. presents:
DREAMS OF THE SON by Herman D. Farrell III; Direction and Set, Herman D. Farrell III; Production Manager, Kevin J. Watson; Choreographer, Monique Farrell; Costumes, Carol Squadra; Lighting, Paul Bartlett; Stage Managers, David A. Schwartz, Nikki Wiesner; Press, Dow Flint Kowalczyk
CAST: Gina Bonati, Charles Butler, John Combs, Thomas Dillon, Robinet Flynn, Mel Jurdem, Eleanora Kaye, Dow Flint Kowalczyk, Donald Linahan, Stephanie Martine, Barbara Nolan, Charles Potts, Jack Ramey, Kristin Reeves, Ian David Smith, Vernon Spencer

(Perry Street Theatre) Thursday, July 26,–August 5, 1984 (13 performances and 27 previews). John Glines and Lawrence Lane present:
CARLA'S SONG by Michelle Morris; Based on her book "If I Should Die Before I Wake"; Director, John Glines; Lighting, Jeff Davis; Set, Leon Martin; Costume Coordinator, Kathy Powers; Original Music, Bill Brohn; Puppets, Randy Carfagno; General Manager, Lawrence Lane; Company Manager, Lisa Seldin; Technical Director, Peter Waldron; Stage Managers, William Castleman, David Kerin; Press, Hunt/Pucci Associates, James Sapp
CAST: Kym Le Mon (Carla), David Hayward (Jay), David Kerin (Dean), Jeanne Schlegel (Mrs. Forsythe/Sister Marietta/Elise)
   A drama in two acts.

David Hayward, Kym LeMon
in "Carla's Song"
(Gerry Goodstein Photo)

61

(INTAR Theatre) Tuesday, August 7–September 23, 1984 (48 performances). Artistic New Directions presents:
RELATIVELY SPEAKING by Alan Ayckbourn; Director, Rick Meyer; Production Design, Marc D. Malamud; Executive Producer, Jim Wemett; Stage Manager, Peter Kent
CAST: James Kirsch (Greg), Kristine Niven (Ginny), Thomas Barbour (Philip), Kathleen Claypool (Sheila)
 A play in 2 acts and 4 scenes. The action takes place during a summer weekend in London and in the country.

(Lambs Theatre) Wednesday, August 8–26, 1984 (21 performances). Louis D. Pietig in association with Mary Gaston presents:
COUPLE OF THE YEAR by Sam Havens; Director, Edward Stern; Set, Bob Barnett; Lighting, Lisa Grossman; Costumes, Mary-Anne Aston; Technical Director, Joseph Connell; Stage Manager, Denise Laffer
CAST: William Van Hunter (Lionel), Gordana Rashovich (Jill), Tom McGreevey (Father McShane), Amelia David (Merle)
 A drama in two acts. The action takes place at the present time on Easter Sunday.

(Village Gate/Downstairs) Tuesday, August 21, 1984–April 20, 1985 (226 performances and 3 previews). Tony Conforti and Jerry Saperstein in association with Brian Winthrop present:
SHADES OF HARLEM, a Cotton Club Cabaret Musical; Director, Mical Whitaker; Set, Linda Lombardi; Lights, Robert Strohmeier; Costumes, Sharon Alexander; Hairstylist, Phyllis Della; Choreography, Ty Stephens; Created by Jeree Palmer; Musical Direction/Arrangement/Additional Concepts, Frank Owens; Stage Manager, Pam Osman; Company Manager, Conley Richards; Associate Producers, Howard Effron, Robert Roth, Richard Scarlato, Hank Thomas; Executive Producers, Sal Surace, George Tassone; Press, Max Eisen, Maria Somma, Madelon Rosen, Deborrah Karim
CAST: Branice McKenzie, Jeree Palmer, Ty Stephens, Renaissance Ladies: Ludie Jones, Juanita Boisseau, Alice Wilkie, Renaissance Girls: Sheila Barker, Doris Bennett, Melanie Daniels, Alyson Lang, Band Leader/Pianist, Frank Owens
MUSICAL NUMBERS: Shades of Harlem, Take the A Train, I Love Harlem, Sweet Georgia Brown, Madame Alberta K. Johnson, Right Key Wrong Keyhole, Satin Doll, I Got It Bad and That Ain't Good, Black Coffee, Jitterbug, Harlem Hop, Georgia Camp Meeting, If You Wanna Keep Your Man, Diga Diga Doo, Stowaway, I'm Just Simply Full of Jazz, My Man, On the Sunny Side of the Street, Body and Soul, I Got Rhythm, Perdido, It Don't Mean a Thing, God Bless the Child, Finale

(Promenade Theatre) Wednesday, September 5–16, 1984 (18 performances). Bill Miller and I.A.I Presentations present:
THE CHINESE MAGIC REVUE OF TAIWAN under the supervision of Ben Sprecher; Lighting, Alvin Ho; Technical Director, Tom Shilhanek; Company Manager, David Musselman; Press, Jeffrey Richards, C. George Willard, Bob Ganshaw, Toby Mailman, Naomi Grabel, Bill Shuttleworth
PROGRAM: Act I: Opening Ceremony, Dragon Dance, Comedy Contortion, Juggling Cycle, Balancing Fantasy, Chinese Magic, Feet Balancing, Chinese Kung-Fu Act II: Precision Balancing, Flaming Circle, Chinese Comedy, High Act, Tower of Chairs, Human Pyramid, Bicycle Act, Finale

(18th Street Playhouse) Sunday, September 9–23, 1984 (12 performances). BTA Productions and D. A. Dorwart present:
THE RIGHT DECISION by Eliza Wyatt; Director, Tony Alicata; Set, Roger Mooney; Lighting, Richard Clausen; Stage Managers, Candace J. Coons, Sandy Musolf; Press, FLT/Francine Trevens, Andrew P. Shearer
CAST: Anthony Inneo (Al), Judith Elaine (Marion), Joel Rooks (Joe), Jean Anderson (Brenda), Anthony St. Martin (Arthur)
 A drama in two acts. The action takes place at the present time in the apartment of Al and Marion.

(Cubiculo) Monday, September 10,–October 7, 1984 (28 performances and 6 previews). Evelyn Powers and Kent Productions present:
LESTER SIMS RETIRES TOMORROW by William Curtis; Director, Louis Erdmann; Set, Kay Coughenour; Lighting, Jim Mayo; Costumes, Eugenia Erdman; General Management, Evelyn Powers; Stage and Company Manager, Deborah Teller; Press, Jeffrey Richards, C. George Willard, Bob Ganshaw, Bill Shuttleworth, Toby Mailman
CAST: George Murdock (Lester Sims), Jennifer Rhodes (Margaret Beauchamp), Karl Erdmann (Harold Yurtz/Delivery Boy)
 A play in two acts. The action takes place at the present time in Lester Sims' apartment in a small Midwestern college town in Mid-May.

Branice McKenzie, Jeree Palmer, Ty Stephens
in "Shades of Harlem"

(Minetta Lane Theatre) Thursday, September 6, 1984–January 6, 1985 (143 performances). Brent Peek, Rhoda Herrick, James C. Ezzes, Circle Repertory Company, Steppenwolf Theatre Company present the Steppenwolf Theatre Company of Chicago's production of:
BALM IN GILEAD by Lanford Wilson; Director, John Malkovich; Set & Lighting, Kevin Rigdon; Costume Supervision, Glenne Headly; Sound, John Malkovich; Sound Supervision, Chuck London Media/Stewart Werner; General Management, Brent Peek Productions; Management Associate, Scott Green; Company Manager, Sally Campbell; Technical Supervisor, Jim Fainberg; Production Manager, Kate Stewart; Wardrobe, Taryn Trappe; Production Assistant, Timothy Hawkins; Casting, Hughes/Moss; Stage Managers, Teri McClure, Anne Marie Paolucci; Press, Fred Nathan, Anne Abrams, Leslie Anderson, Ted Killmer, Bert Fink.*
CAST: Betsy Aidem (Kay), Steven Bauer succeeded by Vincent Spano (Tig), Paul Butler (John), Adam Davidson (Child), Eben Davidson (Child), Debra Engle (Babe), Giancarlo Esposito (Ernesto), Francis Guinan (Franny), Glenne Headly (Ann), Jonathan Hogan (Martin), Terry Kinney (Fick), Samantha Kostmayer (Child), Zane Lasky succeeded by Lazaro Perez (Frank), Charlotte Maier (Judy), Jodie Markel (Understudy), Bruce McCarty (Bob), S. Epatha Merkerson (Understudy), Laurie Metcalf (Darlene), D. W. Moffett (Stranger), Mario A. Moreno (Understudy), Billie Neal (Rust), Burke Pearson (Al), Lazaro Perez succeeded by Mario Moreno (Carlo), James Pickens, Jr. (Rake), Michael Rispoli (Understudy), Karen Sederholm (Terry), Gary Sinise (Dopey), Danton Stone (Joe), Brian Tarantina (David), Lynne Thigpen (Bonnie), Mick Weber (Tim), Tom Zanarini (Xavier)
 A drama in two acts. The action takes place during October of 1972 in an all-night coffee shop and the street corner outside on Upper Broadway in New York City.
*The company received a Drama Desk Award for Ensemble Acting, and John Malkovich for Best Direction of a Play. Laurie Metcalf received a Theatre World Award for Outstanding New Talent.

Danton Stone, Gary Sinise, Laurie Metcalf
in "Balm in Gilead"

(Morse Center Trinity Theatre) Wednesday, September 12–22, 1984 (10 performances and 4 previews). The Morse Center at Trinity School presents:
THE NEW YORKERS by Murray Schisgal; Director, Peter Maloney; Producer/Artistic Director, John Dooley; Sets, Brian Martin; Lighting, Daniel C. Abrahamsen; Costumes, Tina Watson Lang; Production Assistant, Cassandra Scott; Stage Managers, Lisa Fleischman, Elizabeth Dubelman; Press, Shirley Herz, Pete Sanders
CAST: "The Pushcart Peddlers": Allen Swift (Cornelius J. Hollingsworth III), Adolph Green (Shimmel Shitzman), Amanda Green (Maggie Cutwell). The action takes place at the turn of the century on New York City's waterfront. "Jealousy": Adolph Green (Jerry Hollingsworth), Phyllis Newman (Nina Stone Hollingsworth), Allen Swift (Robert Ginsberg). The action takes place at the present time in a NYC East Side co-op apartment.

(TOMI Park Royal Theatre) Tuesday, September 12,–30, 1984 (15 performances). Berry Productions presents:
TRESPASSES by Barbara Santee; Director, Don Signore; Set, Evelyn Sakash; Lighting, Victor En Yu Tan; Costumes, Ricardo Morin; Sound, Tom Gould; Stage Manager, Janet P. Callahan; Wardrobe, Karen Christie; Press, Free Lance Talents/Francine L. Trevens, Andrew Shearer
CAST: Irene Schaeffer (Maggie), Renette Zimmerly (Rose, Maggie's mother), Regina David (Momma, Maggie's grandmother), Kim Keating (Velma, Maggie's aunt), Peter Bogyo (Jim, Velma's husband)
A drama in 2 acts, 12 scenes, with prologue and epilogue. The action takes place from July of 1940 to the present.

(Village Performers Theatre) Wednesday, September 12,–October 28, 1984 (32 performances). Village Performers Theatre Ltd. (Reena Heenan, Artistic Director) presents:
REHEARSAL FOR MURDER by John Patrick Hart; Directed by Mr. Hart; Assistant Director, Frank Brancaccio; Lighting, Rob Birarelli; Stage Managers, Elaine O'Donnell, Melissa Neenan
CAST: Paul Rosson (Florin Thatcher), Sylvester Rich (Iago), Stanton Marchbanks (Brad Evans), Malcolm Gray (Marshall Fonda), Nancie Phillips (Susan Brent), T. W. Miller (Andy McGuire), Carol Lee Shahid (Jill), Joan Jacqueney (Rachel Howard).
A drama in two acts, with prologue. The action takes place in Sing Sing Prison (present time), in a Broadway Theatre in NYC (a few years earlier), and in a cottage in Devonshire, England during World War II.

(Lamb's Theatre) Friday, September 14, 1984–January 6, 1985, and transferred to Samuel Beckett Theatre Tuesday, January 8,–April 13, 1985 (209 performances and 6 previews). Jack Garfein and Byron Lasky present:
AVNER THE ECCENTRIC a solo performance by Avner Eisenberg; Production Designer, Gordon A. Juel; Lighting, Kevin Rigdon; General Manager, Kevin W. Dowling, Proscenium Services; Company Managers, Craig S. Dorfman, Claudette Sutton; Production Assistant, Fred Berning, Jr.; Stage Manager, Gordon A. Juel; Press, Jeffrey Richards, C. George Willard, Robert Ganshaw, Eileen McMahon, Ben Morse, Toby Mailman, Bill Shuttleworth

(One Sheridan Square) Wednesday, Sept. 19, 1984 – still playing May 31, 1985. The Ridiculous Theatrical Company (Artistic Director, Charles Ludlam; General Manager, Steven Samuels) presents:
THE MYSTERY OF IRMA VEP written and directed by Charles Ludlam; Original Music, Peter Golub; Settings, Charles Ludlam; Costumes, Everett Quinton; Lighting, Lawrence Eichler; Dressers, Deborah Petti, Mary Ann Quinton; Hairstylist, Ethyl Eichelberger; Stage Manager/Technical Director, Lawrence Eichler; Press, Steven Samuels
CAST: Charles Ludlam (Nicodemus Underwood/Lady Enid Hillcrest/Alcazar/Irma Vep), Everett Quinton (Jane Twisden/Lord Edgar Hillcrest/An Intruder)
A mystery in 3 acts performed with one intermission.

(Promenade Theatre) Wednesday, September 19–30, 1984 (14 performances). ICM Artists presents the Center Theatre Group/Mark Taper Forum production of:
VIVA VITTORIO! conceived and directed by Vittorio Gassman; Set & Lighting, John De Santis; Original Music, Fiorenzo Carpi; General Manager, Leonard Stein; Company Manager, Marvin Schofer; Stage Manager, James T. McDermott; Press, Marilynn LeVine/P. R. Partners, Merle Frimark, Meg Gordean, Fran Colgan, Francesca Rodolfi
CAST: Vittorio Gassman, Rhonda Aldrich, Neil Bagg, Nino Prester
PROGRAM: Part I: "A Report to an Academy" by Franz Kafka, "Kean" (Fragments) by Alexandre Dumas adapted by Jean-Paul Sartre, "The Man with the Flower in His Mouth" by Luigi Pirandello, performed in Italian Part II: "On the Harmfulness of Theatre" by Luciano Codignola

Top: Avner Eisenberg Below: Everett Quinton, Charles Ludlam in "The Mystery of Irma Vep" (*S&S Labs Photo*)

Vittorio Gassman, Neil Bagg in "Viva Vittorio!"

(Samuel Beckett Theatre) Sunday, September 23,–October 7, 1984 (17 performances and 8 previews). Jack Garfein and Kilian C. Ganly present:
ALL STRANGE AWAY by Samuel Beckett; Director, Gerald Thomas; Setting and Costume, Daniela Thomas; Lighting, Howard Thies; General Manager, Craig S. Dorfman; Assistant to Director, Richard Bach; Technical Director, Marc D. Malamud; Production Assistant, Horacio Palacio; Stage Manager, Glen Hauser; Press, Jeffrey Richards, C. George Willard, Robert Ganshaw, Ben Morse, Eileen McMahon, Bill Shuttleworth, Toby Mailman
CAST: Robert Langdon-Lloyd. Performed without intermission.

(Harold Clurman Theatre) Sunday, Sept. 23,–October 6, 1984 (19 performances). Irish Arts Center (Jim Sheridan, Artistic Director; Nye Heron, Executive Director) in association with Kathleen Grace presents:
MR. JOYCE IS LEAVING PARIS by Tom Gallacher; Director, Jordan Deitcher; Set, Rick Butler; Lighting, Victor En Yu Tan; Costumes, David Loveless; General Manager, Nye Heron; Assistant to Producer, Siobhan Kennedy; Stage Manager, Kurt Wagemann; Press, FLT/Francine L. Trevens, Andrew P. Shearer
CAST: Vincent Carroll (Man), Robin Howard (Woman), Brian Mallon (Young Man), Rory Sullivan (Stanislaus), Neil Vipond (James Joyce)
    A play in two acts. The action takes place in Trieste in February of 1908, and in Paris in December of 1939.

(Jack Lawrence Theatre) Tuesday, September 25,–October 14, 1984 (24 performances and 5 previews). The Denver Center for the Performing Arts, The John F. Kennedy Center for the Performing Arts, The American National Theatre and Academy and Brockman Seawell present:
QUILTERS by Molly Newman and Barbara Damashek; Music and Lyrics, Miss Damashek; Based on book "The Quilters: Women and Domestic Art" by Patricia Cooper and Norman Bradley Allen; Director, Barbara Damashek; Set, Ursula Belden; Costumes, Elizabeth Palmer; Lighting, Allen Lee Hughes; Casting, Hughes/Moss; General Manager, Robert Buckley Associates; Company Manager, Susan Bell; Wardrobe, Crystal Chapman; Assistant Director, Charles Otte; Stage Managers, Bruce A. Hoover, Diana M. Scott, Charles Otte; Press, Patt Dale, Julianne Waldheim
CAST: Lenka Peterson (Sarah), Daughters: Evalyn Baron, Marjorie Berman, Alma Cuervo, Lynn Lobban, Rosemary McNamara, Jennifer Parsons, Musicians/Daughters/Sons: Emily Knapp Chatfield, Melanie Sue Harby, John S. Lionarons, Joseph A. Waterkotte, Catherine Way, Understudies: Eda Seasongood (Sarah), Daughters: Catherine Way, Eda Seasongood, Jennifer Parsons, Rosemary McNamara, Lynn Lobban, Alma Cuervo
SONGS: Pieces of Lives, Rocky Road, Little Babes That Sleep All Night, Thread the Needle, Cornelia, The Windmill Song, Are You Washed in the Blood of the Lamb?, The Butterfly, Green, Hoedown, Quiltin' and Dreamin', Every Log in My House, Land Where We'll Never Grow Old, Who Will Count the Stitches, The Lord Don't Rain Down Manna, Dandelion, Everything Has a Time, Hands Around. A musical in two acts.

(Apple Corps Theatre) Thursday, September 27,–October 7, 1984 (12 performances). Belltolls Productions present:
A STEP OUT OF LINE by Enid Rudd; Director, Joan Vail Thorne; No other credits available.
CAST: Ralph Bell, Michael Tolan, Patricia Roe, Verona Barnes, Glenn Bristow, Bryan Clark, John Connolly, Barry Cullison, Kit Flanagan, Vincent Grant, Linda Lee Johnson

(Perry Street Theatre) Sunday, September 30,–October 7, 1984 (8 performances and 12 previews) The Iris Group in association with Lori Wasserman and Michael Lewis presents:
ENTER A FREE MAN by Tom Stoppard; Director, Dean Button; Sets, Rick Dennis; Costumes, Gregg Barnes; Lighting, John Gleason; Sound, Peter Kallish; General Manager, Sherman Gross; Stage Managers, Diane Ward, Elizabeth Miller; Press, Jeffrey Richards Associates, Bill Shuttleworth
CAST: Jerome Kilty (George Riley), Helen Stenborg (Persephone), Deanna Deignan (Linda), W. T. Martin (Harry), Jeremiah Alexander (Able), Jill Larson (Florence), Curt Williams (Brown), Charles M. Kray (Carmen), Understudies: Charles M. Kray, Elizabeth Miller
    A play in two acts. The action takes place sometime in the early 1960's in the Riley home and the neighborhood pub of a working-class London suburb.

(top) Marjorie Berman, Evalyn Baron, Lenka Peterson, Alma Cuervo, (bottom) Rosemary McNamara, Jennifer Parsons, Lynn Lobban in "Quilters"
(Martha Swope Photo)

(Village Gate Upstairs) Wednesday, Oct. 3,–Nov. 11, 1984 (69 performances). Rosita Sarnoff presents:
RAP MASTER RONNIE with Music by Elizabeth Swados; Lyrics, Garry Trudeau; Director, Caymichael Patten; Set, Neil Peter Jampolis; Costumes, David Woolard; Lighting, Anne Militello; Sound, Tom Gould; Choreography, Ronni Stewart; Music Arranger/Director, John Richard Lewis; Casting, Elisa Meyers; General Manager, David Lawlor; Associate General Manager, Helen L. Nickerson; Assistant to Producer, Bonnie Grossman; Wardrobe, Carlena Stone; Stage Managers, Nancy Harrington, Richard Hester, Abigail Koreto; Press, Shirley Herz, Sam Rudy, Peter Cromarty, Pete Sanders, Gary Lawrence
CAST: Reathel Bean, Catherine Cox, Ernestine Jackson, Mel Johnson, Jr., Richard Ryder
MUSICAL NUMBERS: Rap Master Ronnie, Take That Smile Off Your Face, The Class of 1984, You're Not Ready, The Majority, Self-Made Man, O Grenada, The Assistant Understudy of State for Human Rights, Nine to Twelve, Thinking the Unthinkable, Cheese, Facts, The Empire Strikes First, New Year's in Beirut 1983, The Roundup, Something for Nothing
    A partisan revue.

Ernestine Jackson, Richard Ryder, Reathel Bean, Catherine Cox, Mel Johnson, Jr. in "Rap Master Ronnie" *(Carol Rosegg Photo)*

(Playhouse 91) Thursday, Oct. 4,–Dec. 2, 1984 (67 performances and 28 previews).
Roger Berlind and Ray Larsen present:
AFTER THE FALL by Arthur Miller; Director, John Tillinger; Set, John Lee Beatty; Costumes, William Ivey Long; Lighting, Dennis Parichy; Sound, Gary Harris; Wigs, Paul Huntley; Casting, Deborah Brown; General Management, R. Tyler Gatchell, Peter Neufeld; Company Manager, David Conte; Wardrobe, Mary Lou Rios; Hairstylist, Ron Frederick; Stage Managers, Trey Hunt, Anne Marie Kuehling; Press, Solters/Roskin/Friedman, Joshua Ellis, Cindy Valk, Jackie Green
CAST: Frank Langella (Quentin), Dianne Wiest (Maggie), Rose Arrick (Nurse/Carrie), William Cain (Man), Lisa Dunsheath (Felice), Henderson Forsythe (Lou), Delphi Harrington (Elsie), Benjamin Hendrickson (Mickey), Tresa Hughes (Mother), Laurie Kennedy (Holga), Salem Ludwig (Father), Mary-Joan Negro (Louise), Understudies: Paul Collins (Quentin), Lisa Dunsheath (Maggie), William Cain (Father/Lou), Lauren Klein (Holga/Elsie/Felice/Louise), Rose Arrick (Mother), Anne Marie Kuehling (Carrie/Nurse)

A drama in two acts. The action takes place in the mind, thought and memory of Quentin.

(Westbeth Theater Center) Thursday, Oct. 4–21, 1984 (12 performances). The Harbor Shakespeare Festival with the assistance of the Westbeth Theater Center presents:
THE TAMER TAMED by John Fletcher; Director, R. Jeffrey Cohen; Design, Alexis Siroc; Lighting, John Enea; Costumes, Jacqueline Hart; Stage Manager, Emily Oberman; Press, Patt Dale Associates
CAST: Charles Anderson (Pedro/Apothecary), Andrew Barnicle (Rowland), Brian Evers (Petruchio), Rorri Feinstein (Country Wife), Alexandra Fendell (Maid 1), Hugh Hodgin (Tranio), Bill Hooper (Jacques/Doctor/Drunken Servant), Lisa Levine (Maid 3), Jill MacKavey (Maria), Steven J. Parris (Petronius), Cristine Reid (Byancha), Kayla Serotte (Livia), Rick Tolliver (Sophocles), Patrick Tull (Moroso), Gwenne Wilcox (Maid 2), Debbie Wojcik (City Wife).

A comedy performed with one intermission.

(Audrey Wood Theatre) Tuesday, Oct. 9. 1984–Apr. 21, 1985 (298 performances and 5 previews). The Jewish Repertory Theatre and Jarick Productions present:
KUNI-LEML or THE MISMATCH with Book by Nahma Sandrow; Based on "The Fanatic or the Two Kuni-Lemls" by Avrom Goldfadn; Music, Raphael Crystal; Lyrics, Richard Enquist; Director, Ran Avni; Musical Staging, Haila Strauss; Sets, Joel Fontaine; Costumes, Karen Hummel; Lighting, Dan Kinsley; Orchestrations, Raphael Crystal; General Management, Dorothy Olim, George Elmer; Wardrobe, Sheryl Joshua; Casting, Susan Haskins; Stage Managers, Gay Smerek, Joanne Baum; Press, Shirley Herz, Peter Cromarty, Pete Sanders, Sam Rudy, Gary Lawrence
CAST: Steve Sterner (Simkhe/Sasha), Adam Heller succeeded by Jack Savage (Yankl/Yasha), Mark Zeller (Reb Pinkhos), Barbara McCulloh succeeded by Patricia Ben Petersen (Carolina), Gene Varrone (Kalmen), Scott Wentworth succeeded by Adam Heller (Max), Susan Friedman succeeded by Liz Larsen (Libe), Stuart Zagnit (Kuni-Leml), Understudies: Joanne Baum, Adam Heller, Joel Kramer, Steve Sterner, Jack Savage, Daniel Pevsner
MUSICAL NUMBERS: Celebrate!, The Boy Is Perfect, Carolina's Lament, The World Is Getting Better, Cuckoo, The Matchmaker's Daughter, A Meeting of the Minds, A Little Learning, Nothing Counts But Love, What's My Name?, Purim Song, Do Horses Talk to Horses?, Lovesongs and Lullabies, Be Fruitful and Multiply, Finale

A musical in 2 acts and 8 scenes. The action takes place in Odessa in the Ukraine, before and during the holiday of Purim in 1880.

(Theatre Off Park) Tuesday, Oct. 9,–Nov. 18, 1984 (36 performances) Theatre Off Park (Bertha Lewis, Producing Director; Albert Harris, Artistic Director) presents:
THE POKER SESSION by Hugh Leonard; Director, Albert Harris; Set, Philipp Jung; Costumes, Christina Giannini; Lighting, Jeremy Craig Johnson; Sound, Kenn Dovel; Original Music, Michael Valenti; Technical Director, James Knight; Stage Managers, John M. Atherlay, Alice Farrell; Press, Howard Atlee, Barbara Atlee
CAST: Keith McDermott (Billy), Ruby Holbrook (Mrs. Beavis), Keliher Walsh (Irene), Colm Meany (Kevin), Jessie K. Jones (Fran), Stephen Vinovich (Teddy), Matthew Smith (Des)

A drama in 2 acts and 3 scenes. The action takes place at the present time in the conservatory of the Beavis home in Dublin, Ireland.

(South Street Theatre) Thursday, Oct. 11,–Nov. 25, 1984 (32 performances and 20 previews) New Writers presents:
BETWEEN RAILS by Eric Hertz; Producer-Director, Hal Scott; Set, Mark Haack; Costumes, Karen Perry; Lighting, Shirley Pendergast; Production Assistant, David DeCastro; Wigs and Makeup, Daniel Maddux; Stage Managers, Joseph DePauw, Paul Botchis; Press, Philip Rinaldi, Max Eisen, Irene Gandy, Maria Somma
CAST: Thelma Louise Carter (Willie-Mae). Performed without intermission.

Frank Langella, Dianne Wiest in "After the Fall" *(Peter Cunningham Photo)*

Stephen Vinovich, Keith McDermott (seated) in "The Poker Session" *(Martha Swope/Carol Rosegg Photo)*

Susan Friedman, Stuart Zagnit in "Kuni-Leml" *(Adam Newman Photo)*

(Promenade Theatre) Friday, Oct. 12, 1984–January 27, 1985 (109 performances).
The Shubert Organization (Gerald Schoenfeld, Chairman; Bernard B. Jacobs, President), McCann & Nugent present:
PACIFIC OVERTURES with Music & Lyrics by Stephen Sondheim; Book, John Weidman; Additional Material, Hugh Wheeler; Director, Fran Soeder; Scenery, James Morgan; Lighting, Mary Jo Dondlinger; Costumes, Mark Passerell; Additional Costumes, Eiko Yamaguchi; Musical Director, Eric Stern; Orchestrations, James Stenborg; Choreographer, Janet Watson; General Management, McCann & Nugent; Production Coordinator, Mary T. Nelson; Company Manager, David Musselman; Management Associates, Patricia Taylor, Daniel Kearns, Jeffrey Hillock, Edward Nelson; Technical Director, Tom Shilhanek; Wardrobe, Jenna Krempel; Props, Deborah Alix Martin, John Hodge; Sound, T. Richard Fitzgerald; Production Assistants, Laura Heller, Beth Pollack; Stage Managers, Peter J. Taylor, Elisabeth Farwell; Press, Fred Nathan, Ted Killmer, Anne Abrams, Leslie Anderson, Bert Fink
CAST: Ernest Abuba (Reciter), Tony Marino (Lord Abe), Chuck Brown (Shogun's Mother/British Admiral), Kevin Gray (Kayama Yesaemon), Timm Fujii (Tamate/British Sailor), John Caleb (John Manjiro/Fisherman/French Admiral), Ronald Yamamoto (Merchant), Tim Ewing (Thief), John Bantay (Commodore Perry), Thomas Ikeda (Madam/Russian Admiral), John Baray (Old Man/American Admiral), Francis Jue (Boy/Dutch Admiral/British Sailor), Ray Contreras (Warrior/British Sailor), Tom Matsusaka (Imperial Priest), Allan Tung (Fencing Master's Daughter), Proscenium Servants: Gerri Igarashi, Gayln Kong, Diane Lam, Christine Toy, Understudy: John Aller
MUSICAL NUMBERS: The Advantages of Floating in the Middle of the Sea, There Is No Other Way, Four Black Dragons, Chrysanthemum Tea, Poems, Welcome to Kanagawa, Someone in a Tree, Lion Dance, Please Hello, A Bowler Hat, Pretty Lady, Next
   A musical in 2 acts and 12 scenes. The Action takes place in Japan, from July 1853 and from then on.

(Samuel Beckett Theatre) Friday, Oct. 12–28, 1984 (20 performances) The Barbara Barondess Theatre Lab presents:
MEDEA AND THE DOLL by Rudy Gray; Director, Randy Frazier; Production Design, Don Jensen; Producing Director, Lily Turner; Stage Manager, Otis White; Press, Jeffrey Richards, Ben Morse, C. George Willard, Robert Ganshaw, Eileen McMahon, Leo Stern, Toby Mailman, Bill Shuttleworth
CAST: Maria E. Ellis (Nilda Belmont), Morgan Freeman (Winston Crews, M.D.), Understudies: Cherron Hoye, Dean Irby
   A drama in two acts.

(Judith Anderson Theatre) Friday, Oct. 12–28, 1984 (12 performances and 4 previews). Randy Finch and Stage Arts Theater Company (Nell Robinson, Ruth Ann Norris, Artistic Directors) present:
CAP AND BELLS by Luigi Pirandello; Translated by Norman A. Bailey; Director, John Ferraro; Set, Toby Corbett; Costumes, Shay Cunliffe; Lighting, Greg MacPherson; Casting, Ellen Novack; General Manager, Erik Murkoff; Production Manager, Woji Gero; Wardrobe, Lynn Van Wagener; Stage Managers, Jono Gero, Adam Storke; Production Assistant, Amy Miller; Press, Henry Luhrman Associates
CAST: Jay Acovone (Fifi), Frank Gero (Ciampa), Carolyn Green (Nina), Tom Mardirosian (Spano), Frederica Meister (La Saracena), Lucrezia Norelli (Assunta), Angela Pietropinto (Beatrice), Fiddle Viracola (Fana)
   A comedy in two acts. The action takes place in the Fiorica salon in a small town in the interior of Sicily.

(Off Center Theatre) Sunday, October 14–27, 1984 (12 performances and 9 previews). Irondale Ensemble (James Louis Niesen, Artistic Director; Terry Greiss, Executive Director) presents:
JASON AND THE ARGONAUTS from the classic Greek myth as told by Euripides, Robert Graves, Edith Hamilton, Bullfinch and others; Director, James Louis Niesen; Set, Kennon Rothchild; Costumes, Elena Pellicciaro; Lighting, Richard Dorfman; Movement, Annie B. Parson; Dramaturg, Jonathan Ward; Technical Director, Michael Yarborough; Press, G. Theodore Killmer
CAST: Paul Bonner, Josh Broder, Catherine A. Chad, Terry Greiss, Paul Lazar, Harry Primeau, Jody Reiss, Pat Russell

(Lamb's Little Theatre) Monday, Oct. 15–Nov. 11, 1984 (12 performances and 3 previews) Lamb's Theatre Company (Carolyn Rossi Copeland, Executive Director) presents:
PORCH by Jeffrey Sweet; Director, Nan Harris; Sets, Michael C. Smith; Lighting, Marc D. Malamud; Costumes, Neal Bishop; Casting, McCorkle Casting; Stage Manager, Steve Zorthian; Press, Patt Dale, Julianne Waldheim
CAST: Clarke Gordon (Herbert), Lianne Kressin (Lorraine), Jill Eikenberry (Amy), Gary Bayer (Sam)
   A play with prologue and performed without intermission. The action takes place in Springfield, Ohio.

**Ernest Abuba (center) and company
in "Pacific Overtures"
*(Martha Swope Photo)***

(New York University Theatre) Monday, October 15–21, 1984 (7 performances) New York University presents:
THE AMERICAN MIME THEATRE: Founder/Director, Paul J. Curtis; Managing Director, Jean Barbour; Stage Manager, Dale Fuller. CAST: Jean Barbour, Charles Barney, Joseph Citta, Paul J. Curtis, Dale Fuller, Kevin Kaloostian, Erica Sarzin, and Mr. Bones. Repertory: Dreams, The Lovers, The Scarecrow, Hurly-Burly, Evolution, Sludge, Six, The Unitaur (World Premiere)

(Westside Arts Center/Cheryl Crawford Theatre) Monday, Oct. 15, 1984–Jan. 20, 1985 (113 performances and 13 previews). The Gero Organization (Frank Gero, President), Stephen Graham, Joan Stein present the Manhattan Theatre Club production of:
THE MISS FIRECRACKER CONTEST by Beth Henley; Director, Stephen Tobolowsky; Set, John Lee Beatty; Costumes, Jennifer von Mayrhauser; Lighting, Dennis Parichy; Sound, Stan Metelits; General Management, The Gero Organization; Company Manager, Erik Murkoff; Production Assistant, Amy Miller; Technical Director, Derald Plumer; Wardrobe, Winsome McKay, Mary Justice; Casting, Mary Jo Slater; Stage Managers, Louis D. Pietig, Daniel Kanter; Press, Henry Luhrman, Terry M. Lilly, Helene Greece, David Mayhew
CAST: Holly Hunter succeeded by Christina Moore (Carnelle Scott), June Stein (Popeye Jackson), Claire Malis (Elain Rutledge), Mark Linn-Baker succeeded by Gary Roberts (Delmount Williams), Budge Threlkeld (Mac Sam), Joyce Reehling Christopher (Tessy Mahoney), Standbys: Donna Davis, Michael Countryman
   A comedy in two acts. The action takes place in Brookhaven, Mississippi, a small southern town, at the end of June and the beginning of July.

**June Stein, Holly Hunter
in "The Miss Firecracker Contest"
*(Gerry Goodstein Photo)***

(TOMI Park Royale Theatre) Wednesday, Oct. 17–Nov. 3, 1984 (16 performances and 4 previews). The Actors Producing Company presents:
A PERFECT DIAMOND by Don Rifkin; Director, Philip Giberson; Scenery, Reagan Cook; Lighting, Michael Gebhardt; Costumes, Jo-Dee Mercurio; Managing Director, John Weinstein; Production Manager, Melissa Davis; Technical Director, Greg Haydock; Fight Choreography, Jim Manley; Stage Managers, Deborah A. Friedman, Jocelyn N. Stern; Press, Fred Nathan, Anne Abrams, Bert Fink
CAST: Steve Beauchamp (The Kid), Jayne Bentzen (Tess Gallagher), Thomas Blum (Mark Haftel), Michael Bofshever (Legs Lannigan), Dan Desmond (Beauregard), John Anthony Lack (Gentleman Jim Wilson), Todd Michael Lewis (Buster Ziltz), Allan Wasserman (Dollar Bill Brunowski)

A play in two acts. The action takes place in an office deep in the bowels of a major league ball park, on a Sunday afternoon in late July of this season.

(The Triplex) Wednesday, Oct. 17–Nov. 17, 1984 (40 performances). The Triplex (William Soencer Reilly, Executive Director; Lindsay Gambini, Managing Director) presents Lincoln Center Institute's production of:
TWELFTH NIGHT by William Shakespeare; Director, Andy Wolk; Scenery and Costumes, Karen Gerson; Lighting, Toshiro Ogawa; Music, John Richard Lewis; Press, Howard Atlee, Barbara Atlee
CAST: Mark Benninghofen (Sebastian), Hewitt Brooks (Sir Andrew Aguecheek), Amanda Carlin (Viola), Peter Crombie (Orsino), Jack Hallett (Sir Toby Belch), Thomas Kopache (Sea Captain/Antonio), Madeleine Potter (Olivia), David Purdham (Malvolio), Willie Reale (Feste), Brian Reddy (Fabian), Charlaine Woodard (Maria)

A comedy performed with one intermission. The action takes place during the summer in Illyria, a coastal resort on the Mediterranean.

(Courtyard Playhouse) Thursday, Oct. 18–Nov. 11, 1984 (16 performances). The Actors Collective (Cathy Russell, Marcus Lutsky, Producers) presents:
THE LUNCH GIRLS by Leigh Curran; Director, Stuart Ross; Set, Dick Block; Costumes, Randall Ouzts; Lighting, Heather Sacco; Technical Director, Peter Bendevski; Assistant to Director, Lisa Lindstrom; Props, Ann Corley; Sound, Ed Porter; Stage Manager, Deirdre Sinnott; Press, Craig Fols, Harriet Bass
CAST: Kathryn Stalter (Claire), Jan Leslie Harding (Kate), Harriet Bass (Charlene), Carrie Nodella (Danusha), Cyndi Raftus (Vicky), Karen Gilliatt (Rhonda), Cathy Russell (Edie), Marc Lutsky (Chef), W. McGregor King (Henri), Ramon Franco (Jesus)

A play in 3 acts. The action takes place in October of 1969 in the girls' locker room and kitchen of a key club in mid-town Manhattan.

(Chelsea Playhouse) Thursday, Oct. 18,–Dec. 16, 1984.
Keller Theater Associates (Jerry Keller/Noel L. Silverman) presents:
THE COUNTRY GIRL by Clifford Odets; Director, Richard Thomsen; Set, Jack Chandler; Costumes, Julie Schwolow; Lighting, Phil Monat; General Manager, Douglas E. Ellis; Assistant Director, Marcia Milgrom Meeker; Props, Dawn Eaton; Production Assistant, Mary-Susan Gregson; Hairstylist, Vito Mastrogiovanni; Stage Managers, Ginny Martino, Marc Umile; Press, Shirley Herz, Sam Rudy, Peter Cromarty, Pete Sanders, Mary Bryant, Gary Lawrence
CAST: Jeffrey DeMunn (Bernie Dodd), Richard Zobel (Larry), Victor Raider-Wexler (Phil Cook), Gus Kaikkonen (Paul Unger), Jennifer Joyce (Nancy Stoddard), Hal Holbrook (Frank Elgin), Christine Lahti (Georgie Elgin), Marc Umile (Ralph), Understudies: Victor Raider-Wexler (Frank), Gus Kaikkonen (Bernie), Richard Zobel (Phil), Marc Umile (Paul/Larry)

A drama in 2 acts and 8 scenes. The action takes place in the autumn of 1950 in New York and Boston.

(18th Street Playhouse) Thursday, Oct. 18,–Nov. 4, 1984 (12 performances). Eccentric Circles Theatre (Producing Directors: Janet Bruders, Barbara Bunch, Rosemary Hopkins, Paula Kay Pierce) presents:
LOVE GAMES by Elaine Denholtz; Director, Paula Kay Pierce; Music and Lyrics, Musical Direction and Arrangements, Sound Supervision, Leslie Steinweiss; Production Manager, Gary Miller; Lighting, Richard Clausen; Set, Gary Miller, Randy Ingram, Kathy Zoumis; Stage Manager, Kathy Zoumis; Press, Patt Dale, Julianne Waldhelm
CAST: Aurelia De Felice (Monica), Paula Ewin (Carly), Martha Greenhouse (Mrs. Forzhammer), Eric Himes (Emerson), Johnnie Mae (Pearline Dee), Muriel Mason (Mrs. Bosworth)

A play in 3 acts. The action takes place at the present time on a Saturday in June in a garden apartment in South Orange, N.J.

Hal Holbrook, Jeffrey DeMunn, Christine Lahti in "The Country Girl" *(Martha Swope Photo)*

(Vineyard Theatre) Friday, Oct. 19–Nov. 11, 1984 (24 performances). Vineyard Theatre (Barbara Zinn Krieger, Executive Director) presents:
WE'RE HOME with Words and Music by Bob Merrill; Adaptation by Douglas Aibel, Stephen Milbank; Conceived and Directed by Douglas Aibel; Choreography, Pamela Sousa; Musical Direction/Arrangements, Stephen Milbank; Set, James Wolk; Lighting, Richard Lund; Costumes, Amanda J. Klein; Production Manager, Susan Wilder; Technical Director, Greg Laird; Dance Captain, Larry Keith; Stage Managers, Crystal Huntington, Deborah Natoli; Press, Bruce Cohen
CAST: Peter Frechette (Paul), Rita Gardner (Anne), Larry Keith (Ted), Ann Talman (Evelyn)
MUSICAL NUMBERS: I'm in a Tree, Nine O'Clock, Here I Am, Make Yourself Comfortable, Traveling, You Are Woman, I'm Naive, My Place, My Red Riding Hood, Mira, The Girl with Too Much Heart, A Woman in Love, Stay with Me, People Watchers, Nothing Is New in New York, The Rich, Party People, I've Got a Penny, To a Small Degree, How Could I Know?, Knights on White Horses, Breakfast at Tiffany's, Home for Wayward Girls, Company of Men, She Wears Red Feathers, Pittsburgh Pennsylvania, Sunshine Girls, Flings, Grade "A" Treatment, Staying Young, We're Home, Better Together, But Yours, Waltz, When Daddy Comes Home, Do You Ever Go to Boston?, Alone in the World, People

A musical performed with one intermission. The action takes place in a small city park on an evening this spring.

Peter Frechette, Ann Talman in "We're Home"

(West Side Y Arts Center) Thursday, Oct. 19,–Nov. 11, 1984 (16 performances). American Kaleidoscope (Joan Rice Franklin, Rebecca Dobson, Nicholas Benton, Richard Bell, Producing Artistic Directors) presents:
BEAGLEMAN & BRACKETT by Linda Segal; Director, Tom Crawley; Scenery, Eric Veenstra; Lighting, Jayne Dutra; Costumes, Mary Marsicano; Props, Melanie Demetrie; Stage Managers, Carolyn Caldwell, Anne Veenstra; Press, Kevin P. McAnarney
CAST: Peter Jolly (Dan), Pamela Moller (Ellie), Joel Rooks (Claude), David Rosenbaum (Brackett), Pamela Pascoe (Maria), Tom Bade (Whitaker-Smith), Obie Story (Mike), Sally Parrish (Muriel), Albert Ratcliffe (Rugoff), Paul Mantell (Bauman)
   A comedy in 2 acts. The action takes place during the Summer of 1972 in the law offices of Beagleman & Brackett on Court Street in Brooklyn, NY.

(Actors Repertory Theater) Friday, Oct., 19–Nov. 11, 1984 (21 performances) Actors Repertory Theatre (Warren Robertson, Artistic Director; Janet Merry Doeden, Artistic Manager) presents:
SNOWMAN by Douglas Braverman; Director, Warren Robertson; Set, Craig Rosenberg; Lighting, Doug Dubitsky; Stage Manager, Anne Colby; Production Assistants, Joni Falk, Frans Bloem; Press, Howard Atlee, Barbara Atlee
CAST: Anna Stuart (Gail Blumenthal), Jesse Doran (Vinnie Tagliari)
   A comedy in two acts. The action takes place at the present time in a studio apartment on Staten Island, NY.

(New York University Deutsches Haus) Saturday, Oct. 20–Nov. 18, 1984 (14 performances)
ON THE CHIMBORAZO by Tankred Dorst; Director, Gregorij von Leitis; Set, Beate S. Kessler; Lights, Bill Bartlett; Costumes, Katrin Kalveram; Stage Manager, Pierre Shrady; Press, Henry S. R. Alford
CAST: Hope Cameron (Dorothea Merz), Matthew Murphy (Tilman Merz), Mark Ethan (Heinrich Merz), Gayle Greene (Klara Falk), Mary Sellers (Irene)
   The action takes place in Franconia, West Germany, overlooking the East-German border in the early 1970's.

(Riverwest Theatre) Monday, Oct. 22–Nov. 11, 1984 (21 performances). CHS Productions in association with Riverwest Management Company presents:
JUMP, I'LL CATCH YOU! by Cy Young; Director, Loukas Skipitaris; Set, James Noone; Lighting, Matt Ehlert; Costumes, Karen Gerson; Sound, David Lawson; Technical Director, Christopher Cole; Stage Managers, Marcia Simon, Jonathan Shulman, Raymond Haboush, Chris Svendsen, Rick Smith; Press, FLT/Francine L. Trevens
CAST: Sharon Ullrick (Merriam), Tony Miratti (Bennie)
   A romantic comedy in 2 acts and 9 scenes. The action takes place at the present time.

(American Place Theatre) Tuesday, Oct. 23–Nov. 10, 1984 (20 performances and 21 previews). Fred Kolo presents:
ZELDA by William Luce; Based on the writings of Mrs. F. Scott Fitzgerald; Director, Paul Roebling; Set & Costumes, Fred Kolo; Lighting, Kirk Bookman; Projections, Pete Buchin; General Management, Brent Peek, Scott Green; Company Manager, Marshall B. Purdy; Dance Consultant, Karen Lewis Brown; Sound, Peter Bengtson; Production Assistant, Lisa Randleman; Press, David Powers
CAST: Olga Bellin (Zelda Fitzgerald). Performed without intermission.

(Raft Theatre) Wednesday, Oct. 24–Nov. 19, 1984 (20 performances). Catherine Roberts presents:
OBLOMOV by John Ginman; Based on the novel by Ivan Goncharov; Director, Franklyn Lenthall; Lighting, William J. Plachy; Scenery, Peter Hackman; Costume, Martin Pakledinaz; Press, Welton Smith
CAST: Robin Swados (Oblomov)

(Inroads Theatre) Wednesday, Oct. 24–Nov. 17, 1984 (20 performances). The Bandit Company presents:
HAUNTED LIVES (Three One-act Plays) by John Pielmeier; Sets, David Banner; Costumes, C. Claire Robertson; Lighting, Lemming Brothers; Original Music, Doug Dowling; Sound, Fullhouse Productions; Stage Managers, Cynthia M. Mazzant, Carol Sussman; Press, Bob Burrichter, Lisa DeJager
CAST: "A Witch's Brew" directed by Frank Licato; with Paul D'Amato (Daedulus), Nancy Rothman (Jule), Larry Banner (Tucker). The action takes place at 2 A.M. in the darkened basement of Daed's farmhouse. "A Ghost Story" directed by Robert Clem; with Paul D'Amato (Hackett), Frank Licato (Oswald), Nancy Rothman (Soma). The action takes place in a cabin in the woods of Maine. "A Gothic Tale" directed by Frank Licato; with John Haag (Isaac), Larry Banner (Morten), Joanne Hoersch (Eliza). The action takes place in the spring of 1898 in the tower room of an old house on an island.

Olga Bellin in "Zelda"

(Norman Thomas Theatre) Saturday, Oct. 27, 1984–Mar. 31, 1985 (70 performances). Art D'Lugoff, Moishe Rosenfeld present:
THE GOLDEN LAND an English-Yiddish Musical created by Zalmen Mlotek and Moishe Rosenfeld; Directed and Staged by Howard Rossen; Set, Abe Lubelski; Costumes, Natasha Landau; Lighting, Victor En Yu Tan; Musical Arrangements/Musical Direction, Zalmen Mlotek; Orchestrations, Peter Sokolow; Sound, Tom Gould; Golden Land Klezmer Orchestra conducted by Zalmen Mlotek; Production Assistants, Allen Dolgener, Greg Kostroff, Samara Lubelski, Rena Frymer; Stage Managers, Doug Laidlaw, Ira Belgrade
CAST: Bruce Adler succeeded by Bernardo Hiller, Phyllis Berk, Joanne Borts, Avi Hoffman, Betty Silberman, Standbys: Shifee Lovitt, Ira Belgrade
MUSICAL NUMBERS: Mir Forn Kayn Amerike, Vi Shver S'iz Tsu Sheydn, Troyerik Zayn Darf Men Nit, Amerike Hurrah for Onkl Sem, Ellis Island, Lozt Arayn, Give Me Your Tired Your Poor, Vatch Your Step, Gebentsht Iz Amerike, Fonye Ganev, Koyft A Tsaytung!, Dem Peddlers Brivele, A Brivele Der Mamen, Lekho Dodi, Fifty Fifty, The Wheels Turn Quickly, Motl the Operator, Working Women, Rebel Girl, Ballad of the Triangle Fire, Elegy on the Triangle Fire Victims, Bread and Roses, Long Live Columbus, Three Cheers for Yankee Doodle, Yankee Doodle Rides Uptown, Flag of Freedom, She'll Be Coming from the Mountains, Fun Downtown-Uptown, I Am a Boarder at My Wife's House, When Rosie Lived on Essex Street, Ovinu Malkeynu, God and His Judgment Are Right, Where Shall We Find the Witnesses?, The Wedding, I Bring You Greetings from the Trenches, Steam, Joe and Paul's, Levine and His Flying Machine, Come Dance Leybke, The Yidisha Charleston, How Do I Make a Living?, Brother Can You Spare a Dime?, As Long as You Are Healthy, Everything Is Spoiled, Buy Cigarettes, Rumania, Yiddle with His Fiddle, Dear Brothers Help, The Jewish People Live
   A musical in 2 acts and 10 scenes.

Joanne Borts, Phyllis Berk, Avi Hoffman, Betty Silberman in "The Golden Land"
(Curt Kaufman Photo)

(Ballroom Theater) Monday, Oct. 29–Dec. 2, 1984 (32 performances and 10 previews). Henry Luhrman presents:
I HEAR MUSIC. . . .OF FRANK LOESSER AND FRIENDS staged by Donald Saddler; Musical Director/Arrangements, Colin Romoff; Gowns, Robert Mackintosh; Sound, Sandor Margolin; Production Coordinator/Lighting Design, Gene McCann; General Management, Alan C. Wasser; Company Manager, Beth Riedmann; Press, Henry Luhrman, Terry M. Lilly, Helene Greece, David Mayhew
CAST: Jo Sullivan, Greg Utzig, Brian Slawson, Douglas Romoff, Ed Joffe, Colin Romoff

(The Acting Studio) Wednesday, Oct. 31–Nov. 17, 1984 (12 performances). Metro Artists presents:
DELIRIOUS by J. Bunzel; Director, Leah Joki; Set, Chris Baskous, Jerome Butler; Lighting, James Brembt; Stage Manager, Mary Ellen Allison; Press, Chris Hanckel
CAST: Peter Toran (Nick), John Means (Mr. Richfield), Robert Michael Tomlinson (Hart Stephens), Jerome Butler (Real Cool), Kymberly Dakin (Naomi), John Bigham (Cliff), Gregory Welch (Scott), Richard Ziman (Lenny), Lolita Lorre (Didi)
   A play in two acts. The action takes place at the present time in and around Mr. Richfield's house, high in the canyons above Beverly Hills, California.

(Perry Street Theatre) Thursday, November 1–25, 1984 (20 performances/5 performances of each play). New York Theatre Workshop (Jean Passanante, Artistic Director; Nancy Kassak Diekmann, Managing Director; Stephen Graham, Executive Director) presents:
THE NEW DIRECTORS PROJECT of four new plays directed by emerging new directors. Sets, Sally de Valenzuela; Sound, Stan Metelits, Deena Kaye; Costumes, Muriel Stockdale, Gene Lakin; Lighting, Susan Chute; Stage Managers, Michele Hinrichs, Richard Costabile. (Nov. 1–3) *"War on the Third Floor"* by Pavel Kohout; Translated and Directed by Elizabeth Diamond; Advisor, Andre Gregory. CAST: Mary Lou Rosato (Mrs. Blaha), Thomas Carson (Emile Blaha), Charles Randall (Doctor/Karl Muller), Brian Hargrove (Mailman/Soldier/General), Zach Grenier (General/Policeman), Robert Stephen Ryan (Plainclothesman), Jonathan Freund (Soldier). The action takes place in the bedroom of Mr. and Mrs. Blaha. (Nov. 7–10) *"The Grand Hysteric"* and *"The Box"* by Sheldon Rosen; Director, T. Riccio; Advisor, Steven Katz. CAST: David Pierce (Game), Ann Sachs (Clara) in "The Grand Hysteric"; Frankie Faison (Man 2), Tom Wright (Man 1) in "The Box." (Nov. 14–17) *"My Life in Art"* by Victor Steinbach; Director, Rebecca Harrison; Advisor, A. J. Antoon. CAST: Don Plumley (Clement Tyrrell), Neil Vipond (Sigmund Hoffman), Victor Steinbach (Alexander Barescu), David Strathairn (Nehemia Byron), Paul Guilfoyle (William Tyrrell). The action takes place at the present time in New York City. (Nov. 21–25) *"A Fool's Errand"* by Chris Ceraso; Director, Jim Peskin; Advisor, James Lapine. CAST: Edward Baran (Brighella), Johann Carlo (Columbina), Zach Grenier (Capitano), Stephen Hanan (Arlecchino), Lolita Lorre (Isabella), Graeme Malcolm (Pantalone), Carla Meadows (Gibon), Musicians: Iris Brooks, Peter Griggs.

(The Spanish Institute) Thursday, November 1–11, 1984 (8 performances). American Indian Community House in collaboration with The Americas Society, Canadian Affairs Division presents:
THE ECSTASY OF RITA JOE by George Ryga; Director, Gordon McCall; Assistant Director, Gloria Miguel; Set, Gordon McCall; Lighting, Allen Stillman; Music, Willy Dunn, Ann Mortifee; Lyrics, George Ryga; Musical Director, Bernard Grobman; Costumes, Pena Bonita; Sound, Randy Adler; Technical Director, Machiste Quintana; Stage Manager, Peter Wolf; Press, Fred Nathan, Ted Killmer, Anne Abrams, Leslie Anderson, Bert Fink
CAST: Pearl Tama (Rita Joe), Tom Jackson (Jamie Paul), Gary Farmer (David Joe), Jane Lind (Eileen Joe), Norman Brown (Johnny), Marie Antoinette Rogers (Old Indian Woman), Mark Melymick (Magistrate), Bill Nunnery (Homer), Mike Lisenco (Priest/Witness), Joshua Cruze (Policeman/Witness), Diane Fraher (Singer)
   A play in two acts.

(Astor Place Theatre) Thursday, Nov. 1, 1984, and still playing May 31, 1985. John A. McQuiggan presents:
THE FOREIGNER by Larry Shue; Director, Jerry Zaks; Associate Producers, Nancy B. Hoover, Douglas M. Lawson, Gina Rogak; Set, Karen Schulz; Costumes, Rita Ryack; Lighting, Paul Gallo; Sound, Aural Fixation; Casting, Deborah Brown; General Manager, Ellen Sorrin; Management Associate, Jean May Spence; Assistant to Director, Dani Klein; Props, Karen McDuffee, Sara Gormley Plass; Wardrobe, Patricia White; Dialogue Coach, Arden Sampson; Stage Managers, George Darveris, Chet Leaming; Press, Patricia Krawitz, Robert W. Larkin, Keith Aaron
CAST: Larry Shue succeeded by Ian Trigger, Ian Stuart ("Froggy" LeSueur), Anthony Heald succeeded by Larry Shue (Charlie Baker), Sudie Bond succeeded by Kathleen Claypool (Betty Meeks), Robert Schenkkan (Rev. David Marshall Lee), Patricia Kalember (Catherine Simms), Christopher Curry (Owen Musser), Kevin Geer (Ellard Simms), Understudies: Chet Leaming (Froggy/Charlie), Kathleen Claypool (Betty), Donna Bullock (Catherine), Stephen Ahern (Rev./Ellard/Owen)
   A comedy in 2 acts and 4 scenes. The action takes place in the recent past in Betty Meeks' Fishing Lodge Resort, Tilghman County, Georgia, U.S.A.

Jo Sullivan, Ed Joffe in "I Hear Music . . ."
(Martha Swope Photo)

(Billie Holiday Theatre) Thursday, Nov. 1, 1984–Feb. 10, 1985 (90 performances and 24 previews) The Billie Holiday Theatre (Marjorie Moon, Executive Producer) presents:
INACENT BLACK AND THE BROTHERS by A. Marcus Hemphill; Director, Mikell Pinkney; Set and Costumes, Felix E. Cochren; Wardrobe, Ardis Johnson; Stage Managers, Avan Littles, James Carter; Press, Howard Atlee, Barbara Atlee
CAST: Louise Stubbs (Mama Essie Rydell), Jay Aubrey Jones (Marv Rydell), Richard Williams (Helwin Rydell), Maurice Carlton (Percy Rydell), Gwendolyn Nelson-Fleming (Ruby), Gwendolyn Ricks-Spencer (Inacent Black), Clifton Powell (Pretty Pete), Kim Weston-Moran (Carmen Casteel), Karen Charles (Sally Baby Washington), Understudies: Gwendolyn Nelson-Fleming (Mama), Avan Littles (Percy/Marv/Pretty Pete), Karen Charles (Carmen), Carol Mitchell-Smith (Sally/Ruby)
   A "spiritual mystery comedy" in 2 acts and 8 scenes. The action takes place at the present time on a weekend in spring in Old Westbury, Long Island, and in New York City.

(Provincetown Playhouse) Thursday, Nov. 8, Mary Keil and Don Leslie present:
LOSING IT by Jon Klein; Director, Andrew Cadiff; Scenery & Lighting, Paul Wonsek; General Management, Marshall B. Purdy; Casting, Leonard Finger; Company Manager, David Jannone; Costume Coordinator, Rosemary Keough; Props, Chris Mealey; Stage Manager, Arlene Grayson; Press, Becky Flora
CAST: Larry Nicks (Arch Leighton), Richard Karn (Cutty Moore), Jeff Alan-Lee (The Kid)
   The action takes place on a recent October in a hollow about 40 miles west of Nashville, Tennessee, and is performed without intermission.

Anthony Heald, Larry Shue
in "The Foreigner"
(Van Williams Photo)

69

(Joyce Theatre) Sunday, Nov. 11, 1984–Jan. 6, 1985 (17 performances and 3 previews). Lee Gross Associates presents:
ANN REINKING. . . .MUSIC MOVES ME with Direction and Choreography by Alan Johnson; Musical Supervision/Vocal Arrangements/Original Material, Larry Grossman; Musical Direction/Dance Arrangements, Ronald Melrose; Set, Thomas Lynch; Costumes, Albert Wolsky; Lighting, Ken Billington; Sound, Charles Bugbee III; Assistant Director/Choreographer, Stephen Jay; Orchestrations, Joseph Gianono, Michael Gibson, Harold Wheeler; Special Lyrics, Ellen Fitzhugh; General Management, Frank Scardino Associates; Hairstylist/Makeup, Hiram Ortiz; Company Manager, Phil Leach; Dance Captain/Swing, Stephen Jay; Wardrobe, Mary Lou Rios; Stage Managers, Perry Cline, Randall Whitescarver; Press, Mark Goldstaub, Kevin P. McAnarney, Daniel Kellachan, Philip Butler
CAST: Ann Reinking, Gary Chryst, Reed Jones, Michael Kubala, Rob Marshall, Sara Miles, Christina Saffran
MUSICAL NUMBERS: Another Mr. Right, Anything Goes, Ballin' the Jack, Higher and Higher, Hit Me with a Hot Note, I Can't Turn You Loose, If Love Were All, Isn't It Romantic, Just Once, Moonlight Sonata, Music Moves Me, Nowhere to Run, Oh Baby Won't You Please Come Home, Rescue Me, Satin Doll, Sing Sing Sing, Stompin' at the Savoy, Tea for Two, Unchained Melody, Why Not?, Wild Women, You and Me. Presented in two acts.

(18th Street Playhouse) Sunday, November 11–28, 1984 (12 performances) A benefit performance was given at Symphony Space. The Greensboro Civil Rights Fund presents:
JERICHO. . . . a musical legend Book and Lyrics, Judy Brussell; Music, Buck Brown; Director, Jerry Campbell; Set, Bob Phillips; General Manager, George Slowik; Stage Managers, James M. Sigler, Stu Goldman; Press, Judith Davidson
CAST: Eugene Key (Joshua), Buck Brown (Mayor), Mark Cohen (Paul Berliner), Kate Hunter Brown (Katy Berliner), Juanda LaJoyce Holley (Sandy Johnson), Evelyn Blakey (Evylyn), Molly Stark (Johanna Berliner), Kevin Glenn (Matt Cane), Marcus Neville (Frank/Wayne), Richard Rohan (Fred/Police Chief), Mimi Wyche (Billie Jo Klyde), Larry Campbell (Rev. Darwin Johnson)
MUSICAL NUMBERS: Spinning Song, But I Hear, A Decent Job, In Good Old Colony Times, Jericho Cotton Mill Blues, Devoted to the Cause, One Step at a Time, My Son, Song of the United Racist Front, Song of Escape, If It All Were True, In Love with the Expert Red, A Kind of Power, Hard Times in the Mill, Strike!, Joshua's Rap, Come Back to Brooklyn, One Step Forward Two Steps Back, The Douglass Decree, Gentle People, The Necessity of Being Cruel, Song of the Nazi Dogs, Operation Flea, Song of Identification, We Have to Lead the Fight, Nothing Left but the Rope, Remember Nov. 3rd, Our Kids, The Union Is Behind Us, Jericho Massacre, Nothing Else to Do, We Are No Longer Strangers, Beware the Thunder and the Light
A musical in 3 acts and 40 scenes.

(Parsons/May Auditorium) Monday, November 12, 1984 (One performance only). American Shaw Festival (Bruce Wall, Artistic Director/Founder) presents a concert performance of:
A LITTLE BIT MORE OF PYGMALION by G. B. Shaw; with artists Carole Shelley, Remak Ramsay, Gordon Chater, Brenda Forbes, Margaret Hilton, Richard Neilson, Patricia Matthews, Bruce Wall

(Riverwest Theatre) Monday, Nov. 19–Dec. 2, 1984 (16 performances). CHS Productions in association with Riverwest Management Company presents:
STARTING IN THE MIDDLE a musical story by Sally-Jane Heit; Director, Leslie Eberhard; Music and Lyrics, Shirley Grossman; Musical Director, Stuart Malina; Setting, Leslie Eberhard; Lighting, Karen Wenderoff; Costume Consultant, Karen Gerson; Technical Director, Christopher Cole; Stage Manager, Charles Davisson; Press, FLT/Francine Trevens, Andy Shearer
CAST: Sally-Jane Heit

(St. Clement's Theatre) Tuesday, Nov. 20, 1984–
Music Theatre Group/Lenox Arts Center (Lyn Austin, Producing Director) with the New York Shakespeare Festival (Joseph Papp, Producer), and Robert de Rothschild presents:
THE GARDEN OF EARTHLY DELIGHTS based on Hieronymus Bosch's painting; Conception and Direction, Martha Clarke; Created in collaboration with Robert Barnett, Felix Blaska, Robert Faust, Marie Fourcaut, Margie Gillis, Polly Styron; Music, Richard Peaslee; In collaboration with Eugene Friesen, Bill Ruyle, Steven Silverstein; Lighting, Paul Gallo; Costumes, Jane Greenwood; Flying, Foy; Consultant, Peter Beagle; Managing Director, Diane Wondisford; Production Associate, Vanessa Palmer; Wardrobe, Amy Gennello; Stage Managers, Steven Ehrenberg, David Carriere; Press, Louise Ment, Monina von Opel
CAST: Felix Blaska, Martha Clarke or Lila York, Robert Faust, Marie Fourcaut, Eugene Friesen, Margie Gillis, Bill Ruyle, Steven Silverstein, Polly Styron, Tim Wengerd
Performed in four parts without intermission: Eden, The Garden, The Seven Scenes, Hell.

Gary Chryst, Ann Reinking
in "Music Moves Me"

(Circle in the Square Downtown) Friday, Nov. 23, 1984–March 31, 1985 (122 performances). Stephen G. Martin, Harold DeFelice, Louis W. Scheeder, Kenneth John Productions Inc. in association with Frank Basile present:
DIAMONDS with Book by Bud Abbott, Ralph G. Allen, Roy Blount, Jr., Richard Camp, Jerry L. Crawford, Lou Costello, Lee Isenberg, Sean Kelly, Jim Wann, John Lahr, Arthur Masella, Harry Stein, John Weidman, Alan Zweibel; Music, Gerard Allessandrini, Craig Carnelia, Cy Coleman, Larry Grossman, John Kander, Doug Katsaros, Alan Menken, Jonathan Sheffer, Lynn Udall, Albert Von Tilzer, Jim Wann; Lyrics, Gerard Alessandrini, Howard Ashman, Craig Carnelia, Betty Comden, Fred Ebb, Ellen Fitzhugh, Adolph Green, Karl Kennett, Jack Norworth, Jim Wann, David Zippel; Director, Harold Prince; Choreography, Theodore Pappas; Setting, Tony Straiges; Costumes, Judith Dolan; Lighting, Ken Billington; Sound, Tom Morse; Associate Producer, Len M. Collara; Musical Direction/Orchestrations, Paul Gemignani; Assistant Director, Arthur Masella; General Management, De-Felice-Scheeder Productions, Kathryn Frawley; Technical Supervisor, Lizard Zimmerman; Props, Katherine Conklin, Tom Swift; Wardrobe, Patricia Brundage; Production Assistants, Rob Weiner, Daniel Lewin; Publicity Consultant, David Powers; Stage Managers, Beverley Randolph, Bill McComb; Press, Fred Nathan, Leslie Anderson, Anne Abrams, Ted Killmer, Bert Fink
CAST: Loni Ackerman, Susan Bigelow, Jackee Harry, Scott Holmes, Dick Latessa, Dwayne Markee, Wade Raley, Larry Riley, Nestor Serrano, Chip Zien, Bill McComb (Stadium Announcer); Standbys and Understudies: Bill McComb, Gordon Stanley, Mark Zimmerman, Valerie Perri, Zelda Pulliam
SCENES & MUSICAL NUMBERS: Winter in New York, Batting Order, In the Cards, Favorite Sons, Warner Wolf #1, Song for a Pinch Hitter, Vendors, Fanatics #1, What You'd Call a Dream, Kasi Atta Bat, Ballparks of the Gods, Escorte-Moi, The Dodger Game, He Threw Out the Ball, Hundreds of Hats, Warner Wolf #2, 1919, P.A. Announcement, Let's Play Ball, Warner Wolf #3, Psyched Out, Fanatics #2, Five Ives, Boys of Summer, Fanatics #3, Song for a Hunter College Graduate, Warner Wolf #4, Who's on First, Stay in Your Own Back Yard, Chief Surgeon, Ka-Razy, Famous People Quotes, Batting Order, Diamonds Are Forever
A musical in two acts.

Loni Ackerman (front center) and
cast of "Diamonds" (Martha Swope Photo)

(Town Hall) Sunday, Nov. 28–Dec. 30, 1984 (55 performances and 5 previews). Shalom Yiddish Musical Comedy Theatre (Raymond Ariel, Producer) presents:
OY MAMA! AM I IN LOVE! with Music by Ed Linderman; Lyrics, Yakov Alper; Director, Michael Greenstein; Dances/Musical Numbers Staged by Derek Wolshonak; Music Direction/Dance Music/Orchestrations, Barry Levitt; Book, Moshe Blum; Scenery, Gary Prianti; Costumes, Mary Marsicano; Lighting, Paul McDonagh; English translation, Bella Mysell Yablokoff; Production Supervisor, Sandy Levitt; Executive Manager, Ruth V. Ellin; Hair and Makeup, Jeff Cate; Stage Manager, Paul McDonagh; Press, Max Eisen, Maria Soma, Madelon Rosen
CAST: Mary Soreanu (Malkele), Max Perlman (Meir Mordche), Yankele Alperin (Fayvish), Reizl Bozyk (Zeesl/Suzy), David Ellin (Leybl/Mr. Green), Stewart Figa (Sidney), Shifra Lerer (Sure Feyge), Sandy Levitt (George/Pesach), Michael Michalovic (Moishe/Morris), Barbara Niles (Annie), Eleanor Reissa (Millie), Alec Timerman (Simchele), Tara Tyrrell (Malkele), Ensemble: Catherine Caplin, Carolyn Goor, Elisa Heinsohn, Tara Tyrrell, Nick Harvey, Stanley Kramer, David Reitman, Alec Timerman
   A musical in two acts with a prologue. The action takes place in Poland in 1905, and in New York City in 1923.

(The Lighthouse Auditorium) Thursday, November 29–December 1, 1984 (5 performances). The Lighthouse (The New York Association for the Blind) presents the Peacock Players in the Bernard Gavzer production of:
RAINDANCE by M. Z. Ribalow; Director, Thomas Babe; Sets, Ray Recht; Lighting, Susan White; Costumes, Vel Riberto, Karen Roston; Choreography, Chris Fleming; Musical Director, Karl Jurman; Stage Managers, Ed Isser, Randy Charnin, Marc Dietrich; Press, Barbara and Howard Atlee
CAST: John Hambrick (John Wesley Hardin), Reggie Harris (Jim Crow), Chauncey Howell (George), Pia Lindstrom (Wicked Falina), Jim Ryan (J. P. Standard), Liz Smith (Chief Sitting Bull), Karl Jurman (Saloon Pianist)
   A comedy in two acts. The action takes place in and around a saloon somewhere in the mythical American southwest during the legendary last half of the 19th Century sometime.

(Courtyard Playhouse) Thursday, Nov. 29–Dec. 23, 1984 (16 performances). MDR Productions (Michael Del Rio, Artistic Director) presents:
LONELY STREETS by January Stevens; Director, Dan McKereghan; Press, Bob Burrichter, Lisa De Jager.
CAST: Ben Jacobs, Michael Lekain, Joey Maldonado, Lory Marcosson, Debra Lynn Reichler, Anthony Spina, David J. Youse

(Lamb's Theatre) Monday, Dec. 13, 1984–Jan. 6, 1985 (35 performances and 3 previews). Lamb's Theatre (Carolyn Rossi Copeland, Executive Director) presents:
THE GIFTS OF THE MAGI with Book and Lyrics, Mark St. Germain; Co-Lyricist and Music, Randy Courts; Director, Christopher Catt; Sets, Michael C. Smith; Lighting, Heather Carson; Costumes, Hope Hanafin; Choreography, Piper Pickrell; Musical Director, Steve Alper; Casting, McCorkle Casting; Stage Managers, Steve Zorthian, Maude Brickner; Press, Patt Dale, Julianne Waldhelm
CAST: Brick Hartney (City Man), Lynne Wintersteller (City Woman), Michael Brian (Willy), Jeff McCarthy (Jim), Leslie Hicks (Della), Bert Michaels (Soapy)
MUSICAL NUMBERS: Light Our Way, Gifts to the Magi, Christmas Is to Blame, How Much to Buy My Dream, The Restaurant, Who Needs Presents, Bum Luck, Greed, Pockets, The Same Girl
   A musical performed without intermission. The action takes place in New York City on December 23 through 25, 1905.

(Actors Outlet) Thursday, December 6–16, 1984 (15 performances) Stage Arts Theater Company (Nell Robinson, Ruth Ann Norris, Artistic Directors) presents:
SULLIVAN & GILBERT by Kenneth Ludwig; Music, Arthur Sullivan; Lyrics, W. S. Gilbert; Director, Larry Carpenter; Musical Staging, Michael Connolly, Larry Carpenter; Musical Direction, Herbert Kaplan; Scenery, John Falabella; Costumes, David Murin; Lighting, John Gisondi; Casting, Binder-Jennings; Technical Director, John Saltonstall; Hair and Makeup, David Lawrence; Stage Managers, Sally Hassenfelt, Roy Meachum; Press, Shirley Herz, Sam Rudy, Peter Cromarty, Pete Sanders
CAST: George Ede (William Schwenck Gilbert), Jonthan Moore (Sir Arthur Sullivan), Etain O'Malley (Kitty Gilbert), Gordon Stanley (Courtice Pounds), John Keane (Durward Lely), Christopher Coucill (Rutland Barrington), Catherine Gaines (Sybil Grey), Tina Shafer (Jessie Bond), Mary Leigh Stahl (Rosina Brandram), Thomas Carson (Richard D'Oyly Carte), Herbert Kaplan (Francois Cellier), Connie Coit (Violet Russell), Gary Krawford (Alfred, Duke of Edinburgh), Michael Connolly (George Grossmith), Stuart Ryder (Stagehand)
MUSICAL NUMBERS: Brightly Dawns Our Wedding Day, The Battle's Roar Is Over, You Understand?, In Sailing O'er Life's Ocean Wide, When You're Lying Awake, If You Go In, Young Man Despair, So Please You Sir, Three Little Maids from School, Would You Know the Kind of Maid, Never Mind the Why and Wherefore, I Know a Youth Who Loves a Little Maid, When I Go Out of Door, Hail Poetry, For He's Gone and Married Yum-Yum, For the Threatened Cloud Has Passed Away
   A musical in 2 acts and 13 scenes with prologue and epilogue. The action takes place in December of 1890, most of it at the Savoy Theatre, London, England.

John Hambrick, Pia Lindstrom, Liz Smith
in "Raindance" *(Martha Swope Photo)*

(Riverwest Theatre) Monday, December 10–30, 1984 (21 performances). CHS Productions, RoseAnn and Jack Adolfi in association with Riverwest Management Co. present:
HORIZONS by Jack Adolfi; Music, Carlos Davidson; Lyrics, Kathleen True; Additional Music and Lyrics, Jack Adolfi; Musical and Vocal Arrangements/Direction, J. T. Thomas; Director, Paul Eiseman; Set, Christopher Cole; Costumes, Susan Rosenberg; Lighting, Nancy Collings; Choreography, Ron Bohmer; Props, M. Paige Miller; Stage Managers, Jonathan Shulman, M. Paige Miller, Chris Stevenson, Michael Kinnie; Press, FLT/Francine Trevens, Andy Shearer
CAST: Deborah Smith (Candi), Clayton Prince (Marvin), Jamie Zee Eisner (Lucy), Leslie Kincaid (Santa), Ron Bohmer (Keith), Sundra Jean Williams (Jo), Anthony Abbriano (Billy), Bob Ferreri (Drug Dealer/"John")
MUSICAL NUMBERS: I See the Light, I See the Streetlights, Your Time Has Come, Turned Off to Turning On, Ladies of the Night, Why Can't It Be?, Listen to the Children, Grow Up Little Girl, Don't Live in Yesterday
   A musical drama in two acts. The action takes place at the present time in any major city in the United States (New York City), and alternates between the street and Horizons, a lodging house for teenagers.

Jonathan Moore, Etain O'Malley, George Ede
in "Sullivan & Gilbert" *(Carol Rosegg Photo)*

71

(Westside Arts Theatre/Downstairs) Thursday, December 13–16, 1984 (5 performances and 18 previews). Charles Paul Kopelman, Mark B. Simon, Gary P. Steuer present:
TOTAL ECLIPSE by Christopher Hampton; Director, John Tillinger; Scenery, Marjorie Bradley Kellogg; Lighting, Richard Nelson; Costumes, Bill Walker; Music, Nick Bicat; Casting, Johnson-Liff; Projections, Lucie D. Grosvenor; Sound, Gary Harris; Fights, J. Allen Suddeth; Associate Producer, Mike Tolman; General Management, Gatchell & Neufeld, Ltd.; Company Manager, David Conte; Technical Coordinator, Tom Shilhanek; Wardrobe, Mary Lou Rios; Props, David Smith; Hairstylist, Tek West; Assistant to Producers, Rod Kates; Stage Managers, Marjorie Horne, Claire Beckman; Press, Solters/Roskin/Friedman, Cindy Valk, Joshua Ellis, Adrian Bryan-Brown, Keith Sherman
CAST: Peter Evans (Paul Verlaine), Michael Cerveris (Arthur Rimbaud), Marissa Chibas (Mathilde Verlaine), Caitlin Clarke (Isabelle Rimbaud), Lynn Cohen (Eugenie Krantz), Ann Hillary (Mme. Maute de Fleurville), I. M. Hobson (M. Maute de Fleurville/Etienne Carjat/Judge), Adrian Sparks (Jean Aicard), Adam Storke (Charles Cros/Barman)
A drama in 2 acts and 12 scenes. The action takes place in Paris, Brussels, and London, from Sept. 10, 1871 to Feb. 29, 1982.

(Harold Clurman Theatre) Monday, Dec. 17, 1984–Apr. 21, 1985 (130 performances). The Harold Clurman Theatre (Jack Garfein, Artistic Director) and Byron Lasky present:
A KURT WEILL CABARET performed by Martha Schlamme and Alvin Epstein, with Steven Blier at the piano. Presented with one intermission.
SONGS: Moritat, Barbara Song, Alabama Song, Herr Jakob Achmidt, Ich Habe Gelernt, Ballad of Sexual Slavery, There Was a Time, Pirate Jenny, Kanonensong, Soldatenweib, Eating, That's Him, The Saga of Jenny, September Song, Le Roi d'Aquitaine, Moon-Faced Starry-Eyed, It Never Was You, Tschaikowsky, Bilboa Song, Sailor's Tango, Surabaya Johnny, Survival Song, Finale

(Musical Theatre Works) Wednesday, January 9–27, 1985 (12 performances and 2 previews).
DOWNRIVER with Music and Lyrics by John Braden; Book, Jeff Tambornino; Based on "The Adventures of Huckleberry Finn" by Mark Twain; Producer-Director, Michael Maurer; Scenery, Karl Eigsti; Lighting, Neil Peter Jampolis; Costumes, Karen Roston; Sound, Gary Harris; Arrangements, Jeff Waxman; Musical Director, Michael Ward; Casting, Mary Jo Slater/Dennis D' Amico; Choreographer, Mary Jane Houdina; Technical Director, David Kraatz; Production Assistant, Nell Balaban; Dance Arrangements, Michael Dansicker; Production Coordinator, Dorris Carr; Wardrobe, Chris Sanders; Stage Managers, Robert Vandergriff, John Weeks; Press, Patt Dale, Julianne Waldhelm
CAST: John Scherer (Huckleberry Finn), Todd Heughens (Tom Sawyer), Joe Lynn (Jim), Jack Fletcher (King of France), Don Harrington (Duke of Bridgewater), Frank Vohs (Tim Collins), Suzanne Bedford (Mary Jane), Cara Lunden (Susan), Andi Henig (Joanna), Timothy Jecko (Dr. Robinson), Ted Forlow (Silas Phelps), Helon Blount (Aunt Sally Phelps), Ensemble: Jack Brenton, Jayne Cacciatore, Tom Kosis, Kathy Lynn, Mark Manley, Teressa Wylie
MUSICAL NUMBERS: Bound Away, 'Til Our Good Luck Comes Along, It's a Hard Life, The Musicale: Introduction, Waltz of the Cameleopard, Fare-Thee-Well, You've Brightened Up My Day, Come Home Runaway, Hallelujah He's On His Way, River Rats, Just Like Love, What a Fine Day for an Auction Sell, Downriver, Every Other Saturday Night, Tom and Huck's Argument, Shine Down Lord
A musical in 2 acts and 12 scenes. The action takes place along the Mississippi River before the Civil War.

(Theatre Off Park) Tuesday, Jan. 15, –March 2, 1985 (48 performances). Theatre Off Park (Albert Harris, Artistic Director; Bertha Lewis, Producing Director) and the Community Church of New York present:
HONEY, I'M HOME by Julie Goldsmith Gilbert; Director, Albert Harris; Set, Alan Kimmel; Lighting, Victor En Yu Tan; Costumes, Arnold S. Levine; Sound, Kenn Dovel; Technical Director, E. F. Morrill; Production Assistant, Tony Powell; Wardrobe, Barbara Sullivan; Hairstylist/Makeup, Esther Price Johnson; Stage Managers, John M. Atherlay, David Paupaw; Press, Michael Alpert, Ruth Jaffe
CAST: Haviland Morris (Helen), Ray Blackburn (Rick), Susan Plaksin (Shalom)
A drama in 2 acts and 3 scenes. The action takes place in 1968–1969 in Rick and Helen Baracini's apartment somewhere in New Jersey.

(Puerto Rican Traveling Theatre) Thursday, Jan. 17,–Feb. 17, 1985 (42 performances). The Puerto Rican Traveling Theatre (Artistic Director, Miriam Colon; Managing Director, Arthur Conescu) presents:
ORINOCO by Emilio Carballido; Director, Vicente Castro; Set, Carl A. Baldasso; Lighting, Rachel Budin; Costumes, Maria Contessa; Composer, Julio Gutierrez; Translator, Margaret Peden; Choreographer, Jimmy Del Rio; Stage Manager, Stacey Fleischer; Press, Max Eisen, Maria Somma
CAST: Ivonne Coll (Mina), Miriam Colon (Fifi)
A play in two acts. The action takes place on board the "Stella Maris" on the Orinoco River.

Peter Evans, Michael Cerveris, Marissa Chibas,
I. M. Hobson, Ann Hillary in "Total Eclipse"

(18th Street Playhouse) Thursday, Jan. 24,–Feb. 17, 1985 (16 performances). Eccentric Circles Theatre presents:
ALL SOULS' DAY by Cate Ryan; Director, Ben Janney; Production Manager, Gary Miller; Lighting, Richard Clausen; Props, Randy Ingram; Press, Patt Dale Associates; Stage Manager, Gary Miller
CAST: Margaret Ritchie (Elsie), Jeanne Cullen (Esther), Joseph Rose (Frank)
A drama in 2 acts and 6 scenes. The action takes place at the present time in a town in the U.S.A.

Martha Schlamme, Alvin Epstein
in "A Kurt Weill Cabaret"
(Martha Swope Photo)

(Studio 54) Sunday, January 27, 1985–
Bert Stratford Productions in association with Gene Cates, Doug Leeds, Christine Mortimer Biddle, Rex Farr present:
STREETHEAT based on an original concept by Michele Assaf and Rick Atwell; Music and Songs produced by Michael G. Millius and James Gregory for M.C.A. Music; Songs developed and supervised by Michael G. Millius; Direction and Choreography, Rick Atwell; Associate Producer, Judee Wales; Costumes, Franne Lee; Lighting, John McLain; Sound, Bob Kerzman; Scenery and Costumes, Dianna Freas, Michael Rizzo; Casting, Slater-Wilson/MCL; General Manager, Malcolm Allen; Orchestrations/Dance Arrangements/Underscoring/Special Music, Frank Owens, James Gregory; Assistant Director, Joanna Noble; Assistant Choreographer/Dance Captain, Aimee Covo; Assistant Musical Director, Peter Lurye; Technical Director, Howard Feinman; Wardrobe, Alison Lances; Hair and Makeup, Arron Quarles; Props, Henry Blumenthal, Lilly Blumenthal, Tracy Crum, Karen Eisenstadt; Stage Managers, Mark Baltazar, Eric J. Scheps, Susan Willett; Press, Betty Lee Hunt, Maria Cristina Pucci, James Sapp
CAST: Michael DeLorenzo (Spinner), James Arthur Johnson (Leon), Vicki Lewis (Victoria), Ron Lee Savin (Character Man), Glenn Scarpelli (Lucky Louie), Tico Wells (Picasso), Ensemble: Bryant Baldwin, Nora Cherry, Cecilia Marta, Troy Myers, Rick Negron, Daryl Richardson, Louis Ritarossi, Robin Summerfield, Jorge Vasquez, Understudies: Rick Negron (Picasso/Leon), Louis Ritarossi (Spinner/Louie), Aimee Covo (Victoria), Swings: Aimee Covo, Alan Stuart
MUSICAL NUMBERS: We Paint Life, Picasso's Theme, Uptown Dreamer's Express, Hold On, To Dance Is to Fly, Power, I'm a Wow, Lucky Louie, Full Circle, Streetheat, I Want a Real Man, Sacrifice Your Body, The King Becomes a Clown, Nirvana, Danger Men Working, Today I Found Me, Power Lies Within

Michael Allinson, Paul Ukena, Jr., Beulah Garrick
in "A Loud Bang on June the First"
(Allan Gassman Photo)

(INTAR Stage 2) Saturday, February 2–24, 1985 (16 performances). Sovereign Productions (Patricia Schmidt, Line Producer) presents:
STUD SILO by Tom White; Director, Dennis Logan; Set, Cam Lorendo; Lighting, Sally Small; Sound, Larry Basinski; Costumes, Nina Percy; Fight Master, Michael Monks; Stage Manager, Barry Barish; Press, Bill Evans, Sandra Manley, Jim Baldassare
CAST: Doug Barron (Jimmy Tolliver), Jeff Beach (Chip McAlister), Cynthia Exline (Judy Holcomb), Lisa Griffith (Linda Perkins), Ed Grimes (Burt Kleghorn), Jane MacFie (Paulette Holcomb), Lewis Musser (Tom Blackmore), Bill Reynolds (Edward Williams), Patrick Roche (Witt Holcomb), Bonnie Brown Smith (Maureen Holcomb), Dennis Sook (Mitch Mitchell), Jim Tully (Ben Rigby)
A drama in two acts. The action takes place in Fakir Switch, Texas.

(DON'T TELL MAMA) Saturday, February 2–March 2, 1985 (20 performances). David Drummond in association with Therese Orkin presents:
SWEET WILL by Lance Mulcahy; Director, John Olon; Musical Direction, Michael Wand; General Manager, Paul B. Berkowsky; Management Associate, Sheala N. Berkowsky; Musical Arrangements, Michael Ward; Production Coordinator, Anita Ross; Press, Jeffrey Richards Associates
CAST: Stephanie Cotsirilos, Carol Dennis, Stephen Lehew, Byron Utley, Steve Postel, Anita Ross
PROGRAMME: Hey Ho the Wind and the Rain, When Icicles Hang by the Wall, Hark Hark the Lark, Where the Bee Sucks, It Was a Lover and His Lass, Who Is Sylvia?, When Daisies Pied, Sigh No More, O Mistress Mine, Sea Song, Over Hill Over Dale, Take Oh Take Those Lips Away, Full Fathom Five, And Will He Not Come Again?, Under the Greenwood Tree, Touch But My Lips, Farewell Dear Love

(Minetta Lane Theatre) Tuesday, Feb. 5–June 30, 1985 (160 performances and 20 previews). James B. Freydberg, Stephen Wells, Max Weitzenhoffer in association with Richard Maltby, Jr. present:
3 GUYS NAKED FROM THE WAIST DOWN with Book and Lyrics by Jerry Colker; Music, Michael Rupert; Director, Andrew Cadiff; Choreography, Don Bondi; Scenery/Projections, Clarke Dunham; Costumes, Tom McKinley; Lighting, Ken Billington; Sound, Tony Meola; Orchestrations, Michael Starobin; Musical Director/Conductor, Henry Aronson; Associate Producers, Ray Larsen, Karen Howard; Original Cast recording by Polydor Records; General Manager, Fremont Associates, Maria Di Dia; Casting, Leonard Finger; Company Manager, Dana Sherman; Production Assistant, Debbie Levy; Production Associate, Henry Taliaferro; Wardrobe, Curtis Hay; Stage Managers, Brian Kaufman, Virginia Jones; Press, Jeffrey Richards, C. George Willard, Robert Ganshaw, Ben Morse, Toby Mailman, Bill Shuttleworth
CAST: Scott Bakula (Ted Klausterman), John Kassir (Kenny Brewster), Jerry Colker (Phil Kunin)
MUSICAL NUMBERS: Promise of Greatness, Angry Guy/Lovely Day, Don't Wanna Be No Superstar, Operator, Screaming Clocks, The History of Stand-Up Comedy, Dreams of Heaven, Kamikaze Kabaret, The American Dream, What a Ride, Hello Fellas, A Father Now, "Three Guys Naked from the Waist Down" Theme
A musical in two acts. The action takes place in New York City and in Southern California.

(No Smoking Playhouse) Wednesday, February 6–17, 1985 (14 performances and 11 previews). The Modern Romance Company presents:
MODERN ROMANCE by F. LaTour; Director, Bernard Barrow; Set, Don Jensen; Lighting, John Branon; Costumes, Jane Aire; General Manager, Lily Turner; Production Assistant, Meg Slavin; Casting, Mark Fleischman; Sound, Ian Toll; Props, Rochelle Blank; Stage Manager, Otis White; Press, David Lipsky, Avivah Simon
CAST: Alix Elias (Nicky), Jim Desmond (Tom), Mark Hofmaier (Robert), Geoffrey Wade (Dennis Howard), John Fleming (Jonathan), Joseph Ragno (Ralphie), Nicolas Klar (Chuck), Musical Bridges, Gerald Cook
A comedy in 2 acts and 13 scenes. The action takes place at the present time in New York City and environs.

(13th Street Playhouse) Thursday Feb. 7,–March 3, 1985 (16 performances)
A LOUD BANG ON JUNE THE FIRST by Wesley Burrowes; Director, William E. Hunt; Set, John Robert Lloyd; Lighting, Dan Kotlowitz; Costumes, Marla Speer; Original Music, Hank Levy; Lighting, John Koshell; Sound, Ian Toll; Sculpture, Inocente Del Sol; Stage Managers, William Michael Maher, Steve Cassidy; Press, Audrey Ross
CAST: Michael Allinson (King Solomon), Beulah Garrick (Queen Porphyria), Paul Ukena, Jr. (Joe/Fred)
A comedy in two acts. The action takes place at the present time in the ancient underground palace apartments of the King and Queen.

Jerry Colker, John Kassir, Scott Bakula
in "3 Guys Naked from the Waist Down"
(Diana Kassir Photo)

73

(Lamb's Theatre) Thursday, Feb. 7,–March 3, 1985 (28 performances and 10 previews). Norma and David Langworthy present:
CLIFFHANGER by James Yaffe; Director, David McKenna; Scenery, Leo B. Meyer; Costumes, Merrily Murray-Walsh; Lighting, Jeff Davis; Sound, Paul Garrity; Casting, Elizabeth Woodman; General Management, Dorothy Olim, George Elmer; Assistant Company Manager, Colin Fraser; Production Assistant, Nan Siegmund; Props, David Malvin; Sound, Lia Vollack; Wardrobe, Joy Alpern; Stage Managers, Ellen Raphael, J. R. MacDonald; Press, Jeffrey Richards, C. George Willard, Robert Ganshaw, Ben Morse, Bill Suttleworth, Toby Mailman
CAST: Henderson Forsythe (Henry Lowenthal), Lenka Peterson (Polly Lowenthal), Natalia Nogulich (Edith Wilshire), Keith Reddin (Melvin McMullen), Tom Mardirosian (Dave DeVito)
A drama in 2 acts and 4 scenes. The action takes place at the present time during late May, in the Lowenthal house in a small college town somewhere in the Rockies.

(Inroads Theatre) Sunday, Feb. 10,–March 3, 1985 (16 performances). George Grec, David Singer, Frank Laraia present:
HAVE I GOT A GIRL FOR YOU! with Book by Joel Greenhouse, Penny Rockwell; Music and Lyrics, Dick Gallagher; Director, Bruce Hopkins; Choreography, Felton Smith; Set, Herman C. Arnholt; Costumes, Kenneth M. Yount; Lighting, Annette DeMeo; Wigs, Michael DiCesare; Sound, Dave Schneider; Musical Director, Dick Gallagher; Stage Manager, Richard Coumbs; Press, FLT/Francine Trevens, Andrew Shearer
CAST: Rick Stanley (Dr. John Frankenstein), Chris Tanner (The Monster), Semina DeLaurentis (Mary Phillips), Susan Borneman (Effie), J. P. Dougherty (Dr. Pretorius), Ruby Rims (Little Girl/Gypsy/Blindman), Robert I. (Igor), and Tom Matthews, Anne Marie McElroy, Maria Morreale, Constance Pachl, Steve Pinzer
MUSICAL NUMBERS: Peasant's Song, Don't Open the Door, Always for Science, Hollywood, Last Lullaby, The Way I Look at You, I Love Me, Have I Got a Girl for You, If This Is How It Ends, The Opera, I'll Take It from Here
A musical in two acts. The action takes place "a long time ago" in a Bavarian forest just east of Hollywood.

(West Side Y Arts Center) Sunday, Feb. 10,–March 2, 1985 (13 performances and 3 previews). American Kaleidoscope present:
CHAOS AND HARD TIMES by Brandon Cole; Director, Richard Bell; Scenery, Eric Veenstra; Lighting, Robert F. Strohmeier; Costumes, Marcy Grace Froehlich; Technical Director, Geoffrey Freeman; Production Assistant, Celia Braxton; Company Manager, Deirdre Moynihan; Stage Managers, Anne Veenstra, Paul A. Kochman; Press, FLT/Francine L. Trevens, Gail Dawson, Jessica Greene, Diane Swanson
CAST: Joel Rooks (Morrow), Michael Badalucco (Ralph), Warren Keith (Booker), Josephine Nichols (Ema), John Turturro (Jesse)
A drama in three acts. The action takes place at the present time in the common room of a large suburban house.

(Courtyard Playhouse) Thursday, Feb. 14,–Mar. 10, 1985 (16 performances) and returned Thursday, Apr. 25,–May 26, 1985 (25 performances). The Actors Collective presents:
CREEPS by David Freeman; Director, Stuart Ross; Set, Dick Block; Lighting, Jeffrey McRoberts; Incidental Music, John Simon; Technical Director, Clive MacDonald; Sound, Tom Textor, Stuart Ross; Costume Coordinator, Carol Wenz; Vocals, Mary Testa; Movement Consultant, May Kesler; Stage Managers, Meaghan O'Connell, Richard Hauenstein, Donna Stone; Press, Patt Dale, Julianne Waldhelm
CAST: W. McGregor King (Pete), Don de Franco succeeded by Jim O'Malley (Michael/M.C./Shriner), William Carrigan (Tom), Perry Jon Pirkkanen (Sam), Cynthia Raftus (Sally/Majorette/Thelma), Craig Fols (Jim), Kathryn Stalter (Saunders/Puffo), Glenn Alterman (Shriner/Carson)
A drama performed without intermission; The action takes place at the present time in Toronto, Canada, in the men's room of a sheltered workshop for people with cerebral palsy.

(Theatre of the Riverside Church) Friday, Feb. 15,–Mar. 3, 1985 (12 performances). Theatre of the Riverside Church (David K. Manion, Artistic Director) presents:
PERE GORIOT based on the novel by Balzac; Music, Gary Levinson; Director,/ Libretto, Alan Mokler; Sets, Marina Draghici; Costumes, Isabelle Ring; Choreography, Ricky Schussel; Musical Direction, William Graham; Stage Managers, David Ganon, Byrne Clark; Press, Mary Galaty
CAST: Mark Wolff (Eugene de Rastignac), Richard Frisch (Goriot), Robert Grossman (Vautrin), Claudia O'Neill (Victorine), Laura Sighinolfi (Madame Vauquer), Bob Strickland (Christophe), Margery Cohen (Claire de Beausseant), Leena Tucker (Anastasie de Restaud), Sarah Wohlenhaus (Delphine de Nucingen), William Broderick (Maxime de Trailles), Gerry Dieffenbach (Count de Restaud), Michael Lengel (Marquis d'Ajuda), Ensemble: Bary Barber, William Bonecutter, Susan Borofsky, Peter Buchi, Julia Davidson, Lorraine Goodman
MUSICAL NUMBERS: In the City Paris!, Today's the Day, I Said Hello, So Nice, Chamber of the Heart, The Love Letter, The New World, The Polonaise, At the Opera: Mozart, My Own Way of Loving, Don't Come Back, How Can We Know?, Joy, What Are Fathers For?, Becoming Becoming, Let Happen, I Dreamed, Finale
A musical drama in 3 acts and 17 scenes. The action takes place in Paris in 1820.

Henderson Forsythe, Keith Reddin, Lenka Peterson
in "Cliffhanger" (*Bert Andrews Photo*)

(18th Street Playhouse) Thursday, Feb. 21,–March 17, 1985 (16 performances). Eccentric Circles Theatre presents:
DANCING TO DOVER by Judith Fein; Producer-Director, Paula Kay Pierce; Assistant Director-Choreographer, Albert Makhtsier; Original Music, Leslie Steinweiss; Set and Costumes, Randy Ingram; Lighting, Richard Clausen; Wardrobe, Johnnie Mae; Stage Managers, David Lawrence Folender, Kathy Zoumis; Press, Patt Dale Associates
CAST: Vera Lockwood (Bella at 80), Holly Hawkins (Young Bella), Phyllis Hedeman (Her Mother), L. Paul Watson (Her Father), Marianne McNamara (Bella's older daughter), Marianne Murphy (Bella's younger daughter), Eric Himes (Ralph Sooter), Robert O'Neill (Isidore, Bella's husband), Martha Greenhouse (Winnie Elton)
A drama in two acts. The action covers about four months in the life of Bella Vroncha, ballet teacher extraordinaire, beginning in the present.

(Westbeth Theatre Center) Friday, February 22,–April 7, 1985 (18 performances). Stonewall Repertory Theater presents.
8 × 10 GLOSSY by Sarah Dreher; Director, Jacqueline Allen; Sets, Robert Edmonds; Lighting, Ed Matthews; Costumes, Brenda Jones
CAST: Barbara Bornmann, Catherine Cannon, Claire Clark, Anne DuPont, Charlotte Durham

Josephine Nichols, Joel Rooks, John Turturro
in "Chaos and Hard Times"
(*Anita & Steve Shevett Photo*)

(Harold Clurman Theatre) Monday, Feb. 25,–March 16, 1985 (11 performances). The Harold Clurman Theatre (Jack Garfein, Artistic Director) and Lucille Lortel present:
AN EVENING WITH EKKEHARD SCHALL with Karl-Heinz Nehring at the piano. Program One: From Laughing at the World to Living in the World; Program Two: Questions, Laments, Answers. Both programs with words of Bertolt Brecht. General Manager, Craig S. Dorfman; Associate Producer, Naomi Koncius; Company Manager, Ed Hambleton; Press, Henry Luhrman, Terry M. Lilly, David Mayhew, Andrew P. Shearer

(Theater for the New City) Thursday, February 28,–March 24, 1985 (16 performances). Theater for the New City (George Bartenieff, Crystal Field, Artistic Directors) presents:
THE CONDUCT OF LIFE by Maria Irene Fornes; Directed by Ms. Fornes; Set, T. Owen Baumgartner; Lighting, Anne Militello; Costumes, Sally J. Lesser; Stage Manager, Karen Moore; Press, Bruce Cohen, Kathleen von Schmid
CAST: Sheila Dabney (Nena), Crystal Field (Leticia), Pedro Garrido (Orlando), Alba Oms (Olimpia), Hermann Lademann (Alejo)
A drama in one act without intermission.

(Cubiculo) Thursday, Feb. 28,–March 17, 1985 (12 performances). The Classic Theatre (Nicholas John Stathis, Executive Director; Maurice Edwards, Artistic Director) presents:
THE IMAGINARY INVALID by Moliere; Adapted by Owen S. Rackleff; Director, Maurice Edwards; Producer, Nicholas John Stathis; Producing Director, Ron Daley; Set, Bob Phillips; Costumes, Bari Odom; Lighting, Lisa Grossman; Music, David Hollister; Technical Director, Edmond Ramage; Stage Managers, Robert Verini, David S. Cohen; Press, Howard Atlee, Barbara Atlee
CAST: David Carlyon (Thomas), Kathryn Graves (Angelique), Eleni Kelakos (Purgon/Dancer), Joseph O'Brien (Notary Bonnefoy), Daniel Pollack (Beralde), Owen S. Rackleff (Argan), David Snizek (Dr. Diafoirus), Maggie Topkis (Toinette), Susan Winter (Beline), Craig Paul Wrol (Cleante)
A comedy in two acts. The action takes place in Argan's house in Paris.

(Actors Outlet) Thursday, Feb. 28,–March 10, 1985 (8 performances and 4 previews). Stage Arts Theater Company (Nell Robinson, Ruth Ann Norris, Artistic Directors) presents:
SNOW LEOPARDS by Martin Jones; Director, Licia Colombi; Set, Daniel Proett; Costumes, Sheila Kehoe; Lighting, Bob Bessoir; Hairstylist, Laura Blood; Sound, Tom Gould; Stage Manager, Mary Ann Chance; Press, Shirley Herz, Peter Cromarty, Pete Sanders
CAST: Giulia Pagano (Sally), Alice White (C. J. "Claire"), Understudy, Mary Ann Chance
A comedy in two acts. The action takes place at the present time and a year later in Chicago's Lincoln Park Zoo.

(Hartley House Theater) Thursday, Feb. 28,–March 16, 1985 (12 performances). Playwrights Preview Productions presents:
AAH REFRESHING: Three New Comedies. Production Design, Jim Horton; Lighting, Richard Comfort; Costume Coordinators, Harty Platt, Bebe Shmash; Production Assistant, Linda Shary; Stage Managers, Ben Fuchs, Ann Hollywood. *"Thirty Years in Sixty Seconds"* by J. Paul Porter; Director, Frances Hill. CAST: Timothy Estin, Linda Shary (60's Couple), Joe O'Connor, Jayne Chamberlin (70's Couple), Bill Carmichael, Laura Henry (80's Couple). *"Success Story"* by Arthur Kopit; Director, Joe Paradise. CAST: Annie Weiss Mauer (Mrs. Hoffensberg), Evan McHale (Mr. Krum), Phyllis Chase (Woman). *"Wacs in Khaki"* by Mary Steelsmith; Director, Paul Dervis. CAST: Nancy Rothman (Loretta), Marcy Kaplin (Veronica), Janet Kenney (Dotty), Jayne Chamberlin (Betty Good), Joel Spineti (Bernie), Ann Hollywood (Ann Hollywood)

(Open Space/Apple Corps Theatre) Friday, March 1–25, 1985 (20 performances). The Open Space Theatre Experiment (Lynn Michaels, Artistic Director; Harry Baum, Administrative Director) presents:
THE OTHER SIDE OF NEWARK by Enid Rudd; Director, Nancy Gabor; Lights, Jackie Manassee; Costumes, Gail Brassard; Sound, Mike Cohen; Technical Director, Michael Schutte; Props, Ken Young; Stage Managers, Lawrence Berrick, Linda Riley, Jenelle Pointer; Press, Bruce Cohen, Kathleen von Schmid, Naomi Cahn Puiter
CAST: Laurinda Barrett (Rose Alcott), Louise Stubbs (Dinah), Ralph Bell (Dr. Lenn), W. T. Martin (Alan Tremont), Richards (Young Dinah)
A play in two acts. The action takes place at the present time in a hospital room, and in a teachers' lounge in the late 1930's.

Ekkehard Schall

(Palsson's) Monday, March 4,–May 13, 1985 (11 performances, Mondays only) Steven McGraw presents:
TABOO IN REVUE written by Peggy Gordon, Robin Lamont, Leslie Ray; Director, Michael Leeds; Musical Director, Jeffrey Klitz; Technical Director, Lynn McCracken; Press, Patt Dale, Julianne Waldhelm
CAST: James Gleason, Peggy Gordon, Robin Lamont, Leslie Ray
PROGRAM: I'm Okay, Indifference, Live from WKGB, Up Front, The Box, Celibate, Cosmo's Angels, Special Guy, Working It Out, Carter Kliner, The Chorus, Group Singles, It Wasn't Me, Beat the Clock, Oh Helen!

(Top of the Village Gate) Thursday, March 7–17, 1985 (14 performances and 3 previews). Mike Houlihan presents:
A COUPLE OF BLAGUARDS by and with Frank McCourt and Malachy McCourt. A cabaret comedy in two parts. General Management, Fremont Associates; Stage Manager, Thom Mangan; Production Coordinator, Mark Haack; Company Manager, Debbie Levy; Stage Manager, Thom Mangan; Press, Patt Dale, Julianne Waldhelm

(Shakespeare Center) Friday, March 8,–31, 1985 (17 performances). The Riverside Shakespeare Company (Artistic director, W. Stuart McDowell; Executive Director, Gloria Skurski; Assistant Artistic Director, Timothy Oman; Press, Lisa Salomon)
THE HISTORY OF KING LEAR by William Shakespeare with Nahum Tate's adaptation; Director, W. S. McDowell; Music, John Aschenbrenner; Set, Norbert Kolb; Costumes, Ellen Seeling; Dramaturg, Seymour Isenberg; Lighting, Sam Scripps; Fights, Richard Raether; Associate Director, Maureen Clarke; Stage Managers, Marc Ramsey, Jill Bailey, Alice A. Farrell
CAST: Edwin Bordon (Cornwall), Daniel Daily (Kent), Saunder Finard (Albany), Don Fischer (Edgar), Sandra Proctor Gray (Arante), Margo Gruber (Regan), Buck Hobbs (Burgundy), Eric Hoffman (Garrick), Freda Kavanagh (Freda), Frank Muller (Bastard), Gene Santarelli (Gentleman), Barbara Tirrell (Goneril).

Alice White, Giulia Pagano
in "Snow Leopards"
(Carol Rosegg/Martha Swope Photo)

**Perry Arthur (top), Mary-Cleere Haran,
Camille Saviola in "Hollywood Opera"**
(Kenn Duncan Photo)

(Vineyard Theatre) Friday, March 8–25, 1985 (20 performances). Vineyard Theatre (Barbara Zinn Krieger, Executive Director; Douglas Aibel, Artistic Director) presents:
RESPONSIBLE PARTIES by Jeffrey Sweet; Director, Thomas Gruenewald; Scenery, James Wolk; Lighting, Phil Monat; Costumes, Pamela Scofield; Sound, Bruce Ellman; Production Manager, Susan Wilder; Technical Director, David Raphel; Production Assistant, Gabriel Harris; Stage Managers, Roy Harris, Linda Young; Press, Bruce Cohen, Kathleen von Schmid
CAST: Larry Block (Randolph), Matthew Penn (Cornell), Tim Halligan (Fred Chaney), Fred Sanders (Marshall), Mary Joy (Joanne Reese), Dave Florek (A. J. Reese), Helen Slater (Tina)
    A comedy/drama in three scenes performed without intermission. The action takes place in May in the lobby of the Ventura Oasis Motel in Los Angeles, California.

(Raft Theatre) Friday, March 8–30, 1985 (20 performances). American Road Production Corp. presents:
'TIL JASON COMES by Dan Lauria; Director, Gerald Anthony; Set, J. Newton White; Costumes, R. L. Bross, Jr.; Lighting, Tony Quintovalla; General Manager, Malita Barron; Technical Director, D. Scott Gagnon; Assistant Director, Hank Liebeskind; Assistant Producer, Shirley Brown; Production Assistants, Cameron Taylor, Jerry Rodgers; Stage Manager, Amy A. C. Coombs; Press, Lou Gordon Associates
CAST: Maggie Baird (Ellie), Roger Serbagi (Carmondy), Jane Culley (Bea), George Spelvin (Jason)
    A drama in two acts. The action takes place on an autumn afternoon and evening in 1929 in a Victorian mansion on the outskirts of Boston.

**Norman Snow, Lorraine Morgan
in "The Fantod"** *(Susan Cook/Martha Swope Photo)*

(South Street Theatre) Sunday, March 10–31, 1985 (27 performances). Michael Loeb presents:
HAVEN by Joel Gross; Director, Bruce Ornstein; Scenery, Brian Martin; Costumes, David Toser; Lighting, Barry Arnold; Associate Producer, Susan Forney; Sound, Lia Vollack; General Management, Whitbell Productions (J. A. Whitcomb/Gail Bell); Associate General Manager, Lee Blattau; Assistant to Director, Roy Friedland; Technical Director, Ted Reinert; Props, Nan Siegmund; Wardrobe, Kenneth Warks; Hairstylist, Jerry Mafarone; Stage Managers, Denise A. Laffer, Michael Spier; Press, Bruce Cohen, Kathleen von Schmid, Naomi Cahn Pewter
CAST: Ellen Barber (Marie), Lane Brinkley (Honey), Stephen McHattie (Jack), Anita Keal (Mrs. Horowitz), David Lynn Chandler (Jimmy)
    A play in 2 acts and 8 scenes. The action takes place during the summer of 1948 in Marie's apartment, in a diner, and in an empty store, all in Forest Hills, Queens, NY.

(The Ballroom) Wednesday, March 13,–May 18, 1985 (40 performances and 4 previews). Wendell Minnick, Bob Smith and Entertainment Ventures Ltd. present:
HOLLYWOOD OPERA conceived by Barry Keating; Musical Staging/Special Material, Stuart Ross; Music and Lyrics, Barry Keating; Additional Lyrics, David Schechter; Director, Barry Keating; Musical Director/Vocal Arrangements, John Spalla; Orchestrations, Jim MacElwaine; Costumes, Bosha Johnson; Puppets, Perry Arthur; Lighting, Matthew Ehlert; Decor, Dick Block; Wigs, James Amaral; Stage Managers, Myron Moore, Ron Woodall
CAST: Camille Saviola succeeded by Lynne Eldredge, Mary-Cleere Haran, Perry Arthur
MUSICAL NUMBERS: Hollywood Opera, D'Oyly Carte Blanche, Citizen Kong, Three Phases of Eve, Opera in 3-D, Delle Rose's Turn, Das Exorcist, How Now Voyager, Tippy's Immolation, Finale

(Actors Outlet) Thursday, March 14,–April 21, 1985 (50 performances in repertory). Echo Stage Company (Martin Nordal, Artistic Director; Mitchell Mills, Managing Director) presents in repertory:
HELLO DALI by Andrew Dallmeyer; Director, Martin Nordal; with Sam Tsout-souvas as Dali; **ABEL'S SISTER** by Timerlake Wertenbaker; Based on material by Yolande Bourcier; Director, Martin Nordal; with Richard Abernethy (Howard), Cynthia Hayden (Laura), Donald Most (Chris), Mim Solberg (Sandra).
THE LAND OF OTHERWISE by Tor Aage Bringsvaerd; Translated by Anthony Martin; Co-Directors, Martin Nordal, Anne Beck; with Jessica Lockhart (Keri), Mitchell Mills (Father), Molly Noble (Mother), Victor Stone (Andy). Sets, Bruce Monroe; Costumes, Marla Kaye; Lighting, Leon DiLeone, Pierette Pillone; Sound, Judy Baldwin; Projections, Philip Nye; General Manager, Mitchell Mills; Stage Fights, T. J. Glenn; Stage Managers, Ken Simmons, Heather Montanye; Music Arranged by Woody Regan, Judy Baldwin; Press, David Lipsky, Avivah Simon

(Perry Street Theatre) Monday, March 18,–April 1, 1985 (26 performances). New York Theatre Workshop (Jean Passanante, Artistic Director; Nancy Kassak Diekmann, Managing Director) presents:
THE FANTOD by Amlin Gray; Director, Stephen Katz; Production Manager, Michael Moody; Set, Richard Hoover; Costumes, Andrew B. Marlay; Lighting, John Gisondi; Stage Manager, Joseph De Pauw; Press, Milly Schoenbaum, Marc Routh
CAST: Jeanne Cullen (Mrs. Hannah Marryat), Lorraine Morgan (Rachel Marryat), Mark Moses (Arthur Loscombe), Charles Gregory (Maj. Leonidas Marryat), Burke Pearson (Vicar Didbin), Norman Snow (Sir Tristam Northmoor), Martha Miller (Selina Darch), Charles Gregory (John Connor)
    A drama in two acts. The action takes place during 1854 in the Pavilion Room at Garden Close, England.

(Players Theatre) Monday, March 18–24, 1985 (8 performances). On the Street Productions presents:
THE MUGGER by Steven J. Sher; Director, Phillip Price; Set, Don Jensen; Costumes, Mary Brecht; Lighting, Beverly Emmons; Fights, Randy Kovitz; General Manager, Lily Turner; Stage Managers, Ruth Kreshka, Walter Teper; Press, Patricia Krawitz, Keith Aaron
CAST: Stewart J. Zully (Man with the gun), John Di Carlo (Young Man), Jaime Perry (Radio Man), Evelyn Orbach (Shopping Bag Lady), Walter Teper (Cop)
    A drama in two acts. The action takes place at the present time on a street in New York City

(Parsons School May Auditorium) Monday, March 18, 1985 (one performance only)
MEMORIES OF AN IMMORTAL SPIRIT: TENNESSEE WILLIAMS, a celebration of the late, great American playwright's works, read by Tom Spackman, Rosemary Prinz and Tandy Cronyn

(Playhouse 91) Thursday, March 21–24, 1985 (4 performances and 11 previews). Jessica Levy presents:
CROSSING THE BAR by Michael Zettler; Director, Jerry Zaks; Set, Loren Sherman; Costumes, Sally Lesser; Lighting, Paul Gallo; Casting, Stuart Howard; General Management, Jay Kingwill/Larry Goossen; Assistant Company Manager, Susan Sampliner; Assistant Producer, Kate Loewald; Assistant to Director, Jonathan Freund; Props, Art Hansen; Wardrobe, Allison Sommers; Stage Managers, T. L. Boston, Ira Klein; Press, Jeffrey Richards, Robert Ganshaw, Ben Morse, Bill Shuttleworth, Toby Mailman
CAST: Betsy Aidem (Peggy), Dick Latessa (Rudi), Frank Hamilton (Kelly), George Guidall (John), Stan Lachow (Tony), Ed Setrakian (Augie), Jay Devlin (Jim), Brian Hartigan (Freddie), Don Perkins (Fitz), Understudy: Dani Klein (Peggy)

A drama in 2 acts and 3 scenes. The action takes place on a winter's day in Windgap, Pennsylvania.

(American Place Theatre) Sunday, March 24–31, 1985 (8 performances and 16 previews). Rick Hobard presents:
BEFORE THE DAWN by Joseph Stein; Director, Kenneth Frankel; Adapted from "A Ladies' Tailor" by Aleksandr Borshchagovsky; Translated by Lev Loseff, Dennis Whelan; Associate Producer, Joan Firestone; General Manager, Marvin A. Krauss; Set, Andrew Jackness; Costumes, Jennifer von Mayrhauser; Lighting, Stephen Strawbridge; Sound, Gary Harris; Technical Director, Jeff Turner; Props, Charlie Zuckerman, Al Steiner; Wardrobe, Mary Jestice; Production Assistant, Laura Bellomy; Stage Managers, Tammy Taylor, John Amedro; Press, Milly Schoenbaum, Michael Alpert, Ruth Jaffee, Marc Routh
CAST: Peter Michael Goetz (Isaak Moiseevich Starkman), Deborah Hedwall (Sonia Isaakovna), Roberta Maxwell (Irina), David Leary (Anton Gorbunov), Elisa Loti (Natalia), Jennie Dundas (Masha), Jeremy Peter Johnson (Alyosha Yermakov), Jodi Thelen (Rosa Spivak), Katherine Borowitz (Polina Fyodorovna), Betty Miller (Yevdokia Ivanovna), L. R. Hults (Ukranian Polizei), German Soldiers: John Amedro, Pollard Brown

A drama in two acts. The action takes place in the basement apartment occupied by Sonia, Masha and Irina on the night of Sept. 28 and the morning of Sept. 29, 1941.

(Riverwest Theatre) Monday, March 25,–April 14, 1985 (20 performances). Robert Lissauer and CHS Productions with Blanche Miller in association with Riverwest Management Company present:
JACK AND JILL with Book and Lyrics by Bob Larimer; Music, Hal Schaefer; Direction/Musical Staging, Miriam Fond; Set, Bob Phillips; Lighting, Mark DiQuinzio; Costumes, David C. Woolard; Computer Programming, Neil Larimer; Musical Director/Arrangements, Hal Schaefer; Assistant Musical Director, Mark Lipman; Technical Director, Anthony Ross; Props, Shelley Ginsberg; Wardrobe, Jeanne Ward; Production Assistants, Abigail Koleto, Penny Potenz; Stage Managers, Nancy Harrington, Jonathan Shulman; Press, Jeffrey Richards Associates.
CAST: Lara Teeter (Jack Miller), Jennifer Naimo (Janet Miller), Raymond Thorne (Ben Miller), Sheila Smith (Ruth Miller), Ernestine Jackson (Jill Donovan), David Pendleton (Brad Donovan), Edye Byrde (Ruby Donovan), Daniel B. Wooten, Jr. (Gary Donovan)
MUSICAL NUMBERS: Jazz, Getting Ahead of Yourself, The First Time I Heard Ella, The First Time I Heard Ellington, Woulda Coulda Shoulda, D Blues, There Ain't Nothing Wrong with Me, The Old Mom and Pop Lament, You Can Be a Little Bit, Waltzing Me Around, But Not You, At 16, In-Between Gigs, Without a Doubt, By the Numbers

A musical in 2 acts and 18 scenes. The action takes place at the present time.

(Promenade Theatre) Tuesday, March 26,–April 7, 1985 (16 performances and 16 previews). Roger Berlind, Franklin R. Levy, Gregory Harrison present:
IN TROUSERS by William Finn; Director, Matt Casella; Set, Santo Loquasto; Lighting, Marilyn Rennagel; Costumes, Madeline Ann Graneto; Musical Direction, Roy Leake, Jr.; Orchestrations, Michael Starobin; Sound, Tom Morse; Casting, Julie Hughes/Barry Moss; General Management, R. Tyler Gatchell, Jr., Peter Neufeld, Nina Lannan; Company Managers, Jodi Moss, J. Anthony Magner; Assistant to Director, Michael Cooper; Wardrobe, Cynthia Boardman; Assistant to Producers, Bill Hutton; Production Associates, David R. Brymer, Jeanne Troy; Stage Manager, Rebecca Klein; Press, Solters/Roskin/Friedman, Joshua Ellis, Keith Sherman, Adrian Bryan-Brown, Cindy Valk, Jackie Green
CAST: Tony Cummings (Marvin), Catherine Cox (His Wife), Sherry Hursey (His High School Sweetheart), Kathy Garrick (Miss Goldberg, His Teacher), Understudies: Carol Dilley (Wife/Sweetheart), Mary Bond Davis (Teacher)
MUSICAL NUMBERS: I Can't Sleep, Time to Wake Up, I Have a Family, How Marvin Eats His Breakfast, Marvin's Giddy Seizures, My High School Sweetheart, Set Those Sails, I Swear I Won't Ever Again, High School Ladies at 5 O'clock, The Rape of Miss Goldberg, Love Me for What I Am, I Am Wearing a Hat, Wedding Song, Three Seconds, How the Body Falls Apart, I Feel Him Slipping Away, Whizzer Going Down, I'm Breaking Down, Packing Up, Breakfast Over Sugar, How America Got Its Name, Scrubby Dubby, Another Sleepless Night, Without You, No Hard Feelings

A musical performed without intermission.

Sheila Smith, Ernestine Jackson, Lara Teeter, David Pendleton in "Jack and Jill"
(Peter Cunningham Photo)

(Cubiculo) Tuesday, March 26,–April 14, 1985 (21 performances). The Classic Theatre (Maurice Edwards, Artistic Director; Nicholas John Stathis, Executive Director) in association with the National Shakespeare Company (Ron Daley, Producing Director) presents:
ROUNDHEADS AND THE POINTHEADS by Bertolt Brecht; Director, Jerry Roth; Original Score, Hanns Eisler; New English translation, Michael Feingold; Musical Director, Erich K. Rausch; Producers, Nicholas John Stathis, Adda C. Gogoris; Assistant Director, Keith Miller; Set, Bob Phillips; Lighting, Lisa Grossman; Costumes, Bary Odom; Masks and Makeup, Thomas J. Wilson; Choreography, Thomas Nichols; Pianist, Erich K. Rausch; Technical Director, Edmond Ramage; Managing Director, Owen S. Rackleff; Stage Manager, Denise A. Albright; Press, Howard Atlee
CAST: Bill Maloney (Callas), Amy Brentano (Nana), Jade Kameron (Angela), Elise Dewsberry (Emma), William Snovell (Viceroy), Alan Walworth (Missena), Joan Crowe (Lawyer), Joe MacDonald (Saz), Ray Collins (Judge), Peter Manos (Callamassi), David Sharps (Parr), Paul Tumbleson (Palmosa), Laura Tewksbury (Madam Tomaso), Michael Rush (Emanuel), Ellen Boggs (Isabella), Paul Tumbleson (Lopez), Daniel Large (Peruiner), Laura Tewksbury (Lawyer), Paul Edwards (Hat-Knocker), Amy Hohn (Chorus)
MUSICAL NUMBERS: Change the World, Hymn of Yahoo's Awakening, Nana's Song, Whitewash Song, Sickle Song, Ballad of Button Flipping, Urging of the Flesh, See-What-You-Want-Grab-It Song, Song of the Stimulating Effect of Money, Ballad of the Mill Wheel, Pimping Song, Poverty Chastity Obedience, Song of Wealth and Power, Landlord's Round

A musical in 2 acts and 11 scenes.

Catherine Cox, Sherry Hursey, Tony Cummings, Kathy Garrick in "In Trousers"
(Martha Swope Photo)

77

(INTAR Hispanic American Theatre) Wednesday, April 3–28, 1985 (34 performances). International Arts Relations (Max Ferra, Artistic Director; Dennis Ferguson-Acosta, Managing Director) presents:
COLD AIR by Virgilio Pinera; Translated and Adapted by Maria Irene Fornes; Director, Miss Fornes; Scenery, Ricardo Morin; Lighting, Anne E. Militello; Costumes, Gabriel Berry; Casting, Janet L. Murphy; Technical Director, Tom Carroll; Props, Dor Green; Stage Managers, Susan D. Greenbaum, Raul Aranas, Armando Molina; Press, Bruce Cohen, Kathleen von Schmid
CAST: Ivonne Coll (Luz Marina), Leo Garcia (Oscar), Al Casas (Angel), Miriam Cruz (Ana), Raul Aranas (Enrique), Armando Molina (Luis), Katrina Ramos, Jennifer Valle (Children)
   A drama in 3 acts and 12 scenes. The action takes place in a living room in Havana from 1940 to 1954.

(TOMI Park Royal Theatre) Wednesday, April 10–28, 1985 (12 performances). City Rep/Hedi Molnar present:
THE EDUCATION OF ONE MISS FEBRUARY: SHARON TWANE by Ralph Pezzullo; Director, Dana Bate; Set, Mark Marcante, John Paino; Lighting, Edward R. F. Matthews; Music and Lyrics, Ralph Pezzullo; Pianist, David Cummings; Guitarist, Scott Wakefield; Choreography, Lisa Bottalico; Fight, Edward Easton; Costumes Coordinator, Pamela Ross; Stage Manager, Dan Da Silva; Press, FLT/Francine L. Trevens, Gail Dawson, James Mayer
CAST: John Bigham (Ron), Stacy Courtney (Rhonda), Kevin Cutts (Biff), Nicholas B. Daddazio (Pompeii), Edward Easton (Louie), Jean Hackett (Sharon), Robert McFarland (Gorman), Maureen McGinnis (Bunny Mother), Kim Merrill (Petula), Warner Schreiner (Stu Heffer), Scott Wakefield (Chuck)
   A comedy in two acts. The action takes place at the present time in the United States.

(Latin Quarter) Wednesday, April 10,–May 18, 1985 (46 performances and 8 previews). Arnie Socher presents:
CAROUSSEL DES FOLLES conceived by Michael Andrews; Choreography, Richard Pierlon, Luis Arriaga; Executive Producer, Robert Roth; Press, Shirley Herz, Pete Sanders, Peter Cromarty, David Roggensack, Gary Lawrence
CAST: Pudgy, Michael Andrews (Ann-Margaret/Cyndi Lauper), Stephen McCall (Donna Summer/Diana Ross/Dionne Warwick), Elgin Kenna (Cher/Barbra Streisand), Danee Russo (Shirley Bassey/Tina Turner), Joey Skelbred (Dolly Parton/Charo), David Christopher (Sheila) and the Caroussel Des Folles Dancers
   A musical cabaret entertainment in two acts.

(Cherry Lane Theatre) Wednesday, April 10,–August 18, 1985 (161 performances). William Ross and Perry Bruskin in association with Daniel Neiden present The Writers Theatre Production of:
HANNAH SENESH by David Schechter; Developed in collaboration with Lori Wilner; Based on the Diaries and Poems of Hannah Senesh; English Translation, Marta Cohn, Pater Hay; Director, David Schechter; Music Composed and Arranged by Steven Lutvak; Additional Music, Elizabeth Swados, David Schechter; Set, Jennifer Gallagher; Lighting, Vivien Leone; Costumes, David Woolard; Production Supervisor, Christopher Santee; General Manager, Leonard A. Mulhern; Company Manager, James Hannah; Wardrobe, Candace Miller; Production Assistant, Wayne Hoffman; Stage Managers, Daniel S. Lewin, John Fistos; Press, Max Eisen, Maria Somma, Madelon Rosen
SONGS: The Rainbow Song, Eli Eli, Blessed Is the Match, Soon, Shtil Di Nacht, Zog Nit Keyn Mol, One Two Three
CAST: Lori Wilner (Catherine/Hannah Senesh), David Schechter (Voice of George Senesh), John Fistos (Young Man), Understudy: Susan Gabriel
   A drama in two acts.

(Actors Playhouse) Sunday, April 14,–May 19, 1985 (56 performances). Rick Seeber presents:
THE SINGULAR DOROTHY PARKER conceived and adapted by Rory Seeber from the works of Dorothy Parker; Director, Laura Cuetara; Scenery and Lighting, Neil Prince; Costumes, Deborah Bays; Sound, Bruce Odland; Associate Producers, Entertainment Ventures, Thomas Hardy; General Management, Edgewood Organization, Lewis Friedman, Richard Martini, Dick Grayson; Company Manager, Melinda Palmore; Wardrobe, Ginnie Weidmann; Press, Jacqueline Burnham, Edward Callaghan, David Lotz, Jeanne Browne, Melissa Davis, Ina Goldberg, Jill Larkin, Gary Murphy
CAST: Jane Connell as Dorothy Parker.
   The action takes place during the early 1950's and other ill-remembered periods of the not-so-legendary past in Mrs. Parker's rooms. Presented in two acts.

Stephen Joyce, Ron Randell in "Maneuvers"
(Carol Rosegg/Martha Swope Photo)

(South Street Theatre) Sunday, April 14,–May 12, 1985 (28 performances and 5 previews). The Montecito Company (David Knapp, President; Richard Ross, Vice President) present:
MANEUVERS by Catherine Muschamp; Director, Fielder Cook; Set, Loy Arcenas; Lighting, John Hickey; Costumes, David Loveless; Fight Choreography, Randy Kovitz; Casting, Mary Colquhoun; Associate Producer, Cheryl Faraone in association with the New York Theatre Studio; Assistant to Director, Sally Burnett; Props, Charlie Eisenberg; Technical Director, Tom Pavelka; Production Assistants, Lisa Bemel, Deirdre Sinnott; Wardrobe, Elizabeth Call; Stage Manager, Joanna Ward; Press, Patt Dale, Julianne Waldhelm
CAST: Stephen Joyce (Pvt. John Brown), Lise Hilboldt (Clarissa Holden), David Purdham (Maj. George Bradley), Edmond Genest (Lt. Col. Guy Holden), Ron Randell (Major-General Anderson-Greene), William Campbell (Sutherland)
   A drama in 2 acts and 3 scenes. The action takes place at the present time in the living room of Guy and Clarissa's married quarters in the Camberly area in the south of England.

(Lamb's Theatre) Monday, April 15,–May 26, 1985 (36 performances and 5 previews). Lamb's Theatre Company (Carolyn Rossi Copeland, Executive Director) presents:
EPISODE 26 by Howard Korder; Director, Christopher Catt; Scenery, Michael C. Smith; Costumes, Andrea N. Carini; Lighting, Heather Carson; Production Associate, Eric Booth; Props, Amy Darnton; Stage Managers, Robert Mark Kalfin, Maude Brickner; Press, Patt Dale, Julianne Waldhelm
CAST: A. C. Weary (Buzz Gatecrasher), Diane Heles (Hillen Dale), Eric Booth (Vaknor, Emperor of the Universe), Jack Schmidt (Dr. Arthur Deco), Marek Johnson (Walaneeba/Female Servant), James W. Monitor (Arno/Mr. Gatecrasher/Photographer/Guard), Daniel Wirth (Zugdish/Zargo Phildrooni/Ghost of Biedermier/Voice of Komo), Dan Delafield (Garga/Wild-eyed Man/Worker), Tom Flagg (Dave/Guard from the Lost Asteroid/Etherscope Operator/Scribe/Guard/Announcer)
   A comedy in two acts. The action takes place on and in the vicinity of the distant planet Darvon.

Lori Wilner in "Hannah Senesh"   **Jane Connell as Dorothy Parker**
(Martha Swope Photo)   *(Marc Raboy Photo)*

(Westside Arts Theatre/Downstairs) Thursday, April 18, 1985 and still playing May 31, 1985. Richard Frankel and Ivy Properties (Thomas Viertel, Steven Baruch, Jeffrey Joseph) present:
PENN & TELLER: "two eccentric Guys who have learned to do a few cool things"; Set, John Lee Beatty; Lighting, Dennis Parichy; Sound, Chuck London Media/Stewart Werner; General Management, Richard Frankel Productions; Company Manager, Patricia Butterfield; Technical Director, Gordon Huff; Props, Walter Johnsen; Stage Manager, Marc Garland; Press, Solters/Roskin/Friedman, Joshua Ellis, Cindy Valk, Adrian Bryan-Brown, Keith Sherman, Jackie Green
CAST: Penn Jillette and Teller (no last name) performing with one intermission.

(All Souls Church) Friday, April 19,–May 5, 1985 (16 performances). All Souls Players present:
ROBERTA with music by Jerome Kern; Book and Lyrics, Otto Harbach; Additional Lyrics, Dorothy Fields; Director, Jeffery K. Neill; Musical Director, Wendell Kindberg; Costumes, Charles W. Roeder, Sy Robin; Producers, Marie and Walter Landa, Harry Blum; Settings, Norb Joerder; Lighting, David Bean; Assistant to Director, Suzanne Kaszynski; Wardrobe, Leslie Murtha; Stage Managers, Cynthia Hart, Declan Weir; Props, Julia Parisi; Press, Marie Landa
CAST: Norb Joerder (Huckleberry Haines), Richard Reuter-Smith (John Kent), Dave DeChristopher (Dave), James T. Erwin (Jim), George Hutchison (George), Peter Klein (Pete), Steven Riddle (Steve), John Dennis Sullivan (Jack), Melissa Ann Green (Sophie Teale), Joyce Lynn (Aunt Minnie), Olie Karlsson (Claudine), John Dennis Sullivan (Ladislaw), Jean McClelland (Stephanie), Anna Spaven (Marie), Nancy Meadows (Countess Clementina), Dave DeChristopher (M. Laval/M. Le Roux), Barbarell Hughes (Luella LaVerne), Victoria Dryden (Victoria), Pamela Galvin (Pamela), Barbarell Hughes (Luella), Olie Karlsson (Claudine), Liyako Matsuda (Liyako), Caroline Surface (Caroline)
MUSICAL NUMBERS: Let's Begin, Lafayette, Yesterdays, Something Had to Happen, You're Devastating, The Touch of Your Hand, I Won't Dance, Hold 'Em High, The Most Exciting Night, Smoke Gets in Your Eyes, Don't Ask Me Not to Sing, She Didn't Say Yes, Who?, Why Was I Born?, Bill, They Didn't Believe Me, You Couldn't Be Cuter, Armful of Trouble, I'll Be Hard to Handle, I Dream Too Much, Lovely to Look At
    A musical in 2 acts and 6 scenes.

(Village Gate) Wednesday, April 24,–June 30, 1985 (79 performances and 14 previews). Ken Kragen, Lewis Friedman, Albert Nocciolino, Ken Yates, Stuart Oken, Jason Brett present:
LIES & LEGENDS, THE MUSICAL STORIES OF HARRY CHAPIN with Musical Direction and Arrangements by Stephen Chapin, Tom Chapin; Director, Sam Weisman; Musical Numbers Staged by Tracy Friedman; Scenery and Lighting, Gerry Hariton, Vicki Baral; Costumes, Marsha Kowal; Pianist/Conductor, Karl Jurman; Sound, Christopher "Kit" Bond; Original Concept, Joseph Stern; Creative Consultant, Sandy C. Chapin; Associate Producers, Richard Martini, Richard Grayson; General Manager, Edgewood Organization; Company Managers, Richard Grayson, Alice Bernstein; Technical Director, Rick Bloom; Wardrobe, Margaret Shan Jensen, Nancie R. Picinich; Production Associate, Nan Tooker; Stage Managers, Kim Beringer, John Leslie Wolfe; Press, Jeffrey Richards, C. George Willard, Robert Ganshaw, Ben Morse, Toby Mailman, Bill Suttleworth
CAST: Joanna Glushak, John Herrera succeeded by Mark Fotopoulos, Terri Klausner, Ron Orbach, Martin Vidnovic, Understudies: John Leslie Wolfe, Victoria Forster
MUSICAL NUMBERS: Circle/Story of a Life, Corey's Coming, Salt and Pepper, Mr. Tanner, The Rock, Old College Avenue, Taxi, Get on with It, Bananas, Shooting Star, Sniper, Dance Band on the Titanic, W*O*L*D, Dogtown, Mail Order Annie, Odd Job Man, Dreams Go By, Tangled Up Puppet, Cat's in the Cradle, Halfway to Heaven, Better Place to Be, You Are the Only Song/Circle
    A musical in two acts.

(Puerto Rican Traveling Theatre) Wednesday, April 24,–June 2, 1985 (42 performances)
SIMPSON STREET by Eduardo Gallardo; Producer-Director, Miriam Colon; Set, Carl Baldasso; Lights, Rachel Budin; Sound, Gary Harris; Stage Manager, Stacey Fleischer
CAST: Miriam Colon (Lucy), Iraida Polanco (Rosa), Laura Elena Surillo (Angela), Marta De La Cruz (Elva), Freddy Valle (Michael), Eva Lopez (Sonia)

Penn Jillette and Teller
(Gerry Goodstein Photo)

Barbara Schottenfeld, John Wesley Shipp in "Sit Down and Eat . . ."
(Bert Andrews Photo)

(West Side Y Arts Center) Friday, May 3–17, 1985 (11 performances and 9 previews). American Kaleidoscope (Joan Rice Franklin, Rebecca Dobson, Nicholas Benton, Richard Bell, Producing Artistic Directors) presents:
SIT DOWN AND EAT BEFORE OUR LOVE GETS COLD with Book, Music and Lyrics, Musical and Vocal Arrangements by Barbara Schottenfeld; Director, Anthony McKay; Musical Director, David Loud; Scenery, Duke Durfee; Lighting, Rachel Budin; Costumes, Christina Weppner; Orchestrator, John McKinney; Assisted by Bruce Doctor; Choreographer, David Storey; Company Manager, Henry Kuryla; Production Manager, Roni Schwartz; Technical Director, Beau Kennedy; Props, Susan Vosburgh; Wardrobe, John Michael Reefer; Stage Managers, Ruthanne Patterson, Susan Vosburgh; Press, FLT/Francine L. Trevens, Gail Dawson
CAST: Bev Larson (Sue), Barbara Schottenfeld (Abby), John Wesley Shipp (Josh)
MUSICAL NUMBERS: First Child by 33, Boy to Love, I Don't Want Anymore Good Friends, Legalese, How Did I Come Across, Losing Touch, Simple Things, I Don't Want to Hold Back, Sit Down and Eat before Our Love Gets Cold, I'm So Happy for Her, I Want You to Be, Why Should We Talk, Why Do I Only, Revisions, When You Find Somebody
    A musical in two acts. The action takes place at the present time in New York City.

Martin Vidnovic, Joanna Glushak, Ron Orbach, Terri Klausner, John Herrera in "Lies and Legends . . ." *(Martha Swope Photo)*

(St. Clement's Theatre) Tuesday, May 7–18, 1985 (23 performances). Music-Theatre Group/Lenox Arts Center (Lyn Austin, Producing Director) in association with Val and Jack Evans presents:
THE COURTROOM conceived, written and staged by Bill Irwin; Music, Doug Skinner; Set, Loren Sherman; Costumes, Ann Emonts; Lighting, Jan Kroeze; Puppets, Julie Taymor; Props, John Kahn; Assistant Director, Nancy Harrington; Production Assistant, Liz Sherman; Wardrobe, Sara Davis; Stage Manager, Steven Ehrenberg, Carroll L. Cartwright; Press, Shirley Herz, Peter Cromarty
CAST: Bob Berky, Brenda Bufalino, Lloyd Davis, Jr., Bill Irwin, Rory Mitchell, Michael Moschen, M. C. O'Connor, Bill Ruyle, Kario Salem, Doug Skinner

(Westside Arts Theatre/Cheryl Crawford Theatre) Tuesday, May 7, 1985 and still playing May 31, 1985. Wolfgang Productions, Dasha Epstein, Joan Cullman, The Steppenwolf Theatre Company present:
ORPHANS by Lyle Kessler; Director, Gary Sinise; Set and Lighting, Kevin Rigdon; Sound, Gary Sinise; Sound Supervision, Chuck London Media/Stewart Werner; Costumes, Cookie Gluck; Props, Lori S. Sugar; General Management, Albert Poland; Company Manager, Russ Smith; Technical Director, J. Michael McBride; Production Assistants, Christopher Fields, William Hamilton, Fred Bainbridge; Stage Managers, Douglas Bryan Bean, Anne Marie Paolucci; Press, Milly Schoenbaum, Kevin Patterson, Marc Routh
CAST: Kevin Anderson (Phillip), Terry Kinney (Treat), John Mahoney (Harold), Understudies: Christopher Fields (Phillip/Treat), William Wise (Harold)
   A drama in two acts. The action takes place at the present time in an old row house in North Philadelphia, Pennsylvania.

(Piccolo Theatre) Thursday, May 9–26, 1985 (12 performances). American Commedia Theatre (Sabin Epstein, Artistic Director) presents:
BLIND VENETIANS or the Making of the Master; By Lorraine Thompson; Director, Fred Sanders; Associate Producer, Cappy Enterprises; Scenery, Marshall Watson; Lighting, David M. Shepherd; Costumes, Nancy Boensch; Fight Choreography, Steve Ommerle; General Manager, Douglas Capozzalo; Technical Director, David M. Shepherd; Stage Managers, Liz Dreyer, Liz Kessler; Press, FLT/Francine Trevens, Gail Dawson
CAST: Paul Bates (Santino), Debra Cardona (Zerbinetta), David Friedlander (Al), David J. Goewey (Gianni), Deborah Laufer (Adriana), Jim L'Ecuyer (Nero), Stephen Ommerle (Leo DeMarco), Bill Phillips (Lorenzo), Phil Prestamo (Donato), Kate Redway (Celia), Michele Waxman (Angelino), Renette Zimmerly (Pollina)
   A comedy in two acts. The action takes place in 1791 in Venice.

(Perry Street Theatre) Thursday, May 9–26, 1985 (30 performances). New York Theatre Workshop (Jean Passanante, Artistic Director; Nancy Kassak Diekmann, Managing Director) presents:
SALLY'S GONE, SHE LEFT HER NAME by Russell Davis; Director, Tony Giordano; Set, Jane Clark; Costumes, Linda Fisher; Lighting, John Gisondi; Sound, Stan Metelits; Production Manager, Michael Moody; Casting, David Tochterman; Props, Charlie Eisenberg; Stage Manager, Tracy B. Cohen; Press, Milly Schoenbaum, Marc Routh
CAST: Robert Leonard (Christopher Decker), Cynthia Nixon (Sally Decker), David Canary (Henry Decker), Michael Learned (Cynthia Decker)
   A drama in two acts. The action takes place at the present time during August in a suburban home.

(McBurney YMCA) Sunday, May 12,–June 2, 1985 (12 performances and 4 previews). Venture Stage Artists' Chelsea Players, William Osborn in association with McBurney YMCA presents:
GLORY! by Glenn Allen Smith; Director, Kate Gifford; Sound, Robert Raines; Associate Producer, G. Theodore Killmer; Assistant Director, Maggie Eldred; Production Coordinator, John Bill Jones; Props, Brynn Edyn; Stage Managers, Joan Valentina, Barbra-Anne Carter; Press, G. Theodore Killmer
CAST: Mary Bozeman (Sister Ferguson), Robert Caccomo (Prosecutor), Barbara-Anne Carter (Sister Moss), Bart Darby (Ed McKee), Brynn Edyn (Susanna), Maggie Eldred (Sister Liller), Jamie Martin Forbes (Brother Jessop), John Bill Jones (Brother Cobbs), Selma Lieb (Mother Fletcher), Michael McMahon (Robert Campbell), Noel Novack (Jack Hirschel), Timothy Rule (Reporter), Belle Maria Wheat (Opal)

**Terry Kinney, John Mahoney, Kevin Anderson
in "Orphans"** *(Lisa Ebright Photo)*

(Top of the Gate) Monday, May 13, 1985 and still playing May 31, 1985. Martin Richards, Jerry Kravat, Mary Lea Johnson with the New York Music Company/Sid Bernstein present:
MAYOR with Book by Warren Leight; Based on "Mayor" by Mayor Edward I. Koch; Music and Lyrics, Charles Strouse; Director, Jeffrey B. Moss; Choreography, Barbara Siman; Sets and Costumes, Randy Barcelo; Musical Director/Arranger, Michael Kosarin; Lighting, Richard Winkler; Orchestrations, Christopher Bankey; Associate Producer, Sam Crothers; General Management, Maria Productions; Company Manager, Thomas Shovestull; Assistant to Director, Karen Robinson; Production Assistant, Richard Hester; Hairstylists, Lloyd Kindred, Gerry Leddy; Wardrobe, Nancy Lawson; Sound, Lewis Mead; Original Cast Album by NY Music Company; Press, Henry Luhrman, Terry M. Lilly, David Mayhew, Andrew P. Shearer
CAST: Lenny Wolpe (Mayor), Douglas Bernstein, Marion J. Caffey, Keith Curran, Nancy Giles, Ken Jennings, Ilene Kristen, Kathryn McAteer
MUSICAL NUMBERS AND SCENES: Mayor, You Can Be A New Yorker Too!, Board of Estimate, You're Not the Mayor, March of the Yuppies, The Ribbon Cutting, Hootspa, What You See Is What You Get, In the Park, Ballad, On the Telephone, I Want to Be the Mayor, The Last 'I Love New York' Song, We Are One, How'm I Doin'?, My City
   A musical in two acts.

**Nancy Giles, Lenny Wolpe
in "Mayor"**
(Martha Swope Photo)

(Cubiculo) Wednesday, May 15,–June 2, 1985 (16 performances). The Classic Theatre presents a staged concert version of:
SAMSON AGONISTES by John Milton; Director, Maurice Edwards; Producer, Nicholas John Stathis; Production Coordinator, Gerald A. Carter; Music, David Hollister; Lighting, Patricia Elaine Bainer; Set, Makuta and Carter; Stage Manager, Heidi Seifert; Press, Howard Atlee
CAST: Owen S. Rackleff (Samson), Maurice Edwards, Eric Kramer (Chorus of Danites), Chris Gampel (Manoa), Martitia Palmer (Dalila), Gilbert Stafford (Harapha/Publick Officer), Eric Kramer (Messenger)
Performed with one intermission. The action takes place before the prison in Gaza.

(Harold Clurman Theatre) Wednesday, May 15,–June 2, 1985 (22 performances and 9 previews). The Harold Clurman Theatre (Jack Garfein, Artistic Director) presents:
ROMMEL'S GARDEN by Harvey Gabor; Director, Jack Garfein; Set, Charles Henry McClennahan; Lighting, Jackie Manassee; Costumes, Ruth Morley; Casting, David Tochterman; General Management, Albert Poland; General Manager, Craig S. Dorfman; Company Manager, Edward Hambleton; Technical Director, Production Assistant, Richard Goodis; Stage Manager, Robert I. Cohen; Special Effects, Joachim and Meeh; Special Consultant, SFC. Robert E. Sunshine; Press, Joe Wolhandler, Megan Svensen
CAST: Lonny Price (Private Ackenbaum), Jay O. Sanders (Sergeant Wolff)
A drama performed without intermission. The action takes place in 1944 in North Africa during World War II.

**Lonny Price, Jay O. Sanders
in "Rommel's Garden"**
(Martha Swope Photo)

(Judith Anderson Theatre) Thursday, May 16–25, 1985 (16 performances). David C. Gold presents:
BE HAPPY FOR ME by Jerry Sterner; Director, John Ferraro; Set, Toby Corbett; Costumes, Shay Cunliffe; Lighting, Greg McPherson; General Manager, Allan Francis; Casting Director, Ronnie Yeskel; Technical Director, Bruce Buchanan; Sound, Scott Lehrer; Wardrobe, Jill Moray; Musical Arranger, Margaret Pine; Stage Manager, R. Nelson Barbee; Press, Betty Lee Hunt
CAST: David Groh (Phil), Philip Bosco (Norman), Priscilla Lopez (Elizabeth), Russ Pennington (Dealer)
A drama in two acts. The action takes place at the present time on Aruba, an island in the Caribbean.

(INTAR Stage 2) Saturday, May 18,–June 9, 1985 (24 performances). International Arts Relations (Max Ferra, Artistic Director; Dennis Ferguson-Acosta, Managing Director) presents:
SAVINGS with Book and Lyrics by Dolores Prida; Music, Leon Odenz; Director, Max Ferra; Set and Lighting, Robert McBroom; Costumes, Karen Barbano; Choreography, Frank Pietri; Musical Direction/Arrangements, Leon Adenz; Casting, Janet Murphy; Dance Captain, Ricci Reyes Adan; Production Assistant, Richard Maldonado; Stage Managers, Jesse Wooden, Jr., Edward M. Rodriguez; Press, Bruce Cohen, Kathleen von Schmid
CAST: D'Yan Forest (Leila Zukov), Lawrence Reed (Marcello Mofetti), Al Ferrer-Rodriguez (Fred Gonzalez), Georgia Galvez (Mrs. Sylvia Cabrera), Judith Granite (Mrs. Borestein), Carmen Rosario (Mrs. Gloria Dominguez), Edward M. Rodriguez (Mailman), Peter Jay Fernandez (Leroy Young), Marilyn Schnier (Teller/Peggy/Victoria/Paramedic), Ricci Reyes Adan (Teller/Jane/Ms. Wong)
MUSICAL NUMBERS: There Goes the Neighborhood, Subtleties, Tutti Tofutti, Savings, Iron Pumping Woman, Leila's Theme, Dear Postmaster General, Son to "La Virgen", Good Afternoon, Gentrification, Leila at Noontime, Aerobics, Make Me Believe, One Last Song, We Won't Be Moved
A musical in 2 acts and 3 scenes with an overture. The action takes place in the lobby of The Neighborhood Savings Bank at the present time.

**Michael Learned, Cynthia Nixon
in "Sally's Gone, She Left Her Name"**
(Susan Cook/Martha Swope Photo)

(Susan Bloch Theatre) Sunday, May 19,–June 2, 1985 (16 performances). New Directions Theater (Joseph Holloway, Executive Director) presents:
DOCTOR FAUSTUS by Christopher Marlowe; Adapted by Daniel Gerroll, Samuel Blackwell; Director, Samuel Blackwell; Scenery, Jim Steere; Lighting, Phil Monat; Costumes, Tom McAlister; Sound/Music, Auroal Fixation; Magic, Peter Samelson; Technical Director, Les Forshey; Props, Cindy Dout; Stage Managers, Jill Larmett, Ellen Simsarian; Press, DeJager/Burrichter
CAST: Hewitt Brooks (Chorus/Cardinal/Friar), Daniel Gerroll (John Faustus), Gwyllum Evans (Wagner), John Shepard (Valdes/Bruno/Friar/Seven Deadly Sins), Jarlath Conroy (Mephistophilis), Rick Lawless (Dick/Friar), Alisha Das (Helen), Thom McCleister (Pope)
A drama in two acts.

**Gwyllum Evans, Daniel Gerroll, Jarlath Conroy
in "Dr. Faustus"** *(Tom Bloom Photo)*

(Chelsea Playhouse) Monday, May 20,–July 7, 1985 (57 performances and 15 previews). Keller Theatre Associates (Jerry Keller/Noel L. Silverman) in association with Kenny Karen present:
THE RETURN OF HERBERT BRACEWELL by Andrew Johns; Director, Geraldine Fitzgerald; Set, James Wolk; Costumes, Julie Schwolow; Lighting, Phil Monat; General Manager, Douglas E. Ellis; Assistant to Producers, Richard Thomsen; Assistant to Director, John Bowman; Technical Director, David Raphel; Hairstylist, Vito Mastrogiovanni; Props/Wardrobe, Andrea Nugit; Production Assistant, Kate Riddle; Stage Manager, Dawn Eaton; Press, Shirley Herz, Peter Cromarty, David Roggensack, Pete Sanders, Gary Lawrence
CAST: Milo O'Shea (Herbert Bracewell), Frances Sternhagen (Florence), Understudies: Andrew Johns, Peggy Cowles.

A play in two acts. The action takes place on a New Year's Eve in the early 1900's in the attic of Herbert Bracewell's home in New York City.

(Marymount Manhattan Theatre) Tuesday, May 21–26, 1985 (8 performances in repertory). The Acting Company (John Houseman, Producing Artistic Director), Margot Harley (Executive Producer), Michael Kahn, Artistic Director) presents:
A NEW WAY TO PAY OLD DEBTS by Philip Massinger; Director, Michael Kahn; Sets, John Kasarda; Lighting, Dennis Parichy; Stage Managers, Giles F. Colahan, Liza C. Stein; **AS YOU LIKE IT** by William Shakespeare; Director, Mervyn Willis; Sets/Costumes, Stephen McCabe; Lights, Dennis Parichy; Composer, Jeffrey Taylor; Choreography, Primavera Boman; Fight Choreographer, Bjorn Johnson; **THE SKIN OF OUR TEETH** by Thornton Wilder; Director, Gerald Freedman; Set, Joel Fontaine; Costumes, Jeanne Button; Lights, Dennis Parichy
COMPANY: Laura Brutsman, Terrence Caza, Libby Colahan, Aled Davies, Matt deGanon, Albert Farrar, Susan Finch, Julie Fishell, Philip Goodwin, David Manis, Phil Meyer, Joel F. Miller, Anthony Powell, Derek David Smith, Ana Valdes

(Manhattan Theatre Club) Tuesday, May 21,–June 2, 1985 (11 performances). Trujo Company (Trudy Cranston Chamlin, Joel Portnoy, Producers) presents:
"D." by Michael Stewart; Director, Dan Held; Set, Peter Harrison; Costumes, Karen Hummel; Lighting, Steve Pollock; Sound, Tom Gould; General Management, McCann & Nugent; Company Manager/Production Coordinator, Mary T. Nealon; Technical Director, Michael Yarborough; Wardrobe, Scott Mortimer; Props, Dan Paul; Casting, Elissa Myers; Musical Interludes, Wayne Abravanel; Stage Manager, Douglas Laidlaw; Press, FLT/Francine L. Trevens, Gail Dawson
CAST: Lynne Thigpen (Cora), Jane Fleiss (Jenny), Bobo Lewis (Maudie), Michael Zaslow (D.), Jason Alexander (Billy), Max Chalawsky (Callers), Sam Gray (Uncle Herman), Grace Keagy (Aunt Lily), Rosalind Harris (Honey Kauffman)

A drama in 2 acts and 15 scenes, with a prologue and epilogue. The action takes place in the living room of D's apartment on the Upper West Side of Manhattan from August 1938 to May 1945.

(New Vic Theatre) Thursday, May 23,–June 16, 1985 (16 performances). Jani Group/New World Previews (Jane Stanton, James Wilson, Producers) present:
TEN LITTLE INDIANS by Agatha Christie; Director, Gary Canier; Stage Manager, Anne Diggs
CAST: Edwin Bordo, Howard Davidson, Thomas Dorff, Martha Farrar, Stephen Gruwell, Kathi Levitan, Marilyn McDonald, Marcus Neville, Keith Perry, Robert Sonderskov, Bill Steele

(INTAR Theatre) Thursday, May 23,–July 7, 1985 (56 performances)
Patricia Daily and Arthur Master Productions present:
CURSE OF THE STARVING CLASS by Sam Shepard; Director, Robin Lynn Smith; Setting, Brian Martin; Costumes, Frances Nelson; Lighting, Mark W. Stanley; General Management, Brent Peek Productions; Company Manager, Scott Green; Assistant to Director, Blake Hansen; Wardrobe, Kristin Ames; Props, Victoria Greer; Production Assistant, Stuart Richardson; Stage Manager, Penny Marks; Press, Burnham-Callaghan Associates, Gary Murphy
CAST: Kathy Bates (Ella), Stephen Bradbury (Malcolm/Slater), Dan Patrick Brady (Emerson), Jude Ciccolella (Ellis), James Gleason (Taylor), Eddie Jones (Weston), Bill Pullman (Wesley), Karen Tull (Emma), Understudies: Jude Ciccolella (Weston), Dan Patrick Brady (Wesley), Stephen Bradbury (Taylor), Rick Dean (Ellis/Emerson/Slater/Malcolm), Carlotta Schoch (Emma/Ella)

A drama in three acts. The action takes place at the present time in Southeast California.

**Milo O'Shea, Frances Sternhagen
in "The Return of Herbert Bracewell"**
(Carol Rosegg/Martha Swope Photo)

(Samuel Beckett Theatre) Wednesday, May 29,–June 30, 1985 (38 performances and 6 previews). The Harold Clurman Theatre (Jack Garfein, Artistic Director) presents:
CHILDHOOD after the book by Nathalie Sarraute; Adapted by Simone Benmussa; and **FOR NO GOOD REASON** by Nathalie Sarraute; Director, Simone Benmussa; Scenery and Lighting, Simone Benmussa, Antoni Taule; Costumes, Gail Brassard, Sonia Rykiel; Casting, David Tochterman; General Management, Albert Poland; Company Manager, Edward Hambleton; Technical Director, Mark Porter; Assistant Director, Valerie Lumbroso; Wardrobe, Katherine Haniskewicz; Stage Managers, Raymond Chandler, Lynn Johnson; Press, Jeffrey Richards, C. George Willard, Robert Ganshaw, Ben Morse, Bill Shuttleworth, Toby Mailman, Naomi Grabel
CAST: "For No Good Reason" translated by Kate Mortley: Stephen Keep (Man 1), Max Wright (Man 2), Michael Grodenchik, Marek Johnson (Neighbors). "Childhood" translated by Barbara Wright: Glenn Close (Actress), Andrea Weber (Mother), Stephen Keep (Father), Marek Johnson (Vera), Voice of Nathalie Sarraute, Understudies: Judith Novgrod, Michael Grodenchik

(Colonnades Theatre) Wednesday, May 29,–June 15, 1985 (12 performances). DD Productions presents:
THE TAMING OF THE SHREW by William Shakespeare; Director, Christopher Markle; Set and Lights, David Birn; Music Director, Leslie Steinweiss; Assistant Director, Blake Hanson; Stage Managers, Jonathan Shulman, Amy Coombs; Producer, Debra Davis
CAST: Kenneth Abisror, Seth Barrish, Paul Binotto, Christopher Britton, Paul Caruso, Drew Eliot, Davis Hall, Kenneth Lazebnik, Douglas Mancheski, Paula Marmon, Jeff Meyer, Frank Muller, James Newcomb, Patrizia Norcia, Stephen Spinella, Diana Sutherlin, Daniel Tamm, Time Winters

clockwise from left: Karen Tull, Bill Pullman,
Eddie Jones, Kathy Bates in "Curse of the
Starving Class" *(Carol Rosegg/Martha Swope Photo)*

OFF-BROADWAY SERIES

AMAS REPERTORY THEATRE

Sixteenth Season

Founder/Artistic Director, Rosetta LeNoire; Administrator/Business Manager, Gary Halcott; Administrator, Jerry Lapidus; Development, Richard Hunter; Technical Director, Alex LaBianca; Press, Fred Nathan Associates, Bert Fink

(AMAS Repertory Theatre) Thursday, Oct. 25–Nov. 18, 1984 (16 performances)
ANONYMOUS with Book, Lyrics and Music by Vincenzo Stornaiuolo; Additional Music, Giancarlo De Matteis; Additional Lyrics, Jack Everly; Director, Vincenzo Stornaiuolo; Choreographed and Staged by Gui Andrisano; Musical Director/Arrangements, Jack Everly; Set, Janice Davis; Costumes, Robert Locke; Lighting, William H. Grant III; Production Manager, Ronald L. McIntyre; Wardrobe, Ernest Mossiah; Stage Managers, Jim Griffith, Katie Stevens

CAST: Ed Battle (Motivator), Steven Cates (Black Pope/Ensemble), Sarah C. Clark (Ensemble), Michael Duran (Secretary of State/Father Cardinal/Ensemble), Ivy Fox (Ensemble), Lisa LaCorte (Holy Ghost/Ensemble), Paul Loper (Cardinal/Son/Ensemble), Janice Lorraine (Ensemble), Dirk Lombard (Pope Anonymous), Jayne Ackley Lynch (Ensemble), Maura Miller (Motivator), Mark Pennington (Cardinal/Ensemble), Phillip Perry (Cardinal/Ensemble), Kevin Ramsey (Ensemble), Tug Wilson (Cardinal/Ensemble)

MUSICAL NUMBERS: Overture, Anonymous, Conclave, What Can It Be, Church of the World, Smoke Smoke, Praised Be the Lord Our Savior, Brothers, Figli, God I Beg Your Forgiveness, Come with Us, Fire, They're Killing the Pope, New York, Monotheism, How Much Love, Mon Marte, Trinity, Vatican, Our Decision, We Want the Pope, I Shall Condemn, I Bless You, We Have the Pope, Finale

A musical in 2 acts and 27 scenes. The action takes place sometime in the future in Rome and New York.

Thursday, Feb. 14–Mar. 10, 1985 (16 performances)
NORTHERN BOULEVARD with Book by Kevin Brofsky; Music and Lyrics, Carleton Carpenter; Director, William Martin; Set, Tom Barnes; Lighting, Deborah Tulchin; Costumes, Judy Dearing; Wardrobe, Ernest Mossiah; Choreography, Dennis Dennehy; Musical Director/Arrangements, James Steven Mironchik; Production Manager, Ronald L. McIntyre; Assistant Choreographer, Jose De La Cuesta; Stage Managers, Lynda Field, Rick Lucero

CAST: Alice Cannon (Roslyn), Jose De La Cuesta (Time Changer), Dolores Garcia (Mrs. D'Angelo/Mrs. Hernandez), Regina Reynolds Hood (Time Changer), Audrei-Kairen (Mrs. Golden/Mrs. McSherry), Curtis LeFebvre (Michael/George), Rosetta LeNoire (Mrs. Washington), Luke Lynch (Donald), Morgan Mackay (Jerry), Miriam Miller (Celia), Brian Noodt (Mikey/Modke), Art Ostrin (Saul), Kelley Paige (Margo/Connie), Kelly Sanderbeck (Dorothy)

MUSICAL NUMBERS: Get Up and Dance, He Loves Her, Half a World Away, Plus One, Growing, Northern Boulevard, Living in Luxury, Master, Priorities, A Silvery Song, Fathers and Sons, Let's Not Miss the Boat, Whoa Baby

A musical in 2 acts and 13 scenes. The action takes place from October 1941 to October 1981 on Northern Boulevard in Jackson Heights, Queens, NY, and in Simon's delicatessen there.

Thursday, April 18–May 12, 1985 (16 performances)
MANHATTAN SERENADE a revue based on the music of Louis Alter; Compiled and Arranged by Alfred Heller; Written by Karen Cottrell, Alfred Heller; Lyrics, Frank Loesser, Stanley Adams, and others; New Lyrics, Stanley Adams, Karen Cottrell; Direction and Choreography, Bob Rizzo; Ballet Choreography, David Anderson; Musical Direction/Arrangements, Alfred Heller; Sets, Mina Albergo; Lighting, Gregg Marriner; Costumes, Christina Giannini; Wardrobe, Ernest Mossiah; Assistant Choreographer, Jennifer Thorsby; Tap, Horace Turnbull; Dance Captain, Michael Biondi; Hairstylist, Morey Greenberg; Stage Managers, Marygrace Tardi, Douglas Bergman, Iris Gregory-Helfand

CAST: Michael Biondi, Cliff Hicklen, Connie Kunkle, Janice Lorraine, Luke Lynch, Richie McCall, Marie McKinney, Kelly Patterson, Mark Pennington, Michele Pigliavento, Brad J. Reynolds, Andrea Sandall, Sally Ann Swarm, Robert Torres, Carrie Wilder, Mona Yvette Wyatt, Sally Yorke

MUSICAL NUMBERS: Manhattan Serenade, Piano Phun, Lopeziana, Melody from the Sky, Blue Shadows, New Love for Old Love, My Kinda Love, That Tired Feeling, Throw It Out the Window, Blow Hot Blow Cold, Metropolitan Nocturne, You Turned the Tables on Me, Up to Your Ears in Souvenirs, The Rain Falls on Everybody, Wonderworld, Autumn Night, Something's Come Over Me, Dolores, Love Me as I Am, The Blues Are Brewin', Hello Manhattan!, Star Crazy, We Can't Go on Like This, We Worked the Whole Thing Out, Seeing Things

A musical revue in 2 acts, 9 vignettes, a prologue and entr'acte.

Top Right: Dirk Lombard (C) in "Anonymous"
Below: Art Ostrin, Rosetta LeNoire
in "Northern Boulevard"
(Gilbert Johnson Photos)

Cliff Hicklen, Michele Pigliavento
in "Manhattan Serenade"

AMERICAN JEWISH THEATRE
Fifth Season

Artistic Director, Stanley Brechner; Business Manager, Gene Terruso; Development, Norman Golden; Technical Director, Floyd R. Swagerty, Jr.; Literary Manager, Susan Nanus; Production Coordinator, Alice Perlmutter; Stage Manager, Lori M. Doyle; Press, Lois Cohen, Helene Davis, Krista Altok

(92nd Street Y) Wednesday, Sept. 19–Nov. 4, 1984 (36 performances). *World Premiere.*

JESSE'S LAND by Ernest Joselovitz; Director, Jeff Martin; Set, George Tsypin; Costumes, Stephan Rotondaro; Sound, Dan Rogers; Lighting, Amy Richards; Assistant to Director, Michael Bates. CAST: Gary S. Nathanson (Jesse Kletchik), Sylvia Gassell (Romola, his wife), R. Michael Baker (Sammi), Sophie Schwab (Willa). A drama in two acts. The action takes place in Jesse's home in the dairy farmland of the Connecticut River Valley during 1941–42.

Saturday, Dec. 1, 1984–Jan. 13, 1985 (36 performances)
ENTER LAUGHING by Joseph Stein; Based on book by Carl Reiner; Director, Dan Held; Set, Dan Conway; Costumes, Arnold S. Levine; Lighting, Amy Richards; Sound, Dan Welsh; Stage Manager, Stephanie Keyser. CAST: R. Michael Baker (David), Doug Baldwin (Roger/Don), Carl Don succeeded by David S. Howard (Foreman), Joseph Dineen (Don Darwin/Waiter/Lawyer), Joey Faye (Father), Joie Gallo (Wanda), Louan Gideon (Miss B), Norman Golden (Pike), Estelle Harris (Mother), Frederica Meister (Angela), Owen Rackleff (Marlowe), Jeff Rochlin (Marvin)

Saturday, February 9–March 24, 1985 (36 performances)
THE RACHEL PLAYS by Leah K. Friedman; Director, Susan Einhorn; Set, Audrey Hemenway; Costumes, Karen Gerson; Lighting, Victor En Yu Tan; Assistant to Director, Terri Klestzick; Production Liaison, Constance Trapani; Stage Manager, Janet Gillespie. CAST: *"I'm Hiding! I'm Hiding!"* with Maia Danziger (Rachel), Regina Baff (Dorothy), Lisabeth Bartlett (Rachel's Mother). *"Running Home"* with Lisabeth Bartlett (Rachel), Maia Danziger (Anna), Richie Allan (Joseph), Regina Baff (Gussie), Paul Stolarsky succeeded by Frank Anderson (Stranger/Insurance Man)

Saturday, April 20–June 16, 1985 (36 performances)
MY OLD FRIENDS by Mel Mandel and Norman Sachs; Director, Philip Rose; Choreography, Robert Tucker; Set, Paul Wonsek; Lighting, Dennis Size; Costumes, Don Newcomb; Assistant Director/Casting, Lynda Watson; Musical Director, Norman Sachs; Stage Manager, Janet Gillespie. CAST: King Donovan (Catlan), Norman Golden (Fineberg), Robert Weil (Slocum), Norberto Kerner (Arias), Grace Carney (Mrs. Polianoffsky), Maxine Sullivan (Mrs. Cooper), Imogene Coca (Heloise), Peter Walker (Peter), Jean Taylor (Mrs. Stone), John Danelle (Carpenter/Gettlinger)

Saturday, June 15–23, 1985 (6 performances)
A BROADCAST BABY by Isaiah Sheffer; Director, Dan Held; Set, Eugene Gurlitz; Lighting, Bob Bessoir; Costumes, Karen Hummel; Musical Supervisor, Stan Free; Stage Manager, Alice Perlmutter; Casting, David Tochterman. CAST: Marilyn Sokol (Becky Barrett), Henderson Forsythe (Hastings Hamilton), Stan Free (Julius Mishkin), Mart Hulswit (Vinnie Vincent)

Joie Gallo, Joseph Dineen, R. Michael Baker in "Enter Laughing" Top: Lisa Goodman, Sylvia Gassell, R. Michael Baker in "Jesse's Land"

84

Richie Allan, Maia Danziger, Regina Baff in "The Rachel Plays"
(Gerry Goodstein, Ken Howard Photos)

R. Michael Baker (standing), Estelle Harris, Joey
Faye in "Enter Laughing"

Paul Stolarsky, Richie Allan, Lisabeth Bartlett
in "The Rachel Plays"

Imogene Coca, Maxine Sullivan
in "My Old Friends"
(Gerry Goodstein Photos)

Henderson Forsythe, Marilyn Sokol, Mart Hulswit
in "A Broadcast Baby"

85

AMERICAN PLACE THEATRE

Twenty-first Season

Director, Wynn Handman; Associate Director, Julia Miles; Business Manager, Joanne Vedder; Literary Advisors, Chris Breyer, Myra Velasquez; Literary Manager/Women's Project, Suzanne Bennett; Production Manager, Nancy Harrington; Technical Director, Carl Zutz; Press, Jeffrey Richards Associates, Ben Morse, Robert Ganshaw

(American Place Theatre) Sunday, Oct. 21–Nov. 11, 1984 (21 performances and 10 previews).

WHAT'S A NICE COUNTRY LIKE YOU STILL DOING IN A STATE LIKE THIS? with Music by Cary Hoffman; Lyrics, Ira Gasman; Directed and Choreographed by Miriam Fond; Set, Neil Peter Jampolis; Lighting, Anne Militello; Costumes, David C. Woolard, Marcy Grace Froehlich; Musical Director, John Spalla; Production Assistant, Pamela Keogh; Props and Costumer, Melissa Croom; Stage Manager, Marc Ramsey

CAST: Brent Barrett, Jack Landron, Krista Neumann, Patrick Richwood, Diana Szlosberg

MUSICAL NUMBERS: Get Out of Here, Hello Mr. Church, I'm in Love With, What the Hell, Greatest Performance, Johannesberg, Who Put the Glitz in Fritz, It's Hard to Be a Liberal Today, Changing Partners, Male Chauvinist Pig, Street Suite, Runaways, It's Getting Better, I Like Me, Carlos Juan & Miguel, Button A, Nuclear Winter, There's No Such Thing, New York Suite, But I Love New York, I Found the Girl of My Dreams on Broadway, A Mugger's Work Is Never Done, How'm I Doing?, Why Do I Keep Going to the Theatre?, Keeping the Peace, God Is Not Finished with Me Yet, America You're Looking Good, They Aren't There, Farewell, I'm Not Myself Anymore, Porcupine Suite, People Are Like Porcupines, I'm Not Taking a Chance on Love, Threesome, Scale of 1 to 10, The Four R's, Take Us Back, Come On Daisy, Finale

A musical revue in two acts.

Wednesday, Feb. 6–17, 1985 (14 performances) The Women's Project (Julia Miles, Director) presents:

FOUR CORNERS conceived, directed and designed by Gina Wendkos; Co-written by Gina Wendkos, Donna Bond; Associate Director, Richard Press; Original Music, Jim Farmer; Lighting, Anne Militello; Costumes, Donna Bond; Sound, Tom Gould; Stage Managers, Nancy Harrington, Paul Garten

CAST: Margaret Harrington (Anna), Josh Hamilton (Jimmy), Ryan Cutrona (Ralph)

The action takes place in Missouri, and is performed without an intermission.

Friday, Feb. 8–24, 1985 (16 performances)

RUDE TIMES by Stephen Wylie; Director, Gordon Edelstein; Set, Pat Woodbridge; Costumes, David C. Woolard; Lighting, John Gisondi; Sound, Gary Harris; Wardrobe, Mary Jestice; Stage Managers, W. Scott Allison, Lloyd Caldwell

CAST: Tom McDermott (Old Man), Willie Carpenter (Bert), Peter J. Saputo (Clarence), Kate Wilkinson (Mrs. Crystal), Mara Hobel (Cherry)

The action takes place in an inner city YMCA boarding house during the summer and fall, and is performed without an intermission.

Thursday, April 11–28, 1985 (21 performances) The Women's Project (Julia Miles, Director) presents:

PADUCAH by Sallie Bingham; Director, Joan Vail Thorne; Set, Karen Schulz; Costumes, Mimi Maxmen; Lighting, Anne Militello; Casting, Elissa Myers/Mark Teschner; Assistant to Director, Paul Garten; Props, Chris Mealey, Priscilla Huddleston; Wardrobe, Joy Alpern; Stage Managers, Peggy Peterson, Thomas J. Podiak

CAST: William Cain (Clay Baker), Tammy Grimes (Julia Baker), Laura Hicks (Suzi Baker), Lou Myers (Clete), Carrie Nye (Angela Langtry), Standby for Julia and Angela, Patricia O'Connell.

A play in 2 acts and 5 scenes. The action takes place at the present time during the spring in a house outside Paducah, Kentucky.

Tuesday, May 14–June 24, 1985 (91 performances of 4 presentations in the American Place Theatre complex)

JUBILEE! A BLACK THEATRE FESTIVAL: "M.L.K." a play by Al Eaton about the life and times of Martin Luther King, Jr., with the author portraying all the roles. "Celebration", a musical journey from the beginning of the African American tradition to the present. Directed by Shauneille Perry, and performed by Carolyn Byrd, Fran Salisbury, Andre Robinson, Jr., guitarist Clebert Ford, and pianist Thomas Riggsbee. "Love to All, Lorraine" a play by Elizabeth Van Dyke with the playwright portraying the late playwright Lorraine Hansberry. Ebony Jo-Ann presenting her cabaret performance, singing jazz, blues and gospel.

Martha Holmes Photos

Top Left: Jack Landron, Diana Szlosberg, Brent
Barrett, Krista Neumann, Patrick Richwood in
"What's a Nice Country. . . ." Below: Ryan Cutrona,
Josh Hamilton, Margaret Harrington
in "Four Corners"

Willie Carpenter, Tom McDermott
in "Rude Times"

Carrie Nye, William Cain
in "Paducah"

William Cain, Tammy Grimes
in "Paducah"

Elizabeth Van Dyke
in "Love to All, Lorraine"

Al Eaton in "M.L.K."

87

AMISTAD WORLD THEATRE
Fourth Season

Artistic Director, Samuel P. Barton; Managing Director, Shirley Fishman; Board of Directors, Richard G. Dudley, Jr., Rev. Frederick B. Williams, Micki Grant; Press, Shirley Fishman

(INTAR Stage Two) Thursday, June 14–July 1, 1984 (12 performances)
TIES THAT BIND by Walter Allen Bennett, Jr.; Director, Samuel P. Barton; Set, Daniel Proett; Lighting, John Senter; Production Assistant, Gordon T. Skinner; Stage Manager, Jerry Cleveland
CAST: Walter Allen Bennett, Jr. (Billy Pittman), Kim Yancey (Tanya Pittman), Breena Clarke (Jean Pittman), Debrah Ann Holland (Lisa Pittman), Ellis "Skeeter" Williams (William Pittman)
 A drama in 3 acts. The action takes place at the present time in Harlem, New York City, before, during, and after Mother's Day.

Thursday, Oct. 25–Nov. 18, 1984 (16 performances)
THE REHEARSAL a dramatization of an actual event, conceived and developed by members of the Amistad World Theatre company; Director, Samuel P. Barton; Set, Mr. Barton; Lighting, Sylvester N. Weaver; Production Assistant, Ruben D. Scott; Stage Manager, Janine Trevens. CAST: Pamela Tucker-White (Pat), Mizan Nunes (Azania), Sol (Carmen), Kent C. Jackman (Paul/Director), Antonio Aponte (Carlos), Anthony Carrion (Felipe), Joey Maldonado (Jimmy Mercado), Ruben D. Scott (Ralphy/Production Assistant), Mary Lum (Liz/Company Manager), Phil DiPietro (Orlando), Maryce Carter (Louise), Jose Febus (Marti)
 A drama in two acts with an epilogue. The action takes place at the present time in an old dirty rehearsal hall on Saturday and Sunday.

Thursday, Nov. 29–Dec. 14, 1984 (12 performances)
KINDRED SPIRITS with Direction and Set by Samuel P. Barton; Lighting, Sylvester N. Weaver; Production Assistant, Ruben D. Scott; Sound, Terry Gabis; Stage Manager, Janine Trevens. CAST: Steven Gary Simon (Seth Schwartz), Jose Febus (Miguel Angel)
 A play in two acts. The action takes place at the present time in a warehouse.

Thursday, Mar. 28–Apr. 14, 1985 (12 performances)
BODYBAGS by Tee Saralegui; Director, Samuel P. Barton; Set, Mr. Barton; Sound, Mr. Barton and Phil Lee; Lighting, Sylvester N. Weaver; Production Assistant, Ruben D. Scott; Stage Manager, Diane B. Greenberg. CAST: Leo V. Finnie III (Lou), Felipe Gorostiza (Johnny), Sharon Taylor (Anita), Phil Nee (Vietnamese Soldier), Soldiers: Alfredo Chevere, Ruben D. Scott, Gordon T. Skinner
 A play in two acts. The action takes place during 1981 in a bar in East Harlem, New York City.

Austin Trevett Photos

**Right: Walter Allen Bennett, Jr., Ellis Williams
in "Ties That Bind" Top: Maryce Carter,
Joey Maldonado in "The Rehearsal"**

**Felipe Gorostiza, Leo V. Finnie III
in "Bodybags"**

**Steven Gary Simon, Jose Febus
in "Kindred Spirits"**

ARK THEATRE COMPANY

Seventh Season

Directors, Bruce Daniel, Donald Marcus, Lisa Milligan; Development, Carol Ochs; Production Supervisor, Peter J. Monahan; Literary Manager, Elizabeth Margid; Press, Jeffrey Richards Associates

(Ark Theatre) Sunday, Jan. 27–Feb. 17, 1985 (20 performances)
CHARLEY BACON AND HIS FAMILY by Arthur Giron; Director, Donald Marcus; Scenery, Derek McLane; Costumes, Catherine Zuber; Lighting, Richard Dorfman; Sound, Daryl Bornstein; Choreography, Jose Coronado; Casting, David Tochterman; Technical Director, Scott Wolfeil; Wardrobe, Drew Meyers; Stage Managers, Mark Rhodes, Joshua Brown
CAST: Jonathan Hadary (Charley), Pat Lavelle (Dusty), Leslie Geraci (Dorothy), James Handy (Fred), Stan Lachow (Uncle Harvey/Mr. O'Malley/Dr. Fisher/Seth Scanlon), Voices of Senor Coco Morales (Al Casas), David Pogrebin (Woody), Eddie Shapiro (Edgar)

A comedy in two acts. The action takes place in Hollywood in the late '50's and early '60's, and in Manhattan in the late '60's and early '70's.
Sunday, March 24–April 14, 1985 (20 performances)
LIFE IS A DREAM by Pedro Calderon de la Barca; English Translation, Edwin Honig; Director, James Simpson; Scenery, John Arnone; Costumes, Kurt Wilhelm; Lighting, Frances Aronson; Dramaturg, Alisa Solomon; Original Music, Kim Sherman; Musical Director, Rocco Matone; Technical Director, David Tasso; Wardrobe, Michael Darling; Production Assistant, Sophie Munger; Stage Managers, Patrice Thomas, Margaret Conley
CAST: Laura Innes (Rosaura), Thomas Richards (Clarin), Rocco Sisto (Segismundo), Jeremiah Sullivan (Clotaldo), Jeff Shoemaker, Brian Crawley (Guards), Michael Cerveris (Astolfo), Kristine Nielson (Estrella), John Heppenstall (Servant), Warren Manzi (Basilio), Mark Tankersley (Courtier), Daniel Moran (Rebel Leader), Rebels: Simon Allen, Charles Campo, Brian Crawley, Todd Field, Bart Gardy, Terrence McDonnell, Tony Raiford
Sunday, May 12–June 9, 1985 (25 performances)
CHOPIN IN SPACE by Phil Bosakowski; Director, Rebecca Guy; Scenery, Anne Servanton; Costumes, Catherine Zuber; Lighting, Bruce Daniel; Sound, Daryl Bornstein; Assistant Director, Judy Goldman; Wigs, Barbara Somerville; Technical Director, Robin Guarino; Wardrobe, Claudia Dunagan; Props, Lisa Morgan; Production Assistant, Sophie Munger; Stage Managers, Mark Rhodes, Linda Bryce
CAST: Noble Shropshire (Chopin/Lech), Nancy Mette (Marya/Danuta), Paul Romero (Bear/Waiter), Phil Lenkowsky (Tank/Waiter/Chopin II), William Mesnik (Hitler/Delacroix/Stash), Mary Lou Rosato (Beezo/Nancy Reagan), Rick Thomas (Tank/Waiter/Harry), William Duff-Griffin (Pope/FDR/Reagan), Sylvia Short (Babci/Eleanor). Performed without intermission.

Carol Rosegg, C. Rossi Photos

Leslie Geraci, Jonathan Hadary in "Charley Bacon . . ." Top Right: Thomas Richards, Rocco Sisto, Laura Innes in "Life Is a Dream"

Leslie Geraci, Jonathan Hadary in "Charley Bacon . . ." Above: Mary Lou Rosato, Noble Shropshire, Nancy Mette in "Chopin in Space"

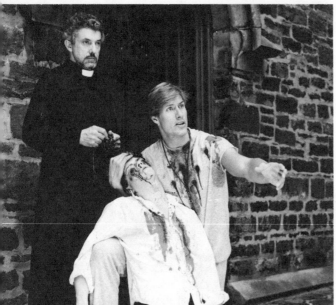

Marc Corum, Dayton Callie, Shane
O'Neill in "The Weekend"

APPLE CORPS THEATRE

Sixth Season

Artistic Director, John Raymond; Managing Director, Neal Arluck; Assistant Administrator, Bob Del Pazzo; Press, Aviva Cohen

(Apple Corps Theatre) Thursday, July 5–29, 1984 (20 performances)
CHILD'S PLAY by Robert Marasco. Director, Philip Giberson; Set, Marc Scott; Costumes, Maria Kaye; Lighting, Wayne S. Lawrence; Sound, Judy Baldwin; Makeup, Daniel Frye; Stage Manager, Max Storch.
CAST: Mart McChesney (Paul), Richard Niles (Father Penny), Richard Voigts (Father Griffin), Richard Fancy (Jerome), Sam Gary (Dobbs), C. J. Bau (Father Mozian), J. P. Chartier (Carre), Jeffrey Solberg (Medley), Bjorn Teheran (Banks), Joseph Donohue (Jennings), Cesar Cabrera (Cabrera), Steve Rogers (Shea), Frank Dowd (McArdle), Tony DeAngelis (Travis)
    Thursday, Aug. 9–Sept. 2, 1984 (20 performances)
LADIES IN RETIREMENT by Reginald Denham and Edward Percy; Director, William MacDuff; Lighting, Deborah Constantine; Costumes, Marie Hilgemann; Sound, Elliott Forrest; Stage Manager, Kara Sheridan. CAST: Kathryn C. Sparer (Lucy), Mary Orr (Leonora), Helen Marcy (Ellen), Gary Richards (Albert), Ruby Payne (Louisa), Kathleen Roland (Emily), Janet Kingsley (Sister Teresa)
    Wednesday, Oct. 17–Nov. 4, 1984 (20 performances)
OUTWARD BOUND by Sutton Vane. Director, Harold J. Kennedy; Set, Marc Scott; Lighting, William J. Plachy; Costumes, MaryAnn D. Smith; Sound, Elliott Forrest; Stage Manager, Kara Sheridan. CAST: Skipp Lynch (Scrubby), Meg Huston (Ann), Steve Tschudy (Henry), Farley Granger (Prior), Lucille Patton (Mrs. Cleveden-Banks), Peter Waldren (Rev. Duke), Imogene Coca (Mrs. Midgit), Henry Morgan (Lingley), Harold J. Kennedy (Rev. Thompson)
    Thursday, Nov. 15–Dec. 9, 1984 (20 performances)
THE WEEKEND by Christopher Jones; Director, John Raymond; Set, Marc Scott; Sound, Elliott Forrest; Costumes, MaryAnn D. Smith; Lighting, William J. Plachy; Stage Manager, Douglas Salzinger. CAST: Carmen Bau (Tommy), Dayton Callie (Mike), Shane O'Neill (Jimmy), Peter G. Morse (Red), Mark Corum (Buzzy), Jaye Stewart (Clyde), Tony Carlin (Billy)
    Thursday, Dec. 27, 1984–Feb. 11, 1985 (16 performances)
POE IN PERSON with Set by Marc Scott; Lighting, Deborah Constantine. CAST: Conrad Pomerleau in a solo performance as Edgar Allan Poe.
    Thursday, Jan. 15–Feb. 17, 1985 (24 performances)
DR. COOK'S GARDEN by Ira Levin; Director, William MacDuff; Set, Marc Scott; Sound, Elliott Forrest; Lighting, Deborah Constantine; Costumes, MaryAnn D. Smith; Stage Manager, Kara Sheridan.
CAST: Steve Tschudy (Dr. Jim Tennyson), Helen Marcy (Bea Schmidt), Lois Nelson (Dora Ludlow), Bob Del Pazzo (Elias Hart), Sam Gray (Dr. Leonard Cook)
    Monday, March 4–26, 1985 (8 performances)
THE FACES OF LOVE and PORTRAIT OF AMERICA with Music composed and adapted by Lee Norris; Lighting, Deborah Constantine; Stage Manager, Kara Sheridan. CAST: Barbara Feldon, Michael Tolan
    Thursday, April 11–28, 1985 (16 performances)
SOMETHING OLD, SOMETHING NEW two programs of one-act plays: Program A: *"The Boor"* by Anton Chekhov; Director, Edward Farley; with Maureen Kenny (Mrs. Popov), Quinton Wiles (Luka), George Holmes (Smirnov). *"The Rats"* by Agatha Christie; Director, Elliott Forrest; with Anne Barrett (Sandra), Janet Kingsley (Jennifer), Bruce McDonnell (David), Keith Williams (Alec). *"The Caravan"* by Louis Phillips; Director, John A. C. Kennedy; with Curt Williams (Hoyle), Eric Kornfeld (Hopwood), D. E. Fletcher (Abdul). Program B: *"Slambook"* written and directed by Gary Richards; with Catherine Natale (Debbie), Mary Cushman (Linda). *"The Doctor in spite of Himself"* by Moliere; Director, Kara Sheridan; with Neal Arluck (Sganarelle), Laurine Towler (Martine), Frank Dowd (M. Robert), John C. Jenson (Valere), Mart McChesney (Lucas), Wendy Waterman (Jacqueline), Susanna Frazer (Lucinde), Dick Roper (Geronte), Kevin Moran (Leandre). *"Post Office"* by Lory Frankel; Director, Penelope Hirsch; with Estelle Green (Kathie), Lois Raebeck (Millie), Deidre Westervelt (Joanie), Ruby Payne (Snooks), Vickie Usher (Alice), Kricker James (Joe), Judith Scarpone (Barb)
    Sunday, May 19–June 16, 1985 (33 performances and 9 previews). Presented in association with RSM Productions and Pequod Productions.
MAN ENOUGH by Patty Gideon Sloan; Director, Steve McCurdy; Set/Lighting, Clark Middleton; Costumes, Joy Alpern; Casting, Alan Coleridge; Stage Manager, Nereida Ortiz. CAST: Aideen O'Kelly (Josie), Bruce Roberts King (Joey), Peter Noel Duhamel (Donal), Alissa Alban (Kit), David S. Howard (Jack), Tudi Roche (Sheila), Richard Karn (Tom), Jay Keye (Frank)

Austin Trevett Photos

**Top Left: Carmen Bau, John Cartier,
Mart McChesney in "Child's Play"
Below: Peter Waldren, Farley Granger
in "Outward Bound"**

Conrad Pomerleau
as Edgar Allan Poe

Barbara Feldon

Michael Tolan

Bruce Roberts King, Marilyn Chris, David S. Howard, Will Jeffries
in "Man Enough" *(Susan Cook Photo)*

CIRCLE REPERTORY COMPANY

Sixteenth Season

Artistic Director, Marshall W. Mason; Associate Artistic Director, B. Rodney Marriott; Managing Director, Richard Frankel; Casting, Eve Battaglia; Associate Literary Manager, William Hemming; Business Manager, Valerie Tomaselli; Marketing Director, Lynn Landis; Development, Christine S. Peck; Production Manager, Kate Stewart; Stage Managers, Fred Reinglas, Jody Boese, Earl R. Hughes; Technical Director, Jim Fainberg; Hats and Headresses, Frances E. Rosenthal; Hairdresser, Joan E. Weiss; Props, Eric Nightengale, Emily Rymland; Sound, Leslie Loeb; Wardrobe, Patricia Fletcher, Michelle Summerline; Press, Richard Frankel, Reva Cooper

(Circle Repertory Theatre) Tuesday, Oct. 2–Nov. 11, 1984 (32 performances)
LOVE'S LABOR'S LOST by William Shakespeare; Director, Toby Robertson; Set, Franco Colavecchia; Lighting, Dennis Parichy; Costumes, Laura Crow; Music/Instrumental and Vocal Arrangements, Norman L. Berman; Sound, Chuck London Media/Stewart Werner; Dances, Jessica Sayre; Stage Manager, Earl Hughes
CAST: Michael Ayr (Berowne), Kelly Connell (Forester/Marcade), Jack Davidson (Dull), Amy Epstein (Maria), Colin Fox succeeded by Roger Chapman (Sir Nathaniel), Christopher Goutman (King of Navarre), Charlotte Graham (Rosaline), Charles T. Harper (Dumaine), Trish Hawkins (Princess), Michael Higgins (Holofernes), Ken Kliban (Armado), Ben Lemon (Longaville), Joseph Mydell (Costard), Lisa Pelikan (Katharine), Eric Schiff (Moth), Sharon Schlarth (Jacquennetta), Edward Seamon (Boyet)

Sunday, Dec. 2–30, 1984 (33 performances and 13 previews)
BING AND WALKER by James Paul Farrell; Director, Dan Bonnell; Set, David Potts; Lighting, Mal Sturchio; Costumes, Deborah Shaw; Sound, Chuck London Media/Stewart Werner; Original Music, Kevin Bartlett; Stage Manager, Denise Yaney
CAST: Jack Davidson (Arthur Walker), Stephanie Musnick (Ellie Walker), Edward Power (Eddie Bing), Samantha Atkins (Diane Bing). A play in two acts. The action takes place in the Walker backyard in Woods Hole, Massachusetts, during late summer of the present time.

Thursday, Jan. 10–Feb. 17, 1985 (45 performances)
DYSAN by Patrick Meyers; Director, B. Rodney Marriott; Set, Christopher Barreca; Lighting, Dennis Parichy; Costumes, Fran Rosenthal; Original Music, Robert Tomaro; Lyrics, Patrick Meyers; Sound, Chuck London Media/Stewart Werner; Assistant to Director, Emily Rymland; Wardrobe, Pat Fletcher; Stage Manager, Les Cockayne
CAST: Jimmie Ray Weeks (Jake), Danton Stone (Eddie Pataco), Charles T. Harper (Spider Veloci), Katherine Cortez (Dysan), Steven Gregan (Merwan), Mark Myers
A drama in two acts. The action takes place early in September of 1987 in a beach home on the northern coast of California.

Wednesday, Feb. 27–Apr. 22, 1985 (62 performances). Transferred to Broadway, Friday, Apr. 26, 1985. Circle Repertory Co. and The Glines present:
AS IS by William M. Hoffman; Director, Marshall, W. Mason; Set, David Potts; Lighting, Dennis Parichy; Costumes, Michael Warren Powell; Associate Director, George Boyd; Sound, Chuck London Media/Stuart Werner; Stage Manager, Fred Reinglas
CAST: Claris Erickson (Hospice Worker/Business Partner/Nurse), Steven Gregan (Chet), Jonathan Hadary (Saul), Jonathan Hogan (Rich), Ken Kliban (Brother/Barney), Lily Knight (Lily), Lou Liberatore (Clone/Pat/Orderly), Mark Myers (Clone)
A drama performed without intermission. The action takes place in New York City at the present time.

Wednesday, May 8–12, 1985 (6 previews only. Opening was canceled)
ANGELO'S WEDDING by Julie Bovasso; Director, Marshall W. Mason; Set, John Lee Beatty; Lighting, Dennis Parichy; Costumes, Jennifer von Mayrhauser; Sound, Chuck London Media/Stewart Werner; Stage Manager, Ginny Martino
CAST: Scott Glenn (Larry), Cliff Gorman (Benny), Mari Gorman (Pigeon), William Hickey (Uncle Salvatore), Lynn Cohen (Vera)
A play in three acts. The action takes place on a Saturday in March in the Perrone house on Staten Island.

Gerry Goodstein Photos

Top Left: Christopher Goutman, Michael Ayr, Charles T. Harper, Ben Lemon, and below: Trish Hawkins, Amy Epstein, Charlotte Graham in "Love's Labour's Lost"

Jack Davidson, Samantha Atkins in "Bing and Walker"

Jonathan Hogan, Jonathan Hadary in "As Is" Top: (L) Scott Glenn, Mari Gorman, and
(R) William Hickey, Cliff Gorman in "Angelo's Wedding" Center: (L)
Claris Erickson in "As Is" (R) Katherine Cortez, Jimmie Ray Weeks in "Dysan"

ENSEMBLE STUDIO THEATRE

Thirteenth Season

Artistic Director, Curt Dempster; Managing Director, David S. Rosenak; Artistic Associate, John McCormack; Assistant to Artistic Director, Jackie Reingold; Literary Manager, Stuart Spencer; Literary Associate, D. S. Moynihan; Casting, Billy Hopkins, Lisa Peterson; Production Manager, Cornella Twitchell; Technical Director, Jack Wilkoff; Production Coordinator, Jared F. Tausing; General Manager, Teresa Elwert; Development, Lucy Mayer Harrop; Press, Bruce Cohen, Kathleen von Schmid

Saturday, November 17–December 16, 1984 (27 performances)
THE BLOODLETTERS by Richard Greenberg; Director, Shirley Kaplan; Set, Edward T. Gianfrencesco, Jr.; Costumes, Bruce Harrow; Lighting, Richard Lund; Sound, Bruce Ellman; Stage Managers, Diane Ward, Michael L. Allwine, Melissa L. Burdick
CAST: Nancy Franklin (Faye Sutter), Bruce MacVittie (Defe Hagemeyer), Corey Parker (Corky Sutter), Garrett M. Brown (Reid Sutter), Cheryl McFadden (Annie Sutter), William Carden (Callie van der Vlis), Stephen Pearlman (Jake Abrams)
A dark comedy in three acts with one intermission. The action takes place in the living room/dining room of Faye Sutter's home in Levittown, Long Island, on a Saturday and Sunday.
Friday, December 7–23, 1984 (26 performances) Re-opened Thursday, January 10–February 11, 1985 for 28 additional performances.
ONCE ON A SUMMER'S DAY with Book and Lyrics by Arthur Perlman; Music, Jeffrey Lunden; Director, John Henry Davis; Producer, Diane de Mailly; Choreography, Elizabeth Keen; Musical Direction, Ronald Clay Fullum; Orchestrations, Jeffrey Lunden, Michael Harrison; Setting, Philipp Jung; Costumes, Donna Zakowska; Lighting, Michael Orris Watson; Projections, Fran Albin; Technical Director, Adam Hart; Props, Shelley Barclay; Wardrobe, Sandra McAllister; Stage Managers, David Allen Pfeiffer, Diane Ward
CAST: Kimi Morris (Alice Liddell), Martin Moran (Mad Hatter), David Purdham (Charles Dodgson), Carolyn Mignini (Older Alice/Mrs. Liddell), Nicholas Wyman (Caterpillar), Mimi Wyche (Duchess), Polly Pen (White Rabbit), David Green (Robinson Duckworth), Understudy: Kay Walbye
MUSICAL NUMBERS: Once on a Summer's Day, Don't Depend on Watches, The Angles of Geometry, Wonderland, Fairy Child, No, The Music Box, See What Mr. Dodgson Gave Me, The Tea Party, Jabberwocky, The Equation Cannot Be Solved, The Trial, Rules Shall Not Be Broken
A musical in two acts. The action takes place in Victorian England over a 30-year period, and shows the relationship between Lewis Carroll and Alice.
Friday, February 1–March 17, 1985 (52 performances)
THE CRATE by Shel Silverstein; Director, Art Wolff; Scenery, Sally de Valenzuela; Costumes, Isis C. Mussenden; Lighting, Karl E. Haas; Sound, Bruce Ellman; Technical Director, Adam Hart; Wardrobe, Michael Astor, Julia Prud'homme; Assistant to Director, Bill Tenenbaum; Stage Managers, Lauren Class Schneider, Susan Selig
CAST: Bill Cwikowski, John Fiedler, Heather Lupton, Deborah Reagan, Raynor Scheine, Howard Sherman, Robert Trebor, Janet Zarish
ACT I: The Performers, Dracula Drag, We'll Call You, Best Daddy, The Brioche, Jack, Magic Pen
ACT II: Curse of the Idol's Eye, Do I Know Him, Big Bigger Biggest, Hamlet, French Toast, Rah, Santa Claus Comes to Death Row, Mirror Mirror, Moby and Me

Carol Rosegg Photos

**Top Left: Bruce McVittie, Evan Handler,
Nancy Franklin in "The Bloodletters"**

**David Purdham, Kimi Morris
in "Once on a Summer's Day"**

Wednesday, May 8–June 17, 1985 (52 performances)

MARATHON '85: Eighth annual festival of one-act plays; Producers, Risa Bramon, Billy Hopkins; Unit Set, Johniene Papandreas; Lighting, Greg MacPherson; Sound, Bruce Ellman; Associate Producer, John McCormack.

SERIES A: Stage Manager, Pamela Edington; Sets, Dana Hasson; Costumes, Martha Hally. *"Mariens Kammer"* by Roger Hedden; Adaptation of Georg Buchner's "Wozzeck"; Director, Billy Hopkins; Original Music, David Rickets; Assistant Director, Michael Astor; Stage Manager, Susan Selig. CAST: Alex Neil (Marie), Andrew McCarthy (Franz), James Ryan (Major), Mary Joy (Margret/Grandmother/Policewoman). *"The Frog Prince"* by David Mamet; Director, Peter Maloney; Assistant, Christa K. Page; Stage Manager, Anne Singer. CAST: Garrett M. Brown (Prince), John Fiedler (Servingman), Jane Hoffman (Witch), Kristin Griffith (Milkmaid). *"Men Without Dates"* by Jane Willis; Director, Shirley Kaplan; Stage Manager, Michael L. Allwine. CAST: Kevin Bacon (Murph), John Turturro (Sal), James Murtaugh (Bartender). *"Life Under Water"* by Richard Greenberg; Director, Don Scardino; Assistant, Monica Kling; Stage Manager, Dom Ruggiero. CAST: Alexa Kenin (Amy-Joy), Amanda Plummer (Amy-Beth), Andrew McCarthy (Kip), Jill Eikenberry (Jinx), Larry Bryggman (Hank).

SERIES B: Stage Manager, Diane Ward; Sets, Marlene Marta; Costumes, Deborah Shaw. *"Aggressive Behavior"* by Stuart Spencer; Director, Jane Hoffman; Stage Manager, Paul J. Smith. CAST: Garrett M. Brown (Doug), Peter Phillips (Fisher). *"Desperadoes"* by Keith Reddin; Director, Mary B. Robinson; Stage Manager, Roy Harris. CAST: Karen Young (Rebecca), Michael Kaufman (Walt), Sam McMurray (Phil). *"Between Cars"* by Alan Zweibel; Director, Risa Bramon; Stage Manager, Denise Laffer. CAST: Perry Lang (Jerry), Elizabeth Perkins (Robin). *"The Road to the Graveyard"* by Horton Foote; Director, Curt Dempster; Assistant, Howie Demere; Stage Manager, Ted Altschuler. CAST: Frank Girardeau (Sonny), Carolyn Coates (Lyda), Roberta Maxwell (India), Margaret Thomson (MissLillie), Emmett O'Sullivan Moore (Mr. Hall).

SERIES C: Stage Manager, Pamela Edington; Sets, Brian Martin; Costumes, Colleen Muscha. *"The Semi-Formal"* by Louisa Jerauld; Director, Billy Hopkins; Assistant, Peter Hopkins; Stage Managers, Susan Selig, Lenny Wagner. CAST: Dara Levy (Lynn), Samantha Atkins (Janice), Corey Parker (Patrick), Debra Piver (Lynn's Mother). *"North of Providence"* by Edward Allan Baker; Director, Risa Bramon; Assistant, Jackie Reingold; Stage Manager, Denise Laffer. CAST: Lucinda Jenney (Carol), Bruce MacVittie (Bobbie), Matthew Cowles (Radio D.J.). *"One Tennis Shoe"* by Shel Silverstein; Director, Art Wolff; Stage Manager, Madeline S. Katz. CAST: Janet Zarish (Sylvia), James Tolkan (Harvey). *"Painting a Wall"* by David Lan. Director, Joe Gilford; Stage Manager, Nan Siegmund; Fight Director, Randy Kovitz; Dialogue Consultant, Liz Smith, Timothy Monich. CAST: Jason Parris Fitz-Gerald (Willy), Raymond Anthony Thomas (Samson), Alvin Alexis (Peter), Harsh Nayyar (Henry)

Carol Rosegg Photos

Top: Nicholas Wyman, Kimi Morris in "Once on a Summer's Day"

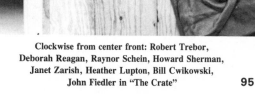

Clockwise from center front: Robert Trebor, Deborah Reagan, Raynor Schein, Howard Sherman, Janet Zarish, Heather Lupton, Bill Cwikowski, John Fiedler in "The Crate"

95

EQUITY LIBRARY THEATRE

Forty-second Season

Managing Director, George Wojtasik; Production Director, Lynn Montgomery; Business Manager, Janice E. Sager; Development, Michael P. Lynch; Assistant Managing Director, Rebecca Kreinen; Production Coordinators, Stephanie Brown, Randy Becker; Technical Directors, Michael Yarborough, Jason Townley; Associate Production Director, Randy Becker; Costumer, Ken Brown; Staff Musician, Paul Johnson; Informals Producer, Gregg Stebben; Sound and Audio, Hal Schuler; Press, Lewis Harmon

(Master Theatre) Thursday, September 27–Oct. 14, 1984 (22 performances).
TRIBUTE by Bernard Slade; Director, William Hopkins; Scenery, Janice Davis; Lighting, Craig Kennedy; Costumes, Julie Doyle; Original Music, Al Carmines; Wardrobe, Rose Olivito; Stage Managers, Ellen Sontag, Mike Stevens
CAST: Matthew Lewis (Lou Daniels), Dolores (Dodi) Kenan (Dr. Gladys Petrelli), Charles Major (Scottie Templeton), Cynthia Babak (Sally Haines), Caroline Aaron (Maggie Stratton), Mark Rogers (Jud Templeton), Nancy Youngblut (Hilary)
 A comedy in 2 acts and 6 scenes. The action takes place at the present time in the living room of a New York City townhouse, and on the stage of a New York theatre.
 Thursday, October 25–November 18, 1984 (30 performances)
BELLS ARE RINGING with Music by Jule Styne; Book and Lyrics, Betty Comden, Adolph Green; Directed and Staged by Charles Abbott; Choreography, Ed Nolfi; Scenery, Joseph Barga; Lighting, Andrew Taines; Costumes, Konnie Kittrell; Musical Direction, Francis P. Minarik; Dance Captain, Michael B. Tapley; Stage Managers, Lawrence Berrick, Colleen Janich, Carolyn Jordan
CAST: George Emch (Announcer/Larry Hastings), Lorna Erickson (Sue), Becky Garrett (Gwynne), K. K. Preece (Ella), Linda Milani (Mrs. Mallett/M.C.), Bill Milvaney (Phone Voices/Businessman), Jean Cantrell (Mme. Grimaldi), Kelly Woodruff (Carl), Donald McGrath (Insp. Barnes), Herbert Mark Parker (Francis), Lawrence Raiken (Sandor), Mark Jacoby (Jeff Moss), Barbara Passolt (Michelle), Jack Stuart (Telephone Man/Nightclub Singer), Paul Tardi (Charles Bessemer/Man from Corvello Mob), Cameron MacDonald (Mobster/Subway Drunk), Erica L. Paulson (Carol), David Jordan (Paul Arnold), Susan Sarber (Hooker), Melanie Mitchell (Cheer Leader)
MUSICAL NUMBERS: Bells Are Ringing, It's a Perfect Relationship, Independent, You've Got to Do It, Simple Little System, Is It a Crime?, Hello There, I Met a Girl, Long Before I Knew You, Mu-Cha-Cha, Just in Time, Drop That Name, The Party's Over, Salzburg, The Midas Touch, I'm Going Back, Finale. A musical in 2 acts and 22 scenes.
 Thursday, November 29–December 16, 1984 (22 performances)
THE DESK SET by William Marchant; Director, Lise Liepmann; Scenery, Barry Axtell; Lighting, John Culver; Costumes, John Deering; Sound, Hal Schuler; Production Assistant, Adele Bove; Research, William Isaacs; Stage Managers, Lawrence Berrick, Michael Prevulsky, Lori Rosecrans

CAST: Denise Bessette (Ruthie Saylor), George Bohler (Kenny), Jonathan Brody (Burt Ferris/Pianist), Christine Campbell (Sadel Meyer), Nada Despotovich (Cleaning Lady/Cheri), Robert Fass (Trumpeter/Photographer), Merry Flershem (Miss Warriner), William Isaacs (Mr. Bennett), Laine Jastram (Elsa), Brian Kosnik (Corbin), Mary Libertucci (Helen), Gloria Maddox (Bunny Watson), Cleve Roller (Old Lady), Anthony St. Martin (Richard Summer), Celia Tackaberry (Peg Costello), Jeremy Trexler (Abe Cutler)
 A comedy in 3 acts. The action takes place in the Reference Department of a large radio broadcasting company in Manhattan in the early 1950's.
 Thursday, January 3–27, 1985 (30 performances)
JACQUES BREL IS ALIVE AND WELL AND LIVING IN PARIS with Conception, English Lyrics, Additional Material, Eric Blau, Mort Shuman; Based on Brel's lyrics and commentary; Music, Jacques Brel; Director, Stephen Bonnell; Musical Direction, Benjamin Whiteley; Scenery, J. Robin Modereger; Lighting, Mark DiQuinzio; Costumes, Margarita Delgado; Choreography, Piper Pickrell; Wardrobe, Barbara Weber; Hairstylist, Osmani Garcia; Stage Managers, Peter Wolf, David Lawrence Folender, Jack Doulin
CAST: Louise Edeiken, Richard Hilton, Jan Horvath, J. C. Sheets
SONGS: Marathon, Alone, Madeleine, I Loved, Mathile, Bachelor's Dance, Timid Frieda, My Death, Girls and Dogs, Jackie, Statue, The Desperate Ones, Sons of, Amsterdam, The Bulls, Old Folks, Marieke, Brussels, Fanette, Funeral Tango, Middle Class, No Love You're Alone, Next, Carousel, If we Only Have Love. Performed with one intermission.
 Thursday, February 7–24, 1985 (22 performances)
THE COMEDY OF ERRORS by William Shakespeare; Director, Kent Thompson; Set, Jefferson Sage; Lighting, Mark W. Stanley; Costumes, Mary L. Hayes; Original Music, Duane Nelsen; Makeup, Michael Laudati; Hairstylist, Scott A. Mortimer; Stage Managers, Robert John Ulrich, Dominique Carron, Margaret Rose, Jacqueline Owens

CAST: Janet Aldrich (Courtesan), N. Erick Avari (Balthazar/Dr. Pinch), Bonnie Black (Luciana), Chet Carlin (Solinus), David Dario (Merchants), Howard Friedland (Messenger/Ensemble), Richard Grubbs (Dromio of Ephesus), David Holbrook (Jailer/Officer/Nell), J. C. Hoyt (Egeon), James Jenner (Antipholus of Syracuse), Elizabeth Pearson (Adriana), Sam Pond (Dromio of Syracuse), Steven Riedel (Merchant/Ensemble), Wesley Stevens (Antipholus of Ephesus), Maxine Taylor-Morris (Emilia/Lady Abbess), Mitch Ebo (Angelo). Performed with one intermission.

Evan Cohen Photos
Top Right: Charles Major, Mark Rogers, Caroline Aaron in "Tribute"
Below: Mark Jacoby, Lorna Erickson, Lawrence Raiken,
K. K. Preece in "Bells Are Ringing"

Jan Horvath, Richard Hilton, Louise Edeiken,
J. C. Sheets in "Jacques Brel . . ." Above:
Celia Tackaberry, Anthony St. Martin, Gloria
Maddox in "The Desk Set"

Thursday, March 7–31, 1985 (30 performances)
VERY WARM FOR MAY with Music by Jerome Kern; Book and Lyrics, Oscar Hammerstein II; Staged and Directed by Worth Howe; Scenery, Victor Capecce; Lighting, Clarke W. Thornton; Costumes, Deborah Newhall; Musical Direction, Lawrence W. Hill; Choreographer, Dee Dee Sandt; Assistant Musical Director, Paul Johnson; Dance Captain, Tom Condon; Wardrobe, Maureen Frey; Stage Managers, John W. Calder III, Colleen Janich, Noel Stern
CAST: Brian Arsenault (Watson), Tom Condon (McGee/Dream Ogdon), Robert Cooner (Pratt), Nick Corley (Lowell Pennyfeather), Daniel Davie (Johnny Graham), Valerie DePena (May Graham), Lorraine Goodman (Carol), Robert Grossman (Will Graham/Jethro/Eddie Schlessinger), Michael Latimer (Kenny/Smoothy), Kirsten Lind (Miss Hude), Karen Longwell (Elizabeth Spofford), Glenn Mure (Quiller), Beth Musiker (Miss Randall), Jennifer S. Myers (Mrs. Wasserman), Doug Tompos (Raymond Sibley), Dana Walker (Maxime), P. J. Wilson (Sonny Spofford)
MUSICAL NUMBERS: In Other Words Seventeen, Finaletto, That Lucky Fellow, L'Histoire de Madame de La Tour, That Lucky Lady, The Strange Case of Adam Standish, In the Heart of the Dark, All in Fun, High Up in Harlem, Finale
A musical in 2 acts and 5 scenes.
Thursday, April 11–28, 1985 (22 performances)
DEATHTRAP by Ira Levin; Director, Robert Bridges; Set, John Charles Kenny; Lighting, Richard Latta; Costumes, Sue Ellen Rohrer; Original Music, Duane Nelsen; Fight Director, Thomas Schall; Special Effects, Emile Husson; Props, Mimi Cohen; Wardrobe, Geraldine Teagarden; Stage Managers, D. C. Rosenberg, David Lawrence Folender, Arlene Mantek
CAST: Lewis Morgan (Sidney Bruhl), Maryanne Dempsey (Myra Bruhl), John Donahoe (Clifford Anderson), Judith Tillman (Helga ten Dorp), James Bormann (Porter Milgrim)
A drama in 2 acts and 6 scenes. The action takes place in Sidney Bruhl's study, in the Bruhl home in Westport, Connecticut.
Thursday, May 9–June 2, 1985 (30 performances)
A LITTLE NIGHT MUSIC with Music and Lyrics by Stephen Sondheim; Book, Hugh Wheeler; Director, Susan H. Schulman; Scenery, Linda Hacker; Costumes, C. L. Hundley; Lighting, Ruth Roberts; Musical Director, Phil Reno; Wardrobe, Linda Panzner; Stage Managers, James D'Asaro, Camille Calman, Linda Riley, Sandy Shannon
CAST: Judith Blazer (Anne), Judith Brio (Mrs. Anderson), Maris Clement (Charlotte), Sarah Combs (Petra), Avril Gentles (Mme. Armfeldt), Carolyn Goor (Osa), Kathryn Hays (Desiree), Eric Johnson (Lindquist), Eddie Korbich (Henrik Egerman), Bryan John Landrine (Erlanson), Marty McDonough (Frid), Nita Moore (Mrs. Segstrom), Daniel Pelzig (Bertrand), Ross Petty (Fredrik Egerman), Patrick Quinn (Carl-Magnus), Barbara Scanlon (Mrs. Nordstrom), Ellen Troy (Malla), Karen Wald (Fredrika)
MUSICAL NUMBERS: Night Waltz, Now, Later, Soon, The Glamorous Life, Remember?, You Must Meet My Wife, Liasons, In Praise of Women, Every Day a Little Death, A Weekend in the Country, The Sun Won't Set, It Would Have Been Wonderful, Perpetual Anticipation, Send in the Clowns, The Miller's Son, Finale.
A musical in 2 acts and 15 scenes. The action takes place in Sweden during the early 1900's.

EQUITY LIBRARY THEATRE INFORMALS

(Bruno Walter Auditorium/Lincoln Center) Producer, Rebecca Kreinen; Each production presented for three performances. Sept. 17–19, 1984: TRADING IN FUTURES by Robert Clyman; Director, Gregg L. Stebben; Lighting, Cindy Dout; Stage Manager, Delila Pearson. CAST: Valerie Beaman, James D'Apollonia. Oct. 15–17, 1984: CONSENTING ADULTS by Ralph Hunt; Director, Gregg L. Stebben; Lighting, Cindy Dout. CAST: Anthony John Lizzul, Gale Galione, John David Barone. Jan. 21–23, 1985: DONUTS by James Nicola; Director, Gregg L. Stebben; Lighting, Cindy Dout. CAST: David Pierce, David Trim. Feb. 25–27, 1985: WRITERS BLOC by Geoffrey Gordon; OF MACE AND MEN by Gregg L. Stebben; Staged by Gregg L. Stebben; Lighting, Raymond J. Hardy; Stage Manager, Christine Carter. CAST: William Ellis, Leo Ferstenberg, Michael Iannucci, David Lough, Nancy Richards, Kathleen Marie Robbins, Christine Carter, Anita Montgomery, Victoria Page. March 18–20, 1985: WHAT COMES AFTER OHIO by Daniel Meltzer; Director, William Sevedge, Jr; Lighting, Raymond J. Hardy. CAST: Arland Russell, Michael Waldron. Apr. 22–23, 1985: Cabaret performed by Deborah Arters, Kevin Maguire, Merrie Rich; Musical Directors, Dan Wolgemuth, Wes McAffee. May 20–21, 1985: PAULA OF THE GREEN CLOUDS by Faustino Rothman; Director, Rebecca Kreinen; Lighting, Rebecca Kreinen, Fran Miksits; Stage Manager, Joseph Callari. CAST: Grace Bentley, Martin Curland, Dan Gershwin, Cornelia Mills, Stephen Moser, Bee-be Smith

Top Right: Karen Longwell, Valerie Depena, P. J. Wilson, Michael Latimer, Daniel David in "Very Warm for May" Below: Lewis Morgan, John Donahoe, Maryanne Dempsey in "Deathtrap"

Dan Gershwin, Grace Bentley in "Paula of the Green Clouds" Above: cast of "A Little Night Music"

HUDSON GUILD THEATRE
Tenth Season

Producing Director, David Kerry Heefner; Associate Director, Daniel Swee; Production Manager/Technical Director, John B. Marean; Production Stage Manager, Carol Klein; Marketing Director, Chrissie Hines; Business Manager, James Abar; Literary Manager, Fritz Erti; Press, Jeffrey Richards, Bob Ganshaw, C. George Willard, Ben Morse, Eileen McMahon, Toby Mailman, Bill Shuttleworth

(Hudson Guild Theatre) Wednesday, Oct. 24,–Nov. 18, 1984 (28 performances)
BURKIE by Bruce Graham; Director, Lynn M. Thomson; Set, William Barclay; Costumes, Ann Morrell; Lighting, Phil Monat; Sound, Ed Fitzgerald; Production Assistant, Anne Cowett; Props, Charlotte Eisenberg
CAST: Jeffrey Hayenga (Jonathan Burke), Eddie Jones (Ed Burke), Sam Coppola (Dom), Caryn West (Jess Burke)
  A drama in two acts. The action takes place during autumn of the present time in and around the Burke home in South Philadelphia.
  Wednesday, Dec. 5,–30, 1984 (28 performances)
THE ACCRINGTON PALS by Peter Whelan; Director, Daniel Gerroll; Set, Robert Thayer; Costumes, Pamela Scofield; Lighting, Phil Monat; Sound, Ed Fitzgerald; Production Assistant, Camille Calman; Props, Chris Meely; Wardrobe, Rosalyn Brunner; Pianist, David Gaines; Hairstylist, Scott Green
CAST: Anthony Fusco (Tom), Amelia White (May), Ian Stuart (Arthur), E. Keyishian (Reggie), Thomas Virtue (Ralph), Kate Burton (Eva), Veronica Castang (Annie), Denise Stephenson (Sarah), Amanda Carlin (Bertha), George Taylor (C. S. M. Rivers)
  A drama in two acts. The action takes place between 1914 and 1916 in Accrington, an industrial town in Lancashire, England, and on the battlefields of the Western Front.
  Wednesday, Jan. 30,–Feb. 24, 1985 (28 performances)
OUTSIDE WACO by Patricia Browning Griffith; Director, June Rovenger; Set, Daniel Proett; Costumes, Patricia Adshead; Lighting, Phil Monat; Sound, Ed Fitzgerald; Production Assistant, Camille Calman; Wardrobe, Rosalyn Brunner
CAST: Susan Mansur (Sarah Matthews Phillips), Carlin Glynn (Georgia Lee Matthews), Kate Skinner (Juanita Matthews Buchanan), Elizabeth Berridge (Lashondra Phillips), Edward Power (George Harold Matthews)
  A comedy in 2 acts and 5 scenes with a prologue. The action takes place at the present time in the Matthews home in Bright Light, Texas.
  Wednesday, March 27,–April 21, 1985 (24 performances)
SEPTEMBER IN THE RAIN by John Godber; Director, David Kerry Heefner; Costumes, Mary L. Hayes; Lighting, Phil Monat; Assistant to Director, Evanne Christian; Production Assistant, Julie Swenson; Stage Manager, Carol Klein
CAST: Susan Greenhill (Liz), Steve Ryan (Jack)
  A play in two acts. The action takes place in Yorkshire and Lancashire, England at the present time and in the late 1940's.
  Wednesday, May 22,–June 16, 1985 (28 performances)
SUBMARINERS by Tom McClenaghan; Director, David Kerry Heefner; Set, Daniel Proett; Costumes, Pamela Scofield; Lighting, Phil Monat; Sound, Ed Fitzgerald; Assistant to Director, Evanne Christian; Production Assistant, Jeffrey Hilburn; Dialect Consultant, Daniel Gerroll; Hairstylist, Michael di Cesare; Props/Wardrobe, Chris Mealy; Stage Manager, Carol Klein
CAST: John Bowman (Able Seaman "Cock" Roach), Tim Choate (Chief Petty Officer "Spider" Webb), Adam LeFevre (Chief Petty Officer "Housey" Houseman), Kevin O'Rourke (Chief Petty Officer "Splash" Brady), Ralph Williams (Rev. Ian Butler, Chaplain)
  A comedy in 2 acts and 6 scenes. The action takes place aboard the nuclear submarine HMS Superior in the Chief Petty Officers' mess room at the present time.

Charles Marinaro Photos

**Top Left: Jeffrey Hayenga, Eddie Jones,
Caryn West in "Burkie" Below: Kate
Burton, Thomas Virtue in "The Accrington Pals"**

**Amanda Carlin, Kate Burton, Denise Stephenson,
Amelia White in "The Accrington Pals"**

Kevin O'Rourke, Tim Choate, John Bowman in "Submariners" Top: (L) Kate Skinner,
Susan Mansur, Carlin Glynn in "Outside Waco" (R) Susan Greenhill,
Steve Ryan in "September in the Rain"

JEWISH REPERTORY THEATRE
Eleventh Season

Artistic Director/Producer, Ran Avni; Associate Director, Edward M. Cohen; Casting, Susan Haskins; Technical Director, Jonathan Goldstein; Press, Bruce Cohen, Kathleen von Schmid

(Emanu-El Midtown YM-YWHA) Saturday, June 9,–July 29, 1984 (30 performances). Moved to Audrey Wood Theatre Tuesday, Oct. 9, 1984.
KUNI LEML based on Avrom Goldfadn's farce; Book, Nahma Sandrow; Music, Raphael Crystal; Lyrics, Richard Engquist; Director, Ran Avni; Sets, Joel Fontaine; Costumes, Karen Hummel; Lighting, Dan Kingsley; Musical Staging, Haila Strauss; Musical Director, Raphael Crystal; Stage Manager, Gay Smerek
CAST: Daniel Marcus (Yankl/Yasha), Jack Savage (Simkhe/Sasha), Mark Zeller (Reb Pinkhos), Barbara McCulloh (Carolina), Gene Varrone (Kalmen), Scott Wentworth (Max), Susan Victor (Libe), Stuart Zagnit (Kuni Leml)
MUSICAL NUMBERS: Celebrate, The Boy Is Perfect, Carolina's Lament, The World Is Getting Better, Cuckoo, Matchmaker's Daughter, A Meeting of the Minds, A Little Learning, Nothing Counts but Love, What's My Name?, Purim Song, Do Horses Talk to Horses?, Lovesongs and Lullabies, Be Fruitful and Multiply, Finale
   A musical in 2 acts and 8 scenes. The action takes place in Odessa in the Ukraine during the reign of Czar Alexander II, before and during the holiday of Purim in 1880.
   Saturday, Oct. 13,–Nov. 18, 1984 (31 performances)
SHLEMIEL THE FIRST by Isaac Bashevis Singer; Edited for the stage by Sarah Blacher Cohen; Director, Edward M. Cohen; Sets, Ray Recht; Costumes, Debra Stein; Lighting, Dan Kinsley; Music/Sound Effects, Margaret Rachlin Pine; Sound, Paul Garrity; Wardrobe, Lisa Baron; Stage Managers, D. C. Rosenberg, Williamson Vedder
CAST: Michael Slade (Chaim Rascal), Ray Xifo (Gronam Ox), Richard Doran (Shmendrick), Peter Shuman (Yold), Helen Hanft (Yente Pesha), Karen Ludwig (Tryna Rytza), Zane Lasky (Shlemiel), Scott Brazer (Feivish), Heather Kristin (Keile Beile)
   A play in two acts. The action takes place in the village of Chelm in the middle of the 19th Century, or any century.
   Saturday, Dec. 8, 1984–Jan. 6, 1985 (27 performances)
COLD STORAGE by Ronald Ribman; Director, Len Cariou; Set, Jeffrey Schneider; Costumes, Shay Cunliffe; Lighting, Dan Kinsley; Stage Managers, G. Franklin Heller, Elizabeth Sherman.
CAST: Jay Thomas (Richard Landau), Odalys Dominguez (Miss Madurga), Joe Silver (Joseph Parmigian)
   A comedy in two acts. The action takes place at the present time on a hospital roof garden in New York City.
   Saturday, Feb. 2, 1985–
CITY BOY based on stories by Leonard Michaels; Adaptation and Direction, Edward M. Cohen; Sets, Geoffrey Hall; Costumes, Edie Giguere; Lighting, Dan Kinsley; Sound, Paul Garrity
CAST: Max Cantor (Myron), DeLane Matthews (The Women), Scott G. Miller (Ikstein)
   Saturday, April 13,–May 12, 1985 (30 performances)
CROSSING DELANCEY by Susan Sandler; Director, Pamela Berlin; Set, Jeffrey Schneider; Lighting, Bennet Averyt; Costumes, Lindsay Davis; Music, Robert Dennis; Stage Manager, Alice Dewey
CAST: Melanie Mayron (Isabelle), Sylvia Kauders (Bubbie), Shirley Stoler (Hannah), Geoffrey Pierson (Tyler), Jacob Harran (Sam)
   A comedy in two acts. The action takes place at the present time on both sides of Delancey Street on the Lower East Side of Manhattan, and Upper West Side.

Adam Newman Photos

**Top Left: Scott Wentworth, Stuart Zagnit
Below: Scott Wentworth, Barbara McCulloh
in "Kuni-Leml"**

Mark Zeller, Barbara McCulloh
in "Kuni-Leml"

Scott G. Miller, Max Cantor, DeLane Matthews in "City Boy" Top: (L) Paul Stolarsky
(bottom), Peter Shuman, Ray Xifo in "Shlemiel the First" (R) Jacob Harran,
Melanie Mayron in "Crossing Delancey"

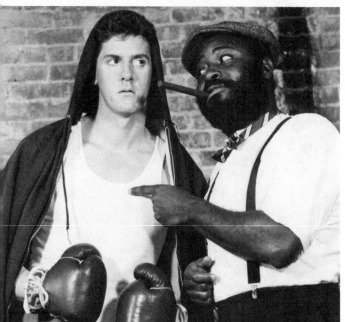

MANHATTAN PUNCH LINE

Seventh Season

Artistic Director, Steve Kaplan; Executive Director, Mitch McGuire; Managing Director, Patricia Baldwin; Development, Ferne A. Farber; Production Manager, Pamela Singer; Props, Helen Bielak; Press, Bruce Cohen, Harold L. Marmon

(Susan Bloch Theatre) Thursday, Nov. 8,–Dec. 9, 1984 (24 performances).
KID PURPLE by Donald Wollner; Director, Don Scardino; Producing Directors, Steve Kaplan, Mitch McGuire; Set, Steve Saklad; Costumes, Mimi Maxmen; Lighting, Joshua Dachs; Sound, Bruce Ellman; Casting, Alexa Fogel; Fight Coordinator, Danny Aiello III; Technical Coordinator, Marc D. Malamud; Props, Jaqueline Roberts; Production Assistants, Michael Mooers, Peter Adolf; Stage Manager, K. Siobhan Phelan
CAST: Sam McMurray (Benjamin "Kid Purple" Schwartz), Melodie Somers (Mrs. Schwartz/Judge Hannah May Fulcrum), Lyn Greene (Michelle Schwartz), Joyce Leigh Bowden (Charlotta Watkins/Julie Schneider/Round Girl), Ellis "Skeeter" Williams (Willie Hogan), Daryl Edwards ("Sweet Eddie" Kareem), Michael Tucker (Announcer's Voice), Debbie Ellis, Dayna Clark (Children's Voices)
   A comedy in two acts. The action takes place in Benjamin "Kid Purple" Schwartz's mind as he runs through his memoirs.
(Judith Anderson Theatre) Saturday, Jan. 19,–Feb. 24, 1985 (28 performances)
FESTIVAL OF ORIGINAL ONE-ACT COMEDIES with Settings by Jane Clark, Christopher Stapleton; Costumes, David Loveless, Gail Brassard; Lighting, Scott Pinkney; Sound, Bruce Ellman; Original Music, Louis Rosen; Artistic Director, Steve Kaplan; Associate Producer, Kathi Levitan; Managing Director, Patricia Baldwin; Technical Director, Rob Oakley; Production Manager, Pamela Singer; Casting, Alexa Fogel; Stage Managers, David Lansky, Lori Rosecrans
PROGRAM A: "*Women and Shoes*" by Nina Shengold; Director, Mitch McGuire; with Matthew Locricchio succeeded by Mitch McGuire (Seb), Paul Geier (Willis). The action takes place at the present time in a bar in Queens, NY. "*The Art of Self Defense*" by Trish Johnson; Director, Steven D. Albrezzi; with Peter Webster (Dennis), Denise Bessette (Jan), Helen Harrelson (Ruth), Kathrin King Segal (Frannie), Gina Barnett (C.Y.), Caryn West (Elizabeth). The action takes place at the present time in and around a downtown health club. "*Finger Food*" by Nina Shengold; Director, William Hopkins; with Mark Morocco (Denny), Helene Spitzer (Mona). The action takes place at the present time in a photographer's studio. "*Backbone of America*" by Mark D. Kaufmann; Director, Porter Van Zandt; with Cameron Charles Johann (S.A.), Stephen Hamilton (Chase). The action takes place at the present time in an executive living room at 7:30 P.M.
PROGRAM B: "*Falsies*" by Richard Gott; Director, Robert S. Johnson; with Joseph Daly (Jimmy), Barbara Colton (Nurse), Stefan Hartman (Clancey), Taylor Davidson (Orderly). The action takes place at the present time in St. Elizabeth Hospital in Boston. "*Mongolian Idiot*" by Fredric Sirasky; Director, John Schwab; with Rick Lawless (Alex Henderson), Patricia Mauceri (Myra Payton). The action takes place in Akron, Ohio, during the spring of 1965. "*Life on Earth*" by Howard Korder; Director, Robin Saex; with Jack Stehlin (Jack), Lisa Barnes (Maggie). The action takes place at the present time in Central Park, New York City. "*Sleeping Beauty*" by Laurence Klavan; Director, Steve Kaplan; with Amy Beth Williams (Louise), Brad Bellamy (Malcolm), Peter Webster (Richard), Steve Skrovan (Tony), Mitch McGuire (Radio Announcer). The action takes place at the present time on Staten Island, NY.
(Judith Anderson Theatre) Thursday, Feb. 21,–March 25, 1985 (20 performances)
RETURN OF THE CREATURE FROM THE BLUE ZALOOM, a one-man show by Paul Zaloom
(Theatre Guinevere) Monday, April 22,–May 19, 1985 (24 performances)
ALMOST IN VEGAS by Janet Neipris; Director, Susan Einhorn; Setting, Harry Feiner; Lighting, Marc D. Malamud; Costumes, Donna Zakowska; Sound, Phil Lee; Assistant Production Manager, David Lansky; Assistant to Director, Lauren Class Schneider; Technical Director, Charlie Lagola; Production Assistants, Jeff Corrick, Peter Adolf; Stage Manager, Sondra R. Katz
CAST: Mitch McGuire (Felix), Susan Cash (Margie), April Shawhan (Alma), David Little (Louis)
   A comedy in 2 acts and 4 scenes. The action takes place at the present time in the Birdcage Bar of a large hotel in Las Vegas, Nevada, and in Room 1222 in the Fantasy Tower on an evening in December.

Phyllis Reison, Jim Moore, Cathryn Williams Photos

Top Left: Sam McMurray, Ellis "Skeeter" Williams in "Kid Purple" Below: Peter Webster, Amy Beth Williams, Brad Bellamy in "Sleeping Beauty"

Stephen Hamilton, Cameron Charles Johann in "Backbone of America"

April Shawhan, David Little, Susan Cash, Mitch McGuire in "Almost in Vegas"
Top: (L) Paul Zaloom in "Return of the Creature from the Blue Zaloom"
(R) Patricia Mauceri in "Mongolian Idiot"

103

MANHATTAN THEATRE CLUB

Thirteenth Season

Artistic Director, Lynne Meadow; Managing Director, Barry Grove; General Manager, Connie L. Alexis; Artistic Associate/Literary Manager, Jonathan Alper; Casting Director, Donna Isaacson; Development, Judith L. DeMott; Marketing Director, Virginia Louloudes; Press Assistant, Howard Sherman; Business Manager, Victoria B. Bailey; Production Manager, Tom Aberger; Technical Director, Nicholas R. Miller

(The Space at City Center) Tuesday, Oct. 30,–Dec. 2, 1984 (39 performances)
IN CELEBRATION by David Storey; Director, Lindsay Anderson; Set, John Lee Beatty; Costumes, Linda Fisher; Lighting, Dennis Parichy; Sound, Stan Metelits; Props, Denise Laffer; Wardrobe, Otis Gustafson; Stage Managers, Peggy Peterson, Travis DeCastro
CAST: Frank Grimes (Steven Shaw), Robert Symonds (Mr. Shaw), Margaret Hilton (Mrs. Burnett), Pauline Flanagan (Mrs. Shaw), Malcolm McDowell (Andrew Shaw), John C. Vennema (Colin Shaw)
  A drama in 2 acts and 4 scenes. The action takes place at the present time in the living room of Mr. and Mrs. Shaw's house in the north of England.

(MTC/DownStage) Tuesday, Nov. 27,–Dec. 22, 1984 (30 performances)
HUSBANDRY by Patrick Tovatt; Director, Jon Jory; Set, David Jenkins; Costumes, Marcia Dixcy; Lighting, F. Mitchell Dana; Props, Renee Gahn, David Warren; Wardrobe, Winsome McKoy; Stage Managers, Johnna Murray, Anne S. King
CAST: Gloria Cromwell (Dee), Richard Hamilton (Les), James Rebhorn (Harry), Deborah Hedwall (Bev)
  The action takes place in an old farmhouse on an evening in early spring, and is performed without an intermission.

(The Space at City Center) Tuesday, Dec. 11, 1984–Jan. 13, 1985 (37 performances)
MESSIAH by Martin Sherman; Director, David Leveaux; Set, Tony Straiges; Costumes, Linda Fisher; Lighting, James F. Ingalls; Composer, Robert Dennis; Assistant to Director, Bruce Colville; Sound, Jill Merzon; Props, Ted Altschuler, David Warren; Wardrobe, Otis Gustafson; Makeup, Kevin Hanley; Wigs, David Laurence; Stage Managers, William Chance, Karen Armstrong
CAST: Diane Venora (Rachel), Verna Bloom (Rebecca), Karen Ludwig (Tanta Rose), David Warrilow (Reb Ellis), Mark Blum (Asher), Margaret Gibson (Sarah)
  A drama in two acts. The action takes place during 1665 in Yultishk, a small village on what was once the Ukrainian border of Poland.

(The Space at City Center) Tuesday, Jan. 22,–Feb. 24, 1985 (39 performances)
HANG ON TO THE GOOD TIMES conceived by Richard Maltby, Jr., Gretchen Cryer, Nancy Ford; Songs by Gretchen Cryer, Nancy Ford; Director, Richard Maltby, Jr.; Set/Projections, James Morgan; Costumes, Karen Gerson; Lighting, Mary Jo Dondlinger; Sound, Sound Associates; Choreography, Kay Cole; Musical Director, Cheryl Hardwick; Orchestrations/Arrangements, Cheryl Hardwick, Steven Margoshes; Assistant to Director, Stephen Lloyd Helper; Props, David Warren; Wardrobe, Otis Gustafson; Stage Managers, Peggy Peterson, Karen L. Carpenter
CAST: Terri Klausner, Cass Morgan, Don Scardino, Charlaine Woodard, Standbys: Kirsti Carnahan, Scott Robertson
MUSICAL NUMBERS: Big Bill Murphy, In a Simple Way I Love You, Strong Woman Number, You Can Never Know My Mind, Do Whatcha Gotta Do, Too Many Women in My Life, You Can Kill Love, She's My Girl, Dear Tom, Joy, Changing, Happy Birthday, Goin' Home with My Children, Mary Margaret's House in the Country, White Trash Motel, Last Day at the Job, The News, Rock Singer, Put in a Package and Sold, Lonely Lady, Blackberry Wine, Old Friend, Hang on to the Good Times
  A musical in two acts.

(MTC/DownStage) Tuesday, Jan. 29,–Feb. 23, 1985 (22 performances)
WHAT'S WRONG WITH THIS PICTURE? by Donald Margulies; Director, Claudia Weill; Set, Adrianne Lobel; Costumes, Rita Ryack; Lighting, Beverly Emmons; Props, Renee Gahn, David Warren; Wardrobe, Winsome McKoy; Stage Managers, Travis DeCastro, Marianne Cane
CAST: Florence Stanley (Bella), Evan Handler (Artie), Marcia Jean Kurtz (Ceil), Bob Dishy (Mort), Salem Ludwig (Sid), Madeline Kahn (Shirley)
  A comedy in two acts. The action takes place at the present time in a middle-class apartment in Brooklyn, NY.

Gerry Goodstein Photos

**Top Right: Pauline Flanagan, Malcolm McDowell,
Frank Grimes, Robert Symonds, John C. Vennema
in "In Celebration" Below: Deborah Hedwall,
Richard Hamilton in "Husbandry"**

Diane Venora, Mark Blum
in "Messiah"

(The Space at City Center) Monday, January 28, 1985 (1 performance only)
SUNG AND UNSUNG SONDHEIM a tribute to the works of the composer and lyricist, Stephen Sondheim;
CAST: Patricia Elliott, John McMartin
(The Space at City Center) Friday, March 8,–April 8, 1985 (37 performances)
DIGBY by Joseph Dougherty; Director, Ron Lagomarsino; Set, James Leonard Joy; Costumes, Rita Ryack; Lighting, Curt Ostermann; Sound, Lawrence White; Props, Renee Gahn, Lynn Moffat; Wardrobe, Katrina Jeffries; Winsome McKoy; Production Assistant, Sean Gavigan; Fights, J. Allen Suddeth; Stage Managers, Johnna Murray, Trey Hunt
CAST: Anthony Heald (Digby Merton), Keith Szarabajka (Harry Crocker), Bernie McInerney (Carl Evert), Roxanne Hart (Faye Greener), John Glover (Nelson Worth), Marilyn Redfield (Mrs. Grace Evert), Tony Goldwyn (Alfred Becker), Jon Polito (Lester Delehanty)

A comedy in two acts. The action takes place at the present time in and around New York City.
(MTC) Tuesday, March 19,–24, 1985 (8 performances). A Musical Development Project.
THE PORTABLE PIONEER AND PRAIRIE SHOW with Book by David Chambers; Music, Mel Marvin; Lyrics, David Chambers, Mel Marvin; Director, Stephen Zuckerman; Musical Director, Robert Grusecki; Choreography, Danute Miskinis; Costume Coordinator, Debra Tennenbaum; Lights, Kimberly Kruger; Stage Manager, Michael S. Mantel
CAST: David Asher (Tyrone), Joe Barrett (Johnny Slade), Ned Coulter (Paul/Lars), Jim Lauderdale (Karl), Nancy Mayans (Annie), Donna Murphy (Cordelia), Mary Catherine Wright (Karin)
(MTC) Tuesday March 26,–31, 1985 (8 performances). A Musical Development Project.
A BACKERS' AUDITION with Book, Music and Lyrics by Douglas Bernstein and Denis Markell; Director, Daniel Gerroll; Musical Director, William Roy; Stage Manager, Toby Simpkins
CAST: Mary Anne Dorward (Kim), Beau Gravitte (Don), John Horton (Peter), Nathan Lane (Leonard/Haji Rahaji/Jed Rubin), Phyllis Newman (Esther), Scott Robertson (Arthur), William Roy (Andrew/Musical Director), Claudette Sutherland (Nellie/Maxine Rubin)
(The Space at City Center) Tuesday, April 16,–May 19, 1985 (40 performances)
CALIFORNIA DOG FIGHT by Mark Lee; Director, Bill Bryden; Set, Santo Loquasto; Costumes, Rita Ryack; Lighting, Andy Phillips; Sound, Stan Metelits; Animals, William Berloni; Assistant to Director, Lynn Moffat; Props, Jeffrey Hilburn; Wardrobe, Winsome McKoy; Stage Managers, Scott LaFeber, Susi Mara; Casting, Deborah Brown
CAST: Mariel Hemingway (Sarah), Bruce MacVittie (Skip), Darren McGavin (Vern), Sheree North (Lillian), James Remar (Pete), Jimmy Ray Weeks (Rawley)

A drama in two acts. The action takes place at the present time on the Sacramento delta in California.
(MTC/UpStage) Wednesday, April 24,–May 11, 1985 (18 performances)
SECRETS OF THE LAVA LAMP adapted from characters and stories created by Camille Saviola; Written by Adriana Trigiani; Direction/Musical Staging, Stuart Ross; Musical Direction, Joel Silberman; Lighting, Jackie Manassee; Sound, Steven Alias; Wardrobe, Katrina Jeffries; Stage Manager, Anne S. King
CAST: Camille Saviola, Tommy Hollis, Stephen Lehew, Scott Robertson
MUSICAL NUMBERS: There's No Business Like Show Business, Three Coins in the Fountain, Della Rosa's Turn, Ten Commandments of Soul, River Deep Mountain High, Moments to Remember, I'll Follow the Boy, Catch a Falling Star, Round and Round, Temptation, Papa Loves Mambo, God Save the City

An entertainment in two acts.

Cass Morgan, Charlaine Woodard, Don Scardino,
Terri Klausner in "Hang on to the Good Times"

Roxanne Hart, Anthony Heald
in "Digby"

(clockwise) Camille Saviola, Scott
Robertson, Stephen Lehew, Tommy Hollis
in "Secrets of the Lava Lamp"

Sheree North, James Remar, Jimmie Ray Weeks,
Darren McGavin, Mariel Hemingway in "California
Dog Fight"

105

MEAT & POTATOES COMPANY
Ninth Season

Artistic Director, Neal Weaver; Administrative Director, Lisa Kofod, Andrew Sackin; Resident Lighting Designer, David L. Arrow; Studio Manager, Kevin Osborne; Press, Lisa Kofod

(Alvina Krause Theatre) Thursday, June 21,–July 22, 1984 (20 performances)
THE HOLLOW by Agatha Christie; Director, Herbert DuVal; Set, David Birn; Stage Manager, David Keats
CAST: Nan Wray (Henrietta), Cornelius Redmond succeeded by Herbert DuVal (Sir Henry Angkatell), Megan Hunt (Lady Angkatell), Tom Morrissey (Gudgeon), William Blair (John Cristow), Martha McMahon (Gerda Cristow), Bob Diamond (Edward Angkatell), Laura Neal (Midge), Patricia Denny (Doris), Marilise Tronto (Veronica), Vernon Morris (Inspector Colquhoun), Douglas Edwards (Sgt. Penny)
 A drama in 3 acts and 5 scenes. The action takes place in the garden room of Sir Henry's house. The Hollow, about 18 miles from London in early summer.
 Friday, July 27,–Aug. 19, 1984 (20 performances)
LULU by Frank Wedekind; Adapted and Directed by Neal Weaver; Costumes, Madeleine McEvoy, Rosemary Ponzo; Lighting, Janet Herzenberg; Set, Neal Weaver; Stage Managers, Walter Ulasinski, Terrence McDonnell
CAST: Lucien Douglas (Ringmaster/Alva Schon), Gwendolyn Lewis (Lulu), Richard Bourg (Dr. Schon), Douglas Tobin Edwards (Walter Schwarz/Jack), Vernon Morris (Dr. Goll/Prince Escerny/Puntschu), Ashley Shepherd (Henriette/Bianetta), Frank Nastasi (Schigold), Jeff Post (Fritz Escherich/Policeman/African Prince), Mark Rowen (Sandwich Man/Bob/Dr. Hilti), Terrence McDonnell (Newsboy/Stage Manager), Frances Ford (Countess Geschwitz), John Harnagel succeeded by Ed Hyland (Rodrigo Quast), Gerard Hausheer (Albert Hugenberg), Alan Nebelthau (Marquis), Stephanie Beswick (Magelone), Anne Gartrell (Kadidja), Toby O'Brien (Heilmann), Catherine A. Hayes (Ludmilla)
 A drama in 3 acts and 7 scenes with a prologue. The action begins in Berlin in 1892.
 Wednesday, Sept. 5,–30, 1984 (20 performances)
YOU NEVER CAN TELL by George Bernard Shaw; Designed and Directed by Neal Weaver; Stage Managers, Joseph Barry, Jill Larmett
CAST: Barbara Callander (Dolly Clandon), Neal Canavan (Valentine), Jill Larmett (Maid), Timothy Dolan (Phillip Clandon), Jean Gennis (Mrs. Clandon), Barbara Leto (Gloria), Ronald Willoughby (Fergus), Stephan Yarian (Finch), Philip Wentworth (Waiter), Joseph Barry (Waiter), Oliver Dixon (Bohun)
 A play in 3 acts and 4 scenes. The action takes place during August of 1896 at a seaside resort on the coast of torbay in Devon, England.
 Thursday, Oct. 11,–Nov. 11, 1984 (20 performances)
WHY MARRY? by Jesse Lynch Williams; Direction/Design, Neal Weaver; Costume Coordinator, Georgea Pace; Stage Manager, Tom Farrell
CAST: Karen Rizzo (Jean), John Heppenstall (Rex), Jayne Chamberlin (Lucy), Laura Neal (Helen), Terrence McDonnell (Butler), Tom Farrell (Footman), Donald Pace (Uncle Everett), Elliott Landen succeeded by Neal Weaver (Cousin Theodore), Ronald Willoughby (John), Richard McWilliams (Ernest), Doug MacCowan (Cousin Charlie), Jill Larmett (Cousin Margaret), Kenneth Gray (Uncle Willard), Karli Dwyer (Aunt Susan)
 A play in 3 acts. The action takes place at John's country house on a weekend in September of 1917.
 Friday, Nov. 23,–Dec. 23, 1984 (20 performances)
LADY WINDERMERE'S FAN by Oscar Wilde; Director/Designer, Neal Weaver; Technical Director, Tom Farrell; Costume Coordinator, Carol Squadra; Lighting, Janet Herzenberg; Stage Managers, Rocco Matone, Jill Larmett, Kenneth Gold
CAST: Jean Tafler (Lady Windermere), Ken E. Gray (Parker), Casey Kizziah (Lord Darlington), Kenneth Gold (Footman), Tessa Mills (Arabella), Babs Gray (Lady Agatha), John A. O'Hern, Jr. (Lord Windermere), Larry Morris (Arthur Bowden), Jill Larmett (Mrs. Bowden), Kathleen Darcy (Mrs. Cowper-Cowper), Carole Mailman (Lady Stutfield), Rocco Matone (Sir James Royston), Steven Georgio (Dumby), Harriet Gold (Lady Plymdale), Ursula King (Lady Jedburgh), Karli Dwyer (Miss Graham/Rosalie), John E. Brady (Hopper), Vernon Morris (Lord Augustus Lorton), Leon Head (Cecil), Nancy Killmer (Mrs. Erlynne), Douglas MacCowan (Lord Paisley), Dana Kuznetzkoff (Lady Paisley)
 A comedy in 3 acts and 4 scenes. The action takes place in early August of 1891.

Herbert Fogelson Photos

**Top Right: William Blair, Nan Wray
in "The Hollow" Below: Gwendolyn Lewis,
Lucien Douglas in "Lulu"**

**Tim Dolan, Barbara Callender
in "You Never Can Tell"**

Thursday, Jan. 10,–Feb. 10, 1985 (20 performances)

A DOLL'S HOUSE by Henrik Ibsen; Director, Herbert DuVal; Set, David Birn; Costumes, Ewa Ritchie; Lighting, Kathleen Latimer; Technical Director, Tom Farrell; Stage Manager, James H. Sweeney

CAST: Laura Neal (Nora), Sea Glassman (Helene), David Barron (Torvald), Mimi Bensinger (Kristin), John Bakos (Nils), William Ellis (Dr. Rank), Ruth Neuman (Anne Marie), Amy Crickenberger (Emmy), Benji Crickenberger (Robert), Morna Neal (Inga)

A drama in 3 acts. The action takes place in Torvald's home in a large Norwegian town in December of 1879.

Thursday, Feb. 21,–March 24, 1985 (20 performances)

A SUMMER OF EDUCATION by Neal Weaver; Director, Mr. Weaver; Costumes, Ewa Ritchie; Set, Neal Weaver; Stage Managers, James Braly, Tom Farrell, Jill Larmett

CAST: Ed Wintle (Larry), Raymond Proscia (Ben), John E. Brady (Bobby), Michael Raymond (Kevin), Stephen Weihs (Rocky), David Press (Mickey), Barbara Leto succeeded by Laura Neal (Andrea), Ken Gold (Ziggy), Edna Dix (Neighbor/Muriel), Stephanie Beswick (Kate), Jill Larmett (Mimi), Theresa Aceves succeeded by Babs Gray (Canada), Jan Meredith (Samantha), Ruth Neuman (Mrs. Mazucca)

A play in 3 acts and 9 scenes. The action takes place in a parlor-floor apartment of a brownstone in Manhattan's West 40's during June and July of a summer in the late 1950's.

Wednesday, April 10,–May 5, 1985 (20 performances)

FERRY TALES by Don and Rich Werbacher; 3 one-act comedies; Director, Judd Silverman; Set, Susan Bolles; Costumes, Liz Barcia; Sound, Jeffrey H. Allgeier, Judd Silverman; Stage Managers, Peter Andrew Rosenberg, Doug Ryan

CAST: Eugene J. Anthony, Alice Spivak

Thursday, May 16,–June 16, 1985 (20 performances)

NIGHT MUST FALL by Emlyn Williams; Designed and Directed by Neal Weaver; Costumes, Liz Barcia, Charlotte Wagster; Stage Managers, Jackie Goldhammer, Andrew R. Rosenthal

CAST: Tessa Mills (Mrs. Bramson), Jean Gennis (Olivia), Andrew Boyer (Hubert), Kathleen Darcy (Nurse Libby), Jan Meredith (Mrs. Terence), Dorothy Brooks succeeded by Barbara Callander (Dora), Joel Parsons (Inspector), Alan Brooks (Dan)

A drama in 3 acts and 5 scenes. The action takes place in the sitting room of Mrs. Bramson's bungalow in Essex, England, in the fall of 1935.

Herbert Fogelson Photos

**Right: Eugene J. Anthony, Alice Spivak
in "Ferry Tales" Above: Ed Wintle,
Michael Raymond in "A Summer of Education"
Top: John A. O'Hern, Jr. Nancy Killmer
in "Lady Windermere's Fan"**

**Richard McWilliams, Laura Neal
in "Why Marry?"**

**Alan Brooks, Tessa M. Mills
in "Night Must Fall"**

MIRROR REPERTORY COMPANY
Second Season

Artistic Director, Sabra Jones; Producing General Management, Weiler/Miller Associates; Manager, Marshall B. Purdy; Marketing/Development, John Blinstrub Fisher; Technical Director, Jess Klarnet; Props, Charlie Eisenberg; Wardrobe, Frank Sabino; Hairstylist, Teddy Jenkins; Scenic Designer, James Tilton; Stage Managers, Lewis Rosen, Nicholas Dunn, Kate Hancock; Press, Mary Bryant, Becky Flora, Susan Chicoine

(Theatre at Saint Peter's Church) Monday, January 14, 1985–May 19, 1985 (135 performances)

COMPANY: Mason Adams, Haru Aki, Margaret Barker, Kristofer Batho, Peter Bloch, Tom Brennan, Ivar Brogger, W. B. Brydon, Alexander D. Carney, Frank Comacho, Maxwell Caulfield, Randy William Charnin, Bryan Clark, Matthew Cowles, David Cryer, John David Cullum, Marc Dietrich, Michael DiGioia, William Driscoll, Brandon Ellis Doemling, Nicholas Dunn, Terry Finn, Clement Fowler, Laura Galusha, Francois de la Giroday, Rose Gregorio, Grayson Hall, Frank Hamilton, Kate Hancock, William Ha'o, Baxter Harris, Ann Hillary, Anthony Hopkins, Meg Hosey, Katharine Houghton, Timothy Jenkins, Sabra Jones, Tad Jones, Lilah Kan, Jose Kendall, Jim Knobeloch, Sofia Landon, Omar Lotayef, Joan MacIntosh, David May, Thomas McAteer, Gordon McConnell, George McGuiness, Clark Middleton, Juliet Mills, Camilla Moore, David Moreland, Nancy J. Nichols, Carrie Nye, F. J. O'Neil, Jess Osuna, Geraldine Page, James Pritchett, Phillip Pruneau, Ellis Rabb, James Rebhorn, Charles Regan, Lewis Rosen, Donna M. Sacco, Madeleine Sherwood, Fred G. Smith, Michael O. Smith, Victor Slezak, Denise Stephenson, John Strasberg, Thomas G. Waites, Todd Waring, Steven Weber

DIRECTORS: Stephen Porter, Ellis Rabb, Arthur Storch, John Strasberg, Porter Van Zandt

DESIGNERS: Rob Gorton, Gail Cooper-Hecht, Heidi Holliman, Ron Placzek, Steve Shapiro, Mal Sturchio, James Tilton

PRODUCTIONS IN REPERTORY: *The Madwoman of Chaillot* by Jean Giraudoux; Adapted by Maurice Valency; Director, Stephen Porter; Opened Jan. 14, 1985 and played 67 performances; *Clarence* by Booth Tarkington, directed by Arthur Storch; Opened Feb. 7, 1985 and played 29 performances; *Vivat! Vivat Regina!* by Robert Bolt, directed by John Strasberg; Opened March 8, 1985 and played 39 performances.

Barbara Carrellas, Henry Grossman, Martha Swope Photos

Left: Tad Jones, W. B. Brydon, Tom Brennan, Geraldine Page, David Cryer Top Left: Carrie Nye, Geraldine Page, Jane White, Madeleine Sherwood in "The Madwoman of Chaillot"

Carrie Nye, Geraldine Page, Madeleine Sherwood in "The Madwoman of Chaillot"

Jess Osuna, Baxter Harris, Geraldine Page, (Top Right) James Pritchett, Elijah
William Burkhardt, Sabra Jones in "Vivat! Vivat Regina!" Top Left: John David
Cullum, Phillip Pruneau, Geraldine Page, and (below) Page, Laura Galusha, Ivar
Brogger, Pruneau in "Clarence"

NEGRO ENSEMBLE COMPANY
Seventeenth Season

Artistic Director, Douglas Turner Ward; Managing Director, Leon B. Denmark; General Manager, Stephanie S. Hughley; Production Supervisor, John M. Lucas; Administrative Manager, William Edwards; Director of Development, Ben Patterson; Press, Burnham-Callaghan, David Lotz

(Theatre Four) Thursday, June 7,–October 14, 1984 (147 performances and 16 previews) Presented by Philip Rose, Gus Fleming, John McDonald in cooperation with The Negro Ensemble Company.

SPLIT SECOND by Dennis McIntyre; Director, Samuel P. Barton; Set, Daniel Proett; Lighting, Leo Gambacorta; Costumes, Judy Dearing; Original Music, Jimmy Owens; General Manager, Robert I. Goldberg; Casting, Lynda Watson; Wardrobe, Marie McKinney; Stage Managers, Dwight R. B. Cook, Robert Aberdeen; Press, Henry Luhrman, Terry M. Lilly, Keith Sherman, Kevin P. McAnarney. Originally produced by Amistad World Theatre.
CAST: Bill Cwikowski (Willis), John Danelle (Val Johnson), Helmar Augustus Cooper (Parker), Peter Jay Fernandez (Charlie), Michele Shay (Alea Johnson), Norman Matlock (Rusty Johnson), Understudies: Count Stovall (Val/Charlie), Marie Thomas (Alea), Irving Barnes (Rusty/Parker), Robert Aberdeen (Willis).
    A drama in two acts. The action takes place at the present time on July 4th.
    Tuesday, Nov. 13 1984,–Jan. 1, 1985 (60 performances).
DISTRICT LINE by Joseph A. Walker; Director, Douglas Turner Ward; Set, Charles Henry McClennahan; Costumes, Myrna Colley-Lee; Lighting, William H. Grant 3rd; Sound, Bernard Hall; Stage Manager, Jerry Cleveland.
CAST: Graham Brown (Actor 9), C. Dumas (Actor 6), Frankie Faison (Actor 2), Richard Gant (Actor 3), John Harnagel (Actor 1), Samuel L. Jackson (Actor 7), Saundra McClain (Actor 4), John D. McNally (Actor 10), Peggy Schoditsch (Actor 8), Larry Sharp (Actor 5)
    A drama in two acts. The action takes place at the taxi stand at the district line, the boundary between Washington, D.C., and its Maryland suburbs.
    Friday, Jan. 18,–March 10, 1985 (60 performances)
HENRIETTA by Karen Jones-Meadows; Director, Samuel P. Barton; Set, Llewellyn Harrison; Lighting, Sylvester N. Weaver; Costumes, Karen Perry; Stage Manager, Jerry Cleveland; Production Supervisor, John Mark Lucas; Music, Cornelia J. Post
CAST: Frances Foster (Henrietta), Elain Graham (Sheleeah), William Jay (Thomas)
    A play in two acts. The action takes place in Harlem.
    Saturday, April 6,–May 5, 1985 (32 performances)
TWO CAN PLAY by Trevor Rhone; Director, Clinton Turner Davis; Set, Llewellyn Harrison; Lighting, Sylvester Weaver; Sound, Bernard Hall; Costumes, Julian Asion; Stage Manager, Jerry Cleveland
CAST: Hazel J. Medina (Gloria), Sullivan H. Walker (Jim)
    A play in 2 acts and 9 scenes. The action takes place in the late 1970's in the home of Jim and Gloria Thomas in Kingston, Jamaica, West Indies.
    Thursday, May 9,–June 30, 1985 (44 performances)
CEREMONIES IN DARK OLD MEN by Lonne Elder III; Director, Douglas Turner Ward; Set, Charles Henry McClennahan; Lighting, Shirley Prendergast; Sound, Dennis Ogburn; Costumes, Judy Dearing; Production Supervisors, John Mark Lucas, Llewellyn Harrison; Stage Manager, Ed DeShae
CAST: Douglas Turner Ward (Russell Parker), Graham Brown (William Jenkins), Ruben Hudson (Theopolis Parker), Walter Allen Bennett, Jr. (Bobby Parker), Patty Holley (Adele Parker), Keith David (Blue Haven), Tracy Camila Johns (Young Girl)
    A drama in 2 acts and 4 scenes. The action takes place in the late 1950's in a barbershop in Harlem.

Bert Andrews Photos

**Top Left: Bill Cwikowski, John Danelle
in "Split Second" Below: Michele Shay,
Norman Matlock, John Danelle in
"Split Second"**

**Peggy Schoditsch, Graham Brown
in "District Line"**

Frances Foster
in "Henrietta"

Sullivan H. Walker, Hazel J. Medina
in "Two Can Play"

Douglas Turner Ward, William Jay,
Arthur French (seated) in "Ceremonies
in Dark Old Men"

Douglas Turner Ward, Graham Brown
in "Ceremonies in Dark Old Men"

NEW YORK SHAKESPEARE FESTIVAL PUBLIC THEATER

Producer, Joseph Papp; General Manager, Laurel Ann Wilson; Casting, Rosemarie Tichler; Development, Jane Gullong; Assistants to Mr. Papp, Mary Kelley Leer, Tom Ross; Associate Producer, Jason Steven Cohen; Production Manager, Andrew Mihok; Props, Joe Toland; Press, Merle Debuskey, Richard Kornberg, Barbara Carroll, Bruce Campbell, Don Summa

(Public/Other Stage) Tuesday, Oct. 2,–Nov. 25, 1984 (62 performances). Joseph Papp presents the Interart Theatre and Mabou Mines production of:
THROUGH THE LEAVES by Franz Xaver Kroetz; Translated by Roger Downey; Director, JoAnne Akalaitis; Scenery, Douglas Stein; Lighting, Frances Aronson; Dramaturg, Colette Brooks; Costumes, Kurt Wilhelm; Sound, L. B. Dallas; Technical Director, Richard Meyer; Props, Susan Block; Production Assistant, Catherine Smith; Associate Producer, Jason Steven Cohen; Supervising Producer for Interart Theatre, Byeager Blackwell; Presented in cooperation with Goethe House New York; Stage Manager, Paula Gordon
CAST: Ruth Maleczech (Annette), Frederick Neumann (Victor), Jonesey (Ralphie the dog)

A drama in two acts. The action takes place in Annette's apartment back of her butcher shop.

(Public/Newman Theater) Monday, Nov. 12,–Dec. 2, 1984 (24 performances and 39 previews)
THE BALLAD OF SOAPY SMITH by Michael Weller; Director, Robert Egan; Scenery, Eugene Lee; Costumes, Robert Blackman; Lighting, Jennifer Tipton; Music, Norman Durkee; Songs, Michael Weller; Fight Direction, B. H. Barry; Hairstylist/Makeup, Marlies Vallant; Associate Producer, Jason Steven Cohen; Stage Managers, Stephen McCorkle, Mitchell Lemsky; Props, John Masterson, Frances Smith; Wardrobe, Susan Freel
CAST: William Andrews (Maj. James Strong), Denis Arndt (Jefferson Randolph "Soapy" Smith), Nesbitt Blaisdell (Charlie "Reverend" Bowers), Larry Bryggman (Calvin Barkdull), Timothy Carhart (Billy "Red" Gibbs), Lori Tan Chinn (Pearl), Hortensia Colorado (Mrs. Whitmore), Christopher Cooper (Paul Anthony MacAleer), Jon DeVries (George Wilder), James Eckhouse (Jensen/Photographer), Pierre Epstein (Rev. Dickey), Annette Helde (Mrs. Dickey), James Hilbrandt (Jedediah "Tripod" Schultz), Cherry Jones (Kitty Chase), Olek Krupa (Fritz), Stephen Markle (Syd Dixon), Kevin McClarnon (Cpl. Egan), John C. McGinley (J. D. Stewart), Peter McRobbie (William H. "Doc" Jackson), Marjorie Nelson (Mattie Silks), E. Claude Richards (Tagish Sam), Peter Rogan (Clancy), Jimmy Smits (Frenchie Villiers), John Spencer (Burke Gallagher/Commissioner Shelbrede), Brad Sullivan (William Whitmore), Kevin Tighe (Frank Reid), Dierk Torsek (Mike Sherpy), Joseph Warren (Gov. Brady), Marisa Zalabak (Mollie Fewclothes), Nancy Waldman (Pianist)

(Public/Anspacher Theater) Thursday, Nov. 29,–Dec. 30, 1984 (38 performances and 30 previews).
LA BOHEME with Music by Giacomo Puccini; Music Supervised and Conducted by William Starobin; Orchestrations, Michael Starobin; Director, Wilford Leach; Associate Producer, Jason Steven Cohen; Adaptation and New Lyrics, David Spencer; Original Libretto, Giuseppe Giacosa, Luigi Illica, based on novel by Henri Murger; Scenery, Bob Shaw; Costumes, Jane Greenwood; Lighting, Paul Gallo; Sound, Tom Morse; Assistant Conductor, Edward Strauss; Production Assistant, Connie Drew; Props, Evan Canary, Nathaniel Hussey; Wardrobe, Hannah Murray; Wigs, Paul Huntley; Hair and Makeup, Daniel Paul Platten; Stage Managers, James Harker, Robin Herskowitz
CAST: Howard McGillin (Marcel), David Carroll/Gary Morris (Rodolfo), Keith David (Colline), Neal Klein (Schaunard), Joe Pichette (Benoit/Porter), Patti Cohenour/Linda Ronstadt/Caroline Peyton (Mimi), Cass Morgan (Musette), Merwin Goldsmith (Alcindoro), John Herrera (Maitre d'/Sweeper), Bill Carmichael (Waiter/Sweeper), Daniel Marcus (Waiter/Night Clerk), James Judy (Trumpet Vender/Head Sweeper), Marcie Shaw (Bonnet Vendor/Dairymaid), Nancy Heikin (Lady with pearls/Dairymaid), Margaret Benczak (Student/Dairymaid), Carol Dennis (Student/Dairymaid), Caroline Peyton (Student/Dairymaid), Michael Willson (Parpignol/Porter), Understudies: Margaret Benczak (Mimi), Bill Carmichael (Marcel), Carol Dennis (Musette), John Herrera (Rodolfo), James Judy (Schunard), Daniel Marcus (Benoit/Alcindoro), Michael Willson (Colline)

An opera in four acts, performed with one intermission. The action takes place in Paris.

Martha Swope Photos

**Top: (L) Ruth Maleczech, Frederick Neumann
in "Through the Leaves"** *(Donna Grey Photo)*
**(R) Christopher Cooper, Cherry Jones
in "The Ballad of Soapy Smith" Below:
Denis Arndt (L), Jon DeVries (C) in "The
Ballad of Soapy Smith"**

**Gary Morris, Patti Cohenour
in "La Boheme"**

**David Carroll, Linda Ronstadt
in "La Boheme"**

(Public/Martinson Hall) Sunday, Feb. 3,–March 31, 1985 (65 performances and 23 previews).

COMING OF AGE IN SOHO by Albert Innaurato; Directed by the author; Scenery, Loren Sherman; Costumes, Ann Emonts; Lighting, James F. Ingalls; Wardrobe, Sheri Peterson; Props, Lisa Venezia; Stage Managers, Jim Bernardi, Evan Canary
CAST: John Procaccino (Beatrice), Mercedes Ruehl (Patricia), Evan Miranda (Danny), Scott DeFreitas (Dy), Ward Saxton (Puer), Stephen Rowe (Pasquale), Michael Dolan (Trajan). A comedy in 2 acts and 3 scenes. The action takes place at the present time in Beatrice's loft in SoHo.

(Public/LuEsther Hall) Wednesday, Feb. 6,–March 10, 1985 (37 performances and 7 previews). Joseph Papp presents the Royal Court Theatre production of:

TOM AND VIV by Michael Hastings; Director, Max Stafford-Clark; Scenery and Costumes, Antony McDonald and Jock Scott; Lighting, Robin Myerscough-Walker; Associate Producer, Jason Steven Cohen; Props, Frances Smith; Wardrobe, Hannah Murray; Hairstylist, Vanessa Witt; Stage Managers, Kate Salberg, Bethe Ward
CAST: Edward Herrmann (Tom), Julie Covington (Viv), David Haig (Maurice), Michele Copsey (Louise), Margaret Tyzack (Rose), Richard Butler (Charles/William Leonard Janes), Edward Herrmann (Charles), Marion Todd
A play in 2 acts and 7 scenes. The action takes place from 1915 to 1947.

(Public/Newman Theater) Monday, March 4,–April 14, 1985 (35 performances and 11 previews).

VIRGINIA by Edna O'Brien; from the lives and writings of Virginia and Leonard Woolf; Director, David Leveaux; Scenery and Costumes, Santo Loquasto; Lighting, Arden Fingerhut; Props, John Masterson, Than Hussey; Wardrobe, Judith Holland; Production Assistant, Abbe Levin; Stage Managers, William Chance, Karen Armstrong
CAST: Kate Nelligan (Virginia), Kenneth Welsh (Virginia's father/Leonard Woolf), Patricia Elliott (Vita)
A play in two acts. The action takes place from 1882 to 1942 in London and the English countryside.

(Public/Anspacher) Tuesday, April 2,–May 19, 1985 (56 performances and 24 previews).

SALONIKA by Louise Page; Director, John Madden; By arrangement with Hume Cronyn; Set, Andrew Jackness; Costumes, Dunya Ramicova; Lighting, Paul Gallo; Associate Producer, Jason Steven Cohen; Props, Susan Prime Kappel; Wardrobe, Carol Gant; Stage Managers, Stephen McCorkle, Robin Herskowitz
CAST: Jessica Tandy (Charlotte), Elizabeth Wilson (Enid), David Strathairn (Ben), Thomas Hill (Leonard), Maxwell Caulfield (Peter)
A play in two acts. The action takes place at the present time in Greece on the beach at Salonika after a tide.

Martha Swope Photos

**Right: Margaret Tyzack, David Haig,
Julie Covington, Edward Herrmann
in "Tom and Viv"**

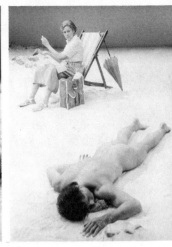

**Jessica Tandy, Maxwell Caulfield
in "Salonika"**

**Elizabeth Wilson, Maxwell Caulfield
in "Salonika"**

**Kate Nelligan, Patricia Elliott
in "Virginia"**

**Scott DeFreitas, John Procaccino
in "Coming of Age in Soho"**

113

NYSF PUBLIC THEATER

(Public/LuEsther Hall) Sunday, April 21, and still playing May 31, 1985.
THE NORMAL HEART by Larry Kramer; Director, Michael Lindsay-Hogg; Scenery, Eugene Lee, Keith Raywood; Costumes, Bill Walker; Lighting, Natasha Katz; Associate Producer, Jason Steven Cohen; Props, Frances Smith; Wardrobe, Bruce Brumage; Stage Managers, Kathleen Blair Costello, Alan R. Traynor
CAST: Phillip Richard Allen (Ben Weeks), David Allen Brooks (Bruce Niles), Brad Davis succeeded by Stephen Rowe, Joel Grey (Ned Weeks), William DeAcutis (Tommy Boatwright), Robert Dorfman (Mickey Marcus), Lawrence Lott succeeded by Tom Mardirosian (David/Hiram Keebler/Examining Doctor), D. W. Moffett succeeded by Donald Berman (Felix Turner), Michael Santoro succeeded by Richard Ziman (Craig Donner/Grady/Orderly), Concetta Tomei (Dr. Emma Brookner)
A drama in two acts. The action takes place in New York City between July 1981 and May 1984.

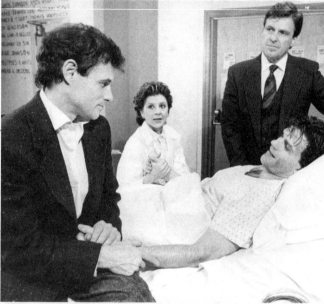

(Public/Newman Theater) Thursday, May 16,–July 28, 1985 (86 performances and 18 previews)
THE MARRIAGE OF BETTE AND BOO by Christopher Durang; Director, Jerry Zaks; Set, Loren Sherman; Costumes, William Ivey Long; Lighting, Paul Gallo; Original Music, Richard Peaslee; Hairstylist, Ron Frederick; Associate Producer, Jason Steven Cohen; Production Assistant, Roger Smith; Music Director, Amy Rubin; Stage Managers, James Harker, Pamela Singer
CAST: Joan Allen (Bette), Graham Beckel (Boo), Olympia Dukakis (Soot Hudlocke), Patricia Falkenhain (Margaret Brennan), Kathryn Grody (Emily Brennan), Bill McCutcheon (Paul Brennan), Bill Moor (Karl Hudlocke), Mercedes Ruehl (Joan Brennan), Richard B. Shull (Father Donnally/Doctor), Christopher Durang (Matt)
(Public/Martinson Hall) Tuesday, May 21,–June 23, 1985 (39 performances and 6 previews). Joseph Papp presents the Royal Court Theatre production of:
RAT IN THE SKULL by Ron Hutchinson; Director, Max Stafford-Clark; Scenery and Costumes, Peter Hartwell; Lighting, Andy Phillips; Associate Producer, Jason Steven Cohen; Wardrobe, Peter White; Props, Lisa Venezia; Stage Managers, Bethe Ward, Judi Wheway
CAST: Colum Convey (Roche), Philip Jackson (Harris), Gerard Horan (Naylor), Brian Cox (Nelson)
A drama performed without intermission.

Martha Swope Photos

**Right: Brad Davis, Concetta Tomei,
Phillip Richard Allen, D. W. Moffett
in "The Normal Heart"
Top: Kathryn Grody, Mercedes Ruehl, Patricia
Falkenhain, Bill McCutcheon, Joan Allen,
Richard B. Shull, Graham Beckel, Olympia
Dukakis, Bill Moor in "The Marriage of
Bette and Boo"**

**Brad Davis, D. W. Moffett
in "The Normal Heart"**

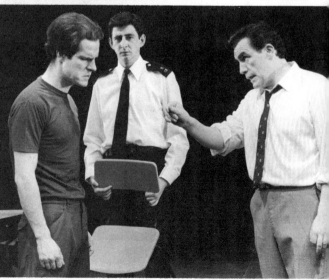

**Colum Convey, Gerard Horan, Brian Cox
in "Rat in the Skull"**

THE NEW THEATRE OF BROOKLYN/TNT

First Season

Artistic Director, Deborah J. Pope; Managing Director, Lillie Bellin; Technical Director, Jesse Herman; Assistant to Artistic Director, Paula Singer; Costume Consultant, Alyce Gilbert Briggs; Lighting Consultant, Victor En Yu Tan; Sound Consultant, Bill Dreisbach; Video Consultant, Erik Lewis; Development Consultant, Sheila Wood

(800 Union Street) TNT/The New Theatre of Brooklyn presents:
ARTISTS AND ADMIRERS by Alexander Ostrovsky; Translated by Alex Bayer, Deborah J. Pope; Director, Deborah J. Pope; Sets, Daniel Conway; Costumes, Kenneth M. Yount; Lighting, Victor En Yu Tan; Props, Paula Singer; Stage Managers, Evan A. Georges, Deborah L. Peavey
CAST: Joan Penn (Domna Pantelevna), Michael Sutton (Martin Prokofich Narokov), Elek Hartman (Prince Irakly Stratonich Dulebov), Barry Klassel (Grigory Antonich Bakin), Gayle Harbor (Alexandra Nikolavna "Negina"), Jayne Bentzen (Nina Vasilyevna Smelskaya), Alex Paul (Ivan Semyonich Velikatov), Mitchell Gossett (Pyotr Yegorich Meluzov), Hal Studer (Erast Gromilov), John Baird (Vasya), Richard Cosentino (Gavril Petrovich Migaev), Michael Blanc (Porter), Paula Singer (Waitress)
   A play in 4 acts with one intermission. The action takes place during the summer in the late 1870's in Bryakhimov, a Russian town.
   Wednesday, Nov. 14,–Dec. 9, 1984 (20 performances)
THE NEST by Franz Xaver Kroetz; Translated by Roger Downey; Director, Grafton Mouen; Sets, Christopher Barreca; Costumes, Connie Singer; Lighting, Victor En Yu Tan; Production Manager, Greg Buch; Wardrobe, Emily Pinsker; Stage Managers, Nicholas Dunn, Joseph M. Petrillo, Jr.
CAST: Amanda McTigue (Martha), Warren Keith (Kurt)
   A play in two acts. The action takes place at the present time in a city in Bavaria.
   Wednesday, March 6,–31, 1985 (20 performances)
PANTOMIME by Derek Walcott; Director, Kay Matschullat; Set, Daniel Conway; Sound, Tom Gould; Lighting, Christina Gianelli; Costumes, Marybeth McCabe; Dance Consultant, Kelvin Rotardier; Assistant Director, Susan Fenichell; Musical Arranger, Deena Kaye; Wardrobe, Emily Pinsker; Stage Manager, Kenneth Bridges
CAST: Chuck Stransky (Harry Trewe), Count Stovall (Jackson Phillip)
   A play in two acts. The action takes place during the mid 1970's at Castaways Guest Hotel in Tobago, West Indies
   Thursday, May 23,–June 16, 1985 (20 performances)
THE MAN WHO KILLED THE BUDDHA by Martin Epstein; Director, Christian Angermann; Sets, Daniel Conway; Costumes, Martha Kelly; Lighting, Victor En Yu Tan; Sound, Tom Gould; Stage Manager, Leslie Moore
CAST: Geoffrey Owens (Kenji), Bill Cohen (Misou Roshi), Ian Blackman (Ouushoo), Susana Tubert (Kenshi), Mark Diekmann (Majiama), Lenny Pass (Buddha)
   A play in two acts.

Jessica Katz Photos

**Alex Paul, Barry Klassel, Hal Studer,
John Baird in "Artists and Admirers"**

NEW YORK THEATRE STUDIO

Eighth Season

Artistic Director, Richard Romagnoli; Managing Director, Cheryl Faraone; Associate Director, James Petosa; Literary Managers, David Kelley, Elizabeth Swain; Assistant Administrator, Ann Batdorf; Press, Patt Dale Associates, Julianne Waldhelm

(New Dramatists) Thursday and Friday, September 19–20, 1984 (2 performances). The Playwrights, Actors and Directors Developmental Project presents:
PADD two works-in-progress: Stage Manager, Ann Batdorf
TOM BITES HARD WITH HIS TEETH developed and performed by Tom Carder; Director, Sam Ellis
NO DIRECTION HOME by Jack Shannon; Director, David Tochterman; Assistant Director, Margi R. Saraco
CAST: John Newton (Donald), Mark Metcalf (Hank), Cordis Heard (Grace), Daren Kelly (Milan), Claudia Sherman (Vicki), Patricia Hodges (Sarah), Michael Medeiros (Bobby)
   A play in two acts. The action takes place during September of 1980 on the Bucks County farm belonging to Donald.
(TOMI Park Royal Theatre) Wednesday, December 5–23, 1984 (15 performances)
THE MAIDS by Jean Genet; Director, James Petosa; Set, Gerard P. Bourcier; Lights, John Hickey; Costumes, Walker Hicklin; Sound, Tommy Hawk. CAST: Susan Sharkey (Claire), Patricia Oetken (Solange), Demetra Karras (Madame). The action, without intermission, takes place in the inner room of Madame's boudoir in Paris.
FOR HER OWN GOOD by Thomas G. Dunn; Director, Cheryl Faraone; Set, Gerard P. Bourcier; Lights, John Hickey; Costumes, Walker Hicklin; Sound, Tommy Hawk; Stage Managers, Michael Magenta, James Mountcastle, Ann Batdorf; Technical Director, James Mountcastle. CAST: Nick Cosco (Bruce), Susan Greenhill (Wanda), K. C. Kelly (Brian). Performed without intermission. The action takes place at the present time in a courthouse in St. Cloud, Minnesota, with flashbacks in various locales in Minnesota and California.
(TOMI Park Royal Theatre) Saturday, February 2–24, 1985 (16 performances)
THE CRUELTIES OF MRS. SCHNAYD by David Suehsdorf; Director, John Pepper; Set, Stephen McCabe; Lighting, David N. Weiss; Costumes, Gene K. Lakin; Sound, Elizabeth Heddens; Props, Gregory W. Galway; Fight Direction, Rany Kovitz; Casting, Tracy Lilienfield; Hairstylist, Justin; Production Manager, James Mountcastle; Stage Manager, Deirdre Sinnott
CAST: Frank Hankey (Garret Boynton), Charles Shaw Robinson (Douglas Boynton), Alex Neil (Madeleine Boynton), James Harper (Frehlich), Dion Anderson (Hogan)
   A dark comedy in 2 acts and 8 scenes. The action takes place at the present time in an urban brownstone house.
(TOMI Park Royal Theatre) Saturday, May 18,–June 16, 1985 (20 performances)
SUMMIT CONFERENCE by Robert David MacDonald; Director, Richard Romagnoli; Set, Gerard P. Bourcier; Lighting, John Hickey; Costumes, Walker Hicklin; Associate Costumer, Mary Gottlieb; Sound, Tommy Hawk; Hairstylist/Makeup, Michael Kriston; Production Manager, Joanna Ward; Stage Managers, Deirdre Sinnott, Maureen Barnes; Props, Charlie Eisenberg; Technical Director, Tom Pavelka; Production Assistant, George P. Choma
CAST: Laurence Overmire (Soldier), Susan Sharkey (Eva Braun), Mary Jay (Clara Petacci)
   A drama in two acts. The action takes place during the summer of 1941 in a room in the Chancellery in Berlin.

**Susan Sharkey
in "Summit Conference"
*(Gerard Bourcier Photo)***

**Charles Shaw Robinson, Frank Hankey
in "Cruelties of Mrs. Schnayd"
*(Carol Rosegg/Martha Swope Photo)***

PAN ASIAN REPERTORY THEATRE

Eighth Season

Artistic/Producing Director, Tisa Chang; Managing Director, Elizabeth A. Hyslop; Development/Marketing Director, Jon Nakagawa; Press, G. Theodore Killmer

(Actors Outlet) Wednesday, Oct. 10,–Nov. 4, 1984 (28 performances).
CHIP SHOT by Donald G. McNeil, Jr.; Director, Raul Aranas; Set, Bob Phillips; Lighting, Victor En Yu Tan; Costumes, Eiko Yamaguchi; Foliage/Landscaping, Modern Artificial; Stage Manager, Jon Nakagawa
CAST: Gerald Lancaster (Maxwell Robinson), Mel Duane Gionson (Hajime Takai), Stanford Egi (Shusaku Kamiyama), Michael Arkin (George Seitz), Susan Gordon-Clark (Patricia Riley), Bea Soong (Cindy Takai), Erol Tamerman (Howard)

A play in two acts. The action takes place on the green of the Hakone Golf Course, owned by a Japanese company, Hibachi Enterprises, in Silicon Valley, California, and at various computer terminals in the homes and offices of the characters.

Wednesday, Nov. 14,–Dec. 9, 1984 (28 performances)
STATE WITHOUT GRACE by Linda Kalayaan Faigao; Director, Aida Limjoco; Set, Robert Bullock; Lighting, Victor En Yu Tan; Costumes, Linda Taoka; Choreographer, Joy Coronel; Wardrobe, Cindy Boyle; Stage Manager, Ronald A. Koenig
CAST: Mia Katigbak (Celia), John Quincy Lee (Ponce), Adrienne Telemaque (Laura), Makalina (Rosa), Jaime Sanchez (Leon), Tysan (Nene), Ching Valdes (Lola), Luna Borromeo (Elise)

A play in two acts. The action takes place in a city in the Philippines during May of 1978.

Wednesday, Feb. 20,–March 24, 1985 (35 performances)
MANOA VALLEY by Edward Sakamoto; Director, Kati Kuroda; Lighting, Richard Dorfman; Set, Bob Phillips; Costumes, Eiko Yamaguchi; Incidental Music, Aaron Loo; Foliage/Landscaping, Modern Artificial; Stage Manager, Ronald A. Koenig
CAST: Alvin Lum (Tosh Kamiya), Carol A. Honda (Fumiko), Lori Tanaka (Debbie, their youngest daughter), Stanford Egi (Spencer, their son), Lily Sakata (Laura, their eldest daughter), Jeffrey Akaka (Toku, Laura's husband), Mel Duane Gionson (Uncle Aki, Tosh's brother), Kati Kuroda (Auntie Tomi, Aki's wife), Eric Miji (Nobu, their son), Barbara Pohlman (Susan, Nobu's wife)

A comedy performed without intermission. The action takes place in the back yard of Tosh's home in Manoa Valley on the island of Oahu, Hawaii, during August of 1959, the year of statehood.

Wednesday, April 17,–May 12, 1985 (28 performances)
EAT A BOWL OF TEA by Ernest Abuba; Based on novel by Louis Chu; Directors, Ernest Abuba, Tisa Chang; Set, Alex Polner; Lighting, Richard Dorfman; Costumes, Eiko Yamaguchi; Stage Manager, Ronald A. Koenig
CAST: Tom Matsusaka (Wong Wah Gay), Ron Nakahara (Lee Gong), Michael G. Chin (Ben Loy), Les J. N. Mau (Chong Loo), Donald Li (Ah Song), Richard Lee-Sung (Fay Lo), Elizabeth Sung (Mei Oi), Mary Lum (Wong Eng Shee), Sandy Hom (Wong Chuck Ting)

A drama in 2 acts and 10 scenes. The action takes place in 1949 in Chinatown, New York City.

Carol Rosegg Photos

Jaime Sanchez, Makalina, and
Above: John Lee, Mia Katigbak,
Luna Borromeo in "State without Grace"

Bea Soong, Erol Tamerman and
Top Left: Stanford Egi, Gerald Lancaster,
Mel Duane Gionson in "Chip Shot"

Ron Nakahara, Les J. N. Mau, Donald Li, Richard Lee-Sung, and (Top Right) Elizabeth
Sung, Mary Lum in "Eat a Bowl of Tea" Top Left: Carol A. Honda, Lily Skata, Kati
Kuroda in "Manoa Valley"

THE PEARL THEATRE COMPANY
Premiere Season

Artistic Director, Shepard Sobel; Company Manager, Susannah Hewson; Development, Juan C. Dandridge; Dramaturg, Dale Ramsey; Production Assistant, Kathleen Ireton; Press, Robert Goodman

(Nameless Theatre) Thursday, October 11–28, 1984 (16 performances)
THE MERCHANT OF VENICE by William Shakespeare; Director, Shepard Sobel; Scenery, James Noone; Costumes, Wallace G. Lane, Jr.; Lighting, Edward R. F. Matthews; Sound, Richard Sirois; Technical Director, Ronald Selke; Stage Managers, Robert Verini, Richard Buchsbaum
CAST: James Nugent (Antonio), Pinkney Mikell (Salerio), Peter G. Morse (Salanio), Kenneth Meseroll (Bassanio), Patrick Turner (Lorenzo), Robert Zukerman (Gratiano), Joanne Camp (Portia), Robin Westphal (Nerissa), Shelley Frew (Bellanca), Joel Bernstein (Shylock), Eric R. Moreland (Prince of Morocco), Robert Emmet (Launcelot/Tubal), Frank Geraci (Old Gobbo/Duke of Venice), Christopher Lonstrup (Leonardo), Laura Margolis-Region (Jessica), Michael Govan (Prince of Arragon/Jailer). Performed with one intermission.
    Saturday, November 3–25, 1984 (16 performances)
THE MOLLUSC by Hubert Henry Davies; Director, Henry Fonte; Set, James Noone; Costumes, Wallace G. Lane, Jr.; Sound, Richard Sirois; Technical Director, Ronald Selke; Assistant Director, Susan Farwell; Stage Manager, Lee J. Copenhaver
CAST: Robin Leslie Brown (Miss Roberts), Jesse Caldwell (Mr. Baxter), Donnah Welby (Mrs. Baxter), Dugg Smith (Tom Kemp)
    A play in three acts. The action takes place in Mrs. Baxter's sitting room in the early summer of 1911.
    Friday, Nov. 30,–Dec. 23, 1984 (20 performances)
THE THREE ZEKS by Marvin Pletzke; Set, James Noone; Lighting, Edward R. F. Matthews; Technical Director/Production Coordinator, Richard Sirois; Stage Manager, Pam Weinstein
CAST: Rose Stockton (Masha), David Pierce (Ivan), Frank Geraci (Alexander)
    A comedy in two acts. The action takes place at the present time on a stage.
    Thursday, April 25,–May 24, 1985 (15 performances in repertory with "Taming of the Shrew").
ARMS AND THE MAN by George Bernard Shaw; Director, Terence Lamude; Set, James Morgan; Lighting, Edward R. F. Matthews; Sound, Richard Sirois; Costumes, Barbara Forbes; Stage Manager, Richard Buchsbaum
CAST: Robert Emmet, Bonnie Horan, Laura Margolis-Region, James Nugent, Michael M. Ryan, Rose Stockton, Robert Zukerman
    Wednesday, May 1–31, 1985 (15 performances in repertory with "Arms and the Man").
THE TAMING OF THE SHREW by William Shakespeare; Director, Bruce Cornwell; Set, James Morgan; Lighting, Edward. R. F. Matthews; Costumes, John Carver Sullivan; Stage Manager, Robert Verini
CAST: Joel Bernstein, Robin Leslie Brown, Albert Corbin, Joseph Daly, Shelley Frew, Frank Geraci, Michael Govan, Pinkney Mikell, Judith Reagan, Daniel Region, Dugg Smith, Patrick Turner, Donnah Welby, Robin Westphal

Ann Blackstock Photos

**Top Left: Joanne Camp, Joel Bernstein
in "Merchant of Venice" Below: Donnah
Welby, Jesse Caldwell, Robin Leslie Brown
in "The Mollusc"**

**Donnah Welby
in "The Mollusc"**

David Pierce, Frank Geraci, Rose Stockton in "The Three Zeks" (also Top left)
Top Right: Dugg Smith, Jude Reagan in "The Taming of the Shrew"

PLAYWRIGHTS HORIZONS
Fourteenth Season

Artistic Director, Andre Bishop; Managing Director, Paul Daniels; General Manager, James F. Priebe; Development Director, Carolyn Stolper; Special Projects, Carol Lawhon; Production Manager, Pat DeRousie; Casting, John Lyons, Amy Introcaso; Technical Director, Robert Usdin; Costumer, Laurie Buehler; Literary Manager, Eric Overmyer; Assistant to Artistic Director, Rachel Chanoff; Press, Bob Ullman, Oliver Goldstick

Wednesday, November 14, 1984–January 6, 1985 (52 performances and 25 previews)
ROMANCE LANGUAGE by Peter Parnell; Director, Sheldon Larry; Original Music and Lyrics, Jack Eric Williams; Set, Loren Sherman; Costumes, Sheila McLamb; Lighting, Jeff Davis; Sound, Scott Lehrer; Orchestrations/Musical Direction, Jack Eric Williams; Fights, B. H. Barry; Saloon Movement, Marcia Milgrom Dodge; Wardrobe, Lynn Nickels; Wardrobe/Hairdressers, Jill Anderson, Diane Swanson; Props, Virginia Addison, Gail Fitzgibbons, Thomas Beall; Stage Managers, Morton Milder, Carroll L. Cartwright
CAST: Al Carmines (Walt Whitman), Jon Matthews succeeded by John David Cullum (Huckleberry Finn), Steve Ryan succeeded by Peter Crombie (Dan'l/Lt. Varnum), Frances Conroy (Louisa May Alcott), Hechter Ubarry (Kooloo/Raincloud), William Duell (Alcott/Lonesome Charley), Cynthia Harris (Charlotte Cushman), Marcia Lewis (Emma Stebbins/Ellen Emerson/Dancehall Girl), Marc Castle (Tommy/Mme. Nash), Ben Siegler (Autie Reed), Valerie Mahaffey (Emily Dickinson), Philip Pleasants succeeded by William Hickey (Ralph Waldo Emerson/Mitch Bouyer), William Converse-Roberts succeeded by Frank Maraden (Henry David Thoreau/George Armstrong Custer), John Noonan (Tom Sawyer), Carroll L. Cartwright succeeded by David Warshofsky (Bloody Knife), Townspeople: Larry Attile, Janet Borrus, Laurence Gleason, Christopher Grove, Glenn Karant, Greg Pake, David Warshofsky, Understudies: Josh Hamilton (Huck Finn/Tom Sawyer/Kooloo/Bloody Knife), Tom Brennan (Emerson/Whitman/Alcott/Lonesome Charlie/Mitch), David Warshofsky (Thoreau/Custer/Reed/Dan'l/Varnum/Mme. Nash)
A play in 2 acts and 16 scenes. The action takes place in 1876.
Thursday, Jan. 24,–Feb. 17, 1985 (30 performances and 17 previews).
LIFE AND LIMB by Keith Reddin; Director, Thomas Babe; Set, John Arnone; Costumes, David C. Woolard; Lighting, Stephen Strawbridge; Sound, Tom Gould; General Manager, James Priebe; Assistant to Director, David Briar; Choreography, Christopher Fleming; Wardrobe, Valerie Joyce; Stage Managers, Melissa Davis, Pam Edington
CAST: Robin Bartlett (Doina), Patrick Breen (Tod), Benjamin Hendrickson (Sam/Erik), Robert Joy (Franklin Roosevelt Clagg), Elizabeth Perkins (Effie), J. David Rozsa (Chris), Thomas Toner (Jerry/Grandfather)
A dark comedy in two acts. The action takes place during the years 1952–1956.
Monday, Feb. 18,–March 3, 1985 (14 performances)
CARMINES SINGS WHITMAN SINGS CARMINES conceived and directed by Al Carmines; Lighting, David N. Weiss; Stage Manager, Carroll L. Cartwright; Poems by Walt Whitman, passages from "Romance Language" by Peter Parnell, and original passages by Al Carmines; Music and Lyrics, Abel Baer, Irving Berlin, Anne Caldwell, Al Carmines, David Epstein, Maria Irene Fornes, L. Wolfe Gilbert, Jerome Kern, Gertrude Stein, Mao Tse Tung, P. G. Wodehouse
CAST: Al Carmines; performed with one intermission.
Wednesday, April 10,–28, 1985 (26 performances). The Foundation of the Dramatists Guild's production of:
THE YOUNG PLAYWRIGHTS FESTIVAL: Producing Director, Peggy C. Hansen; Sets, Loren Sherman; Costumes, Jennifer von Mayrhauser; Lighting, Stephen Strawbridge; Production Coordinator, Melissa Davis; Sound, Scott Lehrer; Stage Managers, M. A. Howard, Kate Stewart. *"Field Day"* by Leslie Kaufman; Directed by Don Scardino; with Stephen Ahern (Man #1), Robert Joy (Man #2). *"Sonata"* by Elizabeth Hirschhorn; Director, Shelly Raffle; with Jonathan Harold Gabriel (Little Boy), Wendy Rockman (Little Girl), John Spencer (Joseph Wallace), Stacey Glick (Lisa Amory), Robin Groves (Judy Amory), John Martinuzzi (Clark Amory), Brian Smiar (Man's Voice/Chief). *"True to Life"* by Marc Ratliff; Director, Ben Levit; with Steven Flynn (Dallas), Don Plumley (Max), Lucinda Jenney (The Woman), Brian Smiar (Jack). The action takes place at the present time on a Sunday afternoon in October at Jack's Supper Club Bar and Grill in a small town in South Dakota. *"The Ground Zero Club"* by Charlie Schulman; Director, John Ferraro; with Thomas Ikeda (Tourist), Tom Mardirosian (Guard), Bill Schoppert (Voice/Bob), Elizabeth Berridge (Angela), Larry Joshua (Sal), Polly Draper (Fiona), Lucinda Jenney (Tanya). The action takes place later tonight on the Observation Deck of the Empire State Building.
Wednesday, May 22,–June 16, 1985 (15 performances and 15 previews).
FIGHTING INTERNATIONAL FAT by Jonathan Reynolds; Director, David Trainer; Set, Tony Straiges; Costumes, Rita Ryack; Lighting, Frances Aronson; Sound, Scott Lehrer; Production Manager, Carl Mulert; Stage Managers, M. A. Howard, Peter J. Downing; Production Assistant, Jane Roth; Wardrobe, Mary Jestice; Props, Maureen Boler
CAST: Jessica Walter (Rosalind Gambol), Ann McDonough (Vi Wickers), Ruth Jaroslow (Lillian Rapkin), B. Constance Barry (Auntie Pram), Stephen Ahern (Jacques LaFace), John Gabriel (Shep Bradley Diedricksen), Lisa Banes (D. Raleigh Bell)
A comedy in two acts. The action takes place at the present time in the Versailles Room of Olney's, an elegant New York City hotel.

Philip Pleasants, Marcia Lewis, and (top)
Cynthia Harris, Valerie Mahaffey, Al
Carmines in "Romance Language"

Elizabeth Perkins, Robert Joy
in "Life and Limb"

Gerry Goodstein Photos

Robert Joy, Stephen Ahern
in "Field Day" Top: Al Carmines

Don Plumley, Steven Flynn, Brian Smiar,
Lucinda Jenney in "True to Life" Top: Larry
Joshua, Elizabeth Berridge, Polly Draper,
Bill Schoppert in "Ground Zero Club"

Lisa Banes, John Gabriel
in "Fighting International Fat"

John Gabriel, Jessica Walter
in "Fighting International Fat"
(Susan Cook Photos)

121

Lawrence Joshua, Maureen Silliman
in "Blue Window"

THE PRODUCTION COMPANY

Eighth Season

Artistic Director, Norman Rene; Managing Director, Abigail Franklin; Production Supervisor, Margi Rountree; Technical Director, Derald Plumer; Marketing, Bill Schaeffer; Press, Jeffrey Richards Associates

(Theatre Guinevere) Tuesday, June 12,–December 9, 1984 (207 performances). Gero Organization, Force Ten Productions present the Production Company's:

BLUE WINDOW by Craig Lucas; Director, Norman Rene; Set, Loy Arcenas; Lighting, Debra J. Kletter; Costumes, Walker Hicklin; General Management, Gero Communications, Erik Murkoff, Amy Miller; Props/Sound, Bob Morrissey; Stage Manager, M. A. Howard

CAST: Maureen Silliman (Emily), Lawrence Joshua (Tom), Randy Danson (Libby), Matt Craven (Norbert), Jane Galloway (Boo), Brad O'Hare (Griever), Margo Skinner (Alice), Understudies: Susan Blommert, Dan Butler

Sunday, Jan. 13,–27, 1985 (14 performances and 26 previews)

PRIVATE SCENES by Joel Homer; Director, Maggie L. Harrer; Set, Andy Stacklin; Costumes, Nan Cibula; Lighting, Barbara DuBois; Sound, Nat Fast, Terry Hunter; Casting, Hughes/Moss; Technical Director, Russ Stevens; Stage Manager, Chris Fielder

CAST: Michael French (Young Man), Donna Snow (Young Woman)

A play in two acts. The action takes place at the present time.

Thursday, Jan. 31,–Feb. 18, 1985 (22 performances)

LEVERAGE/BABY STEPS with Sets by Loy Arcenas; Costumes, Walker Hicklin; Lighting, David N. Weiss; Stage Manager, Paula Gordon. "*Leverage*" by Ara Fitzgerald; Director, Carey Perloff; Text, Richard Appleman; Music, Max Rapkin, Perry Iannone; with Ara Fitzgerald, Lesley Wise, Candace Derra, Lesley Farlow, Erin Martin, Jane E. Macdonald, Coco McPherson, Barbara Sieck Taylor "*Baby Steps*" by Deborah Fortson; Director, Steve Seidel; Performed by Miss Fortson.

Wednesday, March 13,–April 14, 1985 (35 performances)

WALK THE DOG, WILLIE by Robert Auletta; Director, Norman Rene; Set, Mike Boak; Costumes, Walker Hicklin; Lighting, Debra J. Kletter; Sound, David Gotwald; Dramaturg, Colette Brooks; Fight Choreography, Richard Randig; Technical Director, Russ Stevens; Assistant to Director, John Swanbeck; Props, Susan Block; Stage Manager, Jack Doulin

CAST: Larry Bryggman (Bijou Billins), Amy Steel (Jennifer), Evan Thompson (Browfield), Lilene Mansell (Rose Billins), Kathleen Mahony-Bennett (Lou Ann), Dan Butler (Ronnie Billins), William Converse-Roberts (Willie)

A dark comedy in two acts. The action takes place at the present time somewhere in the midwest on a Saturday morning.

Peter Cunningham Photos

Donna Snow, Michael French
in "Private Scenes"

Donna Snow, Michael French
in "Private Scenes"

Larry Bryggman, Amy Steel in "Walk the Dog, Willie" *(Jean-Paul Picard Photo)*
Top Left:
Leslie Wise, Ara Fitzgerald in "Leverage" Top Right: Ara Fitzgerald in "Babysteps"

QUAIGH THEATRE

Tenth Season

Artistic Director, Will Lieberson; Managing Director, Peggy Ward, Anna Elman; Administrative Consultant, Anna Ellman; Production Coordinator, Ruth Preven; Development, Iris Posner; Sound, George Jacobs; Press, Max Eisen, Maria Somma, Madeline Rosen, Henry Luhrman Associates, Susan Bloch Company

(Harold Clurman Theatre) Saturday, June 23,–Aug. 12, 1984 (44 performances)
SACRAMENTS by Jo Ann Tedesco; Director, Sherwood Arthur; Producer, Richard Mancini; Set, Bob Phillips; Lighting, Harry F. Sangmeister; Costumes, Maureen Hogan; Stage Managers, Sheila Bam, Joanna Allen
CAST: Julie Pepper (Ginevra), Gregory Salata (Father Michael), Kricker James (Bishop), Richard Dahlia (Rocco), Judith Scarpone (Carmella), Marcia Savella (Stacy), Denise Assante (Delia), Vera Lockwood (Ma), Cosmo Canale (Vinnie), Rutanya Alda (Ern), Rosanne Sorrentino (Young Ginevra), Max Cantor (Frank), Dina Mattei (Carla)
A dramatic comedy in three acts. The action takes place from 1946 through 1960.
(Quaigh Theatre) Saturday, Oct. 27,–Nov. 17, 1984 (20 performances)
MAN ENOUGH by Patty Gideon Sloan; Director, Steve McCurdy; Props, Milo Kevin Sloeter, Penny Robson; Lighting, Clark Middleton; Stage Managers, Michelle E. Tatum, Chuck Ferrero, Nereida Ortiz
CAST: Bruce King (Joey Delaney), Florence Anglin (Josie Delaney), Ron Woods (Donal Delaney), Kerry Kienzle (Kit Delaney), Jack O'Reilly (Jack Delaney), Alissa Alban (Sheila McCardle), Michael Dalby (Tom McCardle), Dan Brady (Father Frank Quinn)
A drama in 2 acts and 4 scenes. The action takes place at the present time in the Delaney home.
Wednesday, Nov. 28,–Dec. 16, 1984 (20 performances)
AN OCCASION OF SIN by Deborah Lundy; Director, Will Lieberson; Set, Thomas Wood; Lighting, Donnalee Katz; Stage Manager, Nancy Rutter; Producers, Ruth Preven, Judith Rubin
CAST: Keith Michl (Robert Hayden), Susan Monts (Armeson Kazan), Mike Champagne (Father Edward), Howard Mungo (Attorney), Pat Squire (Nellie), Robert Haufrecht (Guard)
A drama in two acts.
Saturday, December 29,–31, 1984.
DRAMATHON '84: 57 hours of continuous theatrical entertainment. Producers, Michelle E. Tatum, Ted Mornell; Set, Lisa Watson; Lighting, Deborah E. Matlack; Sound, George Jacobs; Production Coordinator, Anne Cowett; Production Consultants, Al Brower, Adam Kraar; Stage Managers, Saundra L. Guglieme, A. J. Geddes, Lucia J. Minguia, Karen Christino, Sharon L. Reich, Elizabeth Dreyer, Jim Griffith.
ENTERTAINMENT: "The Shaved Monkey" by Charles Pulaski; Director, Joel Winston; with David Braselman, Laura Christi, Karen Leslie Gerst, Forest Hamilton, Al Nazario Hunter, April Lang, Peter Lang, Marion Covit. "Really Rosie" with Book by Maurice Sendak; Music and Lyrics, Carole King; Director, Jean Carillo; with Donna Donaldson (Rosie), Roseanne Guccione (Chicken Soup), Ed Freidman (Pierre), Jill Conklin (Alligator), Nina Gabriele (Kathy), Benny Longarino (Johnny) "Courage" by Christine Nieland; Director, Carl Arnold; with Robert Haufrecht (Neil), Elizabeth Pearson (Arlene), Robin Tate (Timmy), John Galluzzi (Larry), Frank Montella (Senator), Conni Brunner (Helene), Robin Tate (Wayne). "A Pretty Blue" by Resa Alboher, Noreen Ellis, Daniel Donnelly; Director, Resa Alboher; with Daniel Donnelly (Paul), Laura Rebecca (Claire), Joe Weston (Alan). "The Pelican" by August Strindberg; Director, Peter Hardy; with Mark Campbell, Mary Cushman, Maryann Ronksley, Simon Reynolds, Ann Wilson. "Still Beat Noble Hearts" by Laurie James; Director, Clifton James; with Laurie James, Margaret Fuller. "A Good Time" by Ernest Thompson; Director, Leslie (Hoban) Blake; with Susanne Frazer (Mandy), Jeff Breslaur (Rick), Marty Fluger (Voice). "Simon of Cyrene" by Joseph Hart; Director, Richard Trousdell; with Harry Mahnken (Simon), Ronald Willoughby (Thomas), Karen Christino (Mira), Bill Pullman (Reuben), Frank Powers (Soldier). "The Actress and the I. R. S." by Dick Zybtra; Director, Bruce Biggins; with Raymond Reichenberg (Don), Christina Roberts (Greta). "Down the Drain" by Steve Shilo; Director, Stewart Schwartz; with Debrah Walsh, Edmund Day, Gus Demos, Wendy Matthews. Vincent Gerardi in cabaret. "Parkchester Oval" by Stephen Holt who directed; with Virginia Aquino (Didi), Jeffrey Marcus (Joey), Ellaxis Smith (Policewoman). Patsy Meck & Bob Rumnock. "Convulsions: A Neuro Comedy" by Wendy Marie Goodman; Director, Charles Rudd; with Christine Onterlante (Mimi), Leo Farley (Dr. Fitz), John Harnion (Dan), Sal Tassone (Tom), Phillip Stansburg (Prof. Cortex), Staci Jacobson, Susan Cicarelli, Matthew Rudd (Doctors). "Siblings" by Demmy Tambakos; Director, Cynthia Stokes; with Kevin Floeter (Michael), Karen Rizzo (Jean). "Configurations" by Kent R. Brown; Director, Fern Bachman; with Adele Cabot (Karen), Michael Barbary (Andrew), Rachel Hancock (Sandra), Pete Palazo (Leon). "Hopscotch" by Israel Horovitz; Director, Cynthia Marie; with Carmel Callan (Elsa), Rema Portelli (Will). "Food" by Ross Maclean; Director, Ellen Nickles. "Trial Run" by John Mighton; Director, David Pratt; with Edward Hyland (Stewart), Marcus Olson (DeWayne). "Happy Hour" by Poty Oliveira; Director, Allen Frame; with Mary Kozy, Butch Walker, Frank Franza, Laurence Rawlins, Susan Willet. "Ladies Room" by Kassianni Bradoc; Director, Sheldon Deckelbaum; with Miriam Miller, Keith A. Bradoc, Mary Elizabeth Michel, Marilyn Lerche, Sarah Dupuy, David Benioff, Sheldon Deckelbaum, Melanie Jeanne Bradoc, Estelle Wallach. "Rosaline" by Michael Hill; Director, Will Cantler; with Michael Hill (Ben), Anne Newhall (Rosaline). "Egomania" by Peter LaVilla and directed by him; with Ron Leir (Herbie), Denise Cintron (Marge), Hank Henry

(Maurice), Meg Masse (Lily), Paul Kamfe (Andre), Ed Greene (Morgan), Barbara Sobczyk (Lesley). "Shakespeare: Our Contemporary" by Becca Mavnery, Joe Millet; Director, Linda M. Pilz. "Mrs. Claus to the Rescue" by Steven Ottfinoski; Directors, George Hansel, Mary Lang; Music, Karl Blumenkranz; with Richard Abair (Santa), Mary Lang (Mrs. Claus), George Hansel (Shopkeeper), Jaime Baroni (Elmer), Eileen Toth (Egbert). "Storytime" by Mary Lang; with Richard Abair, Kate Ernst, George Hansel, Mary Lang. "The Alexandra Municipal Reading Library" by Saragail Katzman; "The Night Before Christmas" by Clement Moore; Directors, Dina Hoffman, Carol Strauss; with Deena Hoffman, Carol Strauss; "Sunset" by Ruth Pearl; Director, Michelle Schacherer; with Joniruth White (Lionel), Ralph Douglas (Berthel). "The Judgement of Paris" by Risa Victoria Greenberg; with Debi L. Hawkins, Ron Golding, Janelle Keane, John Blair, Debra Cardona, Elizabeth Cade, Timothy Durkin, Robert Fama, Mike Jankowitz. "Winning the Angry American River Race" by Denise Springer; Director, Ellen Lewis. "Metamorphosis" an adaptation of Kafka's short story by Ralph Hunt; Director, Gregg L. Steben; with Tom Morrissey (Mr. Samsa), Harriet Bigus (Mrs. Samsa), Anita Montgomery (Gretta), John David Barone (Albert). "Who's Holding the Elevator" by Tony DeNonno, Donald Margolies; with Lois Barth (Phillis), David Dellinger (Michael), Edna Dix (Audrey), Ron Greene (Peter), Vera Lockwood (Rosalie), Frank Nastasi (Sam), Devon O'Brien (Marilyn), Daniel Freedman (Marvin), Robert S. Gregory (Walter), Olivia Negron (Cynthia). "Third Singles" by Thomas G. Dunn; Director, Liz Wright; with Ben Stiller (Michael), Merit MacKay (Coach). "Present Company" directed by Robert Martin; with Leslie Ann Welles, Harry Peerce, Robert Raines Martin, Shane Franz, Stephanie Hofer, Roy Cohen, Don Kaplan. "Nurse on Terror Island!!!" by Doris Knight; Adapted and Directed by Susan Vosburgh; with Alex Bernstein, Jeanne Willcoxon, Susan Cargill. "The Man with the Flower in His Mouth" by Luigi Pirandello; Director, Lou Jacob; with Lou Jacob (The Man), Bruce Kerman (Commuter), Greta Donovan (Wife). "Funs-a-Pop-in'" written and directed by Tom Murphy. "The Man with the Flower in His Mouth #2" by Luigi Pirandello; Director, Muriel Burre; with Michael Field (Man), Terrence Frawley (Commuter). "Stage Directions" by Israel Horovitz; Director, Gary Canier; with Steve Skrovan (Richard), Kathi Levitan (Ruth), Virginia Thomas (Ruby). Ann Berman. "The Lady in 5" by James Himelsbach; Director, G. Michael Trupiano; with Paul Spencer (Nick), Susan Crippen (Arlene). "A Dim Capacity for Wings" by William Thompson; Director, Craig Butler; with Jane Hamilton (Miss Hall), Gene Morra (Charley), Scott Sherman (Scott). "No Stone Left Unturned" by Mitchell S. Kobren; Directed by author; with Dennis Wit (Lester/Benny), Barry Greenberg (Michael), Betsy Wingfield (Grandmother), Nicolas Glaeser (Robbie), Marianne McNamara (Mrs. Ferguson), Debra Zane (Gloria). "Holding Out" written and directed by Adam Kraar; with Phiamma Elias (Nora), Timothy Hunter (Kurt), Bill Watkins (Cupid). "The Snore Therapist" by Steve Shilo; Director, Rita Tiplitz; with John Mean (Dr. Xavier), Kitty Dunn (Miss Zener), Richard Dahlia (Youngblood). "The Lady Wants No Children" by Oliver Goldstick; Director, Scoobie Patterson; with Barbara Lehman (Charlie), Kricker James (Braverman). "A Short Visit to El Salvador" by James Castagna; with James Castagna (Priest), Leslie Duncan (Woman). "Total Honesty" by Kricker James; Director, Mr. James; with JoAnn Watkins (Karen), Bill Frischman (Herb). "Pornography Is More Honest Than Teaching Any Day" by Marvin D. Resnick; Director, Mr. Resnick; with Judy Cole (Ruby), Karl Schroeder (Harry), Mel Silverman (Doc), Gary Singer (Mark), Roman Brice (James). "A Hell of a Heavenly Time" by Matthew Witten; Director, Barbara Head; with Richard Spore (Dr. Marcus), Ed Royce (Bill). "Sweet Sweet Monique" by George Ghirlando; Director, James Manos, Jr.; George Ghirlando (Dr. Lombardi), Wendy Nute (Mrs. Jacobson). "The Beauty Show Part I" by Karen Fox, Amielle Zemach; Director, Amielle Zemach; with Karen Fox. "It's All in the Eyes" by Ray Alvin; with Rick Dean, Ray Alvin. "Barbie Don't Got Nappy Hair" by Charles Dumas; Director, Meleesa Wyatt; with Howard Mungo (Cliff), Susan Stralion (Ann), Victoria Platt (Rosa), Jeanette Freeman (Thelma), Alexandra Dumas (Selma). "The Love Vodoo" by Novalynne Ellis; Director, Renee Gahn; with Renee Gahn (Yvonne), Kathy Rogers (Marie). "Longfellow Returns" with Humphrey Davis. "Born Again American" by James T. McCartin; Director, C. C. Catanese; Kala Kaminsky (Jane), Terri Kehoe (Madeline), David Gilbert (Tom), Michael Juzwak (Henry), Charlie Sullivan (George), Gordon Kupperstein (Pat). "Medusa in the Suburbs" directed by David Steven Rappoport; Director, Alan Langdon; with Mary Tharp (Marietta). "Ratman and Wilbur" by Jules Feiler; Director, Charles Gemmill; with Alex Wipf (Ratman), Daniel Nuden (Wilbur), Anne Pasquale (Kathy). "Muzeeka" by John Guare; Director, Elizabeth Margid; with Doug Tompos (Jack), Henry Dardenne (#2), Connie Brenner (Sally-Jane), Ellen McQueen (Evelyn). "It's Time" by Richard Cory; Director, Robert Watson. with Ric E. Anderson (Bob), Julia Glander (Jane), Eric Kramer (John), Nick Pippin (David), Leslie Quinn (Jill), Paul Ravich (Jack). Nancy Molnar. "The Card Table" byMichael Ladenson, and directed by him; with Thomas Mills (Jason), John Ewanuik (Squash), David Castro (Tony), John Lawton (Vito), Greg Wood (John), Susan Cinoman-Castro (Sarah). "12:21 P.M." by F. J. Hartland; Director, Peter Gordon; with John Wool, Tennyson Bendwell, Maureen Quigley. Bruce Vernon Bradley. "An Irish New Year with Synge & Dunsany" directed by Carole Start; "The Jest of Hahalaba" by Lord Dunsany; with Ron Keith (Sir Arthur), Richard Drumm (Snaggs), Richard Creamer (Alchemist), Mary Barto (Hahalaba). "In the Shadow of the Glen" by John M. Synge; with Richard Creamer (Dan Burke), Mary Barto (Nora), Ron Keith (Tramp), Richard Drumm (Michael)., Lana Forrester. Happy New Year!

Tuesday, April 2,–May 19, 1985 (36 performances)
BLESSED EVENT by Manuel Seff and Forrest Wilson; Director, Will Lieberson; Producers, Ruth Preven, Judith Rubin; Set, Thomas R. Wood; Lighting, Deborah Matlack; Costumes, Lillian Pan; Sound, George Jacobs; Stage Manager, Ann M. Chitwood
CAST: Jack Mahoney (Alvin), John Barone (Tommy), Rende Rae Norman (Miss Stevens), Susan Monts (Gladys), Lee Moore (George), Paul Hart (Louis), Mary Ellen Brady (Miss Baumann), Richard Dahlia (Herbert), George Ghirlando (Emil), John Dorish (Frankie), Lezlie Dalton (Amelia), Belinda Munsell (Dorothy), Joyce Renee Korbin (Mrs. Roberts), Dickson Shaw (Sam), James A. Pyduck (Reilly), Robert Haufrecht (Cooper), Gene Morra (Boldt), Louie Mustillo (Louis DeMarco), Patrick Ferraro (Joe), Charles Gemmill (Policeman), Pat Freni (Detective), Jerry Silverstein (Announcer)

A comedy in 3 acts, and a prologue. The action takes place in 1930 in an office of "The Daily Express".

**Right: Gregory Salata (C) and cast
in "Sacraments"**

**Keith Michl, Susan Monts, Pat Squire
in "An Occasion of Sin"**

**Rende Rae Norman, Lee Moore, Jack Mahoney
in "Blessed Event"** *(Adam Newman Photo)*

125

ROUNDABOUT THEATRE
Nineteenth Season

Artistic Director, Gene Feist; Managing Director, Todd Haimes; Development, Shelley Jane Grossberg; Marketing, Susan B. Grossman; Literary Manager, Eileen Cowel; Business Manager, Ellen Richard; Casting and Research, Mitzi Metzl-Pazer; Technical Director, Patrick Kelly; Costumes, Richard Hieronymus; Musical Director/Sound, Philip Campanella; Press, Adrian Bryan-Brown

(Roundabout Stage One) Thursday, July 12,–September 2, 1984 (71 performances and 27 previews).
COME BACK, LITTLE SHEBA by William Inge; Director, Paul Weidner; Set, Lowell Detweiler; Costumes, Jeanne Button-Eaton; Lighting, Judy Rasmuson; Sound, Philip Campanella; Stage Managers, Mimi Apfel, Kathy J. Faul, Matthew Mundinger, Debbie Larkin; Production Assistants, Mimi Cohen, Terry Perkins, Sonja Dove, Lorraine Algozer; Casting, David Tochterman
CAST: Philip Bosco (Doc), Shirley Knight (Lola), Mia Dillon (Marie) succeeded by Kate Hopkins (Marie), Kevin Conroy (Turk), William Newman (Postman/Elmo Huston), Patricia O'Connell (Mrs. Coffman), Michael Corbett (Milkman), Steven Weber (Bruce)
  A drama in 2 acts and 3 scenes. The action takes place in Doc and Lola's home in a run-down neighborhood of a mid-western city.
(The Triplex) Wednesday, October 17,–November 4, 1984 (32 performances)
SHE STOOPS TO CONQUER by Oliver Goldsmith; Director, Daniel Gerroll; Set, Robert Thayer; Costumes, Eloise Lunde; Lighting, Allen Lee Hughes; Sound, Philip Campanella; Wigs, Charles LoPresto, Richard Hieronymus; Props, Gary Wissner; Stage Managers, Kathy J. Faul, Matthew Mundinger; Press, Solters/Roskin/Friedman, Joshua Ellis, Adrian Bryan-Brown, Keith Sherman, Cindy Valk
CAST: Kaye Ballard (Mrs. Hardcastle), E. G. Marshall (Mr. Hardcastle), Nathan Lane (Tony Lumpkin), Tovah Feldshuh (Kate Hardcastle), Cynthia Dozier (Constance Neville), W. Erik Maeder, Derek Conte (Fellows at inn/Servants), Maggi-Meg Reed (Pimple), Norman Snow (Marlow), John Bedford-Lloyd (Hastings), Dane Knell (Diggory), Matthew Mundinger (Roger), Gordon Chater (Landlord/Sir Charles Marlow)
  A comedy in two acts. The action occurs in the English countryside at a place over 50 miles west of London in September of 1774.
(Haft Theatre) Sunday, December 22, 1984–February 3, 1985 (53 performances). Moved to Broadway March 21, 1985.
A DAY IN THE DEATH OF JOE EGG by Peter Nichols; Director, Arvin Brown; Set, Marjorie Bradley Kellogg; Costumes, Bill Walker; Lighting, Ronald Wallace; Sound, Philip Campanella; Stage Managers, Kathy J. Faul, Matthew Mundinger; Production Assistant, Debbie Larkin
CAST: Jim Dale (Bri), Stockard Channing (Sheila), Tenney Walsh (Joe), Joanna Gleason (Pam), Gary Waldhorn (Freddie), Margaret Hilton (Grace)
  A comedy in two acts. The action takes place on a winter evening of the late 1960's in the living room of Bri's and Sheila's home.
(New Roundabout Theatre) Wednesday, February 13,–March 17, 1985 (55 performances)
THE PLAYBOY OF THE WESTERN WORLD by J. M. Synge; Director, Joe Dowling; Set, Michael Sharp; Costumes, A. Christina Giannini; Lighting, Judy Rasmuson; Sound, Philip Campanella; Stage Managers, Kathy J. Faul, K. Siobhan Phelan
CAST: Kate Burton (Margaret "Pegeen Mike" Flaherty), Jarlath Conroy (Shawn Keogh), Rex Everhart (Michael James Flaherty), Danny Sewell (Jimmy Farrell), Stephen Daley (Philly Cullen), Ken Marshall (Christopher "Christy" Mahon), Caroline Kava (Widow Quin), Brenda Foley (Susan Brady), Leslie E. Daniels (Honor Blake), Maggi-Meg Reed (Sara Tansey), James Greene (Old Mahon), W. Erik Maeder, David Spaulding (Villagers)
  A comedy in 3 acts. The action takes place near a village on the coast of Mayo, Ireland, at the turn of the century.
  Wednesday, March 27,–May 12, 1985 (55 performances).
AN ENEMY OF THE PEOPLE by Henrik Ibsen; English version by Frank Hauser with Anna Bamborough; Director, Frank Hauser; Set, Bob Mitchell; Costumes, A. Christina Giannini; Lighting, Dennis Parichy; Sound, Guy Sherman; Stage Managers, K. Siobhan Phelan, Matthew Mundinger
CAST: Barrett Heins (Billing), Ruby Holbrook (Katrine Stockmann), Paul Sparer (Peter Stockmann), Mark Capri (Hovstad), Roy Dotrice (Dr. Thomas Stockmann), DeVeren Bookwalter (Capt. Horster), Janet Zarish (Petra Stockmann), Bart Acocella (Morten Stockmann), Sean H. M. Reynolds (Eilif Stockmann), Jack Bittner (Morten Kiil), Townspeople: Robert Brownstein, Jared Roy, Alex Stuhl, Brian Tomlinson, Understudy: Luke Reiter
  A drama in 5 acts performed with 2 intermissions. The action takes place in a small Norwegian town in the 1880's.
  Wednesday, May 22,–July 7, 1985 (56 performances).
THE VOICE OF THE TURTLE by John Van Druten; Director, Robert Berlinger; Set, Michael Sharp; Costumes, Bary Odom; Lighting, Ronald Wallace; Sound, Philip Campanella; Casting, David Tochterman; Stage Managers, Matthew Mundinger, K. Siobhan Phelan; Press, Solters/Roskin/Friedman, Joshua Ellis, Adrian Bryan-Brown, Keith Sherman, Cindy Valk, Jackie Green
CAST: J. Smith-Cameron (Sally Middleton), Patricia Elliott (Olive Lashbrooke), Chris Sarandon (Bill Page)
  A comedy in 3 acts and 6 scenes. The action takes place over a weekend in early April of 1943 in an apartment in the East Sixties, near Third Avenue, in New York City.

Mia Dillon, Philip Bosco, and (above) Shirley Knight, Philip Bosco in "Come Back, Little Sheba"

Tovah Feldshuh, Kaye Ballard, Nathan Lane, E. G. Marshall (seated) in "She Stoops to Conquer"

Martha Swope Photos

**Stockard Channing, Jim Dale
in "Joe Egg"**

**Patricia Elliott, J. Smith-Cameron, Chris
Sarandon in "Voice of the Turtle"**

**Paul Sparer, Ruby Holbrook, Roy Dotrice,
Janet Zarish in "An Enemy of the People"**

**Kate Burton, Ken Marshall
in "Playboy of the Western World"**

**John Glover, Carol Kane
in "Linda Her and the Fairy Garden"**

THE SECOND STAGE
Fifth Season

Artistic Directors, Robyn Goodman, Carole Rothman; Managing Director, Rosa I. Vega; Associate Director, Andrew Farber; Casting, Simon/Kumin; Production Supervisor, Kim Novick; Literary Manager/Dramaturg, Kim Powers; Technical Director, Dale Harris; Administrative Associate, Beth Clearfield; Production Associate, John Moser; Press, Richard Kornberg

(Walter McGinn/John Cazale Theatre) Tuesday, June 19,–July 1, 1984 (30 performances)
LINDA HER and THE FAIRY GARDEN by Harry Kondoleon; Director, Carole Rothman; Sets, Andrew Jackness; Lighting, Frances Aronson; Costumes, Mimi Maxmen; Sound, Gary Harris; Hairstylist, Antonio Soddu; Produced in association with Tony Kiser; Production Manager, Kristina Kinet; Music, Gary Fagin; Props, John Thew; Wardrobe, David Craven; Stage Managers, Robin Rumpf, Stacey Fleischer, Amanda Marks
CAST: *"Linda Her"*: Brooke Adams (Carol), Patrick Kilpatrick (Matt), Brenda Currin (Janet), Tannis Vallely (Hillary). The action takes place in the middle of the night in the bedroom of a summer house. *"The Fairy Garden"*: Anne Lange (Dagney), John Glover (Roman), Mark Soper (Mimi), Carol Kane (The Fairy), Robert Weil (Boris), Rick J. Porter (Mechanic). The action takes place on a summer afternoon in a garden.
Monday, November 26,–December 31, 1984 (46 performances)
SHORT EYES by Miguel Pinero; Director, Kevin Conway; Produced in association with Tony Kiser; Set, David Jenkins; Lighting, Marc B. Weiss; Costumes, V. Jane Suttell; Sound, Gary Harris; Fight Direction, J. Allen Suddeth; Assistant Director, Nancy Panzarella; Wardrobe, Clare Gosney; Props, Jefferson Sage; Stage Managers, Paul Schneeberger, Laura Heller
CAST: Paul Calderon (Juan), Bari K. Willerford (Morrison), Larry Fishburne (Ice), Ving Rhames (Omar), David Patrick Kelly (Longshoe), Reggie Montgomery (El Raheem), Arnaldo Santana (Paco), Esai Morales (Cupcakes), Richard Bright (Nett), Michael O'Keefe (Davis), John Bentley (Allard)
A drama in two acts and epilogue. The action takes place in the dayroom of one of the floors in a house of detention.
Sunday, March 31,–April 14, 1985 (34 performances)
THE VIENNA NOTES by Richard Nelson; Director, Carole Rothman; Sets, Andrew Jackness; Lighting, Frances Aronson; Costumes, Shay Cunliffe; Sound, Gary Harris; Hairstylist, Antonio Soddu; Special Effects, Jauchem & Meeh; Props, Patricia Hoffman; Stage Managers, Kit Liset, Sondra R. Katz, Maggie Zellner
CAST: Mia Dillon (Georgia), Lois Smith (Rivers), James Noble (Stubbs), Gwyllum Evans (Gunter) Performed without intermission. The action takes place in an intimate hotel in Vienna, and in a country house outside Vienna.
Tuesday, May 28,–June 9, 1985 (39 performances)
JUNO'S SWANS by E. Katherine Kerr; Director, Marsha Mason; Set, Kate Edmunds; Lighting, Frances Aronson; Costumes, Ann Roth; Sound, Gary Harris; Music and Lyrics, Julie Janney; Technical Director, William B. Allison III; Assistant to Director, Nancy Simon; Wardrobe, Clare Gosney; Props, Richard Lollo; Stage Managers, Melody Kirkwagner, Allison Sommers, Maggie Zellner
CAST: Mary Kay Place (Cary Davis), Daniel Hugh-Kelly (Douglas Deering), Betty Buckley (Cecilia Miller)
A comedy in two acts. The action takes place at the present time in a one-room apartment in the West Seventies of Manhattan.

Stephanie Saia Photos

**Michael O'Keefe
in "Short Eyes"**

Lois Smith, Mia Dillon, James Noble in "The Vienna Notes"

Daniel Hugh-Kelly, Betty Buckley, and above
with Mary Kay Place in "Juno's Swans"

Mary Kay Place
in "Juno's Swans"

**Mark Margolis, Robin Haynes, Suzanne Ford
in "The Crimes of Vautrin"**

**Stephen Mellor, Deirdre O'Connell,
Reg E. Cathey, Olek Krupa
in "Energumen"**

SOHO REPERTORY THEATRE
Tenth Season

Artistic Directors, Jerry Engelbach, Marlene Swartz; Business Manager/Resident Stage Manager, Deborah A. Friedman; Dramaturg, Victor Gluck

(410 East 29th Street) Friday, February 1–24, 1985 (20 performances)
THE CRIMES OF VAUTRIN by Nicholas Wright; Based on novel by Honore de Balzac; Director, Carol Corwen; Sets/Costumes, Marek Dobrowolski; Lighting, Chaim Gitter; Assistant Director, Kathleen King; Hats/Wigs/Masks, Susan Ruddie; Sound, Kathleen King; Technical Director, Jennifer L. Brehn; Stage Manager, Deborah A. Friedman
CAST: Helen Zelon (Prudence/Coquart), John Shepard (Topinard/Corentin/Louchard/Bibi-Lupin), Tom Crawley (Baron Mucingen/Camusot/99), Mark Margolis (Abbe Carlos Herrera), Suzanne Ford (Esther van Gobseck), Robin Haynes (Lucien de Rubempre/Theodore Calvi), Sybil Lines (Jacqueline Collin/Katt/Countess de Serisy), Dustin Evans (Peyrade/Dr. Desplain/Count de Granville; LeBiffon), Cynthia Hayden (Lydia/Val-Noble/Mme. Camusot)
    American premiere of a play in two acts based on "Splendeurs et Miseres des Courtisanes" by Balzac.
    Friday, March 15–31, 1985 (15 performances)
ENERGUMEN by Mac Wellman; Director, Rebecca Harrison; Sets, Felix E. Cochren; Costumes, Gabriel Berry; Lighting, Dan Kotlowitz; Stage Manager, Nina Stachenfeld; "Internationale" Arrangement/Electronic Sounds, Michael S. Roth; Props, Dara O'Brien; Technical Director, Keith A. Hoovler
CAST: Reg E. Cathey (Jacques Petit), Deirdre O'Connell (Deborah Martin), Stephen Mellor (Samuel Nutley), Nicholas Saunders (Mr. Feather), Karen Young (Megan Feather), Olek Krupa (Master of Many Perfections/John Sleight), Mark Kindschi (Santa/Disciple/Waiter), Betty LaRoe (Santa/Disciple/Bartender), Kim Van Dyke (Santa/Disciple)
    Premiere of a one-act play set in 1980 at various locations in Washington, D. C.
    Friday, April 12,–May 5, 1985 (20 performances)
ALMOS' A MAN by Paris Barclay; Based on short story by Richard Wright; Director, Tazewell Thompson; Musical Direction/Arrangements, Dianne Adams; Set/Lighting, Steve Saklad; Costumes, Daniel Boike; Stage Managers, Thomas Spence, David Gaines; Technical Director, Beau Kennedy; Rehearsal Pianist, David Gaines.
CAST: LaDonna Mabry (Jenny), Todd A. Rolle (Dave), Vernon Bush (Big Boy), Todd Oleson (Jim Hawkins), Kobie Powell (Billy), Fred Hardy (Jake/Ernie), David Daly (Peach Fuzz), Raynor Scheine (Bo), Joshua Astrachan (Joe), B. F. Jefferson (Ma), David Toney (Pa), Tamara Tunie (Mabel), Paul Garrett (Fieldhand/Chain Gang/Traveler), Lewis Anthony Jordan (Fieldhand/Chain Gang/Traveler)
    Premiere of a musical drama in two acts. The action takes place on two consecutive days in the summer of 1933, on a drought-stricken patch of Arkansas farmland and some miles away in Little Rock.
    Friday, May 24,–June 16, 1985 (20 performances)
THE WINTER'S TALE by William Shakespeare; Director/Incidental Music/Songs, Anthony Bowles; Sets, Steve Saklad; Costumes, Gabriel Berry; Lighting, Dan Kotlowitz; Stage Managers, Donald L. Brooks, Carrie Breeding; Assistant Director, Jonathan Nossiter
CAST: Robert Shampain (Archidamus/Jailer/Dion/Clown/Gentleman), James Denton (Camillo/Court Officer), Frank Dwyer (Polixenes/Cleomenes), Erick Devine (Leontes/Old Shepherd), Suzanne Ford (Hermione/Perdita), Katherine Elizabeth Neuman (Mamillius/Servant/Bohemian Servant/Second Woman), Mary Testa (First Lady/Bear/Mopsa/First Woman), Sharon Watroba (Second Lady/Dorcas/Third Woman), Craig Paul Wroe (Lord/Mariner/Florizel), Steve Sterner (Antigonus/Autolycus), Helen Zelon (Paulina), Ellen Nickles (Emilia/Time)
    A romance in two parts.

Gerry Goodstein Photos

THEATER OF THE OPEN EYE

Fourteenth Season

Producing Artistic Director, Jean Erdman; Associate Artistic Director, Amie Brockway; Managing Director, Richard Heeger; Marketing/Development, William C. Martin; Production Manager/Technical Director, Adrienne J. Brockway; Press, FLT/Francine L. Trevens

(Theater of the Open Eye) Friday, Oct. 12,–Nov. 4, 1984 (23 performances)
SCAPIN by Moliere; Director, Amie Brockway; Original Music, Paul Shapiro; Set/Lighting, Adrienne J. Brockway; Costumes, David Mickelsen; Assistant Director, Alice Hale; Stage Managers, Karen Terry, Susan Banks
CAST: Mark Johannes (Octavio), Stephen Cowie (Silvester), Graeme Malcolm (Scapin), Heather Hollingsworth (Hyacintha), Edward Hyland (Argante), Richard Henson (Geronte), Mark Kapitan (Leander), Susan Banks (Zerbinetta), Anne Fox (Nerine)
    A comedy performed without intermission. The action takes place long ago in the city of Naples.
    Friday, February 8,–March 3, 1985 (22 performances)
SHE ALSO DANCES by Kenneth Arnold; Director, Amie Brockway; Composer, Nikki Stern; Choreography, Susan Tenney; Production Design, Adrienne J. Brockway; Saxophone, John Nichols; Stage Manager, Richard Costabile
CAST: James Dutcher (Ted), Susan Jacobson (Lucy)
    A play in two acts, performed without intermission.
    Friday, March 22,–April 14, 1985 (21 performances)
THE DREAM OF KITAMURA by Philip Kan Gotanda; Directed and Choreographed by Jean Erdman; Set, Adrienne J. Brockway; Design Consultant, Isamu Noguchi; Lighting, Victor En Yu Tan; Masks, Ralph Lee; Costumes, Eiko Yamaguchi; Music Composed by Origin; Stage Manager, James Sweeney
CAST: Chris Odo/Maureen Williams (Karma), James Pax (Paolo), Glenn Kubota (Sam), William Ha'o (Rosanjin), Jodi Long (Zuma), Lauren Tom (Otsu), Understudy: June Angela, Musician, Yukio Tsuiji
    A play in two acts.
    Monday, May 13,–June 2, 1985 (21 performances)
MISS JULIE by August Strindberg; Translated by Harry Carlson; Director, Kent Paul; Original Music, Michael Bacon; Scenery, William Barclay; Lighting, Phil Monat; Costumes, Adrienne J. Brockway; Choreography, Anthony Abbriano; Stage Manager, Richard Costabile
CAST: Megan Gallagher (Miss Julie), Marko Maglich (Jean), Susan Boehm (Kristine), Alexander Peck (Fiddler), Dancers: Dawn-Marie Marano, Tom Hinkley, Albert Porcius
    Performed without intermission. The action takes place in the count's kitchen on midsummer eve.

Ken Howard Photos

**Left: Susan Jacobson, James Dutcher
in "She Also Dances" Top: Heather
Hollingsworth, Graeme Malcolm, Mark
Johannes in "Scapin"**

**Jodi Long, Maureen Williams,
Chris Odo in "The Dream
of Kitamura"**

**Megan Gallagher, Marko Maglich
in "Miss Julie"**
(S & S Labs Photo)

131

WPA THEATRE
Eighth Season

Artistic Director, Kyle Renick; Managing Director, Wendy Bustard; Casting Director/Literary Advisor, Darlene Kaplan; Designer, Edward T. Gianfrancesco; Lighting, Craig Evans; Production Manager, Ross A. Wilmeth; Props/House Manager, Leah Menken; Press, Milly Schoenbaum, Marc Routh

(WPA Theatre) Wednesday, Oct. 17,–Nov. 18, 1984 (38 performances)
FEATHERTOP based on the short story by Nathaniel Hawthorne; Book, Bruce Peyton; Music and Lyrics, Skip Kennon; Director, Susan H. Schulman; Choreography, Michael Lichtefeld; Setting, Edward T. Gianfrancesco; Lighting, Craig Evans; Costumes, David Murin; Musical Direction, Sand Lawn; Props, Jennifer Burchett; Magic Consultant, Peter Maloney; Hair & Wigs, David Lawrence; Stage Manager, Mary Fran Loftus
CAST: Alexandra Korey (Rigby), David Barron (Justice Groutt), Charles Bari (Dickon), Stephen Bogardus (Lord Feathertop), Laura Dean (Polly), Jason Graae (Tom Fulham)
MUSICAL NUMBERS: The New World, Here I Am, The Incantations, They Had to Change, Spring Day, Home, One Two Three, Better, Happily the Days Are Running By, Alleluia, Marvelous Curious and Strange, Something Different, It's Only the Best Yet, The Last Incantation
   A musical in two acts. The action takes place during the springtime of the middle 1700's in the Colony of Massachusetts.
   Wednesday, Dec. 12, 1984–Jan. 13, 1985 (35 performances)
THE INCREDIBLY FAMOUS WILLY RIVERS by Stephen Metcalfe; Director, Stephen Zuckerman; Set, James Fenhagen; Lighting, Richard Winkler; Costumes, Mimi Maxmen; Music, Denny McCormick; Sound, Aural Fixation; Music Produced and Arranged by Don Markowitz, Denny McCormick; Lyrics, Stephen Metcalfe; Wigs, Bruce Geller; Stage Manager, Michael S. Mantel
CAST: Jay O. Sanders (Willy Rivers), John Bedford-Lloyd (Friend/Reporter/TV Director/Gypsy Davie/Husband), Elizabeth Berridge (Subway Girl/Friend's Wife/Reporter/Groupie), John Bowman (Beggar/Killer/TV Host/Paramedic), Lois Chiles (Mom/Reporter/Darlene), Dave Florek (Anchorman/Actor/Roadie/Trenchcoat 1/Paramedic), James McDaniel (Reporter/Goatman Jango/Cop/Trenchcoat 2/Guard), Kathy Rossetter (Subway Girl 2/Blond), Hansford Rowe (Suit/Announcer/Dad)
   A play with music in two acts.
   Tuesday, Feb. 19,–March 24, 1985 (35 performances)
THE HITCH-HIKERS by Eudora Welty; Adapted to the stage by Larry Ketron; Director, Dann Florek; Set, Edward T. Gianfrancesco; Lighting, Phil Monat; Costumes, Don Newcomb; Sound, Aural Fixation; Stage Manager, Michael S. Mantel
CAST: John Anthony Lack (Sanford), Peter Zapp (Sobby), Timothy Carhart (Tom), Elizabeth McGovern (Carol), Wyman Pendleton (Mr. Gene), William Jihmi Kennedy (Cato), Edward Cannan (Sheriff), Frances Fisher (Ruth)
   A play in two acts. The action takes place during 1939 in Mississippi.
   Tuesday, April 23,–May 19, 1985 (28 performances)
OUT OF GAS ON LOVERS LEAP by Mark St. Germain; Director, Elinor Renfield; Set, Edward T. Gianfrancesco; Lighting, Craig Evans; Costumes, Don Newcomb; Sound, Aural Fixation; Stage Manager, Michael S. Mantel
CAST: Melissa Leo (Myst), Fisher Stevens (Grouper)
   Performed without intermission. The action takes place at the present time on senior commencement night at White Oaks Academy, at Eagle Point, overlooking the New England town of Grosset Bay

Ken Howard Photos

**Top Left: David Barron, Laura Dean,
Stephen Bogardus, Charles Bari, and below:
Alexandra Korey, Stephen Bogardus
in "Feathertop"**

**John Bedford-Lloyd, Elizabeth Berridge,
Jay O. Sanders in "The Incredibly Famous
Willy Rivers"**

Lois Chiles, Kathy Rossetter,
Elizabeth Berridge, Jay O. Sanders in
"The Incredibly Famous Willy Rivers"

Frances Fisher, Elizabeth McGovern,
Timothy Carhart in "The Hitch-Hikers"

Fisher Stevens, Melissa Leo
in "Out of Gas on Lovers Leap"

Melissa Leo, Fisher Stevens
in "Out of Gas on Lovers Leap"

**John Newton, Anne Gartlan, Juliette
Kurth in "The Miser"**

**Mary Hara, Kermit Brown, Patricia
Falkenhain, Robert Gerringer
in "Home"**

YORK THEATRE COMPANY
Sixteenth Season

Producing Director, Janet Hayes Walker; Literary Manager, Ralph David Westfall; Artistic Advisors, James Morgan, John Newton; Press, Keith Sherman

(Church of the Heavenly Rest Theatre) Wednesday, November 7–25, 1984 (16 performances)
THE MISER by Moliere; Adapted by Miles Malleson; Director, Janet Hayes Walker; Scenery, James Morgan; Lighting, Mary Jo Dondlinger; Costumes, Holly Hynes; Music, Jed Feuer; Technical Director, Deborah Alix Martin; Production Manager, Molly Grose; Stage Manager, Victor Lukas
CAST: Sally Dunn (Mariane), Brian Evers (La Fleche), Philip Garfinkel (Brindavoine/Clerk), Anne Gartlan (Frosine), Timothy Hall (Jacques), Robin Haynes (Valere), David Kroll (Cleante), Juliette Kurth (Elise), John Rainer (Seigneur Anselm), Eric Schussler (Master Simon), John Newton (Harpagon), Robert Warren (La Merluche), Ralph David Westfall (Justice)
Performed in two acts and four scenes. The action takes place during one day in the house of Monsieur Harpagon in Paris in the year 1668.
Thursday, Feb. 14,–March 3, 1985 (16 performances)
HOME by David Storey; Director, Alex Dmitriev; Set, James Morgam; Costumes, Holly Hynes; Lighting, Mary Jo Dondlinger; Technical Director, Deborah Alex Martin; Production Manager, Molly Grose; Stage Manager, Nereida Ortiz
CAST: Kermit Brown (Harry), Robert Gerringer (Jack), Mary Hara (Marjorie), Patricia Falkenhain (Kathleen), Paul Perri (Alfred)
A drama in two acts.
Wednesday, March 20,–April 14, 1985 (20 performances)
THE BAKER'S WIFE based on "La Femme du Boulanger" by Marcel Pagnol and Jean Giono; Book, Joseph Stein; Music and Lyrics, Stephen Schwartz; Director, Stephen Schwartz; Musical Director, Tim Weil; Choreography, Lynne Taylor-Corbett; Scenery, James Morgan; Costumes, Holly Hynes; Lighting, Mary Jo Dondlinger; Technical Director, Deborah Alix Martin; Casting, Judy Henderson; Orchestrations, David Siegel, Kevin Stites; Dance Arrangements, Michael Abbott; Stage Managers, Susan Whelan, Victor Lukas
CAST: Florence Anglin (Therese), Gabriel Barre (Priest), Joyce Leigh Bowden (Genevieve), Pamela Clifford (Simone), Bert Fraser (Antoine), Charles Goff (M. LeMarquis), Kevin Gray (Dominique), Judith Lander (Denise), Mayla McKeehan (Inez), Paul O'Keefe (Phillipe), Gail Pennington (Nicole), Hal Robinson (Claude), Jack Weston (Aimable Castagnet)
MUSICAL NUMBERS: Chanson, Voila, Bread, Proud Lady, Gifts of Love, Serenade, Meadowlark, Any-Day-Now-Day, I Could Never Get Enough of You, Feminine Companionship, If I Have to Live Alone, New Musketeers, Where Is the Warmth?
A musical in two acts. The action takes place in a small village in the south of France.
Sunday, May 5, 1985 (One performance only)
JOAN OF ARC AT THE STAKE by Arthur Honegger; Text, Paul Claudel; Director, Janet Hayes Walker; Choreography, Rodney Griffin; Set, James Morgan; Lighting, Mary Jo Dondlinger; Costumes, Karen Gerson; Technical Director, Deborah Alix Martin, Sally Smith; Wardrobe, Robert Swasey; Sound, David Gotwald, Kurt Fischer; Stage Managers, Victor Lukas, Ivana Mestrovic; Conductor, Charles Dodsley Walker
CAST: Glenn Close (Joan of Arc), William Hurt (Brother Dominic), Mary Burgess (The Virgin), Mary Shearer (St. Margaret), Patricia Miller (St. Catherine), Marcus Haddock (Porcus/Herald/Cleric), John Ostendorf (The Ass/Herald/Voice), Jonathan Rigg (Herald/Priest), Randolph Lindel (Usher/Miller Trusty), Jane Coleman (Mother O'Barrels), Helen Donald (Child), Barbara A. Peters (Soloists), Jim Fredericks (Soloists), Gil Koppel (King of France), Julia Basile (Stupidity), Paul Pecko (King of England), Kathleen Lowry (Pride), William Gabriner (Duke of Burgundy), Mary Kathryn Barnes (Avarice), Gerry McIntyre (Death), Diane Caputo (Lasciviousness), Martha Hirschman (Duke of Bedford), Cate Caplin (John of Luxembourg), Steve Kadel (Regnault de Chartres), John Bantay (Guillaume de Flavy), The Canterbury Choral Society (Charles Dodsley Walker, Founder-Conductor), Youth Choir of the Church of the Heavenly Rest (J. Michael Bart, Director), The Day School Singers (Barbara Wright Lindow, Director)
A dramatic oratorio performed without intermission.
(Paul Mazur Theatre) Friday, May 17,–June 1, 1985 (16 performances)
CHEROKEE COUNTY by Alan Ball; Director, Roger T. Danforth; Sets, James Morgan; Costumes, Robert Swasey; Lighting, Mary Jo Dondlinger; Sound, Deena Kaye; Technical Directors, Deborah Alix Martin, Sally Smith; Stage Manager, Victor Lukas
CAST: Clark Brown (Rusty), Carol McCann (Jean Ann), Karen Sederholm (Brenda), Ellen Whyte (Jackie), Ashley Gardner (Debba), Lea Floden (Sissy), Bob Kratky (Carl)
A comedy in 3 acts. The action takes place during 1967 in Cherokee County, Georgia, in the Dog 'n' Suds Drive-in, Cherokee High School parking lot, Tommy Bradshaw's backyard.

Carol Rosegg Photos

**Top Left: John Newton, Anne Artlan
in "The Miser"**

Kevin Gray, Joyce Leigh Bowden,
Jack Weston, and (Top) Bowden,
Weston in "The Baker's Wife"

William Hurt, Glenn Close
in "Joan of Arc at the Stake"

Lea Floden, Ellen Whyte, Ashley
Gardner in "Cherokee County"

Karen Sederholm, Clark Brown
in "Cherokee County"

BLUES IN THE NIGHT

Conceived and Directed by Sheldon Epps; Choreography, Mercedes Ellington; Producing Director, Mitchell Maxwell; Presented by Blues Tours; Associate Producer, Elaine Brownstein; Vocal Arrangements, Chapman Roberts; Musical Arrangements/Orchestrations, Sy Johnson; Musical Direction, Clem Moorman; Musical Supervision; David Brunetti; Set, Randel Wright; Costumes, Patty Greer McGarity; Lighting, Doug Kolbo; Production Supervisor, Bruce Kagel; General Management, M2 Entertainment; Company Manager, Andrea Ladik; Technical Director, David Lansky; Production Assistant, Douglas Kane; Press, Jane M. Shannon. Opened Monday, March 4, 1985 in Blacksburg, Va., and closed March 24, 1985 in Woodlands, Texas. For original Bdwy production, see *Theatre World* Vol. 36.

CAST

Girl with a date .... Liz Larsen
Woman of the World .... Eartha Kitt
Lady from the road .... Carrie Smith
Saloon Singer .... Clem Moorman

MUSICAL NUMBERS: Blue Blues, Four Walls Blues, I've Got a Date with a Dream, New Orleans Hop Scop Blues, Stompin' at the Savoy, Taking a Chance on Love, It Makes My Love Come Down, Lush Life, Take Me for a Buggy Ride, Wild Women Don't Have the Blues, Lover Man, Willow Weep for Me, Kitchen Man, Low, Take It Right Back, Jams Session, Blues in the Night, Dirty NoGooders Blues, When a Woman Loves a Man, Am I Blue, Rough and Ready Man, Reckless Blues, Wasted Life Blues, Baby Doll, Nobody Knows You When You're Down and Out, I Gotta Right to Sing the Blues, Finale

A musical in two acts. The action takes place in Chicago in the late 1930's in a cheap hotel.

Terry Zinn Photos

Right: Eartha Kitt

Carrie Smith, Eartha Kitt, Liz Larsen

BRIGHTON BEACH MEMOIRS

By Neil Simon; Director, Gene Saks; Set, David Mitchell; Costumes, Patricia Zipprodt; Lighting, Tharon Musser; Company Manager, Jane Robison; Props, Patrick Harmeson; Wardrobe, Jeanne Frisbie; General Manager, Robert Kamlot; Production Supervisor, Martin Herzer; Technical Supervisor, Theatrical Services; Stage Managers, Thomas P. Carr, Lisa M. Hogarty; Press, Bill Evans, Sandra Manley, Jim Baldassare, Harry Davies. Opened Monday, Nov. 21, 1983 and still touring May 31, 1985. For original Broadway production, see *Theatre World* Vol. 39.

CAST

Eugene	Jonathan Silverman
Blanche	Barbara Caruso
Kate	Joan Copeland
Laurie	Olivia Laurel Mates[1]
Nora	Elizabeth Perkins[2]
Stanley	Mark Nelson[3]
Jack	Charles Cioffi

STANDBYS: Geoffrey Sharp (Eugene/Stanley), Wendy Gazelle (Nora), Judy Unger (Laurie), Rocky Parker (Kate/Blanche), Jack R. Marks (Jack)

A play in two acts. The action takes place in Brighton Beach, Brooklyn, NY., during September of 1937 in the home of Jack and Kate.

Succeeded by: 1. Erin Leigh Peck, 2. Wendy Gazelle, 3. Brian Drillinger

Right: (seated) Erin Leigh Peck, Barbara Caruso, Jonathan Silverman (on floor), Mark Nelson, Joan Copeland, (standing) Wendy Gazelle, Charles Cioffi

Mark Nelson, Jonathan Silverman

Joan Copeland, Charles Cioffi

CATS

Based on "Old Possum's Book of Practical Cats" by T. S. Eliot; Music, Andrew Lloyd Webber; Presented by Cameron Mackintosh, The Really Useful Co., David Geffen and the Shubert Organization; Executive Producers, R. Tyler Gatchell, Jr., Peter Neufeld; Orchestrations, David Cullen, Andrew Lloyd Webber; Musical Directors, Stanley Lebowsky, Thomas Helm; Sound, Martin Levan; Lighting, David Hersey; Design, John Napier; Associate Director/Choreographer, Gillian Lynne; Director, Trevor Nunn; Production Supervisor, David Taylor; Dance Supervisor, T. Michael Reed; Company Managers, Martin Cohen, Nina Lannan; Assistant Musical Director, Susan Anderson; General Management, Gatchell & Neufeld; Production Assistant, Jay Raibourn; Props, George Green, Jr., John Alfredo, Sr., Paul Bach; Wardrobe, Adelaide Laurino, Robert Daily; Hairstylists, Leon Gagliardi, Wayne Herndon, Jodi Denn, Linda Goggin; Wigs, Paul Huntley; Makeup, Candace Carell; Stage Managers, Jake Bell, Dan Hild, Maureen C. Donley; Press, Fred Nathan, Leslie Anderson, Anne Abrams, Bert Fink, Judi Davidson, Tim Choy. Opened in Boston's Shubert Theatre on Wednesday, Dec. 21, 1983 and still touring May 31, 1985. For original Broadway production, see *Theatre World* Vol. 39.

CAST

Alonzo/Rumpus Cat	Jamie Patterson
Bustopher Jones/Asparagus/Growltiger	Sal Mistretta
Bombalurina	Cindi Klinger
Cassandra	Charlotte d'Amboise
Coricopat	Allen Hidalgo
Demeter	Pamela Blasetti
Grizabella	Diane Fratantoni
Jellylorum/Griddlebone	Jennifer Butt
Mistoffelees	Jaime Torcellini
Munkustrap	Mark Dovey
Old Deuteronomy	Calvin E. Remsberg
Plato/Macavity	Russell Warfield
Pouncival	Barry K. Bernal
Rum Tum Tugger	Rich Hebert
Rumpleteazer	Kelli Ann McNally
Sillabub	Tina Decker
Skimbleshanks	Anthony Whigas
Tantomile	Tori Brenno
Tumblebrutus	Thomas McManus
Victoria	Susan Zaguirre
Cats Chorus	John Dewar, Janene Lovull, Bill Nolte, Susanna Wells

George Anthony Bell (center) and cast

CATS

For additional credits, see preceding listing; Musical Director, Martin Levan; Production Supervisor, David Taylor; Dance Supervisor, T. Michael Reed; Company Manager, Barbara Seinfeld; General Management, Gatchell & Neufeld Ltd.; Dance Captains, Greg Minahan, Leigh Webster; Assistant Conductor, John Berkman; Production Assistant, Beth Peterson; Props, George Green, Jr., Edward Schneck, John Alfredo, Jr.; Wardrobe, Adelaide Laurino, Dorothy Priest; Hairstylists, Carol Shurley, Henri Coultas; Stage Managers, Scott Faris, J. A. Mayo, Maureen Donley; Press, Fred Nathan, Leslie Anderson, Anne Abrams, Bert Fink, Ted Killmer, Judi Davidson, Tim Choy. Opened at the Shubert Theatre in Los Angeles, and still playing there May 31, 1985.

CAST

Alonzo/Rumpus Cat	Derryl Yeager
Bustopher/Asparagus/Growltiger	Norman A. Large
Bombalurina	Edyie Fleming
Cassandra	Leigh Webster
Coricopat	Serge Rodnunsky
Demeter	Sheri Cowart
Grizabella	Kim Criswell
Jellylorum/Griddlebone	Sally Spencer
Jennyanydots	Marsha Mercant
Mistoffelees	George De La Pena
Mungojerrie	Don Johanson
Munkustrap	Mark Morales
Old Deuteronomy	George Anthony Bell
Plato/Macavity	Jeff Adkins
Pouncival	Phineas Newborn III
Rum Tum Tugger	Michael Alan-Ross
Rumpleteazer	Kristi Lynes
Sillabub	Kathleen Dawson
Skimbleshanks	Thom Keeling
Tantomile	Adrea Gibbs Muldoon
Tumblebrutus	Kenneth Jezek
Victoria	J. Kathleen Lamb
Cats Chorus	Vincent Pirillo, Lance Roberts, Deborah Shulman, Linden Waddell

STANDBYS & UNDERSTUDIES: Gregory Donaldson/Steve Moore/Greg Minahan (Alonzo/Rumpus), Vincent Pirillo (Bustopher/Asparagus), Beth Cloninger/Karen Babcock (Bombalurina/Cassandra), Steven Moore/Dean Scott/Greg Minahan (Coriocopat), Sally Spencer (Grizabella), Karen Babcock/Deborah Shulman (Jellylorum/Griddlebone), Linden Waddell/Janie Walton (Jennyanydots), Don Johanson/Dean Scott (Mistoffelees), T. Clarke Bennett/Dean Scott/Greg Minathan (Munkustrap/Plato/Macavity), Lance Roberts (Old Deuteronomy), T. Clarke Bennett/Dean Scott (Pouncival), Steven Moore/Derryl Yeager/Greg Minahan (Rum Tum Tugger), Nikki D'Amico/Susan Carr George/Janie Walton (Rumpleteazer/Sillabub), T. Clarke Bennett/Gregory Donaldson/Greg Minahan (Skimbleshanks), T. Clarke Bennett, Dean Scott (Tumblebrutus), Karen Bobcock/Janie Walton (Victoria)
MUSICAL NUMBERS: See Broadway calendar.

Kim Criswell

CAMELOT

Book and Lyrics, Alan Jay Lerner; Music, Frederick Loewe; Devised, Staged and Directed by Richard Harris; Scenery, Tom Barnes; Lighting, Ruth Roberts; Sound, Bruce Greenhut; Additional Costumes, Michael Bottari, Ronald Case; Dance Captain/Choreographer, Norb Joerder; Musical Director, Terry James; Presented by Jamar Productions, Larry Tarnofsky, Dino J. Santangelo; General Manager, Bob Young; Company Managers, Alan Zullo, Cyndi Christian; Stage Managers, J. Thomas Vivian, Dianne Trulock, Mark Schorr; Assistant Musical Director, John Visser; Props, Glenn Belfer; Wardrobe, James M. Kabel, Shirley Bird; Production Associate, Martin Shelby; Press, Cynthia Snyder. Opened in Boston's Orpheum Theatre, Tuesday, May 15, 1984 and closed Sept. 9, 1984 in the Denver Auditorium. For original Bdwy production, see *Theatre World* Vol. 17.

CAST

Arthur	Richard Harris
Sir Sagramore	Andy McAvin
Merlyn/King Pellinore	James Valentine
Merlyn's Sprites	Nick Harvey, Norb Joerder, Phil LaDuca
Guenevere	Betsy Joslyn
Sir Dinadan	Patrick Godfrey
Nimue/Lady Sybil	Linda Milani
Nimue's Nymphs	Nancy Meadows, Sally Stotts, Martha Traverse
Lancelot Du Lac	Richard Muenz
Mordred	Mark Martino
Tom of Warwick/Young Arthur	William Thomas Bookmyer
Musician/Sir Castor of Cornwall	Dean G. Watts
Lady Anne	Mary Gaebler
Lady Margaret	Marcia Brushingham
Sir Lionel	William James
Jester	Tony Jaeger
Squire Dap/Turquine of Glenfield	Robert Ousley
Horrid	Sean Sable Belevedere
Herald	Nick Harvey
Sagramore's Squire/Sir Bliant	John Deyle
Sir Dinadan's Squire	Chip Huddleston
Lord Chancellor/Forest Merlyn	Martin Van Treuren
Court Dancer	Norb Joerder
Wenches	Darleigh Miller, Deborah Rhodes

KNIGHTS, LORDS, LADIES: Marcia Brushingham, John Deyle, Mary Gaebler, Patrick Godfrey, Nick Harvey, Chip Huddleston, Tony Jaeger, William James, Norb Joerder, Phil LaDuca, Andy McAvin, Nancy Meadows, Linda Milani, Darleigh Miller, Robert Ousley, Douglas J. Portillo, Deborah Rhodes, Sally Stotts, Martha Traverse, Martin Van Treuren, Dean G. Watts, Swings: Eric Alderfer, Karen Luschar

MUSICAL NUMBERS: Guenevere, I Wonder What the King Is Doing Tonight, The Simple Joys of Maidenhood, Camelot, Follow Me, Madrigal, C'Est Moi, The Lusty Month of May, Take Me to the Fair, How to Handle a Woman, The Jousts, Before I Gaze at You Again, If Ever I Would Leave You, The Seven Deadly Virtues, Fie on Goodness, What Do the Simple Folk Do?, I Love You Once in Silence
A musical in 2 acts and 16 scenes with prologue.

**Richard Harris
in "Camelot"**

DOONESBURY

Book and Lyrics, Garry Trudeau; Music, Elizabeth Swados; Based on comic strip "Doonesbury" by Garry Trudeau; Presented by James Walsh in association with Universal Pictures; Director, Jacques Levy; Choreography, Margo Sappington; Set, Peter Larkin; Costumes, Patricia McGourty; Lighting, Beverly Emmons; Sound, Tom Morse; Orchestrations, Elizabeth Swados; Arrangements/Musical Direction, Jeff Waxman; Casting, Juliet Taylor, John Lyons; General Management, James Walsh; Company Manager, Stanley D. Silver; Puppets, Edward G. Christie; Stage Managers, Warren Crane, Lewis Rosen, Jonathan Simmons; Props, Robert Saltzman; Wardrobe, Claudia Kaneb; Assistant to Producer, Richard Alfredo; Dance Captain, Elizabeth Sung; Press, Jeffrey Richards Associates, Solters/Roskin/Friedman Inc. Opened Friday, Oct. 12, 1984 in the Warner Theatre, Washington, D.C., and closed Nov. 11, 1984 in the Wilshire Theatre, Los Angeles, CA. For original Broadway production, see *Theatre World* Vol. 40.

CAST

Roland	Hal Robinson
Mike Doonesbury	Gregg Edelman
Mark	Stuart Bloom
B. D.	Mark T. Fairchild
Boopsie	Marin Mazzie
Zonker	Martin Moran
Duke	Paul Kandel
Honey	Elizabeth Sung
J. J.	Julie Boyd
Joanie	Laura Gardner
Provost	Jonathan Simmons
(all cast members play multiple roles)

UNDERSTUDIES: Jody Abrahams (Boopsie/Honey/J. J.), Bradford Minkoff (Mark/Mike/Zonker), Jonathan Simmons (Duke/Roland/B. D.), Judith Thiergaard (Joanie)
MUSICAL NUMBERS: Graduation, I Came to Tan, Guilty, I Can Have It All, The Chairman's Song, Just One Night, Baby Boom Boogie Boy, Another Memorable Meal, Just a House, Complicated Man, Real Estate, Mother, It's the Right Time to Be Rich, Muffy and the Topsiders.
A musical in 2 acts and 13 scenes. The action takes place at the present time in Walden, an off-off campus house in late spring.

Martha Swope Photos

**Julie Boyd, Gregg Edelman
in "Doonesbury"**

42nd STREET

Book, Michael Stewart/Mark Bramble; Based on novel by Bradford Ropes; Music, Harry Warren; Lyrics, Al Dubin; Choreography, Gower Champion; Reproduced by Karin Baker/Randy Skinner; Director, Lucia Victor from Gower Champion's original; Set, Robin Wagner; Musical Direction, Stephen Bates; Vocal Arrangements, John Lesko; Lighting, Tharon Musser; Costumes, Theoni V. Aldredge; Orchestrations, Philip J. Lang; Hairstylists, Anne Sampogna, Ron Scott, Sherri Bramiett; Props, Leo Herbert, Michael Gallagher; Wardrobe, Robin B. Robillard; Furs, Oscar Loewy; General Manager, Leo K. Cohen; Company Manager, Kim Sellon; Dance Captain, Christopher Lucas; Presented by David Merrick; Stage Managers, Harold Goldfaden, Pat Trott, David Hansen, John Salvatore; Press, Solters/Roskin/Friedman, Joshua Ellis, Cindy Valk, Adrian Bryan-Brown, Keith Sherman, Jackie Green, Morris Yuter. Opened at the Forrest Theatre, Philadelphia, Pa., Tuesday, Nov. 9, 1983, and still touring May 31, 1985. For original Broadway production, see *Theatre World,* Vol. 37.

CAST

Andy Lee	Barry Preston
Oscar	Chuck Hunnicut
Mac/Thug/Doctor	Igors Gavon[1]
Annie	Beth Leavel[2]
Maggie Jones	Bibi Osterwald[3]
Bert Barry	Don Potter
Billy Lawlor	Jim Walton[4]
Peggy Sawyer	Clare Leach[5]
Lorraine	Sandra Yarish[6]
Phyllis	Bonnie Patrick[7]
Julian Marsh	Barry Nelson
Dorothy Brock	Dolores Gray
Abner Dillon	J. Frank Lucas
Pat Denning	Randy Phillips
Thug	Al Micacchion

ENSEMBLE: Linda Marie Brenz, Marietta Clark, T. Michael Dalton, Debbie DiBiase, Deanna Dys, Suzie Jary, Monica Kelly, Wade Laboissonniere, Kim Larese, Rosemary Loar, Laura Menhart, Al Micacchion, Steven Minning, Ann Nieman, Vicky Nitchie, Doug Okerson, Tina Parise, Chris Peterson, Russell Rhodes, Richard Lee Ruth, Anne Rutter, Greg Schanuel, Jeanna Schweppe, Robin Stephens, Elizabeth Stover, Karen Toto, Mary Chris Wall, James Walski, Melodie Wolford, Carol Lynn Worcell, Michael Worcell.
UNDERSTUDIES & STANDBYS: Rosemary Loar/Marge Sires (Dorothy/Maggie), Randy Phillips (Julian), Jeanna Schweppe/Carol Lynn Worcell (Peggy), Russell Rhodes/Doug Okerson (Billy), Christopher Lucas (Bert), Al Micacchion/Greg Schanuel (Andy), Lew Resseguie (Abner/Pat), Ann Nieman/Mary Chris Wall (Annie), Jay Alger (Oscar), Suzie Jary/Deanna Dys (Phyllis/Lorraine), Ensemble: Christopher Lucas, John Salvatore, Lynn Marlowe, Brenda Pipik.
MUSICAL NUMBERS: see Broadway Calendar
Succeeded by: 1. Lew Resseguie, 2. Sandra Yarish, Denise Lor, Kevin Daly, 5. Gail Benedict, 6. Anne Rutter, 7. Ann Nieman.

Martha Swope Photos

Dolores Gray, Barry Nelson   **Barry Nelson, Gail Benedict**
(Carol Rosegg Photos)

42nd STREET

See credits for preceding listing; Musical Direction, Jack Gaughan; Hairstylist, Russell Smith; Sound, Jan Nebozenko; Company Manager, John Corkill; Dance Captain, Jon Engstrom; Props, Leo Herbert; Wardrobe, Frank Tauss; Assistant Musical Director, Edward Morris; Stage Managers, George Martin, John Grigas, William O'Brien, Luke Stallings; Press, Solters/Roskin/Friedman, Joshua Ellis, Cindy Valk, Jackie Green, Violet Welles, Jim Kerber. Opened in the Golden Gate Theatre, San Francisco, Ca., on Sunday, Feb. 24, 1985, and still playing May 31, 1985.

CAST

Andy Lee	James Dybas
Oscar	Sand Lawn
Mac/Thug/Doctor	Michael Vita
Annie	Cathy Susan Pyles
Maggie Jones	Bibi Osterwald
Bert Barry	Ted Pritchard
Billy Lawlor	Jim Walton
Peggy Sawyer	Cathy Wydner
Phyllis	Nancy Bickel
Lorraine	Bonnie Patrick
Julian Marsh	Gary Marshal
Dorothy Brock	Elizabeth Allen
Abner Dillon	Steve Lincoln
Pat Denning	Michael Dantuono
Thug	Paul Del Vecchio

ENSEMBLE: Charles E. Baker, Marcella Betz, Nancy Bickel, John Bazzell, Jim Carey, Sterling Clark, Candy Cook, Kelly Crafton, Janie Dale, Paul Del Vecchio, James Darrah, Carla Earle, Lloyd Gordon, Jill B. Gounder, Victoria Kent, Terry Mason, Susan Banks McGonegle, Lucille Naar, Jeanne O'Connell, Bonnie Patrick, Kay Perry, Anne Marie Roller, Patricia Ruck, Deborah Seitz, William Strickland, Lynn Sullivan, Scott Willis, Truett Wright.
STANDBYS & UNDERSTUDIES: Elizabeth French, Terry Mason (Dorothy/Maggie), Michael Dantuono, Jim Carey (Julian), Patricia Ruck/Cathy Susan Pyles (Peggy), James Darrah/Sterling Clark (Billy), Lloyd Gordon (Bert), John Bazzell (Andy), Michael Vita (Abner/Pat), Bonnie Patrick (Annie), Paul Del Vecchio (Mac), Donalin Patton (Phyllis/Lorraine), Edward Morris (Oscar), Ensemble: Jon Engstrom, Donalin Patton, Pamela Prescott, Luke Stallings.

Cathy Wydner (center)

LA CAGE AUX FOLLES

See credits for Broadway listing; Musical Director, Larry Blank; General Manager, Marvin A. Krauss; Company Managers, Drew Murphy, Michael Gill; Management Associates, Allan Williams, Sue Frost; Dance Captain, Bob Brubach; Props, Charles Zuckerman, Gregory Martin, Joe Schwartz, Alan Steiner; Wardrobe, Gayle Patton, Max Hager; Makeup/Hairstylist, Robert DiNiro; Press, Shirley Herz, Sam Rudy, Peter Cromarty, Pete Sanders, Gary Lawrence, Judi Davidson, Tim Choy; Stage Managers, Janet Beroza, Robert Bennett, Jay Adler. Opened in San Francisco's Golden Gate Theatre Sunday, June 10, 1984 and still touring May 31, 1985. For original Broadway production see *Theatre World* Vol. 40.

CAST

Georges	Keith Michel†
Les Cagelles:	
Dermah	Kevin Backstrom
Bitelle	Lynn Faro
Odette	Kyle Whyte
Lo Singh	Michael Jon Black
Mercedes	Randy Doney
Monique	Larry Lynd
Clo Clo	Tommy Peel
Hanna	Bill Burns
Chantal	Mark Knowles
Angelique	Cady Huffman
Nicole	Eric Underwood
Phaedra	A. Michael McKee
Francis	Bob Brubach
Jacob	Darrell Carey
Albin	Walter Charles
Jean-Michel	Joseph Breen
Anne	Mollie Smith
Poppie	Bradd Wong
Babette	Amelia Haas
Yves	Larry Wray
Paulette	Lynn Rose
Hercule	Dan McCoy
Etienne	Stephen Pender
Colette	Sylvia Rhyne
Mme. Renaud	Leslie Chain
Jacqueline	Carol Teitel
M. Renaud	Steeve Arlen
Edouard Dindon	Robert Burr
Mme. Dindon	Laurel Lockhart

UNDERSTUDIES: Stephen Pender (Albin/Renaud), Steeve Arlen (Georges/Dindon), Dan McCoy (Jean-Michel), Bradd Wong (Jacob), Amelia Haas (Mme. Dindon), Lynn Rose (Anne), Leslie Chain (Jacqueline), Flynn McGrath/Deborah Stone (Mme. Renaud/Colette/Paulette/Babette/Angelique), Wade Collings (Francis/Les Cagelles), Reece Holland (Etienne/Hercule/Poppie/Hanna/Mercedes/Yves/Phaedra), Reece Holland/Flynn McGrath (Dermah)
MUSICAL NUMBERS: see Broadway calendar
†Succeeded by Gene Barry.

Gene Barry, Walter Charles

LA CAGE AUX FOLLES

See credits for Broadway listing; Musical Director, Donald W. Chan; General Management, Marvin A. Krauss Associates; Company Managers, Mark Andrews, Michael Sanfilippo; Management Associates, Allan Williams, Jeff Capitola; Dance Captain, Shannon Lee Jones; Props, Charles Zuckerman, Paul Mazurek, Colleen Mazurek, Alan Steiner; Wardrobe, Gayle Patton, Jerry Wolf, Mario Brera; Hairstylist, Lamara Jackson; Music Coordinator, John Monaco; Associate Conductor, James May; Assistant Choreographers, Richard Balestrino, Linda Haberman; Makeup, Max Factor of Hollywood; Stage Managers, Kathleen A. Sullivan, Jeanne Fornadel, Allan Sobek; Press, Shirley Herz, Sam Rudy, Peter Cromarty, Mary Bryant, Pete Sanders, Gary Lawrence. Opened Thursday, Dec. 27, 1984 at Theatre of Performing Arts, Miami Beach, FL., and still touring May 31, 1985. For original Broadway production, see *Theatre World* Vol. 40.

CAST

Georges	Peter Marshall
Les Cagelles:	
Clo Clo	Harrison Beal
Bitelle	Deborah Roshe
Odette	John Clonts
Dermah	Louie M. Trisoliere
Monique	John Anzalone
Hanna	Keith Allen
Chantal	Philip Clayton
Angelique	Karen Byers
Nicole	Andrew A. Currie
Phaedra	Thomas C. Stoehr
Francis	Joseph L. Taylor
Jacob	Ronald Dennis
Albin	Keene Curtis
Jean-Michel	Peter Reardon
Anne	Juliette Kurth
Jacqueline	le Clanche du Rand
M. Renaud	Mace Barrett
Mme. Renaud	Melody Jones
Paulette	Leslie Ellis
Hercule	Joe Joyce
Etienne	Scott Sigler
Colette	Mary Ellen Thomas
Pepe	Bryce Ward
Mme. Dindon	Pamela Hamill
Edouard Dindon	Bob Carroll

STANDBYS & UNDERSTUDIES: Mace Barrett (Georges/Albin), Bryce Ward (Jean-Michel), John Anzalone (Jacob), Leslie Ellis (Anne), Melody Jones (Jacqueline), Bob Carroll (Georges), Scott Sigler (Dindon/Renaud), Mary Ellen Thomas (Mme. Dindon/Mme. Renaud), Mark Edward (Francis/Pepe/Etienne/Phaedra/Hanna), Michael Joseph Berglund (Hercule/Chantal/Dermah), Shannon Lee Jones (Colette/Paulette/Angelique/Bitelle), Swings: Michael Joseph Berglund, Mark Edward, Shannon Lee Jones
MUSICAL NUMBERS: see Broadway Calendar.

Peter Marshall, Keene Curtis

Martha Swope Photos

SOUTH PACIFIC

Music, Richard Rodgers; Lyrics, Oscar Hammerstein II; Book, Oscar Hammerstein II, Joshua Logan; Based on "Tales of the South Pacific" by James Michener; Director, A. J. Antoon; Choreography, Richard Levi; Scenery, Andrew Jackess; Costumes, Linda Fisher; Lighting, Paul Gallo; Orchestrations, Robert Russell Bennett; Musical Supervisor, Paul Gemignani; Musical Director, Jim Coleman; Sound, Sound Associates; Presented by Don Gregory, Jon Cutler, Irving Mansfield in association with Kenneth F. Martel and Martel Media Productions; Hairstylist, Werner Sherer; Casting, Julie Hughes/Barry Moss; General Management, Joseph P. Harris Associates; Company Manager, Kathryn Frawley; Associate Producers, Paul Levine, John Jacobs; Assistant Conductor, Marc Pressel; Props, Paul Biega, Kevin Swanke; Wardrobe, Sally D. Smith; Stage Managers, Peter Lawrence, Jim Woolley, Barrie Moss; Press, Martin Shwartz, Keith Aaron. Opened in the Dorothy Chandler Pavilion/Music Center, Los Angeles, CA., on Thursday, May 14, 1985, and closed there July 6, 1985. For original Broadway production, see *Theatre World* Vol. V.

CAST

Ngana	Ruby Cheng
Jerome	Max Barabas
Henry	Peter Yoshida
Ensign Nellie Forbush	Meg Bussert
Emile de Becque	Richard Kiley
Bloody Mary	Novella Nelson
Marcel	Peter Yoshida
Stewpot	Andrew Hammond
Luther Billis	Al Mancini
Professor	Leslie Feagan
Lt. Joseph Cable, USMC	Brent Barrett
Capt. George Brackett, USN	Walter Flanagan
Cmdr. William Harbison USN	Gary Holcombe
Yeoman Herbert Quale	Russ Jolly
Radio Operator Bob McCaffrey	Dan Shaheen
Liat	Jade Go
Lt. Buzz Adams	Al DeCristo

NURSES, NATIVES: Catherine Campbell, Mary-Pat Green, Terry Iten, Jacquey Maltby, Barbara McCulloh, Kathleen Moore, Alison Morgan
SAILORS, MARINES, NATIVES: John Aller, Al DeCristo, Leslie Feagan, Andrew Hammond, Peter Heuchling, Nick Jolley, Russ Jolly, Anthony Mastrorilli, Paul Nunes, William Ryall, Joel Sager, Dan Shaheen, Gordon Weiss
STANDBYS AND UNDERSTUDIES: Gary Holcombe (Emile), Terry Iten (Nellie), Mary-Pat Green (Bloody Mary), Leslie Feagan (Henry/Marcel/Brackett), Dan Shaheen (Cable), Nick Jolley (Billis), Jacquey Maltby (Liat), William Ryall (Harbison), Swings: Lynn Keeton, Nathan Hurlin, Jay Tramel
MUSICAL NUMBERS: Dites-moi, Cockeyed Optimist, Twin Soliloquies, Some Enchanted Evening, Bloody Mary, There Is Nothin' Like a Dame, Bali Ha'i, I'm Gonna Wash That Man Right Out of My Hair, A Wonderful Guy, Younger Than Springtime, This Is How It Feels, Thanksgiving Day Follies, Happy Talk, Honey Bun, You've Got to Be Carefully Taught, This Nearly Was Mine

A musical in 2 acts and 18 scenes. The action takes place on two islands in the South Pacific during World War II.

Richard Kiley, Meg Bussert
in "South Pacific"

SUGAR BABIES

Conceived by Ralph G. Allen and Harry Rigby; Book, Ralph G. Allen; Based on traditional material; Music, Jimmy McHugh; Lyrics, Dorothy Fields, Al Dubin; Additional Music and Lyrics, Arthur Malvin; Staged/Choreography, Ernest O. Flatt; Sketches directed by Rudy Tronto; Production supervision, Ernest O. Flatt; Scenery/Costumes, Raoul Pene du Bois; Lighting, Gilbert V. Hemsley, Jr.; Vocal Arrangements, Arthur Malvin, Hugh Martin, Ralph Blane; Music Director, Sherman Frank; Orchestrations, Dick Hyman; Dance Music Arrangements, Arnold Gross; Presented by Terry Allen Kramer, and Harry Rigby in association with Columbia Pictures; Associate Producers, Frank Montalvo, Thomas Walton Associates; General Management, Alan Wasser; Company Managers, Barbara Seinfeld, Don Joslyn, Alexander Holt, Mitzi Harder; Stage Managers, Robert Vandergriff, Kay Vance, Bill Braden, Thom Mitchell; Assistant to Producers, David Campbell; Assistant Choreographer, Eddie Pfeiffer; Associate Conductor, Jon Olson; Wardrobe, Mario Brera, Joy Macpherson-Ortiz, Lyn Gilsbach; Hairstylist, Stephen LoVullo, Antonio Belo, Mel McKinney, Grant Kocontes; Press, Henry Luhrman, Bill Miller, Terry M. Lilly, Opened at the Arie Crown Theatre, Chicago, IL, Monday, Nov. 8, 1982 and still touring May 31, 1985. For original Broadway production see "Theatre World" Vol. 36.

CAST

Mickey	Mickey Rooney
Jay	Jay Stuart
Gail	Gail Dahms†1
Mickey D	Mickey Deems
Phil	Phil Ford
Ann	Ann Miller†2
Frank	Frank Olivier
Jeff	Jeff Dunham
Gaiety Quartet	Jonathan Aronson, David Brownlee†3, Kirby Ward†4, Barry Woodruff, Hank Brunjes (Alternate)

SUGAR BABIES: Carol Ann Basch†5, Dani Brownlee, Betsy Chang†6, Kimberly Dean, Margaret Francis†7, Millie Garvey, Sarah Grove†8, Katherine Hopkins, Cindi Johnson†9, Kym Kaminsky, Melanie Montana, Susie Nelson, Andrea Rose, Kathy Skizlak, Topaz†10, Beverly Ward†11, Andrea Cohen (alternate)†12
STANDBYS & UNDERSTUDIES: Toni Kaye/Julie Miller/Jane Summerhays (Ann), Mickey Deems (Mickey), Barry Woodruff (Mickey D./Phil), David Brownlee/Dale Hensley (Jay), Katherine Hopkins (Gail)
SKITS & MUSICAL NUMBERS: A Good Old Burlesque Show, Let Me Be Your Sugar Baby, I Want a Girl, In Louisiana, I Feel a Song Comin' On, Goin' Back to New Orleans, Broken Arms Hotel, Sally, Scenes from Domestic Life, Don't Blame Me, Monkey Business, Orientale, Little Red Schoolhouse, Frank Olivier, Mme. Rentz and Her All Female Minstrels, Down at the Gaiety Burlesque, Mr. Banjo Man, Candy Butcher, I'm Keepin' Myself Available for You, Exactly Like You, Court of Last Retort, I'm in the Mood for Love, Presenting Mme. Alla Gazaza, Cuban Love Song, Cautionary Tales, I Can't Give You Anything but Love, I'm Shootin' High, When You and I were Young Maggie Blues, On the Sunny Side of the Street, Frank Olivier, You Can't Blame Your Uncle Sammy

A musical in 2 acts and 24 scenes.
†Succeeded by: 1. Julie Miller, 2. Jane Summerhays (4/2–5/31/85) during Miss Miller's recovery from knee injury, 3. Dale Hensley, 4. Gary Kirsch, 5. Carole Cotter, 6. Meridith Johnson, 7. Terry Nelson, 8. Kimberly Campbell, 9. Teresa Puente, 10. Barbara Tobias, 11. Kate Murtagh, 12. Joan Aslund

Mickey Rooney, Ann Miller
in "Sugar Babies"

Martha Swope Photos

ACT/A CONTEMPORARY THEATRE

Seattle, Washington
June 3, 1984–June 2, 1985
Twentieth Season

Producing Director, Gregory A. Falls; Producing Manager, Phil Schermer; Administrative Manager, Susan Trapnell Moritz; Marketing, Julie Anderson; Development, Ann-Marie Spata; Press, Michael Eagan, Jr.; Stage Managers, Bonita M. Ernst, Joan Kennedy

PRODUCTIONS & CASTS

TOP GIRLS by Caryl Churchill; Director, Sharon Ott; Set, Robert Dahlstrom; Costumes, Alexandra B. Bonds; Lighting, Jody Briggs; Sound, David Hunter Koch. CAST: Gayle Bellows (Griselda/Nell), Kathleen Chalfant (Isabella/Joyce/Mrs. Kidd), Megan Cole (Marlene), Mary Ewald (Lady Nijo/Jeanine), Kathryn Mesney Hetler (Dull Gret/Angie), Liann Pattison (Waitress/Win), Jeanne Paulsen (Pope)
ANGELS FALL by Lanford Wilson; Director, Fred Chappell; Set, Karen Gjelsteen; Costumes, Josie Gardner; Lighting, Rick Kennedy-Paulsen; Sound, Robert Bulkley. CAST: Clayton Corzatte (Niles Harris), Katherine Ferrand (Vita Harris), Rudy Goldschmidt (Zappy), Rene Moreno (Don Tabaha), Jeanne Paulsen (Marion Clay), Ben Tone (Father Doherty)
THIRTEEN by Lynda Myles; World Premiere; Director, Gregory A. Falls; Set, Bill Forrester; Costumes, Sally Richardson; Lighting, A. W. Nelson; Sound, David Hunter Koch. CAST: Peter Marklin (Norman), Anne O'Sullivan (Patsy), Stefan Schnabel (Marcus), Joan Shangold (Jo), Barbara Sohmers (Honey), Catherine Wolf (Eleanor)
FOOL FOR LOVE by Sam Shepard; Director, Gary Gisselman; Set/Costumes, Shelley Henze Schermer; Lighting, Donna Grout; Sound, James Verdery. CAST: Christine Healy (May), Robert Loper (Old Man), John Procaccino (Martin), Stephen Yoakam (Eddie)
THE COMMUNICATION CORD by Brian Friel; American Premiere; Director, Mel Shapiro; Set, Bill Forrester; Costumes, Sarah Nash Gates; Lighting, James Verdery; Sound, Bill Carswell. CAST: Dorothy Brooks (Susan), Mary Diveny (Nora), Katherine Ferrand (Evette), Davis Hall (Tim), Daren Kelly (Jack), Peter Lohnes (Barney), Michael Morgan-Dunne (Sen. Donovan), Liann Pattison (Claire), Understudy: Michael J. Smith
UNCLE BONSAI & NONE OF THE ABOVE with original music and improvisational comedy. Uncle Bonsai: Arni Adler, Ashley Eichrodt, Andrew Ratshin, None of the Above: Floyd Giannone, Van Buskirk, Paul Gladstone, Roberta Maguire, Barry Press, Edward Sampson, David Silverman, Andrea Stein, D. J. Wilson
A CHRISTMAS CAROL by Charles Dickens; Adapted by Gregory A. Falls; Music, Robert MacDougall; Director, Ann-Denise Ford; Set, Bill Forrester; Costumes, Nanrose Buchman; Lighting, Jody Briggs; Choreography, Susan Glass Burdick; Stage Manager, Jorie Wackerman. CAST: Elizabeth Carter (Elizabeth Cratchit), Amy Crumpacker (Martha Cratchit), B. J. Douglas (Mrs. Fezziwig), Nathan Haas (Fred), Kevin C. Loomis (Grocer), Christopher Marks (Dick Wilkens), Brian Martin (Ali Baba), Glenn Mazen (Marley's Ghost), Helene McCardle (Niece), Ursula Meyer (Belle), Jeanne Paulsen (Ghost of Christmas Past), Larry Paulsen (Fezziwig), David Pichette (Bob), Ethan Sandler (Boy Singing), Michael Santo/Peter Silbert (Scrooge), Adam Silver (Young Scrooge), Ben Silver (Master Fezziwig), Casey Smith (Peter), Lara A. Smith (Belinda), Vern Taylor (Ghost of Christmas Present), Casey Trupin (Tiny Tim), Robert John Zenk (Undertaker's Assistant)
THE PERSIAN PRINCESS by Gregory A. Falls; Director, Anne-Denise Ford; Design, Shelley Henze Schermer; Stage Manager, Jorie Wackerman. CAST: Steve Brush (Beaumont/Bahman), Melissa Gray (Perizade), Scott Honeywell (Genie/Shah), Helene McCardle (Sarah/Queen), Mitchell Patrick (Bulbul-al-Hazar), Andy Taylor (Perry/Farez)
BEAUTY AND THE BEAST by Gregory A. Falls; World Premiere; Music, Chad Henry; Director, Gregory A. Falls; Set, Shelley Henze Schermer; Costumes, Anne Thaxter Watson; Lighting, Jody Briggs; Stage Manager, James Verdery. CAST: Roderick Aird (Merchant), Gayle Bellows (Allevia), Hugh Hastings (Beast), Katherine Klekas (Gwendolen), Rikki Ricard (Alexia), Rebecca Stucki (Beauty), Bill terKuile (Gnomera)
STEP ON A CRACK by Suzan Zeder; Director, Anne-Denise Ford; Set, Bruce Jackson; Costumes, Sheryl Collins; Lighting, Donna Grout; Stage Manager, James Verderly. CAST: Gayle Bellows (Lucille), Shana Bestock (Ellie), Rikki Ricard (Lana), Daniel Singer (Frizbee), Bill terKuile (Max), Mary Thielen (Ellie's other voice)
THE ODYSSEY by Homer; Adapted by Gregory A. Falls, Kurt Beattie; Director, Jeff Steitzer; Set, Scott Weldin; Costumes, Rose Pederson; Lighting, Jennifer Lupton; Sound, David Hunter Koch; Stage Manager, James Verdery. CAST: Roderick Aird (Entinous/Eurylocus), Gayle Bellows (Penelope), Ki Gottberg (Pallas Athena), Hugh Hastings (Leodes/Perites), Kevin C. Loomis (Ktessipos/Peremides), Alvin Lee Sanders (Eurymachus/Polites), Daniel Singer (Telemachus), Bill terKuile (Odysseus)

WHAT'S IN IT FOR ME? a World Premiere musical revue; Director, Bruce Sevy; Choreography, Susan Glass Burdick; Set, Patti Henry, Wendy Ponte; Costumes, Mary Ellen Walter; Lighting, Peter Allen; Stage Manager, Bruce Elsperger; Songs by Arni Adler, Michelle Beaudry, John Engerman, Jean Burch Falls, John Gray, Suzanne Grant, Chad Henry, Shakeh Herbekian, Stephen Randoy, Andrew Ratshin, Carl Sander, Howard Weinberg; Sketches by A. M. Collins, B. J. Douglas, Joe Guppy, Roberta Maguire, Carl Sander. CAST: Jill Klein, David Hunter Koch, Liann Pattison, Mark Perry
KING LEAR by William Shakespeare; Director, Arne Zaslove; Assistant, Craig Huisenga; Musical Director, Robert Davidson; Set, Shelley Henze Schermer; Costumes, Julie James; Lighting, Phil Schermer; Stage Manager, Michael Wise. CAST: Mark Anders (Fool), John Aylward (Lear), Mark Drusch (Edmund), Allen Galli (Gloucester), Eric Hagerman (Oswald), Randy Hoffmeyer (Edgar), Daniel Mayes (King of France), David Mong (Duke of Cornwall), Stephen Randoy, Andrew Ratshin, Gretchen Orsland (Goneril), Michael V. Schauermann (Duke of Burgundy), David Stettler (Duke of Albany), Rick Tutor (Earl of Kent), Joe Vetter (Regan), Kevin Lynch (Old Man), David Mainer (Doctor), Chorus: Rex E. Allen, Susan Finque, Dylan Marshall, Frank Smith, Eric Sumearll, Robert E. Taeschner, G. Valmont Thomas, Carolyn Ayres, Kelly Cresap, Robert Ellis, Eric Newman, Micha Rice

Chris Bennion Photos

John Gilbert, Brian Hargrove, Ki Gottberg in "Amadeus"

Right Center: Jeanne Paulsen, Rudy Goldschmidt, Clayton Corzatte, Katherine Ferrand in "Angels Fall"

ACTORS THEATRE OF LOUISVILLE

Louisville, Kentucky
Twenty-first Season

Producing Director, Jon Jory; Administrative Director, Alexander Speer; Associate Director, Marilee Hebert-Slater; Sets, Paul Owen, Miklos Feher, Laura Luisa Cowell; Costumes, Marcia Dixcy, Katherine Bonner, Ann Wallace, Karen Anderson-Fields; Lighting, Jeff Hill, Geoff Korf, Joe Ragey; Props, Diann Fay, Sam Garst; Sound, James M. Bay; Technical Director, Tom Rupp; Fight Director, Steve Rankin; Composers, Ja'nos Gonda, Mark DiPalma; Production Manager, Frazier Marsh; Stage Managers, Craig Weindling, Margaret Castleman, Geoffrey T. Cunningham, Richard A. Cunningham, Phebe A. Day, Alan Duke, Cynthia A. Hood, Bob Hornung, Anne King, Larry Varvel, Chip Washabaugh, Frank Wicks; Press, Jenan Dorman, Mina S. Davis, Chris Boneau, Ginny Pfeiffer; Literary Managers, Julie Beckett, Nancy Beverly; Dramaturg, Bill Thomas; Development, James R. Luigs, Karen Phelps

COMPANY: John Anania, Walter Atamaniuk, Andy Backer, Kathy Bates, Peter Bergman, Wanda Bimson, Nesbett Blaisdell, Cheryl Lynn Bruce, Susan Bruyn, Leo Burmester, Bob Burrus, Tim Carroll, Susan Cash, Kathleen Chalfant, Thom Christopher, Lynn Cohen, Paul Collins, Melody Combs, Maury Cooper, Shelley Crandall, Leigh Curran, Richard M. Davidson, Steve Decker, Louis DiVincenti, Beth Dixon, Cara Duff-MacCormick, Alan Duke, George Dvorsky, Cornelia Evans, Lee Anne Fahey, Lanny Flaherty, Lili Flanders, Robert Foster, Patricia Frontain, Ray Fry, Sam Fulkerson, Marita Geraghty, Virgil Gibson, Janna Gjesdal, Donna Harrison, Suzanna Hay, Nina Hennessey, Gary Leon Hill, Dorothy Holland, Anna Maria Horsford, Patrick Husted, Laura Innes, Zoe Jackson, Ken Jenkins, Craig Johnson, Jessica Jean Jory, Victor Jory, Christian Kauffmann, Gretchen Kehde, Michael Kevin, George Kimmel, Rob Knepper, Sofia Landon, Raye Lankford, Larry Larson, Levi Lee, Delroy Lindo, Jodi Long, Frederic Major, Ellen Mareneck, Linda Margules, Norman Matlock, Beverly May, Dana Mills, Debra Monk, Elizabeth Moore, Joe Morton, Kelly McBride, Vaughn McBride, Christopher McCann, Steven McCloskey, Joe McCullough, William McNulty, Karen Nyre, Adale O'Brien, Will Oldham, Dink O'Neal, AnneMarie Potter, Steve Rankin, Kevin Read, Ryan Reid, Marilyn Rockafellow, Harriet Rogers, Jeannie Rogers, Marcell Rosenblatt, Fred Sanders, Sloane Shelton, Sylvia Short, Gary Sloan, Bill Smitrovich, Margaret Terranova, William Verderber, Doug Wert, Gretchen West, Jennifer Weiner, Steve Wise, Nan Wray, Tom Wright, Peter Zapp

PRODUCTIONS: True West by Sam Shepard, The Caine Mutiny Court-Martial by Herman Wouk, The Dining Room by A. R. Gurney, Jr., The Gift of the Magi by Peter Ekstrom from the O'Henry story, A Christmas Carol adapted from Dickens' novel by Barbara Field, The School for Wives by Moliere, Uncle Vanya by Chekhov, 'night Mother by Marsha Norman, Wait until Dark by Frederick Knott, K2 by Patrick Meyers, Tent Meeting by Larry Larson, Levi Lee and Rebecca Alworth Wackler

'84 SHORTS: (Festival of One-act plays/All *World Premieres*) Advice to the Players by Bruce Bonefede, The American Century by Murphy Guyer, The Black Branch by Gary Leon Hill with Jo Hill, The Cool of the Day by Wendell Berry, That Dog Isn't Fifteen by Roy Blount, Jr., My Early Years by Charles Leipart, I'm Using My Body as a Roadmap by Patrick Tovatt, The Love Suicide at Schoefield Barracks by Romulus Linney, The Person That I Once Was by Cindy Lou Johnson, Private Territory by Christopher Davis, The Root of Chaos by Douglas Soderberg, Summer by Jane Martin

HUMANA FESTIVAL OF NEW AMERICAN PLAYS: Available Light by Heather McDonald, Days and Nights Within by Ellen McLaughlin, Ride the Dark Horse by J. F. O'Keefe, Two Masters by Frank Manley, The Very Last Lover of the River Cane by James McLure, War of the Roses by Lee Blessing

David S. Talbott Photos

Left Center: Christian Kauffmann, Dana Mills, Debra Monk in " '84 Shorts" Top: Frederic Major, Thom Christopher, Lee Anne Fahey in "Uncle Vanya" Below: Andy Backer, Kathy Bates in "Two Masters (The Rain of Terror)"

Leigh Curran, Sloane Shelton in " 'night, Mother"

ACTORS THEATRE OF ST. PAUL

St. Paul, Minnesota
November 2, 1984–May 19, 1985

Artistic Director, Michael Andrew Miner; Managing Director, Jan Miner; Associate Director, Jeff Steitzer; Associate Artistic Director, David Ira Goldstein; Design, Chris Johnson; Costumes, Nayna Ramey; Stage Manager, Jeff Couture; Press, Andrew Brolin
RESIDENT COMPANY: Paul Boesing, D. Scott Glasser, Tim Goodwin, Barbara Kingsley, David M. Kwiat, David Lenthall, Faye Price, Barbara Reid, Sally Wingert, Alan Woodward
GUEST ARTISTS: Jeff Steitzer, Stephen Peabody, Marc Ira Goldstein, Janice Lee, John Seibert, Alison Stair Neet, Dolores Noah, Dick Leerhoff, Tom Butsch, Mary Helen Horty, Doug Pipan, Randall Davidson, Gary Rue
PRODUCTIONS: Awake and Sing! by Clifford Odets, Season's Greetings by Alan Ayckbourn, Faith Healer by Brian Friel, We Won't Pay! We Won't Pay! by Dario Fo, Scapin by Moliere, and *Premieres* of Careless Love by John Olive, Bully by Paul D'Andrea

Connie Jerome Photos

**Right: John Seibert, David M. Kwiat
in "Scapin" Top: David Lenthall, Tim
Goodwin, Paul Boesing, Sally Wingert,
David M. Kwiat, Faye Price in "Awake and Sing!"**

**June Gibbons, Maeve McGuire, Moultrie Patten,
Terry Layman, Marshall Borden in "Noises Off"
Above: Julian Rivers, Roy Brocksmith,
Philip Pleasants in "Pantagleize"**

ALASKA REPERTORY THEATRE

Anchorage/Fairbanks, Alaska
October 14, 1984–March 23, 1985
Ninth Season

Artistic Director, Robert J. Farley; Producing Director, Paul Brown; General Manager, Bennett Taber; Sound, Jerry Summers; Company Manager, Jim Woodard; Fiscal Manager, Alice Chebba; Development, Judith Bankston; Marketing, Erick Borland; Stage Manager, Jim Woodard
NOISES OFF by Michael Frayn; Director, Robert J. Farley; Scenery, Connie Lutz; Costumes, Cathleen Edwards; Lighting, Spencer Mosse; Sound, Jerry Summers. CAST: June Gibbons, Marshall Borden, Terry Layman, Tracy Shaffer, Annie Schooler, Douglas Fisher, Maeve McGuire, Richard Riehle, Moultrie Patten
TRANSLATIONS by Brian Friel; Director, Michael Murray; Scenery, Karl Eigsti; Costumes, Mariann Verheyen; Lighting, Neil Peter Jampolis. CAST: John Finn, Maggie Baird, Dermot McNamara, Nancy Boykin, John Conley, Jean McNalley, Robert Donley, Eric Tull, Edward Conery, Patrick O'Connell
BRIGHTON BEACH MEMOIRS by Neil Simon; Director, Clayton Corzatte; Scenery, Karen Gjelsteen; Costumes, Sally Richardson; Lighting, Judy Rasmuson. CAST: Marc Riffon, Katherine Ferrand, Catherine Wolf, Perrin Morse, Annie Schooler, Rudy Goldschmidt, Alan Mixon
PANTAGLEIZE by Michel de Ghelderode; Director, Robert J. Farley; Scenery/Props, Michael Olich; Costumes, Deborah Dryden; Lighting, Robert Peterson. CAST: Philip Pleasants, Gerald Gilmore, John Morrow, Jr., Joe Meek, Jack Murdock, Zack Grenier, Betsy Scott, Roy Brocksmith, Richard Ussery, Glenn Mazen, Peter Josephson, Dan Millen, Jody Morse, Guy Payne, J. Courtney Pollard, Michael Purcell, Julian Rivers, Dennis Sullivan
BILLY BISHOP GOES TO WAR by John Gray and Eric Peterson; Director, Robert J. Farley; Scenery, Connie Lutz; Costumes, Jennifer Svenson; Lighting, Lauren MacKenzie Miller. CAST: Clayton Corzatte, K. C. Helmeid

Chris Arend Photos

145

ALLEY THEATRE

Houston, Texas
July 12, 1984–June 23, 1985
Thirty-eighth Season

Artistic Director, Pat Brown; Managing Director, Tom Spray; Associate Artistic Director, George Anderson; Production Manager, Richard Earl Laster; Scenery, Dale F. Jordan; Lighting, Richard W. Jeter; Costumes, Ainslie G. Bruneau; Wardrobe, Bernadette Schmeits; Props, Suzanne Kaplor; Sound, Tony Johnson; Stage Managers, Richard Earl Laster, Katherine M. Goodrich, Glenn Bruner, Robert S. Garber, Ann Arganbright, Cathy A. Fank; General Manager, Michael Tiknis; Development, Clare Dowdall; Marketing/Press, Carl Davis, Bob Feingold.

PRODUCTIONS & CASTS

ANGEL STREET by Patrick Hamilton; Director, John Vreeke. CAST: Richard Poe (Manningham), Pamela Lewis (Mrs. Manningham), Lillian Evans (Elizabeth), Lawr Means (Nancy), K. Lype O'Dell (Inspector), Fritz Dickmann, David Williams (Police)

TALES FROM THE ARABIAN NIGHTS by Michael Bigelow Dixon; Director, John Vreeke; Original Score/Musical Direction, Jan Cole; Set, Michael Holt; Costumes, Fontini Dimou; Choreography, Lea Geeslin, Terrence Karn, Abiatha Simpson; Stage Manager, Mark Tynan. CAST: "*Scheherazade and the Sultan*" with Jeff Bennett, Kayce Glasse, Raan Lewis, Bob Rumsby, Scott Fults, Mary Agen Cox, Luisa Amaral-Smith; "*The Fisherman and His Wife*" with Gregory Ruhe, Luisa Amaral-Smith; "*Ali Baba and the 40 Thieves*" with Raan Lewis, Bob Rumsby, Luisa Amaral-Smith, Scott Fults, Gregory Ruhe; "*The Snake Charmer and His Wife*" with Michael Normandy, Kayce Glasse; "*Shukat and the Princess*" with Bob Rumsby, Kayce Glasse, Gregory Ruhe, Scott Fults, Michael Normandy, Raan Lewis

THE SORROWS OF FREDERICK by Romulus Linney; Director, Pat Brown; Set, Michael Holt; Costumes, Fotini Dimou; Music, Jan Cole. CAST: Robert Cornthwaite (Frederick II), Bruce Norris (Prince Frederick), Todd Duffey (Frederick as a boy), Paul C. Thomas (Frederick William I), Cynthia Lemmel (Elizabeth Christine), K. Lype O'Dell (General), Philip Fisher (Doctor), Jim Bernhard (Chancellor), William Simington (Bishop), Bob Rumsby (Lt. Nocklin-Grantz), Michael Alan Gregory (Katte/Lt. Kort), Rick Hamilton (M. G. Fredersdorf), Timothy Arrington (Voltaire), Donn Whyte (Executioner/Potsdam Giant), Soldiers: Charles E. Sanders, Jeff Bennett, Michael Normandy, Gregory Ruhe

SEASON'S GREETINGS by Alan Ayckbourn; Director, Pat Brown; Sound, Jan Cole. CAST: Robert Cornthwaite (Harvey Bunker), Dale Helward (Dr. Longstaff), Fredi Olster (Belinda), Cynthia Lemmel (Pattie), Richard Poe (Neville), Rick Hamilton (Eddie), Lawr Means (Rachel), Lillian Evans (Phyllis), Michael Alan Gregory (Clive)

A CHRISTMAS MEMORY Adapted from Truman Capote's story by Bettye Fitzpatrick and Beth Sanford; Director, Beth Sanford; Music, Jan Cole; Lighting, Pam Gray; Sound, John Michener. CAST: Charles E. Sanders (Buddy), Bettye Fitzpatrick (Sook)

FINDING HOME with Book and Lyrics by Michael Bigelow Dixon, Jerry Patch; Music, Jan Cole; Director, John Vreeke; Choreography, Lea Geeslin, Luisa Amaral-Smith; Set, Byron Taylor; Costumes, Joanie Canon; Stage Managers, Mark Tynan, Gregory J. Ruhe. CAST: Luisa Amaral-Smith, Raan Lewis, Scott Fults, Mary Agen Cox, Gregory J. Ruhe, Kayce Glasse (Understudy)

STARRY NIGHT by Monte Merrick; Director, George Anderson; Set, Mo Holden; Stage Manager, Cathy A. Frank. CAST: Jeff Bennett (Bo), Brandon Smith (Len), Johanna Leister (Katie)

EXTREMITIES by William Mastrosimone; Director, Beth Sanford; Costumes, Mo Holden. CAST: Susan Pellegrino (Marjorie), Steven Marcus (Raul), Lawr Means (Terry), Fredi Olster (Patricia)

SWEET BIRD OF YOUTH by Tennessee Williams; Director, Joan Vail Thorne. CAST: Mark Soper (Chance), Patricia Roe (Princess Kosmonopolis), Raan Lewis (Fly), Richard Poe (George Scudder), Charles Sanders (Hatcher), Paul C. Thomas (Boss Finley), Michael Alan Gregory (Tom Junior), Bettye Fitzpatrick (Aunt Nonnie), Tracy Thorne (Heavenly), Dennis Lebby (Charles), Rick Hamilton (Stuff), Carolyn Cope (Miss Lucy), Timothy Arrington (Heckler), Kayce Glasse (Edna), Brandon Smith (Scotty), James Belcher (Bud), Scott Fults (Page), Jeff Bennett, Gregory Ruhe, Dennis Wells (Men in bar)

FOOL FOR LOVE by Sam Shepard; Director, Lee Shallat. CAST: Robin Moseley (May), Arliss Howard (Eddie), Blue Deckert (Martin), Robert Cornthwaite (Old Man)

Top: (L) Ray Stricklyn in "Confessions of a Nightingale" (R) Patricia Roe, Mark Soper in "Sweet Bird of Youth" Below: Blue Deckert, Arliss Howard, Robin Moseley in "Fool for Love" Bottom: (L) Rick Hamilton, Fredi Olster in "Much Ado about Nothing" (R) Susan Pellegrino, Richard Poe in ". . . And a Nightingale Sang"

MUCH ADO ABOUT NOTHING by William Shakespeare; Director, Mervyn Willis; Set, Charles Stanley Kading; Dances, Lea Geeslin. CAST: K. Lype O'Dell (Leonato), Jim Bernhard (Antonio), Cynthia Lemmel (Hero), Lawr Means (Margaret), Kayce Glasse (Ursula), Mary Agen Cox (Attendant), Fredi Olster (Beatrice), William Simington (Friar), Gregory Ruhe (Boy), Richard Poe (Don Pedro), Timothy Arrington (Don John), Brandon Smith (Claudio), Rick Hamilton (Benedick), Paul Hope (Borachio), Michael Alan Gregory (Conrade), Jeff Bennett, Raan Lewis (Messengers), Michael Normandy (Balthasar), Paul C. Thomas (Dogberry), Harold Suggs (Verges), Charles Sanders (Sexton)

CONFESSIONS OF A NIGHTINGALE conceived and arranged by Ray Stricklyn from interviews with Tennessee Williams by Charlotte Chandler and C. Robert Jennings; Performed by Ray Stricklyn as Tennessee Williams.

QUARTERMAINE'S TERMS by Simon Gray; Director, Neil Havens. CAST: Dale Helward (St. John Quartermaine), Cynthia Lemmel (Anita Manchip), Rick Hamilton (Mark Sackling), Robert Cornthwaite (Eddie Loomis), Michael Alan Gregory (Derek Meadle), Richard Poe (Henry Windscape), Lillian Evans (Melanie Garth)

OPEN ADMISSIONS by Shirley Lauro; Director, George Anderson. CAST: Carolyn Cope (Alice Miller), Daryl Edwards (Calvin Jefferson); with **SIZWE BANZI IS DEAD** by Athol Fugard, John Kani, Winston Ntshona; Director, Jim O'Connor. CAST: Lou Ferguson (Styles/Buntu), Stephen McKinley Henderson (Sizwe Banzi)

AND A NIGHTINGALE SANG . . . by C. P. Taylor; Director, Beth Sanford; Set, James Franklin. CAST: Susan Pellegrino (Helen Stott), Lawr Means (Joyce Stott), Jim Bernhard (George), Bettye Fitzpatrick (Peggy), Robert Cornthwaite (Andie), Michael Alan Gregory (Eric), Richard Poe (Norman)

ALLIANCE THEATRE COMPANY

Atlanta, Georgia
September 5, 1984–May 11, 1985
Sixteenth Season

Artistic Director, Fred Chappell; Associate Director, Kent Stephens; Managing Director, Edith Love; General Manager, William B. Duncan; Development, Betty Blondeau; Marketing/Press, Cynthia Harman Conner, Kim Resnik, G. Brock Haley; Literary Manager, Sandra Deer; Production Manager, Billings Lapierre; Technical Manager, Stephen Reardon; Wardrobe, Margaret E. Keller; Props, Sharon Braunstein; Wigs, Dorothy Durden; Hairstylist, Forbici; Sound, David M. Lyons; Stage Managers, Dale C. Lawrence, Kathy Richardson, John Kirman, Rixon Hammond

PRODUCTIONS & CASTS:

CYRANO DE BERGERAC by Edmond Rostand; Adapted by Emily Frankel; Music, Michael Jay; Director, Arthur Storch; Set, Victor A. Becker; Costumes, Jennifer von Mayrhauser; Lighting, Marc Weiss; Sound, Michael Jay; Fights, Erik Fredricksen. CAST: John Cullum (Cyrano), David Wasman (Bellerose/Marquand), Suzanne McCalla (Orange Girl/Sister Claire), Lisabeth Bartlett (Roxane), Timothy Davis-Reed (Christian/Bertran), Richard Cottrell (DeGuiche), Mary Nell Santacroce (Duenna/Mother Margaret), John Perkins (Ragueneau), Sean G. Griffin (LeBret), Al Hamacher (Marquis/Musketeer), Richard Bowden (Ligniere/Vadim/Monk), John Purcell (Brissaille), Jon Menick (Busybody/Gentleman/Leon), Laura Whyte (Lady/Lise/Mme. Aubrey/Sister Ann), Darren Stephens (Baron/Gentleman/Page/Sentry), Marc Clement (Montfleury/Ullman), Marcus Smythe (Christian)

FOXFIRE by Susan Cooper, Hume Cronyn; Director, Skip Foster; Set, Paul Wonsek; Music Director, Bob McDowell; Costumes, J. Thomas Seagraves; Lighting, Greg Mariner. CAST: Collin Wilcox Paxton (Annie Nations), Robert Blackburn (Hector Nations), Marc Clement (Prince Carpenter), Clarinda Ross (Holly Burrell), Harry Guffee (Dillard Nations), Al Hamacher (Doctor)

SHE LOVES ME with Book by Joe Masteroff; Based on play by Miklos Laszlo; Music, Jerry Bock; Lyrics, Sheldon Harnick; Director, Fred Chappell; Choreography, Ken Ellis; Musical Director, Michael Fauss; Set, Mark William Morton; Costumes, Susan Hirschfeld; Lighting, Jason Kantrowitz. CAST: Brian White (Arpad Laszlo), John Purcell (Ladislav Sipos), Victoria Tabaka (Ilona Ritter), John Sloman (Steven Kodaly), Jeffrey Dreisbach (Georg Nowack), Peter Johl (Mr. Maraczek), Felicia Hernandez (Shopper/Customer), Valerie Kassel, Jr. (Shopper/Customer), Holly Graham, Robby Preddy, Lulu Downs, Diana Kavilis, Kristin Galloway (Customers), Lulu Downs (Nurse), Nancy Ringham (Amalia Balash), Tony Lawson (Keller), Ed Romanoff (Waiter), Tony Lillo (Busboy), Chip Epstein (Violinist), Cafe Couples: Kenny Bruce Morris, Diana Kavilis, Dennis Bell, Felicia Hernandez, Scott Martin, Kristin Galloway, Tony Lawson, Holly Graham

MASTER HAROLD . . . and the boys by Athol Fugard; Director, Stephen Hollis; Set, Mark Loring; Costumes, Yvonne Lee; Lighting, Dante Cardone. CAST: Paul Butler (Sam), Kenneth Leon (Willie), T. Scott Cunningham (Halley)

AND A NIGHTINGALE SANG . . . by C. P, Taylor; Director, Kent Stephens; Set, Richard Hoover; Costumes, J. Thomas Seagraves; Lighting, Gregg Marriner. CAST: Carol Schultz (Helen), Gavin Reed (George), Dennis King, Jr. (Andie), Betty Leighton (Mam), Audrey Jacques (Joyce), Christian Hesler (Eric), David Reinhardsen (Norman)

HIGH STANDARDS by Tom Huey; World Premiere; Director, Skip Foster; Set, Johnny Thigpen; Lighting, Liz Lee. CAST: Al Hamacher (Crimmer), Jay McMillan (Parboil), Brenda Bynum (Shuford). A play in two acts. The action takes place in an abandoned warehouse in downtown Greensboro, N.C.

CAT ON A HOT TIN ROOF by Tennessee Williams; Director, Fred Chappell; Set, Michael Stauffer; Costumes, Joyce Andrulot; Lighting, Paulie Jenkins. CAST: Al Garrison (Lacey), Ginnie Randall (Sookey), Pat Nesbit (Maggie), David W. Head (Brick), Linda Stephens (Mae), Ken Strong (Gooper), Marian Baer (Big Mama), Valerie Vanis (Dixie), Justin Nowell (Buster), Jeff Kolesky (Sonny), April Vanis (Trixie), David Sabin (Big Daddy), Rob Roper (Rev. Tooker), John Purcell (Dr. Baugh)

PAINTING CHURCHES by Tina Howe; Director, Malcolm Morrison; Set, Tom Lee; Costumes, J. Thomas Seagraves. CAST: Mary Nell Santacroce (Fanny Sedgewick Church), Max Jacobs (Gardner Church), Linda Stephens (Margaret Church)

THE TEMPEST by William Shakespeare; Director, Kent Stephens; Set, Mark William Morton; Costumes, Susan Hirschfeld; Lighting, William B. Duncan; Music, Hal Lanier; Movement, Ellen Ishino Rankart.
CAST: Richard Andrew (King of Naples; John Purcell (Sebastian), David Schramm (Prospero), John Ammerman (Antonio), Mark Chamberlin (Ferdinand), Al Hamacher (Gonzalo), Christian Hesler (Adrian/Male Spirit), Chuck Cooper (Caliban), Jeff Brooks (Trinculo), Raymond Xifo (Stephano), Bruce Evers (Boatswain), Jean Taylor (Miranda), Scott Ellis (Ariel), Randy Thomas Kemp (Male Spirit), Female Spirits: Sue Hannen, Stefanie Thompson

SO LONG ON LONELY STREET by Sandra Deer; World Premiere; Director, Kent Stephens; Costumes, Joyce Andrulot; Lighting, David Brewer; Set, Mark William Morton. CAST: Stephen Markle (Raymond Brown), Lizan Mitchell (Annabel Lee), Pat Nesbit (Ruth Brown), Tambra Smith (Clairice Vaughnum), Stephen Root (King Vaughnum III), Ken Strong (Bobby Stack). A play in two acts. The action takes place during late August at Honeysuckle Hill a few miles outside a small Southern town.

THE EMPEROR AND THE NIGHTINGALE adapted from Hans Christian Andersen's story by Sandra Deer and Kent Stephens. CAST: John Ammerman, Lynn Brown, Scott Douglas, Dennis King, John Forrest Ferguson, Lizan Mitchell, Ken Strong, Teresa Texiera, Seth R. Ghitelman, Sarah Trowbridge

THE PRINCE AND THE PAUPER adapted from Mark Twain's story by John Vreeke. CAST: John Ammerman, Deborah Anderson, Suzi Bass, Suzanne Calvert, Dennis Durrett-Smith, Joe Everett, Pat Hurley, Alan Kilpatrick, Jay McMillan, Buck Newman, Pamella O'Connor, Brad Sherrill

THE BEAST by Skip Foster/**THE LAND BETWEEN** by Elizabeth Sams; Director, Skip Foster. CAST: Lynn Brown, Christopher Curmick, Bill Nunn, Tina Smith

Charles Rafshoon Photos

Jay McMillan, Al Hamacher
in "High Standards"

Brad Sherrill, Joe Everett
in "The Prince and the Pauper"

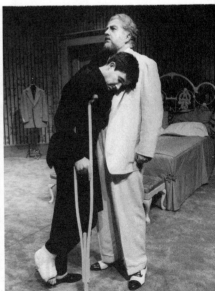

David Head, David Sabin
in "Cat on a Hot Tin Roof"

147

AMERICAN CONSERVATORY THEATRE

San Francisco, California
October 24, 1984–June 1, 1985
Nineteenth Season

General Director, William Ball; Managing Director, Benjamin Moore; Production Managers, John Brown, Eric Shortt; Designers, Joseph Appelt, Robert Blackman, Michael Casey, Ralph Funicello, Richard Goodwin, Katharine E. Kraft, Dawn Line, Christopher Moore, Robert Morgan, David Percival, Robert Peterson, Duane Schuler, Richard Seger, Greg Sullivan, Debra Booth, Rick Shrout; Stage Managers, James Haire, Eugene Barcone, James L. Burke, Karen Van Zandt; Props, Oliver C. Olsen; Wardrobe, Donald Long-Hurst, Thea Heinz; Composer, Lee Hoiby; Music Director, Richard Hindman; Administrative Director, Adrian Stewart; Communications/Marketing, Dennis Powers, Ralph Hoskins; Stage Directors, William Ball, Eugene Barcone, Edward Hastings, Lawrence Hecht, Janice Hutchins, Nagle Jackson, Laird Williamson
COMPANY: Linda Aldrich, Annette Bening, Joseph Bird, Scot Bishop, Kate Brickley, George Deloy, Barbara Dirickson, Peter Donat, Geoffrey Elliott, Drew Eshelman, Jill Fine, Scott Freeman, Wendell Grayson, Lawrence Hecht, Scott Hitchcock, Nancy Houfek, Janice Hutchins, Johanna Jackson, Jane Jones, Douglas Martin, Dakin Matthews, Deborah May, Carolyn McCormick, Judith Moreland, Mark Murphey, Frank Ottiwell, William Paterson, Jim Poyner, Ray Reinhardt, Richard Riehle, Stephanie Shroyer, Rosemarie Smith, Francine Tacker, Bernard Vash, Sydney Walker, Marrian Walters, J. Steven White, Bruce Williams, Henry Woronicz

Mark Amarotico, Scot Bishop, Michelle Casey, Nike Doukas, Amy Freed, Stephen Hough, Lisa Ivary, Todd Jackson, Peter Jacobs, Kay Kostopoulos, Brianna Lewis, David Maier, Richard Mason, Elizabeth Padilla, Marty Pistone, Marcia Pizzo, Stephen Pratt, Jill Romero, Douglas Sills, Mark Simpson, Kenn Watt, Teresa Williams, Alicia Wollerton, Taylor Young
PRODUCTIONS: Old Times by Harold Pinter, The School for Wives by Moliere, A Christmas Carol by Charles Dickens, Translations by Brian Friel, Macbeth by William Shakespeare, Our Town by Thornton Wilder, Painting Churches by Tina Howe, Mass Appeal by Bill C. Davis

Larry Merkle Photos

**Janice Hutchins, Barbara Dirickson,
William Paterson in "Painting Churches"**

**Robert Drivas, Priscilla Smith, Thomas
Derrah in "Jacques and His Master"
Above: "The Civil Wars"**

AMERICAN REPERTORY THEATRE

Cambridge, Massachusetts
November 23, 1984–June 2, 1984
Sixth Season

Artistic Director, Robert Brustein; Managing Director, Robert J. Orchard; Literary Director, Jonathan Marks; Production Manager, Jonathan Miller; Marketing, Jeanne Brodeur; Press, Jan Geidt; Technical Director, Donald R. Soule; Lighting, Jennifer Tipton; Production Coordinator, Thomas C. Behrens; Stage Managers, John Grant-Phillips, Abbie H. Katz, Antony Rudie

PRODUCTIONS & CASTS:
THE KING STAG by Carlo Gozzi; English version, Albert Bermel; and **THE LOVE OF THREE ORANGES** with Text and Music by Sergei Prokofiev, from a scenario by Carlo Gozzi; English version, Albert Bermel; Director, Andrei Serban; Sets, Michael H. Yeargen; Costumes/Puppets/Masks, Julie Taymor; Original Music, Elliot Goldenthal. CAST: Thomas Derrah, Diane D'Aquila, Richard Grusin, Lynn Chausow, Jeremy Geidt, Priscilla Smith, Dennis Bacigalupi, Harry S. Murphy, Rodney Hudson, Christopher Moore, John Bottoms
ENDGAME by Samuel Beckett; Director, JoAnne Akalaitis; Set, Douglas Stein; Costumes, Kurt Wilhelm; Incidental Music, Philip Glass, produced by Kurt Munkacsi. CAST: Ben Halley, Jr., John Bottoms, Rodney Hudson, Shirley Wilber
JACQUES AND HIS MASTER by Milan Kundera; *American Premiere;* English translation, Michael Henry Heim; Director, Susan Sontag; Set, Douglas Stein; Costumes, Jane Greenwood; Original Music, Elizabeth Swados. CAST: Thomas Derrah, Robert Drivas, Priscilla Smith, Jeremy Geidt, Richard Grusin, Harry S. Murphy, Diane D'Aquila, Dennis Bacigalupi, Frances Shrand, Lynn Chausow
CIVIL WARS by Robert Wilson, Heiner Muller; *American Premiere;* English translation, Christopher Martin, Danile Woker; Director, Robert Wilson; Set, Robert Wilson, Tom Kamm; Costumes, Yoshio Yabara; Composition and Sound, Hans Peter Kuhn; Assistant to Director, Ann-Christin Rommen. CAST: Priscilla Smith, Ben Halley, Jr., Thomas Derrah, Diane D'Aquila, Shirley Wilber, Jeremy Geidt, Seth Goldstein, Frances Shrand
LOVE'S LABOUR'S LOST by William Shakespeare; Director, Jerome Kilty; Set, Michael H. Yeargan; Costumes, Constance R. Wexler; Lighting, Spencer Mosse; Music, Conrad Susa. CAST: Thomas Derrah, Cherry Jones, Diane D'Aquila, Rodney Hudson, John Bottoms, Jerome Kilty, Ben Halley, Jr., Jeremy Geidt, Harry S. Murphy, Jack Stehlin, Gregory Welch
GILLETTE by William Hauptman; Director, David Wheeler; Set, Karen Schulz; Costumes, Lynn Jeffery; Lighting, Thom Palm; Sound, Randolph C. Head. CAST: John Bottoms, Jack Stehlin, Diane D'Aquila, Rodney Hudson, Harry S. Murphy, Cherry Jones, Gayle Keller
CLAPTRAP by Ken Friedman; Director, Robert Drivas; Set, Karen Schulz; Costumes, Karen Eister; Lighting, Thom Palm; Sound, Randolph C. Head. CAST: Harry S. Murphy, Cherry Jones, Treat Williams, Rose Arrick, Ursula Drabnik

Richard Feldman Photos

AMERICAN THEATRE ARTS

Hollywood, California
November 8, 1984–August 31, 1985

Artistic Director, Don Eitner; Executive Director, James Hildebrandt; Production Manager, Margaret Perry; Company Manager, Barbara Stewart; Literary Manager, Oren Curtis; Art Director, Robert Green; Costumes, Armand Coutu; Sound, Warren Teel; Props, Dena Williams; Press, Wesley Harris, Todd Durwood

PRODUCTIONS & CASTS

THE COUNTRY WIFE by William Wycherly; Producer-Director, Tom Henschel; Music, Elaine Vaan Hogue; Lighting, Magda Gonzalez. CAST: Kerry Calkins, Patrick D. Tanzillo, Sandy Becker, Charles Berendt, Dale Reynolds, Sara Shearer, Dena Marie Williams, Jay Louden, Stephen Workman, Steve Yudson, Joseph Ruskin, Bridget Markusfeld, Nita McKenzie, Victoria Herrick, Doug Johnstone, Jeannie Sherry

INNER/INTER CHANGES a series of one-act plays in repertory, by Conrad Bromberg, Michael Frayn, Oliver Hailey, Israel Horovitz, Harvey Perr, John Rechy. Directors: Ron Ames, Armand Coutu, Jim Drake, Howard Penn, Sue Wolfe; Sets, N.J. Benedetti; Lights, Geoffrey Rinehart; Costumes, Reve Richards, Susanne L. Holland. CAST: Pamela Printy, Marc Tuber, Kelly Bailey, Maura Albertson, Tim Durkee, Sandy Becker, Michael Richardson, Doug Johnstone, N. Kelly Cole, Don Amendolia, Elaine Nalee, Jeannie Sherry, Barbara Stewart, John Scott, Stevie Michaels, Peter Parros, Harriette McCauley, Tanya George, Lee Ryan

BLOOD RELATIONS by Sharon Pollock; Director, Don Eitner; Producer, Barbara Stewart; Set, Dan Dryden; Costumes, Elena Del Rio; Lighting, Geoffrey Rinehart; Choreography, Sonja Haney. CAST: Elaine Nalee, Jeanne Hepple, Dale Reynolds, Michael Richardson, Sally J. Sommer, Lisa Figus, Ron Ray

THE DIARY OF A MADMAN by Nikolai Gogol; Adapted by Don Eitner, Tom Troupe; Original translation, Rodney Patterson; Director, Don Eitner; Set, Owen Williams; Lighting, Geoffrey Rinehart. CAST: Tom Troupe

THE SCARECROW by Percy MacKaye; Director, Ed Waterstreet; Lighting, Paul Mitchell; Translation, Bob Daniels, Fredda Norman; Adapted by Rico Peterson; Set/Costumes, Armand Coutu. CAST: Fredda Norman, Joy Pankin, Lou Fant, Frank Warner, Linda Bove, Genni Klein, Tim Johnson, Brad Green, Dean Sheridan, Christopher Dakin, Robert Daniels, Ian Kelly, Ron Kleiger, Frances Ripplinger, Roxanne Baker

A SCRAP OF PAPER by Victorien Sardou; Translation, Leonie Gilmour; Director, Tom Henschel; Set, Robert Green; Lighting, Magda Gonzalez; Costumes, Suzanne Cranfil; Speech Coach, Jessica Drake.
CAST: Sandy Becker, Mary Bomba, Cary Calkins, Lou Fant, Cindy Friedl, Jeanne Hepple, Eric Poppick, Cathryn Purdue, David Sage, Barbara Stewart, Leda Siskind

Rick Moffitt Photos

Elaine Nalee, Jeanne Hepple
in "Blood Relations"

ARENA STAGE

Washington, D.C.
October 5, 1984–June 16, 1985
Thirty-fourth Season

Producing Director, Zelda Fichandler; Executive Director, Thomas C. Fichandler; Associate Producing Director; Administrative Director, JoAnn M. Overholt; Production Coordinator, Guy Bergquist; Development, Elspeth Udvarhelyi; Technical Director, David M. Glenn; Directors, Garland Wright, Lee Breuer, Elinor Renfield, Douglas C. Wager, Christopher Markle, Lucian Pintilie, Amy Saltz, Douglas C. Wager; Sets, John Arnone, Alison Yerxa, Loren Sherman, Adrienne Lobel, David Jenkins, Radu Boruzescu, Patricia Woodbridge, Ming Cho Lee; Costumes, Jared Aswegan, Ghretta Hynd, Alison Yerxa, Marjorie Slaiman, Miruna Boruzescu, Mary Ann Powell; Lighting, Frances Aronson, Julie Archer, Allen Lee Hughes, Paul Gallo, Beverly Emmons, Nancy Schertler; Stage Managers, Rita Calabro, Sal Rasa, Ann Matthews, Robin Rumpf, Martha Knight, Bill Gregg, Pat Cochran; Press, Richard Bryant, Shawn Fraser, Teresa Balkam

COMPANY: Stanley Anderson, Richard Bauer, Marilyn Caskey, Terrence Currier, Mark Hammer, John Leonard, Henry Strozier, Halo Wines

GUEST ARTISTS: Jorge Abreu, Brooks Baldwin, Mark Berman, Pamela Bierly, Casey Biggs, Wesley Boyd's Gospel Music Choir, Fran Brill, Pamela Brown, Sam Butler, Jr., Michael Chaban, Colonus Messengers, Melody Combs, Ralph Cosham, Brian Cousins, Kevin Davis, Francois de la Giroday, Gillian Doyle, Elizabeth DuVall, J. J. Farley and the Original Soul Stirrers, Clarence Fountain and the Five Blind Boys of Alabama, Peter Francis-James, Gina Franz, Morgan Freeman, Martin Goldsmith, Lisa Goodman, Carla Hall, Dorothea Hammond, June Hansen, Harriet Harris, Jeffrey Hayenga, Jayne Haynes, Tom Hewitt, Butch Heyward, Tana Hicken, James Hild, Terry Hinz, Christopher Hurt, Richard S. Iglewski, Max Jacobs, Martin Jacox, Keith Johnson, Robert Earl Jones, Ben Kapen, Katherine Leask, Joseph Lee, Steve Lejnar, Marty Lodge, Carl Lumbly, Walt MacPherson, Sarah Marshall, Earl F. Miller, Isabell Monk, Patrick T. O'Brien, Gerry Paone, Gregory Procaccino, Willie Rogers, Rick Sabatini, Ned Schmidtke, Joanne Schmoll, Cary Anne Spear, Jeanne Sprague, Kim Staunton, J. D. Steele Singers, Jevetta Steele, Jearlyn Steele-Battle, Carolyn Swift, Pamela Tomassetti, Stephen Wade, Scott Wentworth, Carolyn Johnson White, Carl Williams, Jr., Michael Willis, Rudolph Willrich, Maggie Winn-Jones, Harris Yulin

PRODUCTIONS: The Tempest by William Shakespeare with Music by John McKinney, The Gospel at Colonus conceived, adapted, directed by Lee Breuer with Music composed and arranged by Bob Telson, Passion Play by Peter Nichols, Man and Superman by George Bernard Shaw, Tartuffe by Moliere with translation by Richard Wilbur, Isn't It Romantic by Wendy Wasserstein, Execution of Justice by Emily Mann, and *American Premiere* of Real Estate by Louise Page.

Joan Marcus, George de Vincent Photos

Francois de la Giroday, Harriet Harris
in "Man and Superman"

ARIZONA THEATRE COMPANY

Tucson/Phoenix, Arizona
October 27, 1984–June 9, 1985
Sixth Season

Artistic Director, Gary Gisselman; Associate Artistic Director, Ken Ruta; Resident Director, Walter L. Schoen; Managing Director, David Hawkanson; General Manager, Mitch Oomens; Marketing/Press, Sharon Griggins, Gary Bacal; Development, Barbara R. Levy; Company Manager, Mary Nelson; Wardrobe, Margi Shaw, Peggy Hinsley, Elaine Radovich; Sound, Rob Cumberledge; Technical Director, Mark Freij; Props, James N. Clark, Michael Armstrong; Production Coordinator, Philip J. Fleming; Production Assistant, Ken Bahn; Stage Managers, Sara Lee Howell, Jay Rabins

PRODUCTIONS & CASTS
AND A NIGHTINGALE SANG . . . by C. P. Taylor; Director, Gary Gisselman; Set, Don Yunker; Lighting, Vivian Robson; Musical Director, Sandi Schroads; Costumes, David Mickelsen; Sound, Jeff Ladman; Choreography, Gail Chodera. CAST: Jane Murray (Helen), Christine Carter (Joyce), Alfred M. Anderson (George), Patricia Fraser (Peggy), Paul Ballantyne (Andie), Marco Barricelli (Eric), Kevin McGuire (Norman)
MASTER HAROLD . . . and the boys by Athol Fugard; Director, Walter L. Schoen, Jr.; Lighting, Don Hooper; Set, Don Yunker; Costumes, Bobbi Culbert; Stage Manager, Ken Heer; Choreography, Gail Chodera. CAST: Sullivan Walker (Sam), Earl Billings (Willie), Duane Black (Hally)
THE LEARNED LADIES by Moliere; Translated by Richard Wilbur; Director, Ken Ruta; Set, Vicki Smith; Lighting, Don Darnutzer; Costumes, Lewis Brown; Sound, Jeff Ladman. CAST: Michael Keenan (Chrysale), Jeanette Landis (Philaminte), Jenna Cole (Armande), Melissa Stern (Henriette), Ray Rodriguez (Ariste), Peggy Roeder (Belise), Michael Lueders (Clitandre), William Roesch (Trissotin), Gary P. Clark (Vadius), Darrie Lawrence (Martine), Peder Melhuse (Lepine), Marco Barricelli (Notary)
DEATH OF A SALESMAN by Arthur Miller; Director, Gary Gisselman; Set, Vicki Smith; Lights, Don Darnutzer; Sound, Warren Hogan; Costumes, David Mickelsen; Original Music, Ken LaFave. CAST: James J. Lawless (Willy Loman), Darrie Lawrence (Linda), Peder Melhuse (Biff), Marco Barricelli (Happy), Michael Lueders (Bernard), Peggy Roeder (The Woman), Michael Keenan (Charley), William Roesch (Uncle Ben), Ray Rodriguez (Howard), Jeanette Landis (Jenny), Gary P. Clark (Stanley), Melissa Stern (Miss Forsythe), Jenna Cole (Letta)
GOODBYE FREDDY by Elizabeth Diggs; Director, Ken Ruta; Set, William Bloodgood; Lighting, Vivian Robson; Costumes, David Mickelsen. CAST: Henry J. Jordan (Hank), Katherine Ferrand (Kate), Tony DeBruno (Paul), Peggy Schoditsch (Alice), Dan Kern (Andy), Jenifer Parker (Nessa)
THE ROBBER BRIDEGROOM with Book and Lyrics by Alfred Uhry; Adapted from the novella by Eudora Welty; Music, Robert Waldman; Direction/Choreography, Gary Gisselman/Myron Johnson; Set, Dahl Delu; Costumes, Jared Aswegan; Musical Director, Roberta Carlson. CAST: William Bruce Miller (Jamie), Michael Ellison (Clement), Barbara Davidson (Salome), Molly Sue McDonald (Rosamund), Stephen Yoakam (Little Harp), Richard Glover (Big Harp), Bruce Nelson (Goat), Janice Robillard (Goat's Mother), JoEllen Geske (Airie), Devi Piper (Raven), Pamela Beitman (Rebecca), Tim Mathistad (Ephraim), Karen Rouse (Sarah), Don Weingust (Ezekiel)

Tim Fuller Photos

**Peggy Schoditsch, Tony DeBruno
in "Goodbye Freddy"**

ASOLO STATE THEATER

Sarasota, Florida
June 1, 1984–May 31, 1985
Twenty-sixth Season

Executive Director, Richard G. Fallon; Associate Executive Director, Stephen Rothman; Artistic Director, John Ulmer; Assistant to Artistic Director, John Gulley; Press, Edith N. Anson; Sets, Kenneth L. Kurtz, Robert Barnes, John Doepp, Jeffrey Dean, John Ezell, Bennet Averyt, Peter Harvey; Costumes, Catherine King, Peter Harvey, Sally Kos Harrison; Lighting, Martin Petlock, Kenton Yeager; Technical Director, Victor Meyrich; Stage Managers, Marian Wallace, Stephanie Moss, Juanita Munford, Dan Carter
COMPANY: (through July 1984): Randy Clements, Kay Daphne, Daria Dolan, Joleen Fodor, Jayne Houdyshell, Richard Hoyt-Miller, Jerry Allan Jones, Katie Karlovitz, Marcie Stringer, Eric Tavares, Isa Thomas, Bradford Wallace, Carol Williard, and Diane Compton, Joan Crowe, Paul J. Ellis, Neil Lee Friedman, Coleen Kane, Tim O'Neal Lorah, Patrick Manley, Holly Methfessel, Cynthia Newman, Pam Taylor, William L. Thomas, Jack Willis, Marc Ciokajlo, Jody Kielbasa, Susan Jones Mannino, Carol Martini, Michael Piontek, Kenn Rapczynski, Karen Rasch, Kathryn Riedman, Jennifer Riggs, Steve Spencer. (through January 1985): Howard Brunner, Judith Halek, Lisa P. Hermatz, Chuck Rosenow, Howie Seago, Isa Thomas, Mary Colleen Vreeland. (through March 1985): Louis Beachner, Lydia Bruce, A. D. Cover, Douglas Jones, Barbara Lester, Philip Lombardo, Karl Redcoff, Diana Reis, Leon B. Stevens, Eric Tavares, Bradford Wallace, Jane Welch, and Mark Ciokajlo, Jody Kielbasa, Susan Jones Mannino, Carol Martini, Michael Piontek, Kenn Rapczynski, Karen Rasch, Kathryn Riedman, Jennifer Riggs, Steve Spencer, Donna Anderson, Karen Blair, Nancy Hartman, Michael Lee Lariscy, Mary E. Launder, David B. Levine, Lynne Perkins, Parry B. Stewart, Vince Williams. (through July 1985): George Dvorsky, Donna Kane, Dirk Lumbard, Richard Sabelloco, Susan Elizabeth Scott, Donald Buka, A. D. Cover, Stephen Daley, Douglas Jones, Jack Koenig, Carolyn Michel, Karl Redcoff, Barbara Sohmers, Georgia Southcotte, Eric Tavares, Isa Thomas, Bradford Wallace
PRODUCTIONS: The Drunkard, Rashomon, The Importance of Being Earnest, Children of a Lesser God, Amadeus, And a Nightingale Sang, The Little Foxes, Dames at Sea, A Month in the Country, You Can't Take It with You, Twice Around the Park

Gary W. Sweetman Photos

**Jerry Allan Jones, Katie Karlovitz, Richard
Hoyt-Miller, Isa Thomas, Carol Williard
in "The Importance of Being Earnest"**

BARTER THEATRE

Abingdon, Virginia
Fifty-second Season

Producing Director, Rex Partington; Business Manager, Pearl P. Hayter; Press, Lou Flanigan, Christin Whittington; Directors, Pamela Hunt, Geoffrey Hitch, Ken Costigan, Gregory S. Hurst, William Van Keyser; Musical Director, Randy Barnett; Sets, Lynn Pecktal, Daniel Ettinger, Dennis Bradford, Jim Stauder; Costumes, Georgia Baker, Carr Garnett, Martha Hally, Karen Brewster, Sigrid Insull, Barbara Forbes; Lighting, Al Oster; Stage Managers, Champe Leary, Tony Partington

PRODUCTIONS & CASTS
TINTYPES conceived by Mary Kyte with Mel Marvin and Gary Pearle. CAST: Ralph Braun, Babara Niles, David Pevsner, Lynne Wieneke, Mary Yarbrough
CRIMES OF THE HEART by Beth Henley. CAST: Carol Schultz, Katie Grant, Tracy Griswold, Laura Gardner, Barbara Lail, Christopher James Wright
THE GOOD DOCTOR by Neil Simon, adapted from Chekhov. CAST: Ross Bickell, George Hosmer, Laura Gardner, Donald Christopher, Cleo Holladay
ARTICHOKE by Joanna M. Glass. CAST: Donald Christopher, Ken Costigan, Cleo Holladay, Ross Bickell, Catherine Coray, Harry Ellerbe, George Hosmer
MASS APPEAL by Bill C. Davis. CAST: John Bennes, Nick Bakay
PROMENADE, ALL! by David B. Robison. CAST: Tracy Griswold, Cleo Holladay, Chet Carlin, Gwyllum Evans
BELL, BOOK AND CANDLE by John Van Druten. CAST: Joleen Fodor, Ross Bickell, Eve Johnson, Robert B. Putnam, Donald Christopher
World Premiere of **CALLING ON LOU** from the stories and poems of Lou Crabtree, adapted for the stage by Larry Richman; Performed by Cleo Holladay

Dave Grace Photos

BERKELEY REPERTORY THEATRE

Berkeley, California
September 19, 1984–May 26, 1985

Artistic Director, Sharon Ott; Managing Director, Mitzi Sales; Production Manager, Dennis Gill Booth; Technical Director, Richard G. Norgard; Business Manager, Ellen Russell; Stage Managers, Meryl Lind Shaw, Kimberly Mark Webb; Production Assistant, Judith Offer; Wardrobe, Donald M. Smith; Props, Jerry Reynolds; Sound, Don McKennan; Literary Manager, Carole Braverman; Marketing, Jim Royce; Press, Susan Bellows; Development, Susanne K. Dunn, Catie Laufer
COMPANY: Hope Alexander-Willis, Tony Amendola, David Booth, James Carpenter, Charles Dean, Ken Grantham, Irving Israel, Judith Marx, Michelle Morain, Barbara Oliver, Richard Rossi, Brian Thompson
PRODUCTIONS: A Touch of the Poet by Eugene O'Neill, Otherwise Engaged by Simon Gray, Tartuffe by Moliere (Richard Wilbur translation), Kingdom Come by Amlin Gray, Misalliance by George Bernard Shaw, The Tooth of Crime by Sam Shepard, Execution of Justice by Emily Mann

Ken Friedman Photos

CALDWELL PLAYHOUSE

Boca Raton, Florida
July 3, 1984–May 26, 1985
Fifth Season

Producing Director, Michael Hall; Sets, Frank Bennett, James Morgan, Laurel Shoemaker, Joe Gillie; Costumes, Bridget Bartlett; Lighting, Craig R. Ferraro, Laurel Shoemaker, Mary Jo Dondlinger; Stage Managers, Doug Fogel, Chip Latimer, Joe Gillie, Jerome Stone; Press, Patricia Burdett

PRODUCTIONS & CASTS (all directed by Michael Hall)
SAME TIME NEXT YEAR by Bernard Slade. CAST: Pat Nesbit, Geoffrey Wade
WHOSE LIFE IS IT ANYWAY by Brian Clark. CAST: Geoffrey Wade, Pat Nesbit, John Gardiner, Emily Kairalla, Tom Nowicki, Deborah Stern, Jack Hrkach, James McGill, Kate Powers, Harold Bergman, Peter Haig, Annie Stafford, Randolph Del Lago
ISN'T IT ROMANTIC by Wendy Wasserstein. CAST: Becky London, Carole-Ann Scott, Anita Keal, Peter Trencher, Ralph Redpath, David Berk, Ruth Clark-Everitt, Stephen S. Neal
PAINTING CHURCHES by Tina Howe. CAST: Susan Willis, Larry Swansen, Cordis Heard
BENT by Martin Sherman. CAST: Tom Lawson, Anthony Newfield, John Bjostad, Ronald Wendschuh, Miller Lide, Geoff Edholm, Lawrence Tobin, Jeffrey Blair Cornell, Mark Stuart-Howard
THE PLAY'S THE THING by Ferenc Molnar. CAST: James Hillgartner, Elias Eliadis, Barbara Bradshaw, Miller Lide, Curzon Dobell, Ronald Wendschuh, John Bjostad

Joyce Brock Photos

Laura Gardner, Carol Schultz, Barbara Lail
in "Crimes of the Heart"

Ray Reinhardt, Barbara Oliver
in "A Touch of the Poet"

Geoff Edholm, Tom Lawson,
John Bjostad in "Bent"

151

CALIFORNIA REPERTORY THEATRE

Pacific Grove, California
June 1, 1984–May 31, 1985

Producing Director, Ben Benoit; Development Director, Jim Bennett; Literary Manager, Edward Weingold; Stage Managers, Ken Barton, Robin Kevrick, Barbara Lane; Sets, Gene Angell, Ron Pratt, Keith Snider, Noel Uzemack, Cathy Johnstone; Stage Directors, Tony Amendola, Ben Benoit, Cab Covay, Peter Craze, Peter Layton, Julian Lopez-Morillas, Howard Malpas, Edward Weingold; Costumes, Karen S. Ohlmann, Keith Snider, Jule Emerson

COMPANY: Marcia Banks, Barry Boys, Don Bilotti, Patricia Cullen, Michael Flynn, Jean Gilpin, Randy Haege, Susan Hegarty, Ken Hicks, Dana Kelly, Karen Lamb, Wanda McCaddon, Molly Mayock, Jarion Monroe, Douglas Nigh, Kate Rowland, Morgan Stock, Kimberly King
PRODUCTIONS: The Dining Room, Bullshot Crummond, The Good Doctor, Betrayal, The Norman Conquests, A Christmas Carol, Jesse and the Bandit Queen, Who's Afraid of Virginia Woolf?, Private Lives

Kira Godbe Photos

Top Right: Jarion Monroe, Marcia Banks, Dana Kelly in "The Norman Conquests"

Frank Maraden, Stephen McHattie in "Danton's Death" Above: Anne Pitoniak in "Painting Churches"

CENTER STAGE

Baltimore, Maryland
September 21, 1984–June 30, 1985
Sixth Season

Artistic Director, Stan Wojewodski, Jr.; Managing Director, Peter W. Culman; Associate Artistic Director, Jackson Phippin; Artistic Associates, Hugh Landwehr, Irene Lewis, Grace McKeaney, Eric Overmyer; Technical Director, John Horsman; Stage Managers, Amanda Mengden, Robert S. Garber; Press, Jean Brubaker

PRODUCTIONS & CASTS

DANTON'S DEATH by Georg Buchner; *American Premiere* of new version by Howard Brenton; Director, Stan Wojewodski, Jr.; Set, Hugh Landwehr; Costumes, Jess Goldstein; Lighting, Pat Collins; Composer, Claude White; Sound, Janet Kalas. CAST: Stephen McHattie, David Strathairn, David Harum, Damien Leake, Stephen Pelinski, Daniel Szelag, Michael Thompson, Frank Maraden, Jack Stehlin, Ron Dortch, Victor Love, Mark Redfield, Tana Hicken, Jennifer Harmon, Jana Schneider, Elane Denny, Denise Diggs, Harvey Elridge, Steven Tague, Michael Buster, Greg McClure, Emery Battis, Rosemary Knower, Michael Grodenchik, Wil Love, William Duff-Griffin, Berry Cooper
HENRY IV PART I by William Shakespeare; Director, Stan Wojewodski, Jr.; Set, Doug Stein; Costumes, Lawrence Casey; Lighting, Stephen Strawbridge; Fights, Peter Nels, B. H. Barry; Composer, Claude White. CAST: Emery Battis, Tony Soper, Michael Buster, William Duff-Griffin, Nels Hennum, Roland Bull, Jack Stehlin, Lorraine Toussaint, Damien Leake, Steven J. Tague, Donna Pierce, Michael Thompson, Stephen Pelinski, David Harum, Greg McClure, Adam Gish, Michael Egan, Daniel Szelag, Wil Love, Michael Grodenchik, Victor Love, Rosemary Knower, Berry Cooper, Ron Dortch, Mark Redfield
HEDDA GABLER by Henrik Ibsen; New version by Kenneth Cavander; Director, Irene Lewis; Set, Hugh Landwehr; Costumes, Jess Goldstein; Lighting, Stephen Strawbridge; Language Consultant, Irene B. Berman. CAST: Martin LaPlatney, Tana Hicken, Georgia Southcotte, Joanne Camp, Adrian Sparks, Joseph Hindy, Rosemary Knower
A FLEA IN HER EAR by Georges Feydeau; New Adaptation/Direction, Roy Brocksmith; Set, Nancy Winters; Costumes, Jim Buff; Lighting, Pat Collins; Musical Adaptations, Grant Sturiale. CAST: Mary Ellen Ashley, John Bauer, Daniel Szelag, Wil Love, Jennifer Harmon, Mary Beth Fisher, Stephen Pelinski, Rosemary Knower, David O. Petersen, Kim Chan, Susan Beverly, J. Daniel McDonald, Grant Sturiale
PAINTING CHURCHES by Tina Howe; Director, Stan Wojewodski, Jr.; Set, Hugh Landwehr; Costumes, Del W. Risberg; Lighting, Judy Rasmuson. CAST: Anne Pitoniak, Thomas Barbour, Mary Beth Fisher
EXECUTION OF JUSTICE by Emily Mann; Director, Stan Wojewodski, Jr.; Set, Hugh Landwehr; Costumes, Jess Goldstein; Lighting, James F. Ingalls; Sound, Janet Kalas; Photographic Material, Daniel Nicoletta. CAST: Peter Crombie, Stephen Pelinski, Michael Buster, Tony Soper, Elane Denny, Robert Horen, Mark Redfield, Lorraine Toussaint, Daniel Szelag, David O. Petersen, Joan Strueber, David Harum, Michael Thompson, Jennifer Harmon, Walt MacPherson, Steven J. Tague, Rosemary Knower, Nels Hennum, Rebecca Nelson
WORLD PREMIERES
ON THE VERGE OR THE GEOGRAPHY OF YEARNING by Eric Overmyer; Director, Jackson Phippin; Set, Tony Straiges; Costumes, Del W. Risberg; Lighting, James F. Ingalls; Composer, Paul Sullivan; Sound, Paul Sullivan, Janet Kalas; Movement, Kathy Wildberger. CAST: Brenda Wehle, Mary Layne, Marek Johnson, James McDonnell
NATIVE SPEECH by Eric Overmyer; Director, Paul Berman; Set, Hugh Landwehr; Costumes, Jess Goldstein; Lighting, James F. Ingalls; Sound, Janet Kalas. CAST: Kario Salem, Lorey Hayes, Sa'Mi Chester, Khin-Kyaw Maung, Tzi Ma, Robert Salas, Caris Corfman, Samuel L. Jackson, Jimmy Smits, Melinda Mallari, Adam Gish
WHO THEY ARE AND HOW IT IS WITH THEM by Grace McKeaney; Director, Jackson Phippin; Set, Hugh Landwehr; Costumes, Jess Goldstein; Lighting, James F. Ingalls; Sound, Janet Kalas. CAST: James Handy, William Foeller, Anderson Matthews, Brenda Wehle

Richard Anderson Photos

CENTER THEATRE GROUP

MARK TAPER FORUM
August 26, 1984–August 4, 1985
Eighteenth Season

Artistic Director/Producer, Gordon Davidson; Managing Director, William P. Wingate; Associate Artistic Director, Kenneth Brecher; Resident Director, Robert Egan; Producer Taper Too, Madeline Puzo; Dramaturg, Russell Vandenbroucke; Literary Manager, William Storm; Press, Nancy Hereford, Guy Giarrizzo, Robert Wildman, Phyllis Moberly; Lighting, Tharon Musser; Artistic Associate, Jose Quintero; Production Coordinator/Casting Director, Frank Bayer; Technical Director, Robert Routolo; Production Administrator, Don Winton; Stage Managers, Al Franklin, Jonathan Barlow Lee, James T. McDermott, Mary Michele Miner, Michael F. Wolf, Mireya Hepner, Tami Toon, Richard Winnie

PRODUCTIONS & CASTS:

VIVA VITTORIO! An Evening with Vittorio Gassman; *American Premiere;* Conceived and Directed by Mr. Gassman; Set/Lighting, John DeSantis; Original Music, Fiorenzo Carpi; Associate Producer, Madeline Puzo. Part I: "*A Report to an Academy*" by Franz Kafka; "*Kean*" (Fragments) by Alexandre Dumas; Adapted by Jean Paul Sartre; with Rhonda Aldrich (Anna), Neil Bagg (Dresser), Nino Prester (Solomon); "*The Man with the Flower in His Mouth*" by Luigi Pirandello; with Nino Prester (Commuter). Part II: "*On the Harmfulness of Theatre*" by Luciano Codignola.

THE HANDS OF ITS ENEMY by Mark Medoff; *World Premiere;* Director, Gordon Davidson; Set, Michael Devine; Costumes, Carol Brolaski; Lighting, Paulie Jenkins; Assistant Director, Jody McAuliffe; Sign Coaches, Robert Daniels, Fredericka Norman. CAST: Tom Henschel (T. O. Finn), Robert Steinberg (Mel Katzman), Debra Medoff succeeded by Shawnee Smith (Amanda Yerby), Phyllis Frelich (Marieta Yerby), Sharon Madden (Elma Pafko), Jeffrey Tambor (Edgar "Skip" Donner), Richard Dreyfuss (Howard Bellman), Veronica Cartwright succeeded by Patricia McCormack (Diane Newbury), Elizabeth Self (Assistant Stage Manager). A play in 2 acts and 9 scenes. The action takes place from the first day of rehearsal to four weeks later. Production was moved to the Huntington Hartford Theatre for a 9-week run.

PASSION PLAY by Peter Nichols; Director, Gwen Arner; Set, D. Martyn Bookwalter; Costumes, Robert Blackman; Lighting, Martin Aronstein; Sound, Jon Gottlieb. CAST: Roxanne Hart (Kate), Donald Moffat (James), Barbara Babcock (Eleanor), Paddi Edwards (Agnes), John McMartin (Jim), Claudette Nevins (Nell), and June Claman, Janet DeMay, Neil Flanagan, David Hall, Neil Hunt, Jill Johnson, Judith Jordan, Louis Schaefer

TRAVELER IN THE DARK by Marsha Norman; Director, Gordon Davidson; Set, Ming Cho Lee; Costumes, Susan Denison; Lighting, Marilyn Rennagel. CAST: Len Cariou (Sam), Deborah May (Glory), Scott Grimes (Stephen), Claude Akins (Everett)

IN THE BELLY OF THE BEAST by Jack Henry Abbott; Adapted by Adrian Hall; Further Adaptation, Robert Woodruff; Director, Robert Woodruff; Set, John Ivo Gilles; Costumes, Carol Brolaski; Lighting, Paulie Jenkins; Music, Douglas Wieselman; Sound, Stephen Shaffer; Video Design, Chip Lord, Branda S. Miller; Associate Producer, Madeline Puzo. CAST: Andrew Robinson (Jack Henry Abbott), Andy Wood (Reader 1), Carl Franklin (Reader 2). Performed without intermission.

UNDISCOVERED COUNTRY by Arthur Schnitzler in a version by Tom Stoppard; Director, Ken Ruta, Set, Ralph Funicello; Costumes, Sam Kirkpatrick; Lighting, Martin Aronstein; Music, Hiram Titus; Production Coordinator, Frank Bayer. In repertory with **MEASURE FOR MEASURE** by William Shakespeare; Director, Robert Egan; Set, Ralph Funicello; Costumes, Robert Blackman; Lighting, Martin Aronstein; Original Music/Sound, Daniel Birnbaum; Production Coordinator, Frank Bayer. CAST (for both productions): Wayne Alexander (Wahl/Claudio), Vaughn Armstrong (Rosenstock/Gentleman, Abhorson, Guard), Tom Atkins (Dr. Mauer/Angelo), June Claman (Romanian Violinist/Nun), Jenna Cole (Kathi, Italian Girl/Prostitute, Nun), Suzanne Collins (Mrs. Rhon/Nun), Joel Colodner (Provost in MM), Gary Dontzig (Paul Kreindl/Friar Peter), Kelsey Grammer (Demeter Stanzides/Lucio), Michael Keenan (Natter/Froth, Guard), Sally Kemp (Mrs. von Aigner/Francisca), Jeanette Landis (Mrs. Wahl/Mistress Overdone), William Biff McGuire (Dr. von Aigner/Escalus), Marnie Mosiman (Adele Natter/Mariana), Kate Mulgrew (Isabella in MM), Albert Owens (Head Waiter/Craccus, Prisoner, Friar), Edwin Owens (Maestro/Justice), Christina Pickles (Genia Hofreiter in UC), David Prather (Bellboy/Guard), Mark Ruch (Elevator Boy/Eros), Ken Ruta (Director/Vincentio), Don Sparks (Serknitz/Elbow), Granville Van Dusen (Friedrich Hofreiter in UC), Peter Van Norden (Albertus Rhon/Pompey), Laurie Walters (Erna Wahl/Julietta), Carl Weintraub (Penn/Gentleman/Barnardine/Guard), Belinda Wells (Spanish Girl/Prisoner, Prostitute, Nun), Robert Yacko (Otto von Aigner/Varrius/Friar)

**Right Center: Len Cariou, Scott Grimes
in "Traveler in the Dark"**

TAPER, TOO:

TALKING WITH by Jane Martin; Director, Michael Peretzian; Set, Cliff Faulkner; Costumes, Susan Denison; Lighting, Brian Gale; Sound, Stephen Shaffer. CAST: K Callan (Scraps), Virginia Capers (French Fries), Cynthia Carle (Audition), Radha Delamarter (Twirler), Ann Hearn (Handler), Susan Krebs (15 Minutes), Elizabeth Norment (Rodeo), Anabella Price (Dragons), Barbara Townsend (Lamps), Patricia Wettig (Clear Glass Marbles), Grace Zabriskie (Marks)

MANSAMENTE created and performed by Marcos Caetano Ribas and Rachel Ribas; Music, Helena Pinheiro

SWIMMING TO CAMBODIA Parts 1 and 2 written and performed by Spalding Gray

FIVE OF US by Len Jenkins; Director, Tony Abatemarco; Set, Leslie McDonald; Costumes, Susan Denison; Lighting, Greg Sullivan; Sound, Jon Gottlieb. CAST: Richard Frank (Herman), Darrell Larson (Mark), Annabella Price (Lee), Susan Barnes (Crystal), Erich Anderson (Eddie)

IMPROVISATIONAL THEATRE PROJECT: "*A Family Album*" in repertory with "*School Talk*"

SUNDAYS AT THE ITCHEY FOOT: "*Eleanor Roosevelt, First Lady of the World*" adapted from her writings by Russell Vandenbroucke; Director, Jody McAuliffe; with Alice Hirson. "*A Christmas Memory*" by Truman Capote; Adapted by Madeline Puzo; Director, Michael Peretzian; Musician, David Johnson; with Mary Carver and Jay Louden. "*Gimpel the Fool*" by Isaac Bashevis Singer; Translated by Saul Bellow; Adapted by Larry Arrick; Music/Lyrics/Direction, Barbara Damashek; Musicians, Kristina Olsen, J. B. Severin; with Jeff Abbott, Suzanne Collins, Gary Dontzig

**Richard Dreyfuss, Phyllis Frelich
in "The Hands of Its Enemy"**

CENTER THEATRE GROUP

AHMANSON THEATRE
September 29, 1984–May 26, 1985
Eighteenth Season

Artistic Director, Robert Fryer; Managing Director, Michael Grossman; Associate Artistic Director, James H. Hansen; Press, Rick Miramontez; Manager, Tom Jordan; Management Associate, Michelle McGrath; Executive Associate, Joyce Zaccaro; Production Manager, Ralph Beaumont; Technical Director/Production Assistant, Kathleen Horton; Props, Steve Rapollo

PRODUCTIONS & CASTS:

A PATRIOT FOR ME by John Osborne; Director, Ronald Eyre; Set and Costumes, Carl Toms; Lighting, Mark Henderson; Music, Ilona Sekacz; Choreography, Tudor Davies; Fights, Roger Martin; Stage Managers, Jasper Fox, Michael F. Wolf, Joe Cappelli, E. Craig Scott. CAST: Alan Bates (Alfred Redl), George Rose (Baron von Epp), George Murcell (Oblensky), June Ritchie (Countess), David King (von Mohl), Harry Andrews (von Hotzendorf), Nicholas Gecks (von Kupfer), Angela Down (Hilde), David Yelland (Siczynski), Christopher Neame (von Taussig), Bruce French (Stanitsin), Charles Shaughnessy (Steinbauer), Jo Webster (Ferdy), Christopher Murray (Paul), Timothy Shelton (Adjutant), Nameer Kadi (Tsarina), Paul Carleton (Jerzabek), Ian Price (Kunz), Anthony Head (Kovacs), Robert Meadmore (Albrecht), Daniel Trent (Lady Godiva), Douglas Blair, Jack Blessing, Gillian Eaton, Rick Giesie, Gary Imhoff, John Napierala, Gregory Niebel, Terrence O'Connor, James Rich, David Sage, E. Craig Scott, Raymond Skipp, Rosina Widdowson-Reynolds, Stanley Wojno, Jr., Jessica Zaccaro, Craig Zehms

BILOXI BLUES by Neil Simon; *World Premiere;* Director, Gene Saks; Set, David Mitchell; Costumes, Ann Roth; Lighting, Tharon Musser; Stage Managers, Charles Blackwell, Henry Valez. CAST: Matthew Broderick (Eugene), Barry Miller (Epstein), Randall Edwards (Rowena), Penelope Ann Miller (Daisy), Matt Mulhern (Wykowski), Alan Ruck (Carney), Geoffrey Sharp (Hennesey), Brian Tarantina (Selridge)

NOISES OFF by Michael Frayn; Director, Michael Blakemore; Set/Costumes, Michael Annals; Lighting, Martin Aronstein; Stage Managers, Arlene Grayson, Jim Dawson. CAST: Dorothy Loudon (Dottie), Brian Murray (Lloyd), Paxton Whitehead (Frederick), Victor Garber (Garry), Linda Thorson (Belinda), Deborah Rush (Brooke), Douglas Seale (Selsdon), Amy Wright (Poppy), Christian Clemenson (Tim)

THE ODD COUPLE by Neil Simon; Director, Gene Saks; Set, David Mitchell; Costumes, Ann Roth; Lighting, Tharon Musser; Stage Managers, Martin Gold, Bonnie Panson. CAST: Rita Moreno (Olive Madison), Sally Struthers (Florence Unger), Marilyn Cooper (Vera), Kathleen Doyle (Renee), Jenny O'Hara (Sylvie), Tony Shalhoub (Jesus Costazuela), Lewis J. Stadlen (Manolo Costazuela), Mary Louise Wilson (Mickey)

Top Right: Estelle Parsons, Polly Holliday, Jack Lemmon, Clifton James in "A Sense of Humor"

Lonny Price, Donna Bullock in "Amateurs"

CINCINNATI PLAYHOUSE IN THE PARK

Cincinnati, Ohio
October 2, 1984–July 28, 1985

Producing Artistic Director, Robert Kalfin; Managing Director, Baylor Landrum; Casting, D. Lynn Meyers; Literary Manager, Michael Burnham; Production Manager, Errol Selsby; General Manager, Katherine Mohylsky; Development, David Hagar; Stage Managers, Laurie F. Stone, Kimberly Osgood, Tom Lawson; Press, Charlaine Martin, Sue Ann Stein

PRODUCTIONS & CASTS

EMPRESS OF CHINA by Ruth Wolff; Director, Robert Kalfin; Set, Michael Sharp; Lighting, Edward Effron; Costumes, Andrew Marlay; Music, Mel Marvin; Choreographer, Danya Krupska. CAST: Ray Dooley, Jonathan Fuller, Vincenetta Gunn, Ron Nakahara, Joe Palmieri, Freda Foh Shen, Keenan Shimizu, Ching Valdes, Joseph Fuqua, Paula Godsey, Jeffrey Hasler, Ellen Lochhead, Mark Mocahbee, Michael Pollard, Anne Shapland, Juanita Scheyett, Robert Stormont, Mary Kay Wildenhain

SHADES OF BROWN by Michael Picardie; Director, Joan Kemp-Welch; Set, David Ariosa; Lighting, Jay Depenbrock; Costumes, Rebecca Senske; Stage Manager, Leslie Moore. CAST: Michael O'Hare, Count Stovall

THE BIG HOLIDAY BROADCAST by Arne Zaslove, Mary-Claire Burke, the Bathhouse Theatre Co.; Director, Arne Zaslove; Set, Shelley Henze Schermer; Lighting, Judy Wolcott; Costumes, Julie James; Musical Director, Robert Davidson; Production Coordinator, Michael Wise. CAST: Robert Davidson, Mark Drusch, Allen Galli, Randy Hoffmeyer, Craig Huisenga, James Lortz, Demetra Pittman, Joyce Mycka-Stettler, Jaye B. Summers, Jo Vetter

THE SEAGULL by Anton Chekhov; Translated by John Murrell; Director, Robert Kalfin; Set, David Ariosa; Lighting, Jay Depenbrock; Costumes, Steven Jones. CAST: Roger DeKoven, Ray Dooley, Elaine Grollman, Jeffrey Hasler, Gillian Jordan, Mark Mocahbee, Jim Nelson, James Secrest, Robert Stocker, Jeannine Taylor, Angela Thornton, Katherine Udall, Arn Weiner

AMATEURS with Book by Winnie Holzman and David Evans; *World Premiere;* Music, David Evans; Lyrics, Winnie Holzman; Director, Mitchell Ivers; Set, Eduardo Sicangco; Lighting, Spencer Mosse; Costumes, Eduardo Sicangco, Rebecca Senske; Orchestrator, Robby Merkin; Musical Director, Edward Strauss; Musical Staging, David Fredericks. CAST: Donna Bullock, Gregg Edelman, Randy Graff, Arthur Howard, Annette Hunt, Karen MacDonald, Dennis Parlato, Lonny Price

PARADISE! with Music by Robert Forrest; *World Premiere;* Book and Lyrics, George C. Wolfe; Director, Robert Nigro; Musical Director/Orchestrator, Jeffrey Saver; Set, John Yeck; Lighting, Neil Jenkinson; Costumes, Rebecca Senske; Sound, Steve Branch; Stage Manager, Tom Lawson. CAST: Kathel Carlson, Tommy Hollis, Steve Mattila, Dale O'Brien, Jackie Welch, Maryrose Wood

HAVE by Julius Hay; Translated by Peter Hay; *American Premiere;* Director, Robert Kalfin; Set, Wolfgang Roth; Lighting, Edward Effron; Costumes, Sam Kirkpatrick. CAST: Betty Alley, Melissa Budig, Diane Danzi, Roger DeKoven, Dale Doreman, Patrice Donnell, Anna Marie Dwertman, Joseph Fuqua, Igors Gavon, Paula Godsey, Frank Gordon, Elaine Grollman, Pat Straley Grooms, Jeffrey Hasler, Tad Ingram, Gillian Jordan, Tony Lawson, Ellen Lochhead, Paul Milikin, Mark Mocahbee, Jim Nelson, Michael Pollard, Juanita Scheyett, William Schwarber, James Secrest, Anne Shapland, Robert Stormont, Terres Unsoeld, Micah Valdes, Ching Valdes/Aran, Mary Kay Wildenhain, Elliot Wortman, Matthew Ziegler

AMADEUS by Peter Shaffer; Director, Robert Kalfin; Set, Wolfgang Roth; Lighting, Christopher Popowich; Costumes, Rebecca Senske; Production Coordinator, Louise Currie. CAST: Betty Alley, Wanda Cannon, Robert Clinton, Roger DeKoven, Ray Dooley, Ken Dresen, Joseph Fuqua, Paula Godsey, Jeffrey Hasler, Blair Haynes, Peter Kingsley, Diego Matamoros, Peter Messaline, Paul Milikin, Christopher G. Moore, Glenn Nelson, Stellina Rusich, Robert Winslow

SLEUTH by Anthony Shaffer; Director, Robert Boss; Set, Rick Dennis; Lighting, Jay Depenbrock; Costumes, Rebecca Senske. CAST: James Cahill, Don Fischer

Sandy Underwood Photos

154

CLARENCE BROWN COMPANY

Knoxville, Tennessee
February 1,–April 28, 1985

Artistic Director, Wandalie Henshaw; General Manager, Kevin Colman; Producer, Peter Garvie; Stage Directors, Wandalie Henshaw, Albert J. Harris, Robert Mashburn; Costumes, Bill Black, Marianne Custer; Sets, Robert Cothran, Leonard Harmon; Lighting, L. J. DeCuir, Leonard Harmon; Stage Managers, Phebe Day, Jane Rothman, Page Phillips

PRODUCTIONS & CASTS:
RICHARD III by William Shakespeare. CAST: Robert Hock, Barry Mulholland, William Shust, Jim Stubbs, Jonathan Epstein, John Sefton, Al Harris, Bruce Cromer, David McCann, Jonathan Peck, Monique Morgan, Harriet Nichols, Basia McCoy, Connie Rotunda
THE CARETAKER by Harold Pinter. CAST: John Sefton, Barry Mulholland, Jon Epstein
SHE STOOPS TO CONQUER by Oliver Goldsmith. CAST: Jon Lutz, Monique Morgan, Lynn Watson, Ellen Jane Smith, Richard Bowden, Jon Epstein, Barry Mulholland, Paul Carlin
THE QUESTIONS OF HAMLET with Bruce Cromer, Jim Stubbs, Ian Thomson, Lisa Norman, Robert Hick

Nick Myers Photos

**Basia McCoy, William Shust
in "Richard III"**

COCONUT GROVE PLAYHOUSE

Miami, Florida
October 12, 1984–June 9, 1985

Producing Artistic Director, Arnold Mittelman; General Manager, Barry J. W. Steinman; Marketing, Barry Colfelt; Development, Ilene Zweig; Company Manager, Terri Schermer; Production Manager, Marsha Hardy; Press, Iris Ratcliffe; Stage Directors, Miguel Ferrer, Jose Ferrer, B. J. Allen, Bryna Wortman, Woodie King, Jr., Gerald Freedman; Sets, David Trimble, Doug Johnson, Christopher Nowak, Kevin Rupnik; Costumes, Barbara A. Bell, Ellis Tillman, Patricia McGourty, Jeanne Button; Lighting, Michael-Newton Brown, David Goodman, Marsha Hardy, B. J. Allen, Pat Collins; Stage Managers, Robin Gray, Rafael V. Blanco, B. J. Allen, Sandy McConnell, David M. Flasck.

PRODUCTIONS & CASTS:
WHEN YOU COMIN' BACK, RED RYDER? with Harold Bergman (Clark), Lisa Figueroa (Angel), Jackie Earle Haley (Stephen/Red), Dennis Jones (Richard), Emily Kairalla (Clarisse), Terence Knox (Teddy), Rebecca Robertson (Cheryl), Hank Rolike (Lyle)
THE GLASS MENAGERIE with Constance Cummings (Amanda), Laura Hughes (Laura), James McDonnel (Tom), Tom McKinney (Jim)
SLEUTH with Patrick Macnee (Andrew Wyke), Jordan Christopher (Milo Tindle)
PUMP BOYS & DINETTES with Mary Gutzi (Rhetta), Ritt Henn (Eddie), David Keyes (L. M.), Jim Lauderdale (Jim), Richard Perrin (Jackson), Donna Watton (Prudie)
'NIGHT, MOTHER with Carmen Mathews (Thelma Cates), Margo Martindale (Jessie Cates)
HOME with Gilbert Lewis (Cephus Miles), Stephanie Alston (Woman 1/Pattie Mae Wells), Andrea-Michele Smith (Woman 2)
AMERICA'S SWEETHEART with Stephen Vinovich (Al Capone), K. T. Sullivan (Mae Capone), Nicholas Gunn (Jake Bensick), Michael McCormick (Frankie Rivaldo), Tom Robbins (Tony Rivaldo), Wayne Bryan (Officer Zwick/Jerry Allen), Carolyn Casanave (Edna Beal), Lucinda Hitchcock Cone (Lulu Blombeck), Gary-Michael Davies (Barney/Schemer/Krauss/President), Donna English (Bernice/Muriel), Jeff Etjen (Bugs Moran/Attorney General/Judge Fox), Tom Henning (Harry Wilzak/Dion O'Bannion), Richard Levine (Nate Beal/Dr. Bailey), Mimi Wyche (Radio Lady/Gladys), Steve Routman (Hymie Weiss/Frank Wilson), Deanna Wells (Vicki Chase/Fay)

Michele Edelson Photos

**Margo Martindale, Carmen Mathews in " 'night, Mother"
Above: Jackie Earle Haley, Lisa Figueroa in "When
You Comin' Back, Red Ryder?"**

155

CROSSROADS THEATRE COMPANY

New Brunswick, New Jersey
September 22, 1984–May 19, 1985

Founder/Artistic Director, Lee Richardson; Founder/Executive Director, Rick Khan; Press, Christine Butler; Development, Garry Johnson; Technical Director, Sue Barr; Props, Vicki Dittemore; Stage Managers, Kenneth Johnson, Cheri Bogdan-Kechely; Sets, Dan Proett, Felix E. Cochren, Wynn P. Thomas, Bill Motyka; Costumes, Judy Dearing, Alvin Perry, Vicki Esposito-McLaughlin, Anita D. Ellis; Lighting, Susan White, Dan Stratman, Shirley Prendergast, William Grant III, Bernadette Englert; Sound, Rob Gorton, Molly Sue Wedding; Stage Directors, Lee Richardson, Rick Khan, Israel Hicks

PRODUCTIONS & CASTS:
STEAL AWAY by Roman King; with Lydia Hannibal, Minnie Gentry, Leila Danette, Rosanna Carter, Juanita Bethea, Petie Trigg Seale
AMERICAN BUFFALO by David Mamet; with William Jay, Raymond Anthony, Thomas Thommie Blackwell
BUBBLING BROWN SUGAR by Loften Mitchell based on a concept by Rosetta LeNoire; with Jai Oscar St. John, L. Michael Gray, Tina Fabrique, Steven Cates, Maime Duncan, Mary Slater, Wayne McCarthy
WHEN THE CHICKENS CAME HOME TO ROOST and ZORA by Laurence Holder; with Delores Mitchell, Thomas Martell Brimm, Roger Robinson
SLOW DANCE ON THE KILLING GROUND by William Hanley; with Frank Borgman, Lee Richardson, Lisa Goodman
SWEET DADDY LOVE by Don Evans; *World Premiere;* with Petie Trigg Seale, Louise H. Gorham, William Jay, Garry Johnson, Nick Smith, Delores Mitchell, Kenneth Johnson, Minnie Gentry

Harry Rubel Photo

Lydia Hannibal (seated), Leila Danette, Rosanna Carter, Petie Trigg Seale, Minnie Gentry, Juanita Bethea in "Steal Away"

**Barbara Orson, Anne Gerety (front)
in "Passion Play"**

DALLAS THEATER CENTER

Dallas, Texas
October 1, 1984–May 31, 1985

Artistic Director, Adrian Hall; Sets, Eugene Lee; Costumes, Donna Kress; Assistant to Artistic Director, Kimberly Cole; Associate General Manager, Michael Ducharme; Stage Managers, Ken Bryant, David Glynn; Press, Sheron Wyant, Ann Aspenes

COMPANY: John Addington, Bill Bolender, Candy Buckley, Michael Cherkinian, Sa'Mi Chester, Margery Clive, Chris Coleman, Melvin O. Dacus, John S. Davies, Scott Everhart, Dwain Fail, James Fields, Linda Gehringer, Bo Gerard, Robert Graham, Ann Hamilton, Marianne Hammock, Lou Hancock, Dee Hennigan, Sean Hennigan, Marion Jeffery, Tom Key, Daniel Allen Kremer, Jeri Leer, Jo Livingston, Andrea McCall, Jim McQueen, Norma Moore, Randy Moore, John Morrison, Michael O'Hara, Jenny Pichanick, Martin Rayner, Kurt Rhoads, Jane Roberts, Dwight Sandell, David Stump, Jarold Suggs, Gary Taggart, Terry Vandivort, James Werner, Nance Williamson, Lou Williford, Jenna Worthen
GUEST ARTISTS: Stephanie Dunnan, Anne Gerety, David C. Jones, Richard Kavanaugh, Richard Kneeland, Barbara Orson, Ford Rainey, William Swetland, Daniel Von Bargen, Norbert Weisser
PRODUCTIONS: Misalliance by George Bernard Shaw, Amadeus by Peter Shaffer, A Christmas Carol adapted from Charles Dickens, Passion Play by Peter Nichols, Three Sisters by Anton Chekhov, You Can't Take It With You by George S. Kaufman and Moss Hart, Good by C. P. Taylor

Linda Blase Photos

DELAWARE THEATRE COMPANY

Wilmington, Delaware
December 4, 1984–April 28, 1985
Sixth Season

Artistic Director, Cleveland Morris; Managing Director, Dennis Luzak; Business Manager, Ray Barto; Development, Ann Schenck; Press, Marilyn Giammarco; Stage Manager, Patricia Christian; Technical Director, Eric Schaeffer; Sets, Timothy M. Durham, Lewis Folden, Eric Schaeffer; Costumes, E. Lee Florance; Lighting, Ben F. Levenberg, Bruce K. Morriss; Sound, Alan Gardner

PRODUCTIONS & CASTS

THE RIVALS by Richard Brinsley Sheridan; Director, Cleveland Morris. CAST: Charles J. Conway, Nancy Daly, Joan Kendall, Kim Krejus, Iliff McMahan, Paul Milikin, Barry Mulholland, Anthony Newfield, Patricia O'Neil, William Pitts, John Rhein, Peter Roasacker, Fred Royal, Greg Tigani
YOU NEVER KNOW by Cole Porter; Direction and Choreography, Derek Wolshonak; Musical Direction, Judy Brown; Based on play "By Candlelight" by Siegfried Geyer and Karl Farkas; Music, Cole Porter, Robert Katcher; Lyrics, Cole Porter; Additional Lyrics, Rowland Leigh, Edwin Gilbert; Book adapted by Rowland Leigh. CAST: William Brockmeier, Gary Lynch, Michael McGrath, Mary Munger, Virginia Seidel, Debra G. Segal
MEDAL OF HONOR RAG by Tom Cole; Director, Paul Hastings. CAST: Richard M. Davidson, Robert D. Heath, Jr., Hubert Baron Kelly
STAGE STRUCK by Simon Gray; Director, Gavin Cameron-Webb. CAST: Jay E. Raphael, Michael Rhoades, Ian Stuart, Valerie von Volz
A STREETCAR NAMED DESIRE by Tennessee Williams; Director, Cleveland Morris. CAST: David Baffone, David Cassling, Charles J. Conway, Ashley Gardner, Paul Hartel, Chantal Hazeur Jackson, Rory Kelly, Frank Licato, Terri Reamer, Sharon Talbot, Susan M. Webster, Barbara Wilhide

Richard Carter Photos

David Baffone, Sharon Talbot, Ashley Gardner,
Rory Kelly, David Cassling in "A Streetcar
Named Desire"

Louis Oropeza, Julian Gamble, Harold
Surratt (back) in "Accidental Death
of an Anarchist"

DENVER CENTER THEATRE COMPANY

Denver, Colorado
October 29, 1984–June 8, 1985
Sixth Season

Artistic Director, Donovan Marley; Associate Artistic Directors, Peter Hackett (New Play Development), Richard L. Hay (Design); Literary Director, Sylvie Drake; Resident Stage Directors, Allen Fletcher, Peter Hackett, Donovan Marley; Scenic Designer, Richard L. Hay; Lighting, James Sale; Costumes, Andrew V. Yelusich; Executive Director, Sarah Lawless; Administrative Director, Karen Knudsen; Producing Director, Barbara E. Sellers; Technical Director, Dan McNeil; Sound, John E. Pryor; Props, Barbara Craig; Wardrobe, Beth Kendig-McBride; Stage Managers, Kevin Mangan, Lyle Raper, Nancy Thomas; Press, Megan Seacord, Susan Goodell

COMPANY: Stephen Anderson, Henri Bolzon, Libby Boone, Pamela Brook, Maryedith Burrell, Jeff Carey, Craig Diffenderfer, Kay Doubleday, Karen Foster, Patricia Fraser, Julian Gamble, Ann Guilbert, Carol Halstead, Mark Harelik, Jamie Horton, Robert Jacobs, Leticia Jaramillo, Byron Jennings, Lisa Karen Kaufman, Kate Levy, James K. Lewis, Lory Marie, Michael X. Martin, Penelope Miller, Gary Montgomery, Luis Oropeza, Dougald Park, Rebecca Prince, Guy Raymond, Mike Regan, Robynn Rodriguez, Tom Schuch, Archie Smith, Ken Sonkin, Harold J. Surratt, Adrienne Thompson, Howard Thompson, John Townsend, W. Francis Walters, Michael Winters, G Wood, D. Paul Yeuell, Peter Zimmerman, Lori Preisendorf
PRODUCTIONS: Hamlet by William Shakespeare, They Knew What They Wanted by Sidney Howard, Design for Living by Noel Coward, The Time of Your Life by William Saroyan, Painting Churches by Tina Howe, Pericles by William Shakespeare, The Accidental Death of an Anarchist by Dario Fo, Don Juan by Moliere, and *World Premieres* of Ringers by Frank X. Hogan, Lahr and Mercedes by James McClure, The Immigrant: A Hamilton County Album by Randal Myler and Mark Harelik, The Female Entertainer by Elizabeth Levin
PRIMAFACIE I: staged readings of ten new American plays: When the Sun Slides by Stephen D. Parks, November by J Ranelli, Pleasuring Ground by Frank X. Hogan, A Woman without a Name by Romulus Linney, Public Lives by Julia Cameron, Normal Doesn't Mean Perfect by Don Gordon, Deal with a Dead Man by Tom DeMers, Emily and Kate by Ruth Phillips, Hope of the Future by Shannon Keith Kelley, Telling Time by Laura Shamas

Nicholas DeScoise Photos

DETROIT REPERTORY THEATRE

Detroit, Michigan
November 1, 1984–June 23, 1985
Twenty-seventh Season

Artistic Director, Bruce E. Millan; Executive Director, Robert Williams; Development/Press, Dee Andrus; Literary Manager, Barbara Busby; Costumes, Anne Saunders; Music Director, Kelly Smith; Administrative Assistant, Kim Davis; Sets, Bruce Millan, Al Flood; Stage Managers, Dee Andrus, William Boswell; Lighting, Kenneth R. Hewitt, Jr., Marylynn Kacir; Sound, Reuben Yabuku; Props, Dee Andrus; Production Assistants, Willie Hodge, Janette Byrd; Technical Director, Mack Palmer

PRODUCTIONS & CASTS
MASTER HAROLD . . . and the boys by Athol Fugard; Director, Bruce E. Millan. CAST: Darius L. Dudley, Robert Williams-Vogue, Edward Nahhat
GOODNIGHT, GRANDPA by Walter Landau; Director, Dee Andrus. CAST: Andrew Dunn, Mack Palmer, Alma Parks, Robert Williams-Vogue, Camille Price, William Boswell, Mattie Wolf, Ruth Allen, Booker Hinton
J. B. by Archibald MacLeish; Director, Barbara Busby. CAST: Darius L. Dudley, William Boswell, Roy K. Dennison, Dody Brodersen, Wilton Hurtt, Scott McCue, Camille Price, Cornell J. Markham, Desi Coleman, Venti Valdez, Brian Schulz, Cathleen Donahue, Felicia McCoy, Reuben Yabuku
IN THE SWEET BYE AND BYE by Donald Driver; Director, Bruce E. Millan. CAST: Dee Andrus, Bethany Carpenter, Divina Cook, Robert Williams-Vogue, Mack Palmer, Cornell J. Markham

Bruce E. Millan Photos

Desi Coleman, Darius L. Dudley, Scott McCue, Brian Schulz, Camille Price, Cathleen Donahue, Felicia McCoy, Dee Andrus, Dody Brodersen in "J. B."

FORD'S THEATRE

Washington, D.C.
September 11, 1984–May 27, 1985

Executive Producer, Frankie Hewitt; Artistic Director, David H. Bell; Company Manager, Patricia Humphrey; Assistant to Executive Producer, Diana Hart; Business Manager, A. J. Pietrantone; Press, Larisa Wanserski

PRODUCTIONS & CASTS
WILL ROGERS' U.S.A. adapted and directed by Paul Shyre; Design, Eldon Elder; Stage Manager, Gene McFall. James Whitmore in a solo performance.
GREATER TUNA written and performed by Joe Sears and Jaston Williams; Director, Ed Howard; Set, Kevin Rupnik; Costumes, Linda Fisher; Lighting, Judy Rasmuson; Stage Manager, William Hare
A CHRISTMAS CAROL adapted from Charles Dickens by Rae Allen and Timothy Near; Set/Costumes, Christina Weppner; Puppets, Ingrid Crepeau; Lighting, John Gisondi; Musical Direction, Michael Howe; Director, Ted Weiant; Stage Manager, Carroll McKee. CAST: Donal Donnelly (Scrooge), and Adriana Amelias, Marie Bethel, Demetri Callas, John C. Canney, Ingrid Crepeau, Amelia Esten, Catherine Flye, Ronnie Gilbert, Hamilton Gillett, Helen Hedman, Ron Johnston, Roger Keiper, Anne Lalley, Dori Legg, Kevin Murray, Paul Norwood, Stephen Rudlin, Michael Schlesinger, Steve Steiner, Andrew Vaughan
BALLETAP U.S.A. produced by Stanley Kay, Florio Roettger; Artistic Directors, Maurice Hines, Mercedes Ellington; Lighting, Christina R. Giannelli; Scenery, Felix E. Cochren; Sound, John Ceglia; Stage Manager, Michael Harrod; Production Manager, Craig Morton; Dance Captains, Tiffney Lyn Myers, Michael Franks; Wardrobe, Olga Jacques; Administration, Patricia Scana; Production Assistant, Dwight Toliver. COMPANY: Maurice Hines, Mercedes Ellington, Debbie DeMeo, Michael Franks, John Fredo, Jodi Goodman, Lawrence Hamilton, Keith Henderson, John Kasak, Tiffney Lyn Myers, Patty Padula, Lisa Scialabba, Kim Winters, Michael Wright
CEREMONIES IN DARK OLD MEN by Lonne Elder III; Director, Douglas Turner Ward; Set, Charles Henry McClennahan; Costumes, Judy Dearing; Lighting, Shirley Prendergast; Sound, Dennis Ogburn; Stage Managers, Ed DeShae, Femi Sarah Heggie. CAST: Douglas Turner Ward (Russell Parker), Graham Brown (William Jenkins), Ruben Hudson (Theopolis Parker), Walter Allen Bennett, Jr. (Bobby Parker), Patty Holley (Adele Eloise Parker), Keith David (Blue Heaven), Tracy Camila Johns (Young Girl)
GODSPELL with Music and New Lyrics by Stephen Schwartz; Conceived by John-Michael Tebelak; Director/Choreographer, David H. Bell; Set, James Fouchard; Costumes, Doug Marmee; Lighting, Jeff Davis; Musical Direction, Billy Lewis; Stage Manager, Carroll McKee. CAST: Eric Aaron, Janet Aldrich, Robin Baxter, Steve Blanchard, Mary Corcoran, Teresa De Zarn, Jerry Dixon, Romain Fruge, John Ganzer, Edwina Lewis, Betsy True, Sal Viviano

Joan Marcus Photos

**Ford's Theatre stage and auditorium
Above: Eric Aaron, Steve Blanchard
in "Godspell"**

GeVa THEATRE

Rochester, N.Y.
November 3, 1984–July 13, 1985

Producing Director, Howard J. Millman; General Manager, Timothy Norland; Marketing/Press, Adele Fico-McCarthy; Production Manager, James Tinsley; Technical Director, Robb Smith; Business Manager, Dorinda Goggin; Literary Director, Anne Patrice Carrigan; Stage Managers, James Stephen Sulanowski, Catherine Norberg

PRODUCTIONS & CASTS

BILLY BISHOP GOES TO WAR by John Gray, Eric Peterson; Director, John Henry Davis; Set, Ray Recht; Lighting, Mitchell Dana; Costume Coordinator, Sylvia Sheret Newman. CAST: Allan Carlsen (Billy Bishop), Michael Deep (Narrator/Pianist)

ALL MY SONS by Arthur Miller; Director, Howard J. Millman; Set, William Barclay; Lighting, Phil Monat; Costumes, Holly Cole. CAST: Frederick Nuernberg (Dr. Bayliss), Gerald Richards succeeded by James Jeter, Howard J. Millman, (Joe Keller), David Lively (Frank Lubey), Nora Chester (Sue Bayliss), Marcia Nowik (Lydia Lubey), Richard Cottrell (Chris Keller), David Lebowitz/Frank Storace, Jr. (Bert), Sylvia Gassell (Kate Keller), Laurie Klatscher (Ann Deever), Richard Warner (George Deever)

PLANET FIRES by Thomas Babe; *World Premiere;* Director, John Henry Davis; Set, Ray Recht; Lighting, F. Mitchell Dana; Costumes, Pamela Scofield; Sound, Jeffrey Miller; Original Music, John Franceschina. CAST: Kevin O'Connor (Van Amburgh), Michael Genet (Will), Ben Siegler (Henry), Leonard Parker (Frederick Douglass), Donna Haley (Susan B. Anthony), Margaret Colin (Tina), Brad Sullivan (Abraham Lincoln)

THE FOREIGNER by Larry Shue; Director, Walton Jones; Set, Kevin Rupnik; Lighting, Walter R. Uhrmann; Costumes, Connie Singer; Sound, Nicholas Minetor. CAST: John C. Vennema (Charlie Baker), Corey Hansen (Rev. David Lee), Jane Murray (Catherine Simms), Richard Fitzpatrick (Owen Musser), F. J. Pratt (Ellard Simms)

AND A NIGHTINGALE SANG by C. P. Taylor; Director, Gideon Schein; Set, Richard Hoover; Lighting, Victor En Yu Tan; Costumes, Pamela Scofield; Sound, Tom Gould. CAST: Amelia White (Helen), Franklin Brown (George), Richard Ziman (Eric), Brad Sullivan (Andie), Geoffrey Wade (Norman), Angela Thornton (Peggy), Brenda Foley (Joyce)

THE ROYAL FAMILY by George S. Kaufman, Edna Ferber; Director, Howard J. Millman; Set, Holmes Easley; Lighting, Phil Monat; Costumes, Pamela Scofield. CAST: Bernie Engel (Oscar Wolf), Robert Strane (Anthony Cavendish), Margot Stevenson (Fanny Cavendish), Patrick Egan (Jo), Walter Rhodes (Gil Marshall), Thomas Schall (Perry), Matthew Kimbrough (Gunga/McDermott), Devora Millman (Gwen Cavendish), Polly Holliday (Julie Cavendish), Barbara Redmond (Kitty Dean), Eb Thomas (Herbert Dean), Marcia Nowik (Della)

John Rizzo, Brad Bliss Photos

**Top Right: Ben Siegler, Michael Genet
in "Planet Fires"**

GLOBE PLAYHOUSE

Los Angeles, California
May 4, 1984–June 1, 1985

Producer-Director, R. Thad Taylor; Co-Producer, Jay Uhley; Associate Producer, John Roberts; Assistant Director, Sami Kamal; Lighting, David Robkin; Choreographer, Golden Kyle; Costumes, Catherine Tabah; The Shakespeare Society of America presents:

OTHELLO directed by Keith Lawrence. CAST: Bennet Guillory (Othello), Patricia Pearcy (Desdemona), Kathrine Bates, Bob Bieleki, Kevin Carr, Christopher Dakin, Kathy Denton, Russell Fear, James Russell, Nonnie Vishner

SIR THOMAS MORE by William Shakespeare and Others; *American Premiere;* Director, Phoebe Wray; Costumes, Cathy Crane; Stage Manager, John McManus. CAST: Gregory Alan, Tony Allen, Danny Babineaux, John Bremmer, Robert J. Britton, Teddy Cashwell, J. Christopher Cleveland, Jensen Collier, Christopher Dakin, Montrose Hagins, Candice Kelly, Thom Koutsoukos (Sir Thomas More), Loring Leeds, Dan Martin, Steve McGrew, John McManus, Tom Noga, Richard Osborn, Don Paul, William Pfleuger, Scott Reiniger, Jon S. Roe, Philip Ruthstrom, Daniel Sabia, Kit Van Zandt, Randall Wright

ANTONY AND CLEOPATRA directed by R. Thad Taylor; Assistant Director, Sami Kamal; Stage Manager, Robert Brogan. CAST: Gregory Alan, Tony Allen, Ricardo Alvarado, Myra Jo Arvin, Tom Ashworth, Craig Augustine, Tanya Barnes, Robert Brogan, Leslie Doqui, Nora Ekserjan, Larry Evans, Ben Ghaffari, Babe Gilliam, Larry Hooper, Neil Houston, Robert Kincaid, Al Malafronte, John McManus, R. A. Mihailoff, Cedric Minkin, Rodrigo Obregon, Lynne Otis, Francois Pascal, Joe Farris, Kaaren Ragland (Cleopatra), Philip Ruthstrom (Antony), Myron Senkus, Jon Slade (Caesar), John Spatafora, Paul Rene St. Peter, Corey Taylor, Dina Eaxman, Randall Wright

ANZAC I & II by Mary A. Mann; *World Premiere;* Director, Edward Ludlum; Scenery/Lighting, D. Martyn Bookwalter; Sound, Leonora Schildkraut; Costumes, George Kiel; Original Music, Hugh S. Coles. CAST: Terri Amoon, Augie Durell Blunt, Paul Boardman, Daniel Brinkley, Ken Capozzi, Michael Cohen, Kevin Cummings, Ronald L. Cyr, Claire Daks, Frank Daniel, Brian Depew, Garry Leigh Douglas, Jean Field, Christian Golden, Joyce E. Greene, Lloyd H. Heslip, Jeff Hammers, Patricia Huston, Raymond Lack, Barbara Louise, Ernest Lucero, Irene Miracle, Adonny Mitchell, Tim Ottman, Pamela Putnam, Steve M. Ray, J. Michael Raye, Marla Rix, Thomas Matthew Ruggles, Cathy Sandrich, Maria Scott, Dawn Smithfield, Phyllis Deon Upton, John Weighton, Susan D. Zimmerman

ROMEO AND JULIET directed by John Roberts; Fight Directors, James Dalesandro, Greg Michaels; Choreographer, Carl Daugenti; Costumes, Janic Tully, Renee Sacks. CAST: Debbie Gates (Juliet), Vsev Krawczeniuk/Robert Dickey (Romeo), Jay McManus (Benvolio), Glenn Simon (Tybalt), Tony Patellis (Mercutio), Kevin Carr (Tybalt), Diana Bellamy (Nurse), Don Altman (Capulet), Corinne Kason (Lady Capulet), Steve Eastin (Montague), Ellen Cameron (Lady Montague), Jon S. Roe (Paris), Cedric Minkin (Friar Laurence), Myron Senkus (Peter), Randy Trovato (Gregory), Randall Caldwell (Sampson)

TROILUS AND CRESSIDA directed by Robert Prior; Costumes, Barbara Cox; Lighting, Ed Davidson; Stage Manager, Wade Carter. CAST: David Farjeon, Chip Heller (Hector), Arye Gross (Troilus), Tony Maggio (Paris), Marc Reeves, Sean Hannon, Bruce Wilner, Ken Salley, Robert Katims, Robert Winley, Paul Dancer (Menelaus), James Marilley (Achilles), George Saunders, Philip Persons, Arnie Markussen, Larry Acosta, Christopher Barrio, Don Boughton, Leslie Paxton, Delta Giordano, Mary Kahl, Julia Fairbanks (Cressida), Shirley Chin, James Shanahan, Christopher Fritz, Ken McCloud

RICHARD II directed by Simon Kazangian; Assistant Director, Thomas Cole; Costumes, Neal Teguns; Stage Managers, Michael Bershad, Leslie Morris. CAST: Michael Bershad, John Behrens, Barry Burke, Peter J. Crawford, Joan Crosby, Oren Curtis, John Dobbs, Paul Elder, Anthony Embeck, Tom Flynn, Mark Goodman, Michael Hadlow, Eric Heath, Holly Lee Henson, J. Howard Higley, Ralph Lucas, Jeff MacNeill, Steve McGrew, Leslie Morris, Myron Natwick, James Nemec, Gregory Niebel, Richard Osborn, Kay Pattison, Sharon Pierson, Charlene Worthley, Ronald Cream

**Thom Koutsoukos (kneeling), Philip
Ruthstrom in "Sir Thomas More"**

FOLGER THEATRE

Washington, D.C.
September 25, 1984–June 30, 1985
Fifteenth Season

Artistic Producer, John Neville-Andrews; Managing Director, Mary Ann de Barbieri; Production Manager, Elizabeth Hamilton; Administrative Coordinator, Valerie Hanlon; Development, Michael Darling; Press, Susan Glazier, Mary Catherine Resing; Dramaturg, Genie Barton; Literary Manager, Bob Stevens; Technical Director, Tom Whittington; Props, Susan Weiss; Wardrobe, Lisa Johnson; Sound, Paul Langer; Stage Managers, Margaret Hahn, B. Laurie Hunt

PRODUCTIONS & CASTS

KING LEAR by William Shakespeare; Director, John Neville-Andrews; Set, Russell Metheny; Costumes, Ann Hould-Ward; Lighting, Stuart Duke; Fight Director, Michael Tolaydo; Movement, Virginia Freeman
CAST: John Wylie (Lear), Mikel Lambert (Goneril), Vivienne Argent (Regan), Barbara Garrick (Cordelia), Michael Howell (Duke of Albany), Roderick Horn (Duke of Cornwall), Floyd King (Fool), Terrence Riggins (Duke of Burgundy), Frank Groseclose (Earl of Gloucester), Michael Tolaydo (Edgar), Edward Gero (Edmund), Jim Beard (Earl of Kent), Richard Hart (Oswald), Alessandro Cima (King of France/Captain/Servant), Seth Jones (Knight), Reese Stevens (Doctor)

CROSSED WORDS with Book/Music/Lyrics by Hugh Atkins, Mike Laflin; Director, Davey Marlin-Jones; Set/Lighting, Lewis Folden; Costumes, Paige Southard; Musical Arranger/Director, Rob Bowman; Choreographer, Virginia Freeman; Magic, Richard I. Bloch. CAST: Jim Beard (Chukka Gobrotte), Alessandro Cima (Adrian/Spotty), Edward Gero (Jack Stamford-Depletions), Richard Hart (Length), Roderick Horn (Grubbie), Michael W. Howell (Friday the Third), Floyd King (Sir Reginald Stamford-Depletions), Mikel Lambert (Lady Ginger Stamford-Depletions), Terrence Riggins (Knocker Rock/Ron Nematode/Rev. Beverage), Michael Tolaydo (Capt. Ferdinand Tempest/Sir Jeremy Curve-Ball), Paula Burns (Mustapha Drag/Bazza Spatula), Lucinda Hitchcock Cone (Lettice Preigh), David Cromwell (Wally), Hannah Weil (Sally O'Alley/Bunty Tupping), Joan Wells (D S X McHinna/Chas Spatula)

MUCH ADO ABOUT NOTHING by William Shakespeare; Director, John Neville-Andrews; Set, William Barclay; Costumes, John Carver Sullivan; Lighting, Daniel M. Wagner; Musical Director, Rob Bowman; Masks, Michael Eade. CAST: Emory Battis (Leonato), Jim Beard (Dogberry), Alessandro Cima (Conrade), Richard Hart (Chauffeur/Verges), Edward Gero (Don John), Roderick Horn (Benedick), Michael W. Howell (Borachio), Floyd King (Father Francis), Mikel Lambert (Beatrice), Terrence Riggins (Hugh Oatcake), Michael Tolaydo (Claudio), John Wylie (Antonio), Erika Lynn Bogren (Ursula), Rob Bowman (Balthasar), Steven Crossley (Don Pedro), Stephen Hayes (George Seacole), Tara Hugo (Hero), Reginald Metcalf (Harry Starboard), Hannah Weil (Margaret)

HAMLET by William Shakespeare; Director, Lindsay Anderson; Set, John Lee Beatty; Costumes, Judianna Makovsky; Lighting, Jeffrey Beecroft; Fight Direction, Erik Fredricksen. CAST: Emory Battis (Polonius), Jim Beard (1st Player/Clown/Gravedigger), Alessandro Cima (Marcellus/Norwegian Captain), Edward Gero (Guildenstern), Richard Hart (Player Queen/Priest/Gentleman), Roderick Horn (Claudius), Michael W. Howell (Bernardo/Lucianus/Monk), Seth Allan Jones (Voltemand/Fortinbras), Floyd King (Osric), Mikel Lambert (Gertrude), Michael Tolaydo (Laertes), John Wylie (Player King/Ghost), Frank Grimes (Hamlet), Edward Hibbert (Rosencrantz), James Maxwell (Horatio), Ritchie Porter (Player/Courtier/Attendant/Bearer), Madeleine Potter (Ophelia), Rick Sabatini (Cornelius/Courtier/Monk), David Shroder (Francisco/Sailor, Courtier/Captain), Joao de Sousa (Attendant/Monk)

A MIDSUMMER NIGHT'S DREAM by William Shakespeare; Director, John Neville-Andrews; Set, Lewis Folden; Costumes, Elizabeth Covey; Lighting, Richard Winkler; Choreography, Virginia Freeman; Music/Arrangements, Sam McClung; Makeup, Barbara York. CAST: Emory Battis (Egeus), Jim Beard (Bottom), Alessandro Cima (Demetrius), Edward Gero (Oberon), Richard Hart (Puck), Roderick Horn (Snug), Michael W. Howell (Tom Snout), Seth Jones (Lysander), Floyd King (Flute), Michael Tolaydo (Robin Starveling), Louise J. Andrews (Moth), Bonnie Black (Hermia), Erika Lynn Bogren (Mustardseed), Orlagh Cassidy (Lady in Waiting/Peaseblossom), Brian Clark (Goblin), David Cromwell (Peter Quince), Steven Crossley (Theseus), Charlotte Dooling (Lady in Waiting/Cobweb), Franchelle Stewart Dorn (Titania), John Elko (Philostrate), Becky Kemper (Lady in Waiting/Coriander), Rita Litton (Helena), Anne Stone (Hippolyta), Peter Sweeney (Indian Boy/Goblin)

Joan Marcus Photos

**Top Left: Frank Groseclose, Vivienne Argent
in "King Lear" Below: Frank Grimes as Hamlet**

**Michael Tolaydo, Steven Grossley
in "Much Ado about Nothing"**

160

GOODSPEED OPERA HOUSE

East Haddam, Connecticut
June 1, 1984–June 28, 1985

Executive Producer, Michael P. Price; Associate Producer, Warren Pincus; Musical Director, Lynn Crigler; Choreographer, Dan Siretta; Technical Director, Jack Conant; Stage Managers, John J. Bonanni, Brennan Roberts; Casting, Warren Pincus; Company Manager, William S. Nagel; Press, Kay McGrath, Mindy Keskinen; Music Research Consultant, Alfred Simon

PRODUCTIONS & CASTS

FOLLOW THRU with Book by Laurence Schwab, B. G. DeSylva; Music and Lyrics, DeSylva, Brown and Henderson; Adapted by Alfred Uhry; Director, Robert Nigro; Choreography/Musical Staging, Dan Siretta; Scenery, James Leonard Joy; Lighting, Pat Collins; Costumes, David Toser; Dance Music, G. Harrell; Musical Director/Additional Orchestrations/Vocal Arrangements, Lynn Crigler; Special Consultant, Robert Kimball; Assistant Musical Director, Patrick Vaccariello. CAST: Gina Battist, Joel Blum, Donna English, Steven F. Hall, Dale O'Brien, Jana Robbins, Nikki Sahagen, Jim Soriero, Raymond Thorne, Blake Atherton, Kimberly Campbell, David Fredericks, Robert McNeill, David Monzione, Mercedes Perez, Rodney Pridgen, Keith Savage, Rhonda J. White, Suzi Winston

TAKE ME ALONG with Music and Lyrics by Bob Merrill; Book, Joseph Stein, Robert Russell; Based on play "Ah, Wilderness!" by Eugene O'Neill; Director, Thomas Gruenewald; Choreography and Musical Staging, Dan Siretta; Assistant Choreographer, David Fredericks; Technical Director, Jay Nilsen; Scenery, James Leonard Joy; Lighting, Craig Miller; Costumes, David Toser; Orchestrations, Philip J. Lang; Dance Arrangements, Allen Cohen; Additional Orchestrations, Lynn Crigler/Allen Cohen; Assistant Musical Director, Patrick Vaccariello. CAST: Beth Fowler, Maggy Gorrill, Taryn Grimes, Betty Johnson, Kurt Knudson, Stephen McDonough, Sarah Navin, Robert Nichols, Gary Landon Wright, Blake Atherton, Ed Brazo, Richard Dodd, Andy Hostettler, Richard Korthaze, Patrick S. Murphy, Amy O'Brien, David Vosburgh, Joel Whittaker, Betty Winsett, John Witham

YOU NEVER KNOW with Music and Lyrics by Cole Porter; Based on play "By Candlelight" by Siegfried Geyer, Karl Farkas, Robert Katscher; Adapted by Rowland Leigh; Additional Adaptation/Direction, Paul Lazarus; Choreography, Patrice Soriero; Producing Associate, Sue Frost; Musical Director, Jeffrey Saver; Musical Supervision/Orchestrations/Arrangements, Steven Oirich; Produced by arrangement with John Nassivera; Scenery, James Leonard Joy; Lighting, Curt Osterman; Costumes, John Falabella; Technical Director, Jay Nilsen; Stage Manager, Ben Janney. CAST: Humbert Allen Astredo, Kirsti Carnahan, Mitchell Greenberg, Rex D. Hays, Denise Nolin, Marianne Tatum

(NORMA TERRIS THEATRE/Musicals-in-progress)
HARRIGAN 'N HART with Book by Michael Stewart; Based on biographical material compiled by Nedda Harrigan Logan, and "The Merry Partners" by E. J. Kahn, Jr.; Music, Max Showalter; Lyrics, Peter Walker; Songs of the period by Edward Harrigan and David Braham; Director, Edward Stone; Choreographer, D. J. Giagni; Scenery, James Leonard Joy; Lighting, Marilyn Rennagel; Costumes, Ann Hould-Ward; Musical Director, Michael Skloff; Musical Supervision/Orchestrations/Arrangements, John McKinney; Producers, Gerald A. Davis, Warren Pincus. CAST: Kenneth Ames, Cleve Asbury, Clent Bowers, Leslie Cokery, Mark Fotopoulos, Michael Gorman, Mark Hamill, Roxie Lucas, Armelia McQueen, Barbara Moroz, Meredith Murray, Tudi Roche, Marianne Tatum, Christopher Wells, Oliver Woodall

MRS. McTHING with Book and Lyrics by Michael Colby; Based on play by Mary Chase; Music, Jacques Urbont; Director, Edward Stone; Choreography/Musical Staging, Dennis Dennehy; Scenery, Mark Morton; Lighting, Jason Kantrowitz; Costumes, Susan Hirschfeld; Dance Arrangements, John McKinney; Musical Arrangements, Jacques Urbont; Musical Director, Jacques Urbont; Production Supervisor, John Bonanni; Magic Consultant, David Roth; Produced by Gerald A. Davis, Warren Pincus. CAST: G. Brandon Allen, Gibby Brand, Bobby Cavanaugh, Deborah Dotson, Lynn Eldredge, Ray Gill, Danyle Heffernan, Tommy Hollis, Wayne Lancaster, Jeanne Lehman, Dennis Parlato, Donna Pompei, Brian Worley

A BROADWAY BABY with Book by Carl Kleinschmitt; Based on a concept of Sid and Marty Krofft and Irwin Meyer; Music, Arthur Freed; Additional Music, Al Hoffman, Al Goodhart, Gus Arnheim, Abe Lyman; Additional Lyrics, Earl K. Brent, Gus Kahn; Director/Choreographer, Thommie Walsh; Associate Director/Choreographer, Baayork Lee; Scenery, Nicky Nadeau; Costumes, William Ivey Long; Lighting, Marilyn Rennagel; Sound, Otts Munderloh; Arrangements/Orchestrations, Wally Harper; Krofft Puppets, Rolf Roediger; Technical Director, Jay Nilsen; Produced by arrangement with Jerome Minskoff, Kenneth Feld, Krofft Entertainment and Pound Ridge Productions. CAST: Richard Blake, Michael Earl, Bobby Gee, Sandey Grinn, Heather Hope Gryning, Karen Hartman, Kim Hauser, Brandy Hill, Piper Lawrence, Frank Charles Lutkus III, Michael Manasseri, Liza Morris, Kimi Parks, Carolyn Potvin, Joseph Reff, Randi Reynolds, R. D. Robb, Matthew Sears, Van Snowden, Sahana Vyas, Todd Walcott, Lily Nell Warren, Shari Wilson, Kent Zbornak, Jason J. Ziegler

THE DREAM TEAM with Book by Richard Wesley; Based on concept by Joseph Robinette and Thomas Tierney; Music, Thomas Tierney; Lyrics, John Forster; Direction-Choreography, Dan Siretta; Assistant Choreographer, Joel Blum; Technical Director, Jay Nilsen; Musical Direction/Arrangements, William Foster McDaniel; Orchestrations, J. Billy Ver Planck; Scenery, James Leonard Joy; Lighting, Beverly Emmons; Costumes, Judy Dearing; Produced under the supervision of Sue Frost; Stage Manager, Holly DeYoung. CAST: Lynne Clifton Allen, Edwin Battle, Harry L. Burney III, Greg Gunning, Stanley Wayne Mathis, James McDaniel, S. Epatha Merkerson, Wellington Perkins, Larry Riley, Melodee Savage, James Stovall, Reginald VelJohnson, Teddey Brown, Lou Connick, Harrison Le Duke, Wayne Bell Pretlow

**Christopher Wells, Mark Hamill
in "Harrigan 'n Hart"**

**Kirsti Carnahan, Mitchell Greenberg
in "You Never Know"**

**Larry Riley
in "The Dream Team"**

GOODMAN THEATRE
NEW THEATRE COMPANY

Chicago, Illinois
October 1, 1984–July 14, 1985

Director, Gregory Mosher; Producer, Roche Schulfer; Associate Director, David Mamet; Press, Jennifer Boznos

RESIDENT COMPANY: Nan Cibula, Gary Cole, Lindsay Crouse, Kathleen Dennehy, John Guare, Linda Kimbrough, W. H. Macy, David Mamet, Michael Merritt, Gregory Mosher, Mike Nussbaum, Les Podewell, Nessa Rabin, Kevin Rigdon, Peter Riegert, Jose Santana, Lionel Mark Smith, Sheila Welch, Lisa Zane, *Guest Artists:* Douglas Turner Ward, Negro Ensemble Company, Robert Brustein and the American Repertory Theatre
PRODUCTIONS: Candide by Leonard Bernstein, The Adventures of Huckleberry Finn adapted by the Organic Theater Company, Ceremonies in Dark Old Men by Lonne Elder III, The Water Engine by David Mamet, Six Characters in Search of an Author by Luigi Pirandello and adapted by Robert Brustein, The Cherry Orchard by Anton Chekhov and adapted by David Mamet, *World Premiere* of The Spanish Prisoner and The Shawl by David Mamet

Top Right: Peter Riegert, Lindsay Crouse,
Colin Stinton in "The Cherry Orchard"
(Brigitte Lacombe Photo)

O. L. Duke, Robert Gossett,
Graham Brown, Lanyard Williams,
Ruben Hudson in "A Soldier's Play"
(Sandy Underwood Photo)

GUTHRIE THEATRE

Minneapolis, Minnesota
April 4, 1984–April 28, 1985
Twenty-second Season

Artistic Director, Liviu Ciulei; Managing Director, Donald Schoenbaum; Literary Manager/Dramaturg, Mark Bly; Dramaturg, Michael Lupu; Literary Associates, Robert Cowgill, Tom Creamer; Directors, Liviu Ciulei, Christopher Markle, Lucian Pintilie, Terry Schreiber, Peter Sellars, Douglas Turner Ward, Garland Wright; Musical Directors, David Bishop, Paul H. Pfeiffer, Craig Smith; Sets, Jack Barkla, Radu Boruzescu, Liviu Ciulei, Felix H. Cochren, Jack Edwards, Adrianne Lobel, Thomas Lynch, Hal Tine; Costumes, Miruna Boruzescu, Judy Dearing, Jack Edwards, Patricia McGourty, Dunya Ramicova; Lighting, Bill Armstrong, Dawn Chiang, Marcus Dilliard, Beverly Emmons, Allen Lee Hughes, James F. Ingalls, Craig Miller, Paul Scharfenberger; Choreographers, Maria Cheng, Loyce Houlton, Dirk Lumbard; Press, Dennis Behl

PRODUCTIONS & CASTS

A SOLDIER'S PLAY with Gary Armagnac, Graham Brown, O. L. Duke, Ben E. Epps, Goeffrey Ewing, Danny Goldring, Robert Gossett, Mike Hodge, Ruben Hudson, Steven A. Jones, Cedric Turner, Lanyard A. Williams, Stephen Zettler
HANG ON TO ME with Mark Baker, Eve Bennett-Gordon, Roy Brocksmith, Susan Browning, Michael Connolly, Roger DeKoven, Carmen DeLavallade, Richard Frank, Werner Klemperer, James J. Lawless, Robert Nadir, Richard Ooms, Patti Perkins, Deirdre Peterson, David Rasmussen, Priscilla Smith, Marianne Tatum, David Warrilow
THREE SISTERS with Gerry Bamman, Roger DeKoven, Michael Egan, June Gibbons, Trish Hawkins, Richard Howard, Joan MacIntosh, Mary McDonnell, Frances McDormand, Randle Mell, Marianne Owen, Jay Patterson, David Rasmussen, John Madden Towey, Paul Walker
TARTUFFE with Gerry Bamman, Francois de la Giroday, Peter Francis-James, Harriet Harris, Katherine Leask, Isabell Monk, Richard Ooms, David Pierce, Paul Walker, Claudia Wilkens, Harris Yulin
'NIGHT, MOTHER with Veronica Castang, Georgine Hall
TWELFTH NIGHT with Julian Bailey, Lawrence Block, Peter Francis-James, Richard Frank, Richard Howard, Katherine Leask, Isabell Monk, Pamela Nyberg, Gordana Rashovich, David Rasmussen, Rocco Sisto, John Madden Towey, Paul Walker, Nicholas Wyman
A CHRISTMAS CAROL with Julian Bailey, Lawrence Block, Peter Francis-James, Kate Fuglei, Richard Howard, Gene Jundt, Kenneth LaZebnik, Pamela Nyberg, Richard Ooms, Deirdre Peterson, David Rasmussen, Hayden Saunier, Barbara Tirrell, John Madden Towey, Henrietta Valor, Paul Walker, Claudia Wilkens, Frederick Winship
ANYTHING GOES with Maureen Brennan, Jonathan Brody, Tarry Caruso, Teresa DeRose, Madeleine Doherty, Michael Duran, Patricia Everett, Felicia Farone, Andrea Goodman, Steve Goodwillie, Brian A. Grandison, Stephen Hanan, John Hoshko, Eric Hutson, Justine Johnston, Kelby Kirk, Marvette Knight, David Lowenstein, John MacInnis, Jeff McCarthy, Katheryn Meloche, Karen Morrow, Peggy O'Connell, Wendy Oliver, Richard Ooms, Kevin Ramsey, Charles Rule, Richard Stafford, Kelly Strange, Michael Watson, Eric Weitz, Kevin Brooks Winkler, Donna Ingram-Young
FOXFIRE with Helen-Jean Arthur, Julian Bailey, Jonathan Bolt, Sally Dunn, Eve Johnson, Ken Magee, Anne Oberbroeckling, Edward Seamon, Jake Turner

Joe Giannetti Photos

Mark Baker (L), Marianne Tatum (C), Patti
Perkins (R) in "Hang on to Me"
(Joe Giannetti Photo)

162

HARTFORD STAGE COMPANY

Hartford, Connecticut
October 9, 1984–June 30, 1985
Twenty-second Season

Artistic Director, Mark Lamos; Managing Director, William Stewart; Associate Artistic Director, Mary B. Robinson; Business Manager, Vera N. Furdas; Production Manager, Candice Chirgotis; Dramaturg, Helen Sheehy; Literary Manager, Constance Congdon; Stage Managers, H. Lloyd Carbaugh, Katherine Goodrich

PRODUCTIONS & CASTS

ANATOL by Arthur Schnitzler; Director, Mark Lamos; Assistant Director, Kent Thompson; Set/Costumes, John Conklin; Lighting, Pat Collins. CAST: Mark Lamos (Anatol), David Schramm (Max), Carol Calkins (Cora), Mary Layne (Gabrielle), Leslie Geraci (Bianca), Giulia Pagano (Emilie), Michele Farr (Annie), Susan Pellegrino (Elsa), Patricia Mauceri (Ilona)

THE MYSTERY PLAYS in a new version by John Russell Brown; Director, Mary B. Robinson; Set/Costumes, John Conklin; Lighting, Robert Wiertzel; Music, Amy Rubin. CAST: Christopher McCann (God), John Rensenhouse (Adam/Shem/Joseph/Mak), Angela Bassett (Eve/Noah's Wife/Mary/Gill), Peter Crook (Lucifer/Abel/Japhet/Shepherd/Herod), Michael Butler (Cain/Ham/Sheherd), Yusef Bulos (Noah/Shepherd)

PASSION PLAY by Peter Nichols; Director, Mark Lamos; Set, Marjorie Bradley Kellogg; Costumes, Jess Goldstein; Lighting, Pat Collins. CAST: Robert Stattel (James), Pamela Payton-Wright (Eleanor), Lisa Emery (Kate), Janet Sarno (Agnes), George Grizzard (Jim), Jennifer Sternberg (Nell)

AMERICA'S SWEETHEART *(World Premiere)* with Book by John Weidman, Alfred Uhry; Music, Robert Waldman; Lyrics, Alfred Uhry; Director, Gerald Freedman; Choreography, Graciela Daniele; Musical Director, Liza Redfield; Sets, Kevin Rupnik; Costumes, Jeanne Button; Lighting, Pat Collins. CAST: Stephen Vinovich (Al Capone), K. T. Sullivan (Mae Capone), Trevor Keeth (Sonny Capone), Nicholas Gunn (Jake Bensick), Michael McCormick (Frankie Rivaldo), Tom Robbins (Tony Rivaldo), Wayne Bryan (Officer Zwick/Jerry Allen/Badger/Grown Sonny), Carolyn Casanave (Edna Beal), Lucinda Hitchcock Cone (Lulu Blombeck), Gary-Michael Davies (President/Barney/Schemer/Sen. Krauss), Donna English (Bernice Madden/Muriel Wilson), Jeff Etjen (Bugs Moran/Attorney General/Judge Fox), Tom Henning (Harry Wilzak/Dion O'Bannion/Stone), Richard Levine (Nate Beal/Dr. Bailey), K. K. Preece (Radio Lady/Gladys), Steve Routman (Max Chase/Hymie Weiss/Frank Wilson), Deanna Wells (Vicki Chase/Fay/Stern)

DESIRE UNDER THE ELMS by Eugene O'Neill; Director, Mary B. Robinson; Sets, Hugh Landwehr; Costumes, Jess Goldstein; Lighting, Paulie Jenkins; Music, Allyn Benedict. CAST: Victor Slezak (Eben Cabot), David A. Kimball (Simeon Cabot), Matthew Kimbrough (Peter Cabot), James Greene (Ephraim Cabot), Frances Fisher (Abbie Putnam)

THE TEMPEST by William Shakespeare; Director, Mark Lamos; Sets, Michael H. Yeargan; Costumes, Dunya Ramicova; Lighting, Pat Collins; Music, Mel Marvin. CAST: Tom Klunis (Alonso), Doug Stender (Sebastian), Philip Kerr (Prospero), Alan Mixon (Antonio), Morgan Strickland (Ferdinand), George Hamlin (Gonzalo), Mark Wayne Nelson (Adrian), Alan Osburn (Francisco), Justin Deas (Caliban), Paul Redford (Trinculo), Lance Davis (Stephano), Mario Vicenzo (Master of ship), Michael O'Gorman (Boatswain), Laura Innes (Miranda), William O'Leary (Ariel)

Lanny Nagler Photos

Frances Fisher, Victor Slezak
in "Desire under the Elms"

George Grizzard, Lisa Emery
in "Passion Play"

HARTMAN THEATRE

Stamford, Connecticut
September 21, 1984–May 19, 1985
Tenth Season

Producing Artistic Director, Edwin Sherin; Executive Director, Harris Goldman; Company Manager, Kevin Kruse; Literary Manager, Frank Rembach; Development, Ann S. Johnson; Production Manager, David N. Feight; Wardrobe, Jill H. Cochran; Props, Timothy Whitney; Sound, Michael Gurvich; Stage Managers, Don Enoch, Kathleen Iacobacci; Press, Lorraine Bauman

PRODUCTIONS & CASTS

THE TORCH-BEARERS by George Kelly; Director, Elinor Renfield; Set, Victor Capecce; Costumes, Mariann Verheyen; Lighting, Jeff Davis; Stage Manager, April Briggs; Casting, Deborah Brown. CAST: Mark Benninghofen, Robert Boardman, Pamela Brook, Joyce Bulifant, David Cryer, Mary Fogarty, Jane Hoffman, Sofia Landon, Jan Miner, Bernie Passeltiner, James Seymour, Doug Stender

OVER MY DEAD BODY by Michael Sutton and Anthony J. Fingleton; *World Premiere;* Director, Edwin Sherin; Set, Victor Capecce; Costumes, Judianna Makovsky; Lighting, Jeff Davis. CAST: Walter Atamaniuk, Richard Clarke, Tammy Grimes, Mordecai Lawner, Stephen Newman, William Preston, Thomas Toner, Fritz Weaver

BELOVED FRIEND by Nancy Pahl Gilsenan; *World Premiere;* Director, David Chambers; Set, Oliver Smith; Costumes, Marie Anne Chiment; Lighting, Arden Fingerhut; Music, Mel Marvin; Stage Manager, Franklin Keysar. CAST: Richard Backus, David Combs, Sheila Dabney, Dana Delany, Max Jacobs, Robert Jason, Mary Jay, Matthew Lewis, Cheryl Rogers, Barbara Sohmers, Kim Staunton, Kim Sullivan

LIGHT COMEDIES (Two one-acts: The Public Eye and Black Comedy) by Peter Shaffer; Director, Peter Pope; Set, Douglas W. Schmidt; Adapted by David N. Feight; Costumes, Carol Oditz; Lighting, Jeff Davis. CAST: Yusef Bulos, Paddy Croft, Monique Fowler, Daniel Gerroll, Breon Gorman, Don Plumley, Rex Robbins, Ian Trigger

THE TEAM by Terence Feely; *World Premiere;* Director, Edwin Sherin; Set, Guido Tondino; Costumes, Mariann Verheyen; Lighting, Jeff Davis; Casting, Leonard Finger. CAST: Richard Clarke, Richard Dow, Alexandra O'Karma, Lenny von Dohlen

GREATER TUNA by Jaston Williams, Joe Sears, Ed Howard; Director, Darwin Knight; Set, David Crank; Costumes, Lana Fritz; Lighting, Jeff Davis. CAST: Michael McCarty, Trip Plymale

Gerry Goodstein Photos

Thomas Toner (seated), Fritz Weaver,
Tammy Grimes in "Over My Dead Body"

HIPPODROME STATE THEATRE OF FLORIDA

Gainesville, Florida
July 12, 1984–June 15, 1985

Producing Directors, Gregory Hausch, Mary Hausch, Margaret Bachus; Scenery, Carlos Asse; Costumes, Marilyn Wall-Asse

COMPANY: Mariah Reed, Kevin Rainsberger, Mike Beistle, Rusty Salling, Dan Jesse, Mike Doyle, Debbie Laumand, Malcolm Gets
PRODUCTIONS: Pump Boys & Dinettes, Romeo and Juliet, Rosencrantz and Guildenstern Are Dead, Season's Greetings, Period of Adjustment, A Christmas Carol, The Middle Ages

Gary Wolfson Photos

Consuelo Dodge, Kevin Rainsberger, Mariah
Reed, Mike Beistle in "The Middle Ages"

William McManus, John Leighton, Thomas
Apple, Elizabeth McGovern in "Twelfth Night"

Maryann Plunkett, Jack Aranson
in "Uncle Vanya"

HUNTINGTON THEATRE COMPANY

Boston, Massachusetts
September 29, 1984–June 16, 1985
Third Season

Producing Director, Peter Altman; Managing Director, Michael Maso; Business Manager, Mary Kiely; Company Manager, Edwin Light; Marketing/Press, Marty Jones, Elaine Davies, Wendy Pilson, Pam Malumphy, Janet DeJean; Production Manager, Roger Meeker; Technical Director, Jim Ray; Props, Bobby Summerlin; Wardrobe, Mary Ellen Bosche; Sound, Peter Sullivan

PRODUCTIONS & CASTS

YOU NEVER KNOW with Music and Lyrics by Cole Porter; Based on play "By Candlelight"; Adapted by Rowland Leigh, Paul Lazarus; Director, Paul Lazarus; Musical Director, Jeffrey Saver; Musical Supervision/Orchestrations, Steven Oirich; Choreography, Patrice Soriero; Lighting, Craig Miller; Costumes, John Falabella; Set, James Leonard Joy; Stage Managers, Thomas L. Clewell, Karen L. Carpenter. CAST: Rex D. Hays (Baron), Mitchell Greenberg (Gaston), Carolyn Casanave (Ida), Donalyn Petrucci (Maria), George Ede (Herr Baltin), Lynne Wintersteller

TWELFTH NIGHT by William Shakespeare; Director, Thomas Gruenewald; Scenery, Franco Colavecchia, David Sumner; Costumes, Mariann Verheyen; Lighting, William Mintzer; Musical Arrangements, Samuel Headrick; Stage Managers, Karen L. Carpenter, Karin Hartmann. CAST: Gary Armagnac (Orsino), James Bodge (Curio), Thomas Apple (Valentine), Elizabeth McGovern (Viola), Ron Perkins (Sea Captain/Priest), Jack Aranson (Sir Toby Belch), Frances Cuka (Maria), Gary Beach (Sir Andrew Aguecheek), Michael Medeiros (Feste), Margaret Reed (Olivia), Joseph Costa (Malvolio), John Leighton (Antonio), Francis Guinan (Sebastian), Leonard Kelly-Young (Fabian), William McManus (Second Officer/Waiter/Attendant), and Ruth Cataldo, John Macero, Kate Maguire, Michael Pereira

UNCLE VANYA by Anton Chekhov; Director, Jacques Cartier; Scenery, Richard M. Isackes; Costumes, Ann Wallace; Lighting, Roger Meeker; Sound, Richard Sirois; Stage Managers, Scott LaFeber, Stacey Michael. CAST: Sally Chamberlin (Marina), Stephen Markle (Mikhail Lovovich Astrov), Jack Aranson (Ivan Petrovich Voynitsky "Uncle Vanya"), Gwyllum Evans (Alexander Vladimirovich Serebryakov), Jack Poggi (Waffles), Maryann Plunkett (Sonya), Monica Merryman (Yelena Andreyevna), Eunice Anderson (Marya Vassilyevna Voynitsky), James Bodge (Workman)

TERRA NOVA by Ted Tally; Director, Michael Murray; Set, Karl Eigsti; Costumes, Mariann Verheyen; Lighting, Spencer Mosse; Sound, Peter Sullivan; Stage Managers, Thomas Clewell, Stacey Michael. CAST: James A. Stephens (Scott), Stephen Markle (Amundsen), Jean McNally (Kathleen), Sean G. Griffin (Bowers), Eberle Thomas (Wilson), Doug Stender (Oates), Robert Burns (Evans)

THE PLOUGH AND THE STARS by Sean O'Casey; Director, Pamela Berlin; Costumes, Susan Tsu; Set, John Falabella; Lighting, James F. Ingalls; Stage Managers, Peggy Peterson, Mari S. Schatz. CAST: Patrick Clear (Jack), Keliher Walsh (Nora), Wyman Pendleton (Peter), William Carden (Young Covey), Pauline Flanagan (Bessie), Veronica Castang (Mrs. Gogan), Pamela Pascoe (Mollser), Sean G. Griffin (Fluther), Kieran Brennan (Lt. Langon), Brian Connors (Capt. Brennan), John Conley (Cpl. Stoddart), William Perley (Sgt. Tinley), Anne O'Sullivan (Rosie), Paul O'Brien (Bartender), Ingrid Sonnichsen (A Woman), William Perley (Figure in the window)

Gerry Goodstein Photos

ILLINOIS THEATRE CENTER

Park Forest, Illinois
September 28, 1984–May 5, 1985

Artistic Director, Steve S. Billig; Scenery; Stage Manager, Jonathan Roark; Lighting, Richard Peterson; Costumes, Henriette Swearingen; Choreographer, Mark Donaway; Stage Directors, Jonathan Roark, Etel Billig, Richard Pickren, Mark Donaway

PRODUCTIONS & CASTS

THE SHOW-OFF by George Kelly; with Claudia Dalton, David Cameron Anderson, Etel Billig, Robert Koons, Diane Fishbein, Mark Donaway, Steve S. Billig, Brian Leo
FOXFIRE by Susan Cooper and Hume Cronyn; with Richard Pickren, Etel Billig, Steve S. Billig, Cathy Bieber, David Saxe, William A. Miles
CHARLOTTE SWEET by Gerald Markoe and Michael Colby; with Karen Wheeler, Troy Pothoff, Susan LeDuc Wiley, Dan Moore, Steve S. Billig, Scott Bingham, Jeanne Weiland, Claudia Dalton
MY SISTER IN THIS HOUSE by Wendy Kesselman; with Margaret Silk, Peri Kaczmarek, Etel Billig, Franette Liebow
RELATIVELY SPEAKING by Alan Ayckbourn; with Jeanne Weiland, Steve S. Billig, Mark Donaway, Etel Billig
BLITHE SPIRIT by Noel Coward; with Iris Lieberman, Donald Ilko, Kate Johnson, Etel Billig, Cathy Bieber, Judy McLaughlin, Steve S. Billig
PACK UP YOUR TROUBLES by Steve S. Billig; *World Premiere;* with Karen Wheeler, Shole Milos, Etel Billig, Mark Donaway, Jane Petrongelli, Steve S. Billig

Lloyd DeGrane Photos

**Dan Moore, Troy Pothoff
in "Charlotte Sweet"**

**Colleen Dewhurst, Jeffrey Jones in "Rainsnakes"
Above: Peter Weller, Stefan Gierasch in "Cat on
a Hot Tin Roof"**

LONG WHARF THEATRE

New Haven, Connecticut
October 5, 1984–June 9, 1985
Twentieth Season

Artistic Director, Arvin Brown; Executive Director, M. Edgar Rosenblum; Associate Artistic Director, Kenneth Frankel; Literary Manager, John Tillinger; General Manager, John K. Conte; Assistant to Directors, Janice Muirhead; Press, Marta Mellinger; Development, Jacqueline Smaga; Sets, Michael Yeargan, John Lee Beatty, Tom Schwinn, David Jenkins, Loy Arcenas, Hugh Landwehr, Marjorie Bradley Kellogg; Lighting, Ronald Wallace, Judy Rasmuson, John Hastings, Pat Collins, Debra J. Kletter; Costumes, Bill Walker, Jane Greenwood, Linda Fisher, David Murin, Walker Hicklin, Jennifer von Mayrhauser; Technical Director, Randy Engels; Props, David Fletcher; Stage Managers, Anne Keefe, Robin Kevrick, Beverly J. Andreozzi

PRODUCTIONS & CASTS

TOBACCO ROAD by Jack Kirkland adapted from the novel by Erskine Caldwell; Director, Arvin Brown. CAST: Tom Aldredge, Robert Macnaughton, Pamela Payton-Wright, Annalee Jefferies, Margaret Barker, Leo Burmester, Richard Mathews, Joyce Ebert, Lucinda Jenney, Robert Hearn, Robert Swetland
RAINSNAKES by Per Olov Enquist; Translated from Swedish by Harry G. Carlson; Director, Jose Quintero. CAST: Colleen Dewhurst, Myra Carter, William Cain, Jeffrey Jones
OLIVER OLIVER by Paul Osborne; Director, Vivian Matalon. CAST: Charlotte Moore, Stephen James, Alexander Reed, Nancy Marchand, Megan Gallagher, Boyd Gaines, James Greene, Connie Roderick
THE COMMON PURSUIT by Simon Gray; *American Premiere;* Director, Kenneth Frankel. CAST: William Converse-Roberts, Ellen Parker, Michael Countryman, Peter Friedman, Nathan Lane, Mark Arnott
BLUE WINDOW by Craig Lucas; Director, Norman Rene. CAST: Maureen Silliman, Michael Butler, Randy Danson, Stephen Burleigh, Jane Galloway, Brad O'Hare, Margo Skinner
CAT ON A HOT TIN ROOF by Tennessee Williams; Director, Edward Gilbert. CAST: Christine Lahti, Peter Weller, Pamela Payton-Wright, Jan Miner, Stefan Gierasch, Beeson Carroll, Ted van Griethuysen, Alexander Reed, Robert Colston, Carol-Jean Lewis, Rosemarie Gambardella, Nikki Lynn Zanni, J. J. Fiorello, John Sayward
ALBERT HERRING by Benjamin Britten; Libretto, Eric Crozier; Director, Arvin Brown; Musical Director, Murry Sidlin. CAST: Lisa Jablow, Carmen Pelton, Freda Herseth, Marsha Hunter, Vaughn Fritts, Dan Entriken, Bruce Kramer, James Javore, William Sharp, Jon David Gruett, Michael Hume, Kristen Hurst-Hyde, Kathleen Keske, Mary Wescott, Sara Chaiken, Lucinda Adams, Benjamin Billingsley, Thomas Brand, New Haven Symphony Orchestra Ensemble
BULLIE'S HOUSE by Thomas Keneally with Irvin S. Baurer; Director, Kenneth Frankel. CAST: Josef Sommer, Ernie Dingo, Paul Pryor, Justine Saunders, Tommy Lewis, Michael Countryman, Ron Frazier, Richard Walley

T. Charles Erickson Photos

McCARTER THEATRE

Princeton, New Jersey
October 1, 1984–May 1, 1985

Artistic Director, Nagle Jackson; Managing Director, Alison Harris; Associate Artistic Director, Robert Lanchester; Production Manager, John Herochik; Business Manager, Timothy J. Shields; Development, Pamela Vevers Sherin; Press, Linda S. Kinsey, Julia Strohm

PRODUCTIONS & CASTS

THE SCHOOL FOR WIVES by Moliere; Richard Wilbur translation; Director, Nagle Jackson; Scenery, Robert Perdziola; Costumes, Elizabeth Covey; Lighting, Richard Moore. CAST: Ashley Gardner, Judith K. Hart, Nat Warren-White, Robert Lanchester, Richard Risso, Dan Diggles, Francis P. Bilancio, Jay Doyle, Mark A. Brown, Dane Cruz

THE DAWNS ARE QUIET HERE by Boris Vassiliev; *U.S. Premiere;* Translated by Alex Miller; Director, Alex Dmitriev; Set, James Morgan; Costumes, Susan Rheaume; Music, Gregory Piatigorsky; Lighting, Richard Moore. CAST: Mario Arrambide, Amy Stoller, Stacy Ray, Veronique Gusdon, Jana Schneider, Penelope Reed, Jay Doyle, Susanne Marley, Janine Santana, Mary Martello, Judith K. Hart, Richard Risso, Greg Thornton, Liz Fillo, Derry Light, Laura Huntsman, Alan Bailey, Mark A. Brown, Daniel P. Chaddock, Dane Cruz, Matthew H. Wright

A CHRISTMAS CAROL adapted by Nagle Jackson from novel by Charles Dickens; Director, Francis X. Kuhn; Scenery, Brian Martin; Lighting, Richard Moore; Costumes, Elizabeth Covey; Music, Larry Delinger; Musical Staging, Nancy Thiel; Hairstylists, Patrik D. Moreton, Charles Lo Presto. CAST: Robert Lanchester (Scrooge), Barry Boys, Mario Arrambide, Greg Thornton, Randy Lilly, Henson Keys, Derry Light, Richard Risso, Bruce Somerville, Valerie Beaman, Thomas Lee Sinclair, Mark A. Brown, Dane Cruz, Stacy Ray, Emilie Bass, Kent Somerville, Jessica Heidt, Matthew M. Maher, Nicole Citron, Marc Magen, Jessica Woolley, Adam Citron, Susan Jordan, Francis P. Bilancio, Jay Doyle, Jennifer Benton, Nicole Bridgewater, Zachary Knower, John Watson Stewart, Mark Zaki

FAUSTUS IN HELL adapted and directed by Nagle Jackson, based on works of Marlowe, Goethe, Moliere, et al; *World Premiere;* with **THE SHOW OF THE SEVEN DEADLY SINS** by Edward Albee, Christopher Durang, Amlin Gray, John Guare, Romulus Linney, Joyce Carol Oates, Jean Claude van Itallie; Set, Elizabeth K. Fischer; Costumes, Kathleen Blake; Lighting, Richard Moore. CAST: Harry Hamlin, Barry Boys, Jay Doyle, Stacy Ray, Bruce Somerville, Mario Arrambide, Keith Curran, Dan Diggles, Danielia Fulmer, Jason P. Jones, Henson Keys, Randy Lilly, Mary Martello, Janine Santana, Greg Thornton, Kerry Waters

UNDER MILK WOOD by Dylan Thomas; Director, Robert Lanchester; Set, Elizabeth K. Fischer; Costumes, Susan Rheaume; Original Music, Lee Hoiby; Lighting, Richard Moore. CAST: Robert Blumenfeld, Randy Lilly, Jay Doyle, Barry Boys, Bruce Somerville, Mario Arrambide, Jill Tanner, Kimberly King, Georgine Hall, Mary Martello

A RAISIN IN THE SUN by Lorraine Hansberry; Director, Terry Burgler; Set, Charles Caldwell; Costumes, Julie Keen; Lighting, Lynne M. Hartman. CAST: Donna Bailey, Jason Ashton Miller, Jerome Butler, Lydia Hannibal, Marie Goodman Hunter, Nathaniel Ritch, Maury Erickson, Michael S. Guess, Zoran Kovcic, Leonard E. Steinline, Jr.

ACT WITHOUT WORDS/HAPPY DAYS by Samuel Beckett; Director, Robert Lanchester; Set, Joseph C. Anderson; Costumes, Barb Taylor; Lighting, Richard Moore. CAST: Penelope Reed, Nat Warren-White

Cliff Moore Photos

Penelope Reed in "Happy Days"
Top: Bruce Somerville, Harry Hamlin
in "Faustus in Hell"

MEADOW BROOK THEATRE

Rochester, Michigan
October 4, 1984–May 12, 1985

Artistic/General Director, Terence Kilburn; Assistant to Mr. Kilburn, Frank F. Bollinger; Stage Directors, Terence Kilburn, Charles Nolte, Carl Schurr, John Ulmer; Sets, Peter W. Hicks, Barry Griffith; Lighting, Reid Johnson, Barry Griffith, Daniel Jaffe; Stage Managers, Terry Carpenter, Judith Darnton; Technical Director, Barry Griffith; Sound, Tony Vaillancourt; Costume Coordinator, Mary Lynn Crum; Wardrobe, Paula Kalevas; Props, Mary Chmelko-Jaffe; Press, Jane Mosher

PRODUCTIONS & CASTS

SHERLOCK HOLMES: Steven Andres, Debra Bader, Anthony Burdick, Bethany Carpenter, Gary Clason, Donald Ewer, J. Nathan French, George Gitto, Joey L. Golden, Robert Grossman, Robert Herrle, Paul Hopper, Lori Johnson, Lisa McMillan, Andrew Mellen, John W. Puchalski, Karl Redcoff, Jim Sterner, Eric Tavares, Peggy Thorp, Kevin Zeese

ALL MY SONS: Steven Anders, Bethany Carpenter, J. Nathan French, Linda Gehringer, Roy Hall, Jayne Houdyshell, William LeMassena, Phillip Locker, Jane Lowry, Peter Gregory Thomson

A CHRISTMAS CAROL: Judi Ammar, Steven Anders, Andrew Barnicle, Bethany Carpenter, Booth Colman, Thom Haneline, Paul Hopper, Jayne Houdyshell, William LeMassena, Phillip Locker, Wayne David Parker, Joseph Reed, Peter Gregory Thomson

A CASE OF LIBEL: Arthur Beer, Mary Benson, John Eames, David Fox, George Gitto, Paul Hopper, J. C. Howe, Phillip Locker, Maureen McDevitt, Tony Mockus, Ron Samuel, Peter Gregory Thomson

TOYS IN THE ATTIC: Jeanne Arnold, Bethany Carpenter, Michel Cullen, Paul Hopper, Jane Lowry, Priscilla Morrill, Mel Winkler, Robert LeVoyd-Wright

TAKING STEPS: Donald Ewer, George Gitto, Jayne Houdyshell, Henson Keys, William Kux, Jillian Lindig

SPIDER'S WEB: Barbara Barringer, Arthur Beer, David Fox, Randall Godwin, Thom Haneline, Judith Klein, William LeMassena, Joseph Reed, Peter Gregory Thomson, Peggy Thorp, Paul Vincent

THE IMPORTANCE OF BEING EARNEST: Jeanne Arnold, Mary Benson, John Eames, Harry Ellerbe, Thom Haneline, Lynn Mansbach, Maureen McDevitt, Tom Spackman, Peter Gregory Thomson

Richard Hunt Photos

Linda Gehringer, Phillip Locker, William
LeMassena, Jane Lowry in "All My Sons"

MERRIMACK REPERTORY THEATRE

Lowell, Massachusetts
November 1984–June 1985

Producing Director, Daniel L. Schay; Production Manager, Richard Rose; Marketing, Helene Desjarlais; Business Manager, Jacqueline A. Normand; Technical Director, Jaime Dunbar; Costumes, Amanda Aldridge; Lighting, David Lockner; Props, Debora Kingston; Production Assistant, R. Victoria Stangroom; Stage Managers, Hazel Youngs, Eileen McNamara; Press, David Balsom

PRODUCTIONS & CASTS

A CHRISTMAS CAROL by Charles Dickens; Adapted by Larry Carpenter; Director, Mr. Carpenter; Sets, Edward Cesaitis; Stage Manager, Thomas Clewell. CAST: Richard Bowne, Robin Chadwick, Edmund Davys, Elizabeth A. Dickinson, Pat Dougan, Richard Maynard, William Miller, Alice White, Arthur Fascione, Allistair Former, John Griffith, David Hilliard, Melissa Luce, Brent Rourke, Elizabeth Sheehy, Dina Veillette, Laura Veino
MONDAY AFTER THE MIRACLE by William Gibson; Director, Ted Davis; Set, Alison Ford; Costumes, Barbara Forbes. CAST: Jeremiah Kissel, Julia Murray, Sally Prager, Richard Seguin, James Leo Walker
STAGE STRUCK by Simon Gray; Director, Nora Hussey; Set, Leslie Taylor. CAST: Tom Bade, Mary Chalon, George Feaster, Don Leslie
A RAISIN IN THE SUN by Lorraine Hansberry; Director, Daniel L. Schay; Assistant Director, Victoria Howard; Costumes, Virginia Aldous; Lighting, Ted Bohlin. CAST: Cynthia Belgrave, Derek Ellcock, Thomas Grimes, Reggie Montgomery, Wiley Moore, Allen Oliver, Cheryl Rogers, Richard Seguin, Kim Weston-Moran
STRANGE SNOW by Steve Metcalfe; Director, Grey Cattell Johnson; Set, Leslie Taylor. CAST: Michael French, Jonathan Fuller, Roberta Wallach
A LITTLE NIGHT MUSIC with Music and Lyrics by Stephen Sondheim; Book, Hugh Wheeler; Director/Choreographer, Richard Rose; Musical Director, Judy Brown; Co-Choreographer, Amanda Aldridge; Sets, Gary English. CAST: Christopher Coucill, Rhonda Farer, Kevin Gray, Howard Hensel, Nancy Hudson, Glenn Mure, Jo Sullivan, Benay Venuta, Tricia Withim, Kerry Sullivan

Cheryl Rogers, Reggie Montgomery
in "A Raisin in the Sun"

Craig Dudley, Richard Stack
in "Dial 'M' for Murder"

NASSAU REPERTORY THEATRE

Hempstead, New York
October 9, 1984–June 30, 1985

Changed to **LONG ISLAND STAGE** in March 1985; Artistic Director, Clinton J. Atkinson; Managing Director, Kenneth E. Hahn succeeded by Andrew Cohn; Administrative Director, Sally Cohen; Press, Doris Meadows; Technical Director, Michael J. Sapsis; Lighting, John Hickey; Sets, Jack Bell Stewart, Dan Conway, John Iacovelli, Steve Perry; Costumes, Fran Rosenthal, David Navarro Velasquez, Jose Lengson; Props, Richard Prouse, Austin Brown, David Von Salis, Janice Kitchen; Stage Managers, John W. Calder III, Thom Mangan, Melody KirkWagner, J. Barry Lewis

PRODUCTIONS & CASTS

VOLPONE by Ben Jonson; Translated by Ruth Langner; Adapted by Stefan Zweig. CAST: K. T. Baumann, Mimi Bensinger, Richard Campbell, Gene Carey, David H. Cohen, Val Dufour, John Fitzgibbon, Adam Hart, Dennis Helfend, Buck Hobbs, Alan Kass, Rudolph Shaw, Tom Spiller
DIAL 'M' FOR MURDER by Frederick Knott; with Rita Litton, Nicholas Kaledin, Craig Dudley, Richard Stack, George Cavey
THE CARETAKER by Harold Pinter; with Joel Leffert, Dermot McNamara, Felix Van Dijk
CANDIDA byGeorge Bernard Shaw; with K. T. Baumann, Rudy Hornish, Felix Van Dijk, James Hillgartner, Roxana Stuart, Brian Hinson
BABY GRAND by P. J. Barry; *World Premiere;* with Robert Burke, Mary Doyle, John Newton, Wendy Radford, Jack Ryland, Teri Keane succeeded by Ruth Livingston
THE COUNTRY GIRL by Clifford Odets; Director, Norman Hall; with David Brizzolara, David H. Cohen, Sofia Landon, Phillip Lindsay, Stephen McNaughton, Bill Myers, Kelley Paterson, Gordon Rigsby

Cathy Blaivas Photos

NEW PLAYWRIGHTS' THEATRE

Washington, D.C.
October 12, 1984–June 23, 1985
Thirteenth Season

Artistic Director, Arthur Bartow; Managing Director, Robert Wilson

PRODUCTIONS & CASTS

BURIAL CUSTOMS by Phoef Sutton; *World Premiere;* Director, Arthur Bartow; Set, Lewis Folden; Costumes, Georgia O. Baker; Lighting, Daniel M. Wagner; Props, Wendy K. McNeny; Sound, Eric Annis; Production Manager, James J. Taylor; Technical Director, Neil P. Wilson; Stage Manager, Ten Eyck Swackhamer. CAST: Mary Woods (Lee Strayhorn), Dennis Carrig (Ethan Shifflet), Ernie Meier (Paulie Arbogast), Wilson Smith (Charlie Strayhorn), Donald Neal (Jimmy Zirkle), Jack Gwaltney (Kyle Whitesel), Leisa Kelley (Pam Lineweaver), Walt MacPherson (Rev. Obaugh), Petrina Huston (Phyllis (Zirkle))

THE BEAUTIFUL LADY with Book by Elizabeth Swados and Paul Schmidt; *World Premiere;* Poetry Translation, Paul Schmidt; Music and Lyrics, Elizabeth Swados; Director, Elizabeth Swados; Scenery/Lighting, Lewis Folden; Costumes, Jane Schloss Phelan; Props, Wendy L. McNeny; Sculpture, Paul Falcon; Musical Director, Michael Sirotta; Assistant Director/Co-Choreographer, Ronni Stewart; Associate Producers, Michael Lonergan, Marilyn LeVine; Production Manager, James J. Taylor; Technical Director, Neil T. Wilson; Stage Managers, Marybeth Ward, Ten Eyck Swackhamer; Presented by Seymour Morgenstern. CAST: Olga Merediz (Pronin/Boris), Natasha Lutov (Pavlovna/Natalia), Karen Trott (Akhmatova/Anna Andreevna), Jack Guidone (Gumilyov/Nikolai Stepanovich), Daniel Noel (Mandelstam/Osip Emilievich), Deborah Jean Templin (Tsvetaeva/Marina Ivanovna), Stephen Crain (Mayakovsky/Vladimir Vladimirovich), Howard Shalwitz (Khlebnikov/Velimir), Gordon Paddison (Yesenin/Sergei Alexandrovitch)

SPALDING GRAY: Swimming to Cambodia, Sex & Death to the Age 14, A Personal History of the American Theatre, Travels Through New England—Spring '84.

AFTER MY OWN HEART by Paul J. Donnelly, Jr.; *World Premiere;* Director, Arthur Bartow; Assistant Director, Ten Eyck Swackhamer; Set, Lewis Folden; Costumes, Jane Schloss Phelan; Lighting, Steve Summers; Props, Matthew Allen; Production Manager, James J. Taylor; Technical Director, Neil P. Wilson; Piano, Ed Rejuney; Voice, Debra Tidwell.

Doc Courtney Photos

**Elizabeth DuVall, Robert Mailhouse
in "After My Own Heart"**

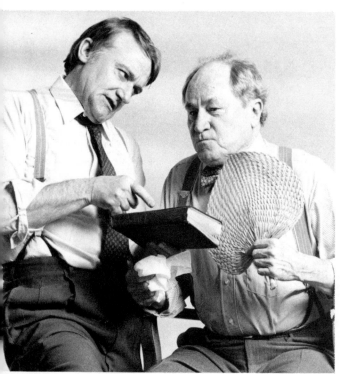

**Robert Vaughn, E. G. Marshall
in "Inherit the Wind"**

PAPER MILL PLAYHOUSE

Millburn, New Jersey
September 19, 1984–June 30, 1985
Forty-fifth Year

Executive Producer, Angelo Del Rossi; General Manager, Wade Miller; Administrative Director, Jim Thesing; Marketing, Debra A. Waxman; Production Manager, David Kissel; Props, Bruce Pollock; Wardrobe, Ralph Fandetta; Dramaturg, Jeffrey A. Solis; Stage Managers, Donald Walters, J. Andrew Burgreen; Press, Albertina Reilly

PRODUCTIONS & CASTS

AMADEUS by Peter Shaffer; Director, Robert Johanson; with Bob Gunton, John Thomas Waite, Sally Ann Flynn

GUYS AND DOLLS with Music and Lyrics by Frank Loesser; Book, Abe Burrows, Jo Swerling; Director, Robert Johanson; with Jack Carter, Larry Kert, Susan Powell, Lenora Nemetz

SIDE BY SIDE BY SONDHEIM with Music and Lyrics by Stephen Sondheim; Music, Leonard Bernstein, Richard Rodgers, Mary Rodgers, Jule Styne; Director, Robert Johanson; with Helen Gallagher, Larry Kert, Judy Kaye, George Rose

INHERIT THE WIND by Jerome Lawrence and Robert E. Lee; Director, John Going; Set, Michael Anania; Lighting, Mimi Jordan Sherin; Costumes, Guy Geoly, Alice S. Hughes; Stage Manager, Donald Walters. CAST: E. G. Marshall (Matthew Harrison Brady), Robert Vaughn (Henry Drummond), James Harper (E. K. Hornbeck), Gavin Troster (Bertram Cates), Sarah Rush (Rachel Brown), Donald Buka (Rev. Brown), Dorothea Hammond (Mrs. Brady), Conrad McLaren (Meeker), William Newman (Mayor Forrester), John Newton (Judge Merle Jenkins), Fritz Sperberg (Tom Davenport), Alec Bauer, Corrie Safris, Jack Stubblefield Johnson, Virginia Downing, Jerry Freeman, John Boyle, Bill Salem, Karl Schroeder, John L. Bryan, Sanford Clark, T. F. Smith, Trinity Thompson, Holly Ritter, Robert Cenedella, Clint Lauber, Gary McGurk, Daniel P. Hannafin, Arden Lewis, Tom Sleeth, David H. Cohen, Alan Walker, Louis Albini, Edward Caliendo, Michael Elich, Steven Rock-Savage, Sarah Marshall, Marc Duncan, Daniel Guggenheim, Barbara Corry, Clay Guthrie

SHOW BOAT based on novel by Edna Ferber; Music, Jerome Kern; Book and Lyrics, Oscar Hammerstein 2nd; Director, Robert Johanson; with Eddie Bracken, Judith McCauley, Richard White, Leigh Berry

EVITA by Tim Rice and Andrew Lloyd Webber; Director, Frank Marino; Starring Loni Ackerman

Terence A. Gili Photos

OLD GLOBE THEATRE

San Diego, California
June 6, 1984–May 12, 1985
Thirty-fifth Season

Executive Producer, Craig Noel; Artistic Director, Jack O'Brien; Managing Director, Thomas Hall; Production Manager, Erica Young; Development, Cassie A. Solomon; Production Stage Manager, Douglas Pagliotti; Wardrobe, Cassandra Carpenter; Props, Ruth Long; Press, William B. Eaton, Charlene Baldridge.

PRODUCTIONS & CASTS

ELEKTRA by Sophocles; Translated by E. F. Watling; Adapted by Diana Maddox with John Sang; Director, Diana Maddox; Scenery, Kent Dorsey; Costumes, Lewis Brown; Lighting, John B. Forbes; Composer, Conrad Susa; Sound, Dan Dugan; Stage Manager, Maria Carrera. CAST: Anne Gee Byrd (Widow), Terrence O'Connor (Wife), Dianne Harper (Maiden), Dudley Knight (Tutor), James Horan (Orestes), James Carpenter (Pylades), Katherine McGrath (Elektra), Nancy Claire Bennett (Chrysothemis), Jill Tanner (Klytemnestra), Vaughn Armstrong (Aigisthos).

RASHOMON by Fay and Michael Kanin; Director, Noel Craig; Scenery, Richard Seger; Costumes, Lewis Brown; Lighting, Kent Dorsey; Original Music, Laurence Rosenthal; Additional Music, Conrad Susa; Sound, Conrad Susa, Tony Tait; Fight Director, Anthony DeLongis; Stage Manager, Douglas Pagliotti. CAST: Jeffrey Alan Chandler (Priest), Mitchell Edmonds (Woodcutter), Jonathan McMurtry (Wigmaker), Andrew J. Traister (Deputy), J. Kenneth Campbell (Bandit), Anthony DeLongis (Husband), Roberta Maxwell (Wife), Susan Shepard (Mother), Mariangela Pino (Medium).

THE MERRY WIVES OF WINDSOR by William Shakespeare; Director, Daniel Sullivan; Set, Steven Rubin; Costumes, Robert Morgan; Lighting, Robert Peterson; Composer, Henry Mollicone; Sound, Dan Dugan; Stage Manager, Anne Marie Salazar. CAST: Oliver Cliff (Shallow), Dennis Bailey (Abraham Slender), Don Sparks (Sir Hugh), Alan Freeman (Page), James Blendick (Falstaff), Charles Fee (Bardolph), Mark Kincaid (Pistol), James Schendel (Nym), Ann-Sara Matthews (Anne Page), Annette Helde (Mistress Ford), Sharon Spelman (Mistress Page), Don R. McManus (Simple), Corey Hansen (Robin), Robert Machray (Host), Rhoda Gemignani (Mistress Quickly), Nathan Haas (Fenton), Mark Hofflund (Jack), Tom Lacy (Caius), Robert Darnell (Ford), Servants: Dianna Berry, Randy Bomer, Carol Flanders, Gregg Ostrin, Greg Porretta, Kathryn Sivak.

BREAKFAST WITH LES AND BESS by Lee Kalcheim; Director, David McClendon; Set, Kent Dorsey; Costumes, Robert Morgan; Lighting, John B. Forbes; Sound, Michael Winston; Stage Manager, Anne Marie Salazar. CAST: Tom Lacy (Voice of Announcer), Anne Gee Byrd (Bess), James Callahan (Les), Dianne Harper (Shelby), Charles Fee (Roger), Don R. McManus (David), Andrew J. Traister (Nate).

SCAPINO! by Frank Dunlop and Jim Dale; Director, David Ogden Stiers; Set, Douglas W. Schmidt; Costumes, Robert Morgan; Lighting, Robert Peterson; Incidental Music, William Perry; Sound, Conrad Susa, Tony Tait; Stage Manager, Maria Carrera. CAST: Mariangela Pina (Waitress), Dennis Bailey (Ottavio), Don Sparks (Sylvestro), Ann-Sara Matthews (Giacinta), Tom Lacy (Argante), G Wood (Geronte), Nathan Haas (Leandro), Alan Freeman (Carlo), Dawn Didawick (Zerbinetta), David Toney (Headwaiter), Randy Bomer, Greg Porretta (Waiters), Carol Flanders (Nurse), Kathryn Sivak (Pizza Person).

OTHELLO by William Shakespeare; Director, Jack O'Brien; Set, Richard Seger; Costumes, Lewis Brown; Lighting, Kent Dorsey; Composer, Conrad Susa; Sound, Roger Gans; Fights, Anthony DeLongis. CAST: Jeffrey Alan Chandler (Roderigo), Jonathan McMurtry (Iago), Oliver Cliff (Brabantio), Paul Winfield (Othello), J. Kenneth Campbell (Cassio), Mitchell Edmonds (Duke of Venice), Robert Machray (Gratiano), James Schendel (Senator), Roberta Maxwell (Desdemona), Katherine McGrath (Emilia), James Carpenter (Montano), Jill Tanner (Bianca), Vaughn Armstrong (Lodovico), Mark Hofflund, Mark Kincaid (Gentlemen), Gregg Ostrin (Bernardo), Corey Hansen (Messenger), Nancy Claire Bennett, Dianna Berry, Jeff Berryman, Cole Miller (Attendants).

FOXFIRE by Susan Cooper and Hume Cronyn; Director, Andrew J. Traister; Set, Alan K. Okazaki; Costumes, Sally Cleveland; Lighting, John B. Forbes; Sound, Michael Winston; Stage Manager, Maria Carrera. CAST: Irene Tedrow (Annie Nations), Wiley Harker (Hector Nations), Mitchell Edmonds (Prince Carpenter), Mary McDonough (Holly Burrell), Don Sparks (Dillard Nations), Gordon Benson (Doctor), Tim Spacek, Chris Vitas (Stony Lonesome Boys).

SEASON'S GREETINGS by Alan Ayckbourn; Director, Jack O'Brien; Set, Kent Dorsey; Costumes, Robert Blackman; Lighting, Robert Peterson; Sound, Michael Holton; Stage Manager, Raul Moncada. CAST: Jonathan McMurtry (Neville), Katherine McGrath (Belinda), Kandis Chappell (Phyllis), Roger C. Carmel (Harvey), Tom Lacy (Bernard), Tandy Cronyn (Rachel), Gary Dontzig (Eddie), Deborah Taylor (Pattie), Laurence Guittard (Clive).

STAGE STRUCK by Simon Gray; Director, David Hay; Set, Alan K. Okazaki; Costumes, Dianne Holly; Lighting, John B. Forbes; Sound, Josef Kucera; Stage Manager, Raul Moncada. CAST: Paul Rudd (Robert), Matthew Dunn (Herman), Gillian Eaton (Anne), Jonathan McMurtry (Widdecombe).

OF MICE AND MEN by John Steinbeck; Director, Craig Noel; Sets/Costumes, Steven Rubin; Lighting, Kent Dorsey; Sound, Michael Holten; Stage Manager, Maria Carrera. CAST: David Huffman (George), Larry Drake (Lennie), Jack Axelrod (Candy), Mitchell Edmonds (The Boss), Johnny Crawford (Curley), Nancy Claire Bennett (Curley's Wife), Philip Reeves (Slim), James Coyle (Carlson), Don Took (Whit), Fred Pinkard (Crooks).

VIKINGS by Stephen Metcalfe; Director, Warner Shook; Set, Fred M. Duer; Costumes, Sally Cleveland; Lighting, Kent Dorsey; Sound, Michael Holten, Adam Tell; Stage Manager, Maria Carrera. CAST: Charles Hallahan (Peter Larsen), Michael McGuire (Yens Larsen), Tegan West (Gunnar Larsen), Karen Hensel (Betsy Simmons).

THE TORCH-BEARERS by George Kelly; Director, Jack O'Brien; Set, Richard Seger; Costumes, Robert Blackman; Lighting, John B. Forbes; Sound, Michael Holten; Stage Manager, Raul Moncada. CAST: George Deloy (Frederick Ritter), Duchess Dale (Jenny), Beth Howland (Paula Ritter), Katherine McGrath (Mrs. Pampinelli), Tom Lacy (Spindler), Kandis Chappell (Nelly), Mitchell Edmonds (Huxley Hossefrosse), Don R. McManus (Teddy), Valerie Karasek (Florence), Jonathan McMurtry (Ralph Twiller), James Coyle (Stage Manager), Anne Gee Byrd (Clara).

Mitchell Edmonds, Jody Gelb, David Ogden Stiers, George Deloy, Jonathan McMurtry in "London Assurance" *(John Peter Weiss Photos)*

Paxton Whitehead, Deborah May in "Richard III"

169

PENNSYLVANIA STAGE COMPANY

Allentown, Pennsylvania
September 19, 1984–June 16, 1985

Producing Director, Gregory S. Hurst; General Manager, Gary C. Porto; Associate Director/Literary Manager, Pam Pepper; Press, Lisa K. Higgins; Production Manager, Peter Wrenn-Meleck; Technical Director, Kevin Wiley; Stage Managers, Peter Del Vecho, Thomas M. Kauffman

PRODUCTIONS & CASTS

HARVEY by Mary Chase; Director, Kevin Kelly; Sets, Richard Hoover; Costumes, David Loveless; Lighting, Rick Gray. CAST: Holly Baumgardner, Helen Lloyd Breed, Robert Cenedella, Donald Christopher, Mary Cooper, John Hallow, Milica Govich, Edwin J. McDonough, Matt McKenzie, Gerald Richards, Shelly Rogers
A CHRISTMAS CAROL adapted and directed by Pam Pepper; Sets, William Barclay; Costumes, Colleen Muscha; Lighting, Curtis Dretsch. CAST: Holly Baumgardner, Stephen C. Bradbury, Lloyd Bass, Susan Louise Decker, Virginia Downing, Milica Govich, Arthur Hanket, Arch Johnson, Michael J. Lorr, Tammie McKenzie, Mary Eileen O'Donnell, Steve Pudenz, Constance Ray, David A. Smith, Tina Stevens, David Tabor, Patrick J. Tull, Chris Van Strander
TRUE WEST by Sam Shepard; Director, Pam Pepper; Set, Richard Hoover; Costumes, Gail Cooper-Hecht; Lighting, Mark Hendren. CAST: Stanja Lowe, Bernie Passeltiner, Jay Patterson, Stephen C. Prutting
EQUUS by Peter Shaffer; Director, Jamie Brown; Choreography, Gabriel Oshen; Set, Quentin Thomas; Costumes, Martha Kelly; Lighting, Curtis Dretsch. CAST: Lisa Barnes, Robert Black, Donald Christopher, Milica Govich, Michael J. Lorr, Stanja Lowe, Jeffrey Marcus, Innes-Fergus McDade, Paul Meacham, Seth Newfeld, Douglas Robb, John Schiappa, Jeff Trachta
STAGE STRUCK by Simon Gray; Director, Gregory S. Hurst; Set, Gary C. Eckhart; Costumes, Karen Gerson; Lighting, Mark Hendren. CAST: Ellen Fiske, Ron Johnston, Terry Layman, Michael Rhoades
JUST SO a musical adaptation of Rudyard Kipling's "Just So Stories"; *World Premiere;* Music, Doug Katsaros; Lyrics, David Zippel; Book, Mark St. Germain; Director, Julianne Boyd; Musical Director, Paul Sullivan; Choreography, Diana Baffa-Brill; Sets, Atkin Pace; Costumes, Lighting, Craig Miller. CAST: Clent Bowers, David Cady, Michael Connolly, Tina Johnson, Larry Marshall, Bebe Neuwirth, Pamala Tyson
A WALK OUT OF WATER by Donald Driver; *World Premiere;* Director, Gregory S. Hurst; Set, Atkin Pace; Costumes, Martha Kelly; Lighting, Curtis Dretsch. CAST: Danny Gerard, Dorrie Joiner, Jacqueline Knapp, John Spencer, Katherine Squire

Gregory M. Fota Photos

**Larry Marshall
in "Just So"**

PITTSBURGH PLAYHOUSE

Pittsburgh, Pennsylvania
September 15, 1984–May 26, 1985

General Director, Mark Lewis; Producer, James O. Prescott; Executive Assistant, Roderick R. Carter; Administrative Assistant, Carole L. Berger; Press, Lee Tommarello; Production Manager, Alan Forino; Technical Director, Mark Somerfield; Scenery, Mary Burt; Costumes, Donald DiFonso, Joan Markert, Mary M. Turner; Lighting, Jennifer Ford, Alan Forino; Props, Mary Burt

PRODUCTIONS & CASTS

A LITTLE NIGHT MUSIC with Music and Lyrics by Stephen Sondheim; Book, Hugh Wheeler; Director, Kenneth Gargaro; Musical Numbers Staged by Ron Tassone; Props, Brian Fitzmorris; Assistant Director, Burton White; Assistant Musical Director, Clay Zambo; Stage Managers, Greg Marcopoulos, Loretta Hurley. CAST: Linda E. Gabler (Fredrika), Ruth Lesko (Mme. Armfeldt), Joseph DiSalle (Frid), Robert Roznowski (Henrik), Lynn Pasteris (Anne), Howard Elson (Fredrik), Pam Shafer (Petra), Rita Stetor (Desiree), James P. McCrum (Count), Robin Walsh (Countess Charlotte), Dinah Mason (Malla)
EXTREMITIES by William Mastrosimone; Director, Don Wadsworth; Sound, Max Weiterhausen. CAST: Helena Ruoti (Marjorie), David Butler (Raul), Maria Barney (Terry), Trish Beatty (Patricia)
JESUS CHRIST SUPERSTAR with Lyrics by Tim Rice; Music, Andrew Lloyd Webber; Director, Kenneth Gargaro; Set, Alison Ford; Musical Staging, Ron Tassone; Stage Managers, Burton White, Christopher Peters. CAST: James P. McCrum (Judas), Anthony DiLeo, Jr. (Jesus), Katie Culzean McCombs (Mary Magdalene), James W. Critchfield (Caiphas), Brian P. Kelly (Annas), William David Beers (Simon), Sam Williams (Pontius Pilate), Paul Zielinski (Peter), Linda Gabler (Maid by the fire), Steve Sirulnik (Old Man), Tom Rocco (King Herod), Carol Adams, Lisa Beatty, Angela Canalungo, Sandra Dowe, Paul Gladora, Eva Jackson, Janice Jarabeck, Mike Jones, Kathy Lash, Jennie Lerch, Elizabeth Matthews, JoAnne Mule, Michelle Mule, Sal Palazzo, Doug Pona, Jane Scutieri, Mark Traxler, Melissa Ventresca, Maura White, Ted Winston, Eileen Wolk, Ted Worsley
BEYOND THERAPY by Christopher Durang; Director, Raymond Laine; Scenery, Judy Staiger; Assistant Director, John Gresh; Stage Managers, Greg Marcopoulos, Sheila McKenna. CAST: David W. Butler (Bruce), Robin Walsh (Prudence), Marty Schiff (Stuart), Susan McGregor-Laine (Charlotte), Chris Josephs (Bob), Kurt Carley (Andrew)
CHILDREN'S THEATRE: *The Emperor's Nightingale* adapted from the Hans Christian Anderson story by Don DiFonso; Director, Jill Wadsworth; Music and Lyrics, Shirley Barasch, Don DiFonso; Choreography, Tammy Petruska. CAST: Peter Enright, Chuck Baker, Kurt Carley, Robert J. Doran, Catherine Fountain, Sarah Worthington. *The Ghost of Mr. Penny* by Rosemary G. Musil; Director, William K. Leech. CAST: Tom Prigorac, Mark Traxler, Sarah Worthington, Debbie Sale, Robin Beruh, T. C. Brown, Wayne H. McCord, James P. McCrum. *A Christmas Carol* with Tom Crawford (Scrooge), Mark J. Dolansky, John T. Mumper, Doug Pona, Marti Gronsky Rami, Debbie Sale, Annie Vernino, Ronald J. Valentino, John Dunmire. *Land of the Dragon* by Madge Miller; Director, Tom McLaughlin. CAST: Cara Marie Gentile, Kathleen Gates, Mary K. Chess, Deborah Sale, Janet Ross, Kimberly J. Martin, Kim Cea, Christopher Peters, C. Vinson Baker, Mike Anderson, Lynn K. Friedland. *Rumplestiltskin* adapted and directed by William K. Leech. CAST: Kurt Carley, Lynn K. Friedland, Jim Huttenhower, Kimberly J. Martin, Donna Meehan, Bernadette Prigorac, Beth Walters. *Beauty and the Lonely Beast* by Eleanor Harder; Director, John Amplas. CAST: Mary K. Chess, Karen L. Sarp, Rosemary Willhide, Sarah Worthington, Charles V. Baker, Daniel Krell

**Dorrie Joiner, Katherine Squire
in "A Walk out of Water"**

PLAYMAKERS REPERTORY COMPANY

Chapel Hill, North Carolina
September 8, 1984–April 21, 1985
Ninth Season

Executive Producer, Milly S. Barranger; Artistic Director, Gregory Boyd; Producing Director, Robert Tolan; Press, Sharon J. Herr

COMPANY: Patti Cohenour, Joe Spano, Nan Jeanette Seitz, William Meisle, Karen Ingenthron, Michael Cumpsty, John Tyson, Hope Alexander-Willis, Wendy B. Wilson, Kieran Connolly, Kathryn Meisle, Caspar Thomson, Nels Hennum, Douglas Johnson, John Franklin Feltch, Ken Grantham, Shelley Williams, Gregory Boyd, Tommy Thompson
PRODUCTIONS: Three Guys Naked from the Waist Down, The Last Song of John Proffit, Loose Ends, Ring Round the Moon, Our Town, Cyrano de Bergerac, Measure for Measure, Cloud 9, Curse of the Starving Class

"Measure for Measure"

REPERTORY THEATRE OF ST. LOUIS

St. Louis, Missouri
September 5, 1984–April 12, 1985

Producing Director, David Chambers; Acting Artistic Director/Managing Director, Steve Woolf; Technical Director, Max DeVolder; Development, Anne B. DesRosiers; Costumes, Arthur Ridley, Dorothy Marshall; Lighting, Max DeVolder, Peter E. Sargent, Glenn Dunn; Stage Managers, Glenn Dunn, T. R. Martin

PRODUCTIONS & CASTS

A RAISIN IN THE SUN by Lorraine Hansberry; Director, Hal Scott; Set, Bill Schmiel. CAST: Brenda Thomas (Ruth), Abe Mills (Travis), Roger Robinson (Walter), Kim Yancey (Beneatha), Esther Rolle (Lena), Lou Ferguson (Joseph), Stephen McKinley Henderson (Bobo), Alan Clarey (Karl)
MASTER HAROLD. . . . and the boys by Athol Fugard; Director, Jim O'Connor; Set and Costumes, Arthur Ridley. CAST: Mike Hodge (Sam), Stephen McKinley Henderson (Willie), Andrew Hill Newman (Hally)
THE 1940's RADIO HOUR by Walton Jones; Director, John Going; Choreographer, Byron Grant; Set, John Roslevich, Jr. CAST: Stan Early (Pops), Steve Chambers (Stanley), Robert Sevra (Clifton), Byron Grant (Zoot), Robert Dorn (Wally), Tony Hoty (Lou), Stephen Berger (Johnny), Dorothy Stanley (Ginger), Christa Germanson (Connie), Jim Walton (B. J.), G. Wayne Hoffman (Neal), Alison Bevan (Ann), Gail Grate (Geneva), Toy Hoylen (Biff)
DIAL "M" FOR MURDER by Frederick Knott; Director, Geoffrey Sherman; Set, Tim Jozwick. CAST: Diana Van Fossen (Margot), Hal Davis (Max), Allan Murley (Tony), Dennis Predovic (Capt. Lesgate), Sam Stoneburner (Inspector)
THE PRICE by Arthur Miller; Director, Edward Stern; Set, John Ezell. CAST: Robert Darnell (Victor Franz), Grace Woodard (Esther Franz), Peter Johl (Gregory Solomon), Alan Mixon (Walter Franz)
THE COMEDY OF ERRORS by William Shakespeare; Director, Geoffrey Sherman; Set, Carolyn L. Ross; Pianist, Richard Roberts. CAST: John Cothran, Jr. (Solinus), Peter Johl (Egeon), John Rensenhouse (Antipholus of Ephesus), Eric Conger (Antipholus of Syracuse), Dennis Predovic (Dromio of Ephesus), Tony Hoty (Dromio of Syracuse), Michael Pierce (Balthasar/Dr. Pinch), Alan Clarey (Angelo), Wayne Salomon (Merchant/Officer), Ken Ross (Merchant/Jailer), Mary Fogarty (Emilia), Lisa McMillan (Adriana), Marsha Korb (Luciana), Kristan Schmidt (Courtesan)
WAITING FOR GODOT by Samuel Beckett; Director, Milton R. Zoth; Set, Tim Jozwick; Costumes, Elizabeth Eisloeffel. CAST: James Paul (Estragon), Brendan Burke (Vladamir), Wayne Salomon (Lucky), Joneal Joplin (Pozzo), Heidi Dorow (Messenger)
STILL LIFE by Emily Mann; Director, Fontaine Syer; Set, Peggy DuPuy; Costumes, Laura Hanson; Stage Manager, Rachael Lindhart. CAST: A. C. Weary (Mark), Deirdre O'Connell (Cheryl), Dolores Kenan (Nadine)
ANNULLA, AN AUTOBIOGRAPHY by Annulla Allen and Emily Mann; Director, Timothy Near; Set/Costumes, Arthur Ridley; Stage Manager, Rachael Lindhart. CAST: Jacqueline Bertrand (Annulla Allen), Jenniffer Russell (Voice of Emily Mann)

Brenda Thomas, Esther Rolle, Abe Mills
in "A Raisin in the Sun" Above: Jim Walton,
Dorothy Stanley, Tony Hoylen, Gail Grate
in "The 1940's Radio Show"

Scott Dine Photos

**Daniel Sullivan, Lori Larsen
in "The Wedding"**

SEATTLE REPERTORY THEATRE

Seattle, Washington
October 24, 1984–May 26, 1985

Producing Director, Peter Donnelly; Artistic Director, Daniel Sullivan; Associate Artistic Director, Douglas Hughes; Technical Director, Robert Scales; Production Manager, Vito Zingarelli; Press, Marnie Andrews, Juli Ann Rae; Marketing, Jerry Sando; Development, Frank Self; Wardrobe, Sally Roberts; Stage Manager, Mary Hunter; Sound, Michael Holten

PRODUCTIONS & CASTS

OUR TOWN by Thornton Wilder; Director, Daniel Sullivan; Set, Karen Gjelsteen; Costumes, Robert Wojewodski; Lights, Pat Collins; Music, Kenneth Benshoof. CAST: Biff McGuire (Stage Manager), William Denis (Dr. Gibbs), Mary Doyle (Mrs. Gibbs), Sally Chamberlin (Mrs. Webb), Campbell Scott (George), Shana Bestock (Rebecca), James Paul Delaney (Wally), Laura Innes (Emily), Pirie Mac-Donald (Mr. Webb), Stuart Duckworth (Simon), Priscilla Hake Lauris (Mrs. Soames), Jason Tanner (Joe/Si), Bill Watson (Prof. Willard/Baseball Player/Sam), Gale McNeeley (Howie/Baseball Player), Glenn Mazen (in auditorium/Joe), Suzy Hunt (in balcony/Dead Woman), William Hall, Jr. (Mr. Carter), Jane Adams (Dead Woman), Dick Arnold (Farmer McCarthy), Townspeople: Jane Adams, Dick Arnold, John Empey, William Hall, Jr., Lizabeth Hinton, Suzy Hunt, Ron Ben Jarrett, Marjorie Kennedy, Stephen Kummerer, Robert E. Taeschner

PASSION PLAY by Peter Nichols; Director, Douglas Hughes; Set, Loren Sherman; Costumes, Jess Goldstein; Lights, Dennis Parichy. CAST: Valerie Karasek (Kate), Ted D'Arms (James), Patricia Gage (Eleanor), Susan Ludlow (Agnes), Sean G. Griffin (Jim), Megan Cole (Nell), and Ken Ballenger, Cristopher Berns, Cathy Bryan, Tina Marie Goff, Suzy Hunt, Gale McNeeley, Victoria Otto, William Earl Ray

I'M NOT RAPPAPORT by Herb Gardner; Director, Daniel Sullivan; Set, Tony Walton; Costumes, Robert Morgan; Lights, Allen Lee Hughes. CAST: Harold Gould (Nat), Cleavon Little (Midge), David Spielberg (Danforth), Liann Pattison (Laurie), Jace Alexander (Gilley), Cheryl Giannini (Clara), David Strathairn (Cowboy)

THE MANDRAKE by Niccolo Machiavelli, adapted by Daniel Sullivan; with **THE WEDDING** by Bertolt Brecht; Translated by Richard Nelson; Director, Daniel Sullivan; Sets, Robert A. Dahlstrom; Costumes, Kurt Wilhelm; Lights, James F. Ingalls; Musical Score, Norman Durkee. CAST: "Mandrake": Daniel Sullivan (Prologue/Timoteo), R. Hamilton Wright (Callimaco), Gale McNeeley (Siro), Ted D'Arms (Nicia), Jack Hallett (Ligurio), Jill Klein (Waitress/Nun), Lori Larsen (Sostrata), Karen Kay Cody (Woman in church), Elizabeth Hess (Lucrezia), "The Wedding": Ted D'Arms (Bride's Father), Jill Klein (Groom's Mother), Elizabeth Hess (Bride), Karen Kay Cody (Her Sister), R. Hamilton Wright (Bridegroom), Gale McNeeley (His Friend), Lori Larsen (Bride's Friend), Daniel Sullivan (Her Husband), Jack Hallett (Young Man)

'night, MOTHER by Marsha Norman; Director, Amy Saltz; Set, Thomas Fichter; Costumes, Sally Richardson; Lights, Robert Peterson. CAST: Helen Harrelson (Thelma), June Daniel White (Jessie)

GUYS AND DOLLS with Music and Lyrics by Frank Loesser; Book, Jo Swerling, Abe Burrows; Director, Paul Giovanni; Choreographer, William Whitener; Musical Director, Stan Keen; Sets, Kate Edmunds; Costumes, Kurt Wilhelm; Lights, Dawn Chiang; Sound, Mac Perkins. CAST: Ray Bussey (Pickpocket), Jerry Coyle (Nicely-Nicely), Charles Whiteside (Benny), Chad Henry (Rusty), Karen Oleson (Martha), Cheryl Massey-Peters (Agatha), Eddie Buffum (Calvin), Yusef Bulos (Arvide), Regina O'Malley (Sarah), Brick Hartney (Harry), Jonathan Simmons (Lt. Brannigan), Sal Mistretta (Nathan), Steven Zediker (Society Max), Stephen Crenshaw (Nick), Ray Bussey (Liver Lips), Jerry Tassin (Scranton Slim), James Horvath (Joey), Faith Prince (Miss Adelaide), Debbie Lehwalder (Kitty), Cindra Avery (Dolores), Alexis Hoff (Wilhelmina), Cheryl Whitener (Joy), Karen Kay Cody (Cutie), Lisa Bell (Irma), Davis Gaines (Sky), Linda Kerns (General Cartwright), Jeffrey Dreisbach (Big Jule), Cuban Dancers: Alexis Hoff, Ray Bussey

NEW-PLAYS-IN-PROCESS SERIES

"*Discovered*" by Anthony Giardina; with John Aylward, Tony Carreiro, R. A. Farrell, Paul Hostetler, Susan Ludlow, Douglas Newell, William Ontiveros, Ben Prager. "*The Nice and Nasty*" by Mark O'Donnell; with Jane Adams, Kurt Beattie, J. V. Bradley, Tony Carreiro, Paul Fleming, Nick Flynn, Ki Gottberg, Peter Lohnes, Kevin Loomis, Liann Pattison, Andrea Stein. "*Cat's Paw*" by William Mastrosimone; with Suzy Hunt, Mark Jenkins, James Sutorius, Jack Young. "*Bearclaw*" by Timothy Mason; with John Eames, Lori Larsen, Donald Mantooth, R. Hamilton Wright

Chris Bennion Photos

**Top Left: Cleavon Little, Jace Alexander,
Harold Gould in "I'm Not Rappaport"
Below: June Daniel White, Helen Harrelson
in " 'night, Mother"**

Randy Rocca, Eileen Seeley in "Shades"
Above: Marc Epstein, Juliana Donald
in "Salt-Water Moon"

SOUTH COAST REPERTORY
Costa Mesa, California
September 6, 1984–June 23, 1985
Twentieth Season

Producing Artistic Director, David Emmes; Artistic Director, Martin Benson; General Manager, Timothy Brennan; Literary Manager, Jerry Patch; Business Manager, Paula Tomei; Development, Bonnie Brittain Hall; Press, John Mouledoux, Cristofer Gross, Corinne Flocken; Production Coordinator, Martin Benson; Production Manager, Paul Hammond; Lighting, Tom Ruzika; Sound, Conny Buczek; Stage Managers, Bill Venom, Julie Haber, Bonnie Lorenger, Andy Tighe; Props, Michael Mora; Technical Director, Ted Carlsson; Wardrobe, Nancy Hamann; Composer, Diane King.

COMPANY: Wayne Alexander, Nathan Adler, Fran Bennett, Ron Boussom, James E. Brodhead, Michael Canavan, Jeffrey Alan Chandler, Sean Coleman, Jeffrey Combs, Peter Crombie, Kenneth Danziger, Steve DeNaut, Ruth de Sosa, Juliana Donald, Diane Doyle, Richard Doyle, Larry Drake, Pamela Dunlap, Dana Elcar, John Ellington, Marc Epstein, Rafael Ferrer, Phyllis Frelich, Marilyn Fox, Wayne Grace, Sam Hamann, Terri Hanauer, Bartha Hartman, Ann Hearn, Karen Hensel, Sydney Hibbert, I. M. Hobson, Patti Johns, Kathryn Johnson, Penny Johnson, John-David Keller, Dan Kern, Art Koustik, Sally Kemp, Hal Landon, Jr., Hal Landon, Sr., Anni Long, Kristen Lowman, Robert Macnaughton, Michael MacRae, Nan Martin, Martha McFarland, Joan McMurtrey, Ron Michaelson, Joanna Miles, Annie Murray, Kerry Noonan, Laurence O'Dwyer, Caitlin O'Heaney, Jenifer Parker, Jennifer Parsons, Tony Plana, Daryl Roach, Tom Rosqui, Diane Salinger, Eileen Seeley, Howard Shangraw, Tom Shelton, Gabrielle Sinclair, Kurtwood Smith, Sally Smythe, Don Took, George Woods, Patti Yasutake, Brad Zerbst.

PRODUCTIONS & CASTS
SAINT JOAN by George Bernard Shaw; Director, John Allison; Sets, Michael Devine; Costumes, Noel Taylor; Lights, Tom Ruzika. CAST: Hal Landon, Jr., Art Koustik, Ruth De Sosa (Joan), Don Took, John-David Keller, James E. Brodhead, John Ellington, Wayne Grace, Dayna Dubrow, Ron Boussom (Dauphin), Richard Doyle, Tom Rosqui (Warwick), Larry Drake, Kay E. Kuter, I. M. Hobson (Inquisitor), Dan Kern.
THE GIGLI CONCERT by Thomas Murphy; *American Premiere;* Director, Martin Benson; Set, Susan Tuohy; Costumes, Barbara Cox; Lights, Cameron Harvey. CAST: Kenneth Danziger, Dana Elcar, Pamela Dunlap.
THE SHOW-OFF by George Kelly; Director, Lee Shallat; Set, Mark Donnelly; Costumes, Shigeru Yaji; Lights, Peter Maradudin. CAST: Nan Martin (Mrs. Fisher), Ron Boussom (Aubrey), Caitlen O'Heaney, Hal Landon, Sr., Kristen Lowman, Steve DeNaut, George Woods, Art Koustik, Rafael Ferrer.
THE IMPORTANCE OF BEING EARNEST by Oscar Wilde; Director, David Emmes; Set, Cliff Faulkner; Costumes, Susan Dennison; Lights, Kent Dorsey. CAST: Wayne Alexander, Howard Shangraw, Sally Kemp, Jennifer Parsons, Sally Smythe, John-David Keller, Tom Rosqui, John Ellington, Annie Murray.
THE DEBUTANTE BALL by Beth Henley; *World Premiere;* Director, Stephen Tobolowsky; Set, Mark Donnelly; Costumes, Robert Blackman; Lights, Tom Ruzika. CAST: Jeffrey Combs, Phyllis Frelich, Penny Johnson, Ann Hearn, Lawrence O'Dwyer, Joanna Miles, Diane Salinger.
MASTER HAROLD. . . . and the boys by Athol Fugard; Director, Martin Benson; Set, Cliff Faulkner; Costumes, Dwight Richard Odle; Lights, Cameron Harvey. CAST: Sydney Hibbert, Robert Macnaughton, Daryl Roach.
TOP GIRLS by Caryl Churchill; Director, David Emmes; Sets, Cliff Faulkner; Costumes, Shigeru Yaji; Lights, Brian Gale. CAST: Jenifer Parker, Karen Hensel, Anni Long, Martha McFarland, Patti Johns, Patty Yasutake, Gabrielle Sinclair.
SHADES by David Epstein; *World Premiere;* Director, John Frank Levey; Set, Mark Donnelly; Costumes, Deborah Slate; Lights, Paulie Jenkins. CAST: Kerry Noonan, Michael MacRae, Randy Rocca, Sean Coleman, Terri Hanauer, Eileen Seeley.
RECKLESS by Craig Lucas; Director, Jan Eliasberg; Set, Cliff Faulkner; Costumes, Barbara Cox; Lights, Tom Ruzika. CAST: Joan McMurtrey, Michael Canavan, Jeffrey Alan Chandler, Ann Hearn, Richard Doyle, Anni Long, Fran Bennett.
SALT-WATER MOON by David French; *U.S. Premiere;* Director, Martin Benson; Set, Michael Devine; Costumes, Sylvia Moss; Lights, Peter Maradudin. CAST: Juliana Donald, Marc Epstein.
RUM AND COKE by Keith Reddin; *World Premiere;* Director, David Emmes; Set, Cliff Faulkner; Costumes, Susan Dennison; Lights, Peter Maradudin. CAST: Peter Crombie, Anni Long, Richard Doyle, Ron Boussom, Tony Plana, John-David Keller, John Ellington, Don Took, Art Koustik.
A CHRISTMAS CAROL by Charles Dickens, adapted by Jerry Patch; Director, John-David Keller; Sets, Cliff Faulkner; Costumes, Dwight Richard Odle; Lights, Tom and Donna Ruzika. CAST: Hal Landon, Jr. (Scrooge), John Ellington (Crachit), Anni Long, Art Koustik, Richard Doyle, Ron Boussom, Martha McFarland, Don Took, Michelle Wallen, Howard Shangraw, Ron Michaelson, Marilyn Fox, Tim Titus.

Stephen Tobolowsky, Steve Sealy Photos

Top Left: Phyllis Frelich, Laurence O'Dwyer, Penny Johnson, Jeffrey Combs, Diane Salinger, Kurtwood Smith in "The Debutante Ball"

173

STAGE #1

Dallas, Texas
September 18, 1984–June 9, 1985

Founder/Artistic Director, Jack Clay; Managing Director, Ernest Fulton; Stage Manager, James Martin; Press, James E. Mitchell; Marketing/Development, Jeff Dannick

PRODUCTIONS & CREDITS (names of actors not submitted)
CURSE OF THE STARVING CLASS by Sam Shepard; Director, David Bassuk; Set, Christopher Rusch; Lighting, Susan Takis; Costumes, A. Dale Nally
NATIVE SPEECH by Eric Overmyer; Director, Cynthia White; Set, Greg Metz; Lighting, Christopher Rusch; Costumes, Ruth Fields, Daniella Maretka; Sound, Will Clay
ANGELS FALL by Lanford Wilson; Director, Pat Kelly; Set, Christopher Rusch; Costumes, Virginia Linn; Sound, Scott Miller
COURTSHIP/VALENTINE'S DAY (*World Premiere*) by Horton Foote; Director, Jack Clay; Set, Michael O'Sullivan; Lighting, Wayne Lambert; Costumes, Rondi Hillstrom Davis; Sound, Rick Peeples, Will Clay
K2 by Patrick Meyers; Director, Jenna Worthen; Set, Roger Farkash; Lighting, David Opper; Costumes, Valerie Jo Grunner, Neil Larson; Sound, Rick Peeples, Will Clay

T. R. Green, Jane Vitus, Jim Fields,
Judy Blue in "Valentine's Day"

174 Rosemary Prinz, Susan Greenhill in "The Glass Menagerie" Above: Antonio Fargas, Mary Beth Fisher in "The Rainmaker" (*Carl Bartels Photos*)

STAGEWEST

Springfield, Massachusetts
October 10, 1984–June 2, 1985

Artistic Director, Timothy Near; Assistant, John McCluggage; Marketing/Development, Sheldon Wolf; Press, Tara K. Becker; Administrative Director, Paul J. Horton; Business Manager, Val Pori; Production Manager, Ken Denison; Technical Director, Joseph W. Long; Props, Steve Rosse; Wardrobe, Sally Schwam; Stage Managers, Nancy Sagosz, Ruth Feldman; Designer, Jeffrey Struckman

PRODUCTIONS & CASTS
THE RAINMAKER by N. Richard Nash; Director, Timothy Near; Lighting, John Gisondi; Fight Choreographer, John McCluggage; Sound, Paul J. Horton/Timothy Near. CAST: Luke Sickle (H. C.), Christopher McHale (Noah), Jace Alexander (Jimmy), Mary Beth Fisher (Lizzie), Brian Connors (File), David O. Petersen (Sheriff), Antonio Fargas (Starbuck)
TRUE WEST by Sam Shepard; Director, James Milton; Costumes, Deborah Shaw; Original Music, James Milton; Stage Manager, N. Anastasia Sagosz. CAST: John Abajian (Austin), Christopher McHale (Lee), William Brenner (Saul), Anna Minot (Mom)
AIN'T MISBEHAVIN' based on an idea by Murray Horwitz and Richard Maltby, Jr.; Conceived by Mr. Maltby; Director, Murray Horwitz; Musical Director, William Foster McDaniel; Set, Ron Placzek; Lighting, Jeremy Johnson; Re-Staged by Lonnie McNeil; Stage Manager, Ruth Feldman. CAST: Leslie Barlow, Evan Bell, Yvette Freeman, Lonnie McNeil, Deborah Lynn Sharpe
THE GLASS MENAGERIE by Tennessee Williams; Director, Timothy Near; Set, Carolyn Ross; Lights, Max DeVolder. CAST: Rosemary Prinz (Amanda Wingfield), Gary Sloan (Tom Wingfield), Susan Greenhill (Laura), Douglas Glenn Clark (Gentleman Caller)
MASTER HAROLD. . . . and the boys by Athol Fugard; Director, Jim O'Connor; Costumes, Kiki Smith; Lighting, Frances Aronson. CAST: Mike Hodge (Sam), Stephen McKinley Henderson (Willie), Andrew Hill Newman (Hally)
THE GOOD DOCTOR by Neil Simon; Director, Stephen Katz; Set, Richard Hoover; Lighting, John Gisondi; Original Music, Michael Bacon. CAST: Reno Roop (Writer); His Family: Charles Antalosky, Davis Hall, Bobo Lewis, Margery Murray
A DOLL'S HOUSE by Henrik Ibsen, adapted by Kathleen Tolan; Director, Timothy Near; Set, Jane Clark; Assistant Director, John Colgan McCluggage. CAST: Holly Hunter (Nora), Paul Walker (Torvald), Cordis Heard (Kristine), Alan Nebelthau (Niels Krogstad), Donald Gantry (Dr. Rank), Vera Johnson (Anne-Marie), Meegan Marasi or Sherreen Harackiewicz (Emmy), Steven Marasi or Michael Degon (Ivar)

STUDIO ARENA THEATRE

Buffalo, New York
September 21, 1984–May 24, 1985
Twentieth Season

Artistic Director, David Frank; Managing Director, Raymond Bonnard; Associate Director/Dramaturg, Kathryn Long; Production Coordinator/Technical Director, Brett Thomas; Stage Managers, Debra A. Acquavella, Christine Michael; Wardrobe, Gail Evans; Props, Jolene Obertin; Sound, Rick Menke; Creative Director, Daniel J. Wasinger; Marketing, Anne E. Conable; Development, Gail Leacy-Kratt; Company Manager, Diana K. Wyatt; Press, Blossom Cohan

PRODUCTIONS & CASTS

A MIDSUMMER NIGHT'S DREAM by William Shakespeare; Directors, David Frank, Robert Morgan; Set, Fred Duer; Costumes, Lorraine Calvert, Mary Nemecek-Peterson; Lighting, Brett Thomas; Music, Terrence Sherman; Stage Managers, Debra A. Acquavella, David Bottrell. CAST: Donna Haley (Hippoluta), Carl Schurr (Philostrate), Monique Fowler (Hermia), Mark Chamberlin (Demetrius), Gilbert Cole (Lysander), Donna Snow (Helena), Timothy Meyers (Quince), John Rainer (Bottom), David Bottrell (Flute), Walter Barrett (Egeus/Starveling), Terrence Sherman (Snout), Brian Keane (Snug), Robert Spencer (Puck), Ludmilla Owcharenko Whearty (First Fairy), Donna Haley (Hippolyta/Titania), Jack Wetherall (Theseus/Oberon), Fairies: Dina Corsetti, Lori Ann Joseph, William Rauch, Sandra Wallace, Shadows: G. Gavin Boyle, Richard Makowski

DARK OF THE MOON by Howard Richardson, William Berney; Directors, David Frank, Robert Morgan; Music, Terrence Sherman; Set, Fred Duer; Costumes, Catherine B. Reich; Lighting, Brett Thomas; Choreography, Linda Swiniuch; Stage Managers, Christine Michael, David Bottrell. CAST: Georgia Southcotte (Mrs. Summey), Jack Wetherall (Boy), Julie White (Dark Witch), G. J. Walsh (Mr. Bergen), Terrence Sherman (Hank Gudger), Philip Banaszak (Burt Dinwitty), Julie White (Edna Summey), Timothy Meyers (Conjur Man/Uncle Smelicue), David Bottrell (Floyd Allen), Mark Chamberlin (Marvin Hudgens), Carl Kowalkowski (Mr. Summey), Tess Spangler (Mrs. Bergen), Bonnie Bowers (Conjur Woman/Miss Metcalf), Melissa Proctor (Fair Witch/Ella Bergen), Monique Fowler (Barbara Allen), Donna Haley (Mrs. Allen), Robert Spencer (Mr. Allen), Carl Schurr (Preacher), Townspeople: Michael Stern, Rosemary Caputi, Glory Ann Dobiesz, Sara Moriarty

THE DOOM OF FRANKSTEIN by Geoffrey Sherman and Paul Wonsk; *World Premiere;* Director, Geoffrey Sherman; Set/Lights, Paul Wonsk; Costumes, Bill Walker; Music, Bob Volkman; Sound, Rick Menke; Production Coordinator, Brett Thomas; Stage Manager, Debra A. Acquavella. CAST: Timothy Meyers (Johann), David Hyde-Lamb (Gregor), Robert Spencer (Victor Frankenstein), Melissa Smith (Elizabeth Abelman), John Curless (Lucian), David Hyde-Lamb (Inspector), Michael Quill (The Monster), Paul A. Connolly or Jonathan Lamb (Kurt), Sarah Lamb or Robin Weiss (Gerda)

MASTER HAROLD. . . . and the boys by Athol Fugard; Director, Kathryn Long; Set, David Potts; Costumes, Janice I. Lines; Lighting, Curt Ostermann; Choreography, Tom Ralabate; Stage Manager, Christine Michael. CAST: Stephen McKinley Henderson (Sam), Basil A. Wallace (Willie), David Bottrell (Hally)

ANYTHING GOES with Music and Lyrics by Cole Porter; Book, Guy Bolton, P. G. Wodehouse, Howard Lindsay, Russel Crouse; Director, Carl Schurr; Choreography, Mary Jane Houdina; Musical Direction, Terrence Sherman; Set, James Joy; Costumes, John Carver Sullivan; Lights, Jeff Davis; Stage Managers, Debra A. Acquavella, Richert Easley. CAST: Steven D. Fazekas (Captain), Gerry Burkhardt (Purser/Crew), Dina Corsetti (Recreation Director), Wil Love (Sir Evelyn), Lora Martens (Hope), Jayne Freeman (Mrs. Harcourt), Richert Easley (Bishop), Ron Chisholm (Ching), Luke Sickle (Elisha), Harvey Evans (Billy), Kathryn Kendall (Bonnie), Robert Spencer (Moonface), Keith Savage (Reporter), David Monzione (Camera Man), Olivia Virgil Harper (Reno Sweeney), Donna Phillip-Miller (Purity), Corinne Melancon (Charity), Blake Atherton (Chastity), Eva Grant (Virtue), Passengers and Crew: Gerry Burkhardt, Ron Chisholm, Joyce Coppola, David Monzione, William Rauch, Mary Beth Robinson, Keith Savage

I OUGHT TO BE IN PICTURES by Neil Simon; Director, David Frank; Set, Gary C. Eckhart; Costumes, Janice I. Lines; Lighting, Brett Thomas. CAST: Anne Gartlan (Steffy), Brenda Daly (Libby), Robert Silver (Herb)

THE GLASS MENAGERIE by Tennessee Williams; Director, Donald Driver; Set, Philipp Jung; Costumes, Janice I. Lines; Lighting, Michael Orris Watson; Original Music, Michael Valenti; Stage Manager, Debra A. Acquavella

K. C. Kratt Photos

Top Right: Anne Newhall (on sofa), Michael Patterson, Scotty Bloch, Andrew Bloch in "The Glass Menagerie" **Below:** Olivia Virgil Harper, Wil Love, Lora Martens, Harvey Evans, Kathryn Kendall, Robert Spencer in "Anything Goes"

David Bottrell, Basil A. Wallace
in "Master Harold . . . and the boys"

175

SYRACUSE STAGE

Syracuse, N.Y.
October 12, 1984–April 21, 1985
Twelfth Season

Producing Artistic Director, Arthur Storch; Managing Director, James A. Clark; Business Manager, Betty Starr; Development, Shirley Lockwood; Marketing, Barbara Beckos; Dramaturg, Tom Walsh; Press, Jenifer Breyer, Zoe Tolone; Production Manager, Bob Davidson; Technical Director, Jeff Vandeyacht; Stage Managers, Cynthia Poulson, Don Buschmann, Barbara Beeching; Sound, Steve Shapiro; Props, Gretchen; Wardrobe, Trish Gryczka

PRODUCTIONS & CASTS

ARMS AND THE MAN by George Bernard Shaw; Director, Arthur Storch; Set, John Doepp; Costumes, Arnold S. Levine; Lighting, Gregg Marriner. CAST: Sherry Skinker (Raina), Yolanda Childress (Catherine Petkoff), Amelia White (Louka), Ivar Brogger (Bluntschli), Timothy Wilson (Soldier), William Ferriter (Nicola), Phillip Pruneau (Maj. Petkoff), Joseph Culliton (Sergius)

CLARENCE by Booth Tarkington; Director, Arthur Storch; Set, John Doepp; Costumes, Arnold S. Levine; Casting, David Tochterman. CAST: Gerardine Clark (Mrs. Martyn), Phillip Pruneau (Wheeler), Yolanda Childress (Mrs. Wheeler), Timothy Wilson (Bobby), Laura Galusha (Cora), Sherry Skinker (Violet), Ivar Brogger (Clarence), Amelia White or Mary Chalon (Della), William Ferriter (Dinwiddie), Joseph Culliton (Hubert)

HANDY DANDY by William Gibson; Director, Arthur Storch; Set, Victor A. Becker; Costumes, Maria Marrero; Lighting, Judy Rasmuson. CAST: James Whitmore (Henry Pulaski), Audra Lindley (Molly Egan)

SHEPARD SETS: "*Angel City,*" "*Back Bog Beast Bait,*" "*Suicide in B Flat*" by Sam Shepard; Director, George Ferencz; Music, Max Roach; Set, Bill Stabile; Costumes, Sally J. Lesser; Lighting, Blu. CAST: Jim Abele, Betsy Aidem, Raul Aranas, Akin Babatunde, Tom Costello, Peter Jay Fernandez, Zivia Flomenhaft, Stephen Mellor, S. Epatha Merkerson

A LESSON FROM ALOES by Athol Fugard; Director, Josephine R. Abady; Set, David Potts; Costumes, Carol Kunz; Lighting, Ann G. Wrightson; Original Music, Chris Binaxas. CAST: Robin Chadwick (Piet Bezuidenhout), Sonja Lanzener (Gladys Bezuidenhout), Herb Downer (Steve Daniels)

PASSION by Peter Nichols; Director, Terry Schreiber; Set, Charles Cosler; Costumes, Maria Marrero; Lighting, Craig Miller. CAST: Kristin Larkin (Kate), Marco St. John (James), Tanny McDonald (Eleanor), Margaret Warncke (Agnes), John C. Vennema (Jim), Maeve McGuire (Nell), Beverly Bluem, Sam Goldsman, William Hynes, Jody Rowell, Mark Wenderlich, Dan Young

Susan Piper Kublick, Lawrence Mason, Jr. Photos

**Top Right: Tanny McDonald, John Vennema,
Kristin Larkin, Marco St. John, Maeve
McGuire in "Passion" Below: William
Ferriter, Timothy Wilson, Laura Galusha,
Yolanda Childress, Ivar Brogger in "Clarence"**

**George Geddes, Caryn West
in "Fool for Love"**

THEATRE BY THE SEA

Portsmouth, New Hampshire
October 4, 1984–May 18, 1985

Artistic Director, Tom Celli; General Manager, Jean Barter; Company Manager, Sharon Fentiman; Development, Donna Meeks; Technical Director, James Murphy; Stage Manager, John Becker

PRODUCTIONS & CASTS

AIN'T MISBEHAVIN' directed by John Montgomery; Musical Director. CAST: Pi Douglass, Lynnie Godfrey, Dwayne Grayman, Trina Thomas, Diane Wilson

IMAGINARY INVALID directed by Larry Carpenter. CAST: Tina Cartmell, Tom Celli, Earle Edgerton, Dean Gardner, Mark Lewis, Judy Nunn, Keith Perry, Jennifer Powers, Darcy Pulliman, Scott Severance

A CHRISTMAS CAROL directed by Peter DeLaurier. CAST: Meredith Allsopp, Sam Blackwell, Amy Burnett, Daniel Clay, Roger Curtis, Earle Edgerton, Nancy Walton-Fenn, Dean Gardner, Nick Mize, Judy Nunn, Ceal Phelan, Tara Schroeder, Scott Severance, James Zvanut

AGNES OF GOD directed by Richard Hughes. CAST: Lynn Goodwin, Tanny McDonald, Sylvia Short

PAINTING CHURCHES directed by Tom Celli. CAST: Robert Blackburn, Victoria Boothby, Dossy Peabody

FOOL FOR LOVE directed by Peter Bennett. CAST: Ward Asquith, George Gerdes, Timothy Wagner, Caryn West

YOU CAN'T TAKE IT WITH YOU directed by Tom Celli. CAST: Ann Brennan, Natalie Brown, Dan Charlton, Charles Dumas, Earle Edgerton, Venida Evans, Kirsten Giroux, Arch Johnson, Nicholas Mize, Paul Mroczka, Budd Peters, Dick Sabol, Maxine Taylor-Morris, Michael Tobin, Tina Young

Northlight Photography

THEATRE/TEATRO

Los Angeles, California
October 3, 1984–June 23, 1985
Sixth Season

A program of the Bilingual Foundation of the Arts (Edward D. Santos, Chairman); Artistic Director, Margarita Galban; Managing Producer, Carmen Zapata; Administrative Director, Edward Lucero; Development, Sue Welsh; Press, Mary de Castro; Technical Director, Robert Fromer; Production Manager, Estela Scarlata

PRODUCTIONS & CASTS

(BFA's Little Theatre) Wednesday, Oct. 3,–Dec. 2, 1984
BLOOD WEDDING/BODAS DE SANGRE by Federico Garcia Lorca; New English translation, Michael Dewell, Carmen Zapata; Director, Margarita Galban; Music, Ian Krouse; Choreography, Linda Dangcil; Sets, Estela Scarlata; Lighting, Robert Fromer; Costumes, Ruth Enriquez; Stage Manager, Jaime Vasquez. CAST: Linda Dangcil/Christine Avila (Death), Raul Espinoza (Woodcutter), Mary Bermudez (Moon), Armando DiLorenzo/Richard Canales (Bridegroom), Carmen Zapata/Myriam Tubert (Mother), Ros Bosley (Neighbor), Lina Montalvo (Mother-in-law), Bonnie Morin/Marie Saint-Clair (Wife), John Vargas/J. Edmundo Araiza/Clay Miller (Leonardo), Lucia Rodriguez (Girl), Angelina Estrada/Margaret Regalado (Maid), Santos Morales/Hecmar Lugo (Father of the bride), Maria Rubell/Elena Martinez (Bride), Rudy Caballero (1st Youth), Heberto Guillen (2nd Youth)
A LA DIESTRA DE DIOS PADRE by Enrique Buenaventura; Director, Jaime John Gil; Scenery, Estela Scarlata; Lighting, Robert Fromer; Choreography, Marco Julio Villegas; Stage Manager, Armando di Lorenzo. CAST: J. Edmund Araiza (Jesus), Brando Bens (Tullido/Mendigo 2), Marilyn Carven (Sobrina), Angelina Estrada (Peraltona), Rosely Flores (Planidera 2/Mujer), Ruben Garfias (Peralta), Jaime John Gil (San Pedro), Heberto Guillen (El Diablo), Maritza Guimet (Planidera 3), Luis Liner (Leproso/Mendigo 3), Rosita Ojeda (Planidera 1/Vieja), Dyana Ortelli (Maruchenga), Ricky Pardon (Ciego/Mendigo 1), Patricia Thomas (La Muerte), Pascual Tibio (Viejo Limosndro), Marco Julio Villegas (Abanderado/Sepulturero)
THE M. C. by Rodolfo Santana; New English translation by Lina Montalvo, Carmen Zapata; Director, Margarita Galban; Set, Estela Scarlata; Lighting, Robert Fromer. CAST: James Victor (Ted Silverstein), John Vargas (Charlie)
THE YOUNG LADY FROM TACNA by Mario Vargas Llosa; Translated and Directed by Joanne Pottlitzer; Producer, Carmen Zapata; Set, Estela Scarlata; Lighting, Robert Fromer; Costumes, Richard D. Smart; Stage Manager, Roy Conboy. CAST: Irene De Bari (Mama-E), Diane Rodriguez (Amelia), Henry Darrow (Belisario), Louie Cruz Beltran (Joaquin), Evelina Fernandez (Grandmother Carmen), Sam Vlahos (Grandfather Pedro), Angela Moya (Carlota), Sal Lopez (Cesar), Richard German (Agustin), Standbys: Michael Sandoval, Angela Moya, Kathleen Salamone

John Vargas, James Victor
in "The M. C."

TRINITY SQUARE REPERTORY COMPANY

Providence, Rhode Island
July 6, 1984–May 26, 1985
Twenty-first Season

Artistic Director, Adrian Hall; Managing Director, E. Timothy Langan; Composer, Richard Cumming; Sets, Eugene Lee, Robert D. Soule; Lighting, John F. Custer; Costumes, William Lane; Production Manager, William Radka; Technical Director, David Rotondo; Wardrobe, Marcia Zammarelli; Props, Robert Schleinig, Michael McGarty; Development, Simone P. Joyaux; Marketing/Press, Anne Marden, Jeannie MacGregor-Jochim, Jerry O'Brien; Stage Managers, Maureen F. Gibson, Wendy E. Cox

COMPANY: Akin Babatunde, Tom Bloom, Barbara Blossom, James Carruthers, Michael Cobb, Timothy Crowe, Richard Cumming, John F. Custer, William Damkoehler, Margot Dionne, Stephanie Dunnum, Richard Ferrone, Anne Gerety, Peter Gerety, Tom Griffin, Ed Hall, Patrick Hines, Richard Hoyt-Miller, Richard Jenkins, Keith Jochim, Vera Johnson, David C. Jones, Richard Kavanaugh, David Kennett, Richard Kneeland, William Lane, Eugene Lee, Geraldine Librandi, Becca Lish, Howard London, Ruth Maynard, Brian McEleney, Derek Meader, Barbara Meek, Philip Minor, Barbara Orson, Ricardo Pitts-Wiley, Ford Rainey, Anne Scurria, Robert D. Soule, David PB Stephens, Cynthia Strickland, Patricia Ann Thomas, Mark Torres, Daniel Von Bargen, Tunc Yalman
PRODUCTIONS: Beyond Therapy by Christopher Durang, What the Butler Saw by Joe Orton, Terra Nova by Ted Tally, Passion Play by Peter Nichols, Tartuffe by Moliere, A Christmas Carol adapted by Adrian Hall and Richard Cumming, Misalliance by George Bernard Shaw, And a Nightingale Sang by C. P. Taylor, The Country Wife by William Wycherly, Master Harold . . . and the boys by Athol Fugard, Present Laughter by Noel Coward

Ron Manville, Tom Bloom, Keith Jochim Photos

Barbara Blossom, Cynthia Strickland, Derek Meader,
Becca Lish, Keith Jochim in ". . . And a Nightingale Sang"

VIRGINIA MUSEUM THEATRE

Richmond, Virginia
October 4, 1984–May 18, 1985
Thirtieth Season

Artistic Director, Terry Burgler; Associate Artistic Director/Musical Theatre, Darwin Knight; General Manager, Edward W. Rucker; Development, Nancy Carmichael; Marketing, Phil Crosby; Press, E. Frazier Millner; Directors, Terry Burgler, Darwin Knight, Robert Lanchester, Tom Markus, Charles Towers; Designers, Candace Cain, Bronwyn Caldwell, Charles Caldwell, Terry Cermak, David Crank, F. Mitchell Dana, Elizabeth K. Fischer, Lana Fritz, Lynne M. Hartman, Julie Keen, Dirk Kuyk, Richard Moore, Susan Rheaume; Stage Managers, Deborah Simon, Jeanne Anich, Doug Flinchum, Donna Stanley

PRODUCTIONS & CASTS:
FINAL TOUCHES by Kenneth O. Johnson; with Frances Helm, Gil Rogers, Anne Sheldon, Jake Turner, Scottie Wilkison
THE MISTRESS OF THE INN by Carlo Goldoni; Adapted by Freyda Thomas, David Carlyon; with Robert Foley, Mark Hattan, Hubert Kelly, Jr., Dan LaRocque, Johanna Morrison, David Pursley, Janet Zarish
A CHRISTMAS CAROL by Charles Dickens, adapted by Tom Markus; with Bev Appleton, Susan Brandner, Donald Christopher, Amanda DiGirolamo, Lucien Douglas, Heather Elizabeth Dunville, Christy Michelle Fairman, Robert Foley, Jan Guarino, Maj-Lis Jalkio, Steven Journey, Will Leskin, Ann MacMillan, Jared Matesky, Joe Terrill Murphy, Jessica Printz, Walter Rhodes, Adrian Rieder, Todd Rodrigues, Ed Sala, Rob Storrs, Freyda Thomas, Robert L. Townes, Gregory S. Womack
GREATER TUNA by Jaston Williams, Joe Sears, Ed Howard; with Michael McCarty, Trip Plymale
CLOUD 9 by Caryl Churchill; with Joseph Culliton, William Denis, Daydrie Hague, Dan LaRocque, Jane Moore, Johanna Morrison, Ian Stuart
A RAISIN IN THE SUN by Lorraine Hansberry; with Donna Bailey, Jerome Butler, John P. Dworak, Maury Erickson, Michael S. Guess, Lycia Hannibal, Marie Goodman Hunter, Brent Jones, Victor Love, Nathaniel Ritch, Dexter Zollicoffer
UNDER MILK WOOD by Dylan Thomas; with Mario Arrambide, Robert Blumfeld (succeeded by Terry Burgler), Barry Boys, Jay Doyle, Georgine Hall, Kimberly King, Randy Lilly, Mary Martello, Bruce Somerville, Jill Tanner
CRIMES OF THE HEART by Beth Henley; with Daniel Ahearn, Alex Bond, Madylon Brans, Debra Dean, Clifford Fetters, Cynthia Mace

Ronald Jennings Photos

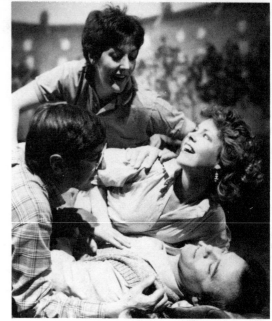

**Ian Stuart, Johanna Morrison, Daydrie Hague,
Joseph Culliton in "Cloud 9"**

**Madylon Brans, Clifford Fetters
in "Crimes of the Heart"**

VIRGINIA STAGE COMPANY

Norfolk, Virginia
October 10, 1984–April 13, 1985
Sixth Season

Artistic Director, Charles Towers; Managing Director, Dan J. Martin; Associate Artistic Director, Christopher Hanna; Development, Stuart Gordon; Marketing, Katie Lincoln-Lively; Business Manager, Caroline F. Turner; Company Manager, Deborah Shumate; Technical Director, Steve Sysko; Props, Christine E. Martis; Costumes, Candice Cain; Sound, Dirk Kuyk; Stage Managers, Dan Sedgwick, Nancy Kay Uffner; Press, Marilyn Meredith

PRODUCTIONS & CASTS
AMADEUS by Peter Shaffer; Costumes, Martha Kelly; Set/Lighting, Joe Ragey; with Lisa Brailoff, Scott Forbes Elliot, Terry Finn, Ron Fitzgerald, Haskell Gordan, Michael Guido, James Harper, Philip LeStrange, David Lively, Edward Morgan, Denis Mullaney, Nancy Mulvey, Jay Oney, Wyman Pendleton, Adam Redfield, Nathan Seymour, Tom Story, Larry Swansen
HUSBANDRY by Patrick Tovatt; Director, Jamie Brown; Set/Lighting, Joe Ragey; with Mary Fogarty, Michael Hartman, Addison Powell, Cecelia Riddett
TAKING STEPS by Alan Ayckbourn; Director, Alex Dmitriev; Set/Lighting, Joe Ragey; with Joyce Fideor, Douglas Fisher, Philip LeStrange, Debra Jo Rupp, Nick Stannard, Stephen Temperley
THE MOUND BUILDERS by Lanford Wilson; Lighting, Spencer Mosse; Set, Joe Ragey; with Joe Barrett, Veronica Castang, Mary Beth Fisher, Jonathan Fuller, Susanne Marley, Terry O'Quinn, Sybil Smith
MOROCCO by Allan Havis; *World Premiere;* Set, Michael Miller; Lighting, Steve Pollock; with Ray Aranha, Larry Pine, Gordana Rashovich
CRIMES OF THE HEART by Beth Henley; Set, Charles Caldwell; with Daniel Ahearn, Alex Bond, Madylon Brans, Debra Dean, Clifford Fetters, Cynthia Mace
ALIAS MARK TWAIN: A VISIT WITH SAMUEL CLEMENS with David Lively

Ellen Forsyth Photos

WALNUT STREET THEATRE COMPANY
Philadelphia, Pennsylvania
November 3, 1984–March 17, 1985
Second Season

Executive Director, Bernard Havard; General Manager, Mary Bensel; Development, Frances R. Bourne; Marketing, Randall J. Voit; Production Manager, William B. Duncan; Assistant, Diana Krauss; Stage Managers, Frank Anzalone, Sherrill deWitt-Howard; Wardrobe, Scott Lesher; Props, Robert F. Wolin; Technical Director, Michael Powers; Press, Robin Wray

PRODUCTIONS & CASTS
CHEKHOV IN YALTA by John Drive and Jeffrey Haddow; Director, John Driver; Set, Loren Sherman; Costumes, Nan Cibula; Lighting, Jim Ingalls; Stage Manager, Marsha Gitkind. CAST: Dara Norman (Fyokla), Stephen Keep (Chekhov), Warren Manzi (Gorky), Charles Gregory (Bunin), Elaine Bromka (Masha Chekhov), Catherine Cox (Olga Knipper), John Connolly (Vladimir Nemirovich-Danchenko), Steve Liebman (Luzhki), David Carlyon (Moskvin), Theresa Saldana (Lilina Stanislavski), Mark Capri (Stanislavski)
THE MUSIC MAN by Meredith Willson; Director, Charles Abbott; Choreographer, Dennis Grimaldi; Musical Director, Elman R. Anderson; Set, Mark W. Morton; Costumes, Kathleen Blake; Lighting, Gregg Marriner. CAST: Joel Craig (Harold Hill), Lynn Fitzpatrick (Marian Paroo), John-Charles Kelly (Charlie Cowell), Charles J. Hicks (Conductor), Irwin Charone (Mayor Shinn), J. B. Adams (Ewart Dunlop), Ralph Braun (Oliver Hix), Dick Decareau (Jacey), Martin J. Walsh (Olin), Michael Cone (Marcellus), Jerry Ziaja (Tommy), Mary Ellen Ashley (Mrs. Paroo), Holly Atlee (Amaryllis), Louis Hirsch (Winthrop), Marian Baer (Eulalie), Tia Riebling (Zaneeta), Johnna Cummings (Gracie), Deborah Bradshaw (Alma), Lynn Albright (Maud), Melissa Bailey (Ethel), Mary Ellen Grant (Mrs. Squires), Charles J. Hicks (Constable), and Kiplee Bell, Paul Charles, Timothy Craskey, Glenn Davish, Stephanie Diienno, Matthew Drennan, Andrea Leigh-Smith, Jennifer McDonough, Gary Mendelson, Nancy Lyn Miller, Donald Newell, Craig North, Cindy Oakes, Daniel Pelzig, Ellen Troy
ANOTHER PART OF THE FOREST by Lillian Hellman; Director, Fred Chappell; Set, Ursula Belden; Costumes, Susan Hirschfeld. CAST: Michele Farr (Regina Hubbard), Charles Gregory (John Bagtry), Mary Nell Santacroce (Lavinia), Olivia Williams (Coralee), David Sabin (Marcus), W. T. Martin (Ben), Rodman Gaillard (Jake), Douglas Wing (Simon), Steve Conway (Oscar), Jane Fleiss (Birdie), Lee Golden (Harold), Harry H. Kunesch (Gilbert), Drucie McDaniel (Laurette)
QUARTERMAINE'S TERMS by Simon Gray; Director, Malcolm Black; Set/Lighting, Paul Wonsek; Costumes, Martha Kelly. Douglas Wing (Quartermaine), Maureen Garrett (Anita), Robert Black (Mark), Richard Curnock (Eddie), David Huband (Derek), John Milligan (Henry), Barbara Barringer (Melanie)
A MIDSUMMER NIGHT'S DREAM by William Shakespeare; Director, Gregory S. Hurst; Set/Costumes, Karen Gerson; Lights, Jane Reisman; Choreography, Schellie Archbold; Composer, John Clifton. CAST: Alan Brooks (Theseus/Oberon), Judith Roberts (Hippolyta/Titania), Josh Clark (Philostrate/Puck), John Hallow (Egeus/Quince), Leslie Hicks (Hermia), Rory Kelly (Demetrius), Alex Corcoran (Lysander), Margaret Reed (Helena), John P. Connolly (Bottom), Time Winters (Flute), Marty Vale (Starveling), Tom Teti (Snout), John Favorite (Snug), Gina Martin (Mustardseed/Attendant), Lisa Merrill McCord (Peaseblossom/Attendant), Charles Grayauskie, Paul Hartel (Fairies), Laura Delano (Cobweb), Tia Riebling (Moth), Jonathan Walsh (Changeling Boy)

Ken Kauffman, Gerry Goodstein Photos

Barbara Barringer, Richard Curnock in
"Quartermaine's Terms" Top: Charles Gregory,
Michele Farr in "Another Part of the Forest"

THE WHOLE THEATRE
Montclair, New Jersey
October 30, 1984–April 28, 1985

Artistic Director, Olympia Dukakis; Managing Director, Patricia K. Quinn; General Manager, Laurence Feldman; Associate Artistic Director, Apollo Dukakis; Technical Director, Mary Orme; Stage Manager, Edward Neuert; Press, Carol J. Coppola; Directors, Apollo Dukakis, Robert Moss, Austin Pendleton, Tom Brennan, Porter Van Zandt; Costumes, Sigrid Insull, Michael Krass, Andrew Marlay; Sets, Michael Miller, Rick Dennis, Reagan Cook, Philipp Jung; Lighting, Rachel Budin, David Noling, Carol Rubinstein, Richard Moore; Stage Managers, Edward Neuert, Suzanne Fry

PRODUCTIONS & CASTS
OF MICE AND MEN by John Steinbeck; with Albert Braun, Thomas Martell Brimm, Andrew Clark, David Clarke, Ron Herzig, Steve Hofvendahl, Terrence Markovich, W. T. Martin, Virginia Meissner, Joseph Ragno
ABSURD PERSON SINGULAR by Alan Ayckbourn; with Tony Aylward, James Cahill, Jane Cronin, Martin LaPlatney, Beth McDonald, Erika Petersen
GHOSTS by Henrik Ibsen; with Scott Burkholder, Apollo Dukakis, Olympia Dukakis, Lucinda Jenney, Louis Zorich
THE SORROWS OF FREDERICK by Romulus Linney; with Linden Ashby, Thomas Barbour, P. L. Carling, Katina Commings, George Ede, Patrick Garner, Max Gulack, Terrence Markovich, George Millenbach, Austin Pendleton, Gay Reed, Edward Zang
THE MIDDLE AGES by A. R. Gurney, Jr.; with Rick Casorla, Margaret Hall, Debra Jo Rupp, Lawrence Weber

Jim Chambers Photos

Debra Jo Rupp, Rick Casorla
in "The Middle Ages"

ANNUAL SHAKESPEARE FESTIVALS

AMERICAN PLAYERS THEATRE

Spring Green, Wisconsin
July 3,–October 7, 1984
Fifth Season

Artistic Director, Randall Duk Kim; Managing Director, Charles J. Bright; Resident Director, Anne Occhiogrosso; Costumes, Nanalee Raphael-Schirmer, Ted Boerner; Movement, Jerry Gardner; Composer, Music Director, Tim Schirmer; General Manager, Francis X. Tobin; Production Manager, Robert Wood; Stage Managers, Dana Graham, Rhoda F. Nathan; Press, Dixie Legler
COMPANY: John Aden, Paul Bentzen, David Cecsarini, Jill Daly, Lee Elmer Ernst, Oksana Fedunyszyn, Steven A. Helmeke, Stephen Hemming, Lucas G. Hendrickson, Suzette Nelson Hendrickson, Jonathan Herold, James Hulin, Leonard Kelly-Young, Terry Kerr, Randall Duk Kim, Howard Lucas, Alexandra Mitchell, Drew C. Noll, Anne Acchiogrosso, Fred Ollerman, Arleigh Richards, Sandra Reigel-Ernst, William Schlaht, Laurie Shaman, Jonathan Smoots, Karl Stoll, Theodore Swetz, Brad Waller, Thomas Winslow
PRODUCTIONS: The Merry Wives of Windsor, A Midsummer Night's Dream, The Taming of the Shrew, Romeo and Juliet, Love's Labour's Lost

**Randall Duk Kim, Arleigh Richards
in "The Merry Wives of Windsor"
(Zane Williams Photo)**

BERKELEY SHAKESPEARE FESTIVAL

Berkeley, California
July 13,–September 23, 1984

Artistic Director, Dakin Matthews; Artistic Manager, Richard E. T. White; Production Manager, Michael Cook; Technical Director, Mark Kessler; Wardrobe, Rick Austin; Props, Eric Landisman; Managing Director, John Maynard, Jr.; Art Director, Bernie Schimbke; Stage Managers, Michael Cook, Carolyn Grigsby; Press, Suzanne Unger

PRODUCTIONS & CASTS

OTHELLO directed by E. T. White; Set, Michael Cook; Musical Director, Linda Laflamme; Costumes, Eliza Chugg; Lighting, James Brentano; Fight Choreographer, Michael Cawelti; Choreographer, Douglas Leach. CAST: Harold Surratt (Othello), Nike Doukas (Desdemona), Geoffrey Elliott (Cassio), Tony Amendola (Iago), Molly Mayock (Emilia), Howard Swain (Roderigo), Francia DiMase (Bianca), Julian Lopez-Morillas (Duke of Venice), Gail Chugg (Brabantio), Tom Ramirez (Lodovico), Mykael O'Sruitheain (Gratiano), Richard Butterfield (Montano), Michael Cawelti (Clown), Katherine Heasley (Columbina), Richard Butterfield (Pantalone)
THE MERCHANT OF VENICE directed by Tony Amendola; Assistant Director, Gillian Shaw; Composer/Music Director, Carl Smith; Set, Shevra Tait; Costumes, Patricia Polen; Lighting, James Brentano; Choreographer, Douglas Leach. CAST: Gail Chugg (Duke of Venice), Harold Surratt (Prince of Morocco), Douglas Leach (Prince of Arragon), Julian Lopez-Morillas (Antonio), Geoffrey Elliott (Bassanio), Mykael O'Sruitheain (Gratiano), Michael Cawelti (Salerio), Richard Butterfield (Solanio), Chiron Alston (Lorenzo), Tom Ramirez (Shylock), Douglas Leach (Tubal), Howard Swain (Launcelot Gobbo), Gail Chugg (Old Gobbo), Carl Smith (Balthasar), Molly Mayock (Portia), Nike Doukas (Nerissa), Francia Di Mase (Jessica)
LOVE'S LABOUR'S LOST directed by Julian Lopez-Morillas; Assistant Director, Cyn Horton; Composer/Musical Director, Carl Smith; Set, Eric Landisman; Costumes, Diana Stone; Lighting, James Brentano; Choreographer, Douglas Leach. CAST: Richard Butterfield (Ferdinand), Chiron Alston (Berowne), Geoffrey Elliott (Longaville), Michael Cawelti (Dumain), Tony Amendola (Don Adriano), Marilyn Prince (Moth), Gail Chugg (Holofernes), Tom Ramirez (Sir Nathaniel), Mykael O'Sruitheain (Dull), Howard Swain (Costard), Molly Mayock (Princess of France), Francia Di Mase (Rosaline), Nike Doukas (Maria), Cheryl Kennedy (Katherine), Douglas Leach (Boyet), Harold Surratt (Marcade)

Allen Nomura Photos

**Nike Doukas, Harold Surratt in "Othello"
Above: Molly Mayock, Geoffrey Elliott
in "The Merchant of Venice"**

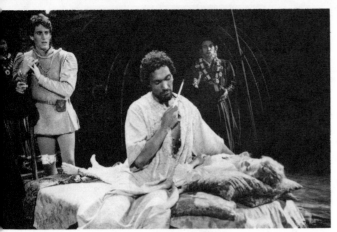

Dan Sturdivant, Jimmy Smits, Katherine
Udall in "Othello"

COLORADO SHAKESPEARE FESTIVAL

Boulder, Colorado
July 12–August 23, 1984
Twenty-seventh Season

Producing Director, Dr. Martin Cobin; Lighting, Richard Devin; Fight Choreographer, Erik Fredricksen; Technical Director, Stancil Campbell; Production Coordinator, Thrim Paulsen; Business Manager, Rona Cantor; Dramaturgs, Paul Edwards, Cynthia Bishop, Assunta Kent; Stage Manager, Tracy Cunningham; Press, Charleen Pappas
COMPANY: Irwin Appel, Judith Aplon, Holly Baumgardner, William Charlton, Jack Cirillo, James DeVita, Tim Douglas, James Drevescraft, Christopher Duncan, Edith Elliott, Linda Edmond, Tom Ford, Thomas Freeland, Gregg Henry, Bill Higham, David Hirvela, Tim Hopper, Bruce Lecuru, Tim Loughrin, Lynn Mathis, William Michie, Carlton Miller, Frank Nall, Samuel Sandoe, Maggie Stewart, Robert Stormont, James Symons
PRODUCTIONS: *Antony and Cleopatra* directed by Libby Appel; Scenery, Robert Schmidt; Costumes, David A. Busse. *The Merry Wives of Windsor* directed by Paul Gaffney; Scenery, Robert Schmidt; Costumes, Gwendolyn Nagle. *Romeo and Juliet* directed by Will York; Scenery, Thrim Paulsen; Costumes, Lee Hodgson

Jerry Stowall Photos

GREAT LAKES SHAKESPEARE FESTIVAL

Cleveland, Ohio
July 6,–October 21, 1984
Twenty-third Season

Producing Director, Vincent Dowling; Managing Director, Mary Bill; Sets, John Ezell; Costumes, Lewis D. Rampino, John Glaser; Lighting, Robert Jared; Stage Managers, Patricia Noto, Katherine M. Goodrich; Production Manager, Olwen O'Herlihy; Press, Bill Rudman
RESIDENT COMPANY: Jeffrey Bihr, Barry Boys, Madylon Branstetter, Bob Breuler, John Q. Bruce, Gale Fury Childs, Rachael Dowling, Robert Elliott, Jonathan Gillard, Neal Jones, Bernard Kates, Kimberly King, Suzanne Petri, Clive Rosengren, Dan Westbrook, William Youmans
GUEST ARTISTS: Edward Duke, Stephen McHattie, Glynnis O'Connor, and directors Larry Arrick, Ken Albers, David Trainer
PRODUCTIONS: The Taming of the Shrew by William Shakespeare, She Stoops to Conquer by Oliver Goldsmith, Our Town by Thornton Wilder, U.S. professional premiere of Thornton Wilder's The Alcestiad, Jeeves Takes Charge by P. G. Wodehouse and Edward Duke, Peg O' My Heart by J. Hartley Manners, A Midsummer Night's Dream by William Shakespeare

Mary Beth Camp Photos

Stephen McHattie, Glynnis O'Connor
in "The Taming of the Shrew"

HOUSTON SHAKESPEARE FESTIVAL

Houston, Texas
July 27,–August 11, 1984

Producing Director, Sidney Berger; Director, Charles Krohn; Scenery, Arch Andrus; Costumes, Barbara Medlicott; Lighting, John A. Gow; Stage Manager, David Fitzgerald; Press, Miriam Strane
PRODUCTIONS & CASTS
HAMLET with James Black (Bernardo/Norwegian Captain), Jeff Baldwin (Francisco), Dante DiLoreto (Horatio), William Gelber (Marcellus), Harry Booker/Gravedigger, Charles Krohn (Claudius), Robin Bradley (Gertrude), Ken Marshall (Hamlet), Richard Hill (Laertes), Luisa Amaral-Smith (Ophelia), Timothy Arrington (Polonius), Jeff Bennett (Rosencrantz), Kent Johnson (Guildenstern), Mary Chovanetz (Player Queen), Sam Russell (Player King), Chuck Hudson (Lucianus), Daniel Christiaens (Osric), and Charles Fuller, Allison Pennel, Carrie Reese, Greg Ruhe, Denise Sebesta, Norman Stewart, R. Alan Wrotenbery
THE TWO GENTLEMEN OF VERONA with Jeff Bennett (Proteus), Richard Hill (Valentine), Vaughn Johnson (Tailor/Outlaw), William Gelber (Tailor/Outlaw/Servant), Dante DiLoreto (Speed), Kathleen Trageser (Julia), Sarah Jane Moody (Lucetta), Harry Booker (Antonio), Kent Johnson (Panthino), Melissa Gray (Silvia), James Black (Launce), Daniel Christiaens (Thurio), Timothy Arrington (Duke of Milan), Allison Pennel (Ursula), R. Alan Wrotenbery (Musician), Dennis Wells (Host), Harry Booker (Eglamore), Charles Fuller (Servant)

Jim Caldwell Photos

Robin Bradley, Ken Marshall
in "Hamlet"

NEW JERSEY SHAKESPEARE FESTIVAL

Madison, New Jersey
June 27,–November 25, 1984
Twentieth Season

Artistic Director, Paul Barry; Producing Director, Ellen Barry; Production Manager, Jon P. Ogden; Lighting Design/Stage Managers, Richard Dorfman, Terry Kaye; Scenery, N. B. Dodge, Jr., Timothy Scalet; Costumes, Mitchell S. Bloom, Jim Buff, Heidi Dollmann; Musical Director, Deborah Martin; General Manager, Donna M. Gearhardt; Press, Kate Wisniewski; Technical Director, Jeff Wisor; Props, David Von Salis
COMPANY: Lisa Bansavage, Ellen Barry, Paul Barry, James Curt Bergwall, Katherine Carlson, Albert Corbin, Regina David, Ed Dennehy, Margaret Emory, Margaret Goodman, Richard Graham, Sandra Proctor Gray, Birdie M. Hale, Fiona Hale, David S. Howard, J. C. Hoyt, Richard Hughes, Alan Jordan, Lydia Laurans, Aaron Lustig, Ronald Martell, Virginia Mattis, Frank Nastasi, Dina Paisner, Don Perkins, Roger Robinson, Scott Schofield, Gedeth Smith, Cal Winn
   Fern Alisa Bachman, Melinda Baker, Susan Rachel Baker, Susan Bernfield, Linda Bisesti, Diana Lynn Bissel, Adele Cabot, Joya Ciciola, Karen Case Cook, David C. Eden, Roxanne Eldred, Denise Elkins, Michael Fields, Tim Foley, Gia Forakis, Susan Forbes, Edward L. Furs, Rebecca Gleason, Randy Herman, Kenneth Hertz, Dorothy A. Hirsch, Kevin Hogan, Erika Johnson, Sharon Johnson, Herman LeVern Jones, Laura Jones, Gail Lelyveld, Scott Lowy, Mary MacDonald, Jill Margolis, Electra McDowell, Marshall McKnight, Bergin Michaels, Deian Miller, Louise Moore, Stephen Moser, Richard O'Brien, Phil Prestamo, Joseph W. Rinaldi, Ken Rosenberg, Maxine Schaffer-Fromm, Linda Shirley, Richard Alan Sinrich, Soryl Stanley, Elizabeth Striker, Darrold Strubbe, Philip Suraci, Jr., Anne Sussman, Anne Torsiglieri, Aviva Twersky, Stephen Waldrup, and Shannon Elizabeth Barry, Donald Kent, Geoffrey Laurie, Jared Laurie
PRODUCTIONS: Othello and The Merchant of Venice by William Shakespeare, The School for Scandal by Richard Brinsley Sheridan, All the Way Home by Tad Mosel, The Sunshine Boys by Neil Simon, The Crucible by Arthur Miller

Jerry Dalia, Gerry Goodstein Photos

**Aaron Lustig, Regina David, Ellen Barry,
Geddeth Smith, Virginia Mattis
in "All the Way Home"**

NEW YORK SHAKESPEARE FESTIVAL

Twenty-ninth Season

(Delacorte Theater/Central Park) Producer, Joseph Papp; General Manager, Laurel Ann Wilson; Executive Assistant, Mary Kelley Leer; Casting, Rosemarie Tichler; Associate Producer, Jason Steven Cohen; Production Manager, Andrew Mihok; Technical Director, Mervyn Haines, Jr.; Props, Joe Toland; Press, Merle Debuskey, Richard Kornberg, Barbara Carroll, Bruce Campbell
   Tuesday, July 3–22, 1984 (16 performances and 11 previews)
HENRY V by William Shakespeare; Director, Wilford Leach; Scenery, Bob Shaw; Costumes, Lindsay W. Davis; Lighting, Paul Gallo; Fight Direction, B. H. Barry; Music, Allen Shawn; Hair and Makeup, Marlies Vallant; Production Assistants, Janet Callahan, Lisa Napoli; Technical Director, Mitchell Yaven; Props, Frances Smith; Wardrobe, Hannah Murray; Stage Managers, Ginny Martino, James Harker.
CAST: Vivienne Argent (Alice), Richard Backus (Constable of France), Loren Bass (English Messenger), John Bauman (Duke of York), Christopher Bradley (French Messenger), Neil Bradley (Messenger), Joseph Costa (MacMorris), Elizabeth Dennehy (Ensemble), Pierre Epstein (French Soldier), Clement Fowler (Bishop of Ely/Erpingham/Governor of Harfleur), Susan Gabriel (Ensemble), Christopher Grove (Lord Scroop), George Guidall (Archbishop of Canterbury/King of France), Paul Guilfoyle (Duke of Orleans), Anthony Heald (Fluellen), Dan Hedaya (Pistol), Earl Hindman (Exeter), Brian Jackson (Jamy), Jeffrey Jones (Montjoy), Eriq Ki LaSalle (Grey), Kevin Kline (Henry V), Adam LeFevre (Bardolph), Robert Macnaughton (Boy), George N. Martin (Chorus), Joseph Maruzzo (Duke of Bourbon), Mary Elizabeth Mastrantonio (Katherine), Peter McRobbie (Gower), David Wayne Nelson (Salisbury), Kristine Nielsen (Hostess Quickly/Queen of France), John Pankow (Williams), Larry Pine (Nym), Robert Schenkkan (Bates), Jack Stehlin (Dauphin), Morgan Strickland (Gloucester), Joseph Urla (Court), David Warshofsky (Bedford), Michael Wetmore (Westmoreland), Jamil Zakkai (Cambridge/Duke of Burgundy). Performed in 2 acts and 17 scenes.
   Friday, August 3,–September 2, 1984 (27 performances)
THE GOLEM by H. Leivick; Translated from the Yiddish by J. C. Augenlight; Director, Richard Foreman; Scenery, Richard Foreman, Nancy Winters; Costumes, Natasha Landau; Lighting, Pat Collins; Music and Sound Composed by Stanley Silverman; Associate Producer, Jason Steven Cohen; Production Assistants, Anne Marie Kuehling, Brendan Smith; Props, John Masterson; Wardrobe, Hannah Murray; Stage Managers, Bonnie Panson, Morton Milder
CAST: F. Murray Abraham (The Rabbi), Mario Arrambide (Spirit of the Golem), Loren Bass (Ensemble), Larry Block (One-Eyed), Wendy Brennan (Ensemble), Judson Camp (Man with cross), Umit Celebi (Ensemble), Melody Combs (Deborah), John P. Connolly (Monk), Ryan Cutrona (Ensemble), Clay Dickinson (Jacob), Carl Don (The Shames), Sam Garcia (Ensemble), David Gregory (Ensemble), George Hamlin (Reb Bosevy), Bette Henritze (Rabbi's Wife), Richard Krohn (Ensemble), James Lieb (Ensemble), Jordan Lund (Ensemble), Daniel Marcus (Isaac), Mark Margolis (The Red One), Christopher McCann (Young Beggar), Parlan McGaw (Ensemble), Conrad McMillan (Ensemble), Clark Middleton (Lame One), Joe Parisi (Ensemble), Moultrie Patten (Blind One), Lenard Petit (Ensemble), Rick Petrucelli (One with the stump), Joel Plotkin (Hunchback), William Preston (Sick One), Randy Quaid (The Golem), David Taylor (Ensemble), Ron Weyand (Old Beggar), Joseph Wiseman (Tadeus), Brita Youngblood (Ensemble), Jamil Zakkai (Tanchum), Vocalists: Ephraim Biran, Richard Frisch, Avery Tracht. Performed with one intermission. The action takes place in the past in Prague.

**Kevin Kline (center)
as "Henry V"**
Martha Swope Photos

SHAKESPEARE & COMPANY

Lenox, Massachusetts
April 30,–November 15, 1984

Artistic Director, Tina Packer; Managing Director, Alan Yaffe; Associate Director, Dennis Krausnick; Director of Fight and Tumbling, B. H. Barry; Movement, John Broome; Sets and Lighting, Bill Ballou; Costumes, Kiki Smith; Production Manager, Bill Ballou; Wardrobe, Georgia Carney; General Manager, Ann Olson; Press, Judy Salsbury, Kathy White, Susannah Rake; Development, Beth Logan Balmuth; Marketing, Eric Pourchot; Assistant to Artistic Director, Diane Prusha; Sound, Janet Kalas

PRODUCTIONS AND CASTS

A MIDSUMMER NIGHT'S DREAM by William Shakespeare; Directors, Tina Packer, Kevin Coleman; Music, Bruce Odland; Choreography, John Broome; Clown Master, Merry Conway; Stage Manager, J. P. Elins.
CAST: Dennis Krausnick (Theseus), Kristin Linklater (Hippolyta), Charles Halden (Philostrate), Lawrence Nathanson (Egeus), Christine Adaire (Hermia), Peter Wittrock (Demetrius), David Ossian (Lysander), Julie Nelson (Helena), N. Erick Avari (Quince), John Talbot (Bottom), Michael Hammond (Flute), Jonathan Croy (Starveling), Louis Colaianni (Snug), Tony Simotes (Puck), Susan Dibble (Mustardseed), Kevin Coleman (Oberon), Natsuko Ohama (Titania), Christine Adaire (Moth), Julie Nelson (Peaseblossom), Wayne Arnold (Cobweb), Fairies: Charles Halden, Timothy Lee
ROMEO AND JULIET by William Shakespeare; Directors, Tina Packer, Dennis Krausnick; Masks, Ralph Lee; Choreography, Susan Dibble. CAST: Tony Simotes (Chorus/Peter), David Ossian (Sampson/Old Man/Servant), Lawrence Nathanson (Gregory/Friar John/Officer/Servant/Musician), Wayne Arnold (Balthasar/Servant), Louis Colaianni (Abram/Officer/Musician), Charles Halden (Benvolio), Peter Wittrock (Tybalt), Dennis Krausnick (Lord Capulet), Craig Toth (Lord Montague/Apothecary/Servant), Christine Adaire (Lady Capulet), Julie Nelson (Lady Montague/Page), Jonathan Croy (Escalus), Michael Hammond (Romeo), Kevin Coleman (Mercutio), Natsuko Ohama (Juliet), Kristin Linklater (Nurse), John Talbot (Paris), N. Erick Avari (Friar Laurence)

Christine Adaire, David Ossian, Julie Nelson, Peter Wittrock in "A Midsummer Night's Dream" *(Robert D. Lohbauer Photo)*

Brian Bedford, Edward Atienza in "Waiting for Godot" Above: "Love's Labour's Lost"

STRATFORD FESTIVAL

Stratford, Ontario, Canada
June 10,–October 27, 1984
Thirty-second Season

Artistic Director, John Hirsch; Associate Directors, Michael Langham, Brian Macdonald; Executive Director, Gerry Eldred; General Manager, Gary Thomas; Literary Manager, Michal Schonberg; Producer, Cecil O'Neal; Director of Production, Richard C. Dennison; General Manager, Gary Thomas; Marketing, April E. Martin; Press, Elizabeth Bradley; Production Manager, Dwight Griffin; Technical Director, Neil McLeod; Lighting and Sound, Peter Lamb; Lighting, Michael J. Whitfield; Music Administrator, Arthur Lang; Company Manager, Robert Beard; Wardrobe, Louise Champion; Props, Frank Holte, Roy Brown, Joy Allan; Production Stage Managers, Paul Shaw, Penelope Sharp, Anne Roper
COMPANY: Edward Atienza, Shaun Austin-Olsen, Brian Bedford, Mervyn Blake, Domini Blythe, Derek Boyes, Simon Bradbury, Benedict Campbell, Douglas Campbell, Torquil Campbell, Les Carlson, Caro Coltman, Patricia Conolly, Holly Dennison, Keith Dinicol, Daniel Dion, Rosemary Dunsmore, David Elliott, Colm Feore, David Ferry, Pat Galloway, Christopher Gibson, Andrew Gillies, Lewis Gordon, Amelia Hall, Mary Haney, Ernest Harrop, Max Helpmann, Bill Johnston, Shane Kelly, Charles Kerr, Danny Kohn, Greg Lawson, Elizabeth Leigh-Milne, Toni LoRaso, Heather MacDonald, Janet Macdonald, Jefferson Mappin, Diego Matamoros, Seana McKenna, Kevin McNulty, Jack Medley, Richard Monette, Susan Morgan, William Needles, John Neville, Tracey Olson, Nicholas Pennell, Kenneth Pogue, Damon Redfern, Ron Rees, David Renton, Maria Ricossa, Stephen Russell, Patrusha Sarakula, Michael Shepherd, Sally Singal, Brent Stait, Tim Whelan, Jan Wood, Joseph Ziegler

Elizabeth Adams, Marie Baron, Stephen Beamish, Aggie Cekuta, Douglas Chamberlain, Tim Cruikshank, Eric Donkin, Maureen Forrester, Paul Gatchell, Allison Grant, Larry Herbert, Debora Joy, John Keane, David Keeley, Avo Kitask, Richard Marsh, Janet Martin, Paul Massell, Katharina Megli, Dale Mieske, Richard McMillan, Lyndsay Richardson, Kelly Robinson, Karen Skidmore, David McMurray Smith, Jean Stilwell, Joy Thompson-Allen, Gwynyth Walsh, Jim White, Sandy Winsby, Karen Wood, Paul Zimet, Kevin Anderwon, David Clark, John Dolan, Peter Donaldson, William Dunlop, Michelle Fisk, Barry Greene, Maggie Huculak, C. David Johnson, Robert McClure, John Moffat, Lucy Peacock, Laurence Russo, Keith Thomas
PRODUCTIONS: A Midsummer Night's Dream, Romeo and Juliet, Love's Labour's Lost, Tartuffe, The Merchant of Venice, Iolanthe, The Gondoliers, The Mikado, A Streetcar Named Desire, Separate Tables, Waiting for Godot, The Two Gentlemen of Verona, Henry IV Part I

David Cooper Photos

183

PULITZER PRIZE PRODUCTIONS

1918-Why Marry? **1919-**No award, **1920-**Beyond the Horizon, **1921-**Miss Lulu Bett, **1922-**Anna Christie, **1923-**Icebound, **1924-**Hell Bent fer Heaven, **1925-**They Knew What They Wanted, **1926-**Craig's Wife, **1927-**In Abraham's Bosom, **1928-**Strange Interlude, **1929-**Street Scene, **1930-**The Green Pastures, **1931-**Alison's House, **1932-**Of Thee I Sing, **1933-**Both Your Houses, **1934-**Men in White, **1935-**The Old Maid, **1936-**Idiot's Delight, **1937-**You Can't Take It with You, **1938-**Our Town, **1939-**Abe Lincoln in Illinois, **1940-**The Time of Your Life, **1941-**There Shall Be No Night, **1942-**No award, **1943-**The Skin of Our Teeth, **1944-**No award, **1945-**Harvey, **1946-**State of the Union, **1947-**No award, **1948-**A Streetcar Named Desire, **1949-**Death of a Salesman, **1950-**South Pacific, **1951-**No award, **1952-**The Shrike, **1953-**Picnic, **1954-**The Teahouse of the August Moon, **1955-**Cat on a Hot Tin Roof, **1956-**The Diary of Anne Frank, **1957-**Long Day's Journey into Night, **1958-**Look Homeward, Angel, **1959-**J. B., **1960-**Fiorello!, **1961-**All the Way Home, **1962-**How to Succeed in Business without Really Trying, **1963-**No award, **1964-**No award, **1965-**The Subject Was Roses, **1966-**No award, **1967-**A Delicate Balance, **1968-**No award, **1969-**The Great White Hope, 1776, **1970-**The Effect of Gamma Rays on Man-in-the-Moon Marigolds, Borstal Boy, Company, **1971-**Home, Follies, The House of Blue Leaves, **1972-**That Championship Season, **1974-**No award, **1975-**Seascape, **1976-**A Chorus Line, **1977-**The Shadow Box, **1978-**The Gin Game, **1979-**Buried Child, **1980-**Talley's Folly, **1981-**Crimes of the Heart, **1982-**A Soldier's Play, **1983-**'night, Mother, **1984-**Glengarry Glen Ross, **1985-**Sunday in the Park with George

NEW YORK DRAMA CRITICS CIRCLE AWARDS

1936-Winterset, **1937-**High Tor, **1938-**Of Mice and Men, Shadow and Substance, **1939-**The White Steed, **1940-**The Time of Your Life, **1941-**Watch on the Rhine, The Corn is Green, **1942-**Blithe Spirit, **1943-**The Patriots, **1944-**Jacobowsky and the Colonel, **1945-**The Glass Menagerie, **1946-**Carousel, **1947-**All My Sons, No Exit, Brigadoon, **1948-**A Streetcar Named Desire, The Winslow Boy, **1949-**Death of a Salesman, The Madwoman of Chaillot, South Pacific, **1950-**The Member of the Wedding, The Cocktail Party, The Consul, **1951-**Darkness at Noon, The Lady's Not for Burning, Guys and Dolls, **1952-**I Am a Camera, Venus Observed, Pal Joey, **1953-**Picnic, The Love of Four Colonels, Wonderful Town, **1954-**Teahouse of the August Moon, Ondine, The Golden Apple, **1955-**Cat on a Hot Tin Roof, Witness for the Prosecution, The Saint of Bleecker Street, **1956-**The Diary of Anne Frank, Tiger at the Gates, My Fair Lady, **1957-**Long Day's Journey into Night, The Waltz of the Toreadors, The Most Happy Fella, **1958-**Look Homeward Angel, Look Back in Anger, The Music Man, **1959-**A Raisin in the Sun, The Visit, La Plume de Ma Tante, **1960-**Toys in the Attic, Five Finger Exercise, Fiorello! **1961-**All the Way Home, A Taste of Honey, Carnival, **1962-**Night of the Iguana, A Man for All Seasons, How to Succeed in Business without Really Trying, **1963-**Who's Afraid of Virginia Woolf?, **1964-**Luther, Hello Dolly!, **1965-**The Subject Was Roses, Fiddler on the Roof, **1966-**The Persecution and Assassination of Marat as Performed by the Inmates of the Asylum of Charenton under the Direction of the Marquis de Sade, Man of La Mancha, **1967-**The Homecoming, Cabaret, **1968-**Rosencrantz and Guildenstern Are Dead, Your Own Thing, **1969-**The Great White Hope, 1776, **1970-**The Effect of Gamma Rays on Man-in-the-Moon Marigolds, Borstal Boy, Company, **1971-**Home, Follies, The House of Blue Leaves, **1972-**That Championship Season, Two Gentlemen of Verona, **1973-**The Hot l Baltimore, The Changing Room, A Little Night Music, **1974-**The Contractor, Short Eyes, Candide, **1975-**Equus, The Taking of Miss Janie, A Chorus Line, **1976-**Travesties, Streamers, Pacific Overtures, **1977-**Otherwise Engaged, American Buffalo, Annie, **1978-**Da, Ain't Misbehavin', **1979-**The Elephant Man, Sweeney Todd, **1980-**Talley's Folly, Evita, Betrayal, **1981-**Crimes of the Heart, A Lesson from Aloes, Special Citations to Lena Horne, "The Pirates of Penzance, **1982-**The Life and Adventures of Nicholas Nickleby, A Soldier's Play, (no musical honored), **1983-**Brighton Beach Memoirs, Plenty, Little Shop of Horrors, **1984-**The Real Thing, Glengarry Glen Ross, Sunday in the Park with George, **1985-**Ma Rainey's Black Bottom, (no musical)

AMERICAN THEATRE WING ANTOINETTE PERRY (TONY) AWARD PRODUCTIONS

1948-Mister Roberts, **1949-**Death of a Salesman, Kiss Me, Kate, **1950-**The Cocktail Party, South Pacific, **1951-**The Rose Tattoo, Guys and Dolls, **1952-**The Fourposter, The King and I, **1953-**The Crucible, Wonderful Town, **1954-**The Teahouse of the August Moon, Kismet, **1955-**The Desperate Hours, The Pajama Game, **1956-**The Diary of Anne Frank, Damn Yankees, **1957-**Long Day's Journey into Night, My Fair Lady, **1958-**Sunrise at Campobello, The Music Man, **1959-**J. B., Redhead, **1960-**The Miracle Worker, Fiorello! tied with The Sound of Music, **1961-**Becket, Bye Bye Birdie, **1962-**A Man for All Seasons, How to Succeed in Business without Really Trying, **1963-**Who's Afraid of Virginia Woolf?, A Funny Thing Happened on the Way to the Forum, **1964-**Luther, Hello Dolly!, **1965-**The Subject Was Roses, Fiddler on the Roof, **1966-**The Persecution and Assassination of Marat as Performed by the Inmates of the Asylum of Charenton under the Direction of the Marquis de Sade, Man of La Mancha, **1967-**The Homecoming, Cabaret, **1968-**Rosencrantz and Guildenstern Are Dead, Hallelujah Baby!, **1969-**The Great White Hope, 1776, **1970-**Borstal Boy, Applause, **1971-**Sleuth, Company, **1972-**Sticks and Bones, Two Gentlemen of Verona, **1973-**That Championship Season, A Little Night Music, **1974-**The River Niger, Raisin, **1975-**Equus, The Wiz, **1976-**Travesties, A Chorus Line, **1977-**The Shadow Box, Annie, **1978-**Da, Ain't Misbehavin', Dracula, **1979-**The Elephant Man, Sweeney Todd, **1980-**Children of a Lesser God, Evita, Morning's at Seven, **1981-**Amadeus, 42nd Street, The Pirates of Penzance, **1982-**The Life and Adventures of Nicholas Nickleby, Nine, Othello, **1983-**Torch Song Trilogy, Cats, On Your Toes, **1984-**The Real Thing, La Cage aux Folles, **1985-**Biloxi Blues, Big River, Joe Egg

1985 THEATRE WORLD AWARD WINNERS

KEVIN ANDERSON
of "Orphans"

PATTI COHENOUR
of "La Boheme" and "Big River"

NANCY GILES
of "Mayor"

RICHARD CHAVES
of "Tracers"

CHARLES S. DUTTON
of "Ma Rainey's Black Bottom"

WHOOPI GOLDBERG

LEILANI JONES
of "Grind"

JOHN MAHONEY
of "Orphans"

BARRY MILLER
of "Biloxi Blues"

LAURIE METCALF
of "Balm in Gilead"

AMELIA WHITE
of "The Accrington Pals"

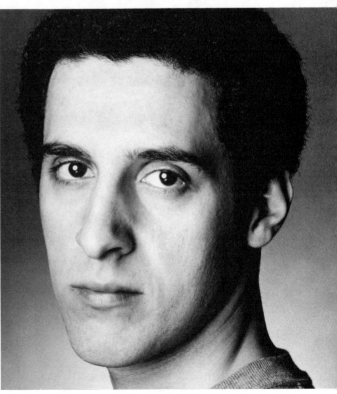

JOHN TURTURRO
of "Danny and the Deep Blue Sea"

THEATRE WORLD AWARDS presentations, Thursday, June 6, 1985. Top: Patricia Elliott, Melba Moore, Giancarlo Esposito, Marianne Tatum, William Hurt; Dorothy Loudon; Rosemary Harris, Harry Groener, Ann Reinking, Len Cariou, Armelia McQueen, John Cullum Below: Walter Willison, John Cullum, Nancy Giles, Armelia McQueen, Charles Dutton Bottom: Kevin Anderson, Ann Reinking, Harry Groener, Patti Cohenour, Rosemary Harris, Jennifer Ehle Above: Charles S. Dutton, Len Cariou, Kevin Anderson, John Mahoney, Dorothy Loudon, Richard Chaves, John Turturro

Alberto Cabrera, Evan Romero, J. M. Viade Photos

188

Top: Marianne Tatum, John Mahoney, William Hurt, Rosemary Harris, Barry Miller, Patricia Elliott Below: Melba Moore, Richard Chaves, Giancarlo Esposito, Ronnie Gesser for Whoopi Goldberg, Leilani Jones, Marianne Tatum Bottom: Lucille Lortel, Clive Barnes, Lucille Lortel (center), Juliette Koka, Rosetta LeNoire, Carleton Carpenter, Lucille Lortel Above: Walter Willison, William Hurt, Ann Reinking, Melba Moore, Leilani Jones, Mark Redanty for Amelia White

Evan Romero, J. M. Viade Photos

| Elizabeth Ashley | Warren Beatty | Carol Burnett | Michael Douglas | Liza Minnelli | Al Pacino |

PREVIOUS THEATRE WORLD AWARD WINNERS

1944-45: Betty Comden, Richard Davis, Richard Hart, Judy Holliday, Charles Lang, Bambi Linn, John Lund, Donald Murphy, Nancy Noland, Margaret Phillips, John Raitt

1945-46: Barbara Bel Geddes, Marlon Brando, Bill Callahan, Wendell Corey, Paul Douglas, Mary James, Burt Lancaster, Patricia Marshall, Beatrice Pearson

1946-47: Keith Andes, Marion Bell, Peter Cookson, Ann Crowley, Ellen Hanley, John Jordan, George Keane, Dorothea MacFarland, James Mitchell, Patricia Neal, David Wayne

1947-48: Valerie Bettis, Edward Bryce, Whitfield Connor, Mark Dawson, June Lockhart, Estelle Loring, Peggy Maley, Ralph Meeker, Meg Mundy, Douglass Watson, James Whitmore, Patrice Wymore

1948-49: Tod Andrews, Doe Avedon, Jean Carson, Carol Channing, Richard Derr, Julie Harris, Mary McCarty, Allyn Ann McLerie, Cameron Mitchell, Gene Nelson, Byron Palmer, Bob Scheerer

1949-50: Nancy Andrews, Phil Arthur, Barbara Brady, Lydia Clarke, Priscilla Gillette, Don Hanmer, Marcia Henderson, Charlton Heston, Rick Jason, Grace Kelly, Charles Nolte, Roger Price

1950-51: Barbara Ashley, Isabel Bigley, Martin Brooks, Richard Burton, Pat Crowley, James Daly, Cloris Leachman, Russell Nype, Jack Palance, William Smothers, Maureen Stapleton, Marcia Van Dyke, Eli Wallach

1951-52: Tony Bavaar, Patricia Benoit, Peter Conlow, Virginia de Luce, Ronny Graham, Audrey Hepburn, Diana Herbert, Conrad Janis, Dick Kallman, Charles Proctor, Eric Sinclair, Kim Stanley, Marian Winters, Helen Wood

1952-53: Edie Adams, Rosemary Harris, Eileen Heckart, Peter Kelley, John Kerr, Richard Kiley, Gloria Marlowe, Penelope Munday, Paul Newman, Sheree North, Geraldine Page, John Stewart, Ray Stricklyn, Gwen Verdon

1953-54: Orson Bean, Harry Belafonte, James Dean, Joan Diener, Ben Gazzara, Carol Haney, Jonathan Lucas, Kay Medford, Scott Merrill, Elizabeth Montgomery, Leo Penn, Eva Marie Saint

1954-55: Julie Andrews, Jacqueline Brookes, Shirl Conway, Barbara Cook, David Daniels, Mary Fickett, Page Johnson, Loretta Leversee, Jack Lord, Dennis Patrick, Anthony Perkins, Christopher Plummer

1955-56: Diane Cilento, Dick Davalos, Anthony Franciosa, Andy Griffith, Laurence Harvey, David Hedison, Earle Hyman, Susan Johnson, John Michael King, Jayne Mansfield, Sara Marshall, Gaby Rodgers, Susan Strasberg, Fritz Weaver

1956-57: Peggy Cass, Sydney Chaplin, Sylvia Daneel, Bradford Dillman, Peter Donat, George Grizzard, Carol Lynley, Peter Palmer, Jason Robards, Cliff Robertson, Pippa Scott, Inga Swenson

1957-58: Anne Bancroft, Warren Berlinger, Colleen Dewhurst, Richard Easton, Tim Everett, Eddie Hodges, Joan Hovis, Carol Lawrence, Jacqueline McKeever, Wynne Miller, Robert Morse, George C. Scott

1958-59: Lou Antonio, Ina Balin, Richard Cross, Tammy Grimes, Larry Hagman, Dolores Hart, Roger Mollien, France Nuyen, Susan Oliver, Ben Piazza, Paul Roebling, William Shatner, Pat Suzuki, Rip Torn

1959-60: Warren Beatty, Eileen Brennan, Carol Burnett, Patty Duke, Jane Fonda, Anita Gillette, Elisa Loti, Donald Madden, George Maharis, John McMartin, Lauri Peters, Dick Van Dyke

1960-61: Joyce Bulifant, Dennis Cooney, Sandy Dennis, Nancy Dussault, Robert Goulet, Joan Hackett, June Harding, Ron Husmann, James MacArthur, Bruce Yarnell

1961-62: Elizabeth Ashley, Keith Baxter, Peter Fonda, Don Galloway, Sean Garrison, Barbara Harris, James Earl Jones, Janet Margolin, Karen Morrow, Robert Redford, John Stride, Brenda Vaccaro

1962-63: Alan Arkin, Stuart Damon, Melinda Dillon, Robert Drivas, Bob Gentry, Dorothy Loudon, Brandon Maggart, Julienne Marie, Liza Minnelli, Estelle Parsons, Diana Sands, Swen Swenson

1963-64: Alan Alda, Gloria Bleezarde, Imelda De Martin, Claude Giraud, Ketty Lester, Barbara Loden, Lawrence Pressman, Gilbert Price, Philip Proctor, John Tracy, Jennifer West.

1964-65: Carolyn Coates, Joyce Jillson, Linda Lavin, Luba Lisa, Michael O'Sullivan, Joanna Pettet, Beah Richards, Jaime Sanchez, Victor Spinetti, Nicolas Surovy, Robert Walker, Clarence Williams III

1965-66: Zoe Caldwell, David Carradine, John Cullum, John Davidson, Faye Dunaway, Gloria Foster, Robert Hooks, Jerry Lanning, Richard Mulligan, April Shawhan, Sandra Smith, Leslie Ann Warren

1966-67: Bonnie Bedelia, Richard Benjamin, Dustin Hoffman, Terry Kiser, Reva Rose, Robert Salvio, Sheila Smith, Connie Stevens, Pamela Tiffin, Leslie Uggams, Jon Voight, Christopher Walken

1967-68: David Birney, Pamela Burrell, Jordan Christopher, Jack Crowder (Thalmus Rasulala), Sandy Duncan, Julie Gregg, Stephen Joyce, Bernadette Peters, Alice Playten, Michael Rupert, Brenda Smiley, Russ Thacker

1968-69: Jane Alexander, David Cryer, Blythe Danner, Ed Evanko, Ken Howard, Lauren Jones, Ron Leibman, Marian Mercer, Jill O'Hara, Ron O'Neal, Al Pacino, Marlene Warfield

1969-70: Susan Browning, Donny Burks, Catherine Burns, Len Cariou, Bonnie Franklin, David Holliday, Katharine Houghton, Melba Moore, David Rounds, Lewis J. Stadlen, Kristoffer Tabori, Fredricka Weber

1970-71: Clifton Davis, Michael Douglas, Julie Garfield, Martha Henry, James Naughton, Tricia O'Neil, Kipp Osborne, Roger Rathburn, Ayn Ruymen, Jennifer Salt, Joan Van Ark, Walter Willison

1971-72: Jonelle Allen, Maureen Anderman, William Atherton, Richard Backus, Adrienne Barbeau, Cara Duff-MacCormick, Robert Foxworth, Elaine Joyce, Jess Richards, Ben Vereen, Beatrice Winde, James Woods

1972-73: D'Jamin Bartlett, Patricia Elliott, James Farentino, Brian Farrell, Victor Garber, Kelly Garrett, Mari Gorman, Laurence Guittard, Trish Hawkins, Monte Markham, John Rubinstein, Jennifer Warren, Alexander H. Cohen (Special Award)

1973-74: Mark Baker, Maureen Brennan, Ralph Carter, Thom Christopher, John Driver, Conchata Ferrell, Ernestine Jackson, Michael Moriarty, Joe Morton, Ann Reinking, Janie Sell, Mary Woronov, Sammy Cahn (Special Award)

1974-75: Peter Burnell, Zan Charisse, Lola Falana, Peter Firth, Dorian Harewood, Joel Higgins, Marcia McClain, Linda Miller, Marti Rolph, John Sheridan, Scott Stevensen, Donna Theodore, Equity Library Theatre (Special Award)

1975-76: Danny Aiello, Christine Andreas, Dixie Carter, Tovah Feldshuh, Chip Garnett, Richard Kelton, Vivian Reed, Charles Repole, Virginia Seidel, Daniel Seltzer, John V. Shea, Meryl Streep, A Chorus Line (Special Award)

1976-77: Trazana Beverley, Michael Cristofer, Joe Fields, Joanna Gleason, Cecilia Hart, John Heard, Gloria Hodes, Juliette Koka, Andrea McArdle, Ken Page, Jonathan Pryce, Chick Vennera, Eva LeGallienne (Special Award)

1977-78: Vasili Bogazianos, Nell Carter, Carlin Glynn, Christopher Goutman, William Hurt, Judy Kaye, Florence Lacy, Armelia McQueen, Gordana Rashovich, Bo Rucker, Richard Seer, Colin Stinton, Joseph Papp (Special Award)

1978-79: Philip Anglim, Lucie Arnaz, Gregory Hines, Ken Jennings, Michael Jeter, Laurie Kennedy, Susan Kingsley, Christine Lahti, Edward James Olmos, Kathleen Quinlan, Sarah Rice, Max Wright, Marshall W. Mason (Special Award)

1979-80: Maxwell Caulfield, Leslie Denniston, Boyd Gaines, Richard Gere, Harry Groener, Stephen James, Susan Kellermann, Dinah Manoff, Lonnie Price, Marianne Tatum, Anne Twomey, Dianne Wiest, Mickey Rooney (Special Award)

1980-81: Brian Backer, Lisa Banes, Meg Bussert, Michael Allen Davis, Giancarlo Esposito, Daniel Gerroll, Phyllis Hyman, Cynthia Nixon, Amanda Plummer, Adam Redfield, Wanda Richert, Rex Smith, Elizabeth Taylor (Special Award)

1981-82: Karen Akers, Laurie Beechman, Danny Glover, David Alan Grier, Jennifer Holliday, Anthony Heald, Lizbeth Mackay, Peter MacNicol, Elizabeth McGovern, Ann Morrison, Michael O'Keefe, James Widdoes, Manhattan Theatre Club (Special Award)

1982-83: Karen Allen, Suzanne Bertish, Matthew Broderick, Kate Burton, Joanne Camp, Harvey Fierstein, Peter Gallagher, John Malkovich, Anne Pitoniak, James Russo, Brian Tarantina, Linda Thorson, Natalia Makaroba

1983-84: Martine Allard, Joan Allen, Kathy Whitton Baker, Mark Capri, Laura Dean, Stephen Geoffreys, Todd Graff, Glenne Headly, J. J. Johnston, Bonnie Koloc, Calvin Levels, Robert Westenberg, Ron Moody

BIOGRAPHICAL DATA ON THIS SEASON'S CASTS

ABRAHAM, F. MURRAY. Born Oct. 24, 1939 in Pittsburgh, PA. Attended UTx. Debut OB 1967 in "The Fantasticks," followed by "An Opening in the Trees," "14th Dictator," "Young Abe Lincoln," "Tonight in Living Color," "Adaptation," "Survival of St. Joan," "The Dog Ran Away," "Fables," "Richard III," "Little Murders," "Scuba Duba," "Where Has Tommy Flowers Gone?," "Miracle Play," "Blessing," "Sexual Perversity in Chicago," "Landscape of the Body," "The Master and Margarita," "Biting the Apple," "The Seagull," "Caretaker," "Antigone," "Uncle Vanya," "The Golem," "Madwoman of Chaillot," Bdwy in "Man in the Glass Booth"(1968), "6 Rms Riv Vu," "Bad Habits," "The Ritz," "Legend," "Teibele and Her Demon."

ABUBA, ERNEST. Born Aug. 25, 1947 in Honolulu, HI. Attended Southwestern Col. Bdwy debut 1976 in "Pacific Overtures," followed by "Loose Ends." OB in "Sunrise," "Monkey Music," "Station J.," "Yellow Fever," "Pacific Overtures," "Empress of China."

ACKERMAN, LONI. Born Apr. 10, 1949 in NYC. Attended New School. Bdwy debut 1968 in "George M.!," followed by "No, No Nanette," "So Long 174th Street," "Magic Show," "Evita," OB in "Dames at Sea," "Starting Here Starting Now," "Roberta in Concert," "Brownstone," "Diamonds."

ADAMS, BROOKE. Born in NYC in 1949. Attended Dalton School. Debut 1974 OB in "The Petrified Forest," followed by "Split," "Key Exchange," "Linda Her."

ADLER, BRUCE Born Nov. 27, 1944 in NYC. Attended NYU. Debut 1957 OB in "It's a Funny World," followed by "Hard to Be a Jew," "Big Winner," "The Golden Land," Bdwy in "A Teaspoon Every Four Hours" (1971), "Oklahoma" (1979), "Oh, Brother!"

AHLIN, MARGIT. Born Feb. 23, 1960 in Chappaqua, NY. Graduate NYU, AMDA. Debut OB 1982 in "Romeo and Juliet," followed by "Social Event," "Vanities," "Standing on the Cheese Line," "Company," "Onlyman."

AIDEM, BETSY SUE. Born Oct. 28, 1957 in Eastmeadow, NY. Graduate NYU. Debut 1981 OB in "The Trading Post," followed by "A Different Moon," "Balm in Gilead," "Crossing the Bar."

AIELLO, DANNY. Born June 20, 1935 in NYC. Bdwy debut 1975 in "Lamppost Reunion" for which he received a Theatre World Award, followed by "Wheelbarrow Closers," "Gemini," "Knockout," "The Floating Light Bulb," "Hurlyburly."

AKERS, KAREN. Born Oct. 13, 1945 in NYC. Hunter College graduate. Bdwy debut 1982 in "Nine" for which she received a Theatre World Award.

ALAN-LEE, JEFF. Born Sept. 8, 1963 in Battle Creek, MI. Attended NYU. Debut 1984 OB in "Losing It."

ALDA, RUTANYA. Born Oct. 13, 1945 in Riga, Latvia. Graduate N. Az. U. Debut 1981 OB in "Every Place Is Newark," followed by "Sacraments."

ALDRICH, JANET. (formerly Aldridge) Born Oct. 16, 1956 in Hinsdale, IL. Graduate UMiami. Debut OB 1979 in "A Funny Thing Happened on the Way to the Forum," followed by "American Princess," "The Men's Group," "Wanted Dead or Alive," "Comedy of Errors," Bdwy in "Annie" (1982), "The Three Musketeers."

ALEXANDER, JACE. Born Apr. 7, 1964 in NYC. Attended NYU. Bdwy debut 1983 in "The Caine Mutiny Court Martial," OB in "I'm Not Rappaport."

ALEXANDER, JASON. Born Sept. 23, 1959 in Irvington, NJ. Attended Boston U. Bdwy bow 1981 in "Merrily We Roll Along," OB in "Forbidden Broadway." "Stop the World . . . ," "D.."

ALJARD, MARTINE. Born Aug. 24, 1970 in Brooklyn, NY. Bdwy debut 1983 in "The Tap Dance Kid" for which she received a Theatre World Award.

ALLEN, ELIZABETH. Born Jan. 25, 1934 in Jersey City, NJ. Attended Rutgers U. Bdwy debut 1957 in "Romanoff and Juliet," followed by "The Gay Life," "Do I Hear a Waltz?," "Sherry!," "42nd Street."

ALLEN, JOAN. Born Aug. 20, 1956 in Rochelle, IL. Attended E. Ill. U., W. ILL. U. Debut 1983 OB in "And a Nightingale Sang" for which she received a Theatre World Award, followed by "The Marriage of Bette and Boo."

ALLEN, PHILIP RICHARD. Born Mar. 26, 1942 in Pennsylvania. Graduate Carnegie Tech. Debut 1970 OB in "Adaptation/Next," followed by "The Village Wooing," "That Championship Season," "The Normal Heart," Bdwy in "Sticks and Bones" (1972).

ALLEN, SETH. Born July 13, 1941 in Brooklyn, NY. Attended AMTA. OB in "Viet Rock," "Futz," "Hair," "Candaules Commissioner," "Mary Stuart," "Narrow Road to the Deep North," "More Than You Deserve," "Split Lip," "The Misanthrope," "Hard Sell," "The Wild Duck," "Jungle of Cities," "Egyptology," "The Lisbon Traviata," Bdwy in "Jesus Christ Superstar," "Accidental Death of an Anarchist."

ALLEN, WALTER. Born July 24, 1940 in NYC. OB in "6 Characters in Search of an Author," "Winter Journey," "Country Girl" (CC), "Ceremonies in Dark Old Men," Bdwy in "Man in the Glass Booth" (1968).

ALLISON DEBORAH. Born Apr. 3 1955 in Miami, Fl. Graduate FlaStateU. Debut 1981 OB in "Tied by the Leg," followed by "Love in the Dark," "The Underlings," Bdwy in "Fools" (1981).

ALLINSON, MICHAEL. Born in London; attended Lausanne U, RADA. Bdwy bow 1960 in "My Fair Lady," (also 1981 revival), followed by "Hostile Witness," "Come Live With Me," "Coco," "Angel Street," "Oliver!," OB in "The Importance of Being Earnest," "Staircase," "Loud Bang on June 1st."

AMENDOLIA, DON. Born Feb. 1, 1945 in Woodbury, NJ. Attended Glassboro State Col., AADA. Debut 1966 OB in "Until the Monkey Comes," followed by "Park," "Cloud 9," Bdwy 1984 in "My One and Only."

ANDERSON, CHRISTINE. Born Aug. 6 in Utica, NY. Graduate UWi. Bdwy debut in "I Love My Wife" (1980), OB in "I Can't Keep Running in Place," "On the Swing Shift," "Red, Hot and Blue," "A Night at Texas Guinan's."

ANDERSON, KEVIN. Born Jan. 13, 1960 in Illinois. Attended Goodman School. Debut 1985 OB in "Orphans" for which he received a Theatre World Award.

ANDERSON, SYDNEY. Born Apr. 4 in Tacoma, WA. Graduate UWa. Debut 1978 OB in "Gay Divorce," Bdwy in "A Broadway Musical" (1978), followed by "Charlie and Algernon," "Oklahoma!," "La Cage aux Folles."

ANDREWS, DAVID. Born in 1952 in Baton Rouge, LA. Attended LSU. Debut 1985 OB in "Fool for Love."

ANDRINI, KATHY. Born May 17, 1958 in San Francisco, CA. Bdwy debut 1979 in "The 1940's Radio Hour," followed by "Take Me Along," OB in "Trixie True."

ANGLIN, FLORENCE. Born Sept. 21 in Brooklyn, NY. Bdwy debut 1945 in "A Bell for Adano," followed by "Skipper Next to God," "Winged Victory," "Lower North," "Street Scene," "Gideon," "Goodbye, Fidel," OB in "Morning, Noon and Evening," "Madame de Sade," "A Doll's House," "Major Barbara," "Me Dandido," "The Little Foxes," "The Baker's Wife."

ARANAS, RAUL. Born Oct. 1, 1947 in Manilla, PI. Graduate Pace U. Debut 1976 OB in "Savages," followed by "Yellow Is My Favorite Color," "49," "Bullet Headed Birds," "Tooth of Crime," "Teahouse," "Shepard Sets," "Cold Air," Bdwy in "Loose Ends" (1978).

ARLISS, DIMITRA. Born in Lorain, OH. Attended Goodman School. Debut 1964 OB in "The Trojan Women," followed by "Antigone," "Pericles," Bdwy in "Indians" (1969), "Arms and the Man."

ARLUCK, NEAL. Born Dec. 4, 1946 in Brooklyn, NY. Graduate Lehigh U., NYU, AADA. Debut 1981 OB in "Catch 22" followed by "Dead Giveaway," "The Hooch," "Something Old Something New."

ARTHUR, PERRY. Born July 23, 1956, in Spirit Lake, LA. Attended Mansfield State Col., Drew U., AMDA. Bdwy debut 1977 in "The Three Musketeers," OB in "Dementos."

ASBURY, CLEVE. Born Dec. 29, 1958 in Houston, TX. Attended L.A. Valley Col. Bdwy debut 1979 in "Peter Pan," followed by "West Side Story," "Bring Back Birdie," "Copperfield," "Harrigan 'n Hart."

ASHFORD, MATTHEW. Born Jan. 29, 1960 in Davenport, IA. Graduate NC School of Arts. Debut 1985 OB in "Surrender," followed by "The Hazard County Wonder."

ASTOR, PHILIP. Born Feb. 17 in Park Ridge, NJ. Graduate WesleyanU. Bdwy debut 1969 in "1776," followed by "All Over Town," "Nuts," "Torch Song Trilogy," OB in "In the Boom Boom Room," "Games," "Troilus and Cressida," "As You Like It."

AUBERJONOIS, RENE. born June 1, 1940 in NYC. Graduate Carnegie Inst. With LCRep in "A Cry of Player," "King Lear," and "Twelfth Night," Bdwy in "Fire," "Coco," "Tricks," "The Good Doctor," "Break a Leg," "Every Good Boy Deserves Favor," "Big River," BAM. Co. in "The New York Idea," "Three Sisters," "The Play's the Thing" and "Julius Caesar."

AVARI, N. ERICK. Born Apr. 13, 1952 in Calcutta, IN. Graduate Col. of Charleston, SC. Debut 1983 OB in "Bhutan," followed by "Comedy of Errors."

AYR, MICHAEL. Born Sept. 8, 1953 in Great Falls, MT. Graduate SMU. Debut 1976 OB in "Mrs. Murray's Farm," followed by "The Farm," "Ulysses in Traction," "Lulu," "Cabin 12," "Stargazing," "The Deserter," "Hamlet," "Mary Stuart," "Save Grand Central," "The Beaver Coat," "Richard II," "Great Grandson of Jedediah Kohler," "Domestic Issues," "Time Framed," "The Dining Room," "The Sea Gull," "Love's Labour's Lost," Bdwy in "Hide and Seek" (1980), "Piaf."

BABATUNDE, OBBA. Born in Jamaica, NY. Attended Brooklyn Col. Debut OB 1970 in "The Secret Place," followed by "Guys and Dolls," "On Toby Time," "The Breakout," "Scottsborough Boys," "Showdown Time," "Dream on Monkey Mt.," "Sheba," Bdwy in "Timbuktu" (1978), "Reggae," "It's So Nice to Be Civilized," "Dreamgirls," "Grind."

BACKUS, RICHARD. Born Mar. 28, 1945 in Goffstown, NH Harvard graduate. Bdwy debut 1971 in "Butterflies Are Free," followed by "Promenade All," for which he received a Theatre World Award, "Ah, Wilderness!," "Camelot" (1981), OB in "Studs Edsel," "Gimme Shelter," "Sorrows of Stephen," "Missing Persons," "Henry V."

BACON, KEVIN. Born July 8, 1958 in Philadelphia, PA. Debut 1978 OB in "Getting Out," followed by "Glad Tidings," "Album," "Flux," "Poor Little Lambs," "Slab Boys," "Men without Dates."

BADE, TOM. Born June 29, 1946 in Brooklyn, NY. AADA graduate. Debut OB 1970 in "Perfect Match," followed by "Nature & Purpose of the Universe," "Play Strindberg," "Peril at End House," "Noon," "My Mother, My Father and Me," "Beagleman & Brackett."

BAFF, REGINA. Born Mar. 31, 1949 in The Bronx, NY. Attended Western Reserve, Hunter Col. Debut 1969 OB in "The Brownstone Urge," followed by "Patrick Henry Lake Liquors," "The Cherry Orchard," "Domino Courts," "The Rachel Plays," Bdwy in "Story Theatre," "Metamorphosis," "Veronica's Room," "West Side Waltz."

BAILEY, DENNIS. Born Apr. 12, 1953 in Grosse Point Woods, MI. UDetroit graduate. Debut 1977 OB in "House of Blue Leaves," followed by "Wonderland," "Head over Heels," "Preppies," Bdwy in "Gemini" (1978), "Leader of the Pack."

BAKER, R. MICHAEL. Born Feb. 28, 1954 in Boston, MA. Attended Boston U, AADA. Debut OB 1984 in "Jessie's Land," "Enter Laughing."

BAKER, RAYMOND. Born July 9, 1948 in Omaha, NE. Graduate UDenver. Debut 1972 OB in "The Proposition," followed by "Are You Now or Have You Ever Been . . . ," "Character Lines," "Lunch Hour," "Legends of Arthur," "War Babies," "Bathroom Plays," "I'm Not Rappaport," Bdwy in "Crimes of the Heart," "Division Street," "Is There Life After High School?," "Torch Song Trilogy."

BAKER-JONES, GLORIA. Born May 22 in NYC. Debut OB 1981 in "The Magic Talisman," followed by "Basin Street," "Busting Out of the Boxes," "The Me Nobody Knows."

BAKER-JONES, SHAUN. Born June 13 in NYC. Attended High School of Performing Arts. Debut OB 1981 in "In De Beginin," followed by "Basin Street," "Mozez," "Huck Finn," "Magic Talisman," "Almost a Man," Bdwy in "My One and Only" (1984).

BALLARD, KAYE. Born Nov. 20, 1926 in Cleveland, OH. Debut 1954 OB in "The Golden Apple," followed by "Cole Porter Revisited," "Hey, Ma, Kaye Ballard," "She Stoops to Conquer," Bdwy in "The Beast in Me" (1963), "Royal Flush," "Molly," "Pirates of Penzance."

BALOU, BUDDY. Born in 1953 in Seattle, WA. Joined American Ballet Theatre in 1970, rising to soloist. Joined Dancers in 1977. Bdwy debut 1980 in "A Chorus Line."

BANES, LISA. Born July 9, 1955 in Chagrin Falls, OH. Juilliard grad. Debut OB 1980 in "Elizabeth I," followed by "A Call from the East," "Look Back in Anger" for which she received a Theatre World Award, "My Sister in This House," "Antigone," "Three Sisters," "The Cradle Will Rock," "Isn't It Romantic," "Fighting International Fat."

BANNER, LARRY. Born Nov. 14, 1945 in Brooklyn, NY. Attended UPittsburgh. Debut 1973 OB in "The Man Who Ate People Raw," followed by "A Hell of a Mess," "Zoo Story," "This Is the Rill Speaking," "Action," "Haunted Lives."

BANTAY, JOHN Born May 10, 1960 in San Francisco, CA. Attended USantaClara. Debut 1984 OB in "Pacific Overtures."

BARANSKI, CHRISTINE. Born May 2, 1952 in Buffalo, NY. Graduate Juilliard Sch. Debut OB 1978 in "One Crack Out," followed by "Says I Says He," "The Trouble with Europe," "Coming Attractions," "Operation Midnight Climax," "Sally and Marsha," "A Midsummer Night's Dream," Bdwy in "Hide and Seek." (1980), "The Real Thing," "Hurlyburly."

BARAY, JOHN. Born Nov. 29, 1944 in San Antonio, TX. Graduate Trinity U. Debut 1981 OB in "The Red Mill," followed by "Babes in Toyland," "Mikado," "Pirates of Penzance," "Pacific Overtures."

BARBER, ELLEN. Born in August, in Brooklyn, NY. Graduate Bard Col. Debut 1970 OB in "The Mod Donna," followed by "Moonchildren," "Apple Pie," "Funeral March for a One Man Band," "Starluster," "Awake and Sing," "Occupations," "Poor Murderer," "Pantagleize," "Modern Ladies of Guanabacoa," "Poisoner of the Wells," "Souvenirs," "Haven," "Shlemiel the First," Bdwy in "The Good Doctor" (1973), "Fame."

BARBOUR, THOMAS. Born July 25, 1921 in NYC. Graduate Princeton, Harvard. Bdwy debut 1968 in "Portrait of a Queen," followed by "Great White Hope," "Scratch," "Lincoln Mask," "Kingdoms," OB in "Twelfth Night," "Merchant of Venice," "Admirable Bashful," "The Lady's Not for Burning," "The Enchanted," "Antony and Cleopatra," "The Saintliness of Margery Kemp," "Dr. Willy Nilly," "Under the Sycamore Tree," "Epitaph for George Dillon," "Thracian Horses," "Old Glory," "Sjt. Musgrave's Dance," Nestless Bird," "The Seagull," "Wayside Motor Inn," "Arthur," "The Grinding Machine," "Mr. Simian," "Sorrows of Frederick," "Terrorists," "Dark Ages," "Royal Bob," "Relatively Speaking."

BARCROFT, JUDITH. Born July 6 in Washington, DC. Attended Northwestern U., Stephens Col. Bdwy debut 1965 in "The Mating Dance," followed by "Plaza Suite," "Dinner at 8," "The Elephant Man," OB in "M. Amilcar," "Cloud 9," "For Sale."

BARDEN, DOUG. Born July 9, 1946 in Honolulu, HA. Debut OB 1985 in "Surf City."

BARI, CHARLES. Born July 15, 1954 in NYC. Attended SUNY/Fredonia. Debut OB 1977 in "Carnival," followed by "Give My Heart an Even Break," "Feathertop."

BARKER, CHRISTINE. Born Nov. 26 in Jacksonville, FL. Attended UCLA. Bdwy debut 1979 in "A Chorus Line."

BARNES, LISA. Born Mar. 5, 1957 in Pasadena, CA. Graduate USCal. Debut OB 1983 in "A Midsummer Night's Dream," followed by "Domino Courts," "Life on Earth."

BARNES, VERONA. Born June 2, 1940 in Wilson, NC. Winston-Salem State Col. graduate. Bdwy debut 1968 in "The Great White Hope," followed by OB's "Sleep," "The Cherry Orchard," "House Party," "All God's Chillun," "Divine Comedy," "Milk of Paradise," "Branches from the Same Tree," "Killings on the Last Line," "A Step out of Line."

BARON, EVALYN. Born Apr. 21, 1948 in Atlanta, GA. Graduate Northwestern., UMinn. Debut 1979 OB in "Scrambled Feet," followed by "Hijinks," "I Can't Keep Running in Place," "Jerry's Girls," "Harvest of Strangers," "Quilters," Bdwy in "Fearless Frank" (1980), "Big River."

BARONE, JOHN. Born March 14, 1954 in Staten Island, NY. Graduate Wagner Col. Debut 1982 OB in "Robin Hood," followed by "The Music Man," "Flesh, Flash & Frank Harris," "Consenting Adults," "Blessed Event."

BARRE, GABRIEL. Born Aug. 26, 1957 in Brattleboro, VT. Graduate AADA. Debut 1977 OB in "Jabberwock," followed by "T.N.T.," "Bodo," "The Baker's Wife."

BARRETT, BRENT. Born Feb 28, 1957 in Quinter, KS. Graduate Carnegie-Mellon. Bdwy debut 1980 in "West Side Story," followed by "Dance a Little Closer," OB in "March of the Falsettos," "Portrait of Jenny," "The Death of Von Richthofen," "Sweethearts in Concert," "What's a Nice Country like You . . ."

BARRETT, LAURINDA. Born in 1931 in NYC. Attended Wellesley Col., RADA. Bdwy debut 1956 in "Too Late the Phalarope," followed by "The Girls in 509," "The Milk Train Doesn't Stop Here Anymore," "UTBU," "I Never Sang For My Father," "Equus," OB in "The Misanthrope," "Palm Tree in a Rose Garden," "All Is Bright," "The Carpenters," "Ah, Wilderness," "The Other Side of Newark."

BARRON, DAVID Born May 11, 1938 in Pilot Point, TX. Graduate Baylor U., Yale, UIll. Debut OB 1976 in "The Fantasticks," followed by "Trouble in Tahiti," "Sound of Music," "A Doll's House," "Feathertop."

BARRON, DOUGLAS. Born Oct. 27, 1953 in Topeka, Ks. Attended AzStateU. Debut OB 1985 in "Stud Silo."

BARRON, HOLLY. Born Feb. 1, 1947 in Oakland, CA. Graduate UCBerkeley. Debut 1977 OB in "Cracks," followed by "Mecca," "Last Summer at Bluefish Cove," Bdwy in "Design for Living" (1984).

BARRY, B. CONSTANCE. Born Apr. 29, 1913 in NYC. Attended Hofstra U., New School. Debut 1974 OB in "Blue Heaven," followed by "Dark of the Moon," "Native Son," "Passing Time," "All the Way Home," "Naomi Court," "Antigone," "Fighting International Fat."

BARRY, GENE. Born June 14, 1919 in NYC. Bdwy in "New Moon," "Rosalinda," "The Merry Widow," "Catherine Was Great," "The Would-Be Gentleman," "Happy as Larry," "Bless You All," "La Cage aux Folles."

BARTENIEFF, GEORGE. Born Jan. 24, 1933 in Berlin, Ger. Bdwy debut 1947 in "The Whole World Over," followed by "Venus Is," "All's Well That Ends Well," "Quotations from Chairman Mao Tse-Tung," "The Death of Bessie Smith," "Cop-Out," "Room Service," "Unlikely Heroes," OB in "Walking to Waldheim," "Memorandum," "The Increased Difficulty of Concentration," "Trelawny of the Wells," "Charley Chestnut Rides the IRT," "Radio (Wisdom): Sophia Part I," "Images of the Dead," 'Dead End Kids," "The Blonde Leading the Blonde," "The Dispossessed," "Growing Up Gothic," "Rosetti's Apologies," "On the Lam," "Samuel Beckett Trilogy."

BARTLETT, ALISON. Born in Massachusetts July 14, 1971. Debut 1984 OB in "Landscape of the Body," Bdwy in "Hurlyburly" (1984).

BARTLETT, LISABETH. Born Feb. 28, 1956 in Denver, CO. Northwestern U. Graduate. Bdwy debut 1981 in "The Dresser," OB in "The Lady's Not for Burning," "The Rachel Plays."

BARTLETT, ROBIN. Born Apr. 22, 1951 in NYC. Graduate Boston U. Bdwy debut 1975 in "Yentl," followed by "The World of Sholem Aleichem," OB in "Agamemnon," "Fathers and Sons," "No End of Blame," "Living Quarters," "After the Fall," "The Sea Gull," "The Philanthropist," "Fen," "Found a Peanut," "Life and Limb," "Isn't It Romantic."

BARTON, FRED. Born Oct. 20, 1958 in Camden, NJ. Graduate Harvard. Debut 1982 OB in "Forbidden Broadway."

BATES, KATHY. Born June 18, 1948 in Memphis, TN, Graduate S. Methodist U. Debut 1976 OB in "Vanities," followed by "The Art of Dining," "The Curse of the Starving Class," Bdwy in "Goodbye Fidel" (1980), "5th of July," "Come Back to the 5 & Dime, Jimmy Dean," " 'night, Mother."

BATTISTA, LLOYD. Born May 14, 1937 in Cleveland, OH. Graduate Carnegie Tech. Bdwy debut 1966 in "Those That Play the Clowns," followed by "The Homecoming," "The Guys in the Truck," OB in "The Flame and the Rose," "Murder in the Cathedral," "The Miser," "Gorky," "Sexual Perversity in Chicago," "King of Schnorrers," "Francis," "The Keymaker," "The Guys in the Truck," "The Cost of Living."

BATTLE, HINTON. Born Nov. 29, 1956 in Neubraecke, Ger. Joined Dance Theatre of Harlem. Bdwy debut 1975 in "The Wiz," followed by "Dancin'," "Sophisticated Ladies," "Dreamgirls," "The Tap Dance Kid."

BAUER, STEVEN. (aka Steven Echevarria, Rocky Bauer) Born Dec. 2, 1956 in Havana, Cuba. Attended UMiami. Debut 1980 OB in "Waiting for Lefty," followed by "Balm in Gilead."

BAYER, GARY. Born June 25, 1944 in Los Angeles, CA. Graduate UEvansville, NYU. Bdwy debut 1978 in "A History of the American Film," followed by "Richard III," with BAM Theatre Co. in "Winter's Tale," "Johnny on a Spot," and "The Barbarians," OB in "Porch."

BEACHNER, LOUIS. Born June 9, 1923 in Jersey City, NJ. Bdwy debut 1942 in "Junior Miss," followed by "No Time for Sergeants," "Georgy," "The Changing Room," "National Health," "Where's Charley?," "Passion," "Oliver," OB in "Time to Burn," "The Hostage," "Savages," "The Overcoat."

BEAN, REATHEL. Born Aug. 24, 1942 in Missouri. Graduate Drake U. OB in "America Hurrah," "San Francisco's Burning," "Love Cure," "Henry IV," "In Circles," "Peace," "Journey of Snow White," "Wanted," "The Faggot," "Lovers," "Not Back with the Elephants," "Art of Coarse Acting," "The Trip Back Down," Bdwy in "Doonesbury" (1983), "Big River."

BEATY, KIM. Born Dec. 1, 1955 in NYC. Yale graduate. Bdwy debut 1980 in "The Philadelphia Story," followed by "Rose," OB in "The Birthday Party," "Some Poe," "Imaginary Lovers," "Old-Fashioned," "The Misanthrope," "Clarence."

BEAUCHAMP, STEVEN. Born March 26 in Watertown, CT. Graduate Wesleyan U. Debut 1981 OB in "Badgers," followed by "Of Mice and Men," "A Perfect Diamond."

BEDFORD, PATRICK. Born May 30, 1932 in Dublin, Ire. Appeared with Dublin Gate Theatre before Bdwy debut (1966) in "Philadelphia Here I Come," followed by "The Mundy Scheme," "Equus," OB in "Small Craft Warnings," "Home."

BEDFORD-LLOYD, JOHN. Born Jan. 2, 1956 in New Haven, CT. Graduate Williams Col., Yale. Debut OB 1983 in "Vieux Carre," followed by "She Stoops to Conquer," "The Incredibly Famous Willy Rivers," "Digby."

BEECHMAN, LAURIE. Born Apr. 4, 1954 in Philadelphia, Pa. Attended NYU. Bdwy debut 1977 in "Annie," followed by "Pirates of Penzance," "Joseph and the Amazing Technicolor Dreamcoat" for which she received a Theatre World Award. "Some Enchanted Evening" (OB), "Pal Joey in Concert," "Cats."

BELL, VANESSA. Born Mar. 20, 1957 in Toledo. OH. Graduate OhioU. Bdwy debut 1981 in "Bring Back Birdie," followed by "El Bravo!," "Dreamgirls," OB in "Take me Along," "A . . . My Name Is Alice.

BELLIN, OLGA. Born Aug. 18, 1932 in Milwaukee, WI. Attended NorthwesternU. Debut 1955 OB in "The Carefree Tree," followed by "A Month in the Country," "Zelda," Bdwy in "Protective Custody" (1956), "A Man for All Seasons."

BENJAMIN, P. J. Born Sept. 2, 1951 in Chicago, IL. Attended Loyola U., Columbia U. Bdwy debut 1973 in "Pajama Game," followed by "Pippin," "Sarava," "Charlie and Algernon," "Sophisticated Ladies," "Torch Song Trilogy."

BENSINGER, MIMI. Born May 5 in Pottsville, PA. Attended Penn State, AmThWing. Debut OB 1961 in "Electra," followed by "Hadrian's Wall," "The Doctor in spite of Himself," "The Eye of a Bird," "A Doll's House."

BENTLEY, GRACE. Born Dec. 1 in NJ. Graduate Hunter Col. Debut 1981 OB in "Suddenly Last Summer," followed by "The Chalk Cross," "Evil Spirit," "Triptych," "Paula of the Green Clouds."

BENTLEY, JOHN. Born Jan. 31, 1940 in Jackson Heights, NY. Graduate AADA. Debut 1961 OB in "King of the Dark Chamber," followed by "As to the Meaning of Words," "West Side Story" (JB), "Short Eyes," Bdwy in "Mike Downstairs" (1968), "Lysistrata," "The Selling of the President," "A Funny Thing Happened on the Way to the Form" (1972), "West Side Story" (1980).

BEREZIN, TANYA. Born Mar. 25, 1941 in Philadelphia, PA. Attended Boston U. Debut OB 1967 in "The Sandcastle," followed by "Three Sisters," "Great Nebula in Orion," "him," "Amazing Activity of Charlie Contrare," "Battle of Angels," "Mound Builders," "Serenading Louie," "My Life," "Brontosaurus," "Glorious Morning," "Mary Stuart," "The Beaver Coat," "Balm in Gilead," Bdwy in "5th of July" (1981), "Angels Fall."

BERGEN, CANDICE. Born May 9, 1946 in Los Angeles, CA. Graduate UPenn. Bdwy debut 1984 in "Hurlyburly."

BERGER, STEPHEN. Born May 16, 1954 in Philadelphia, PA. Attended UCinn. Bdwy debut 1982 in "Little Me," OB in "Nite Club Confidential," "Mowgli," "Isn't It Romantic."

BERNSTEIN, DOUGLAS. Born May 6, 1958 in NYC. Amherst graduate. Debut 1982 OB in "Upstairs at O'Neals," followed by "Backer's Audition," "Mayor."

BERRIDGE, ELIZABETH. Born May 2, 1962 in Westchester, NY. Attended Strasberg Inst. Debut 1984 OB in "The Vampires," followed by "The Incredibly Famous Willy Rivers," "Ground Zero Club," "Outside Waco."

BESSETTE, DENISE. Born Aug. 25, 1954 in Midland, MI. Graduate Marymount Manhattan Col., RADA. Debut 1977 OB in "Fresh Water/Evening at Bloomsbury," followed by "La Ronde," "Admirable Crichton," "War and Peace," "Glory! Hallelujah!," "The Desk Set," "Art of Self Defense."

F. Murray Abraham	Loni Ackerman	Jeff Alan-Lee	Rutanya Alda	Jason Alexander	Martine Allard
Joan Allen	Phillip Richard Allen	Kathy Andrini	Raul Aranas	Dimitra Arliss	Neal Arluck
Cleve Asbury	Regina Baff	R. Michael Baker	Gloria Baker-Jones	Shaun Baker-Jones	Lisa Banes
Ellen Barber	Thomas Barbour	Judith Barcroft	Charles Bari	Christine Barker	David Barron
George Bartenieff	Lisabeth Bartlett	Lloyd Battista	Mimi Bensinger	John Bentley	Candice Bergen

193

BEVELANDER, NANNETTE. Born Jan. 19, 1956 in Holland. Graduate Canadian College of Dance. Bdwy debut 1983 in "Oh! Calcutta!"

BIGELOW, SUSAN. Born Apr. 11, 1952 in Abington, PA. Attended UMd. Bdwy debut 1978 in "Working," followed by "Oklahoma!," OB in "Diamonds."

BITTNER, JACK. Born in Omaha, NE. Graduate UNeb. OB credits: "Nathan the Wise," "Land of Fame," "Beggar's Holiday," "Rip Van Winkle," "Dear Oscar," "What Every Woman Knows," "By Bernstein," "The Philanderer," "Enemy of the People," Bdwy in "Harold and Maude" (1980), "Little Johnny Jones."

BLACK, BONNIE. Born Sept. 21 in Brooklyn, NY. Attended SUNY/Brockport. Debut 1981 OB in "A Song for All Saints," followed by "Comedy of Errors."

BLACK, ROYANA. Born March 1, 1973 in Poughkeepsie, NY. Bdwy debut 1984 in "Brighton Beach Memoirs."

BLAISDELL, NESBITT. Born Dec. 6, 1928 in NYC. Graduate Amherst, Columbia U. Debut 1978 OB in "Old Man Joseph and His Family," followed by "Moliere in spite of Himself," "Guests of the Nation," "Ballad of Soapy Smith."

BLANC, JENNIFER. Born Apr. 21, 1971 in NYC. Attended Professional Children's School. Bdwy debut 1985 in "Brighton Beach Memoirs."

BLANCHARD, STEVEN. Born Dec. 4, 1958 in York, PA. Attended UMd. Bdwy debut 1984 in "The Three Musketeers."

BLAZER, JUDITH. Born Oct. 22, 1956 in Dover, NJ. Graduate Manhattan Sch. of Music. Debut OB 1979 in "Oh, Boy!," followed by "Roberta in Concert," "A Little Night Music."

BLEVINS, MICHAEL. Born Sept. 2, 1960 in Orlando, FL. Attended UNC, NYU. Bdwy debut 1981 in "Bring Back Birdie," followed by "Little Me," "Tap Dance Kid," OB in "Time Pieces," "Bags."

BLOCK, LARRY. Born Oct. 30, 1942 in NYC. Graduate URI. Bdwy bow 1966 in "Hail Scrawdyke," followed by "La Turista," OB in "Eh?," "Fingernails Blue as Flowers," "Comedy of Errors," "Coming Attractions," "Henry IV Part 2," "Feuhrer Bunker," "Manhattan Love Songs," "Souvenirs," "The Golem," "Responsible Parties."

BLOOM, VERNA Born Aug 7 in Lynn, MA. Graduate Boston U. Bdwy debut 1967 in "Marat/deSade," followed by OB's "Kool Aid," "The Cherry Orchard," "Bits and Pieces," "Barbary Shore," "Messiah."

BLOUNT, HELON Born Jan. 15 in Big Spring, TX. Graduate UTx. Bdwy debut 1956 in "Most Happy Fella," followed by "How to Succeed. . . ." "Do I Hear a Waltz," "Fig Leaves Are Falling," "Follies," "Very Good Eddie," "Musical Chairs," "Woman of the Year," OB in "Fly Blackbird," "Riverwind," "My Wife and I," "Curley McDimple," "A Quarter for the Ladies Room," "Snapshot," "Downriver."

BLUM, MARK. Born May 14, 1950 in Newark, NJ. Graduate UPa., UMinn. Debut OB 1976 in "The Cherry Orchard," followed by "Green Julia," "Say Goodnight, Gracie," "Table Settings," "Key Exchange," "Loving Reno," "Messiah."

BODLE, JANE. Born Nov 12 in Lawrence KS. Attended UUtah. Bdwy debut 1983 in "Cats."

BOFSHEVER, MICHAEL. Born Oct. 12, 1950 in Brooklyn, NY. Graduate Boston U. Debut 1981 OB in "Romance," followed by "Saigan Rose," "A Perfect Diamond."

BOGARDUS, STEPHEN. Born Mar. 11, 1954 in Norfolk, Va. Princeton graduate. Bdwy debut 1980 in "West Side Story," OB in "March of the Falsettos," "Feathertop."

BOGGS, ELLEN. Born Mar. 23, 1956 in Palo Alto, CA. Graduate UHawaii. Debut 1984 OB in "The Holy Terror," followed by "Yellow Is My Favorite Color," "Dr. Korczak and the Children," "Roundheads and Pointheads."

BOGYO, PETER. Born Jan. 21, 1955 in Summit, NJ. Yale graduate. Debut 1980 OB in "Hamlet," followed by "Julius Caesar," "The Three Sisters," "After Liverpool," "Trespasses."

BOHLER, GEORGE. Born Sept. 13, 1948 in Hampton, VA. Attended USouthFla., Strasberg Inst. Debut 1984 OB in "The Desk Set."

BOJARSKI, STANLEY. Born June 1, 1950 in Fonda, NY. Graduate Marist Col. Debut 1984 OB in "Red, Hot and Blue," followed by "The Pretender."

BONDS, R. J. Born Nov. 30, 1946 in Detroit, MI. Attended MSU, Neighborhood Playhouse. Debut 1980 OB in "Home of the Brave," followed by "Bury the Dead," "In Pursuit of Liberty," "Icebridge," "Tracers."

BOOCKVOR, STEVEN. Born Nov. 18 1942 in NYC. Attended Queens Col., Juilliard. Bdwy debut 1966 in "Anya," followed by "A Time for Singing," "Cabaret," "Mardi Gras," "Jimmy," "Billy," "The Rothschilds," "Follies," "Over Here," "The Lieutenant," "Musical Jubilee," "Annie," "Working," "The First," "A Chorus Line."

BOOKWALTER, DeVEREN. Born Sept. 8, 1939 in Brun, Austria. Graduate OhioU., AmTh-Wing. Bdwy debut 1967 in "The Promise," OB in "Philosophy in the Boudoir," "Enemy of the People," "Anna K."

BOOTH, ERIC. Born Oct. 18, 1950 in NYC. Graduate Emerson Col., Stanford U. Bdwy debut 1977 in "Caesar and Cleopatra," followed by "Golda," "Whose Life Is It Anyway?," OB in "Taming of the Shrew," "Episode 26."

BORDO, EDWIN. Born May 3, 1931 in Cleveland OH. Graduate Allegheny Col., LAMDA. Bdwy debut 1964 in "The Last Analysis," followed by "Inquest," "Zalmen or the Madness of God," "Annie," OB in "The Dragon," "Waiting for Godot," "Saved," "Ten Little Indians," "King Lear."

BORGES, YAMIL. Born June 8, 1958 in San Lorenzo, PR. Attended HB Studio. Bdwy debut 1980 in "West Side Story," OB in "El Bravo," "The Transposed Heads."

BORMANN, JAMES. Born March 12 in Hot Springs, SD. Graduate UDenver. Debut 1965 OB in "Mackey of Appalachia," followed by "Travelers," "The Tiger," "A Well-Respected Gentleman," "Wonderful Town," "Movie Crazies," "Lovers," "Reckless," "Deathtrap."

BORN, LYNN P. Born Aug. 6, 1956 in Richmond, VA. Attended Northwestern U. Debut 1982 OB in "Catholic School Girls," followed by "Nag and Nell," "Stifled Growls," "Air Conditioned Beach."

BOROWITZ, KATHERINE. Born in Chicago, IL. Graduate Yale, Harvard. Debut 1982 OB in "Cloud 9," followed by "Lennon," "Before the Dawn."

BOSCO, PHILIP. Born Sept. 26, 1930 in Jersey City, NJ. Graduate Catholic U. Credits: "Auntie Mame," "Rape of the Belt," "Ticket of Leave Man," "Donnybrook," "Man for All Seasons," "Mrs. Warren's Profession," with LCRep in "The Alchemist," "East Wind," "Galileo," "St. Joan," "Tiger at the Gate," "Cyrano," "King Lear," "A Great Career," "In the Matter of J. Robert Oppenheimer," "The Miser," "The Time of Your Life," "Camino Real," "Operation Sidewinder," "Amphitryon," "Enemy of the People," "Playboy of the Western World," "Good Woman of Setzuan," "Antigone," "Mary Stuart," "Narrow Road to the Deep North," "The Crucible," "Twelfth Night," "Enemies," "Plough and the Stars," "Merchant of Venice," and "A Streetcar Named Desire," "Henry V," "Threepenny Opera," "Streamers," "Stages," "St. Joan," "The Biko Inquest," "Man and Superman," "Whose Life Is It Anyway," "Major Barbara," "A Month in the Country," "Bacchae," "Hedda Gabler," "Don Juan in Hell," "Inadmissible Evidence," "Eminent Domain," "Misalliance," "Learned Ladies," "Some Men Need Help," "Ah, Wilderness!," "The Caine Mutiny Court Martial," "Heartbreak House," "Come Back, Little Sheba," "Love of Anatole," "Be Happy for Me."

BOVA, JOSEPH. Born May 25 in Cleveland, OH. Graduate Northwestern U. Debut 1959 OB in "On the Town," followed by "Once Upon a Mattress," "House of Blue Leaves," "Comedy," "The Beauty Part," "Taming of the Shrew," "Richard III," "Comedy of Errors," "Invitation to a Beheading," "Merry Wives of Windsor," "Henry V," "Streamers," Bdwy in "Rape of the Belt," "Irma La Douce," "Hot Spot," "The Chinese," "American Millionaire," "St. Joan," "42nd Street."

BOVASSO, JULIE. Born Aug. 1, 1930 in Brooklyn, NY. Attended CCNY. Bdwy in "Monique," "Minor Miracle," "Gloria and Esperanza," OB in "Naked," "The Maids," "The Lesson," "The Typewriter," "Screens," "Henry IV Part I," "What I Did Last Summer," "Angelo's Wedding."

BOYD, JULIE. Born Jan. 2 in Kansas City, MO. Graduate UUtah, Yale. Bdwy debut 1985 in "Noises Off."

BRAZDA, DAVID. Born Sept. 28, 1954 in Weisbaden, Ger. Attended UVa., Circle in the Square. Debut 1985 OB in "Onlyman."

BREEN, J. PATRICK. Born Oct. 26, 1960 in Brooklyn, NY. Graduate NYU. Debut 1982 OB in "Epiphany," Bdwy in "Brighton Beach Memoirs" (1983).

BRENNAN, TOM. Born Apr. 16, 1926 in Cleveland, OH. Graduate Oberlin, Western Reserve. Debut 1958 OB in "Synge Trilogy," followed by "Between Two Thieves," "Easter," "All in Love," "Under Milkwood," "An Evening with James Purdy," "Golden Six," "Pullman Car Hiawatha," "Are You Now or Have You . . .," "Diary of Anne Frank," "Milk of Paradise," "Transcendental Love," "The Beaver Coat," "The Overcoat," "Summer," "Asian Shade," "Inheritors," "Paradise Lost," "Madwoman of Chaillot," Bdwy in "Play Memory" (1984).

BRETT, JEREMY. Born Nov. 3, 1933 in Berkswell, Eng. Attended Eaton. Bdwy debut 1956 with Old Vic's "Troilus and Cressida," "Macbeth," "Richard II," and "Romeo and Juliet," followed by "The Deputy," "Dracula," "Aren't We All?"

BRIAN, MICHAEL. Born Nov. 14, 1958 in Utica, NY. Attended Boston Conservatory. Debut 1979 OB in "Kennedy's Children," followed by "Street Scene," "Death of Von Richthofen as Witnessed from Earth," "Lenny and the Heartbreakers," "Gifts of the Magi," Bdwy in "Baby" (1983), "Big River."

BRIGGS, RICHARD. Born May 28, 1919 in Los Angeles, CA. Graduate College of Pacific, Neighborhood Playhouse. OB in "Blue Is for Boys," "The Cherry Orchard," "Twelfth Night," "Mirrors."

BRIGHT, RICHARD. Born June 28, 1937 in Brooklyn, NY. OB in "The Balcony," "Does a Tiger Wear a Necktie?," "The Beard," "Survival of St. Joan," "Kool Aid," "Gogol," "Short Eyes," Bdwy in "The Basic Training of Pavlo Hummel," "Richard III."

BRILL, FRAN. Born Sept. 30 in PA. Attended Boston U. Bdwy debut 1969 in "Red, White and Maddox," OB in "What Every Woman Knows," "Scribes," "Naked," "Look Back in Anger," "Knuckle," "Skirmishes," "Baby with the Bathwater," "Holding Patterns."

BRITTON, CHRISTOPHER. Born Dec. 23, 1948 in Toronto, Can. Graduate York U. Debut 1985 OB in "The Taming of the Shrew."

BRO, JUDITH. Born Apr. 6, 1954 in Wilmington, DE. Graduate UMd. Debut 1981 OB in "Ka-Boom!," followed by "Florodora," "Opal," "On That Day," "A Little Night Music."

BROCKSMITH, ROY. Born Sept. 15, 1945 in Quincy, IL. Debut 1971 OB in "Whip Lady," followed by "The Workout," "Beggar's Opera," "Polly," "Threepenny Opera," "The Master and Margarita," "Jungle of Cities," "Don Juan," "Dr. Selavy's Magic Theatre," Bdwy in "The Leaf People" (1975), "Stages," "Tartuffe," "Three Musketeers."

BRODERICK, MATTHEW. Born Mar. 21, 1963 in NYC. Debut OB 1981 in "Torch Song Trilogy," Bdwy 1983 in "Brighton Beach Memoirs" for which he received a Theatre World Award, followed by "Biloxi Blues."

BRODY, JONATHAN. Born June 16, 1963 in Englewood, NJ. Debut OB 1982 in "Shulamith," followed by "The Desk Set."

BROGGER, IVAR. Born Jan. 10, 1947 in St. Paul, Mn. Graduate UMn. Debut 1979 OB in "In the Jungle of Cities," followed by "Collected Words of Billy the Kid," "Magic Time," "Cloud 9," "Richard III," "Clarence," "Madwoman of Chaillot," Bdwy in "Macbeth" (1981).

BROOKES, JACQUELINE. Born July 24, 1930 in Montclair, NJ. Graduate UIowa, RADA. Bdwy debut 1955 in "Tiger at the Gates," followed by "Watercolor," "Abelard and Heloise," OB in "The Cretan Woman" for which she received a Theatre World Award, "The Clandestine Marriage," "Measure for Measure," "Duchess of Malfi," "Ivanov," "Six Characters in Search of an Author," "An Evening's Frost," "Come Slowly, Eden," "The Increased Difficulty of Concentration," "The Persians," "Sunday Dinner," "House of Blue Leaves," "A Meeting by the River," "Owners," "Hallelujah," "Dream of a Blacklisted Actor," "Knuckle," "Mama Sang the Blues," "Buried Child," "On Mt. Chimorazo," "Winter Dancers," "Hamlet," "Old Flames," "The Diviners," "Richard II," "Vieux Carre," "Full Hookup."

BROOKS, ALAN. Born July 11, 1950 in Bakersfield, CA. Graduate Occidental Col., FlaStateU. Debut 1978 OB in "Porno Stars at Home," followed by "Dr. Faustus," "Merchant of Venice," "Don Juan," "The Cuchulain Cycle," "The Changeling," "Night Must Fall."

BROOKS, DOROTHY. Born May 23 in Des Moines, IO. Graduate Buffalo State Col., Fla StateU. Debut 1979 OB in "The Underlings," followed by "Hoffman and Co.," "Pigeons on the Walk," "Night Must Fall."

BROWN, CANDY. Born Aug. 19 in San Rafael, CA. Attended MacAlester Col. Bdwy debut 1969 in "Hello, Dolly!," followed by "Purlie," "Pippin," "Chicago," "Grind."

BROWN, CHUCK. Born Oct. 16, 1959 in Cleveland, OH. Attended Baldwin-Wallace Col. Debut 1984 OB in "Pacific Overtures."

BROWN, CLARK. Born Mar. 26, 1958 in Mt. Kisco, NY. Graduate Hampshire Col. Debut OB 1984 in "Magic Time," followed by "Cherokee County."

BROWN, GARRETT M. Born Nov. 7, 1948 in Battle Creek, MI. Graduate Amherst Col. OB in "Noon," "Where Has Tommy Flowers Gone?," "Of Mice and Men," "Touch Black," "Two Hotdogs with Everything," "The Longest Walk," "Bloodletters," Bdwy in "Whoopee!" (1979).

BROWN, GRAHAM. Born Oct. 24 in NYC. Graduate Howard U. OB in "Widower's Houses" (1959), "The Emperor's Clothes," "Time of Storm," "Major Barbara," "Land Beyond the River," "The Blacks," "Firebugs," "God Is a (Guess What?)," "An Evening of One-Acts," "Man Better Man," "Behold! Cometh the Vanderkellans," "Ride a Black Horse," "The Great MacDaddy," "Eden," "Nevis Mountain Dew," "Season Unravel," "The Devil's Tear," "Sons and Fathers of Sons," "Abercrombie Apocalypse," "Ceremonies in Dark Old Men," Bdwy in "Weekend" (1968), "Man in the Glass Booth," "River Niger," "Pericles," "Black Picture Show," "Kings."

BROWN, KERMIT. Born Feb. 3, 1937 in Asheville, NC. Graduate Duke U. With APA in "War and Peace," "Judith," "Man and Superman," "The Show-Off," "Pantagleize" and "The Cherry Orchard," OB in "The Millionairess," "Things," "Lulu," "Heartbreak House," "Glad Tidings," "Anyone Can Whistle," "Facade," "The Arcata Promise," "A Midsummer Night's Dream," "Home."

BROWN, ROO. Born July 22, 1932 in Pittsburgh, PA. Graduate Smith Col. Debut 1984 OB in "A . . . My Name Is Alice."

BROWNING, SUSAN. Born Feb. 25, 1941 in Baldwin, NY. Penn State graduate. Bdwy debut 1963 in "Love and Kisses," followed by "Company" for which she received a Theatre World Award, "Shelter," "Goodtime Charley," "Big River," OB in "Jo," "Dime a Dozen," "Seventeen," "Boys from Syracuse," "Collision Course," "Whiskey," "As You Like It," "Removalists."

BRUMMEL, DAVID. Born Nov. 1, 1942 in Brooklyn, NY. Bdwy debut 1973 in "The Pajama Game," followed by "Music Is," "Oklahoma!," OB in "Cole Porter," "The Fantasticks."

BRUTSMAN, LAURA. Born July 31, 1961 in Cheyenne, WY. Graduate Juilliard. Debut 1984 OB in "Pieces of Eight," followed by "The Skin of Our Teeth," "As You Like It," "A New Way to Pay Old Debts."

BRYDON, W. B. Born Sept. 20, 1933 in Newcastle, Eng. Debut 1962 OB in "The Long, the Short and the Tall," followed by "Live Like Pigs," "Sjt. Musgrave's Dance," "The Kitchen," "Come Slowly Eden," "The Unknown Soldier and His Wife," "Moon for the Misbegotten," "The Orphan," "Possession," "Total Abandon," "Madwoman of Chaillot," Bdwy in "The Lincoln Mask," "Ulysses in Nighttown," "The Father."

BRYGGMAN, LARRY. Born Dec. 21, 1938 in Concord, CA. Attended CCSF, AmThWing. Debut 1962 OB in "A Pair of Pairs," followed by "Live Like Pigs," "Stop, You're Killing Me," "Mod Donna," "Waiting for Godot," "Ballymurphy," "Marco Polo Sings a Solo," "Brownsville Raid," "Two Small Bodies," "Museum," "Winter Dancers," "The Resurrection of Lady Lester," "Royal Bob," "Modern Ladies of Guanabacoa," "The Ballad of Soapy Smith," "Walk the Dog Willie," Bdwy in "Ulysses in Nighttown," "Checking Out," "The Basic Training of Pavlo Hummel," "Richard III."

BRYNE, BARBARA. Born in London, Eng. Attended RADA. NY debut 1981 OB in "Entertaining Mr. Sloane," Bdwy in "Sunday in the Park with George" (1984).

BRYNNER, YUL. Born June 15, 1915 in Sakhalin Island, Japan. Bdwy debut 1946 in "Lute Song," followed by "The King and I" (1951/1977/1984), "Home Sweet Homer."

BUCKLEY, BETTY. Born July 3, 1947 in Big Spring, TX. Graduate TCU. Bdwy debut 1969 in "1776," followed by "Pippin," "Cats," OB in "Ballad of Johnny Pot," "What's a Nice Country Like You . . .," "Circle of Sound," "I'm Getting My Act Together . . .", "Juno's Swans."

BUCKLEY, MELINDA. Born Apr. 17, 1954 in Attleboro, MA. Graduate UMa. Bdwy debut 1983 in "A Chorus Line," OB in "Damn Yankees," "Pal Joey."

BUKA, DONALD. Born Dec. 18, 1921 in Cleveland, OH. Attended Carnegie Tech. Credits include "Twelfth Night," "The Corn is Green" (1950/1983), "Bright Boy," "Helen Goes to Troy," "Sophie," "Live Life Again," "Those That Play the Clowns," "Major Barbara," "Design for Living," OB in "Heritage," "In the Matter of J. Robert Oppenheimer," "Willie."

BURK, TERENCE. Born Aug. 11, 1947 in Lebanon, IL. Graduate S.Ill.U. Bdwy debut 1976 in "Equus," OB in "Religion," "The Future," "Sacred and Profane Love," "Crime and Punishment."

BURKE, MAGGIE. Born May 2, 1936 in Bay Shore, NY. Graduate Sarah Lawrence Col. OB in "Today Is Independence Day," "Lovers and Other Strangers," "Jules Feiffer's Cartoons," "Fog," "Home Is the Hero," "King John," "Rusty & Rico & Lena & Louie," "Friends," "Butterfaces," "Old Times," Bdwy debut 1985 in "Brighton Beach Memoirs."

BURKS, DONNY. Born in Martinsville, VA. Graduate St. John's U. Debut 1964 OB in "Dutchman," followed by "Billy Noname" for which he received a Theatre World Award, "Miracle Play," Bdwy in "Hair" (1968), "The American Clock," "The Tap Dance Kid."

BURNS, CATHERINE. Born Sept. 25, 1945 in NYC. Attended AADA. Bdwy 1968 in "The Prime of Miss Jean Brodie," OB in "Dream of a Blacklisted Actor," "The Disintegration of James Cherry," "Operation Sidewinder," "Dear Janet Rosenberg, Dear Mr. Kooning" for which she received a Theatre World Award, "Two Small Bodies," "Voices," "Jungle of Cities," "One Wedding," "Metamorphosis," "Within the Year."

BURRELL, PAMELA. Born Aug. 4, 1945 in Tacoma, WA. Bdwy debut 1966 in "Funny Girl," followed by "Where's Charley?," "Strider," "Sunday in the Park with George," OB in "Arms and the Man" for which she received a Theatre World Award, "Berkeley Square," "The Boss," "Biography: A Game," "Strider: Story of a Horse," "A Little Madness."

BURRELL, TERRY. Born Feb. 8, 1952 in Trinidad, WI. Attended Pace U. Bdwy debut 1977 in "Eubie!," followed by "Dreamgirls," OB in "That Uptown Feeling."

BURSTYN, ELLEN. Born Dec. 7, 1932 in Detroit, MI. Attended Actors Studio. Bdwy debut 1957 (as Ellen McRae) in "Fair Game," followed by "Same Time Next Year," "84 Charing Cross Road," OB in "The Three Sisters," "Andromeda II," "Park Your Car in Harvard Yard."

BURTON, IRVING. Born Aug. 5, 1923 in NYC. Bdwy debut 1951 in "Peer Gynt," OB in "Three Unnatural Acts," 24 years with the Paper Bag Players, "Pal Joey," "Keegan & Lloyd Again."

BURTON, KATE. Born Sept. 10, 1957 in Geneva, Switz. Graduate Brown U., Yale. Bdwy debut 1982 in "Present Laughter," followed by "Alice in Wonderland," "Doonesbury," OB in "Winners" for which she received a Theatre World Award, "Romeo and Juliet," "The Accrington Pals," "Playboy of the Western World."

BYRDE, EDYE. Born Jan. 19, 1929 in NYC. Bdwy debut 1975 in "The Wiz," OB in "Jam," "Jack and Jill."

CAFFEY, MARION J. Born Jan. 11, 1955 in Hempstead, TX. OB in "Come with Us," "Seeds," "Blackberries," "Dreams of Becoming," "Mayor."

CALDWELL, GISELA. Born Apr. 3 in Enid, OK. Graduate George Washington U. Debut 1972 OB in "The Effect of Gamma Rays . . .," followed by "Cappella," Bdwy in "Three Sisters" (1973), "Beggars Opera," "Measure for Measure," "The Octette Bridge Club."

CALEB, JOHN. Born July 8, 1959 in Mexico City, MX. Bdwy debut 1981 in "My Fair Lady," followed by "Pacific Overtures" (OB 1984).

CALLANDER, BARBARA. Born Mar. 3, 1950 in Washington, D.C. Graduate Oberlin Col. Debut 1980 OB in "The Betrothal," followed by "Period of Adjustment," "Playboy of the Western World," "Spider's Web," "War Games," "Mrs. Warren's Profession."

CAMERON, HOPE Born Feb 21, 1920 in Hartford, Ct. Attended AADA. Bdwy debut 1947 in "All My Sons," followed by "Death of a Salesman," OB in "The Strindberg Brothers," "The Last Days of Lincoln," "Grace," "Skirmishes," "Big Maggie," "Re-Po."

CAMP, JOANNE. Born Apr. 4, 1951 in Atlanta, GA. Graduate FlAtlanticU, Geo WashU. Debut 1981 OB in "The Dry Martini," followed by "Geniuses," for which she received a Theatre World Award, "June Moon," "Painting Churches," "Merchant of Venice."

CANARY, DAVID. Born Aug. 25 in Elwood, IN. Graduate UCin, CinConservatory. Debut 1960 OB in "Kittywake Island," followed by "The Fantastics," "The Father," "Hi, Paisano," "Summer," "Blood Moon," "Sally's Gone, She Left Her Name," Bdwy in "Great Day in the Morning," "Happiest Girl in the World," "Clothes for a Summer Hotel."

CANNON, ALICE. Born June 25 in Rochester, NY. Graduate Cornell U. Debut 1962 OB in "The Fantasticks," followed by "Silent Night Lonely Night," "By Bernstein," "Man with a Load of Mischief," "All in Love," "Sufragette," "Northern Boulevard," Bdwy in "Fiddler on the Roof" (1965), "Johnny Johnson," "Education of Hyman Kaplan," "Company."

CANNON, CATHERINE. Born Apr. 18, 1957 in Boston, MA. Graduate Sarah Lawrence Col. Debut OB 1980 in "Friend of the Family," followed by "8 × 10 Glossy."

CAPRI, MARK. Born July 19, 1951 in Washington, DC. Graduate Stanford U, RADA. Debut 1984 OB in "On Approval" for which he received a Theatre World Award, followed by "An Enemy of the People."

CAPODICE, JOHN C. Born Dec. 25, 1941 in Chicago, IL. Attended Goodman School, Weber-Douglas Academy. Debut 1978 OB in "A Prayer for My Daughter," followed by "Henry V," "Getting Out," Bdwy in "Requiem for a Heavyweight" (1985).

CARDEN, WILLIAM. Born Feb. 2, 1947 in NYC. Attended Lawrence U., Brandeis U. Debut 1974 OB in "Short Eyes," followed by Leaving Home," "Back in the Race," "Thin Ice," "Bloodletters."

CARHART, TIMOTHY. Born Dec. 24, 1953 in Washington, DC. Graduate UIll. Debut 1984 OB in "The Harvesting," followed by "The Ballad of Soapy Smith," "Hitch-Hikers."

CARISTI, VINCENT. Born in 1949 in Brooklyn, NY. Attended Richmond Col. Debut 1985 OB in "Tracers."

CARLIN, AMANDA. Born Dec. 12 in Queens, NY. Graduate Tufts U. Bdwy debut 1980 in "Major Barbara," followed by "The Man Who Came to Dinner," OB in "The Dining Room," "Twelfth Night," "The Accrington Pals," "Comedy of Errors," "Playboy of the Western World."

CARLIN, CHET. Born Feb. 23, 1940 in Malverne, NY. Graduate Ithaca Col., Catholic U. Bdwy debut 1972 in "An Evening with Richard Nixon . . .," OB in "Under Gaslight," "Lou Gehrig Did Not Die of Cancer," "Graffiti!," "Crystal and Fox," "Golden Honeymoon," "Arms and the Man," "Arsenic and Old Lace," "The Father," "Comedy of Errors."

CARMICHAEL, BILL. Born June 18, 1954 in Oceanside, CA. Graduate ConnU. Bdwy debut 1980 in "Peter Pan," OB in "Pirates of Penzance," "La Boheme."

CARNEY, GRACE. Born Sept. 15, 1911 in Hartford, CT. Attended Columbia U., CCNY. Debut OB 1959 in "A Family Portrait," followed by "Billygoat Eddie," "Whitsuntide," "My Old Friends," Bdwy in "Donnybrook," "Eccentricities of a Nightingale," "Vieux Carre," "Angel."

CARRICART, ROBERTSON Born Dec. 28, 1947 in Norfolk, VA. Graduate UCLA. Debut 1974 OB in "Private Ear/Public Eye," followed by "Cromwell," "Out of the Night," "Dr. Faustus," Bdwy in "Oklahoma " (1979), "Design for Living."

CARROLL, DANNY. Born May 30, 1940 in Maspeth, NY. Bdwy bow in 1957 "The Music Man," followed by "Flora the Red Menace," "Funny Girl," "George M!," "Billy," "Ballroom," "42nd Street," OB in "Boys from Syracuse," "Babes in the Woods."

CARROLL, DAVID-JAMES. Born July 30, 1950 in Rockville Centre, NY. Graduate Dartmouth Col. Debut 1975 OB in "A Matter of Time," followed by "Joseph and the Amazing Technicolor Dreamcoat," "New Tunes," "La Boheme," Bdwy in "Rodgers and Hart" (1975), "Where's Charley?," "Oh, Brother!," "7 Brides for 7 Brothers," "Roberta in Concert."

CARROLL, HELENA. Born in Glasgow, Scot. Attended Webster-Douglas Acad. U.S. debut with Dublin Players. Bdwy debut in "Separate Tables" (1956), followed by "Happy as Larry," "A Touch of the Poet," "Little Moon of Alban," "The Hostage," "Oliver!" "Pickwick," "Something Different," "Georgy," "Borstal Boy," "Design for Living," OB in "Three Hand Reel," "Pictures in the Hallway," "Small Craft Warnings," "The Slab Boys."

CARROLL, PAT. Born May 5, 1927 in Shreveport, LA. Attended Catholic U. Debut 1950 OB in "Come What May," followed by "On the Town" (1959), "Gertrude Stein, Gertrude Stein," Bdwy in "Catch a Star" (1955), "Dancing in the End Zone."

CARROLL, VINCENT. Born in Waterford, CT. Graduate Marquette U., Pasadena Playhouse. Debut 1962 OB in "The Hostage," followed by "Even in Laughter," "Mr. Joyce Is Leaving Paris," Bdwy in "Avanti!" (1968).

CARSON, THOMAS. Born May 27, 1939 in Iowa City, IO. Graduate UIo. Debut 1981 OB in "The Feuhrer Bunker," followed by "Breakfast Conversations in Miami," "Sullivan and Gilbert."

CARTER, THELMA LOUISE. Born July 16 in Gary, IN. Debut 1975 OB in "Liberty Call," followed by "The Crucible," "Between Rails," "Long Time Since Yesterday."

CASH, SUSAN. Born Dec. 21, 1956 in Delaware County, PA. Attended Carnegie-Mellon U. Debut 1983 OB in "Talking With," followed by "Almost in Vegas."

CASS, PEGGY. Born May 21, 1926 in Boston, MA. Attended Wyndham Sch. Credits include "Touch and Go," "Live Wire," "Bernardine," "Othello," "Henry V," "Auntie Mame" for which she received a Theatre World Award, "A Thurber Carnival," "Children from Their Games," "Don't Drink the Water," "Front Page" (1969), "Plaza Suite," "Once a Catholic," "42nd Street," "The Octette Bridge Club," OB in "Phoenix '55," "Are You Now or Have You Ever Been," "One Touch of Venus."

CASSERLY, KERRY. Born Oct. 26, 1953 in Minneapolis, MN. Attended UMinn. Bdwy debut 1980 in "One Night Stand," followed by "A Chorus Line," "My One and Only."

CASSIDY, PATRICK. Born Jan. 4, 1961 in Los Angeles, CA. Bdwy debut 1982 in "Pirates of Penzance," followed by "Leader of the Pack."

CASSIDY, TIM. Born March 22, 1952 in Alliance, OH. Attended UCincinnati. Bdwy debut 1974 in "Good News," followed by "A Chorus Line."

CASTANG, VERONICA. Born Apr. 22 in London, Eng. Attended Sorbonne. Bdwy debut 1964 in "How's the World Treating You?," followed by "The National Health," "Whose Life Is It Anyway?," OB in "The Trigon," "Sjt. Musgrave's Dance," "Saved," "Water Hens," "Self-Accusation," "Kaspar," "Ionescapade," "Statements After and Arrest under the Immorality Act," "Ride a Cock Horse," "Banana Box," "Bonjour La Bonjour," "A Call from the East," "Close of Play," "Cloud 9," "After the Prize," "David and Paula," "The Accrington Pals."

CASTLE, MARC. Born Jan. 20, 1952 in NYC. Graduate Pratt Inst. Debut 1962 OB in "Plays for Bleecker Street," followed by "My Great Dead Sister," "Romance Language."

CATLIN, JODY. Born July 6, 1946 in Nebraska. Graduate William and Mary Col. Debut 1977 OB in "Porno Stars at Home," followed by "Colonomos," "The Price of Genius."

CAULFIELD, MAXWELL. Born Nov. 23, 1959 in Glasgow, Scot. Debut 1979 OB in "Class Enemy" for which he received a Theatre World Award, followed by "Crimes and Dreams," "Entertaining Mr. Sloane," "The Inheritors," "Paradise Lost," "Salonika."

CERVERIS, MICHAEL. Born Nov. 6, 1960 in Bethesda, MD. Graduate Yale U. Debut 1983 OB in "Moon," followed by "Macbeth," "Life Is a Dream," "Total Eclipse."

CHALAWSKY, MAX. Born Feb 26, 1956 in Brooklyn, NY. Graduate Bklyn Col. Debut 1980 OB in "D," followed by "I Am a Camera," "Hard to Be a Jew."

CHALFANT, KATHLEEN. Born Jan. 14, 1945 in San Francisco, CA. Graduate Stanford U. Bdwy debut 1975 in "Dance With Me," followed by OB "Jules Feiffer's Hold Me," "Killings on the Last Line," "The Boor," "Blood Relations," "Signs of Life," "Sister Mary Ignatius Explains It All," "Actor's Nightmare," "Faith Healer," "All the Nice People."

CHAMPAGNE, MICHAEL. Born Apr. 10, 1947 in New Bedford, MA. Graduate SMU., MSU. Debut 1975 OB in "The Lieutenant," followed by "Alinsky," "The Hostage," "Livingstone and Sechele," "A Christmas Carol," "Penelope," "An Occasion of Sin."

CHANDLER, DAVID. Born Feb. 3, 1950 in Danbury, CT. Graduate Oberlin Col. Bdwy debut 1980 in "The American Clock," followed by "Death of a Salesman," OB in "Made in Heaven."

CHANNING, STOCKARD. Born in 1944 in NYC. Attended Radcliffe Col. Debut 1970 OB in "Adaptation/Next," followed by "The Lady and the Clarinet," "The Golden Age," Bdwy in "Two Gentlemen of Verona," "They're Playing Our Song," "The Rink," "Joe Egg."

CHARLES, JIM. Born May 4, 1960 in Albany, NY. Debut 1983 OB in "The Fantasticks."

CHARLES, WALTER. Born Apr. 4, 1945 in East Stroudsburg, PA. Graduate Boston U Bdwy debut 1973 in "Grease," followed by "1600 Pennsylvania Avenue," "Knickerbocker Holiday," "Sweeney Todd," "Cats," "La Cage aux Folles."

CHARNIN, RANDY WILLIAM. Born Sept. 1, 1959 in Brooklyn, NY. Graduate CalState/San Bernardino. Debut 1983 OB in "The Inheritors," followed by "Rain," "Paradise Lost," "The Madwoman of Chaillot," "Vivat! Vivat! Regina!"

CHATER, GORDON. Born Apr. 6, 1922 in London, Eng. Debut 1979 OB in "The Elocution of Benjamin," followed by "Learned Ladies," "Major Barbara in Concert," "Pygmalion in Concert," "An Enemy of the People," "She Stoops to Conquer," Bdwy in "Whodunnit" (1982).

CHAVES, RICHARD. Born Oct. 9, 1951 in Jacksonville, FL. Attended Occidental Col. Debut 1985 OB in "Tracers" for which he received a Theatre World Award.

CHEN, TINA. Born Nov. 2 in Chung King, China. Graduate Brown U. Debut 1972 OB in "A Maid's Tragedy," followed by "Family Devotions," "A Midsummer Night's Dream," "Empress of China," Bdwy in "The King and I," "Rashomon."

CHIANESE, DOMINIC. Born Feb. 24, 1932 in NYC. Graduate Brooklyn Col. Debut 1952 OB with American Savoyards, followed by "Winterset," "Jacques Brel Is Alive . . .," "Ballad for a Firing Squad," "City Scene," "End of the War," "Passione," "A Midsummer Night's Dream," "Recruiting Officer," "The Wild Duck," "Oedipus the King," "Hunting Scenes," "Operation Midnight Climax," "Rosario and the Gypsies," "Bella Figura," Bdwy in "Oliver!," "Scratch," "The Water Engine," "Richard III," "Requiem for a Heavyweight."

CHIBAS, MARISSA. Born June 13, 1961 in NYC. Graduate SUNY/Purchase. Debut OB 1983 in "Asian Shade," followed by "Sudden Death," "Total Eclipse," Bdwy in "Brighton Beach Memoirs" (1983).

CHINN, LORI TAN. Born July 7 in Seattle, WA. Bdwy debut 1970 in "Lovely Ladies, Kind Gentlemen," OB in "Coffins for Butterflies," "Hough in Blazes," "Peer Gynt," "The Ing and I," "Children," "Secret Life of Walter Mitty," "Bayou Legend," "Primary English Class," "G. R. Point," "Peking Man," "Ballad of Soapy Smith."

CHOATE, TIM. Born Oct. 11, 1954 in Dallas, TX. Graduate UTx. Bdwy debut 1979 in "Da," followed by "Crimes of the Heart," OB in "Young Bucks," "Comedians," "Hackers," "Submariners."

CHOWDHURY, SAMIR. Born Jan. 4, 1972 in Trenton, NJ. Bdwy debut 1984 in "Oliver!" OB in "Mowgli."

CHRIS, MARILYN. Born May 19 in NYC. Bdwy in "The Office" (1966), "Birthday Party," "7 Descents of Myrtle," "Lenny," OB in "Nobody Hears a Broken Drum," "Fame," "Juda Applause," "Junebug Graduates Tonight," "Man Is Man," "In the Jungle of Cities," "Good Soldier Schweik," "The Tempest," "Ride a Black Horse," "Screens," "Kaddish," "Lady from the Sea," "Bread," "Leaving Home," "Curtains," "Elephants," "The Upper Depths," "Man Enough."

CHRISTOPHER, JOYCE REEHLING. Born Mar. 5, 1949 in Baltimore, MD. Graduate NCSchool of Arts. Debut 1976 OB in "Hot l Baltimore," followed by "Who Killed Richard Cory?," "Lulu," "5th of July," "The Runner Stumbles," "Life and/or Death," "Back in the Race," "Time Framed," "Extremities," "The Miss Firecracker Contest," Bdwy in "A Matter of Gravity" (1976), "5th of July."

CHRYST, GARY. Born in 1959 in LaJolla, CA. Joined Joffrey Ballet in 1968. Bdwy debut in "Dancin' " (1979), OB in "One More Song/One More Dance," "Music Moves Me."

CLARK, BRYAN E. Born Apr. 5, 1929 in Louisville, KY. Graduate Fordham U. Bdwy debut 1978 in "A History of the American Film," followed by "Bent," OB in "Winning Isn't Everything," "Put Them All Together," "Red Rover," "Paradise Lost," "Clarence," "A Step Out of Line," "Madwoman of Chaillot."

CLARK, CHERYL. Born Dec. 7, 1950 in Boston, MA. Attended Ind. U., NYU. Bdwy debut 1972 in "Pippin," followed by "Chicago," "A Chorus Line."

CLARK, SARAH C. Born Jan. 13, 1962 in Rockland, Maine. Graduate Chatham Col. Debut 1984 OB in "Anonymous."

CLARKE, CAITLIN. Born May 3, 1952 in Pittsburgh, PA. Graduate Mt. Holyoke Col., Yale. Debut 1981 OB in "No End of Blame," followed by "Lorenzaccio," "Summer," "Quartermaine's Terms," "Thin Ice," "Total Eclipse," Bdwy in "Teaneck Tanzi" (1983), "Strange Interlude," "Arms and the Man."

CLAYBURGH, JILL. Born Apr. 30, 1944 in NYC. Graduate Sarah Lawrence Col. Bdwy debut 1968 in "The Sudden and Accidental Re-Education of Horse Johnson," followed by "The Rothschilds," "Pippin," "Jumpers," "Design for Living," OB in "It's Called the Sugar Plum," "Calling in Crazy," "The Nest."

CLAYTON, LAWRENCE. Born Oct. 10, 1956 in Mocksville, NC. Attended NC Central U. Debut 1980 OB in "Tambourines to Glory," followed by "Skyline," "Across the Universe," Bdwy 1984 in "Dreamgirls."

CLEAR, PATRICK. Born Apr. 8, 1952 in St. Louis, MO. Graduate Wash.U., PennState U. Bdwy debut 1984 in "Noises Off," followed by OB "Candide in Concert."

CLEMENT, MARIS. Born July 11, 1950 in Philadelphia, PA. Graduate Rollins Col. Debut 1976 OB in "Noel and Cole," followed by "The Great American Backstage Musical," "A Little Night Music," Bdwy in "On the 20th Century," "Copperfield," "Little Me."

CLEMENTE, RENE. Born July 2, 1950 in El Paso, TX. Graduate WestTxStateU. Bdwy debut 1977 in "A Chorus Line," followed by "Dancin'," "Play Me a Country Song," "Cats."

CLOSE, GLENN. Born May 19, 1947 in Greenwich, CT. Graduate William & Mary Col. Bdwy debut 1974 with Phoenix Co. in "Love for Love," "Member of the Wedding," and "Rules of the Game," followed by "Rex," "Crucifer of Blood," "Barnum," "The Real Thing," OB in "The Crazy Locomotive," "Uncommon Women and Others," "Wine Untouched," "The Winter Dancers," "The Singular Life of Albert Nobbs," "Joan of Arc at the Stake," "Childhood."

COCA, IMOGENE. Born Nov. 18, 1908 in Philadelphia, PA. Bdwy debut 1925 in "When You Smile," followed by "Garrick Gaieties," "Flying Colors," "New Faces," "Fools Rush In," "Who's Who," "Folies Bergere," "Straw Hat Revue," "All in Fun," "Concert Varieties," "Janus," "Girls in 509," "On the 20th Century," OB in "Outward Bound," "My Old Friends."

COHEN, LYNN. Born Aug. 10 in Kansas City, MO. Graduate Northwestern U. Debut 1979 OB in "Don Juan Comes Back from the Wars," followed by "Getting Out," "The Arbor," "The Cat and the Canary," "Suddenly Last Summer," "Bella Figura," "The Smash," "Chinese Viewing Pavilion," "Isn't It Romantic," "Total Eclipse," "Angelo's Wedding."

COHEN, MARGERY. Born June 24, 1947 in Chicago, IL. Attended UWisc., UChicago. Bdwy debut 1968 in "Fiddler on the Roof," followed by "Jacques Brel Is Alive. . . . . .," OB in "Berlin to Broadway," "By Bernstein," "Starting Here, Starting Now," "Unsung Cole," "Paris Lights," "Pere Goriot."

COHENOUR, PATTI. Born Oct. 17, 1952 in Albuquerque, NMx. Attended UNMx. Bdwy debut 1982 in "A Doll's Life," followed by "Pirates of Penzance," "Big River," OB in "La Boheme" for which she received a Theatre World Award.

COLAHAN, LIBBY. Born Nov. 8, 1942 in California. Graduate UPacific, UCalSanDiego. Debut 1983 OB in "Pericles," followed by "Tartuffe," "Play and Other Plays," Acting Co. (1985).

COLBERT, CLAUDETTE. Born Sept. 13, 1903 in Paris. Bdwy debut 1925 in "Wild Westcotts," followed by "Ghost Train," "A Kiss in a Taxi," "The Barker," "The Mulberry Bush," "La Gringa," "Tin Pan Alley," "Dynamo," "See Naples and Die," "Janus," "The Marriage-Go-Round," "Jake, Julia and Uncle Joe," "Irregular Verb to Love," "The Kingfisher," "A Talent for Murder," "Aren't We All?"

COIT, CONNIE. Born Apr. 21, 1947 in Dallas, TX. Graduate SMU. Debut 1980 OB in "A Funny Thing Happened on the Way to the Forum," followed by "Promenade," "Sullivan and Gilbert."

COLE, KAY. Born Jan. 13, 1948 in Miami, FL. Bdwy debut 1961 in "Bye Bye Birdie," followed by "Stop the World I Want to Get Off," "Roar of the Greasepaint . . .," "Hair," "Jesus Christ Superstar," "Words and Music," "Chorus Line," OB in "The Cradle Will Rock," "Two If By Sea," "Rainbow," "White Nights," "Sgt. Pepper's Lonely Hearts Club Band," "On the Swing Shift," "Snoopy," "Road to Hollywood," "One-man Band."

COLES, CHARLES HONI. Born Apr. 2, 1911 in Philadelphia, PA. Debut 1933 OB in "Humming Sam," Bdwy in "Gentlemen Prefer Blondes" (1949), "Black Broadway," "My One and Only."

COLKER, JERRY. Born Mar. 16, 1955 in Los Angeles, CA. Attended Harvard U. Debut 1975 OB in "Tenderloin," followed by "Pal Joey," "3 Guys Naked from the Waist Down," Bdwy in "West Side Story," "Pippin," "A Chorus Line."

COLL, IVONNE. Born Nov. 4 in Fajardo, PR. Attended UPR, LACC, HB Studio. Debut 1980 OB in "Spain 1980," followed by "Animals," "Wonderful Ice Cream Suit," "Cold Air," Bdwy in "Goodbye Fidel" (1980).

COLLAMORE, JEROME. Born Sept. 25, 1891 in Boston, MA. Debut 1918 with Washington Square Players in "Salome," and subsequently in "Christopher Bean," "Hamlet," "Romeo and Juliet," "Kind Lady," "Androcles and the Lion," "George Washington Slept Here," "The Would-Be Gentleman," "Cheri," "Abraham Cochrane," "That Hat," BAM Co.'s "New York Idea," "Trouping Since 1912," "The Dresser," "Three Sisters," OB in "That's It, Folks," "Glory!"

COLLET, CHRISTOPHER. Born Mar. 13, 1968 in NYC. Attended Strasberg Inst. Bdwy debut in "Torch Song Trilogy" (1983), followed by OB in "Coming of Age in SoHo."

COLLINS, KATE. Born May 6, 1959 in Boston, MA. Graduate Northwestern U. Debut 1984 OB in "The Danube," Bdwy (1985) in "Doubles."

COLLINS, PAUL. Born July 25, 1937 in London, Eng. Attended LACC. OB in "Say Nothing," "Cambridge Circus," "The Devils," "Rear Column," "Jail Diary of Albie Sachs," "The Feuhrer Bunker," "Great Days," "Courage," "State of the Union," Bdwy in "The Royal Hunt of the Sun" (1965), "A Minor Adjustment," "A Meeting by the River," "Eminent Domain."

COLLINS, STEPHEN. Born Oct. 1, 1947 in Des Moines, IO. Graduate Amherst Col. Bdwy debut 1972 in "Moonchildren," followed by "No Sex, Please, We're British," "The Ritz," "Censored Scenes from King Kong," "Loves of Anatol," OB in "Twelfth Night," "More than You Deserve," "Macbeth," "Last Days of British Honduras," BAMCo.'s "New York Idea," "Three Sisters" and "The Play's the Thing," "Beyond Therapy."

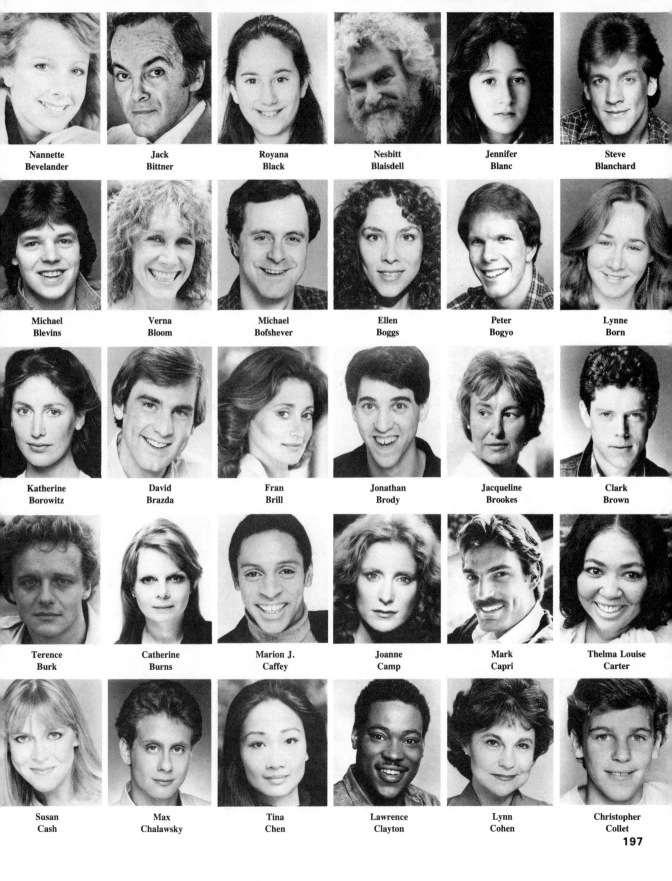

Nannette Bevelander	Jack Bittner	Royana Black	Nesbitt Blaisdell	Jennifer Blanc	Steve Blanchard
Michael Blevins	Verna Bloom	Michael Bofshever	Ellen Boggs	Peter Bogyo	Lynne Born
Katherine Borowitz	David Brazda	Fran Brill	Jonathan Brody	Jacqueline Brookes	Clark Brown
Terence Burk	Catherine Burns	Marion J. Caffey	Joanne Camp	Mark Capri	Thelma Louise Carter
Susan Cash	Max Chalawsky	Tina Chen	Lawrence Clayton	Lynn Cohen	Christopher Collet

197

COLON, MIRIAM. Born in 1945 in Ponce, PR. Attended UPR, Actors Studio. Bdwy debut 1953 in "In the Summer House," OB in "Me, Candido," "The Ox Cart," "The Passion of Antigona Perez," "Julius Caesar," "Fanlights," "Simpson Street."

COLTON, BARBARA. Born July 10, 1938 in NYC. Graduate Boston U. Debut 1980 OB in "The Winslow Boy," followed by "Falsies."

COLTON, CHEVI. Born Dec. 21 in NYC. Attended Hunter Col. OB in "Time of Storm," "Insect Comedy," "The Adding Machine," "O Marry Me," "Penny Change," "The Mad Show," "Jacques Brel Is Alive . . .," "Bits and Pieces," "Spelling Bee," "Uncle Money," Bdwy in "Cabaret," "Grand Tour," "Torch Song Trilogy."

COMBS, DAVID. Born June 10, 1949 in Reno, NV. Graduate UNv, Wayne State U. Bdwy debut 1975 in "Equus," OB in "The Passion of Dracula," "Punch with Judy," "Hamlet Machine."

COMBS, SARAH. Born June 19, 1959 in Durham, NC. Graduate Cincinnati Conservatory. Debut 1985 OB in "A Little Night Music."

COMDEN, BETTY. Born May 3, 1919 in Brooklyn, NY. Graduate NYU. Bdwy debut 1944 in "On the Town," for which she received a Theatre World Award, followed by "A Party with Comden and Green", OB in "A Party with Betty Comden and Adolph Green," "Isn't It Romantic."

CONNELL, GORDON. Born Mar. 19, 1923 in Berkeley, CA. Graduate UCal, NYU. Bdwy debut 1961 in "Subways Are for Sleeping," followed by "Hello, Dolly!," "Lysistrata," "The Human Comedy," "Big River," OB in "Beggar's Opera," "The Butler Did It," "With Love and Laughter."

CONNELL, JANE. Born Oct. 27, 1925 in Berkeley, CA. Attended UCal. Bdwy debut in "New Faces of 1956," followed by "Drat! The Cat!," "Mame" (1966/'83), "Dear World," "Lysistrata," OB in "Shoestring Revue," "Threepenny Opera," "Pieces of Eight," "Demi-Dozen," "She Stoops to Conquer," "Drat!," "The Real Inspector Hound," "The Rivals," "The Rise and Rise of Daniel Rocket," "Laughing Stock," "The Singular Dorothy Parker."

CONNOLLY, JOHN P. Born Sept. 1, 1950 in Philadelphia, PA. Graduate Temple U. Debut 1973 OB in "Paradise Lost," followed by "The Wizard of Oz," "Fighting Bob," "For the Use of the Hall," "The Golem," "A Step Out of Line," "For Sale."

CONNOLLY, MICHAEL. Born Sept. 22, 1947 in Boston, MA. Graduate Fordham U. Bdwy debut 1977 in "Otherwise Engaged," followed by "Break a Leg," "Clothes for a Summer Hotel," "Copperfield," "Amadeus," OB in "Hijinks," "Sullivan and Gilbert."

CONROY, FRANCES. Born in 1953 in Monroe, GA. Attended Dickinson Col., Juilliard, Neighborhood Playhouse. Debut 1978 OB with the Acting Co. in "Mother Courage," "King Lear," "The Other Half," followed by "All's Well That Ends Well," "Othello," "Sorrows of Stephen," "Girls Girls Girls," "Zastrozzi," "Painting Churches," "Uncle Vanya," "Romance Language," Bdwy 1980 in "The Lady from Dubuque."

CONROY, JARLATH. Born Sept. 30, 1944 in Galway, Ire. Attended RADA. Bdwy debut 1976 in "Comedians," followed by "The Elephant Man," "Macbeth," OB in "Translations," "The Wind That Shook the Barley," "Gardenia," "Friends," "Playboy of the Western World."

CONTRERAS, RAY. Born Apr. 14, 1960 in Jersey City, NJ. Attended Strasberg Inst. Debut OB 1977 in "Runaways," followed by "Dispatches," "Street Dreams," "Pacific Overtures," Bdwy in "Runaways" (1978), "West Side Story" (1980).

CONVERSE, FRANK. Born May 22, 1938 in St. Louis, MO. Attended Carnegie-Mellon U. Bdwy debut 1966 in "First One Asleep, Whistle," followed by "The Philadelphia Story" (1980/LC), "Brothers," "Design for Living," OB in "House of Blue Leaves."

COOK, JILL. Born Feb. 25, 1954 in Plainfield, NJ. Bdwy debut 1971 in "On the Town," followed by "So Long, 174th Street," "Dancin'," "Best Little Whorehouse in Texas," "Perfectly Frank," "My One and Only," OB in "Carnival," "Potholes," "Merrily We Roll Along."

COONER, ROBERT. Born Oct. 19, 1956 in Houston, TX. Graduate UHouston. Debut 1985 OB in "Very Warm for May."

COOPER, MARILYN. Born Dec. 14, 1936 in NYC. Attended NYU. Appeared in "Mr. Wonderful," "West Side Story," "Brigadoon," "Gypsy," "I Can Get It for You Wholesale," "Hallelujah Baby!," "Golden Rainbow," "Mame," "A Teaspoon Every 4 Hours," "Two by Two," "On the Town," "Ballroom," "Woman of the Year," "The Odd Couple" (1985), OB in "The Mad Show," "Look Me Up."

COPELAND, JOAN. Born June 1, 1922 in NYC. Attended Brooklyn Col., AADA. Debut 1945 OB in "Romeo and Juliet," followed by "Othello," "Conversation Piece," "Delightful Season," "End of Summer," "American Clock," "The Double Game," "Isn't It Romantic?," Bdwy in "Sundown Beach," "Detective Story," "Not for Children," "Hatful of Fire," "Something More," "The Price," "Two by Two," "Pal Joey," "Checking Out," "The American Clock."

CORBETT, MICHAEL. Born June 20 in Philadelphia, PA. Graduate Boston Conservatory, UPa. Debut OB 1981 in "The Matinee Kids," followed by "Come Back, Little Sheba."

CORBIN, ALBERT. Born Apr. 13, 1926 in New Britain, CT. Graduate Syracuse U. Bdwy debut 1955 in "The Wayward Saint," followed by "Tiger at the Gates," "Cyrano de Bergerac," "Henry IV Part I," OB in "School for Wives," "The White Devil," "Our Town," "Fashion," "The Crucible," "Colombe," "Taming of the Shrew."

CORREIA, DON. Born Aug. 28, 1951 in San Jose, CA. Attended SanJoseStateU. Bdwy debut 1980 in "A Chorus Line," followed by "Perfectly Frank," "Little Me," "Sophisticated Ladies," "5–6–7–8 Dance," "My One and Only," "Singin' in the Rain."

CORREN, DONALD. Born June 5, 1952 in Stockton, CA. Attended Juilliard. Bdwy debut 1980 in "A Day in Hollywood/A Night in the Ukraine," followed by "Tomfoolery" (OB), "Torch Song Trilogy."

CORSAIR, BILL. Born Sept. 5, 1940 in Providence, RI. Debut OB 1984 in "Ernie and Arnie."

CORSAIR, JANIS. Born June 18, 1948 in Providence RI. Debut OB 1984 in "The Coarse Acting Show."

CORTEZ, KATHERINE. Born Sept. 28, 1950 in Detroit, MI. Graduate UNC. Debut 1979 OB in "The Dark at the Top of the Stairs," followed by "Corners," "Confluence," "The Great Grandson of Jedediah Kohler," "A Think Piece," "The Sea Gull," "Dysan," "Fool for Love," "For Sale," Bdwy in "Foxfire" (1982).

COSTALLOS, SUZANNE. Born Apr. 3, 1953 in NYC. Attended NYU, Boston Consv., Juilliard. Debut 1977 in "Play and Other Plays by Beckett," followed by "Elizabeth I," "The White Devil," "Hunting Scenes from Lower Bavaria," "Selma," Bdwy in "Zorba" (1983).

COX, BRIAN. Born June 1, 1946 in Dundee, Scot. Attended LAMDA. Bdwy debut 1985 in "Strange Interlude," followed OB in "Rat in the Skull" (1985).

COX, CATHERINE. Born Dec. 13, 1950 in Toledo, OH. Wittenberg U. graduate. Bdwy debut 1976 in "Music Is," followed by "Whoopee!" "Oklahoma!," "Shakespeare's Cabaret," "Barnum," "Baby," OB in "By Strouse," "It's Better With a Band," "In Trousers."

CRABTREE, DON. Born Aug. 21, 1928 in Borger, TX. Attended Actors Studio. Bdwy bow 1959 in "Destry Rides Again," followed by "Happiest Girl in the World," "Family Affair," "Unsinkable Molly Brown," "Sophie," "110 In the Shade," "Golden Boy," "Pousse Cafe," "Mahagonny" (OB), "The Best Little Whorehouse in Texas," "42nd Street."

CRAIG, BETSY. Born Jan. 5, 1952 in Hopewell, VA. Attended Berry Col. Bdwy debut 1972 in "Ambassador," followed by "Smith," "Brigadoon," "La Cage aux Folles."

CRAIG, NOEL. Born Jan. 4 in St. Louis, MO. Attended Northwestern U., Goodman Theatre, London Guildhall. Bdwy debut 1967 in "Rosencrantz and Guildenstern Are Dead," followed by "A Patriot for Me," "Conduct Unbecoming," "Vivat! Vivat Regina!," "Going Up," "Dance a Little Closer," "A Chorus Line," OB in "Pygmalion," "Promenade," "Family House," "Inn at Lydda."

CRAWLEY, TOM. Born Aug. 4, 1940 in Central Falls, RI. Graduate UNeb., NYU. Debut 1970 OB in "The Persians," followed by "The Measure Taken," "Ghosts," "The Snob," "Heartbreak House," "Life with Father," "Crimes of Vautrin."

CRISCUOLO, LOU. Born Jan. 23, 1934 in NYC. Attended Actors Studio. Debut 1964 OB in "Matty, the Moron and the Madonna," followed by "Hooray! It's a Glorious Day," "Smith," "Rubbers," "Yanks 3, Detroit 0," "The Derby," Bdwy in "Man of La Mancha," "Hurry, Harry," "Ma Rainey's Black Bottom."

CROFOOT, LEONARD JOHN. Born Sept. 20, 1948 in Utica, NY. Bdwy debut 1968 in "The Happy Time," followed by "Come Summer," "Gigi," "Barnum," "Grind," OB in "Circus," "Joseph and the Amazing Technicolor Dreamcoat."

CRONYN, TANDY. Born Nov. 27, 1945 in Los Angeles, CA. Attended London's Central School. Bdwy debut 1969 in "Cabaret," followed by LC's "Playboy of the Western World," "Good Woman of Setzuan," "An Enemy of the People," and "Antigone," OB in "An Evening With the Poet-Senator," "Winners," "The Killing of Sister George," "Memories of an Immortal Spirit."

CROWE, JOAN. Born May 23, 1960 in Wilmar, MN. Graduate Indiana U., FlaStateU. Debut 1985 OB in "Roundheads and Pointheads."

CRYER, DAVID. Born Mar. 8, 1936 in Evanston, IL. Attended DePauw U. OB in "The Fantasticks," "Streets of New York," "Now Is the Time for All Good Men," "Whispers On the Wind," "The Making of Americans," "Portfolio Revue," "Paradise Lost," "The Inheritors," "Rain," "Ghosts," "Madwoman of Chaillot," "Clarence," Bdwy in "110 In the Shade," "Come Summer" for which he received a Theatre World Award, "1776" "Ari," "Leonard Bernstein's Mass," "Desert Song," "Evita."

CRYER, JON. Born Apr. 16, 1965 in NYC. Attended RADA. Bdwy debut 1983 in "Torch Song Trilogy," followed by "Brighton Beach Memoirs."

CUERVO, ALMA. Born Aug. 13 in Tampa, FL. Graduate Tulane U, Yale U. Debut 1977 in "Uncommon Women and Others," followed by "A Foot in the Door," "Put Them All Together," "Isn't It Romantic," "Miss Julie," "Quilters," Bdwy in "Once in a Lifetime," "Bedroom Farce," "Censored Scenes from King Kong," "Is There Life after High School?"

CUKA, FRANCES. Born in London, Eng. Graduate Guildhall School. Bdwy debut 1961 in "A Taste of Honey," followed by "Travesties," "Oliver!," OB in "The Entertainer," "It's Only a Play," "Quartermaine's Terms," "Not Waving."

CULLEN, JEANNE. Born Dec. 21, 1951 in Passaic, NY. Graduate UCon. Debut 1982 OB in "Lysistrata," followed by "Punch with Judy," "The Rivals," "All Soul's Day," "Fantod."

CULLEY, JANE. Born Dec. 3, 1943 in Lawrenceburg, TN. Attended Reed Col. Debut 1964 OB in "Of Mice and Men," followed by "Scuba Duba," "Night of the Iguana," "A Phantasmagoria Historia . . .," "Holy Junkie," "Til Jason Comes."

CULLISON, BARRY. Born Sept. 11, 1949 in Vincennes, IN. Attended Goodman Theatre School. Bdwy debut in "Bedroom Farce" (1979), OB in "Cloud 9," "A Step Out of Line."

CULLUM, JOHN. Born Mar. 2, 1930 in Knoxville, TN. Graduate UTn. Bdwy debut 1960 in "Camelot," followed by "Infidel Caesar," "The Rehearsal," "Hamlet," "On a Clear Day You Can See Forever" for which he received a Theatre World Award, "Man of La Mancha," "1776," "Vivat! Vivat Regina!," "Shenandoah," "Kings," "The Trip Back Down," "On the 20th Century," "Deathtrap," "Doubles," OB in "Three Hand Reel," "The Elizabethans," "Carousel," "In the Voodoo Parlor of Marie Leveau," "The King and I" (JB), "Whistler."

CULLUM, JOHN DAVID. Born Mar. 1, 1966 in NYC. Bdwy debut 1977 in "Kings," followed by "Shenandoah," OB in "Romance Language," "Losing It," "Madwoman of Chaillot," "Clarence."

CUMMINGS, GRETEL. Born July 3 in Bolzano, Italy. Attended Antioch Col. Debut 1964 OB in "Home Movies," followed by "Two Camps by Koutoukas," "Penguin Touquet," "Etiquette," "Egyptology," "The Temptation," Bdwy in "Inner City," "Lolita My Love," "Stages," "Agamemnon."

CUMMINGS, TONY. Born in 1957 in Los Angeles, CA. Juilliard graduate. Debut OB 1985 "In Trousers."

CURTIS, KEENE. Born Feb. 15, 1925 in Salt Lake City, UT. Graduate UUtah. Bdwy bow 1949 in "Shop at Sly Corner," with APA in "School for Scandal," "The Tavern," "Anatole," "Scapin," "Right You Are," "Importance of Being Earnest," "Twelfth Night," "King Lear," "Seagull," "Lower Depths," "Man and Superman," "Judith," "War and Peace," "You Can't Take It With You," "Pantagleize," "Cherry Orchard," "Misanthrope," "Cocktail Party," "Cock-a-Doodle Dandy," and "Hamlet," "A Patriot for Me," "The Rothschilds," "Night Watch," "Via Galactica," "Annie," "Division Street," "La Cage aux Folles," OB in "Colette," "Ride Across Lake Constance."

CWIKOWSKI, BILL. Born Aug. 4, 1945 in Newark, NJ. Graduate Smith and Monmouth Col. Debut 1972 OB in "Charlie the Chicken," followed by "Summer Brave," "Desperate Hours," "Mandrogola," "Two by Noonan," "Soft Touch," "Innocent Pleasures," "3 From the Marathon," "Two Part Harmony," "Bathroom Plays," "Little Victories," "Dolphin Position," "Cabal of Hypocrites," "Split Second."

DADDAZIO, NICHOLAS B. Born May 23, 1943 in Rochester, NY. Graduate SUNY/Buffalo. Debut 1977 OB in "Jockeys," followed by "The Last Chord," "The Education of One Miss February: Sharon Twane."

DALE, JIM. Born in 1936 in Rothwell, Eng. Debut 1974 OB with Young Vic Co. in "Taming of the Shrew," "Scapino" that moved to Bdwy, followed by "Barnum," "Joe Egg."

DALTON, LEZLIE. Born Aug. 12, 1952 in Boston, MA. Attended Pasadena Playhouse, UCLA. Debut 1980 OB in "Annie and Arthur" followed by "After Maigret," "Blessed Event."

DALY, JOSEPH. Born Apr. 7, 1930 in Oakland, CA. Debut 1959 OB in "Dance of Death," followed by "Roots," "Sjt. Musgrave's Dance," "Viet Rock," "Dark of the Moon," "Shadow of a Gunman," "Hamlet," "The Ride Across Lake Constance," "A Doll's House," "Native Bird," "Yeats Trio," "Mecca," "Marching to Georgia," "Comedians," "A Country for Old Men," "Falsies," "Taming of the Shrew."

DANELLE, JOHN. Born July 22, 1944 in Pittsburgh, PA. Graduate Carnegie-Mellon U. Bdwy debut 1972 in "The Sign in Sidney Brustein's Window," followed by "Tough to Get Help," OB in "Split Second," "My Old Friends."

DANIELLE, MARLENE. Born Aug. 16 in NYC. Bdwy debut 1979 in "Sarava," followed by "West Side Story," "Marlowe," "Damn Yankees" (JB), "Cats," OB in "Little Shop of Horrors."

DANIELS, LESLIE E. Born May 27, 1957 in Princeton, NJ. Graduate UPa. Debut 1985 OB in "Playboy of the Western World."

DANSON, RANDY. Born Apr. 30, 1950 in Plainfield, NJ. Graduate Carnegie-Mellon. Debut 1978 OB in "Gimme Shelter," followed by "Big and Little," "The Winter Dancers," "Time Steps," "Casualties," "Red and Blue," "The Resurrection of Lady Lester," "Jazz Poets at the Grotto," "Plenty," "Macbeth," "Blue Window."

DANTUONO, MICHAEL. Born July 30, 1942 in Providence, RI. Debut 1974 OB in "How to Get Rid of It," followed by "Maggie Flynn," "Charlotte Sweet," "Berlin to Broadway," Bdwy 1977 in "Caesar and Cleopatra," "Can-Can" ('81), "Zorba" (84), "The Three Musketeers" ('84).

DANZIGER, MAIA. Born Apr. 12, 1950. Attended NYU. Bdwy debut 1973 in "Waltz of the Toreadors," OB in "Total Eclipse," "Milk of Paradise," "The Rachel Plays."

D'ARCY, MARY. Born in 1956 in Yardville, NJ. Graduate Glassboro State Col. Bdwy debut 1980 in "The Music Man," followed by "Sunday in the Park with George," OB in "Florodora," "Upstairs at O'Neal's," "Backers Audition."

DARIO, DAVID. Born Sept. 11, 1957 in Cleveland, OH. Graduate LeMoyne Col., Catholic U. Debut 1985 OB in "A Comedy of Errors."

DARLING, CANDY. Born March 6, 1954 in Toronto, Can. Bdwy debut 1976 in "Very Good Eddie," followed by "Censored Scenes from King Kong," "Whoopee," "Dreamgirls."

DAVENPORT-RICHARDS, SCOTT. Born in 1960 in NYC. Yale Graduate. Bdwy debut 1984 in "Ma Rainey's Black Bottom."

DAVID, AMELIA. Born Aug. 3, 1958 in NYC. Graduate NYU. Debut 1984 OB in "Couple of the Year."

DAVID, DANIEL. Born May 7, 1960 in Torrance, CA. Attended Carnegie-Mellon U. Bdwy debut 1982 in "Cleavage," OB in "Very Warm for May."

DAVID, REGINA. Born in Denver, CO. Graduate UWy. Debut 1963 OB in "Six Characters in Search of an Author," followed by "Beelch," "Istanboul," "Moondreamers," "Subject to Fits," "Wedding Band," "Confetti and Italian Ice," "True West," "Tropical Fever in Key West," Trespasses."

DAVIDSON, JACK. Born July 17, 1936 in Worcester, MA. Graduate Boston U. Debut 1968 OB in "Moon for the Misbegotten," followed by "Big and Little," "Battle of Angels," "A Midsummer Night's Dream," "Hot 1 Baltimore," "A Tribute to Lili Lamont," "Ulysses in Traction," "Lulu," "Hey, Rube," "In the Recovery Lounge," "The Runner Stumbles," "Winter Signs," "Hamlet," "Mary Stuart," "Ruby Ruby Sam Sam," "The Diviners," "Marching to Georgia," "Hunting Scenes from Lower Bavaria," "Richard II," "The Great Grandson of Jedediah Kohler," "Buck," "Time Framed," "Love's Labour's Lost," "Bing and Walker," Bdwy in "Capt. Brassbound's Conversion" (1972), "Anna Christie."

DAVIS, JEFFREY BRYAN. Born Oct. 6, 1973 in Long Beach, CA. Bdwy debut 1985 in "The King and I."

DAVIS, SHEILA KAY. Born May 30, 1956 in Daytona, FL. Graduate Spelman Col. Debut 1982 OB in "Little Shop of Horrors."

DAVISH, GLENN. Born Jan. 14, 1955 in Philadelphia, PA. Debut OB 1979 in "The Fantasticks," followed by "Godspell," "You're a Good Man, Charlie Brown," "Bells Are Ringing."

DAYKIN, KYMBERLY. Born Dec. 3, 1956 in Denver, CO. Graduate UDenver. Debut 1981 OB in "Prism Blues," followed by "Under the Gaslight," "Delirious," "Running," Bdwy in "The Glass Menagerie" (1984).

DeACUTIS, WILLIAM. Born Sept. 17, 1957 in Bridgeport, CT. Juilliard graduate. Debut 1979 OB in "Spring Awakening," followed by "The Normal Heart."

DEAN, LAURA. Born May 27, 1963 in Smithtown, NY. Debut 1973 OB in "The Secret Life of Walter Mitty," followed by "A Village Romeo and Juliet," "Carousel," "Hey Rube," "Landscape of the Body," "American Passion," "Feathertop," Bdwy in "Doonesbury" (1983) for which she received a Theatre World Award.

De BANZIE, LOIS. Born May 4 in Glasgow, Scot. Bdwy debut 1966 in "Elizabeth the Queen," followed by "Da," "Morning's at 7," "The Octette Bridge Club," OB in "Little Murders," "Mary Stuart," "People Are Living There," "Ride Across Lake Constance," "The Divorce of Judy and Jane," "What the Butler Saw," "Man and Superman," "The Judas Applause," "The Dining Room."

DeFELICE, AURELIA. Born Apr. 2 in NYC. Attended Northwestern U. Debut 1968 OB in "Scarlet Lullaby," followed by "Evenings with Chekhov," "The Anniversary," "On the High Road," "The Wedding," "June Moon," "The Hostage," "The Transgressor Rides Again," "Cold Feet," "Broadway," "Neighbors," "In Agony," "The Killing of Sister George," "Love Games."

DeGANON, MATT. Born July 10, 1962 in NYC. Graduate SUNY/Purchase. Debut 1985 OB in "A New Way to Pay Old Debts," followed by "As You Like It," "The Skin of Our Teeth."

DEIGNAN, DEANNA. Born Oct. 12, 1950 in Lake Geneva, WI. Graduate MichStateU, Goodman School. Debut 1984 OB in "Enter a Free Man," followed by "Love's Labour's Lost."

DeLORENZO, MICHAEL. Born in The Bronx in 1961. Attended NY School of Ballet, HS of Performing Arts. Debut 1985 OB in "Streetheat."

DeMUNN, JEFFREY. Born Apr. 25, 1947 in Buffalo, NY. Graduate Union Col. Debut 1975 OB in "Augusta," followed by "A Prayer for My Daughter," "Modigliani," "Chekhov Sketchbook," "A Midsummer Night's Dream," "Total Abandon," "The Country Girl," Bdwy in "Comedians" (1976), "Bent," "K2."

DENNIS, RONALD. Born Oct. 2, 1944 in Dayton, OH. Debut 1966 OB in "Show Boat," followed by "Of Thee I Sing," "Moon Walk," "Please Don't Cry," Bdwy in "A Chorus Line" (1975), "My One and Only."

DeSAL, FRANK. Born Apr. 14, 1943 in White Plains, NY. Attended AmThWing. Credits include "110 in the Shade," "Marco Millions," "Sherry!," "Sweet Charity," "How Now, Dow Jones," "Fig Leaves Are Falling," "Bring Back Birdie," "Zorba" (1983), OB in "Anything Goes."

DeSHIELDS, ANDRE. Born Jan. 12, 1946 in Baltimore, MD. Graduate UWi. Bdwy debut 1973 in "Warp," followed by "Rachel Lily Rosenbloom," "The Wiz," "Ain't Misbehavin'," "Haarlem Nocturne," OB in "2008½," "Jazzbo Brown," "The Soldier's Tale," "The Little Prince," "Haarlem Nocturne."

DEVINE, LORETTA. Born Aug. 21 in Houston, TX. Graduate UHouston, Brandeis U. Bdwy debut 1977 in "Hair," followed by "A Broadway Musical," "Dreamgirls," OB in "Godsong," "Lion and the Jewel," "Karma," "The Blacks," "Mahalia."

DeVITO, KARLA. Born in 1953 in Oak Lawn, IL. Attended Loyola U. Debut 1974 OB in "El Grande de Coca Cola," followed by "Jubilee," "A Midsummer Night's Dream," Bdwy in "The Pirates of Penzance" (1981), "Big River."

DEVLIN, JAY. Born May 8, 1929 in Ft. Dodge, IA. OB in "The Mad Show," "Little Murders," "Unfair to Goliath," "Ballymurphy," "Front Page," "Fasnacht Day," "Bugles at Dawn," "A Good Year for the Roses," "Crossing the Bar," Bdwy 1978 in "King of Hearts."

DeVRIES, JON. Born Mar. 26, 1947 in NYC. Graduate Bennington Col., Pasadena Playhouse. Debut 1977 OB in "The Cherry Orchard," followed by "Agamemnon," "The Ballad of Soapy Smith," Bdwy in "The Inspector General," "Devour the Snow," "Major Barbara."

DIAMOND, BOB. Born May 10, 1941 in NYC. Attended ACT/San Francisco. Debut 1971 OB in "One Flew over the Cuckoo's Nest," followed by "Les Femme Noire," "The Hollow."

DiCARLO, JOHN. Born Jan. 25, 1958 in Kankakee, IL. Graduate AADA. Debut 1985 OB in "The Mugger."

DIETRICH, MARC. Born Nov. 12, 1951 in Fontana, CA. Graduate CSU/San Bernardino. Debut 1985 OB in "The Madwoman of Chaillot."

DiGIOIA, MICHAEL. Born July 26, 1962 in Niles, IL. Graduate SUNY/Purchase. Debut 1984 OB in "Cricket on the Hearth," followed by "Madwoman of Chaillot," "Vivat! Vivat Regina!"

DILLION, MIA. Born July 9, 1955 in Colorado Springs, CO. Graduate Penn State U. Bdwy debut 1977 in "Equus," followed by "Da," "Once a Catholic," "Crimes of the Heart," "The Corn Is Green," OB in "The Crucible," "Summer," "Waiting for the Parade," "Crimes of the Heart," "Fables for Friends," "Scenes from La Vie de Boheme," "Three Sisters." "Wednesday," "Roberta in Concert," "Come Back, Little Sheba," "Vienna Notes."

DiNOVI, ANTHONY. Born Aug. 13 in NYC. Attended San Francisco State U. Debut OB 1984 in "Flesh, Flash and Frank Harris."

DiPASQUALE, FRANK J. Born July 15, 1955 in Whitestone, NY. Graduate USC. Bdwy debut 1983 in "La Cage aux Folles."

DISHY, BOB. Born in Brooklyn, NY. Graduate Syracuse U. Bdwy debut 1955 in "Damn Yankees," followed by "Can-Can," "Flora the Red Menace," "Something Different," "The Goodbye People," "A Way of Life," "Creation of the World and Other Business," "American Millionaire," "Sly Fox," "Murder at the Howard Johnson's," "Grownups," OB in "Chic," "When the Owl Screams," "Wrecking Ball," "By Jupiter," "The Unknown Soldier and His Wife," "What's Wrong with This Picture?"

DIXON, ED. Born Sept. 2, 1948 in Oklahoma. Attended OkU. Bdwy in "The Student Prince," followed by "No, No, Nanette," "Rosalie in Concert," "The Three Musketeers," OB in "By Bernstein," "King of the Schnorrers."

DODSON, COLLEEN. Born June 29, 1954 in Chicago, IL. Graduate UIl. Debut 1981 OB in "The Matinee Kids," followed by "Pal Joey," "Holding Patterns," Bdwy 1982 in "Nine."

DODSON, JACK. Born May 16, 1931 in Pittsburgh, PA. Graduate Carnegie-Mellon U. Debut 1957 OB in "The Country Wife," followed by "Our Town," "The Balcony," "Under Milk Wood," "Infancy," "Six Characters in Search of an Author," Bdwy in "Hughie" (1964), "You Can't Take It with You."

DOEMLING, BRANDON E. Born Dec. 17, 1958 in Philadelphia, PA. Graduate Westchester State Col. Debut 1985 OB in "Madwoman of Chaillot," followed by "Vivat! Vivat Regina!"

DON, CARL. Born Dec. 15, 1916 in Vitebsk, Russia. Attended Western Reserve U. Bdwy debut 1954 in "Anastasia," followed by "Romanoff and Juliet," "Dear Me, the Sky Is Falling," "The Relapse," "The Tenth Man," "Zalmen," "Wings," OB in "Richard III," "Twelfth Night," "Winterset," "Arms and the Man," "Between Two Thieves," "He Who Gets Slapped," "Jacobowsky and the Colonel," "Carnival," "The Possessed," "Three Acts of Recognition," "The Golem."

DONAHOE, JOHN. Born June 17, 1948 in Norfolk, VA. Graduate UVa. Debut 1985 OB in "Deathtrap."

DORAN, JESSE. Born June 23. Attended AMDA. Bdwy debut 1976 in "The Runner Stumbles," OB in "Goose and Tom-Tom," "Fool for Love," "Spookhouse," "Snowman."

DORFMAN, ROBERT. Born Oct. 8, 1950 in Brooklyn, NY. Attended CUNY, HB Studio. Debut 1979 OB in "Say Goodnight, Gracie," followed by "America Kicks," "Winterplay," "The Normal Heart."

DOTRICE, ROY. Born May 26, 1925 in Guernsey, Channel Islands. Bdwy debut 1967 in "Brief Lives," a return engagement in 1974, "Mr. Lincoln," "A Life," OB in "An Enemy of the People."

DOUGHERTY, J. P. Born July 25, 1953 in Lincoln, IL. Attended S.Ill.U. Debut 1982 OB in "The Frances Farmer Story," followed by "The Little Prince," "The Sound of Music," "The Trojan Women," "Tropical Fever in Key West," "Have I Got a Girl for You," Bdwy in "The Three Musketeers" (1984).

DOUGLAS, LUCIEN. (formerly Lucien Zabielski) Born Aug. 5, 1949 in Torrington, CT. Graduate UCt., RADA. Debut 1972 OB in "Hope Is the Thing with Feathers," followed by "Naked," "Under Milk Wood," "The Tempest," "Candida," "Lulu," Bdwy in "Medea" (1982).

DOUGLASS, PI. Born in Sharon, CT. Attended Boston Consv. Bdwy debut 1969 in "Fig Leaves Are Falling," followed by "Hello, Dolly!," "Georgy," "Purlie," "Ari," "Jesus Christ Superstar," "Selling of the President," "The Wiz," "La Cage aux Folles," OB in "Of Thee I Sing," "Under Fire," "The Ritz," "Blackberries," "Dementos."

DOYLE, KATHLEEN. Born Nov. 7, 1947 in Hyattsville, Md. Graduate Goodman School. Debut 1971 with LCRep in "Ride across Lake Constance," "Mary Stuart," "Twelfth Night" and "The Crucible," Bdwy in "The Odd Couple" (1985).

DRUMMOND, ALICE. Born May 21, 1929 in Pawtucket, RI. Attended Pembroke Col. Bdwy debut 1963 in "Ballad of the Sad Cafe," followed by "Malcolm," "The Chinese," "Thieves," "Summer Brave," "Some of My Best Friends," "You Can't Take It With You," OB in "Royal Gambit," "Go Show Me a Dragon," "Sweet of You to Say So," "Gallows Humor," "American Dream," "Giants' Dance," "Carpenters," "Charles Abbot & Son," "God Says There Is No Peter Ott," "Enter a Free Man," "Memory of Two Mondays," "Secret Service," "Boy Meets Girl," "Savages," "Killings On the Last Line," "Knuckle," "Wonderland," "Endgame."

DUDLEY, CRAIG. Born Jan. 22, 1945 in Sheepshead Bay, NY. Graduate AADA, AmThWing. Debut 1970 OB in "Macbeth," followed by "Zou," "Othello," "War and Peace," "Dial 'M' for Murder."

DUELL, WILLIAM. Born Aug. 30 in Corinth, NY. Attended IllWesleyan, Yale. OB in "Portrait of an Artist. . .," "Barroom Monks," "A Midsummer Night's Dream," "Henry IV," "Taming of the Shrew," "The Memorandum," "Threepenny Opera," "Loves of Cass McGuire," "Romance Language," Bdwy in "A Cook for Mr. General," "Ballad of the Sad Cafe," "Ilya, Darling," "1776," "Kings," "Stages," "The Inspector General."

DUFF-MacCORMICK, CARA. Born Dec. 12 in Woodstock, Can. Attended AADA. Debut 1969 OB in "Love Your Crooked Neighbor," followed by "The Wager," "Macbeth," "A Musical Merchant of Venice," "Ladyhouse Blues," "The Philanderer," "Bonjour, La, Bonjour," "Journey to Gdansk," "The Dining Room," "All the Nice People," "Faulkner's Bicycle," Bdwy in "Moonchildren" (1972) for which she received a Theatre World Award, "Out Cry," "Animals."

DUKAKIS, OLYMPIA. Born in Lowell, MA. Debut 1960 OB in "The Breaking Wall," followed by "Nourish the Beast," "Curse of the Starving Class," "Snow Orchid," "The Marriage of Bette and Boo," Bdwy in "The Aspern Papers" (1962), "Abraham Cochrane," "Who's Who in Hell."

DUMMETT, AUDREY. Born Apr. 22, 1919 in NYC. Graduate UMinn., AADA. Debut 1946 OB in "Juno and the Paycock," followed by "Riders to the Sea," "Strivers Row," "Things Happen But They Change," "Mirrors."

DUNCAN, SANDY. Born Feb. 20, 1946 in Henderson, TX. Attended Len Morris Col. Debut 1965 in CC's revivals of "The Music Man," "Carousel," "Finian's Rainbow," "Sound of Music," "Wonderful Town" and "Life with Father," OB in "Ceremony of Innocence" for which she received a Theatre World Award, "Your Own Thing," Bdwy in "Canterbury Tales" (1969), "Love Is a Time of Day," "The Boy Friend" (1970), "Peter Pan" (1979), "5–6–7–8 Dance," "My One and Only."

DUNDAS, JENNIFER. Born Jan. 14, 1971 in Boston, MA. Bdwy debut 1981 in "Grownups," OB in "Before the Dawn."

DUNSHEATH, LISA. Born March 15 in Trenton, MI. Debut 1984 OB in "After the Fall."

DURAN, MICHAEL J. Born Nov. 25, 1953 in Denver, CO. Graduate UCo. Debut 1981 OB in "Godspell," followed by "Anonymous."

DUTTON, CHARLES S. Born Jan. 30, 1951 in Baltimore, MD. Graduate Yale U. Debut 1983 OB in "Richard III," Bdwy in "Ma Rainey's Black Bottom" (1984) for which he received a Theatre World Award.

EASTON, EDWARD. Born Oct. 21, 1942 in Moline, IL. Graduate Lincoln Col., UIll., Neighborhood Playhouse. Debut 1967 OB in "Party on Greenwich Avenue," followed by "Middle of the Night," "Summer Brave," "Sunday Afternoon," "The Education of One Miss February."

EBERT, JOYCE. Born June 26, 1933 in Homestead, PA. Graduate Carnegie Tech. Debut 1956 OB in "Liliom," followed by "Sing of Winter," "Asmodee," "King Lear," "Hamlet," "Under Milk Wood," "Trojan Women," "White Devil," "Tartuffe," Bdwy in "Solitaire/Double Solitaire" (1971), "The Shadow Box," "Watch on the Rhine" (1980), "Requiem for a Heavyweight."

ECKHOUSE, JAMES. Born Feb. 14, 1955 in Chicago, IL. Graduate Juilliard. Bdwy debut 1982 in "Beyond Therapy," OB in "The Rise and Rise of Daniel Rocker," "Geniuses," "In the Country," "Sister Mary Ignatius Explains It All," "Dubliners," "The Ballad of Soapy Smith."

EDE, GEORGE. Born Dec. 22, 1931 in San Francisco, CA. Bdwy debut 1969 in "A Flea in Her Ear," followed by "Three Sisters," "The Changing Room," "The Visit," "Chemin de Fer," "Holiday," "Love for Love," "Rules of the Game," "A Member of the Wedding," "Lady from the Sea," "A Touch of the Poet," "Philadelphia Story," "Aren't We All?," OB in "The Philanderer," "The American Clock," "The Broken Pitcher," "No End of Blame," "Sullivan and Gilbert."

EDEIKEN, LOUISE. Born June 23, 1956 in Philadelphia, PA. Graduate GeoWashU. Bdwy debut 1982 in "Nine," OB in "Weekend," "Jacques Brel Is Alive . . .," "Ladies and Gentlemen, Jerome Kern."

EDENFIELD, DENNIS. Born July 23, 1946 in New Orleans, LA. Debut 1970 OB in "The Evil That Men Do," followed by "I Have Always Believed in Ghosts," "Nevertheless They Laugh," Bdwy in "Irene" ('73), "A Chorus Line."

EDMEAD, WENDY. Born July 6, 1956 in NYC. Graduate NYCU. Bdwy debut 1974 in "The Wiz," followed by "Stop the World . . .," "America," "Dancin'," "Encore," "Cats."

EDWARDS, BRANDT. Born Mar. 22, 1947 in Holly Springs, MS. Graduate UMiss. NY debut off and on Bdwy 1975 in "A Chorus Line."

EDWARDS, BURT. Born Jan. 11, 1928 in Richmond, VA. Graduate UVa. Debut 1949 OB in "Fifth Horseman of the Apocalypse," followed by "Cenci," Bdwy 1985 in "The King and I."

EDWARDS, RANDALL. Born June 15 in Atlanta, Ga. Attended CalInst of Arts. Debut 1983 OB in "Upstairs at O'Neal's." Bdwy 1985 in "Biloxi Blues."

EDWARDS, SUSAN. Born Aug. 14, 1950 in Levittown, NY. Graduate Hofstra U. Bdwy debut 1976 in "Bubbling Brown Sugar," followed by "The Suicide," "Torch Song Trilogy," OB in "Jazz Babies," "Boys from Syracuse," "Scrambled Feet."

ELDREDGE, LYNN. Born July 25, 1955 in Holden, MA. Graduate San Francisco State U. Debut 1982 OB in "Charlotte Sweet," followed by "Hollywood Opera."

ELIOT, DREW. Born in Newark, NJ. Graduate Columbia, RADA. OB in "The Fairy Garden," "Dr. Faustus," "Servant of Two Masters," "Henry V," "Stephen D," "Sjt. Musgrave's Dance," "Deadly Game," "Taming of the Shrew," Bdwy in "Elizabeth the Queen," "The Physicists," "Romulus."

ELLIOTT, PATRICIA. Born July 21,1942 in Gunnison, CO. Graduate U. Colo., London Academy. Debut with LCRep 1968 in "King Lear," and "A Cry of Players," followed OB in "Henry V," "The Persians," "A Doll's House," "Hedda Gabler," "In Case of Accident," "Water Hen," "Polly," "But Not for Me," "By Bernstein," "Prince of Homburg," "Artichokes," "Wine Untouched," "Misalliance," "Virginia," "Sung and Unsung Sondheim," "Voice of the Turtle," Bdwy bow 1973 in "A Little Night Music" for which she received a Theatre World Award, followed by "The Shadow Box," "Tartuffe," "13 Rue de L'Amour," "The Elephant Man."

ELLIS, FRASER. Born May 1, 1957 in Boulder, CO. Graduate UCo. Bdwy debut 1982 in "A Chorus Line."

ELLIS, WILLIAM. Born Dec. 5, 1929 near Cincinnati, OH. Graduate Goodman School, Columbia, NYU. Debut 1953 OB in "One Foot to the Sea," followed by "Murder in the Cathedral," "Hill of Beans," "Rags to Ruebens," "Hidden Away in Stores," "Today's Children," "The Marriage Proposal," "Much Ado about Nothing," "Writers," "A Doll's House."

ELMORE, STEVE. Born July 12, 1936 in Niangua, MO. Debut 1961 in "Madame Aphrodite," followed by "Golden Apple," "Enclave," Bdwy in "Camelot," "Jenny," "Fade in Fade Out," "Kelly," "Company," "Nash at 9," "Chicago," "42nd St."

EMCH, GEORGE K. Born Oct. 18, 1927 in Poland, OH. Attended New School. Debut 1957 OB in "Macbeth," followed by "Redhead," "How to Succeed in Business . . .," "Up in Central Park," "Ragtime Blues," "Bells Are Ringing," Bdwy in "Capt. Brassbound's Conversion" (1972).

EMMET, ROBERT. Born Oct. 3, 1952 in Denver, CO. Graduate UWash. Debut 1976 OB in "The Mousetrap," followed by "The Seagull," "Blue Hotel," "Miss Jairus," "Hamlet," "Deathwatch," "Much Ado About Nothing," "Songs and Ceremonies," "Mass Appeal," "Macbeth," "Bell, Book and Candle," "Comes the Happy Hour," "The Gift." "Merchant of Venice," "Arms and the Man."

ENGEL, DAVID. Born Oct. 19, 1959 in Orange, CA. Attended UCal/Irvine. Bdwy debut 1983 in "La Cage aux Folles."

ENGLE, DEBRA. Born July 4, 1953 in Baltimore, MD. Graduate IllWesleyanU. Debut 1984 OB in "Balm in Gilead."

EPSTEIN, ALVIN. Born May 14, 1925 in NYC. Attended Queens Col. Appeared on Bdwy with Marcel Marceau, and in "King Lear," "Waiting for Godot" (1956), "From A to Z," "No Strings," "Passion of Josef D," "Postmark Zero," "A Kurt Weill Cabaret," OB in "Purple Dust," "Pictures in a Hallway," "Clerambard," "Endgame," (1958/1984), "Whores, Wares and Tin Pan Alley," "A Place without Doors," "Crossing Niagara," "Beckett Plays." "Kurt Weill Cabaret."

EPSTEIN, PIERRE. Born July 27, 1930 in Toulouse, FR. Graduate UParis; Bdwy debut 1962 in "A Shot in the Dark," followed by "Enter Laughing," "Bajour," "Black Comedy," "Thieves," "Fun City," "Filumena," "Plenty," OB in "Incident in Vichy," "Threepenny Opera," "Too Much Johnson," "Second City," "People vs Ranchman," "Promenade," "Cake with Wine," "Little Black Sheep," "Comedy of Errors," "A Memory of Two Mondays," "They Knew What They Wanted," "Museum," "The Bright and Golden Land," "Manny," "God Bless You, Mr. Rosewater," "The Itch," "Breakfast Conversations in Miami," "The Ballad of Soapy Smith."

ERICKSON, CLARIS. Born Dec. 13, 1940 in Aurora, IL. Graduate Northwestern U., Edinburgh U. Debut 1962 OB in "Little Eyolf," followed by "A Tribute to Lili Lamont," "As Is," Bdwy 1985 in "As Is."

ESPOSITO, GIANCARLO. Born Apr. 26, 1958 in Copenhagen, Den. Bdwy debut 1968 in "Maggie Flynn," followed by "The Me Nobody Knows," "Lost In the Stars," "Seesaw," "Merrily We Roll Along," OB in "Zooman and the Sign" for which he received a Theatre World Award, "Keyboard," "Who Loves the Dancer," "House of Ramon Iglesias," "Do Lord Remember Me," "Balm in Gilead."

ESTEY, SUELLEN. Born Nov. 21 in Mason City, IA. Graduate Stephens Col., Northwestern U. Debut 1970 OB in "Some Other Time," followed by "June Moon," "Buy Bonds Buster," "Smile, Smile, Smile," "Carousel," "The Lullaby of Broadway," "I Can't Keep Running," "The Guys in the Truck," "Stop the World . . .," Bdwy 1972 in "The Selling of the President," followed by "Barnum," "Sweethearts in Concert."

EVANS, PETER. Born May 27, 1950 in Englewood, NJ. Graduate Yale, London Central School of Speech. Debut OB 1975 in "Life Class," followed by "Streamers," "A Life in the Theatre," "Don Juan Comes Back From the War," "The American Clock," "Geniuses," "Transfiguration of Benno Blimpie," "Endgame," "Total Eclipse," Bdwy in "Night and Day" (1979) "Children of a Lesser God."

EVERHART, REX. Born June 13, 1920 in Watseka, IL. Graduate UMo, NYU. Bdwy debut 1955 in "No Time for Sergeants," followed by "Tall Story," "Moonbirds," "Tenderloin," "A Matter of Position," "Rainy Day in Newark," "Skyscraper," "How Now Dow Jones," "1776," "The Iceman Cometh," "Chicago," "Working," "Woman of the Year," OB in "Playboy of the Western World."

EVERS, BRIAN. Born Feb. 14, 1942 in Miami, FL. Graduate Capital U, UMiami. Debut 1979 OB in "How's the House?," followed by "Details of the 16th Frame," "Divine Fire," "Silent Night, Lonely Night," "Uncommon Holidays," "The Tamer Tamed."

EWING, J. TIMOTHY. Born Apr. 3, 1954 in Evansville, IN. Graduate Indiana U. Debut 1983 OB in "Colette Collage," followed by "Promenade," "Pacific Overtures."

EXLINE, CYNTHIA. Born Nov. 22, 1950 in Gladewater, TX. Graduate OkStateU. Debut 1972 OB in "Chamber Music," followed by "Small Craft Warnings," "Anais," "Alma, the Ghost of Spring Street," "The Birthday," "Bremen Coffee," "Moon Cries," "Snow Blind," "Scalp and Dreams," "Stud Silo."

FALKENHAIN, PATRICIA. Born Dec. 3, 1926 in Atlanta, GA. Graduate Carnegie-Mellon, NYU. Debut 1946 OB in "Juno and the Paycock," followed by "Hamlet," "She Stoops to Conquer," "Peer Gynt," "Henry IV," "The Plough and the Stars," "Lysistrata," "Beaux Stratagem," "The Power and the Glory," "M. Amilcar," "Home," "The Marriage of Bette and Boo," Bdwy in "Waltz of the Toreadors," "The Utter Glory of Morrissey Hall," "Once a Catholic."

FANCY, RICHARD. Born Aug. 2, 1943 in Evanston, IL. Attended LAMDA. Debut 1973 OB in "The Creeps," followed by "Kind Lady," "Rites of Passage," "A Limb of Snow," "The Meeting," "Child's Play."

FARWELL, JONATHAN. Born Jan. 9, 1932 in Lansing, MI. Graduate Ithaca Col., Yale. Debut 1961 OB in "A Midsummer Night's Dream," followed by "Home Remedies," Bdwy in "Morning's at 7" (1980), "Amadeus," "The King and I" (1985).

FASS, ROBERT. Born Aug. 15, 1958 in Wantagh, NY. Graduate MacAlester Col. Debut 1984 OB in "The Desk Set."

FAYE, JOEY. Born July 12, 1910 in NYC. Bdwy debut 1938 in "Sing Out the News," followed by "Room Service," "Meet the People," "The Man Who Came to Dinner," "The Milky Way," "Boy Meets Girl," "Streets of Paris," "Allah Be Praised," "The Duchess Misbehaves," "Tidbits of 1948," "High Button Shoes," "Top Banana," "Tender Trap," "Man of LaMancha," "70 Girls 70," "Grind," OB in "Lyle," "Naomi Court," "Awake and Sing," "Coolest Cat in Town," "The Ritz," "Enter Laughing."

FEAGAN, LESLIE. Born Jan. 9, 1951 in Hinckley, OH. Graduate OhU. Debut 1978 OB in "Can-Can," followed by "Merton of the Movies," "Promises Promises," "Mowgli."

FELDON, BARBARA. Born Mar. 12, 1941 in Pittsburgh, PA. Attended Carnegie Tech. Bdwy debut 1960 in "Caligula," followed by "Past Tense," OB in "Faces of Love/Portrait of America."

FELDSHUH, TOVAH. Born Dec. 27, 1953 in NYC. Graduate Sarah Lawrence Col., UMn. Bdwy debut 1973 in "Cyrano," followed by "Dreyfus in Rehearsal," "Rodgers and Hart," "Yentl" for which she received a Theatre World Award, "Sarava," OB in "Yentl the Yeshiva Boy," "Straws in the Wind," "Three Sisters," "She Stoops to Conquer," "Springtime for Henry."

FIEDLER, JOHN. Born Feb. 3, 1925 in Plateville, WI. Attended Neighborhood Playhouse. OB in "The Seagull," "Sing Me No Lullaby," "The Terrible Swift Sword," "The Raspberry Picker," "The Frog Prince," Bdwy in "One Eye Closed," "Howie," "Raisin in the Sun," "Harold," "The Odd Couple," "Our Town."

FIERSTEIN, HARVEY. Born June 6, 1954 in Brooklyn, NY. Graduate Pratt Inst. Debut 1971 OB in "Pork," followed by "International Stud," "Figure In a Nursery," Bdwy 1982 in "Torch Song Trilogy," for which he received a Theatre World Award.

FINARD, SAUNDER. Born Aug. 14, 1919 in Boston, MA. Graduate Lowell U, URochester. Debut 1984 OB in "American Power Play," followed by "King Lear."

FINKEL, FYVUSH. Born Oct. 9, 1922 in Brooklyn, NY. Bdwy debut 1970 in "Fiddler On the Roof" (also 1981 revival), OB in "Gorky," "Little Shop of Horrors."

FIORDELLISI, ANGELINA. Born Mar. 15, 1955 in Detroit, MI. Graduate UDetroit. Bdwy debut 1983 in "Zorba."

FIRE, NORMA. Born June 9, 1937 in Brooklyn, NY. Graduate Bklyn Col. Debut 1982 OB in "3 Acts of Recognition," followed by "Merry Wives of Windsor," "Henry V," "It's All Talk."

FITZGERALD, FERN. Born Jan. 7, 1947 in Valley Stream, NY. Bdwy debut 1976 in "Chicago," followed by "A Chorus Line."

FLAGG, TOM. Born Mar. 30 in Canton, OH. Attended KentStateU, AADA. Debut 1975 OB in "The Fantasticks," followed by "Give Me Liberty," "The Subject Was Roses," "Lola," "Red, Hot and Blue," "Episode 26," Bdwy in "Legend" (1976), "Shenandoah," "Players."

FLANAGAN, KIT. Born July 6 in Pittsburgh, PA. Graduate Northwestern U. Debut 1979 OB in "The Diary of Anne Frank," followed by "An Evening with Dorothy Parker," "Still Life," "Cloud 9," "Alto Part," "A Step Out of Line."

FLANAGAN, PAULINE. Born June 29, 1925 in Sligo, Ire. Debut 1958 OB in "Ulysses in Nighttown," followed by "Pictures in the Hallway," "Later," "Antigone," "The Crucible," "The Plough and the Stars," "Summer," "Close of Play," "In Celebration," Bdwy in "God and Kate Murphy," "The Living Room," "The Innocents," "The Father," "Medea," "Steaming."

FLEISS, JANE. Born Jan. 28 in NYC. Graduate NYU. Debut 1979 OB in "Say Goodnight, Gracie," followed by "Grace," "The Beaver Coat," "The Harvesting," "D.," Bdwy in "5th of July" (1981), "Crimes of the Heart."

FLETCHER, JACK. Born Apr. 21, 1921 in Forest Hills, NY. Attended Yale. Bdwy debut 1947 in "Trial Honeymoon," followed by "She Stoops to Conquer," "Romeo and Juliet," "Ben Franklin in Paris," "Drat! The Cat!," "Lysistrata," "Lorelei," "Sugar Babies," "Can-Can," "Cyrano," "Wonderful Town," OB in "Comic Strip," "Way of the World," "Thieves' Carnival," "The Amorous Flea," "American Hamburger League," "The Time of Your Life," "Music Man" (JB), "Downriver."

FLOREK, DAVE. Born May 19, 1953 in Dearborn, MI. Graduate Eastern MiU. Debut 1976 OB in "The Collection," followed by "Richard III," "Much Ado About Nothing," "Young Bucks," "Big Apple Messenger," "Death of a Miner," "Marvelous Gray," "Journey to Gdansk," "The Last of Hitler," "Thin Ice," "The Incredibly Famous Willy Rivers," "Responsible Parties," "For Sale," Bdwy 1980 in "Nuts."

FOLLANSBEE, JULIE. Born in Sept. of 1919 in Chicago, IL. Graduate Bryn Mawr. Debut 1949 OB in "The Fifth Horseman," followed by "Luminosity without Radiance," "Johnny Doesn't Live Here Anymore," "Epitaph for George Dillon," "Maromichaelis," "Brothers Karamazov," "Excelsior," "In the Summer House," "Road to the Graveyard," "Day of the Dolphin," "Bell, Book and Candle," "Crime and Punishment."

FORBES, BRENDA. Born Jan. 14, 1909 in London, Eng. Bdwy debut 1931 in "The Barretts of Wimpole Street," followed by "Candida," "Lucrece," "Flowers of the Forest," "Pride and Prejudice," "Storm over Patsy," "Heartbreak House," "One for the Money," "Two for the Show," "Three to Make Ready," "Yesterday's Magic," "Morning Star," "Suds in Your Eyes," "Quadrille," "The Reluctant Debutante," "Loves of Cass McGuire," "Darling of the Day," "The Constant Wife," "My Fair Lady," "Aren't We All?," OB in "Busybody," "Pygmalion in Concert."

FORD, CLEBERT. Born Jan 29, 1932 in Brooklyn, NY. Graduate CCNY, Boston U. Bdwy debut 1960 in "The Cool World," followed by "Les Blancs," "Ain't Supposed to Die a Natural Death," "Via Galactica," "Bubbling Brown Sugar," "The Last Minstrel Show," OB in "Romeo and Juliet," "The Blacks," "Antony and Cleopatra," "Ti-Jean and His Brothers," "Ballad for Bimshire," "Daddy," "Gilbeau," "Coriolanus," "Before the Flood," "The Lion and the Jewel," "Branches from the Same Tree," "Dreams Deferred," "Basin Street," "20 Year Friends," "Celebration."

FORD, FRANCES. Born Nov. 10, 1939 in Appleton, WI. Graduate UWis. Debut 1964 OB in "A Midsummer Night's Dream," followed by "The Importance of Being Earnest," "She Stoops to Conquer," "The Maids," "Howling in the Night," "The Marquise," "Lulu," Bdwy in "The Stingiest Man in Town" (1971).

FORD, RUTH. Born July 7, 1915 in Hazelhurst, MS. Bdwy debut 1938 in "Shoemaker's Holiday," followed by "Danton's Death," "Swinging' the Dream," "No Exit," "This Time Tomorrow," "Clutterbuck," "House of Bernarda Alba," "Island of Goats," "Requiem for a Nun," "The Milk Train Doesn't Stop Here Anymore," "Grass Harp," "Harold and Maude," OB in "The Glass Slipper," "Miss Julie," "Madame de Sade," "A Breeze from the Gulf," "Confluence," "Outward Bound."

FORD, SPENCE. Born Feb. 25, 1954 in Richmond, VA. Attended UVa. Debut 1976 OB in "Follies," followed by "Pal Joey," Bdwy in "King of Hearts," "Carmelina," "Peter Pan," "Copperfield," "Dancin'," "Merlin," "La Cage aux Folles."

FORD, SUZANNE. Born Sept. 22, 1949 in Auburn, NY. Attended Ithaca Col., Eastman Sch. Debut 1973 OB in "Fashion," followed by "El Grande de Coca-Cola," "Tenderloin," "A Man between Twilights," "Under the Gaslight," "Mandrake," "Crimes of Vautrin."

FORSYTHE, HENDERSON. Born Sept. 11, 1917 in Macon, MO. Attended UIowa. Debut 1956 OB in "The Iceman Cometh," followed by "The Collection," "The Room," "A Slight Ache," "Happiness Cage," "Waiting for Godot," "In Case of Accident," "Not I," "An Evening With the Poet-Senator," "Museum," "How Far Is It to Babylon," "Wild Life," "Other Places," "Cliffhanger," "Broadcast Baby," "After the Fall,"Bdwy in "The Cellar and the Well" (1950), "Miss Lonelyhearts," "Who's Afraid of Virginia Woolf?," "Malcolm," "Right Honourable Gentleman," "Delicate Balance," "Birthday Party," "Harvey," "Engagement Baby," "Freedom of the City," "Texas Trilogy," "Best Little Whorehouse in Texas."

FOSTER, FRANCES. Born June 11 in Yonkers, NY. Bdwy debut 1955 in "The Wisteria Trees," followed by "Nobody Loves an Albatross," "Raisin in the Sun," "The River Niger," "First Breeze of Summer," OB in "Take a Giant Step," "Edge of the City," "Tammy and the Doctor," "The Crucible," "Happy Ending," "Day of Absence," "An Evening of One Acts," "Man Better Man," "Brotherhood," "Akokawe," "Rosalee Pritchett," "Sty of the Blind Pig," "Ballet Behind the Bridge," "Good Woman of Setzuan" (LC), "Behold! Cometh the Vanderkellans," "Origin," "Boesman and Lena," "Do Lord Remember Me," "Henrietta," "Welcome to Black River."

FOWLER, CLEMENT. Born Dec. 27, 1924 in Detroit, MI. Graduate Wayne State U. Bdwy debut 1951 in "Legend of Lovers," followed by "The Cold Wind and the Warm," "Fragile Fox," "The Sunshine Boys," "Hamlet (1964)," OB in "The Eagle Has Two Heads," "House Music," "Transfiguration of Benno Blimpie," "The Inheritors," "Paradise Lost."

FOX, COLIN. Born Nov. 20, 1938 in Aldershot, Can. Attended UWestern Ontario. Bdwy debut 1968 in "Soldiers," followed by "Pack of Lies," OB in "The Importance of Being Earnest," "Declassee," "Love's Labour's Lost."

FRANCO, RAMON. Born Sept. 12, 1963 in Caguas, PR. Attended Bard Col. Debut 1979 OB in "Sancocho," followed by "Mio," "The Sun Always Shines for the Cook," "Pizza King," "The Lunch Girls."

FRANKLIN, NANCY. Born in NYC. Debut 1959 OB in "Buffalo Skinner," followed by "Power of Darkness," "Oh, Dad, Poor Dad. . .," "Theatre of Peretz," "Seven Days of Mourning," "Here Be Dragons," "Beach Children," "Safe Place," "Innocent Pleasures," "Loves of Cass McGuire," "After the Fall," "Bloodletters," Bdwy in "Never Live over a Pretzel Factory" (1964), "Happily Never After," "The White House," "Charlie and Algernon."

FRANZ, ELIZABETH. Born June 18, 1941 in Akron, OH. Attended AADA. Debut 1965 OB in "In White America," followed by "One Night Stands of a Noisy Passenger," "The Real Inspector Hound," "Augusta," "Yesterday Is Over," "Actor's Nightmare," "Sister Mary Ignatius Explains It All," Bdwy in "Rosencrantz and Guildenstern Are Dead," "The Cherry Orchard," "Brighton Beach Memoirs," "The Octette Bridge Club."

FRASER, BERT. Born Mar. 20, 1940 in Rocky Ford, CO. Graduate UDenver. OB in "The Real Wife Beater," "Life with Father," "The Gang's All Here," "Night of January 16," "The Baker's Wife."

FRATANTONI, DIANE. Born Mar. 29, 1956 in Wilmington, DE. Bdwy debut 1979 in "A Chorus Line," followed by "Cats."

FRAZER, SUSANNA. Born Mar. 28 in NYC. Debut 1980 OB in "Kind Lady," followed by "The Enchanted," "A Doll's House," "Scenes from American Life," "Old Friends and Roommates," "Something Old, Something New."

FREED, SAM. Born Aug. 29, 1948 in York, PA. Graduate PennStateU. Debut 1972 OB in "The Proposition," followed by "What's a Nice Country Like You. . . .," "Dance on a Country Grave," Bdwy in "Candide" (1974), "Torch Song Trilogy."

FREEMAN, MORGAN. Born June 1, 1937 in Memphis, TN. Attended LACC. Bdwy bow 1967 in "Hello, Dolly!" followed by "The Mighty Gents," OB in "Ostrich Feathers," "Niggerlovers," "Exhibition," "Black Visions," "Cockfight," "White Pelicans," "Julius Caesar," "Coriolanus," "Mother Courage," "The Connection," "The World of Ben Caldwell," "Buck," "The Gospel at Colonus," "Medea and the Doll."

FRENCH, ARTHUR. Born in NYC. Attended Brooklyn Col. Debut 1962 OB in "Raisin Hell in the Sun," followed by "Ballad of Bimshire," "Day of Absence," "Happy Ending," "Jonah," "Black Girl," "Ceremonies in Dark Old Men," "An Evening of One Acts," "Man Better Man," "Brotherhood," "Perry's Mission," "Rosalee Pritchett," "Moonlight Arms," "Dark Tower," "Brownsville Raid," "Nevis Mt. Dew," "Julius Caesar," "Friends," "Court of Miracles," "The Beautiful La-Salles," Bdwy in "Ain't Supposed to Die a Natural Death," "The Iceman Cometh," "All God's Chillun Got Wings," "The Resurrection of Lady Lester," "You Can't Take It With You," "Design for Living," "Ma Rainey's Black Bottom."

FRIEDLAND, HOWARD. Born July 1, 1959 in Springfield, IL. Attended IndU., graduate Goodman School. Debut 1985 OB in "The Comedy of Errors."

FRISCH, RICHARD. Born May 9, 1933 in NYC. Graduate Juilliard. Bdwy debut 1964 in "The Passion of Josef D," followed by "Fade Out-Fade In," OB in "Jonah," "Antigone," "The Mother of Us All," "Up from Paradise," "Pere Goriot."

FUJII, TIMM. Born May 26, 1952 in Detroit, MI. Attended CalStateU. Bdwy debut in "Pacific Overtures" (1976), OB in "Pacific Overtures" (1984).

GALLAGHER, PETER. Born Aug. 19, 1955 in NYC. Graduate Tufts U. Bdwy debut 1977 in "Hair," followed by "A Doll's Life" for which he received a Theatre World Award, "The Corn Is Green," "The Real Thing."

GAMPEL, CHRIS/C. M. Born Feb. 19, 1921 in Montreal, Can. Bdwy debut 1950 in "Flight into Egypt," followed by "Capt. Brassbound's Conversion," "Richard II," "St. Joan," "Waltz of the Toreadors," "No Exit," "The Crucible," "Compulsion," "Firstborn," "The Girl Who Came to Supper," "Front Page," OB in "Spoon River," "Samson Agonistes."

GARBER, VICTOR. Born Mar. 16, 1949 in London, Can. Debut 1973 OB in "Ghosts" for which he received a Theatre World Award, followed by "Joe's Opera," "Cracks," Bdwy in "Tartuffe," "Deathtrap," "Sweeney Todd," "They're Playing Our Song," "Little Me," "Noises Off."

GARDENIA, VINCENT. Born Jan. 7, 1923 in Naples, It. Debut 1955 OB in "In April Once," followed by "Man with the Golden Arm," "Volpone," "Brothers Karamazov," "Power of Darkness," "Machinal," "Gallows Humor," "Theatre of the Absurd," "Lunatic View," "Little Murders," "Passing through from Exotic Places," "Carpenters," "Buried Inside Extra," Bdwy in "The Visit" (1958), "Rashomon," "The Cold Wind and the Warm," "Only in America," "The Wall," "Daughter of Silence," "Seidman & Son," "Dr. Fish," "Prisoner of Second Avenue," "God's Favorite," "California Suite," "Ballroom," "Glengarry Glen Ross."

GARFIELD, DAVID. Born Feb. 6, 1941 in Brooklyn, NY. Graduate Columbia, Cornell U. Debut 1964 OB in "Hang Down Your Head and Die," followed by "Government Inspector," "Old Ones," "Family Business," "Ralph Roister Doister," "Actors Deli," Bdwy in "Fiddler on the Roof," "The Rothschilds."

GARRETT, BECKY. Born Mar. 18, 1948 in Pendleton, OR. Bdwy debut 1980 in "Blackstone," OB in "Red, Hot and Blue," "Bells Are Ringing."

GARRICK, BEULAH. Born June 12, 1921 in Nottingham, Eng. Bdwy debut 1959 in "Shadow and Substance," followed by "Auntie Mame," "Juno," "Little Moon of Alban," "High Spirits," "The Hostage," "Funny Girl," "Lovers," "Abelard and Heloise," "Ulysses in Nighttown," "Copperfield," OB in "Little Boxes," "Berkeley Square," "Fallen Angels," "Henry IV Part II," "Candida in Concert," "Loud Bang on June 1st."

GARRICK, KATHY. Born Sept. 4, 1957 in Los Angeles, CA. Graduate Immaculate Heart Col. Debut 1985 OB in "In Trousers."

GARRISON, DAVID. Born June 30, 1952 in Long Branch, NJ. Graduate Boston U. Debut OB in "Joseph and the Amazing Technicolor Dreamcoat," followed by "Living At Home," "Geniuses," Bdwy in "A History of the American Film," "A Day in Hollywood/A Night in the Ukraine," "Pirates of Penzance," "Snoopy," "Torch Song Trilogy," "One Touch of Venus."

GARSIDE, BRAD. Born June 2, 1958 in Boston, MA. Graduate NorthTexState U. Debut 1983 OB in "Forbidden Broadway."

GASSELL, SYLVIA. Born July 1, 1923 in NYC. Attended Hunter Col. Bdwy debut 1952 in "The Time of the Cuckoo," followed by "Sunday Breakfast," "Fair Game for Lovers," "Inquest," OB in "U.S.A.," "Romeo and Juliet," "Electra," "A Darker Flower," "Fragments," "Goa," "God Bless You, Harold Fineberg," "Philosophy in the Boudoir," "Stag Movie," "The Old Ones," "Where Memories Are Magic," "Jesse's Land."

GAVON, IGORS. Born Nov. 14, 1937 in Latvia. Bdwy bow 1961 in "Carnival," followed by "Hello Dolly!" "Marat/deSade," "Billy," "Sugar," "Mack and Mabel," "Musical Jubilee," "Strider," "42 St," OB in "Your Own Thing," "Promenade," "Exchange," "Nevertheless They Laugh," "Polly," "The Boss," "Biography: A Game," "Murder in the Cathedral."

GEFFNER, DEBORAH. Born Aug. 26, 1952 in Pittsburgh, PA. Attended Juilliard, HB Studio. Debut 1978 OB in "Tenderloin," Bdwy in "Pal Joey," "A Chorus Line."

GEIER, PAUL. Born Aug. 7, 1944 in NYC. Graduate Pratt Inst. Debut 1980 OB in "Family Business," followed by "Women in Shoes," Bdwy in "Lunch Hour" (1981).

GELFER, STEVEN. Born Feb. 21, 1949 in Brooklyn, NY. Graduate NYU, IndU. Debut 1968 OB and Bdwy in "The Best Little Whorehouse in Texas," followed by "Cats."

GENEST, EDMOND. Born Oct. 27, 1943 in Boston, MA. Attended Suffolk U. Debut 1972 OB in "The Real Inspector Hound," followed by "Second Prize: Two Months in Leningrad," "Maneuvers," Bdwy in "Dirty Linen/New-Found Land," "Whose Life Is it Anyway?"

GENTLES, AVRIL. Born Apr. 2, 1929 in Upper Montclair, NJ. Graduate UNC. Bdwy debut 1955 in "The Great Sebastians," followed by "Nude with Violin," "Present Laughter," "My Mother, My Father and Me," "Jimmy Shine," "Grin and Bare It," "Lysistrata," "Texas Trilogy," "Show Boat" (1983), OB in "Dinny and the Witches," "The Wives," "Now Is the Time," "Man with a Load of Mischief," "Shay," "Winter's Tale," "Johnny on a Spot," "The Barbarians," "The Wedding," "Nymph Errant," "A Little Night Music."

GERACI, FRANK. Born Sept. 8, 1939 in Brooklyn, NY. Attended Yale, HB Studio. Debut 1961 OB in "Color of Darkness," followed by "Mr. Grossman," "Balm in Gilead," "The Fantasticks," "Tom Paine," "End of All Things Natural," "Union Street," "Uncle Vanya," "Success Story," "Hughie," "Merchant of Venice," "The Three Zeks," "Taming of the Shrew," Bdwy in "The Love Suicide at Schofield Barracks" (1972).

GERRINGER, ROBERT. Born May 12, 1926 in NYC. Graduate Fordham U., Pasadena Playhouse. Debut 1955 OB in "Thieves Carnival," followed by "Home," Bdwy in "Pictures in the Hallway" (1956), "A Flea in Her Ear," "Andersonville Trial," "Waltz of the Toreadors," "After the Fall," "A Doll's House," "Hedda Gabler," "Hide and Seek."

GERROLL, DANIEL. Born Oct. 16, 1951 in London, Eng. Attended Central Sch. of Speech. Debut 1980 OB in "The Slab Boys," followed by "Knuckle" and "Translations" for which he received a Theatre World Award," "The Caretaker," "Scenes from La Vie de Boheme," "The Knack," "Terra Nova," "Dr. Faustus," Bdwy in "Plenty" (1982).

GERSHENSON, SUE ANNE Born Feb. 18, 1953 in Chicago, IL. Attended Ind. U. Debut 1976 OB in "Panama Hattie," followed by "Carnival," "Street Scene," Bdwy in "Sunday in The Park with George" (1984).

GETER, JOHN. Born Sept. 22, 1957 in Wenoka, OK. Graduate Hanover Col. Debut 1980 OB in "The Diviners," followed by "Billy Liar," Bdwy in "Gemini" (1980).

GETTY, ESTELLE. Born July 25, 1923 in NYC. Attended New School. Debut 1971 OB in "The Divorce of Judy and Jane," followed by "Widows and Children First," "Table Settings," "Demolition of Hannah Fay," "Never Too Old," "A Box of Tears," "Hidden Corners," "I Don't Know Why I'm Screaming," "Under the Bridge There's a Lonely Place," "Light Up the Sky," "Pocketful of Posies," "Fits and Starts," Bdwy 1982 in "Torch Song Trilogy."

GIAGNI, D. J. Born Dec. 3, 1950 in NYC. Attended CCNY. Bdwy debut 1983 in "The Tap Dance Kid."

GIANNINI, CHERYL. Born June 15 in Monessen, PA. Bdwy debut 1980 in "The Suicide," followed by "Grownups," OB in "Elm Circle," "I'm Not Rappaport."

GIBSON, JUDY. Born Sept. 11, 1947 in Trenton, NJ. Graduate Rider Col. Bdwy debut 1970 in "Purlie," followed by "Seesaw," "Rachel Lily Rosenbloom," "Rockabye Hamlet," OB in "Sensations," "Manhattan Arrangement," "Two If by Sea," "Let My People Come," "One-Man Band."

GILBORN, STEVEN. Born in New Rochelle, NY. Graduate Swarthmore, Col., Stanford U. Bdwy debut 1973 in "Creeps," followed by "Basic Training of Pavlo Hummel," "Tartuffe," OB in "Rosmersholm," "Henry V," "Measure for Measure," "Ashes," "The Dybbuk," "Museum," "Shadow of a Gunman," "It's Hard to Be a Jew," "Isn't It Romantic."

GILES, NANCY. Born July 17, 1960 in Queens, NYC. Graduate Oberlin Col. Debut 1985 OB in "Mayor" for which she received a Theatre World Award.

GILLETTE, ANITA. Born Aug. 16, 1938 in Baltimore, MD. Debut 1960 OB in "Russell Patterson's Sketchbook" for which she received a Theatre World Award, followed by "Rich and Famous," Bdwy in "Carnival," "All American," "Mr. President," "Guys and Dolls," "Don't Drink the Water," "Cabaret," "Jimmy," "Chapter Two," "They're Playing Our Song," "Brighton Beach Memoirs."

GIOMBETTI, KAREN. Born May 24, 1955 in Scranton, PA. Graduate NYU. Bdwy debut 1978 in "Stop the World, I Want to Get Off," followed by "The Most Happy Fella," "Woman of the Year," "Zorba" (1983).

GIONSON, MEL. Born Feb. 23, 1954 in Honolulu, HI. Graduate UHi. Debut 1979 OB in "Richard II," followed by "Sunrise," "Monkey Music," "Behind Enemy Lines," "Station J," "Teahouse," "A Midsummer Night's Dream," "Empress of China," "Chip Shot," "Manoa Valley."

GIRARDEAU, FRANK. Born Oct. 19, 1942 in Beaumont, TX. Attended Rider Col, HB Studio. Debut 1972 OB in "22 Years," followed by "The Soldier," "Hughie," "An American Story," "El Hermano," "Dumping Ground," "Daddies," "Accounts," "Shadow Man," "Marathon '84."

GLEASON, JAMES. Born Sept. 30, 1952 in NYC. Graduate Santa Fe Col. Debut 1982 OB in "Guys in the Truck," followed by "Corkscrews!," "Patrick Pearse Motel," "Taboo in Revue," "Curse of the Starving Class," Bdwy in "Guys in the Truck" (1983).

GLEASON, JOANNA. Born June 2, 1950 in Toronto, CAN. Graduate UCLA. Bdwy debut 1977 in "I Love My Wife" for which she received a Theatre World Award, followed by "The Real Thing," OB in "A Hell of a Town." "Joe Egg."

GLENN, SCOTT. Born Jan. 26, 1942 in Pittsburgh, PA. Graduate of William & Mary Col. Bdwy debut 1965 in "The Impossible Years," followed by OB's "Collision Course," "Angelo's Wedding."

GLICK, STACEY. Born Dec. 29, 1971 in NYC. Debut 1981 OB in "Twelve Dreams," followed by "Sonata," "Somewheres Better."

GLOVER, JOHN. Born Aug. 7, 1944 in Kingston, NY. Attended Towson State Col. Debut 1969 OB in "A Scent of Flowers," followed by "Government Inspector," "Rebel Women," "Treats," "Booth," "Criminal Minds," "The Fairy Garden," "Digby," Bdwy in "The Selling of the President," "Great God Brown," "Don Juan," "The Visit," "Chemin de Fer," "Holiday," "The Importance of Being Earnest," "Frankenstein," "Whodunnit." "Design for Living."

GLOVER, SAVION. Born Nov. 19, 1973 in Newark, NJ. Bdwy debut 1984 in "The Tap Dance Kid."

GLUSHAK, JOANNA. Born May 27, 1958 in NYC. Attended NYU. Debut 1983 OB in "Lenny and the Heartbreakers," followed by "Lies and Legends," Bdwy in "Sunday in the Park with George" (1984).

GLYNN, CARLIN. Born Feb. 19, 1940 in Cleveland, OH. Attended Sophie Newcomb Col., Actors Studio. Debut 1959 OB in "Waltz of the Toreadors," followed by "Cassatt," "Winterplay," "Outside Waco," Bdwy in "The Best Little Whorehouse in Texas" for which she received a Theatre World Award.

GODFREY, LYNNIE. Born Sept. 11, 1952 in NYC. Graduate Hunter Col. Debut 1976 OB in "I Paid My Dues," followed by "Two Fish in the Sky," "A . . . My Name Is Alice," Bdwy 1978 in "Eubie!"

GOETZ, PETER MICHAEL. Born Dec. 10, 1941 in Buffalo, NY. Graduate SUNY/Fredonia, Southern ILU. Debut 1980 OB in "Jail Diary of Albie Sachs," "Before the Dawn," followed by Bdwy in "Ned and Jack" (1981), "Beyond Therapy," "The Queen and the Rebels," "Brighton Beach Memoirs."

GOLDBERG, WHOOPI. Born Nov. 13, 1949 in NYC. Graduate H.S. of Performing Arts. Bdwy debut 1984 in "Whoopi Goldberg" for which she received a Theatre World Award.

GOLDEN, ANNIE. Born Oct. 19, 1951 in Brooklyn, NY. Bdwy debut 1977 in "Hair," followed by "Leader of the Pack," OB in "Dementos," "Dr. Selavy's Magic Theatre," "A . . . My Name Is Alice," "Little Shop of Horrors."

GOLDSMITH, MERWIN. Born Aug. 7, 1937 in Detroit, MI. Graduate UCLA, Old Vic. Bdwy debut 1970 in "Minnie's Boys," followed by "The Visit," "Chemin de Fer," "Rex," "Chickencoop Chinaman," "Wanted," "Comedy," "Rubbers," "Yankees 3 Detroit 0," "Trelawny of the Wells," "Chinchilla," "Real Life Funnies," "Big Apple Messenger," "La Boheme."

GOLDWYN, TONY. Born May 20, 1960 in Los Angeles, CA. Graduate Brandeis U., LAMDA. Debut 1985 OB in "Digby" followed by "Messiah."

GOODMAN, JOHN. Born June 20, 1952 in St. Louis, MO. Graduate Southwest MoStateU. Debut 1978 OB in "A Midsummer Night's Dream," followed by "The Chisholm Trail," "Henry IV Part II," "Ghosts of the Loyal Oaks," "Half a Lifetime," "Marathon '84," Bdwy in "Big River" (1985).

GOODMAN, LISA. Born in Detroit, MI. Attended UMi. Debut 1982 OB in "Talking With," followed by "The First Warning," "The Show-Off," "Escape from Riverdale," "Jesse's Land," "State of the Union."

GOODMAN, LORRAINE. Born Feb. 11, 1962 in The Bronx, NYC. Graduate Princeton U. Debut 1985 OB in "Very Warm for May."

GOOR, CAROLYN. Born Oct. 11, 1960 in Paris, Fr. Debut 1983 OB in "The Jewish Gypsy," followed by "Oy Mama, Am I in Love," "A Little Night Music."

GORDON, CARL. Born Jan. 20, 1932 in Richmond, VA. Bdwy debut 1966 in "The Great White Hope," followed by "Ain't Supposed to Die a Natural Death," OB in "Day of Absence," "Happy Ending," "The Strong Breed," "Trials of Brother Jero," "Kongi's Harvest," "Welcome to Black River," "Shark," "Orrin and Sugar Mouth," "A Love Play," "The Great MacDaddy," "In an Upstate Motel," "Zooman and the Sign."

GORDON, CLARKE. Born in Detroit, MI. Graduate Wayne State U. Debut 1949 OB in "The Son," followed by "The Philistines," "The Truth," "Porch," Bdwy in "Night Music" (1951), "Pal Joey" (1952), "The Vamp" (1955).

GORDON, PEGGY. Born Dec. 26, 1949 in NYC. Attended Carnegie Tech. Debut OB 1971 in "Godspell," followed by "Taboo in Revue."

GORDON-CLARK, SUSAN. Born Dec. 31, 1947 in Jackson, MS. Graduate Purdue U. Debut 1984 OB in "The Nunsense Story," followed by "Chip Shot."

GORMAN, CLIFF. Born Oct. 13, 1936 in NYC. Attended UCLA. Debut 1965 OB in "Hogan's Goat," followed by "Boys in the Band," "Ergo," "Angelo's Wedding," Bdwy in "Lenny" (1971), "Chapter Two."

GORMAN, MARI. Born Sept. 1, 1944 in NYC. Debut 1966 OB in "The Kitchen," followed by "Walking to Waldheim," "The Memorandum," "Hot 1 Baltimore" for which she received a Theatre World Award, "Angelo's Wedding."

Miriam
Colon

Ray
Contreras

Betsy
Craig

David
Cryer

Jeanne
Cullen

John David
Cullum

Nicholas B.
Daddazio

Lezlie
Dalton

William
DeAcutis

Laura
Dean

Craig
Dudley

Cara
Duff-MacCormick

Audrey
Dummett

James
Eckhouse

Lynn
Eldredge

Drew
Eliot

SuEllen
Estey

Brian
Evers

Richard
Fancy

Angelina
Fiordellisi

Dave
Florek

Spence
Ford

Ramon
Franco

Diane
Fratantoni

Beulah
Garrick

David
Garrison

Sylvia
Gassell

John
Geter

Joanna
Glushak

Clarke
Gordon

GORMAN, MICHAEL. Born July 16, 1954 in Jefferson City, MO. Bdwy debut 1980 in "A Chorus Line," followed by "Copperfield," "Harrigan 'n Hart."

GOULD, GORDON. Born May 4, 1930 in Chicago, IL. Graduate Yale, Cambridge (Eng.). Bdwy debut 1965 in "You Can't Take It with You," followed by "War and Peace," "Right You Are," "The Wild Duck," "Pantagleize," "Exit the King," "The Show-Off," "School for Wives," "Freedom of the City," "Strider," "Amadeus," OB in "Man and Superman," "Scapin," "Impromptu at Versailles," "The Lower Depths," "The Tavern," "Judith," "Naked," "Tatyana Repina," "The Middle Ages," "On Approval."

GOUTMAN, CHRISTOPHER. Born Dec. 19, 1952 in Bryn Mawr, PA. Graduate Haverford Col., Carnegie-Mellon U. Debut 1978 OB in "The Promise" for which he received a Theatre World Award, followed by "Grand Magic," "The Skirmishers," "Imaginary Lovers," "Balm in Gilead," "Love's Labour's Lost."

GOVAN, MICHAEL. Born Sept. 20, 1950 in NYC. Graduate Antioch Col. Debut 1976 OB in "The Bofors Gun," followed by "Twelfth Night," "Winterset," "Importance of Being Earnest," "Count of Monte Cristo," "Merchant of Venice," "Taming of the Shrew."

GRAAE, JASON. Born May 15, 1958 in Chicago, IL. Graduate Cincinnati Consv. Debut 1981 OB in "Godspell," followed by "Snoopy," "Heaven on Earth," "Promenade," "Feathertop," Bdwy 1982 in "Do Black Patent Leather Shoes Really Reflect Up?"

GRAFF, RANDY. Born May 23, 1955 in Brooklyn, NY. Graduate Wagner Col. Debut 1978 OB in "Pins and Needles," followed by "Station Joy," "A . . . My Name Is Alice," "Once on aSummer's Day," Bdwy in "Sarava," "Grease."

GRANGER, FARLEY. Born July 1, 1928 in San Jose, CA. Bdwy debut 1959 in "First Impressions," followed by "The Warm Peninsula," "Advise and Consent," "The King and I" (CC), "Brigadoon" (CC), "The Seagull," "The Crucible," "Deathtrap," OB in "The Carefree Tree," "A Month in the Country," "Sailing," "Outward Bound."

GRANT, VINCENT. Born May 11, 1961 in Denver, CO. Graduate Richland Col. Debut 1984 OB in "A Step Out of Line."

GRAY, KEVIN. Born Feb. 25, 1958 in Westport, CT. Graduate Duke U. Debut 1982 OB in "Lola," followed by "Pacific Overtures," "Family Snapshots," "The Baker's Wife."

GRAY, SAM. Born July 18, 1923 in Chicago, IL. Graduate Columbia U. Bdwy debut 1955 in "Deadfall," followed by "Six Fingers in a Five Finger Glove," "Saturday, Sunday, Monday," "Golda," "A View from the Bridge," OB in "Ascent of F-6," "Family Portrait," "One Tiger on a Hill," "Shadow of Heroes," "The Recruiting Officer," "The Wild Duck," "Jungle of Cities," "3 Acts of Recognition," "Returnings," "A Little Madness," "The Danube," "Dr. Cook's Garden," "Child's Play," "Kafka Father and Son," "D."

GREEN, ADOLPH. Born Dec. 2, 1915 in NYC. Appeared in clubs with "The Revuers" before 1944 Bdwy debut in "On the Town," followed by "A Party with Betty Comden and Adolph Green" (OB) and revived on Bdwy in 1977, "The New Yorkers" (OB).

GREEN, AMANDA. Born Dec. 29, 1963 in NYC. Debut 1984 OB in "The New Yorkers."

GREEN, DAVID. Born June 16, 1942 in Cleveland, OH. Attended KanStateU. Bdwy debut 1980 in "Annie," followed by "Evita," OB in "Once on a Summer's Day."

GREENBERG, MITCHELL. Born Sept. 19, 1950 in Brooklyn, NY. Graduate Harpur Col., Neighborhood Playhouse. Debut 1979 OB in "Two Grown Men," followed by "Scrambled Feet," "A Christmas Carol," "A Thurber Carnival," "Isn't It Romantic." Bdwy in "A Day in Hollywood/A Night in the Ukraine" (1980), "Can-Can" (1981), "Marilyn."

GREENE, JAMES. Born Dec. 1, 1926 in Lawrence, MA. Graduate Emerson Col. OB in "The Iceman Cometh," "American Gothic," "The King and the Duke," "The Hostage," "Plays for Bleecker Street," "Moon in the Yellow River," "Misalliance," "Government Inspector," "Baba Goya," LCRep 2 years, "You Can't Take It With You," "School for Scandal," "Wild Duck," "Right You Are," "The Show-Off," "Pantagleize," "Festival of Short Plays," "Nourish the Beast," "One Crack Out," "Artichoke," "Othello," "Salt Lake City Skyline," "Summer," "The Rope Dancers," "Frugal Repast," "Bella Figura," "The Freak," "Park Your Car in the Harvard Yard," "Pigeons on the Walk," "Endgame," "Great Days," "Playboy of the Western World," Bdwy in "Romeo and Juliet," "Girl on the Via Flaminia," "Compulsion," "Inherit the Wind," "Shadow of a Gunman," "Andersonville Trial," "Night Life," "School for Wives," "Ring Round the Bathtub," "Great God Brown," "Don Juan," "Foxfire," "Play Memory."

GREENE, LYN. Born May 21, 1955 in Boston, MA. Graduate NYU, Juilliard. Debut 1984 OB in "Kid Purple."

GREENHILL, SUSAN. Born Mar. 19 in NYC. Graduate UPa., Catholic U. Bdwy debut 1982 in "Crimes of the Heart," followed OB by "Hooters," "Our Lord of Lynchville," "September in the Rain."

GREENHOUSE, MARTHA. Born June 14 in Omaha, NE. Attended Hunter Col., AmThWing. Bdwy debut 1942 in "Sons and Soldiers," followed by "Dear Me, the Sky Is Falling," "Family Way," "Woman Is My Idea," "Summer Brave," OB in "Clerambord," "Our Town," "3 by Ferlinghetti," "No Strings," "Cackle," "Philistines," "Ivanov," "Returnings," "Love Games," "Dancing to Dover."

GREGORIO, ROSE. Born in Chicago, IL. Graduate Northwestern U., Yale U. Debut 1962 OB in "The Days and Nights of Beebee Fenstermaker," followed by "Kiss Mama," "The Balcony," "Bivouac at Lucca," "Journey to the Day," "Diary of Anne Frank," "Weekends Like Other People," "Curse of the Starving Class," Bdwy in "The Owl and the Pussycat," "Daphne in Cottage D," "Jimmy Shine," "The Cuban Thing," "The Shadow Box," "A View from the Bridge."

GRIER, DAVID ALAN. Born June 30, 1955 in Detroit, MI. Graduate UMich, Yale. Bdwy debut 1981 in "The First" for which he received a Theatre World Award, followed by "Dreamgirls," OB in "A Soldier's Play," "Richard III."

GRIFFITH, LISA. Born June 18 in Honolulu, HI. Graduate Brandeis U., Trinity U. Debut 1977 OB in "The Homesickness of Capt. Rappaport," followed by "The Kennedy Play," "Chalkdust," "Murder at the Vicarage," "Ah, Wilderness!," "Stud Silo."

GRIMES, FRANK. Born in 1947 in Dublin, Ire. Attended Abbey Theatre School. Bdwy debut 1970 in "Borstal Boy," followed by OB's "The Holly and the Ivy," "In Celebration."

GROENENDAAL, CRIS. Born Feb. 17, 1948 in Erie, PA. Attended Allegheny Col, Exeter U, HB Studio. Bdwy debut 1979 in "Sweeney Todd," followed by "Sunday in the Park with George," OB in "Francis," "Sweethearts in Concert," "Oh, Boy "

GROENER, HARRY. Born Sept. 10, 1951 in Augsburg, Ger. Graduate UWash. Bdwy debut 1979 in "Oklahoma!," for which he received a Theatre World Award, followed by "Oh, Brother!," "Is There Life after High School," "Cats," "Harrigan 'n Hart," "Sunday in the Park with George," OB in "Beside the Seaside."

GROVES, ROBIN. Born Nov. 24, 1951 in Neenah, WI. Graduate Hollins Col. Bdwy debut 1976 in "Lady from the Sea," OB in "Vanities" (1978), "Starluster," "Territorial Rites," "The Carpenters," "Weekend Near Madison," "Sonata."

GRUBBS, RICHARD. Born July 27, 1958 in Hamilton, OH. Graduate Denison U., FlaStateU. Debut 1985 OB in "A Comedy of Errors."

GRUBER, MARGO F. Born Jan. 17 in Philadelphia, PA. Graduate UCol. Bdwy debut 1982 in "Fiddler on the Roof," OB in "The King Trilogy," "Starting Here Starting Now," "As You Like It," "Much Ado about Nothing," "Edward II," "King Lear."

GRUSIN, RICHARD. Born Nov. 2, 1946 in Chicago, IL. Graduate Goodman School, Yale U. Debut 1978 OB in "Wings," followed by "Sganarelle," "Heat of Re-Entry," "For Sale."

GUIDALL, GEORGE. Born June 7, 1938 in Plainfield, NJ. Attended UBuffalo, AADA. Bdwy debut 1969 in "Wrong Way Light Bulb," followed by "Cold Storage," OB in "Counsellor-at-Law," "Taming of the Shrew," "All's Well That Ends Well," "The Art of Dining," "Biography," "After All," "Henry V."

GUNN, MOSES. Born Oct. 2, 1929 in St. Louis, MO. Graduate UTenn, AIU, UKan. OB in "Measure for Measure," "Bohikee Creek," "Day of Absence," "Happy Ending," "Baal," "Hard Travelin'," "Lonesome Train," "In White American," "The Blacks," "Titus Andronicus," "Song of the Lusitanian Bogey," "Summer of the 17th Doll," "Kongi's Harvest," "Daddy Goodness," "Cities in Bezique," "Perfect Party," "To Be Young, Gifted and Black," "Sty of the Blind Pig," "Twelfth Night," "Ameri/Cain Gothic," Bdwy in "A Hand Is on the Gate," "Othello," "First Breeze of Summer," "The Poison Tree," "I Have a Dream."

GUNTON, BOB. Born Nov. 15, 1945 in Santa Monica, CA. Attended UCal. Debut 1971 OB in "Who Am I?," followed by "The Kid," "Desperate Hours," "Tip-Toes," "How I Got That Story," "Hamlet," "Death of Von Richthofen," "The Man Who Could See Through Time," Bdwy in "Happy End" (1977), "Working,"'King of Hearts," "Evita," "Passion," "Big River."

HAAG, JOHN. Born Jan. 14, 1947 in NYC. Graduate SUNY/Stony Brook. Debut 1981 OB in "The Rimers of Eldritch," followed by "Haunted Lives."

HACK, STEVEN. Born Apr. 20, 1958 in St. Louis, MO. Attended CalArts, AADA, Debut 1978 OB in "The Coolest Cat in Town," followed by Bdwy in "Cats" (1982).

HACKETT, JEAN. Born Aug. 28, 1956 in York, PA. Graduate NYU, RADA. Debut 1983 OB in "Ah, Wilderness!", followed by "The Education of One Miss February."

HADARY, JONATHAN. Born Oct. 11, 1948 in Chicago, IL. Attended Tufts U. Debut 1974 OB in "White Nights," followed by "El Grande de Coca-Cola," "Songs from Pins and Needles," "God Bless You, Mr. Rosewater," "Pushing 30," "Scrambled Feet," "Coming Attractions," "Tom-foolery," "Charley Bacon and Family," Bdwy in "Gemini," (1977/also OB), "Torch Song Trilogy, "As Is."

HALL, DAVIS. Born Apr. 10, 1946 in Atlanta, GA. Graduate Northwestern U. Bdwy debut 1973 in "Butley," followed by "Dogg's Hamlet and Cahoot's Macbeth," OB in "The Promise," "Dream-boats," "The Taming of the Shrew."

HALL, GEORGE. Born Nov. 19, 1916 in Toronto, Can. Attended Neighborhood Playhouse. Bdwy bow 1946 in "Call Me Mister," followed by "Lend an Ear," "Touch and Go," "Live Wire," "The Boy Friend," "There's a Girl in My Soup," "An Evening with Richard Nixon .," "We Interrupt This Program," "Man and Superman," "Bent," "Noises Off," OB in "The Balcony," "Ernest in Love," "A Round with Rings," "Family Pieces," "Carousel," "The Case Against Roberta Guardino," "Marry Me!" "Arms and the Man," "The Old Glory," "Dancing for the Kaiser," "Casualties," "The Seagull," "A Stitch in Time," "Mary Stuart," "No End of Blame," "Hamlet," "Colette Collage," "The Homecoming," "And a Nightingale Sang."

HALL, GRAYSON. Born in Philadelphia, PA. Attended Temple U. Debut 1953 OB in "Man and Superman," followed by "La Ronde," "Six Characters in Search of an Author," "The Balcony," "Buskers," "The Love Nest," "Shout from the Rooftops," "The Last Analysis," "Friends and Relatives," "The Screens," "Secrets of the Citizens Correction Committee," "The Sea," "What Every Woman Knows," "Jack Gelber's New Play," "Happy End," "Madwoman of Chaillot," Bdwy in "Subways Are for Sleeping," "Those That Play the Clowns," "Leaf People," "Happy End," "Suicide."

HALL, MARGARET. Born in Richmond, VA. Graduate Wm. and Mary Col. Bdwy debut 1960 in "Becket," followed by "High Spirits," "Mame," "The Leaf People," "Sunday in the Park with George," OB in "The Boy Friend," "Fallout," "U.S.A.," "A Midsummer Night's Dream," "Little Mary Sunshine."

HALLETT, JACK. Born Nov. 7, 1948 in Philadelphia, PA. Attended AADA. Debut 1972 OB in "Servant of Two Masters," followed by "Twelfth Night," Bdwy in "The 1940's Radio Show," "The First."

HALLIGAN, TIM. Born May 17, 1952 in Chicago, IL. Graduate UCol. Debut 1985 OB in "Responsible Parties."

HAMILL, MARK. Born Sept. 25, 1952 in Oakland, CA. Attended LACC. Bdwy debut 1981 in "The Elephant Man," followed by "Amadeus," "Harrigan 'n Hart."

HAMILL, MARY. Born Dec. 29, 1943 in Flushing, NY. Graduate UDallas. Debut 1969 OB in "Spiro Who?," followed by "What the Butler Saw," "Siamese Connections," "Trelawny of the Wells," "A Difficult Borning," "Throckmorton, Texas," Bdwy in "4 on a Garden," "P.S. Your Cat Is Dead," "Talley's Folly."

HAMILTON, LAWRENCE. Born Sept. 14, 1954 in Ashdown, AR. Graduate Henderson State U. Debut 1981 OB in "Purlie," Bdwy in "Sophisticated Ladies" (1982), followed by "Porgy and Bess," "The Wiz."

HAMILTON, RICHARD. Born Dec. 31, 1920 in Chicago, IL. Attended Pasadena Jr. Col. Bdwy debut 1952 in "First Lady," (CC), followed by "Cloud 7," "Blood, Sweat and Stanley Poole," "Scratch," "Anna Christie" (77),"A Touch of the Poet," "Morning's at 7," OB in "The Exception and the Rule," "The Bench," "Siamese Connections," "Cream Cheese," "Buried Child," "Fool for Love," "Husbandry."

HAMMOND, MICHAEL. Born Apr. 30, 1951 in Clinton IA. Graduate UIowa, LAMDA. Debut 1974 OB in "Pericles," followed by "The Merry Wives of Windsor," BAM Theatre Co.'s "A Winter's Tale," "Barbarians," "The Purging," "Romeo and Juliet."

HANAN, STEPHEN. Born Jan 7, 1947 in Washington, DC. Graduate Harvard, LAMDA. Debut 1978 OB in "All's Well That Ends Well," followed by "Taming of the Shrew," Bdwy in "Pirates of Penzance" (1978),"Cats."

HANDLER, EVAN. Born Jan. 10, 1961 in NYC. Attended Juilliard. Debut 1979 OB in "Biography: A Game," followed by "Strider," "Final Orders," "Marathon '84," "Found a Peanut," "Bloodletters," "What's Wrong with This Picture?," Bdwy in "Solomon's Child."

HANDY, JAMES. Born Mar. 19 in NYC. Graduate CCNY. Debut 1983 OB in "Big Maggie," followed by "Kerouac," "Ice Bridge," "Charley Bacon and Family."

HAO, WILLIAM. Born Aug. 10, 1953 in Honolulu, HI. Attended Chaminade Col., Leeward Col. Debut 1981 OB in "The Shining House," followed by "Gaugin in Tahiti," "Teahouse," "A Midsummer Night's Dream," "Rain," "Dream of Kitamura."

HARA, MARY. Born in Nebraska. Bdwy debut 1968 in "Rosencrantz and Guildenstern Are Dead," followed by "Waltz of the Toreadors," "The Crucible," "Strange Interlude," OB in "The Kitchen," "Glorious Ruler," "Dona Rosita," "Americans," "Home."

HARDER, JAMES. Born Nov. 19, 1931 in NYC. Graduate Princeton U. Debut 1958 OB in "Bonds of Interest," followed by "The Kitchen," "Dulcy," "Playboy of the Western World," "The Athenian Touch," "By Jupiter," "Lend an Ear," "On the Town," "Isn't It Romantic," Bdwy in "Very Good Eddie" (1975).

HARDING, JAN LESLIE. Born 1956 in Cambridge, MA. Graduate Boston U. Debut 1980 OB in "Album," followed by "Sunday Picnic," "Buddies," "The Lunch Girls."

HARKNESS, SAM. Born Feb. 5 in Abbeville, SC. Bdwy debut 1975 in "The Wiz," followed by "Reggae."

HARNEY, BEN. Born Aug. 29, 1952 in Brooklyn, NY. Bdwy debut 1971 in "Purlie," followed by "Pajama Game," "Tree-Monisha," "Pippin," "Dreamgirls," OB in "Don't Bother Me I Can't Cope," "The Derby," "The More You Get."

HARPER, CHARLES THOMAS. Born Mar. 29, 1949 in Carthage, NY. Graduate Webster Col. Debut 1975 OB in "Down by the River. . .," followed by "Holy Ghosts," "Hamlet," "Mary Stuart," "Twelfth Night," "The Beaver Coat," "Richard II," "Great Grandson of Jedediah Kohler," "Applause," "Love's Labor's Lost," "Dysan," Bdwy in "Passion" (1983).

HARPER, JAMES. Born Oct. 8, 1948 in Bell, CA. Attended Marin Col., Juilliard. Bdwy debut 1973 in "King Lear," followed by "The Robber Bridegroom," "The Time of Your Life," "Mother Courage," "Edward II," OB in "A Midsummer Night's Dream," "Recruiting Officer," "The Wild Duck," "The Jungle of Cities," "The Cradle Will Rock," "All the Nice People," "Cruelties of Mrs. Schnayd."

HARPER, RON. Born Jan. 12, 1936 in Turtle Creek, PA. Princeton graduate. Debut 1955 OB in "3 by Dylan Thomas," followed by "A Palm Tree in a Rose Garden," "Meegan's Game," "Red Rover," "Bone Garden," Bdwy in "Sweet Bird of Youth," "Night Circus," "6 Rms Riv Vu."

HARRELSON, HELEN. Born in Missouri; Goodman Theatre graduate. Bdwy debut 1950 in "The Cellar and the Well," followed by "Death of a Salesman," "Days in the Trees," "Romeo and Juliet," OB in "Our Town," "His and Hers," "House of Atreus," "He and She," "Missing Persons," "Laughing Stock," "The Art of Self-Defense."

HARRINGTON, DELPHI. Born Aug. 26 in Chicago IL. Graduate Northwestern U. Debut 1960 OB in "Country Scandal," followed by "Moon for the Misbegotten," "Baker's Dozen," "The Zykovs," "Character Lines," "Richie," "American Garage," "After the Fall," Bdwy in "Thieves," "Everything in the Garden," "Romeo and Juliet," "Chapter Two."

HARRIS, BAXTER. Born Nov. 18, 1940 in Columbus, KS. Attended UKan. Debut 1967 OB in "America Hurrah," followed by "The Reckoning," "Wicked Women Revue," "More than You Deserve," "Pericles," "him," "Battle of Angels," "Down by the River," "Selma," "Ferocious Kisses," "Three Sisters," "Gradual Clearing," "Dolphin Position," "Paradise Lost," "Ghosts," "Madwoman of Chaillot."

HARRIS, CYNTHIA. Born in NYC. Graduate Smith Col. Bdwy debut 1963 in "Natural Affection," followed by "Any Wednesday," "Best Laid Plans," "Company," OB in "The Premise," "3 by Wilder," "America Hurrah," "White House Murder Case," "Mystery Play," "Bad Habits," "Merry Wives of Windsor," "Beauty Part," "Jules Feiffer's Hold Me," "Second Avenue Rag," "Cloud 9," "Romance Language."

HARRIS, ESTELLE. Born Apr. 22, 1932 in NYC. Debut 1984 OB in "Enter Laughing."

HARRIS, NIKI. Born July 20, 1948 in Pittsburgh, PA. Graduate Duquesne U. Bdwy debut 1980 in "A Day in Hollywood/A Night in the Ukraine," followed by "My One and Only."

HARRIS, RONALD LEW. Born May 29, 1953 in Louisville, KY. Graduate Moorehead State U, AADA. Debut 1976 OB in "Compulsion," followed by "Between Time and Timbuktu," "Going Home," "Midsummer Night's Dream," "Mandrake," "Three Cockolds," "Two Gentlemen of Verona," "Taming of the Shrew," "Julius Caesar," "Henry V."

HARRIS, ROSEMARY. Born Sept. 19, 1930 in Ashby, Eng. Attended RADA. Bdwy debut 1952 in "Climate of Eden" for which she received a Theatre World Award, followed by "Troilus and Cressida," "Interlock," "The Disenchanted," "The Tumbler," APA's "The Tavern," "School for Scandal," "The Seagull," "The Importance of Being Earnest," "War and Peace," "Man and Superman," "Judith," and "You Can't Take It With You," "Lion in Winter," "Old Times," "Merchant of Venice," "A Streetcar Named Desire," "The Royal Family," "Pack of Lies," OB in "The New York Idea," "Three Sisters," "The Seagull."

HARRIS, ROSALIND. Born Dec. 22, in White Plains, NY. Attended Ithaca Col. Debut 1968 OB in "Now," followed by "Do I Hear a Waltz?," "The Rise of David Levinsky," "Crazy Locomotive," "Has Anybody Here Found Love?," "It's Hard to Be a Jew," "Love Songs," "Triptych," "D.," Bdwy in "Fiddler on the Roof" (1968).

HARRISON, REX. Born Mar. 5, 1908 in Huyten, Eng. Attended Liverpool Col. Bdwy debut 1936 in "Sweet Aloes," followed by "Anne of a Thousand Days," "Bell, Book and Candle," "Venus Observed," "Love of Four Colonels," "My Fair Lady" (1956/1981), "Fighting Cock," "Emperor Henry IV," "In Praise of Love," "Caesar and Cleopatra," "The Kingfisher," "Heartbreak House," "Aren't We All?"

HART, CECILIA. Born June 6 in Cheyenne, WY. Emerson Col. graduate. Debut 1974 OB in "Macbeth," followed by "Emperor of Late Night Radio," "The Good Parts," Bdwy in "The Heiress" (1976), "Dirty Linen" for which she received a Theatre World Award, "Othello" (1982), "Design for Living."

HART, KITTY CARLISLE. See Carlisle

HART, PAUL E. Born July 20, 1939 in Lawrence, MA. Graduate Merrimack Col. Debut 1977 OB in "Turandot," followed by "Darkness at Noon," "Light Shines in the Darkness," "Pictures at an Exhibition," "Blessed Event," Bdwy in "Fiddler on the Roof" (1981).

HART, ROXANNE. Born in 1952 in Trenton, NJ. Attended Skidmore, Princton U. Bdwy debut 1977 in "Equus," followed by "Loose Ends," "Passion," OB in "A Winter's Tale," "Johnny On a Spot," "The Purging," "Hedda Gabler," "Waiting for the Parade," "La Brea Tarpits," "Marathon '84," "Digby."

HARTLEY, SUSAN. Born Oct. 20 in Norman, Ok. Graduate Adelphi U. Bdwy debut 1982 in "Annie," followed by "My One and Only."

HARUM, EIVIND. Born May 24, 1944 in Stavanger, Norway. Attended Utah State U. Credits include "Sophie," "Foxy," "Baker Street," "West Side Story" ('68),"A Chorus Line," "Woman of the Year."

HAUDEN, CYNTHIA. Born Dec. 23, 1948 in Memphis, TN. Graduate Adelphi U. Debut 1981 OB in "The Idol Makers," followed by "Occupations," "Absent Friends," "The Crimes of Vautrin," "Abel's Sister."

HAWKINS, TRISH. Born Oct. 30, 1945 in Hartford, CT. Attended Radcliffe, Neighborhood Playhouse. Debut OB 1970 in "Oh! Calcutta!" followed by "Iphigenia," "The Hot l Baltmore" for which she received a Theatre World Award, "him," "Come Back, Little Sheba," "Battle of Angels," "Mound Builders," "The Farm," "Ulysses in Traction," "Lulu," "Hogan's Folly," "Twelfth Night," "A Tale Told," "Great Grandson of Jedediah Kohler," "Time Framed," "Levitations." "Love's Labour's Lost," Bdwy (1977) in "Some of My Best Friends," "Talley's Folly" (1979).

HAYNES, TIGER. Born Dec. 13, 1907 in St. Croix, VI. Bdwy bow 1956 in "New Faces," followed by "Finian's Rainbow," "Fade Out-Fade In," "Pajama Game," "The Wiz," "A Broadway Musical," "Comin' Uptown," "My One and Only," OB in "Turns," "Bags," "Louis," "Taking My Turn."

HEAD, TONY. Born Dec. 16, 1951 in Ft. Sill, OK. Attended Howard U. Debut 1983 OB in "The Basket Case," followed by "After the Rain," "Leather Heart."

HEADLY, GLENNE. Born Mar. 13, 1955 in New London, CT. Graduate AmCol.Switzerland. Debut 1983 OB in "Extremities," followed by "The Philanthropist" for which she received a Theatre World Award, "Balm in Gilead," Bdwy in "Arms and the Man" (1985).

HEALD, ANTHONY. Born Aug. 25, 1944 in New Rochelle, NY. Graduate MiStateU. Debut 1980 OB in "The Glass Menagerie," followed by "Misalliance" for which he received a Theatre World Award, "The Caretaker," "The Fox," "Quartermaine's Terms," "The Philanthropist," "Henry V," "Digby,"Bdwy in "The Wake of Jamey Foster" (1982).

HEALY, CHRISTINE. Born June 13 in Buffalo, NY. Graduate UCSanta Barbara. Debut 1984 OB in "Terra Nova," followed by "Isn't It Romantic."

HEARN, GEORGE. Born June 18, 1934 in St. Louis, MO. Graduate Southwestern Col. OB in "Macbeth," "Antony and Cleopatra," "As You Like It," "Richard III," "Merry Wives of Windsor," "Midsummer Night's Dream," "Hamlet," "Horseman, Pass By," Bdwy in "A Time for Singing," "The Changing Room," "An Almost Perfect Person," "I Remember Mama," "Watch on the Rhine," "Sweeney Todd," "A Doll's Life," "Whodunnit," "La Cage aux Folles."

HECHT, PAUL. Born Aug. 16, 1941 in London, Eng. Attended McGill U. OB in "Sjt. Musgrave's Dance," "MacBird," Bdwy in "Rosencrantz and Guildenstern Are Dead," "1776," "The Rothschilds," "The Ride Across Lake Constance," "The Great God Brown," "Don Juan," "Emperor Henry IV," "Herzl," "Caesar and Cleopatra," "Night and Day," "Noises Off."

HEDAYA, DAN. Born in Brooklyn, NY. Graduate Tufts Col. Debut 1974 OB in "The Last Days of British Honduras," followed by "Conjuring an Event," "Museum," "Scenes from Everyday Life," "Henry V," Bdwy in "The Basic Training of Pavlo Hummel" (1977).

HEDEMAN, PHYLLIS. Born Apr. 26, 1930 in NYC. Graduate Hunter Col. Debut 1985 OB in "Dancing to Dover."

HEIKEN, NANCY. Born Nov. 28, 1948 in Philadelphia, PA. Graduate Sarah Lawrence Col. Bdwy debut 1981 in "Pirates of Penzance," followed by OB in "La Boheme."

HEINS, BARRETT (formerly Barry) Born Dec. 5, 1956 in El Paso, TX. Juilliard graduate. Debut 1978 OB in "Spring Awakening," followed by "Twelfth Night," "The Country Wife," "An Enemy of the People," Bdwy in "Good" (1982).

HEIT, SALLY-JANE. Born Oct. 8, 1938 in NYC. Graduate Hunter Col. Bdwy debut 1979 in "Ballroom," followed by "The World of Sholom Aleichem," OB in "Amidst the Gladiolas," "Starting in the Middle."

HEMINGWAY, MARIEL. Born Nov. 22, 1961 in Portland, OR. Debut 1985 OB in "California Dog Fight."

HENDERSON, JO. Born in Buffalo, NY. Attended WMiU. OB in "Camille," "Little Foxes," "An Evening with Merlin Finch," "20th Century Tar," "A Scent of Flowers," "Revival," "Dandelion Wine," "My Life," "Ladyhouse Blues," "Fallen Angels," "Waiting for the Parade," "Threads," "Bella Figura," "Details without a Map," "The Middle Ages," "Time Framed," "Isn't It Romantic," Bdwy in "Rose" (1981), "84 Charing Cross Road," "Play Memory."

HENDRICKSON, STEVE. Born Sept. 29, 1954 in Schenectady, NY. Yale graduate. Debut 1982 OB in "Herself as Lust," followed by "Lorenzaccio," "Theatre Olympics," Bdwy in "The Misanthrope" (1983).

HENIG, ANDI. Born May 6 in Washington, DC. Attended Yale. Debut 1978 OB in "One and One," followed by "Kind Lady," "Downriver," Bdwy in "Oliver!" (1984), "Big River."

HENNING, DEBBY. Born Jan. 13, 1955 in White Plains, NY. Attended Cooper Union. Bdwy debut 1983 in "Merlin," followed by "World of Magic."

HENNING, DOUG. Born May 3, 1947 in Winnipeg, Can. Graduate McMaster U. Bdwy debut 1974 in "The Magic Show," followed by "Merlin," "World of Magic."

HENRITZE, BETTE. Born May 23 in Betsy Layne, KY. Graduate UTenn. OB in "Lion in Love," "Abe Lincoln in Illinois," "Othello," "Baal," "Long Christmas Dinner," "Queens of France," "Rimers of Eldritch," "Displaced Person," "Acquisition," "Crime of Passion," "Happiness Cage," "Henry VI," "Richard III," "Older People," "Lotta," "Catsplay," "A Month in the Country," "The Golem," Bdwy in "Jenny Kissed Me" (1948), "Pictures in the Hallway," "Giants, Sons of Giants," "Ballad of the Sad Cafe," "The White House," "Dr. Cook's Garden," "Here's Where I Belong," "Much Ado about Nothing," "Over Here," "Angel Street," "Man and Superman," "Macbeth" (1981), "Present Laughter," "The Octette Bridge Club."

HERMAN, DANNY. Born Nov. 2, 1960 in Pittsburgh, PA. Debut 1979 OB in "Big Bad Burlesque," Bdwy in "A Chorus Line" (1981), "Leader of the Pack."

HERNDON, JAN LEIGH. Born Apr. 9, 1955 in Raleigh, NC. Graduate ValntermontCol. Bdwy debut 1982 in "A Chorus Line," followed by "La Cage aux Folles," OB in "Joan and the Devil."

HERRERA, JOHN. Born Sept. 21, 1955 in Havana, Cuba. Graduate Loyola U. Bdwy debut 1979 in "Grease," followed by "Evita," "Camelot," OB in "La Boheme," "Lies and Legends."

HERRMANN, EDWARD. Born July 21, 1943 in Washington, DC. Graduate Bucknell U, LAMDA. Debut 1970 OB in "The Basic Training of Pavlo Hummel," followed by "A Midsummer Night's Dream," "Tom and Viv," Bdwy in "Moonchildren" (1971), "Mrs. Warren's Profession," "The Philadelphia Story."

HEWETT, CHRISTOPHER. Born Apr. 5 in England. Bdwy debut 1957 in "My Fair Lady," followed by "First Impressions," "Unsinkable Molly Brown," "Kean," "The Affair," "Hadrian VII," "Music Is," "Peter Pan" (1980), "Sweethearts in Concert," OB in "Tobias and the Angel," "Trelawny of the Wells," "Finian's Rainbow," "New Jerusalem," "Oh, Boy "

HEYMAN, BARTON. Born Jan. 24, 1937. in Washington, DC. Attended UCLA. Bdwy debut 1969 in "Indians," followed by "Trial of the Catonsville 9," "A Talent for Murder," OB in "A Midsummer Night's Drean," "Sleep," "Phantasmagoria Historia," "Enclave," "Henry V," "A Private View."

HICKEY, WILLIAM. Born in 1928 in Brooklyn, NY. Bdwy debut 1951 in "St. Joan," followed by "Tovarich," "Miss Lonelyhearts," "Body Beautiful," "Make a Million," "Not Enough Rope," "Moonbirds," "Step on a Crack," "Thieves," OB in "On the Town," "Next," "Happy Birthday, Wanda June," "Small Craft Warnings," "Mourning Becomes Electra," "Siamese Connections," "Troilus and Cressida," "Sunday Runners," "Romance Language," "Angelo's Wedding."

HICKS, LAURA. Born Nov. 17, 1956 in NYC. Graduate Juilliard. Debut 1978 OB in "Spring Awakening," followed by "Talking With," "The Cradle Will Rock," "Paducah."

HICKS, LESLIE. Born Oct. 21, 1955 in Providence, RI. Attended CalStateU/Northridge, ACT. Bdwy debut 1983 in "Merlin," OB in "The Gifts of the Magi."

HIGGINS, BOB. Born June 7, 1954 in Tampa, FL. Graduate Georgetown U, AADA. Debut 1979 OB in "Teeth 'n' Smiles," followed by "Holding Patterns."

HIGGINS, DENNIS. Born Aug. 25, 1942 in Washington, DC. Attended Geo. Wash. U, AADA. Debut 1969 OB in "Tom Jones," followed by "Greenwillow," "Isadora Sleeps with the Russian Navy," "The White Crow."

HIGGINS, MICHAEL. Born Jan. 20, 1926 in Brooklyn, NY. Attended AmThWing. Bdwy bow 1946 in "Antigone," followed by "Our Lan'," "Romeo and Juliet," "The Crucible," "The Lark," "Equus," "Whose Life Is It Anyway?," OB in "White Devil," "Carefree Tree," "Easter," "The Queen and the Rebels," "Sally, George and Martha," "L'Ete," "Uncle Vanya," "The Iceman Cometh," "Molly," "Artichoke," "Reunion," "Chieftans," "A Tale Told," "Richard II," "The Sea Gull," "Levitations," "Love's Labour's Lost."

HILBRANDT, JAMES. Born Aug. 13, 1934 in Valley Stream, NY. Graduate Rochester Inst. Debut 1967 OB in "Gorilla Queen," followed by "A Boy Named Dog," "Horse Opera," "Patrick Henry Lake Liquors," "Bus Stop," "Are You Now. . .," "Picnic," "As You Like It," "Get Out!," "What Would Jeanne Moreau Do?," "The Hazard County Wonder," "The Ballad of Soapy Smith."

HILBOLDT, LISE. Born Jan. 7, 1954 in Racine, WI. Attended UWisc., Webber-Douglas Acad. in London. Bdwy debut 1981 in "To Grandmother's House We Go," followed by OB in "Top Girls," "Maneuvers."

HILLARY, ANN. Born Jan 8, 1931 in Jellico, TN. Attended Northwestern U., AADA. Bdwy debut 1953 in "Be Your Age," followed by "Separate Tables," "The Lark," OB in "Dark of the Moon," "Paradise Lost," "Total Eclipse."

HILLNER, NANCY. Born June 7, 1949 in Wakefield, RI. Graduate ULowell. Bdwy debut 1975 in "Dance with Me," followed by OB in "Nite Club Confidential," "Trading Places."

HILTON, MARGARET. Born July 20 in Marple, Cheshire, Eng. Graduate ULondon, LAMDA. Debut 1979 OB in "Molly," followed by "Stevie," "Come Back to the 5 & Dime, Jimmy Dean," "Pygmalion in Concert," "In Celebration," "Joe Egg," Bdwy in "Rose" (1981), "Joe Egg" (1985).

HILTON, RICHARD. Born June 25, 1950 in Kalamazoo, MI. Graduate WMichU. Debut 1981 OB in "Feiffer's People," followed by "Jacques Brel Is Alive. . . ," Bdwy in "Joseph and the Amazing Technicolor Dreamcoat" (1982).

HIRSCH, JUDD. Born Mar. 15, 1935 in NYC. Attended AADA. Bdwy debut 1966 in "Barefoot in the Park," followed by "Chapter Two," "Talley's Folly," OB in "On the Necessity of Being Polygamous," "Scuba Duba," "Mystery Play," "Hot l Baltimore," "Prodigal," "Knock Knock," "Life and/or Death," "Talley's Folly," "The Sea Gull," "I'm Not Rappaport."

HIRSCH, VICKI. Born Feb. 22, 1951 in Wilmington, DE. Graduate UDel, Villanova U. Debut 1985 OB in "Back County Crimes."

HOBEL, MARA. Born June 18, 1971 in NYC. Bdwy debut 1983 in "Moose Murders," followed OB with "Rude Times."

HOCK, ROBERT. Born May 20, 1931 in Phoenixville, PA. Yale graduate. Debut 1982 OB in "Romeo and Juliet," followed by "Edward II," "Macbeth," "The Adding Machine," "Caucasian Chalk Circle," "Kitty Hawk."

HODES, RYN. Born Dec. 28, 1956 in NYC. Graduate NYU. Debut 1979 OB in "Miradolina," followed by "Boy Meets Swan," " A Collier's Friday Night," "Suicide in B Flat," "Kaspar," "Fanshen," "Holy Terrors," "The Hungry Man," "Colonomos."

HOERSCH, JOANNE. Born Dec. 20, 1949 in Jersey City, NJ. Graduate Emerson Col. Debut 1976 OB in "Birdbath," followed by "More Than a Boy's Game," "The Lover," "Angel City," "Action," "Haunted Lives," "The Seagull."

HOFFMAN, DUSTIN. Born Aug. 8, 1937 in Los Angeles, CA. Attended Santa Monica Col., Pasadena Playhouse. Bdwy debut 1963 in "A Cook for Mr. General," followed by "The Subject Was Roses," "Jimmy Shine," "Death of a Salesman" (1984), OB in "A View from the Bridge," "Harry, Noon and Night," 'Journey of the 5th Horse," "Eh?" for which he received a Theatre World Award.

HOFFMAN, JANE. Born July 24 in Seattle, WA. Graduate UCal. Bdwy debut 1940 in "Tis of Thee," followed by "Crazy with the Heat," "Something for the Boys," "One Touch of Venus," "Calico Wedding," "Mermaids Singing," "Temporary Island," "Story for Strangers," "Two Blind Mice," "The Rose Tattoo," "The Crucible," "Witness for the Prosecution," "Third Best Sport," "Rhinoceros," "Mother Courage and Her Children," "Fair Game for Lovers," "A Murderer Among Us," "Murder Among Friends," OB in "American Dream," "Sandbox," "Picnic on the Battlefield," "Theatre of the Absurd," "Child Buyer," "A Corner of the Bed," "Slow Memories," "Last Analysis," "Dear Oscar," "Hocus-Pocus," "Lessons," "The Art of Dining," "Second Avenue Rag," "One Tiger to a Hill," "Isn't It Romantic," 'Alto Part," "Marathon '84," "The Frog Prince."

HOFFMAN, PHILIP. Born May 12, 1954 in Chicago, IL. Graduate UIl. Bdwy debut 1981 in "The Moony Shapiro Songbook," followed by "Is There Life after High School?" "Baby," OB in "The Fabulous '50's," "Isn't It Romantic."

HOFMAIER, MARK. Born July 4, 1950 in Philadelphia, PA. Graduate UAriz. Debut 1978 OB in "A Midsummer Night's Dream," followed by "Marvelous Gray," "Modern Romance."

HOGAN, JONATHAN. Born June 13, 1951 in Chicago, IL. Graduate Goodman Theatre. Debut OB 1972 in "The Hot l Baltimore," followed by "Mound Builders," "Harry Outside," "Cabin 12," "5th of July," "Glorious Morning," "Innocent Thoughts, Harmless Intentions," "Sunday Runners," "Threads," "Time Framed," "Balm in Gilead," Bdwy in "Comedians" (1976), "Otherwise Engaged," "5th of July," "The Caine Mutiny Court Martial," "As Is."

HOGAN, TESSIE. Born Aug. 23, 1957 in Chicago, IL. Graduate UIll, Yale. Debut 1985 OB in "Faulkner's Bicycle."

HOLBROOK, DAVID. Born July 1, 1955 in NYC. Attended Evergreen State Col. Debut 1962 OB in "Abe Lincoln in Illinois," followed by "Comedy of Errors."

HOLBROOK, HAL. Born Feb. 17, 1925 in Cleveland, OH. Denison U. graduate. Bdwy debut 1961 in "Do You Know the Milky Way?," followed by "The Glass Menagerie," "Mark Twain Tonight," "The Apple Tree," "I Never Sang for My Father," "Man of La Mancha," "Does a Tiger Wear a Necktie?," OB in "Henry IV," "Richard II," "Abe Lincoln in Illinois," "Marco Millions," "Incident at Vichy," "Tartuffe," "After the Fall," "Lake of the Woods," "Buried Inside Extra," "The Country Girl."

HOLBROOK, RUBY. Born Aug. 28, 1930 in St. John's,Nfd. Attended Denison U. Debut 1963 OB in "Abe Lincoln in Illinois," followed by "Hamlet," "James Joyce's Dubliners," "Measure for Measure," "The Farm," "Do You Still Believe the Rumor?," "The Killing of Sister George," "An Enemy of the People," Bdwy in "Da" (1979), "5th of July."

HOLGATE, RONALD. Born May 26, 1937 in Aberdeen, SD. Attended Northwestern U., NewEngConserv. Debut 1961 OB in "Hobo," followed by "Hooray, It's a Glorious Day," "Blue Plate Special," Bdwy in "A Funny Thing Happened on the Way. . .," "Milk and Honey," "1776," "Saturday Sunday Monday," "The Grand Tour," "Musical Chairs," "42nd Street."

HOLLIDAY, JENNIFER. Born Oct. 19, 1960 in Houston, TX. Bdwy debut 1980 in "Your Arms Too Short to Box with God," followed by "Dreamgirls" for which she received a Theatre World Award.

HOLLIS, TOMMY. Born Mar. 27, 1954 in Jacksonville, TX. Graduate UHouston. Debut 1985 OB in "Diamonds," followed by "Secrets of the Lava Lamp."

HOLLY, ELLEN. Born Jan. 17, 1931 in NYC. Graduate Hunter Col. Debut 1955 OB in "Two for Fun," followed by "Salome," "Florentine Tragedy," "Tevya and His Daughters," "Othello," "Moon on a Rainbow Shawl," "Antony and Cleopatra," "Funny House of a Negro," "A Midsummer Night's Dream," "Cherry Orchard," "Long Time Since Yesterday," "Henry V," "Taming of the Shrew," Bdwy in "Too Late the Phalarope," "Face of a Hero," "Tiger, Tiger Burning Bright," "A Hand Is on the Gate," "King Lear."

HOLMES, GEORGE. Born June 3, 1935 in London, Eng. Graduate ULondon. Debut 1978 OB in "The Changeling," followed by "Love from a Stranger," "The Hollow," "The Story of the Gadsbys," "Learned Ladies," "The Land Is Bright," "Something Old, Something New."

HOLMES, SCOTT. Born May 30, 1952 in West Grove, PA. Graduate Catawba Col. Bdwy debut 1979 in "Grease," followed by "Evita," "The Rink," OB in "Diamonds."

HONDA, CAROL A. Born Nov. 20 in Kealakekua, HI. Graduate UHi. Debut 1983 OB in "Yellow Fever," followed by "Empress of China," "Manoa Valley."

HOPKINS, KATE. Born Feb. 1, 1964 in NYC. Attended Carnegie-Mellon U. Debut 1984 OB in "Come Back, Little Sheba."

HORAN, BONNIE. Born Aug. 20, 1928 in Dayton, TX. Graduate UHouston, UParis, Geo.Wash.U. Debut 1980 OB in "The Devil's Disciple," followed by "The Mechans," "Arms and the Man."

HORGAN, PATRICK. Born May 26, 1929 in Nottingham, Eng. Attended Stoneyhurst Col. Bdwy debut 1958 in "Redhead," followed by "Heartbreak House," "The Devil's Advocate," "Beyond the Fringe," "Baker Street," "Crown Matrimonial," "Sherlock Holmes," "My Fair Lady," "Deathtrap," "Noises Off," OB in "The Importance of Being Earnest."

HORMANN, NICHOLAS. Born Dec. 22, 1944 in Honolulu, HI. Graduate Oberlin Col., Yale. Bdwy debut 1973 in "The Visit," followed by "Chemin de Fer," "Holiday," "Love for Love," "Rules of the Game," "Member of the Wedding," "St. Joan," "Moose Murders," OB in "Ice Age," "Marco Polo," "Artichoke," "Looking-Glass," "The Dining Room," "A Private View," "Isn't It Romantic."

HORVATH, JAN. Born Jan. 31, 1958 in Lake Forrest, IL. Graduate Cin.Consv. Bdwy debut 1983 in "Oliver!," OB in "Sing Me Sunshine," "Jacques Brel Is Alive and Well.."

HOUGHTON, KATHARINE. Born Mar 10, 1945 in Hartford, CT. Graduate Sarah Lawrence Col. Bdwy debut 1965 in "A Very Rich Woman," followed by "The Front Page" (1969), OB in "A Scent of Flowers" for which she received a Theatre World Award, "To Heaven in a Swing," "Madwoman of Chaillot," "Vivat Vivat Regina "

HOWARD, DAVID. Born Sept. 10, 1928 in Mt. Kisco, NY. Graduate Cornell U. Debut 1964 OB in "Cindy," followed by "Hamp," "Hamlet," "Nude with Violin," "Man Enough."

HOXIE, RICHMOND. Born July 21, 1946 in NYC. Graduate Dartmouth Col., LAMDA. Debut 1975 OB in "Shaw for an Evening," followed by "The Family," "Justice," "Landscape with Waitress," "3 from the Marathon," "The Slab Boys," "Vivien," "Operation Midnight Climax," "The Dining Room," "Daddies," "To Gillian on Her 37th Birthday."

HOYT, J. C. Born Mar. 6, 1944 in Mankato, MN. Graduate UMinn. Debut 1975 OB in "Heathen Piper," followed by "La Ronde," "Two Gentlemen of Verona," "Comedy of Errors."

HOYT, LON. Born Apr. 6, 1958 in Roslyn, NY. Graduate Cornell U. Bdwy debut 1982 in "Rock 'n' Roll: The First 5000 Years," followed by "Baby," "Leader of the Pack."

HUDDLE, ELIZABETH. Born Jan. 20, 1940 in Redding, CA. Attended UPacific. With LCRep (1967) in "Caucasian Chalk Circle," "The Country Wife," "The Alchemist," "Good Woman of Setzuan," "Playboy of the Western World," "Scenes from American Life," Bdwy in "Little Murders," "The Octette Bridge Club."

HUGHES, TRESA. Born Sept. 17, 1929 in Washington, DC. Attended Wayne U. OB in "Electra," "The Crucible," "Hogan's Goat," "Party on Greenwich Avenue," "Fragments," "Passing through from Exotic Places," "Beggar on Horseback," "Early Morning," "The Old Ones," "Holy Places," "Awake and Sing," "Standing on My Knees," "Modern Ladies of Guanabacoa," "After the Fall," Bdwy in "The Miracle Worker," "The Devil's Advocate," "Dear Me, the Sky Is Falling," "The Last Analysis," "Spofford," "Man in the Glass Booth," "Prisoner of Second Avenue," "Tribute," "A View from the Bridge."

HULL, BRYAN. Born Sept. 12, 1937 in Amarillo, TX. Attended UNMx, Wayne State U. Bdwy debut 1976 in "Somethin's Afoot," OB in "The Fantasticks."

HULSWIT, MART. Born May 24, 1940 in Maracaibo, Venz. Attended Hobart Col, AADA. Debut 1961 OB in "Romeo and Juliet," followed by "Richard II," "Merchant of Venice," "The Tempest," "King Lear," "Macbeth," "In Celebration," "Summer People," "Broadcast Baby," Bdwy in "Present Laughter" (1982.)

HUNTER, HOLLY. Born Mar. 20, 1958 in Atlanta, GA. Graduate Carnegie-Mellon U. Debut 1981 OB in "Battery," followed by "Weekend Near Madison," "The Miss Firecracker Contest," Bdwy in "Crimes of the Heart" (1982), "The Wake of Jamey Foster."

HUNTER, KIM. Born Nov. 12, 1922 in Detroit, MI. Attended Actors Studio. Debut 1947 in "A Streetcar Named Desire," followed by "Darkness at Noon," "The Chase," "The Children's Hour," "The Tender Trap," "Write Me a Murder," "Weekend," "Penny Wars," "The Women," "To Grandmother's House We Go," OB in "Come Slowly, Eden," "All Is Bright," "The Cherry Orchard," "When We Dead Awaken," "Territorial Rites," "Faulkner's Bicycle."

HURLEY, JOHN PATRICK. Born May 7, 1949 in Salt Lake City, UT. Graduate UUtah. Debut 1982 OB in "Inserts," followed by "Sharing," Bdwy in "Aren't We All?" (1985).

HURT, WILLIAM. Born Mar. 20, 1950 in Washington, D.C. Graduate Tufts U., Juilliard. Debut 1976 OB in "Henry V," followed by "My Life," "Ulysses in Traction," "Lulu, "5th of July," "The Runner Stumbles." He recieved a 1978 Theatre World Award for his performances with Circle Repertory Theatre, followed by "Hamlet," "Mary Stuart," "Childe Byron," "The Diviners," "Richard II," "The Great Grandson of Jedediah Kohler," "A Midsummer Night's Dream," "Hurlyburly," "Joan of Arc at the Stake," Bdwy in "5th of July," "Hurlyburly."

IANNUCCI, MICHAEL. Born Feb. 3, 1956 in Philadelphia, PA. Graduate Temple U, RADA. Debut 1983 OB in "Waiting for Lefty," followed by "Writers."

IGARASHI, GERRI. Born Nov. 2, in Chicago IL. Graduate Emory U. Debut 1980 OB in "Sunrise," followed by "Monkey Music," "Pacific Overtures."

INGE, MATTHEW. Born May 29, 1950 in Fitchburg, MA. Attended Boston U., Harvard. Bdwy debut 1976 in "Fiddler on the Roof," followed by "A Chorus Line."

INNES, LAURA. Born Aug. 16, 1957 in Pontiac, MI. Graduate Northwestern U. Debut 1982 OB in "Edmond," followed by "My Uncle Sam," "Life Is a Dream."

IRONS, JEREMY. Born Sept. 19, 1948 in Cowes, Eng. Attended Bristol Old Vic School. Bdwy debut 1984 in "The Real Thing."

IRWIN, BILL. Born Apr. 11, 1950 in California. Attended UCLA, Oberlin, Clown Col. Debut 1982 OB in "The Regard of Flight," followed by "The Courtroom," Bdwy in "5-6-7-8 Dance" (1983), "Accidental Death of an Anarchist."

IRWIN, THOMAS (TOM). Born June 1, 1956 in Peoria, IL. Graduate IllStateU. Debut 1984 OB in "Balm in Gilead."

IVEY, DANA. Born Aug. 12, 1941 in Atlanta, GA. Graduate Rollins Col. LAMDA. Bdwy debut 1981 in "Macbeth" (LC), followed by "Present Laughter," "Heartbreak House," "Sunday in the Park with George," "Pack of Lies," OB in "A Call from the East," "Vivien," "Dumping Ground," "Pastorale," "Two Small Bodies," "Candida in Concert," "Major Barbara in Concert," "Quartermaine's Terms," "Baby with the Bathwater."

IVEY, JUDITH. Born Sept. 4, 1951 in El Paso, TX. Bdwy debut 1979 in "Bedroom Farce," followed by "Steaming," "Hurlyburly," OB in "Dulsa, Fish, Stas and Vi," "Sunday Runners," "Second Lady," "Hurlyburly."

JABLONS, KAREN. Born July 19, 1951 in Trenton, NJ. Juilliard graduate. Debut 1969 OB in "The Student Prince," followed by "Sound of Music," "Funny Girl," "Boys from Syracuse," "Sterling Silver," "People in Show Business Make Long Goodbyes," "In Trousers," Bdwy in "Ari," "Two Gentlemen of Verona," "Lorelei," "Where's Charley?," "A Chorus Line."

JACKS, SUSAN J. Born Nov. 5, 1953 in Brooklyn, NY. Graduate SUNY. Debut 1983 OB in "Forbidden Broadway."

JACKSON, ANNE. Born Sept. 3, 1926 in Allegheny, PA. Attended Neighborhood Playhouse. Bdwy debut 1945 in "Signature," followed by "Yellow Jack," "John Gabriel Borkman," "The Last Dance," "Summer and Smoke," "Magnolia Alley," "Love Me Long," "Lady from the Sea," "Never Say Never," "Oh, Men! Oh, Women!," "Rhinoceros," "Luv," "The Exercise," "Inquest," "Promenade All," "Waltz of the Toreadors," "Twice around the Park," OB in "The Tiger," "The Typist," "Marco Polo Sings a Solo," "Diary of Anne Frank," "Nest of the Wood Grouse," "Madwoman of Chaillot."

JACKSON, DAVID. Born Dec. 4, 1948 in Philadelphia, PA. Bdwy debut 1980 in "Eubie!," followed by "My One and Only."

JACKSON, ERNESTINE. Born Sept. 18 in Corpus Christi, TX. Graduate Del Mar Col., Juilliard. Debut 1966 in "Show Boat" (LC), followed by "Finian's Rainbow," "Hello Dolly!," "Applause," "Jesus Christ Superstar," "Tricks," "Raisin" for which she received a Theatre World Award, "Guys and Dolls," "Bacchae," OB in "Louis," "Some Enchanted Evening," "Money Notes," "Jack and Jill."

JACKSON, GLENDA. Born May 9, 1936 in Hoylake, Cheshire, Eng. Attended RADA. Bdwy debut 1965 in "Marat/Sade," followed by "Rose" (1981), "Strange Interlude" (1985).

JACKSON, LEONARD. Born Feb. 7, 1928 in Jacksonville, FL. Graduate Fiske U. Debut 1965 OB in "Troilus and Cressida," followed by "Henry V," "Happy Ending," "Day of Absence," "Who's Got His Own," "Electronic Nigger and Others," "Black Quartet," "Five on the Blackhand Side," "Boesman and Lena," "Murderous Angels," "Chickencoop Chinaman," "Karl Marx Play," "Prodigal Sister," Bdwy in "The Great White Hope," "Lost in the Stars," "Ma Rainey's Black Bottom."

JACKSON, PHILIP. Born June 18, 1948 in Retford, Nottinghamshire, Eng. Graduate Bristol U. Debut 1985 OB in "Rat in the Skull."

JACOBI, DEREK. Born Oct. 22, 1938 in Leytonstone, Eng. Graduate St. John's Col., CambridgeU. Bdwy debut 1980 in "The Suicide," followed by "Cyrano de Bergerac," "Much Ado about Nothing."

JACOBY, MARK. Born May 21 in Johnson City, TN. Graduate GaStateU, FlaStateU, St. JohnsU. Debut 1982 OB in "Eileen in Concert," followed by "Bells Are Ringing."

JAMES, ELMORE. Born May 3, 1954 in NYC. Graduate SUNY/Purchase. Debut 1970 OB in "Moon on a Rainbow Shawl," followed by "The Ups and Downs of Theopholus Maitland," "Carnival," "Until the Real Thing Comes Along," "A Midsummer Night's Dream," "The Tempest," Bdwy in "But Never Jam Today" (1979), "Your Arms Too Short to Box with God," "Big River."

JAMES, KRICKER. Born May 17, 1939 in Cleveland, OH. Graduate Denison U. Debut 1966 OB in "Winterset," followed by "Out of Control," "Rainbows for Sale," "The Firebugs," "Darkness at Noon," "The Hunting Man," "Sacraments."

JAROSLOW, RUTH. Born May 22 in Brooklyn, NY. Attended HB Studio. Debut 1964 OB in "That 5 A.M. Jazz," followed by "Jonah," "Fighting International Fat," Bdwy in "Mame," "Fiddler on the Roof" (1964/'77/'81). "The Ritz."

JASTRAM, LAINE. Born Nov. 28 in Illinois. Attended Hunter Col. Debut 1984 OB in "The Desk Set."

JAY, MARY. Born Dec. 23, 1939 in Brooklyn, NY. Graduate UMe, AmThWing. Debut 1962 OB in "Little Mary Sunshine," followed by "Toys in the Attic," " Telecast," "Sananda Sez," "Soul of the White Ant," "The Quilling of Prue," "Summit Conference," Bdwy in "The Student Gypsy," "Candida" (1981), "Beethoven's Tenth."

JAY, WILLIAM. Born May 15, 1935 in Baxter Springs, KS. Attended Omaha U. Debut 1963 OB in "Utopia," followed by "The Blacks," "Loop the Loop," "Happy Ending," "Day of Absence," "Hamlet," "Othello," "Song of the Lusitanian Bogey," "Ceremonies in Dark Old Men," "Man Better Man," "The Harangues," "Brotherhood," "Perry's Mission," "Rosalee Pritchett," "Sister Sadie," "Coriolanus," "Getting Out," "Henrietta."

JECKO, TIMOTHY. Born Jan. 24, 1938 in Washington DC. Yale graduate. Bdwy debut 1980 in "Annie," followed by "Woman of the Year," OB in "Downriver."

JENNER, JAMES. Born Mar. 5, 1953 in Houston, TX. Attended UTx, LAMDA. Debut 1980 OB in "Kind Lady," followed by "Station J.," "Yellow Fever," "Comedy of Errors."

JENNEY, LUCINDA. Born Apr. 23 in Long Island City, NY. Graduate Sarah Lawrence Col. Debut 1981 OB in "Death Takes a Holiday," followed by "Ground Zero Club," "True to Life," Bdwy in "Gemini" (1981).

JENNINGS, KEN. Born Oct. 10, 1947 in Jersey City, NJ. Graduate St. Peter's Col. Bdwy debut 1975 in "All God's Chillun Got Wings," followed by "Sweeney Todd" for which he received a Theatre World Award, "Present Laughter," OB in "Once on a Summer's Day," "Mayor."

JEROME, TIMOTHY. Born Dec. 29, 1943 in Los Angeles, CA. Graduate Ithaca Col. Bdwy debut 1969 in "Man of La Mancha," followed by "The Rothschilds," "Creation of the World . . . ," "Moony Shapiro Songbook," "Cats," OB in "Beggar's Opera," "Pretzels," "Civilization and Its Discontents," "The Little Prince," "Colette Collage."

JETER, MICHAEL. Born Aug. 26, 1952 in Lawrenceburg, TN. Graduate Memphis State U. Bdwy debut 1978 in "Once in a Lifetime," OB in "The Master and Margarita," "G. R. Point" for which he received a Theatre World Award, "Alice in Concert," "El Bravo," "Cloud 9," "Greater Tuna."

JOHNSON, BETTY. Born Mar. 16, 1929 in Guilford County, NC. Dartmouth Col. graduate. Debut 1983 OB in "Spoon River Anthology," Bdwy in "Take Me Along" (1985).

JOHNSON, DAVID CALE. Born Dec. 28, 1947 in El Paso, TX. Attended AmConTh. Bdwy debut 1975 in "Shenandoah," followed by "My Fair Lady" (1981), "A Doll's Life," "The Human Comedy."

JOHNSON, KURT. Born Oct. 5, 1952 in Pasadena, CA. Attended LACC, Occidental Col. Debut 1976 OB in "Follies," followed by "Walking Papers," "A Touch of Marble," "A Midsummer Night's Dream," Bdwy in "Rockabye Hamlet" (1976), "A Chorus Line," "A Stitch in Time," "Loves of Anatole."

JOHNSON, PAGE. Born Aug. 25, 1930 in Welch, WV. Graduate Ithaca Col. Bdwy bow 1951 in "Romeo and Juliet," followed by "Electra," "Oedipus," "Camino Real," "In April Once," for which he received a Theatre World Award, "Red Roses for Me," "The Lovers," "Equus," "You Can't Take It With You," OB in "The Enchanted," "Guitar," "4 in 1," "Journey of the Fifth Horse," APA's "School for Scandal," "The Tavern," and "The Seagull," "Odd Couple," "Boys In The Band," "Medea," "Deathtrap," "Best Little Whorehouse in Texas," "Fool for Love."

JOHNSON, VAN. Born Aug. 25, 1916 in Newport, RI. Bdwy debut in "New Faces of 1936," followed by "Too Many Girls," "Pal Joey" (1940), "Come on Strong," "Mating Dance," "On a Clear Day You Can See Forever," "La Cage aux Folles."

JOHNSTON, J. J. Born Oct. 24, 1933 in Chicago, IL. Debut 1981 OB in "American Buffalo," and Bdwy 1983 in "American Buffalo" for which he received a Theatre World Award, followed by "Glengarry Glen Ross."

JONES, EDDIE. Born in Washington, PA. Debut 1960 OB in "Dead End," followed by "Curse of the Starving Class," "The Ruffian on the Stairs," "An Act of Kindness," "Big Apple Messenger," "The Skirmishers," "Maiden Stakes," "The Freak," "Knights Errant," "Slacks and Tops," "Burkie," "Curse of the Starving Class" (1985), Bdwy in "That Championship Season" (1974), "Devour the Snow."

JONES, FRANZ. Born Nov. 11, 1951 in Washington, DC. Graduate TxChristianU. Debut 1974 OB in "Holocaust," followed by "Trade-Offs," "Brainwashed," "Pepperwine," "Things of the Heart," Bdwy in "Big River" (1985).

JONES, JAY AUBREY. Born Mar. 30, 1954 in Atlantic City, NJ. Graduate Syracuse U. Debut 1981 OB in "Sea Dream," followed by "Divine Hysteria," "Inacent Black and the Brothers."

JONES, JEFFREY. Born Sept. 28, 1947 in Buffalo, NY. Graduate Lawrence U., LAMDA. Debut 1973 OB in "Lotta," followed by "The Tempest," "Trelawny of the Wells," "Secret Service," "Boy Meets Girl," "Scribes," "Cloud 9," "The Death of Von Richthofen," "Love Letters on Blue Paper," "Henry V."

JONES, JEN. Born Mar. 23, 1927 in Salt Lake City, UT. Attended UUtah. Debut 1960 OB in "Drums under the Window," followed by "The Long Voyage Home," "Diff'rent," "Creditors," "Look at Any Man," "I Knock at the Door," "Pictures in the Hallway," "Grab Bag," "Bo Bo," "Oh, Dad, Poor Dad. . .," Bdwy in "Dr. Cook's Garden," "But Seriously," "Eccentricities of a Nightingale," "The Music Man" (1980), "The Octette Bridge Club."

JONES, LEILANI. Born May 14, in Honolulu, HI. Graduate UHi. Debut 1981 OB in "El Bravo," followed by "The Little Shop of Horrors," Bdwy (1985) in "Grind" for which she received a Theatre World Award.

JONES, REED. Born June 30, 1953 in Portland, OR. Graduate USIU. Bdwy debut 1979 in "Peter Pan," followed by "West Side Story," "America," "Play Me a Country Song," "Cats," "Loves of Anatole," OB in "Music Moves Me."

JONES, SABRA. Born Mar. 22, 1951 in California. Debut 1982 OB in "Joan of Lorraine," followed by "Inheritors," "Paradise Lost," "Ghosts," "Clarence," "Madwoman of Chaillot," "Vivat! Vivat Regina."

JONES, SIMON. Born July 27, 1950 in Wiltshire, Eng. Attended Trinity Hall. Debut 1984 OB in "Terra Nova," followed by Bdwy in "The Real Thing" (1984).

JORDAN, DAVID. Born Mar. 6, 1957 in Raleigh, NC. Graduate SUNY/Oswego. Debut 1982 OB in "The Death of Von Richtofen," followed by "Bells Are Ringing."

JOSHUA, LAWRENCE. Born Feb. 12, 1954 in NYC. Debut 1979 OB in "Tooth of Crime," followed by "Sunday Runners in the Rain," "Middleman Out," "Kid Champion," "One Tiger to a Hill," "Ground Zero Club."

JOY, ROBERT. Born Aug. 17, 1951 in Montreal, Can. Graduate Nfd. Memorial U. Oxford U. Debut 1978 OB in "The Diary of Anne Frank," followed by "Fables for Friends," "Lydie Breeze," "Sister Mary Ignatius Explains It All," "Actor's Nightmare," "What I Did Last Summer," "The Death of Von Richthofen," "Lenny and the Heartbreakers," "Found a Peanut," "Field Day," "Life and Limb."

JOYCE, KIYA ANN. Born Aug. 9, 1956 in Tachikawa, Japan. Attended Miami Dade Jr. Col. Debut 1980 OB in "Innocent Thoughts and Harmless Intentions," followed by "The Harvesting," Bdwy in "Plenty" (1982).

JOYCE, STEPHEN. Born Mar 7, 1933 in NYC. Attended Fordham U. Bdwy debut 1966 in "Those That Play the Clowns," followed by "The Exercise," "The Runner Stumbles," "Devour the Snow," "The Caine Mutiny Court-Martial," OB in "Three Hand Reel," "Galileo," "St. Joan," "Stephen D" for which he received a Theatre World Award, "Fireworks," "School for Wives," "Savages," "Scribes," "Daisy," "Maneuvers."

JUDD, ROBERT. Born Aug. 3, 1927 in NYC. Debut 1972 OB in "Don't Let It Go to Your Head," followed by "Black Visions," "Sweet Enemy," "The Lion Is a Soul Brother," "Welfare," "Zooman and the Sign," Bdwy in "Watch on the Rhine" (1980), "Ma Rainey's Black Bottom."

JULIA, RAUL. Born Mar. 9, 1940 in San Juan, PR. Graduate UPR. OB in "Macbeth," "Titus Andronicus," "Theatre in the Streets," "Life Is a Dream," "Blood Wedding," "Ox Cart," "No Exit," "Memorandum," "Frank Gagliano's City Scene," "Your Own Thing," "Persians," "Castro Complex," "Pinkville," "Hamlet," "King Lear," "As You Like It," "Emperor of Late Night Radio," "Threepenny Opera," "The Cherry Orchard," "Taming of the Shrew," "Othello," "The Tempest," Bdwy in "The Cuban Thing," "Indians," "Two Gentlemen of Verona," "Via Galactica," "Where's Charley?," "Dracula," "Betrayal," "Nine," "Design for Living," "Arms and the Man."

JURDEM, MELIRN. Born June 3, 1919 in NYC. Graduate Neighborhood Playhouse. Debut 1977 OB in "Counsellor-at-Law," followed by "King Trilogy," "Dreams of the Son."

KAHN, MADELINE. Born Sept. 29, 1942 in Boston, MA. Graduate Hofstra U. Bdwy debut in "New Faces of 1968," followed by "Two by Two," "She Loves Me," "On the 20th Century," OB in "Promenade," "Boom Boom Room," "Marco Polo Sings a Solo," "What's Wrong with This Picture?"

KAIKKONEN, GUS. Born May 7, 1951 in Detroit, MI. Attended Georgetown U. Debut 1971 OB in "Dionysus Wants You!," followed by "Private Hicks," "Female Transport," "Casualties," "Cloud 9," "Love," "The Country Girl."

KANSAS, JERI. Born Mar. 10, 1955 in Jersey City, NJ. Debut 1978 OB in "Gay Divorce," Bdwy 1979 in "Sugar Babies," followed by "42nd Street."

KAREL, CHARLES "CHUCK". Born Apr. 22, 1935 in Newark, NJ. Attended USCal. Bdwy debut 1962 in "Milk and Honey," followed by "Hello, Dolly!," "Golden Rainbow," "Dear World," "Zorba (1983), OB in "Chase a Rainbow," "Sing Melancholy Baby," "Heather McBride."

KARN, RICHARD. Born Feb. 17, 1956 in Seattle, WA. Graduate UWash. Debut 1984 OB in "Losing It," followed by "The Other Shore," "Man Enough."

KARPEN, PAT. Born Feb. 21, 1951 in Washington, DC. Graduate Catholic U. Debut 1980 OB in "The Marriage," followed by "The Land Is Bright."

KASSIR, JOHN. Born in 1958 in Baltimore, MD. Debut 1985 OB in "Three Guys Naked from the Waist Down."

KAVA, CAROLINE. Born in Chicago, IL. Attended Neighborhood Playhouse. Debut 1975 OB in "Gorky," followed by "Threepenny Opera," "The Nature and Purpose of the Universe," "Disrobing the Bride," "Marching Song," "Domestic Issues," "Little Victories," "Cloud 9," "Playboy of the Western World," Bdwy in "Stages" (1978).

KAYE, ELEANORA. Born Apr. 4, 1938 in Philadelphia, PA. Attended Villanova U. Debut 1982 OB in "The Way of the World," followed by "The Wife of Bath," "Ghosts," "Lady Windermere's Fan," "Merchant of Yonkers," "Dreams of a Son."

KAYE, JUDY. Born Oct. 11, 1948 in Phoenix, AZ. Attended UCLA, Ariz. State U. Bdwy debut 1977 in "Grease," followed by "On the 20th Century" for which she received a Theatre World Award, "Moony Shapiro Songbook," "Oh, Brother!," OB in "Eileen in Concert," "Can't Help Singing," "Four to Make Two," "Sweethearts in Concert," "Love."

KAYE, STUBBY. Born Nov. 11, 1918 in NYC. Bdwy debut 1950 in "Guys and Dolls," followed by "Li'l Abner," "Everybody Loves Opal," "Good News," "The Ritz," "Grind."

KEAGY, GRACE. Born Dec. 16 in Youngstown, OH. Attended NewEngConsv. Debut 1974 OB in "Call Me Madam," followed by "D.", Bdwy in "Goodtime Charley," "The Grand Tour," "Carmelina," "I Remember Mama," "Musical Chairs," "Woman of the Year."

KEAL, ANITA. Born in Philadelphia, PA. Graduate Syracuse U. Debut 1956 OB in "Private Life of the Master Race," followed by "Brothers Karamazov," "Hedda Gabler," "Witches Sabbath," "Six Characters in Search of an Author," "Yes, My Darling Daughter," "Speed Gets the Poppy," "You Didn't Have to Tell Me," "Val Christie and Others," "Do You Still Believe the Rumor?," "Farmyard," "Merry Wives of Scarsdale," "Exiles," "Fish Riding Bikes," "Haven."

KEEP, STEPHEN. Born Aug. 24, 1947 in Camden, SC. Attended Columbia, Yale U. Bdwy debut 1972 in "Paul Sills Story Theatre," followed by "Metamorphosis," "Shadow Box," OB in "Clarence," "The Cherry Orchard," "Esther," "A Private View," "Childhood."

KELLETT, ROBERT. Born Aug. 29, 1955 in Minneapolis, MN. Attended UIll, Goodman Theatre. Debut 1981 OB in "Oh, Johnny!," followed by "Sex Acts."

KELLY, JOHN-CHARLES. Born Apr. 28, 1946 in Salem, OR. Graduate UOr, UAriz. Debut 1984 OB in "Bells Are Ringing."

KENNEDY, LAURIE. Born Feb. 14, 1948 in Hollywood, CA. Graduate Sarah Lawrence Col. Debut 1974 OB in "End of Summer," followed by "A Day in the Death of Joe Egg," "Ladyhouse Blues," "He and She," "The Recruiting Officer," "Isn't It Romantic," "After the Fall," Bdwy in "Man and Superman" (1978) for which she received a Theatre World Award, "Major Barbara."

KERNER, NORBERTO. Born July 19, 1929 in Valparaiso, Chile. Attended Piscator Workshop, Goodman Theatre. Debut 1971 OB in "Yerma," followed by "I Took Panama," "The F. M. Sale," "My Old Friends," "Sharon Shashanovah," "The Blood Wedding," "Crisp," "The Great Confession," "Cold Air."

KERSEY, BILLYE. Born Oct. 15, 1955 in Norfolk, VA. Bdwy debut 1981 in "42nd Street."

KERSHAW, WHITNEY. Born Apr. 10, 1962 in Orlando, FL. Attended Harkness Joffrey Ballet Schools. Debut 1981 OB in "Francis," Bdwy in "Cats."

KEYES, DANIEL. Born Mar. 6, 1914 in Concord, MA. Attended Harvard. Bdwy debut 1954 in "The Remarkable Mr. Pennypacker," followed by "Bus Stop," "Only in America," "Christine," "First Love," "Take Her, She's Mine," "Baker Street," "Dinner at 8," "I Never Sang for My Father," "Wrong Way Light Bulb," "A Place for Polly," "Scratch," "Rainbow Jones," "Angel," "Passione," "Requiem for a Heavyweight," OB in "Our Town," "Epitaph for George Dillon," "Plays for Bleecker Street," "Hooray! It's a Glorious Day!," "Six Characters in Search of an Author," "Sjt. Musgrave's Dance," "Arms and the Man," "Mourning Becomes Electra," "Salty Dog Saga," "Hot 1 Baltimore," "Artichoke," "Whales of August."

KEYISHIAN, ELIZABETH. Born Oct. 13, 1960 in Brooklyn, NY. Graduate Wesleyan U. Debut 1984 OB in "The Accrington Pals," followed by "A Bonzo Christmas Carol."

KILLMER, NANCY. Born Dec. 16, 1936 in Homewood, IL. Graduate Northwestern U. Bdwy debut 1969 in "Coco," followed by "Goodtime Charley," "So Long, 174th Street," "A Little Night Music," "Sweeney Todd," "Alice in Wonderland," OB in "Exiles," "Mrs. Murray's Farm," "Pillars of Society," "Threads," "A Tale Told," "The Cherry Orchard," "Sea Gull," "Lady Windermere's Fan."

KILMURRAY, MAUREEN. Born July 7, 1953 in Milwaukee, WI. Graduate Marquette U., Southern Methodist U. Debut 1984 OB in "The Pretender."

KILPATRICK, PATRICK. Born Aug. 20 in Orange, VA. Graduate URichmond. Debut 1984 OB in "Linda Her and the Fairy Garden."

KILTY, JEROME. Born June 24, 1922 in Pala Indian Reservation, CA. Attended London's Guildhall Schl. Bdwy debut 1950 in "The Relapse," followed by "Love's Labour's Lost," "Misalliance," "A Pin to See the Peepshow," "Frogs of Spring," "Quadrille," "Othello," "Henry IV," "Moon for the Misbegotten," OB in "Dear Liar," " A Month in the Country," "Enter a Free Man."

KIMBALL, DAVID. Born Feb. 20, 1951 in Memphis, TN. Graduate Carnegie-Mellon U. Debut 1983 OB in "The Last of the Knucklemen," followed by "Crime and Punishment."

KIMBROUGH, CHARLES. Born May 23, 1936 in St. Paul. MN. Graduate IndU, Yale. Bdwy bow 1969 in "Cop-Out," followed by "Company," "Love for Love," "Rules of the Game," "Candide," "Mr. Happiness," "Same Time, Next Year," "Sunday in the Park with George," OB in "All in Love," "Struts and Frets," "Troilus and Cressida," "Secret Service," "Boy Meets Girl," "Drinks Before Dinner," "The Dining Room."

KINCAID, LESLIE. Born Mar. 3, 1961 in Mineola, NY. Graduate SUNY/Purchase. Debut 1983 OB in "War Babies," followed by "He Plays Piano," "Horizons."

KING, BRUCE ROBERTS. Born Apr. 17, 1963 in Houston, TX. Attended UTex, USt. Thomas, UHouston. Debut 1985 OB in "Man Enough."

KING, GINNY. Born May 12, 1957 in Atlanta, GA. Attended NCSch of Arts. Bdwy debut 1980 in "42nd Street."

KING, W. McGREGOR. Born Apr. 1, 1952 in Fitchburg, MA. Graduate Bryant & Stratton Col. Debut 1976 OB in "Lysistrata," followed by "The Lower Depths," "Maid to Marry," "Times Square," "The Ugly Truckling," "The Lunch Girls," "Creeps."

Michael
Gorman

Amanda
Green

Harry
Groener

Margo
Gruber

Richard
Grusin

Jean
Hackett

Helen
Harrelson

Baxter
Harris

Cecilia
Hart

Tony
Head

Phyllis
Hedeman

Steve
Hendrickson

John
Herrera

Laura
Hicks

Bob
Higgins

Tessie
Hogan

Scott
Holmes

Jan
Horvath

Gerri
Igarashi

Bill
Irwin

Judith
Ivey

Kricker
James

Lucinda
Jenney

Page
Johnson

J. J.
Johnston

Jen
Jones

Mel
Jurdem

Jeri
Kansas

Patrick
Kilpatrick

Leslie
Kincaid

209

KIRBY, BRUCE. Born Apr. 28, 1925 in NYC. Debut 1955 OB in "La Ronde." Bdwy 1965 in "Diamond Orchid," followed by "Death of a Salesman" (1984).

KIRK, ALYSON. Born Jan. 14, 1970 in Waldwick, NJ. Bdwy debut 1982 in "Annie," followed by "Take Me Along."

KIRK, LISA. Born Feb. 25 in Brownsville, PA. Bdwy debut 1945 in "Goodnight Ladies," followed by "Are You with It," "Allegro," "Kiss Me, Kate," "Here's Love," "Mack and Mabel," "Me Jack, You Jill," "Design for Living."

KIRSCH, CAROLYN. Born May 24, 1942 in Sheveport, LA. Bdwy debut 1963 in "How to Succeed . . . ," followed by "Follies Bergere," "La Grosse Valise," "Skyscraper," "Breakfast at Tiffany's," "Sweet Charity," "Hallelujah, Baby!," "Dear World," "Promises, Promises," "Coco," "Ulysses in Nighttown," "A Chorus Line," OB in "Silk Stockings," "Telecast."

KLATT, DAVID. Born July 15, 1958 in Martins Ferry, OH. Attended West Liberty State Col. Bdwy debut 1984 in "La Cage aux Folles."

KLIBAN, KEN. Born July 26, 1943 in Norwalk, CT. Graduate UMiami, NYU. Bdwy debut 1967 in "War and Peace," followed by "As Is," OB in "Puppy Dog Tails," "Istanbul," "Persians," "Home," "Elizabeth the Queen," "Judith," "Man and Superman," "Boom Boom Room," "Ulysses in Traction," "Lulu," "The Beaver Coat," "Troilus and Cressida," "Richard II," "Great Grandson of Jedediah Kohler," "It's Only a Play," "Time Framed," "Love's Labour's Lost."

KLINE, KEVIN. Born Oct. 24, 1947 in St. Louis, MO. Graduate IndU, Juilliard. Debut 1970 OB in "Wars of Roses," followed by "School for Scandal," "Lower Depths," "The Hostage," "Women Beware Women," "Robber Bridegroom," "Edward II," "The Time of Your Life," "Beware of the Jubjub Bird." "Dance on a Country Grave," "Richard III," "Henry V," Bdwy in "Theee Sisters," "Measure for Measure," "Beggar's Opera," "Scapin," "On the 20th Century," "Loose Ends," "Pirates of Penzance," "Arms and the Man."

KMECK, GEORGE. Born Aug. 4, 1949 in Jersey City, NJ. Attended Glassboro State Col. Bdwy debut 1981 in "Pirates of Penzance," followed by "On Your Toes," OB in "Surf City."

KNELL, DANE. Born Sept. 27, 1932 in Winthrop, MA. Bdwy debut 1952 in "See the Jaguar," OB in "Ulster," "Moon Dances," "Court of Miracles," "Gas Station," "Zeks," "She Stoops to Conquer."

KNIGHT, LILY. Born Nov. 30, 1949 in Jersey City, NJ. Graduate NYU. Debut 1980 OB in "After the Revolution," followed by "The Wonder Years," Bdwy in "Agnes of God" (1983).

KNUDSON, KURT. Born Sept. 7, 1936 in Fargo, ND. Attended NDStateU, UMiami. Debut 1976 OB in "The Cherry Orchard," followed by "Geniuses," Bdwy in "Curse of an Aching Heart" (1982), "Sunday in the Park with George," "Take Me Along."

KOLINSKI, JOSEPH. Born June 26, 1953 in Detroit MI. Attended UDetroit, HB Studio. Bdwy debut 1980 in "Brigadoon," followed by "Dance a Little Closer," "The Three Musketeers," OB in "Hijinks!", "The Human Comedy" (also Bdwy).

KOLOC, BONNIE. Born Feb. 6, 1946 in Waterloo, IA. Attended U.Northern Iowa. Debut 1983 on and off Broadway in "The Human Comedy" for which she received a Theatre World Award.

KONG, GAYLN. Born Apr. 1, 1952 in Honolulu, HI. Graduate UHi., UOre. Debut 1984 OB in "Pacific Overtures."

KOPACHE, THOMAS. Born Oct. 17, 1945 in Manchester, NH. Graduate San Diego State, Cal. Inst. of Arts. Debut 1976 OB in "The Architect and the Emperor of Assyria," followed by "Brontosaurus Rex," "Extravagant Triumph," "Caligula," "The Tempest," "Macbeth," "Measure for Measure," "Hunting Scenes from Lower Bavaria," "The Danube," "Friends Too Numerous to Mention," "Twelfth Night."

KORDER, HOWARD. Born Nov. 24, 1957 in NYC. Graduate SUNY/Binghamton. Debut 1982 OB in "Booth," followed by "Love in the Dark," "Action," "The Hungry Man."

KOREY, ALEXANDRA. Born May 14 in Brooklyn, NY. Graduate Columbia U. Debut 1976 OB in "Fiorello!," followed by "Annie Get Your Gun," "Jerry's Girls," "Rosalie in Concert," "America Kicks Up Its Heels," "Gallery," "Feathertop," Bdwy in "Hello, Dolly" (1978), "Show Boat" (1983).

KORNFELD, ERIC. Born July 6, 1956 in Reading, PA. Attended Kent State U. Debut 1981 OB in "Catch 22," followed by "The West Street Gang," "Doesn't the Sky Look Green Today?," "The Ventriloquist," "Something Old, Something New."

KORTHAZE, RICHARD. Born Feb. 11 in Chicago, IL. Graduate Chicago Musical Col. Bdwy debut 1953 in "Pal Joey," followed by "Wonderful Town," "Happy Hunting," "Conquering Hero," "How to Succeed in Business. . . ," "Skyscraper," "Walking Happy," "Promises Promises," "Pippin," "Chicago," "Dancin'," "Take Me Along" (1985), OB in "Phoenix '55" (1955).

KOSNICK, BRIAN. Born Nov. 20, 1955 in Cleveland, OH. Graduate Goodman School. Debut 1980 OB in "Ricochet," followed by "Taking in the Grave Outdoors," "The Desk Set."

KOTLISKY, MARGE. Born Feb. 19 in Chicago, IL. Attended Northwestern U, UMiami. Debut 1982 OB in "Edmond," followed by "Isn't It Romantic."

KOVITZ, RANDY. Born Sept 18, 1955 in Arlington, VA. Graduate Carnegie-Mellon U. Debut 1981 in LCRep's "Macbeth," followed by "Othello," OB in "A Prelude to Hamlet," "Romeo and Juliet."

KOZLOWSKI, LINDA. Born Jan 7 in Bridgeport, CT. Attended Juilliard. Debut 1981 OB in "How It All Began," followed by "Henry IV Part I," "The Ballad of Dexter Creed," Bdwy in "Death of a Salesman" (1984).

KRAMER, JOEL. Born July 1, 1943 in The Bronx, NY. Graduate Queens Col., UMich. Debut 1963 OB in "St. Joan of the Stockyards," followed by "Playboy of the Western World," "Measure for Measure," "The Man Who Corrupted Hadleyburg," "Call Me Madam," "Castaways," "Esther," "Bodo," Bdwy in "Animals" (1981).

KRATKY, BOB. Born May 10, 1955 in East St. Louis, IL. Graduate S.Ill.U. FlaStateU. Debut 1985 OB in "Cherokee County."

KRAWFORD, GARY. Born Mar. 23, 1941 in Kitchener, Can. Debut 1968 OB in "The Fantasticks," followed by "Manhattan Apartment," "Dear Oscar," "Anyone Can Whistle," "Sullivan and Gilbert," Bdwy in "Pousse Cafe," "Education of Hyman Kaplan," "Company."

KRESSIN, LIANNE. Born Jan. 5, 1952 in Rochester, PA. Graduate UTenn. Debut 1977 OB in "The Present Tense," followed by "Grand Magic," "Porch."

KUNKLE, CONNIE. Born Apr. 4, 1958 in Memphis, TN. Graduate Ohio U. Debut 1985 OB in "Manhattan Serenade."

KURTZ, MARCIA JEAN. Born in The Bronx, NY. Juilliard graduate. Debut 1966 OB in "Jonah," followed by "America Hurrah," "Red Cross," "Muzeeka," "The Effects of Gamma Rays. . . ," "The Year Boston Won the Pennant," "The Mirror," "The Orphan," "Action," "The Dybbuk," "Ivanov," "What's Wrong with This Picture?," Bdwy in "The Chinese and Dr. Fish," "Thieves."

LACHOW, STAN. Born Dec. 20, 1931 in Brooklyn, NY. Graduate Roger Williams U. Debut 1977 OB in "Come Back, Little Sheba," followed by "Diary of Anne Frank," "Time of the Cuckoo," "Angelus," "The Middleman," "Charley Bacon and Family," "Crossing the Bar," Bdwy in "On Golden Pond."

LAGERFELT, CAROLYN. Born Sept. 23 in Paris. Graduate AADA. Bdwy debut 1971 in "The Philanthropist," followed by "4 on a Garden," "Jockey Club Stakes," "The Constant Wife," "Otherwise Engaged," "Betrayal," "The Real Thing," OB in "Look Back in Anger," "Close of Play," "Sea Anchor," "Quartermaine's Terms," "Other Places."

LaGIOIA, JOHN P. Born Nov. 24, 1937 in Philadelphia, PA. Graduate Temple U. OB in "Keyhole," "Lovers in the Metro," "The Cherry Orchard," "Titus Andronicus," "Henry VI," "Richard III," "A Little Madness," Bdwy in "Henry V" (1969).

LaGRECA, PAUL. Born June 23, 1962 in The Bronx, NY. Graduate AADA. Debut 1983 OB in "Barnum's Last Life," followed by "Really Rosie."

LAHTI, CHRISTINE. Born Apr. 4, 1950 in Detroit, MI. Graduate UMich, HB Studio. Debut 1979 OB in 'The Wood" for which she received a Theatre World Award followed by "Landscape of the Body," "The Country Girl," Bdwy in "Loose Ends" (1980), followed by "Division Street," "Scenes and Revelations," "Present Laughter."

LAM, DIANE. Born Mar. 6, 1945 in Honolulu, HI. Graduate UHi, SMU. Bdwy debut in "Pacific Overures" (1977), followed by "The King and I" (1977), OB in "Anyone Can Whistle," "Pacific Overtures" (1984).

LAM, JENNIFER. Born Feb. 9, 1967 in Honolulu, HI. Bdwy debut in "The King and I" (1977), OB in "Pacific Overtures" (1984).

LAMONT, ROBIN. Born June 2, 1950 in Boston, MA. Attended Carnegie-Mellon U. Debut 1971 OB in "Godspell," followed by "Thoughts," "Taboo in Revue," Bdwy in "Godspell" (1976), "Working."

LANDON, SOFIA. Born Jan 24, 1949 in Montreal, Can. Attended Northwestern U. Debut 1971 OB in "Red, White and Black," followed by "Gypsy," "Missouri Legend," "Heartbreak House," "Peg o' My Heart," "Scenes and Revelations," "The Hasty Heart," "Blue Window."

LANDRON, JACK. Born June 2, 1938 in San Juan, PR. Graduate Emerson Col. Debut 1970 OB in "Ododo," followed by "Mother Courage and Her Children," "If You Promise Not to Learn," "What's a Nice Country Like You. . . ," "Spell 7," "Mondongo," "Ballet Behind the Bridge," Bdwy in "Hurry Harry" (1972), "Dr. Jazz," "Tough to Get Help," "Murderous Angels."

LANE, NANCY. Born June 16, 1951 in Passaic, NJ. Attended Va. CommonwealthU., AADA. Debut 1975 OB and Broadway in "A Chorus Line."

LANE, NATHAN. Born Feb. 3, 1956 in Jersey City, NJ. Debut 1978 OB in "A Midsummer Night's Dream," followed by "Love," "She Stoops to Conquer," Bdwy in "Present Laughter" (1982) "Merlin."

LANG, CHARLEY. Born Oct. 24, 1955 in Passaic, NJ. Graduate Catholic U. Bdwy debut 1978 in "Da," followed by "Once a Catholic," "Mass Appeal," "Strange Interlude," OB in "Class Enemy," "Young Bucks."

LANG, STEPHEN. Born July 11, 1952 in NYC. Graduate Swarthmore Col. Debut 1975 OB in "Hamlet," followed by "Henry V," "Shadow of a Gunman," "A Winter's Tale," "Johnny On a Spot," "Barbarians," "Ah, Men," "Clownmaker," "Hannah," Bdwy in "St. Joan" (1977), "Death of a Salesman" (1984).

LANGE, ANN. Born June 24, 1953 in Pipestone, MN. Attended Carnegie-Mellon U. Debut 1979 OB in "Rat's Nest," followed by "Hunting Scenes from Lower Bavaria," "Crossfire," "Linda Her and the Fairy Garden," Bdwy in "The Survivor" (1981).

LANGELLA, FRANK. Born Jan 1, 1940 in Bayonne, NJ. Graduate Syracuse U. Debut 1963 OB in "The Immoralist," followed by "The Old Glory," "Good Day," "White Devil," "Yerma," "Iphigenia in Aulis,," "A Cry of Players," "Prince of Homburg," "After the Fall," Bdwy in "Seascape" (1975), "Dracula," "Amadeus," "Passion," "Design for Living," "Hurlyburly."

LANNING, JERRY. Born May 17, 1943 in Miami, Fl. Graduate USCal. Bdwy debut 1966 in "Mame" for which he received a Theatre World Award, followed by "1776," "Where's Charley?," "My Fair Lady," OB in "Memphis Store Bought Teeth," "Berlin to Broadway," "Sextet," "Isn't It Romantic."

LANSING, ROBERT. Born June 5, 1929 in San Diego, CA. Bdwy debut 1951 in "Stalag 17," followed by "Cyrano de Bergerac," "Richard III," "Charley's Aunt," "The Lovers," "Cue for Passion," "Great God Brown," "Cut of the Axe," "Finishing Touches," OB in "The Father," "The Cost of Living."

LARSEN, LIZ. Born Jan. 16, 1959 in Philadelphia, PA. Attended Hofstra U, SUNY/Purchase. Bdwy debut 1981 in "Fiddler on the Roof," OB in "Kuni Leml."

LARSON, JILL. Born Oct. 7, 1947 in Minneapolis, MN. Graduate Hunter Col. Debut 1980 OB in "These Men," followed by "Peep," "Serious Bizness," "It's Only a Play," "Red Rover," "Enter a Freeman," Bdwy in "Romantic Comedy" ('80).

LASKY, ZANE. Born Apr. 23, 1953 in NYC. Attended Manhattan Col. HB Studio. Debut 1973 OB in "The Hot 1 Baltimore," followed by "The Prodigal," "Innocent Thoughts, Harmless Intentions," "Time Framed," "Balm in Gilead," "Shlemiel the First." Bdwy in "All Over Town" (1974).

LASSER, LOUISE. Born Apr. 11, 1939 in NYC. Attended Brandeis U. Bdwy debut 1962 in "I Can Get It for You Wholesale," followed by "Henry, Sweet Henry," "The Chinese and Dr. Fish," "Thieves," OB in "The Third Ear," "Are You Now or Have You Ever Been," "Marie and Bruce," "A Coupla White Chicks," "Good Neighbors."

LAURENCE, PAULA. Born Jan. 25 in Brooklyn, NY. Bdwy debut 1936 in "Horse Eats Hat," followed by "Dr. Faustus," "Junior Miss," "Something for the Boys," "One Touch of Venus," "Cyrano de Bergerac," 'The Liar," "Season in the Sun," "Tovarich," "The Time of Your Life," "Beggar's Opera," "Hotel Paradiso," "Night of the Iguana," "Have I Got a Girl for You," "Ivanov," "Rosalie in Concert," OB in "7 Days of Mourning," "Roberta in Concert," "One Touch of Venus," "Coming of Age in SoHo."

LAWRENCE, ELIZABETH. Born Sept. 6, 1922 in Huntington, WVa. Graduate UMich, Yeshiva U. Bdwy debut 1954 in "The Rainmaker," followed by "All the Way Home," "Look Homeward Angel," "A Matter of Gravity," "Strange Interlude," OB in "The Misunderstanding," "Rockaway," "Children."

LaZEBNIK, KENNETH. Born Nov. 11, 1954 in Levittown, PA. Graduate MacAlester Col., RADA. Debut 1985 OB in "The Taming of the Shrew."

LEAGUE, JANET. Born Oct. 13, in Chicago, IL. Attended Goodman Theatre. Debut 1969 OB in "To Be Young, Gifted and Black," followed by "Tiger at the Gates," "The Screens," "Mrs. Snow," "Please Don't Cry and Say No," "Banana Box," "The Brothers," "American Dreams," "Suzanna Andler," "Long Time Since Yesterday," Bdwy in "First Breeze of Summer" (1975), "For Colored Girls Who Have Considered Suicide . . ."

LEARY, DAVID. Born Aug. 8, 1939 in Brooklyn, NY. Attended CCNY. Debut 1969 OB in "Shoot Anything That Moves," followed by "Macbeth," "The Plough and the Stars," "Emigres," "Sus," "Before the Dawn," Bdwy in "The National Health," "Da," "The Lady from Dubuque," "Piaf."

LECESNE, JAMES. Born Nov. 24, 1954 in New Jersey. Debut 1982 OB in "One-Man Band," followed by "Cloud 9," revival of "One-Man Band" (1985).

L'ECUYER, JIM. Born July 21, 1958 in Leominster, MA. Graduate Roger Williams Col. Debut 1981 OB in "Ka-Boom!," followed by "Irma La Douce," "Aladdin," "The Blind Venetians."

LEE, KAIULANI. Born Feb. 28, 1950 in Princeton, NJ. Attended American U. Bdwy debut 1975 in "Kennedy's Children," followed by "Macbeth," "Pack of Lies," OB in "Ballad of the Sad Cafe," "Museum," "Safe House," "Days to Come," "Othello," "Strange Snow."

LeFEVRE, ADAM. Born Aug. 11, 1950 in Albany, NY. Graduate Williams Col., UIowa. Debut 1981 OB in "Turnbuckle," followed by "Badgers," "Goose and Tomtom," "In the Country," "Submariners."

LEIBMAN, RON. Born Oct. 11, 1937 in NYC. Attended Ohio Wesleyan, Actors Studio. Bdwy debut 1963 in "Dear Me, the Sky Is Falling," followed by "Bicycle Ride to Nevada," "The Deputy," "We Bombed in New Haven" for which he received a Theatre World Award, "Cop-Out," "I Ought to Be in Pictures," "Doubles," OB in "The Academy," "John Brown's Body," "Scapin," "The Premise," "Legend of Lovers," "Dead End," "Poker Session," "Transfers," "Room Service," "Love Two," "Rich and Famous," "Children of Darkness," "Non Pasquale."

LEMON, BEN. Born May 21, 1955 in Tarrytown, NY. Graduate Brown U. Debut 1980 OB in "Dulcy," followed by "Love's Labour's Lost."

LENNEY, DINAH. Born Nov. 18, 1956 in NYC. Graduate Yale U. Debut 1982 OB in "Vagabond Stars," followed by "The Winds of Change," "Voice Print," "Colonomos."

LeNOIRE, ROSETTA. Born Aug. 8, 1911 in NYC. Attended AmThWing. Bdwy debut 1936 in "Macbeth," followed by "Bassa Moona," "Hot Mikado," "Marching with Johnny," "Janie," "Decision," "Three's a Family," "Destry Rides Again," "Finian's Rainbow," "South Pacific," "Sophie," "Tambourines to Glory," "Blues for Mr. Charlie," "The Great Indoors," "Lost in the Stars," "The Royal Family," "You Can't Take It with You," OB in "Bible Salesman," "Double Entry," "Clandestine on the Morning Line," "Cabin in the Sky," "Lady Day," "Show Boat," "Cry of Players," "A Streetcar Named Desire," "Northern Boulevard."

LENOX, ADRIANE. Born Sept. 11, 1956 in Memphis, TN. Graduate Lambuth Col. Bdwy debut 1979 in "Ain't Misbehavin'," followed by "Dreamgirls."

LEO, MELISSA. Born Sept. 14, 1960 in NYC. Attended SUNY/Purchase. Debut 1984 OB in "Cinders," followed by "Out of Gas on Lover's Leap."

LEON, JOSEPH. Born June 8, 1923 in NYC. Attended NYU, UCLA. Bdwy debut 1950 in "Bell, Book and Candle," followed by "Seven Year Itch," "Pipe Dream," "Fair Game," "Gazebo," "Julia, Jake and Uncle Joe," "Beauty Part," "Merry Widow," "Henry, Sweet Henry," "Jimmy Shine," "All Over Town," "California Suite," "The Merchant," "Break a Leg," "Once a Catholic," "Fools," "Glengarry Glen Ross," OB in "Come Share My House," "Dark Corners," "Interrogation of Havana," "Are You Now or Have You Ever," "Second Avenue Rag," "Buck," "Ah, Wilderness!"

LEONARD, ROBERT. Born Feb. 28, 1969 in Westwood, NJ. Debut 1985 OB in "Sally's Gone, She Left Her Name," followed by "Coming of Age in SoHo."

LESLIE, MICHAEL. Born Mar. 31, 1952 in Neptune, NJ. Graduate Rutgers U, Cornell U. Bdwy debut 1978 in "Hair," OB in "Butterfingers Angel," "Mowgli."

LEVELS, CALVIN. Born Sept. 30, 1954 in Cleveland, OH. Graduate CCC. Bdwy debut 1984 in "Open Admissions" for which he received a Theatre World Award.

LEWIS, MARCIA. Born Aug. 18, 1938 in Melrose, MA. Attended UCin. OB in "The Impudent Wolf," "Who's Who, Baby," "God Bless Coney," "Let Yourself Go," "Romance Language," Bdwy in "The Time of Your Life," "Hello, Dolly!," "Annie."

LEWIS, TODD. Born May 26, 1952 in Chicago, IL. Graduate Lewis U. Debut 1979 OB in "Flying Blind," followed by "Willy and Sahara," "Sawney Bean," "A Perfect Diamond."

LIBERATORE, LOU. Born Aug. 4, 1959 in Jersey City, NJ. Graduate Fordham U. Debut 1982 OB in "The Great Grandson of Jedediah Kohler," followed by "Threads," "Black Angel," "Richard II," "Thymus Vulgaris," "As Is," Bdwy "As Is" (1985).

LICATO, FRANK. Born Apr. 20, 1952 in Brooklyn, NY. Attended Emerson Col. Debut 1974 OB in "Deathwatch," followed by "Dawn," "Angel City," "Killer's Head," "Haunted Lives."

LINAHAN, DONALD. Born Feb. 22, 1936 in Uniontown, PA. Graduate Wm. & Mary Col. Bdwy debut 1975 in "All God's Chillun Got Wings," followed by "Days in the Trees," "Kingdoms," OB in "Cracks," "Dreams of the Son."

LIND, JANE. Born Nov. 6, 1950 in Hump Back Bay, Perryville, AK. Attended NYU. Debut 1981 OB in "Black Elk Lives," followed by "49," "The Ecstasy of Rita Joe."

LIND, KIRSTEN. Born Feb. 12, in Delft, Holland. Graduate NYU. Debut 1982 OB in "Deep in the Heart," followed by "Very Warm for May."

LINES, SYBIL (aka Marion) Born Feb. 10 in London, Eng. Attended Central School. Debut 1976 OB in "The Philanderer," followed by "Claw," "Penultimate Problem of Sherlock Holmes," "The Team," "The Wit to Woo," "Small Change," "Quartermaine's Terms," "Crimes of Vautrin," Bdwy in "Bedroom Farce" (1979).

LITHGOW, JOHN. Born Oct. 19, 1945 in Rochester, NY. Graduate Harvard U. Bdwy debut 1973 in "The Changing Room," followed by "My Fat Friend," "Comedians," "Anna Christie," "Once in a Lifetime," "Spokesong," "Bedroom Farce," "Division Street," "Beyond Therapy," "Requiem for a Heavyweight," OB in "Hamlet," "Trelawny of the Wells," "A Memory of Two Mondays," "Secret Service," "Boy Meets Girl," "Salt Lake City Skyline," "Kaufman at Large."

LITTLE, CLEAVON. Born June 1, 1939 in Chickasha, OK. Attended San Diego State U., AADA. Debut 1967 OB in "Macbird," followed by "Hamlet," "Someone's Coming Hungry," "Ofay Watcher," "Scuba Duba," "Narrow Road to the Deep North," "Great MacDaddy," "Joseph and the Amazing Technicolor Dreamcoat," "Resurrection of Lady Lester," "Keyboard," "I'm Not Rappaport," Bdwy in "Jimmy Shine," "Purlie," "All over Town," "The Poison Tree."

LITTLE, DAVID. Born Mar. 21, 1937 in Wadesboro, NC. Graduate Wm. & Mary Col., Catholic U. Debut 1967 OB in "MacBird," followed by "Iphigenia in Aulis," "Antony and Cleopatra," "Antigone," "An Enemy of the People," "Three Sons," "Les Blancs," "Almost in Vegas," Bdwy in "Thieves," "Zalmen, or the Madness of God."

LIVINGSTONE, ANNIE. Born Apr. 4, 1963 in San Diego, CA. Attended El Camino Col. Debut 1985 OB in "Surf City."

LIZZUL, ANTHONY JOHN. Born Jan. 11 in the Bronx, NYC. Graduate NYU. Debut 1977 OB in "The Cherry Orchard," followed by "The Prophets," "Lady Windermere's Fan," "Revenger's Tragedy," "Twelfth Night," "Night Talk," "The Butterfingers Angel," "Consenting Adults."

LOBBAN, LYNN. Born Sept. 2, 1949 in Jersey City, NJ. Attended Dartmouth Col. Debut 1975 OB in "Berkeley Square," followed by "Downriver," "Rio Grande," "Quilters."

LONDON, BECKY. Born Feb. 11, 1958 in Philadelphia, PA. Graduate Yale U. Debut 1985 OB in "Isn't It Romantic."

LONG, JODI. Born in NYC. Graduate SUNY/Purchase. Bdwy debut 1963 in "Nowhere to Go but Up," followed by "Loose Ends," "Bacchae," OB in "Fathers and Sons," "Family Devotions," "Rohwer," "Tooth of Crime," "Dream of Kitamura," "A Midsummer Night's Dream."

LONGWELL, KAREN. Born Feb. 7, 1955 in Ithaca, NY. Graduate Fredonia State Col., Ithaca Col. Debut 1983 OB in "The Robber Bridegroom" followed by "Very Warm for May."

LOPEZ, PRISCILLA. Born Feb. 26, 1948 in The Bronx, NY. Bdwy debut 1966 in "Breakfast at Tiffany's," followed by "Henry, Sweet Henry," "Lysistrata," "Company," "Her First Roman," "The Boy Friend," "Pippin," "A Chorus Line," "A Day in Hollywood/A Night in the Ukraine," "Nine," OB in "What's a Nice Country Like you . . . ," "Key Exchange," "Buck," "Extremities," "Non Pasquale," "Be Happy for Me."

LORRE, LOLITA. Born Jan. 25, 1960 in Cleveland, OH. Graduate Boston U. Debut 1984 OB in "La Mulata," followed by "Delirious," "A Fool's Errand."

LOTI, ELISA. Born Aug. 26 in Guayaquil, Ecuador. Vassar graduate. Bdwy debut 1961 in "Rhinoceros," OB in "Come Share My House" (1960) for which she received a Theatre World Award, "The Laundry," "Lucky Rita," "A Murder Is Announced," "Enter Laughing," "Before the Dawn."

LOTT, LAWRENCE. Born Apr. 13, 1950 in Greeley, CO. Graduate UCal/Irvine, UPittsburgh. Debut 1976 OB in "Bingo," followed by "Heartbreak House," "Two Noble Kinsmen," "The Normal Heart."

LOUDON, DOROTHY. Born Sept. 17, 1933 in Boston, MA. Attended Emerson Col., Syracuse U. Debut 1961 in "World of Jules Feiffer," Bdwy 1963 in "Nowhere to Go but Up" for which she received a Theatre World Award followed by "Noel Coward's Sweet Potato," "Fig Leaves Are Falling," "Three Men on a Horse," "The Women," "Annie," "Ballroom," "West Side Waltz," "Noises Off."

LUCAS, ROXIE. Born Aug. 25, 1951 in Memphis, TN. Attended UHouston. Bdwy debut 1981 in "The Best Little Whorehouse in Texas," followed by "Harrigan 'n Hart."

LUCKINBILL, LAURENCE. Born Nov. 21, 1938 in Ft. Smith, AR. Graduate UAr., Catholic U. Bdwy debut 1962 in "A Man for All Seasons," followed by "Beekman Place," "Poor Murderers," "A Meeting by the River," "The Shadow Box," "Chapter Two," "Past Tense," "Dancing in the End Zone," OB in "Oedipus Rex," "There's a Play Tonight," "The Fantasticks," "Tartuffe," "Boys in the Band," "Horseman, Pass By," "Memory Bank," "What the Butler Saw," "Alpha Beta," "A Prayer for My Daughter," "Life of Galileo."

LUDWIG, KAREN. Born Oct. 9 in San Francisco, CA. Bdwy debut 1964 in "The Deputy," followed by "The Devils," "Bacchae," OB in "The Trojan Women," "Red Cross," "Muzeeka," "Huui, Huui," "Our Last Night," "Seagull," "Museum," "Nasty Rumors," "Daisy," "Gethsemene Springs," "After the Revolution," "Before She Is Even Born," "Exiles," "Messiah."

LUDWIG, SALEM. Born July 31, 1915 in Brooklyn, NY. Attended Brooklyn Col. Bdwy debut 1946 in "Miracle in the Mountains," followed by "Camino Real," "Enemy of the People," "All You Need Is One Good Break," "Inherit the Wind," "Disenchanted," "Rhinoceros," "Three Sisters," "The Zulu and the Zayda," "Moonchildren," "American Clock," OB in "Brothers Karamazov," "Victim," "Troublemaker," "Man of Destiny," "Night of the Dunce," "Corner of the Bed," "Awake and Sing," "Prodigal," "Babylon," "Burnt Flower Bed," "American Clock," "Friends Too Numerous to Mention," "What's Wrong with This Picture," "After the Fall."

LUM, ALVIN. Born May 28, 1931 in Honolulu, HI. Attended U Hi. Debut 1969 OB in "In the Bar of a Tokyo Hotel," followed by "Pursuit of Happiness," "Monkey Music," "Flowers and Household Gods," "Station J," "Double Dutch," "Teahouse," "Song for a Nisei Fisherman," "Empress of China," "Manoa Valley," Bdwy in "Lovely Ladies, Kind Gentlemen," "Two Gentlemen of Verona."

LUM, MARY. Born July 26, 1948 in NYC. Graduate Hunter Col. Debut 1982 OB in "Hibakusha: Stories from Hiroshima," followed by "Plaid on Both Sides," "Full-Time Active," "Autumn Dusk," "Afternoon Shower," "Food," "Sister Sister," "Daughters," "Electra Speaks," "Caucasian Chalk Circle," "Julius Caesar," "Eat a Bowl of Tea."

LUNA, BARBARA. Born Mar. 2, 1939 in NYC. Bdwy debut 1951 in "The King and I," followed by "West Side Story," "A Chorus Line," OB in "Fly by Night."

LuPONE, PATTI. Born Apr. 21, 1949 in Northport, NY. Juilliard graduate. Debut 1972 OB in "School for Scandal," followed by "Women Beware Women," "Next Time I'll Sing to You," "Beggar's Opera, "Scapin," "Robber Bridegroom," "Edward II," "The Woods," "Edmond," "America Kicks Up Its Heels," "The Cradle Will Rock," Bdwy in "The Water Engine" (1978), "Working," "Evita," "Oliver!", "Accidental Death of an Anarchist."

LUSTIG, AARON. Born Sept. 17, 1956 in Rochester, NY. Graduate Ithaca Col. Debut 1979 OB in "The Second Man," followed by "Lone Star," "White Boys," "Story of the Gadsbys," "Well of the Saints," "Death Knocks."

LUTSKY, MARC. Born Apr. 15 in NYC. Attended Lehman Col. OB in "The Misanthrope," "The Investigation," "Twelfth Night," "And Baby Makes Four," "The Lunch Girls."

LUZ, FRANC. (aka Frank C.) Born Dec. 22 in Cambridge, MA. Attended NMxStateU. Debut 1974 OB in "The Rivals," followed by "Fiorello!," "The Little Shop of Horrors," Bdwy in "Whoopee!" (1979).

LYMAN, DOROTHY. Born Apr. 18, 1947 in Minneapolis, MN. Attended St. Lawrence Col. Debut OB in "America Hurrah," followed by "Pequod," "American Hamburger League," "Action," "Fefu and Her Friends," "Later," "A Coupla White Chicks," Bdwy in "Dancing in the End Zone" (1985).

LYNCH, LUKE. Born Apr. 23, 1957 in Gardner, MA. Graduate UConn. Debut 1984 OB in "Up in Central Park," followed by "Teddy Roosevelt," "Don 'n Suds," "Bugles at Dawn," "Manhattan Serenade," "Northern Boulevard."

LYND, BETTY. Born In Los Angeles, CA. Debut 1968 OB in "Rondelay," followed by "Love Me, Love My Children," Bdwy in "The Skin of Our Teeth" (1975), "A Chorus Line."

LYNG, NORA MAE. Born Jan. 27, 1951 in Jersey City, NJ. Debut 1981 OB in "Anything Goes," followed by "Forbidden Broadway," "Road to Hollywood."

LYNN, JOE. Born July 4 in Cleveland, OH. Graduate Kent State U. Bdwy debut 1978 in "Timbuktu," followed by "Your Arms Too Short to Box with God," "Ain't Misbehavin'," "Dreamgirls," OB in "Raisin," "Downriver," "In De Beginnin' "

LYNN, JOYCE. Born Nov. 28, 1935 in Norristown, PA. Attended Lamont Sch., AADA. Bdwy debut 1962 in "Milk and Honey," OB in "Jo," "Autumn's Here," "Jane Eyre," "Prisoner of Second Avenue," "Dispatches from Hell," "Roberta."

MACKAY, LIZBETH. Born March 7 in Buffalo, NY. Graduate Adelphi U., Yale. Bdwy debut 1981 in "Crimes of the Heart" for which she received a Theatre World Award.

MACKAY, MORGAN. Born Oct. 13, 1950 in Brooklyn, NY. Graduate Pepperdine U., Yale. Debut 1983 OB in "The Brooklyn Bridge," followed by "Northern Boulevard."

MACNAUGHTON, ROBERT. Born Dec. 19, 1966 in NYC. Debut 1980 OB in "The Diviners," followed by "Henry V."

MacNICOL, PETER. Born April 10 in Dallas, TX. Attended UMn. Bdwy debut 1981 in "Crimes of the Heart" for which he received a Theatre World Award, OB in "Found a Peanut."

MacVITTIE, BRUCE. Born Oct. 14, 1956 in Providence, RI. Graduate Boston U. Bdwy debut 1983 in "American Buffalo," followed by "California Dog Fight."

MAGNUSON, MERILEE. Born June 11, 1951 in Tacoma, WA. Attended UCal/Irvine. Bdwy debut 1973 in "Gigi," followed by "Irene," "The Best Little Whorehouse in Texas," "My One and Only," "Harrigan 'n Hart," OB in "Dancing in the Dark."

MAHAFFEY, VALERIE. Born June 16, 1953 in Sumatra, Indonesia. Graduate UTx. Debut 1975 OB in "Father Uxbridge Wants to Marry," followed by "Bus Stop," "Black Tuesday," "Scenes and Revelations," (also Bdwy), "Twelve Dreams," "Translations," "Butter and Egg Man," "Top Girls," "Romance Language," Bdwy in "Rex," "Dracula," "Fearless Frank," "Play Memory," "Loves of Anatole."

MAHONEY, JOHN. Born June 20, 1940 in Manchester, Eng. Attended Quincy Col., W.Ill.U. Debut 1985 OB in "Orphans" for which he received a Theatre World Award.

MAIS, MICHELE. Born July 30, 1954 in NYC. Graduate CCNY. Debut 1975 OB in "Godspell," followed by "Othello," "Superspy," "Yesterday Continued," "We'll Be Right Back," "Que Ubo?," "El Bravo!," "Opening Night," "Surrender/a flirtation," Bdwy in "Zoot Suit" (1979).

MAKALINA. Born Dec. 9, 1952 on Guam. Graduate Fordham U. Debut 1984 OB in "State without Grace."

MALKOVICH, JOHN. Born Dec. 9, 1953 in Christopher, IL. Attended EastIllU, IllStateU. Debut 1982 OB in "True West" for which he received a Theatre World Award, Bdwy in "Death of a Salesman" (1984).

MALLON, BRIAN. Born May 12, 1952 in Detroit, MI. Attended UMich. Debut 1980 OB in "Guests of the Nation," followed by "Moliere in spite of Himself," "Mr. Joyce Is Leaving Paris," "Shadow of a Gunman."

MANGANO, NICK. Born Oct. 22, 1958 in Brooklyn, NY. Attended Hofstra U. Debut 1981 in "Oh! Calcutta!"

MANN, ALISON. Born Apr. 4 in Lakewood, NJ. Bdwy debut in "A Chorus Line" (1983) followed by "Harrigan 'n Hart."

MANOFF, DINAH. Born Jan. 25, 1958 in NYC. Attended CalArts. Bdwy debut 1980 in "I Ought to Be in Pictures" for which she received a Theatre World Award, followed by "Leader of the Pack," OB in "Gifted Children."

MANTEGNA, JOE. Born Nov. 13, 1947 in Chicago, IL. Attended Goodman Theatre School. Bdwy debut 1978 in "Working," followed by "Glengarry Glen Ross."

MANTELL, PAUL. Born Nov. 21, 1953 in Brooklyn, NY. Graduate Carnegie-Mellon U. Debut 1975 OB in "The Mikado," followed by "Don Juan," "Little Malcolm," "Richard II," "Line," "Moving Day," "Merchant of Venice," "The Key and the Wall," "Lush Life," "Pushcart Peddlers," "Dreamboats," "Beagelman and Brackett," "Walk the Dog, Willie."

MARADEN, FRANK. Born Aug. 9, 1944 in Norfolk, VA. Graduate UMn., MichStateU. Debut 1980 OB with BAM Theatre Co. in "A Winter's Tale," "Johnny on a Spot," "Barbarians," "The Wedding," "Midsummer Night's Dream," "The Recruiting Officer," "The Wild Duck," "Jungle of Cities," "Three Acts of Recognition," "Don Juan," "The Workroom," "Egyptology," "Photographer," "Landscape of the Body," "Pantomime," "Romance Language."

MARCHAND, NANCY. Born June 19, 1928 in Buffalo, NY. Graduate Carnegie Tech. Debut 1951 in CC's "Taming of the Shrew," followed by "Merchant of Venice," "Much Ado about Nothing," "Three Bags Full," "After the Rain," "The Alchemist," "Yerma," "Cyrano de Bergerac," "Mary Stuart," "Enemies," "The Plough and the Stars," "40 Carats," "And Miss Reardon Drinks a Little," "Veronica's Room," "Awake and Sing," "The Octette Bridge Club," OB in "The Balcony," "Children," "Taken in Marriage," "Morning's at 7," "Sister Mary Ignatius Explains It All."

MARCUM, KEVIN. Born Nov. 7, 1955 in Danville, IL. Attended UIll. Bdwy debut 1976 in "My Fair Lady," followed by "I Remember Mama," "Cats," "Sunday in the Park with George."

MARCUS, DANIEL. Born May 26, 1955 in Redwood City, CA. Graduate Boston U. Bdwy debut 1981 in "The Pirates of Penzance," followed OB in "La Boheme," "Kuni Leml."

MARCY, HELEN. Born June 3, 1920 in Worcester, MA. Attended Yale U. Bdwy in "Twelfth Night," "In Bed We Cry," "Dream Girl," "Love and Let Love," OB in "Lady Windermere's Fan," "Verdict," "Hound of the Baskervilles," "Appointment with Death," "Ladies in Retirement," "Dr. Cook's Garden."

MARDIROSIAN, TOM. Born Dec. 14, 1947 in Buffalo, NY. Graduate UBuffalo. Debut 1976 OB in "Gemini," followed by "Grand Magic," "Losing Time," "Passione," "Success and Succession," "Ground Zero Club," "Cliffhanger," "Cap and Bells," Bdwy in "Happy End," "Magic Show."

MARGOLIS, LAURA. Born Sept. 17, 1951 in Kansas City, MO. Graduate Catholic U. Debut 1978 OB in "Laura," followed by "Getting Ready," "Mantikee," "Arms and the Man," "Merchant of Venice."

MARGOLIS, MARK. Born Nov. 26, 1939 in Malta. Attended Temple U. Bdwy debut 1962 in "Infidel Caesar," OB in "Second Avenue Rag," "My Uncle Sam," "The Golem."

MARGULIES, DAVID. Born Feb. 19, 1937 in NYC. Graduate CCNY. Debut 1958 OB in "Golden Six," followed by "Six Characters in Search of an Author," "Tragical Historie of Dr. Faustus," "Tango," "Little Murders," "Seven Days of Mourning," "Last Analysis," "An Evening with the Poet Senator," "Kid Champion," "The Man with the Flower in His Mouth," "Old Tune," "David and Paula," "Cabal of Hypocrites," Bdwy in "The Iceman Cometh" (1973), "Zalmen or the Madness of God," "Comedians," "Break a Leg," "West Side Waltz," "Brighton Beach Memoirs."

MARINOS, PETER. Born Oct. 2, 1951 in Pontiac, MI. Graduate MiStateU, Bdwy debut 1976 in "Chicago," followed by "Evita," "Zorba."

MARKS, KENNETH. Born Feb. 17, 1954 in Harwick, PA. Graduate UPa, Lehigh U. Debut 1978 OB in "Clara Bow Loves Gary Cooper," followed by "Canadian Gothic," "Time and the Conways," "Savoury Meringue," "Thrombo."

MARSHALL, AMELIA. Born Apr. 2, 1958 in Albany, GA. Graduate UTex. Debut 1982 OB in "Applause," Bdwy in "Harrigan 'n Hart" (1985).

MARSHALL, E. G. Born June 18, 1910 in Owatonna, MN. Bdwy debut 1938 in "Prelude to Glory," followed by "Jason," "Skin of Our Teeth," "Petrified Forest," "Jacobowsky and the Colonel," "The Iceman Cometh," "Hope's the Thing," "Survivors," "The Crucible," "Red Roses for Me," "Waiting for Godot," "The Gang's All Here," "The Little Foxes," "Plaza Suite," "Nash at 9," "John Gabriel Borkman," OB in "Mass Appeal," "She Stoops to Conquer."

MARSHALL, KEN (Kenneth). Born in 1953 in Cleveland, OH. Graduate UMi, Juilliard. Debut 1973 OB in "Pericles," followed by "Becoming Memories," "Playboy of the Western World," "Hamlet," "A Midsummer Night's Dream," Bdwy in "West Side Story" (1980).

MARTIN, GEORGE N. Born Aug. 15, 1929 in NYC. Bdwy debut 1970 in "Wilson in the Promise Land," followed by "The Hothouse," "Plenty," "Total Abandon," "Pack of Lies," OB in "Painting Churches," "Henry V."

MARTIN, JARED. Born Dec. 21, 1943 in NYC. Graduate Columbia. Debut 1967 OB in "Hamlet as a Happening," Bdwy in "Torch Song Trilogy" (1983).

MARTIN, LUCY. Born Feb. 8, 1942 in NYC. Graduate Sweet Briar Col. Debut 1962 OB in "Electra," followed by "Happy as Larry," "The Trojan Women," "Iphigenia in Aulis," "Wives," "The Cost of Living," Bdwy in "Shelter" (1973), "Children of a Lesser God."

MARTIN, MILLICENT. Born June 8, 1934 in Romford, Eng. Attended Atalia Conti Sch. Bdwy debut 1954 in "The Boy Friend," followed by "Side by Side by Sondheim," "King of Hearts," "42nd Street."

MARTIN, W. T. Born Jan. 17, 1947 in Providence, RI. Attended Lafayette Col. Debut 1972 OB in "Basic Training of Pavlo Hummel," followed by "Ghosts," "The Caretaker," "Are You Now or Have You Ever Been," "Fairy Tales of New York," "We Won't Pay," "Black Elk Lives," "The End of the War," "A Little Madness," "All the Nice People," "Enter a Free Man," "The Other Side of Newark."

MASTERS, BEN. Born May 6, 1947 in Corvallis, OR. Graduate UOr. Debut 1970 OB in "Boys in the Band," followed by "What the Butler Saw," "The Cherry Orchard," "Key Exchange," "Eden Court," Bdwy in "Capt. Brassbound's Conversion," "Plenty."

MASTRANTONIO, MARY ELIZABETH. Born Nov. 17, 1958 in Chicago, IL. Attended UIll. Bdwy debut 1980 in "West Side Story," followed by "Copperfield," "Oh, Brother!," OB in "Henry V."

MATHERS, JAMES. Born Oct. 31, 1936 in Seattle, WA. Graduate UWA., Beverly Col. Debut 1983 OB in "Happy Birthday, Wanda June," followed by "Uncommon Holidays," "Harvest of Strangers."

MATHEWS, CARMEN. Born May 8, 1918 in Philadelphia, PA. Graduate RADA. Bdwy debut 1938 in "Henry IV," followed by "Hamlet," "Richard II," "Harriet," "Cherry Orchard," "The Assassin," "Man and Superman," "Ivy Green," "Courtin' Time," "My Three Angels," "Holiday for Lovers," "Night Life," "Lorenzo," "The Yearling," "Delicate Balance," "I'm Solomon," "Dear World," "Ring Round the Bathtub," "Ambassador," "Copperfield," "Morning's at 7," OB in "Sunday in the Park with George."

MATSUSAKA, TOM. Born Aug. 8, in Wahiawa, HI. Graduate MiStateU. Bdwy bow 1968 in "Mame," followed by "Ride the Winds," "Pacific Overtures," OB in "Agamemnon," "Chu Chem," "Jungle of Cities," "Santa Anita '42," "Extenuating Circumstances," "Rohwer," "Teahouse," "Song of a Nisei Fisherman," "Empress of China," "Pacific Overtures" (1984), "Eat a Bowl of Tea."

MATTHEWS, DeLANE. Born Aug. 7, 1961 in Cocoa, FL. Graduate FlaStateU. Debut 1984 OB in "Pieces of Eight," "Pericles," "Merry Wives of Windsor," followed by "The Cradle Will Rock," "City Boy."

MAXWELL, ROBERTA. Born in Canada. Debut 1968 OB in "Two Gentlemen of Verona," followed by "A Whistle in the Dark," "Slag," "The Plough and the Stars," "Merchant of Venice," "Ashes," "Mary Stuart," "Lydie Breeze," "Before the Dawn," Bdwy in "The Prime of Miss Jean Brodie," "Henry V," "House of Atreus," "The Resistible Rise of Arturo Ui," "Othello," "Hay Fever," "There's One in Every Marriage," "Equus," "The Merchant."

MAYER, JERRY. Born May 12, 1941 in NYC. Graduate NYU. Debut 1968 OB in "Alice in Wonderland," followed by "L'Ete," "Marouf," "Trelawny of the Wells," "King of the Schnorrers," "Mother Courage," "You Know Al," "Goose and Tomtom," "The Rivals," "For Sale," Bdwy in "Much Ado about Nothing" (1972), "Play Memory."

MAYRON, MELANIE J. Born Oct. 20, 1952 in Philadelphia, PA. Graduate AADA. Bdwy debut 1979 in "The Goodbye People," followed by OB in "Crossing Delancey."

McATEER, KATHRYN. Born Sept. 4, 1949 in Englewood, NJ. Graduate Montclair State Col. Debut 1983 OB in "Upstairs at O'Neal's," followed by "Mayor."

McCANN, CHRISTOPHER. Born Sept. 29, 1952 in NYC. Graduate NYU. Debut 1975 OB in "The Measures Taken," followed by "Ghosts," "Woyzzeck," "St. Joan of the Stockyards," "Buried Child," "Dwelling in Milk," "Tongues," "3 Acts of Recognition," "Don Juan," "Michi's Blood," "Five of Us," "Richard III," "The Golem," "Kafka Father and Son."

McCARTHY, JEFF. Born Oct. 16, 1954 in Los Angeles, CA. Graduate American Consv. Theatre. Bdwy debut 1982 in "Pirates of Penzance," followed by "Zorba" (1983), OB in "Gifts of the Magi."

McCARTHY, KEVIN. Born Feb. 15, 1914 in Seattle, WA. Attended UMn. Bdwy debut 1938 in "Abe Lincoln in Illinois," followed by "Flight to the West," "Winged Victory," "Truckline Cafe," "Joan of Lorraine," "Death of a Salesman," "Anna Christie," "Deep Blue Sea," "Red Roses for Me," "Day the Money Stopped," "Two for the Seesaw," "Advise and Consent," "Something about a Soldier," "Three Sisters," "A Warm Body," "Cactus Flower," "Happy Birthday, Wanda June," "Poor Murderer," "Alone Together," OB in "The Children," "Rapists," "Harry Outside."

McCHESNEY, MART. Born Jan. 27, 1954 in Abilene, TX. Graduate Webster Col Consv. Debut 1979 OB in "Making Pease," followed by "Sometime Soon," "Grunts," "Home Again, Kathleen," "Child's Play."

McCLARNON, KEVIN. Born Aug. 25, 1952 in Greenfield, IN. Graduate Butler U., LAMDA. Debut 1977 OB in "The Homecoming," followed by "Heaven's Gate," "A Winter's Tale," "Johnny on a Spot," "The Wedding," "Between Daylight and Boonville," "Macbeth," "The Clownmaker," "Cinders," "The Ballad of Soapy Smith."

McCOWEN, ALEC. Born May 26, 1925 in Tunbridge Wells, Eng. Attended RADA. Bdwy debut 1951 in "Antony and Cleopatra," followed by "Caesar and Cleopatra," "King Lear," "Comedy of Errors," "After the Rain," "Hadrian VII," "The Philanthropist," "The Misanthrope," "Equus," "Kipling," OB in "St. Mark's Gospel."

McDERMOTT, KEITH. Born in Houston, TX. Attended LAMDA. Bdwy debut 1976 in "Equus," followed by "A Meeting by the River," "Harold and Maude," OB in "Heat of Re-entry," "Misalliance," "The Poker Session."

McDONOUGH, ANN. Born in Portland, ME. Graduate Towson State U. Debut 1975 OB in "Trelawny of the Wells," followed by "Secret Service," "Boy Meets Girl," "Scribes," "Uncommon Women," "City Sugar," "Fables for Friends," "The Dining Room," "What I Did Last Summer," "The Rise of Daniel Rocket," "The Middle Ages," "Fighting International Fat."

McDONOUGH, STEPHEN. Born Oct. 27, 1958 in Brooklyn, NY. Graduate SUNY/Potsdam. Debut 1981 OB in "The Fantasticks," followed by "Teach Me How to Cry," Bdwy in "Take Me Along" (1985).

McDOWELL, MALCOLM. Born June 15, 1943 in Leeds, Eng. Debut 1980 OB in "Look Back in Anger," followed by "In Celebration."

McFARLAND, ROBERT. Born May 7, 1931 in Omaha, NE. Graduate UMi, Columbia U. Debut 1978 OB in "The Taming of the Shrew," followed by "When the War Was Over," "Divine Fire," "Ten Little Indians," "The Male Animal," "Comedy of Errors," "Appointment with Death," "The Education of One Miss February."

McGAVIN, DARREN. Born May 7, 1922 in Spokane, WA. Attended Col. of Pacific. Bdwy debut 1948 in "The Old Lady Says No," followed by "Death of a Salesman," "My Three Angels," "The Rainmaker," "The Innkeepers," "The Lovers," "Tunnel of Love," "Blood, Sweat and Stanley Poole," "The King and I," "Dinner at 8," OB in "Cock-a-doodle-Doo," "The Thracian Horses," "California Dog Fight."

McGINLEY, JOHN C. Born Aug. 3, 1959 in NYC. Graduate NYU. Debut 1984 OB in "Danny and the Deep Blue Sea," followed by "The Ballad of Soapy Smith," "Jesse and the Games."

McGINNIS, MAUREEN. Born Sept. 30, 1957 in Fargo, ND. Attended Noorhead State U. Debut 1983 OB in "Richard II," followed by "The Education of One Miss February."

McGOOHAN, PATRICK. Born Mar. 19, 1928 in NYC. Attended RADA. Bdwy debut 1985 in "Pack of Lies."

McGOVERN, ELIZABETH. Born July 18, 1961 in Evanston, IL. Attended Juilliard. Debut 1981 OB in "To Be Young, Gifted and Black," followed by "Hotel Play," "My Sister in This House" for which she received a Theatre World Award, "Painting Churches," "Hitch-Hikers."

McGRATH, DONALD. Born Mar. 3, 1940 in Pittsburgh, PA. Graduate Duquesne U, NYU, AMDA. Debut 1970 OB in "Madwoman of Chaillot," followed by "Oedipus at Colonnus," "Sigfried in Stalingrad," "Mother & Son & Co.," "Miracle of St. Anthony," "Miss Collins, the English Chairman," "St. Joan," "Myth Oedipus," "Bells Are Ringing," Bdwy in "The Lieutenant" (1975), "Same Time Next Year," "I Ought to Be in Pictures."

McGUIRE, MITCHELL. Born Dec. 26, 1936 in Chicago, IL. Attended Goodman Theatre, Santa Monica City Col. OB in "The Rapists," "Go, Go, God Is Dead," "Waiting for Lefty," "The Bond," "Guns of Carrar," "Oh! Calcutta!," "New York! New York!," "What a Life!," "Butter and Egg Man," "Almost in Vegas."

McGUIRE, RODNEY ALAN. Born Aug. 2, 1959 in Chicago, IL. Attended Juilliard. Debut 1983 in Bdwy's "The Tap Dance Kid."

McHATTIE, STEPHEN. Born Feb. 3 in Antigonish, NS. Graduate Acadia U., AADA. Bdwy debut 1968 in "The American Dream," followed by "The Misanthrope," "Heartbreak House," OB in "Henry IV," "Richard III," "The Persians," "Pictures in the Hallway," "Now There's Just the Three of Us," "Anna K," "Twelfth Night," "Mourning Becomes Electra," "Alive and Well in Argentina," "The Iceman Cometh," "Winter Dancers," "Casualties," "Three Sisters," "Mensch Meier," "Haven."

McINERNEY, BERNIE. Born Dec. 4, 1936 in Wilmington, DE. Graduate UDel, Catholic U. Bdwy debut 1972 in "That Championship Season," followed by "Curse of an Aching Heart," OB in "Life of Galileo," "Losing Time," "Three Friends," "American Clock," "Father Dreams," "Winners," "Digby."

McINTOSH, ANNE. Born June 2, 1953 in Charleston, WVa. Graduate WVaU. Bdwy debut 1984 in "Death of a Salesman."

McKEEHAN, MAYLA. Born Dec. 8 in Barboursville, KY. Graduate FlaStateU. Debut 1979 OB in "Big Bad Burlesque," followed by "God Bless You, Mr. Rosewater," "Anyone Can Whistle," "Facade," "Colette Collage," "The Baker's Wife."

McMARTIN, JOHN. Born in Warsaw, IN. Attended Columbia U. Debut 1959 OB in "Little Mary Sunshine" for which he received a Theatre World Award, followed by "Too Much Johnson," "The Misanthrope," "Sung and Unsung Sondheim," Bdwy in "Conquering Hero" (1961), "Blood, Sweat and Stanley Poole," "Children from Their Games," "Rainy Day in Newark," "Sweet Charity," "Follies," "Great God Brown," "The Visit," "Chemin de Fer," "Love for Love," "Rules of the Game," "Happy New Year," "Solomon's Child," "A Little Family Business."

McMURRAY, SAM. Born Apr. 15, 1952 in NYC. Graduate UWash. Debut 1975 OB in "The Taking of Miss Janie," followed by "Merry Wives of Windsor," "Clarence," "Ballymurphy," "The Connection," "Translations," "Man Overboard," "Comedians," "Kid Purple."

McNAMARA, ROSEMARY. Born Jan. 7, 1943 in Summit, NJ. Attended Newark Col. OB in "The Master Builder," "Carricknabuana," "Rocket to the Moon," "The Most Happy Fella," "Matchmaker," "Anyone Can Whistle," "Facade," "Marya," "A Good Year for the Roses," "Quilters," Bdwy in "The Student Gypsy" (1963).

McNEELY, ANNA. Born June 23, 1950 in Tower Hill, IL. Graduate McKendree Col. Bdwy debut 1982 in "Little Johnny Jones," followed by "Cats."

McQUEEN, ARMELIA. Born Jan 6, 1952 in North Carolina. Attended HB Studio, Bklyn Consv. Bdwy debut 1978 in "Ain't Misbehavin" for which she received a Theatre World Award, followed by "Harrigan 'n Hart," OB in "Can't Help Singing," "5-6-7-8 Dance."

McROBBIE, PETER. Born Jan. 31, 1943 in Hawick, Scot. Graduate Yale U. Debut 1976 OB in "The Wobblies," followed by "The Devil's Disciple," "Cinders," "The Ballad of Soapy Smith," Bdwy in "Whose Life Is It Anyway?" (1979), "Macbeth" (1981).

McWILLIAMS, RICHARD. Born June 27, 1950 in Baytown, TX. Graduate Sam Houston State U. Debut 1983 OB in "Except in My Memory," followed by "Why Marry?"

MEADE, JULIA. Born Dec. 17, 1928 in Boston, MA. Attended Yale U. Bdwy debut 1954 in "The Tender Trap," followed by "Double in Hearts," "Roman Candle," "Mary, Mary," "Front Page" (1969), OB in "Harvest of Strangers," "Isn't It Romantic."

MEADOWS, NANCY. Born July 11, 1953 in Glen Rock, NJ. Debut 1975 OB in "Boy Meets Boy," followed by "Mary," "Nymph Errant," "Roberta," Bdwy in "Oh, Brother!" (1981), "Broadway Follies."

MEANS, JOHN. Born Sept. 8, 1935 in Pittsburgh, PA. Graduate Washington & Jefferson Col. Debut 1984 OB in "Delirious."

MELLOR, STEPHEN. Born Oct. 17, 1954 in New Haven, CT. Graduate Boston U. Debut 1980 OB in "Paris Lights," followed by "Coming Attractions," "Plenty," "Tooth of Crime," "Shepard Sets."

MELOCHE, KATHERINE. Born June 1, 1952 in Detroit, MI. Bdwy debut 1976 in "Grease," followed by "Dancin'," OB in "Street Scene," "Little Shop of Horrors."

MENDILLO, STEPHEN. Born Oct. 9, 1942 in New Haven, CT. Graduate Colo. Col., Yale. Debut 1973 OB in "Nourish the Beast," followed by "Gorky," "Time Steps," "The Marriage," "Loot," "Subject to Fits," "Wedding Band," "As You Like It," "Fool for Love," Bdwy in "National Health" (1974), "Ah, Wilderness," "A View from the Bridge."

MEREDITH, JAN. Born Sept. 21, 1949 in Birmingham, AL. Graduate UAla. Debut 1982 OB in "The Raspberry Picker," followed by "The Ritz," "A Summer of Education," "Night Must Fall."

MERGENTHALER, D. J. Born May 30, 1958 in Pasadena, CA. Attended UCal/Irvine, Santa Clara U. Bdwy debut 1984 in "World of Magic."

MERRELL, RICHARD. Born July 6, 1925 in NJ. Graduate Neighborhood Playhouse. Debut 1953 OB in "Which Way Is Home," followed by "The Investigation," "Feathered Serpent," "Scenes and Revelations," "Busybody," "Family Comedy," "Patrick Pearse Motel," "King Lear," Bdwy in "Viva Madison Avenue" (1960).

MERRILL, DINA. Born Dec. 29, 1925 in NYC. Attended AADA, AMDA, George Washington U. Bdwy in "My Sister Eileen," "Mermaids Singing," "Major Barbara," "Misalliance," "Angel Street," "On Your Toes," OB in "Are You Now or Have You Ever Been," "Suddenly Last Summer."

MESEROLL, KENNETH. Born Apr. 15, 1952 in NJ. Attended UWisc. Debut 1979 OB in "Funeral Games," followed by "Saved," "Flight of the Earls," "Merchant of Venice," Bdwy in "Plenty" (1982).

METCALF, LAURIE. Born June 16, 1955 in Edwardsville, IL. IllStateU graduate. Debut 1984 OB in "Balm in Gilead" for which she received a Theatre World Award.

METCALF, MARK. Born Mar. 11 in Findlay, OH. Attended UMi. Debut 1973 OB in "Creeps," followed by "The Tempest," "Beach Children," "Hamlet," "Patrick Henry Lake Liquors," "Streamers," "Salt Lake City Skyline," "Mr. & Mrs.," "Romeo and Juliet," "Blue Window," "A Midsummer Night's Dream."

METTE, NANCY. Born Jan. 22, 1955 in Pennsylvania. Graduate NCSch. of Arts. Debut 1982 OB in "The Good Parts," followed by "The Alto Part," "Chopin in Space."

MEYER, PHIL. Born in Mar. 6, 1956 in Napoleon, OH. Graduate Bowling Green State U., Temple U. Debut 1984 OB in "Pieces of Eight," followed by "The Cradle Will Rock," "As You Like It," "The Skin of Our Teeth," "New Way to Pay Old Debts."

MEYER, TARO. Born in NYC. Graduate Bklyn. Col. Debut 1972 OB in "Iphigenia," followed by "Circle of Sound," "Astonished Heart," "Snapshots," "Bones," Bdwy in "Two Gentlemen of Verona" (1973), "Zorba" (1983).

MEYERS, T. J. Born July 18, 1953 in Pittsburgh, PA. Graduate Mesa Col. Bdwy debut 1984 in "Sunday in the Park with George."

MICHAELS, BERT. Born Dec. 22, 1943 in NYC. Attended UMiami. Bdwy debut 1965 in "Baker Street," followed by "La Grosse Valise," "Half a Sixpence," "Cabaret," "Man of La Mancha," "Canterbury Tales," "Ulysses in Nighttown," "Mack and Mabel," "On Your Toes," OB in "The Red Eye of Love," "Gifts of the Magi."

MICHELL, KEITH. Born Dec. 1, 1926 in Adelaide, Aust. Attended Aust. School of Arts. Bdwy debut 1960 in "Irma La Douce," followed by "The Rehearsal," "Man of La Mancha," "Abelard and Heloise," "La Cage aux Folles."

MICKENS, JAN. Born Feb. 16, 1939 in NYC. Attended Juilliard. Debut 1973 OB in "Thoughts," followed by "My One and Only" (1983).

MILANI, LINDA. Born Oct. 28, 1946 in Boston, MA. Attended Boston Consv. of Music. Bdwy debut 1983 in "Show Boat," OB in "Bells Are Ringing."

MILES, SYLVIA. Born Sept. 9, 1934 in NYC. Attended Pratt Inst., Actors Studio. Debut 1954 OB in "A Stone for Danny Fisher," followed by "The Iceman Cometh," "The Balcony," "Chekhov Sketchbook," "Matty, Moron and Madonna," "The Kitchen," "Rosenbloom," "Nellie Toole & Co.," "American Night Cry," "It's Me, Sylvia," "Ameri/Cain Gothic," Bdwy in "The Riot Act," "Night of the Iguana."

MILLER, BARRY. Born Feb. 6, 1958 in Los Angeles, CA. Debut 1981 OB in "Forty Deuce," followed by "The Tempest," Bdwy in "Biloxi Blues" (1985) for which he received a Theatre World Award.

MILLER, BETTY. Born Mar. 27, 1925 in Boston, MA. Attended UCLA. OB in "Summer and Smoke," "Cradle Song," "La Ronde," "Plays for Bleecker St.," "Desire Under the Elms," "The Balcony," "The Power and the Glory," "Beaux Stratagem," "Gandhi," "Girl on the Via Flaminia," "Hamlet," "Summer," "Before the Dawn," Bdwy in "You Can't Take It With You," "Right You Are," "The Wild Duck," "The Cherry Orchard," "A Touch of the Poet," "Eminent Domain," "The Queen and the Rebels," "Richard III."

MILLER, COURT. Born Jan. 29, 1952 in Norwalk, CT. Debut 1980 OB in "Elizabeth and Essex," followed by "Welded," "Spookhouse," Bdwy in "The First," "Torch Song Trilogy."

MILLER, MARTHA. Born Aug. 30, 1929 in New Bedford, MA. Graduate Carnegie-Mellon U. Debut 1956 OB in "House of Connelly, followed by "A Place without Morning," "Julius Caesar," "Major Barbara," "In the Summer House," "Merry Wives of Windsor," "Rimers of Eldritch," "Heartbreak House," "The Importance of Being Earnest," "Who'll Save the Plowboy?," "Fantod," Bdwy in "Happy End" (1977), "Morning's at 7."

MILLER, PENELOPE ANN. Born Jan. 13, 1964 in Santa Monica, CA. Attended Menlo Col., HB Studio. Bdwy debut 1985 in "Biloxi Blues."

MILLER, SCOTT GORDON. Born Jan. 21, 1956 in Cleveland, OH. Attended London's Drama Centre. Debut 1983 OB in "Ah, Wilderness!" followed by "City Boy."

MILVANEY, BILL. Born Mar. 10, 1953 in Armonk, NY. Princeton graduate. Debut 1983 OB in "Oh, Baby," followed by "Bells Are Ringing."

MINOT, ANNA. Born in Boston, MA. Attended Vassar Col. Bdwy debut 1942 in "The Strings, My Lord, Are False," followed by "The Russian People," "The Visitor," "The Iceman Cometh," "An Enemy of the People," "Love of Four Colonels," "Trip to Bountiful," "Tunnel of Love," "Ivanov," OB in "Sands of the Niger," "Getting Out," "Vieux Carre," "State of the Union."

MIRATTI, TONY. Born Dec. 6 in Santa Barbara, CA. Attended SBCC, Pasadena Playhouse. Debut 1976 OB in "The Shortchanged Review," followed by "Jump, I'll Catch You!"

MITCHELL, MELANIE. Born May 1, 1961 in Hartford, CT. Graduate NYU. Debut 1984 OB in "Bells Are Ringing."

MOKAE, ZAKES. Born Aug. 5, 1935 in Johannesburg, SAf. Attended St. Peter's Col., RADA. Debut 1970 OB in "Boesman and Lena," followed by "Fingernails Blue as Flowers," "The Cherry Orchard," Bdwy in "A Lesson for Aloes," "Master Harold. . .and the boys."

MOOR, BILL. Born July 13, 1931 in Toledo, OH. Attended Northwestern, Denison U. Bdwy debut 1964 in "Blues for Mr. Charlie," followed by "Great God Brown," "Don Juan," "The Visit," "Chemin de Fer," "Holiday," "P.S. Your Cat Is Dead," "Night of the Tribades," "Water Engine," "Plenty," "Heartbreak House," OB in "Dandy Dick," "Love Nest," "Days and Nights of Beebee Fenstermaker," "The Collection," "The Owl Answers," "Long Christmas Dinner," "Fortune and Men's Eyes," "King Lear," "Cry of Players," "Boys in the Band," "Alive and Well in Argentina," "Rosmersholm," "The Biko Inquest," "A Winter's Tale," "Johnny on a Spot," "Barbarians," "The Purging," "Potsdam Quartet," "Zones of the Spirit," "The Marriage of Bette and Boo."

MOORE, JONATHAN. Born Mar. 24, 1923 in New Orleans, LA. Attended Piscator School. Debut 1961 OB in "After the Angels," followed by "Berkeley Square," "Checking Out," "The Biko Inquest," "Sullivan and Gilbert," Bdwy in "Dylan," "1776," "Amadeus."

MOORE, JUDITH. Born Feb. 12, 1944 in Princeton, WVa. Graduate IndU., Concord Col. Debut 1971 OB in "The Drunkard," followed by "Ten by Six," "Boys from Syracuse," "The Evangelist," Bdwy in "Sunday in the Park with George" (1984).

MOORE, LEE. Born Feb. 19, 1929 in Brooklyn, NY. Debut 1978 OB in "Once More With Feeling," followed by "The Caine Mutiny Court-Martial," "Christopher Blake," "Cat and Canary," "Shrunken Heads," "Raspberry Picker," "Blessed Event."

MOORE, NITA. Born May 25, 1959 in Baton Rouge, LA. Graduate Southeastern La. U., Cincinnati Consv. Debut 1985 OB in "A Little Night Music."

MORAN, DANIEL. Born July 31, 1953 in Corcoran, CA. Graduate NYU. Debut 1980 OB in "True West," followed by "The Vampires," "Tongues and Savage Love," "Life Is a Dream."

MORAN, MARTIN. Born Dec. 29, 1959 in Denver CO. Attended Stanford U., AmConsv Theatre. Debut 1983 OB in "Spring Awakening," followed by "Once on a Summer's Day," Bdwy in "Oliver!" (1984).

MORANZ, BRAD. Born Aug. 29, 1952 in Houston, TX. Bdwy debut in "A Day in Hollywood/A Night in the Ukraine" (1981), OB in "Little Shop of Horrors."

MORANZ, JANNET. (formerly Horsley) Born Oct. 13, 1954 in Los Angeles, CA. Attended CaStateU. Bdwy debut 1980 in "A Chorus Line."

MORELAND, DAVID. Born Feb. 26, 1961 in Buffalo, NY. Attended UMich. Debut 1985 OB in "The Madwoman of Chaillot."

MORFOGEN, GEORGE. Born Mar. 30, 1933 in NYC. Graduate Brown U., Yale. Debut 1957 OB in "The Trial of D. Karamazov," followed by "Christmas Oratorio," "Othello," "Good Soldier Schweik," "Cave Dwellers," "Once in a Lifetime," "Total Eclipse," "Ice Age," "Prince of Homburg," "Biography: A Game," Bdwy in "The Fun Couple," "Kingdoms," "Arms and the Man."

MORENO, RITA. Born Dec. 11, 1931 in Humacao, PR. Bdwy debut 1945 in "Skydrift," followed by "West Side Story," "The Sign in Sidney Brustein's Window," "Last of the Red Hot Lovers," "The National Health," "The Ritz," "She Loves Me," "Wally's Cafe," "The Odd Couple."

MORGAN, LEWIS. Born June 21, 1933 in NYC. Graduate Columbia Col. Debut 1985 OB in "Deathtrap."

MOROZ, BARBARA. Born Feb. 9, 1958 in Dearborn, MI. Bdwy debut 1984 in "Oliver!" followed by "Harrigan'n Hart."

MORRIS, GARY. Born Dec. 7 in Ft. Worth, TX. Debut 1984 OB in "La Boheme."

MORRISEY, BOB. Born Aug. 15, 1946 in Somerville, MA. Attended UWi. Debut 1974 OB in "Ionescapade," followed by "Company," "Anything Goes," "Philistines," Bdwy in "The First" (1981), "Cats."

MORRISON, ANN LESLIE. Born Apr. 9, 1956 in Sioux City, IA. Attended Boston Consv., Columbia U. Debut 1980 OB in "Dream Time," followed by "All of the Above," "Forbidden Broadway," Bdwy in "Merrily We Roll Along" (1981) for which she received a Theatre World Award.

MORSE, PETER G. Born Oct. 9, 1958 in Hanover, NH. Graduate Dartmouth Col., UCal/San Diego. Debut 1983 OB in "That's It, Folks!," followed by "The Weekend," "The Merchant of Venice."

MORSE, ROBIN. Born July 8, 1963 in NYC. Bdwy debut 1981 in "Bring Back Birdie," followed by "Brighton Beach Memoirs."

MORTON, JOE. Born Oct. 18, 1947 in NYC. Attended Hofstra U. Debut 1968 OB in "A Month of Sundays," followed by "Salvation," "Charlie Was Here and Now He's Gone," "G. R. Point," "Crazy Horse," "A Winter's Tale" "Johnny on a Spot," "Midsummer Night's Drean," "The Recruiting Officer," "Oedipus the King," "The Wild Duck," "Rhinestone," "Souvenirs," Bdwy in "Hair," "Two Gentlemen of Verona," "Tricks," "Raisin" for which he received a Theatre World Award, "Oh, Brother!"

MOSES, MARK. Born Feb. 24, 1960 in NYC. Graduate Northwestern U, NYU. Debut 1983 OB in "The Slab Boys," followed by "Fraternity," "Home Remedies," "The Lady and the Clarinet," "Fantod."

MOSIEJ, JAMES E. Born Dec. 14, 1965 in Chicago, IL. Graduate IllWesternU. Debut 1983 OB in "Water Music," Bdwy in "Oh! Calcutta!" (1984).

MOYA, EDDY. Born Apr. 11, 1963 in El Paso, TX. Attended Los Angeles City Col. Debut OB in "Happy Hour."

MULLER, FRANK. Born May 5, 1951 in Beverwijk, Netherlands. Attended UMn, NCSch of Arts. Debut 1980 OB in "Salt Lake City Skyline," followed by "Henry V," "King Lear," "The Taming of the Shrew."

MURAKOSHI, SUZEN. Born May 20, 1958 in Honolulu, HI. Graduate UHawaii. Debut 1980 OB in "Shining House," followed by "Primary English Class," Bdwy in "The King and I" (1984).

MURRAY, BRIAN. Born Oct. 9, 1939 in Johannesburg, SA. Debut 1964 OB in "The Knack," followed by "King Lear," "Ashes," "The Jail Diary of Albie Sachs," "A Winter's Tale," "Barbarians," "The Purging," "Midsummer Night's Dream," "The Recruiting Officer," "The Arcata Promise," "Candida in Concert," Bdwy in "All in Good Time," "Rosencrantz and Guildenstern Are Dead," "Sleuth," "Da," "Noises Off."

MURRAY, MARY GORDON. Born Nov. 13, 1953 in Ridgewood, NJ. Attended Ramapo Col., Juilliard. Bdwy debut 1976 in "The Robber Bridegroom," followed by "Grease," "I Love My Wife," "Little Me," "Play Me a Country Song," OB in "A . . . My Name is Alice," "Blue Plate Special."

MURRAY, PEG. Born in Denver, CO. Attended Western Reserve U. OB in "Children of Darkness" (1958), "Midsummer Night's Dream," "Oh, Dad, Poor Dad . . . ," "Small Craft Warnings," "Enclave," "Landscape of the Body," "A Lovely Sunday for Creve Couer," "Isn't It Romantic," Bdwy in "The Great Sebastians" (1956), "Gypsy," "Blood, Sweat and Stanley Toole," "She Loves Me," "Anyone Can Whistle," "The Subject Was Roses," "Something More," "Cabaret," "Fiddler on the Roof," "Royal Family."

MURRAY, SHARON. Born Dec. 13 in Ann Arbor, MI. Attended ULouisville. Debut 1978 OB in "One and One," Bdwy in "Grind" (1985).

MUSIKER, BETH. Born July 20, 1960 in Chicago, IL. Graduate Northwestern U. Debut 1985 OB in "Very Warm for May."

MUSNICK, STEPHANIE. Born Apr. 12, 1950 in Philadelphia, PA. Graduate Villanova U. Bdwy debut 1977 in "Gemini," followed by "5th of July," OB in "As to the Meaning of Words," "Childe Byron," "Mongoloid Idiot," "Bremen Coffee," "Bing and Walker."

MUSSER, LEWIS. Born Aug. 22, 1953 in Rocky Mount, NC. Attended UNC. Debut 1978 OB in "Rebel without a Cause," followed by "Anna Christie," "End as a Man," "The Winter's Tale," "A Midsummer Night's Dream," "New York City Is Closed," "Stud Silo."

MYDELL, JOSEPH. Born June 30, 1945 in Savannah, GA. Graduate NYU. Debut 1969 OB in "The Ofay Watcher," followed by "Volpone," "Henry IV," "Please Don't Cry and Say No," "Love's Labour's Lost," "Lyrics of the Hearthside."

MYERS, JENNIFER. Born Dec. 21, 1959 in Detroit, MI. Graduate Northwestern U. Debut 1983 OB in "Where's Charley?," followed by "Mighty Fine Music," "Very Warm for May."

MYERS, LOU. Born Sept. 26, 1938 in Charleston, WVa. Graduate WVaStateCol., NYU. Debut 1975 OB in "First Breeze of Summer," followed by "Fat Tuesday," "Do Lord Remember Me," "Paducah," Bdwy in "First Breeze of Summer," "Ma Rainey's Black Bottom."

NAKAHARA, RON. Born July 20, 1947 in Honolulu, HI. Attended UHI. Tenri U. Debut 1981 OB in "Danton's Death," followed by "Flowers and Household Gods," "A Few Good Men," "Rohwer," "A Midsummer Night's Dream," "Teahouse," "Song for Nisei Fisherman," "Eat a Bowl of Tea."

Lisa Kirk	Joseph Kolinski	Marge Kotlisky
Stan Lachow	Paula Laurence	Kenneth LaZebnik
David Leary	Kaiulani Lee	Calvin Levels
Jane Lind	Salem Ludwig	Barbara Luna
Joyce Lynn	Morgan Mackay	Alison Mann
Daniel Marcus	Lucy Martin	James Mathers
Jerry Mayer	Kathryn McAteer	Mitchell McGuire
Mayla McKeehan	Kenneth Meseroll	Taro Meyer
Linda Milani	Tony Miratti	Robin Morse
Joe Morton	Stephanie Musnick	Joseph Mydell

215

NASTASI, FRANK. Born Jan. 7, 1923 in Detroit MI. Graduate Wayne U., NYU. Bdwy debut 1963 in "Lorenzo," followed by "Avanti," OB in "Bonds of Interest," "One Day More," "Nathan the Wise," "The Chief Things,""Cindy," "Escurial," "The Shrinking Bride," "Macbird," "Cakes with the Wine," "Metropolitan Madness,""Rockaway Boulevard," "Scenes from La Vie de Boheme," "Agamemnon," "Happy Sunset Inc." "3 Last Plays of O'Neill," "Taking Steam," "Lulu."

NEAL, BILLIE. Born Dec. 12, 1955 in Little Rock, AR. Attended NYU, Neighborhood Playhouse. Debut 1984 OB in "Balm in Gilead."

NEAL, LAURA. Born Nov. 26 in Dallas, TX. Graduate UTex. Debut 1983 OB in "Under the Gaslight," followed by "A Doll's House," "Why Marry?," "Uncle Lumpy Comes to Visit."

NEGRO, MARY JOAN. Born Nov. 9, 1948 in Brooklyn, NY. Debut 1972 OB in "The Hostage," followed by "Lower Depths," "Women Beware Women," "Ladyhouse Blues," "The Promise," "Modigliani," "Children of Darkness," "Dancing in the End Zone," "After the Fall," Bdwy in "Three Sisters," "Measure for Measure," "Beggar's Opera," "Wings," "Scenes and Revelations," "Loves of Anatol."

NEIL, ROGER. Born Nov. 19, 1948 in Galesburg, IL. Graduate Northwestern U. Debut 1974 OB in "The Boy Friend," followed by "Scrambled Feet," "The Fantasticks."

NEILSON, RICHARD. Born Nov. 30, 1924 in London, Eng. Debut 1959 OB in "Heloise," followed by "O Say Can You See," "Tea Party," "Pygmalion in Concert," Bdwy in "Pickwick" (1964), "Wise Child," "My Fair Lady," "Equus."

NELLIGAN, KATE. Born Mar. 16, 1951 in London, Can. Attended York U, Central Sch. of Speech/Drama. Debut 1982 OB in "Plenty," followed by "Virginia," Bdwy in "Plenty" (1983), "Moon for the Misbegotten"(1984).

NELSON, GAIL. Born Mar. 29 in Durham, NC. Graduate Oberlin Col. Bdwy debut 1968 in "Hello, Dolly!," followed by "Applause,""On the Town,""Music!Music!,""Eubie!," "Rockette Spectacular," "The Tap Dance Kid," OB in "Six," "By Strouse," "Broadway Soul," "Songs You Never Heard Before."

NELSON, MARK. Born Sept. 26, 1955 in Hackensack, NJ. Graduate Princeton U. Debut 1977 OB in "The Dybbuk," followed by "Green Fields," "The Keymaker," Bdwy in "Amadeus" (1981), "Brighton Beach Memoirs."

NELSON, RUTH. Born Aug. 2, 1905 in Saginaw, MI. Attended AmThLab. Bdwy debut 1931 in "House of Connelly," among other Group Theatre productions, and in "The Grass Harp," "Solitaire," "To Grandmother's House We Go," OB in "Collette," "Scenes from the Everyday Life," "3 Acts of Recognition," "Imagination Dead Imagination."

NEUBERGER, JAN. Born Jan. 21, 1953 in Amityville, NY. Attended NYU. Bdwy debut 1975 in "Gypsy," OB in "Silk Stockings," "Chase a Rainbow," "Anything Goes," "A Little Madness," "Forbidden Broadway."

NEWMAN, PHYLLIS. Born Mar. 19, 1935 in Jersey City, NJ. Attended Western Reserve U. Bdwy debut 1953 in "Wish You Were Here," followed by "Bells Are Ringing," "First Impressions," "Subways Are for Sleeping," "The Apple Tree," "On the Town," "Prisoner of Second Avenue," "Madwoman of Central Park West," OB in "I Feel Wonderful," "Make Someone Happy," "I'm Getting My Act Together," "Red River," "The New Yorkers."

NICHOLS, JOSEPHINE. Born Nov. 11, 1913 in Lawrenceville, IL. Graduate UOk., Columbia U. Debut 1960 OB in "The Prodigal," followed by "Roots," "Golden Six," "The Adding Machine," "The Storm," "Uncommon Women and Others," "The Grinding Machine," "Chaos and Hard Times," Bdwy in "On an Open Roof," "The Skin of Our Teeth," "Clothes for a Summer Hotel."

NICHOLS, ROBERT. Born July 20, 1924 in Oakland, CA. Attended Pacific Col., RADA. Debut 1978 OB in "Are You Now . . . ," followed by "Heartbreak House," "Ah, Wilderness!," "Oh, Boy!," Bdwy in "Man and Superman," "The Man Who Came to Dinner," "Einstein and the Polar Bear," "Take Me Along."

NILES, MARY ANN. Born May 2, in NYC. Attended Miss Finchley's Ballet Acad. Bdwy debut in "Girl from Nantucket," followed by "Dance Me A Song," "Call Me Mister," "Make Mine Manhattan," "La Plume de Ma Tante," "Carnival," "Flora the Red Menace," "Sweet Charity," "George M!," "No, No, Nanette," "Irene," "Ballroom," OB in "The Boys from Syracuse," CC's "Wonderful Town" and "Carnival."

NILES, RICHARD. Born May 19, 1946 in NYC. Graduate NYU. Debut 1969 OB in "Sourball," followed by "Innocent Thoughts, Harmless Intentions," "Elephants," "Child's Play," Bdwy in "And Miss Reardon Drinks a Little," "Don't Call Back."

NIXON, CYNTHIA. Born Apr. 9, 1966 in NYC. Debut 1980 in "The Philadelphia Story"(LC) for which she received a Theatre World Award, OB in "Lydie Breeze," "Hurlyburly," "Sally's Gone, She Left Her Name," Bdwy in "The Real Thing" (1983), "Hurlyburly."

NIXON, JAMES. Born Oct. 12, 1957 in Jersey City, NJ. Attended Kean Col. Debut 1982 OB in "The Six O'Clock Boys," followed by "Holy Junkie."

NOBLE, JAMES. Born Mar. 5, 1922 in Dallas, TX. Attended SMU. Bdwy debut 1949 in "The Velvet Glove," followed by "Come of Age," "A Far Country," "Strange Interlude," "1776," "The Runner Stumbles," OB in "Wilder's Triple Bill," "Night of the Dunce," "Rimers of Eldritch," "The Acquisitions," "A Scent of Flowers," "A Touch of the Poet," "Vienna Notes."

NOLEN, TIMOTHY. Born July 9, 1941 in Rotan, TX. Graduate Trenton State Col., Manhattan School of Music. Debut in "Sweeney Todd" (1984) with NYC Opera, Bdwy in "Grind" (1985).

NOODT, BRIAN. Born Mar. 13, 1973 in Freehold, NH. Bdwy debut 1984 in "Oliver!" OB in "Northern Boulevard."

NORCIA, PATRIZIA. Born Apr. 6, 1954 in Rome, Italy. Graduate Hofstra U., Yale. Debut 1978 OB in "Sganarelle," followed by "The Master and Margarita," "The Loves of Cass McGuire," "Fanshen," "The Price of Genius," "The Taming of the Shrew."

NORMAN, DARA. Born Aug. 8 in NYC. Attended UCin, UMiami. Bdwy debut 1975 in "The Magic Show," followed by "Oh! Calcutta!," OB in "Dr. Selavy's Magic Theatre," "Beggar's Opera," "The Boys in the Live Country Band," "Talking Dirty."

NORTH, ALAN. Born Dec. 23, 1927 in NYC. Attended Columbia U. Bdwy bow 1955 in "Plain and Fancy," followed by "South Pacific," "Summer of the 17th Doll," "Requiem for a Nun," "Never Live over a Pretzel Factory," "Dylan," "Spofford," "The American Clock," "Marilyn," OB in "Finian's Rainbow," "The Music Man," "Annie Get Your Gun," "The American Clock," "Comedians."

NORTH, SHEREE. Born Jan. 17, 1933 in Los Angeles, CA. Attended UCLA. Bdwy debut 1953 in "Hazel Flagg" for which she received a Theatre World Award, followed by "I Can Get It for You Wholesale," OB in "California Dog Fight" (1985).

NUGENT, JAMES. Born June 22, 1940 in The Bronx, NY. Graduate UFla. Debut 1984 OB in "Air Rights," followed by "The Merchant of Venus," "Arms and the Man," "Mme. Colombe," "Two Gentlemen of Verona," "Days to Come," "The Good Doctor."

NUNNERY, BILL. Born Nov. 23, 1942 in Sanford, NC. Attended Lees-McRae Col., UNC. Bdwy debut 1978 in "The Inspector General," OB in "Smoking Newports," "Mirrors," "The Ecstasy of Rita Joe."

NUTE, DON. Born Mar. 13, in Connellsville, PA. Attended Denver U. Debut OB 1965 in "The Trojan Women" followed by "Boys in the Band," "Mad Theatre for Madmen," "The Eleventh Dynasty," "About Time," "The Urban Crisis," "Christmas Rappings," "The Life of a Man," "A Look at the Fifties."

NYE, CARRIE. Born in Mississippi, attended Stephens Col., Yale U. Bdwy debut 1960 in "Second String," followed by "Mary, Mary," "Half a Sixpence," "A Very Rich Woman," "Cop-Out," "The Man Who Came to Dinner," OB in "Ondine," "Ghosts," "The Importance of Being Earnest," "The Trojan Women," "The Real Inspector Hound," "a/k/a Tennessee," "The Wisteria Trees," "Madwoman of Chaillot."

O'CONNOR, KEVIN. Born May 7, 1938 in Honolulu, HI. Attended UHi., Neighborhood Playhouse. Debut 1964 OB in "Up to Thursday," followed by "Six from La Mama," "Rimers of Eldritch," "Tom Paine," "Boy on the Straightback Chair," "Dear Janet Rosenberg," "Eyes of Chalk," "Alive and Well in Argentina," "Duet," "Trio," "The Contractor," "Kool Aid," "The Frequency," "Chucky's Hutch," "Birdbath," "The Breakers," "Crossing the Crab Nebula," "Jane Avril," "Inserts," "3 by Beckett," "The Dicks," "A Kiss Is Just a Kiss," "Last of the Knucklemen," "Thrombo," Bdwy in "Gloria and Esperanza," "The Morning after Optimism," "Figures in the Sand," "Devour the Snow," "The Lady from Dubuque."

O'DELL, K. LYPE. Born Feb. 2, 1939 in Claremore, OK. Graduate Los Angeles State Col. Debut 1972 OB in "Sunset," followed by "Our Father," "Ice Age," "Prince of Homburg," "Passion of Dracula," "M. Amilcar," "Fly by Night."

O'HARA, JENNY. Born Feb. 24 in Sonora, CA. Attended Carnegie-Tech U. Bdwy debut 1964 in "Dylan," followed by "The Odd Couple" (1985), OB in "Hang Down Your Head and Die," "Play with a Tiger," "Arms and the Man," "Sambo," "My House Is Your House," "The Kid," "The Fox."

O'HARA, PAIGE. Born May 10, 1956 in Ft. Lauderdale, FL. Debut 1975 OB in "The Gift of the Magi," followed by "Company," "The Great American Backstage Musical," "Oh, Boy!," Bdwy in "Show Boat" (1983).

O'KEEFE, MICHAEL. Born Apr. 24, 1955 in Westchester, NY. Attended NYU. Debut 1974 OB in "The Killdeer," followed by "Christmas on Mars," "Short Eyes," Bdwy in "5th of July," "Mass Appeal" for which he received a Theatre World Award.

O'KEEFE, PAUL C. Born Apr. 27, 1951 in Boston, MA. Graduate Columbia U. Bdwy debut 1958 in "The Music Man," followed by "Sail Away," "Oliver," "A Texas Trilogy," OB in "Passing Game," "The Baker's Wife."

O'KELLY, AIDEEN. Born in Dalkey, IR. Member of Dublin's Abbey Theatre. Bdwy debut 1980 in "A Life," followed by "Othello," OB in "The Killing of Sister George" (1983). "Man Enough."

O'MALLEY, ETAIN. Born Aug. 8 in Dublin, Ire. Attended Vassar Col. Debut 1964 OB in "The Trojan Women," followed by "Glad Tidings," "God of Vengeance," "A Difficult Borning," "In the Garden," "Sullivan and Gilbert," Bdwy in "The Cherry Orchard" (1968), "The Cocktail Party," "The Misanthrope," "The Elephant Man," "Kingdoms," "The Queen and the Rebels," "84 Charing Cross Road."

OMS, ALBA. Born Nov. 6, 1936 in NYC. Attended Actors Studio. Debut 1958 OB in "Comrades," followed by "Sancocho," Young Playwrights Festival, "Conduct of Life."

O'NEILL, CLAUDIA. Born June 8, 1955 in Nuremberg, Ger. Graduate PennStateU. Debut 1979 OB in "HMS Pinafore," followed by "Pirates of Penzance," "The Desert Song," "The Mikado," "Babes in Toyland," "Pere Goriot."

ORBACH, EVELYN. Born July 25, 1932 in NYC. Attended Brooklyn Col. Debut 1953 OB in "The Plough and the Stars," followed by "Lilliom," "The Corn Is Green," "The Mugger."

ORBACH, JERRY. Born Oct. 20, 1935 in NYC. Attended Northwestern U. Bdwy debut 1961 in "Carnival," followed by "Guys and Dolls," "Carousel," "Annie Get Your Gun," "The Natural Look," "Promises Promises," "6 Rms Riv Vu," "Chicago," "42nd Street," OB in "Threepenny Opera," "The Fantasticks," "The Cradle Will Rock," "Scuba Duba."

O'REILLY, CIARAN. Born Mar. 13, 1959 in Ireland. Attended Carmelite Col., Juilliard. Debut 1978 OB in "Playboy of the Western World," followed by "Summer," "Freedom of the City," "Fannie," "Interrogation of Ambrose Fogarty," "King Lear," "Shadow of a Gunman," Bdwy in "The Corn Is Green" (1983).

O'ROURKE, KEVIN. Born Jan. 25, 1956 in Portland, OR. Graduate Williams Col. Debut 1981 OB in "Declassee," followed by "Sister Mary Ignatius . . . ," "Submariners," "A Midsummer Night's Dream," Bdwy in "Alone Together" (1984).

ORR, MARY. Born Dec. 21, 1918 in Brooklyn, NY. Attended Syracuse U, AADA. Bdwy debut 1938 in "Bachelor Born," followed by "Jupiter Laughs," "Wallflower," "Dark Hammock," "Sherlock Holmes," "The Desperate Hours," OB in "Grass Widows," "Appointment with Death," "Ladies in Retirement."

O'SHEA, MILO. Born June 2, 1926 in Dublin, IRe. Bdwy debut 1968 in "Staircase," followed by "Dear World," "Mrs. Warren's Profession," "Comedians," "A Touch of the Poet," "Mass Appeal," OB in "Waiting for Godot," "Mass Appeal," "The Return of Herbert Bracewell."

OSTRIN, ART. Born Aug. 30, 1935 in NYC. Bdwy in "The Time of Your Life," "Carnival," "Finian's Rainbow," "South Pacific," "Promenade," "Beggar on Horseback," "Irma La Douce," "Slapstick Tragedy," OB in "A Funny Thing Happened on the Way. . . .," "Northern Boulevard."

OSUNA, JESS. Born May 28, 1933 in Oakland, CA. OB in "Blood Wedding," "Come Share My House," "This Side of Paradise," "Bugs and Veronica," "Monopoly," "The Infantry," "Hamp," "The Biko Inquest," "The American Clock," "Roads to Home," "The Inheritors," "Rain," "The Madwoman of Chaillot," Bdwy in "The Goodbye People," "That Championship Season," "An Almost Perfect Person."

OVERMIRE, LAURENCE. Born Aug. 17, 1957 in Rochester, NY. Graduate Muskingum Col., UMn. Debut 1982 OB in "Don Juan," followed by "Summit Conference," Bdwy in "Amadeus."

OWENS, GEOFFREY. Born Mar. 18, 1961 in Brooklyn, NY. Yale Graduate. Debut 1985 OB in "The Man Who Killed the Buddha."

OWSLEY, STEVE. Born Aug. 2, 1957 in Michigan City, IN. Graduate Western Mich. U. Debut 1984 OB in "Red, Hot and Blue," Bdwy in "Grind" (1985).

OYSTER, JIM. Born May 3, 1930 in Washington, DC. OB in "Coriolanus," "The Cretan Woman," "Man and Superman," "Fallen Angels," "The Underlings," Bdwy in "Cool World" (1960), "Hostile Winners," "The Sound of Music," "The Prime of Miss Jean Brodie," "Who's Who in Hell."

PAGAN, PETER. Born July 24, 1921 in Sydney, Aust. Attended Scots Col. Bdwy in "Escapade," "Portrait of a Lady," "The Dark Is Light Enough," "Child of Fortune," "Hostile Witness," "Aren't We All?," OB in "Busybody."

PAGANO, GIULIA. Born July 8, 1948 in NYC. Attended AADA. Debut 1977 OB in "The Passion of Dracula," followed by "Heartbreak House," "The Winslow Boy," "Miss Julie," "Playing with Fire," "Out of the Night," "Snow Leopards," "Zoology," Bdwy in "Medea" (1982).

PAGE, GERALDINE. Born Nov. 22, 1924 in Kirksville, MO. Attended Goodman Theatre. Debut 1945 OB in "Seven Mirrors," followed by "Yerma," "Summer and Smoke," "Macbeth," "Look Away," "The Stronger," "The Human Office," "The Inheritors," "Paradise Lost," "Ghosts," "Madwoman of Chaillot," "Clarence," "Vivat! Vivat Regina!," Bdwy in "Midsummer" (1953) for which she received a Theatre World Award. "The Immoralist," "The Rainmaker," "Innkeepers," "Separate Tables," "Sweet Bird of Youth," "Strange Interlude," "Three Sisters," "P.S. I Love You," "The Great Indoors," "White Lies," "Black Comedy," "The Little Foxes," "Angela," "Absurd Person Singular," "Clothes for a Summer Hotel." "Agnes of God."

PAGE, KEN. Born Jan. 20, 1954 in St. Louis, MO. Attended Fontbonne Col. Bdwy debut 1976 in "Guys and Dolls" for which he received a Theatre World Award followed by "Ain't Misbehavin'," "Cats," OB in "Louis," "Can't Help Singing."

PAIGE, JANIS. Born Sept. 16, 1922 in Tacoma, Wa. Bdwy debut 1951 in "Remains to Be Seen," followed by "Pajama Game," "Mame," "Alone Together."

PAIGE, KELLEY. Born May 30, 1960 in Rio, Brazil. Graduate IndU. Debut 1984 OB in "Arabesque," followed by "Insanity of Mary Girard," "Northern Boulevard."

PARKER, COREY. Born July 8, 1965 in NYC. Attended NYU. Debut 1984 OB in "Meeting the Winter Bikerider," followed by "Red Storm Flower," "Been Taken," "Losing Battles," "The Bloodletters."

PARKER, ELLEN. Born Sept. 30, 1949 in Paris, Fr. Graduate Bard Col. Debut 1971 OB in "James Joyce Liquid Theatre," followed by "Uncommon Women and Others," "Dusa, Fish, Stas and Vi," "A Day in the Life of the Czar," "Fen," Bdwy in "Equus," "Strangers," "Plenty."

PARKER, HERBERT MARK. Born Dec. 2, 1954 in Louisville, KY. Graduate Stephens Col., Ohio U. Debut 1984 OB in "Bells Are Ringing."

PARKER, ROXANN. Born Apr. 24, 1948 in Los Angeles, CA. Graduate USCal. Debut 1979 OB in "Festival," followed by "New Faces of 1952," "Looking for Love."

PARRIS, STEVE. Born in Athens, Greece. Graduate CCNY. Debut 1964 OB in "The Comforter," followed by "Consider the Lilies," "A Christmas Carol," "The Man with the Flower in His Mouth," "King David and His Wives," "3 by Pirandello," "Nymph Errant," "The Tamer Tamed."

PARRY, WILLIAM. Born Oct. 7, 1947 in Steubenville, OH Graduate Mt. Union Col. Bdwy debut 1971 in "Jesus Christ Superstar," followed by "Rockabye Hamlet," "The Leaf People," "Camelot" (1980/1981), "Sunday in the Park with George," OB in "Sgt. Pepper's Lonely Hearts Club Band," "The Conjurer," "Noah," "The Misanthrope," "Joseph and the Amazing Technicolor Dreamcoat," "Agamemnon," "Coolest Cat in Town," "Dispatches," "The Derby."

PASEKOFF, MARILYN. Born Nov. 7, 1949 in Pittsburgh, PA. Graduate Boston U. Debut 1975 OB in "Godspell," followed by "Words," "Forbidden Broadway."

PASKOW, KAREN. Born Jan. 8, 1954 in Irvington, NJ. Bdwy debut 1978 in "A Broadway Musical," followed by "My Fair Lady" (1982), "The Tap Dance Kid."

PATINKIN, MANDY. Born in Nov. 30, 1952 in Chicago, IL. Attended Juilliard. OB in "Henry IV," "Leave It to Beaver Is Dead," "Rebel Women," "Hamlet," "Trelawny of the Wells," "Savages," "The Split," Bdwy in "Evita" (1979), "Sunday in the Park with George."

PATTERSON, KELLY. Feb. 22, 1964 in Midland, TX. Attended Southern Methodist U. Debut 1984 OB in "Up in Central Park," followed by "Manhattan Serenade."

PATTERSON, RAYMOND. Born Oct. 1, 1955 in Richmond, VA. Graduate UMd. Bdwy debut in "Hair" (1977), followed by "Comin' Uptown," "Rock 'n' Roll: The First 5000 Years," "The Three Musketeers," OB in "The Tempest," "The Architect and the Emperor of Assyria," "A Book of Etiquette," "Arturo Ui," "Battle of the Giants." "American Heroes," "Child of the Sun," "Cummings and Goings."

PATTON, LUCILLE. Born in NYC, attended Neighborhood Playhouse. Bdwy debut 1946 in "A Winter's Tale," followed by "Topaz," "Arms and the Man," "Joy to the World," "All You Need Is One Good Break," "Fifth Season," "Heavenly Twins," "Rhinoceros," "Marathon '33," "The Last Analysis," "Dinner at 8," "La Strada," "Unlikely Heroes," "Love Suicide at Schofield Barracks," OB in "Ulysses in Nighttown," "Failures," "Three Sisters," "Yes Yes No No," "Tango," "Mme. de Sade," "Apple Pie," "Follies," "Yesterday Is Over," "My Prince My King," "I Am Who I Am," "Double Game," "Love in a Village."

PEARLMAN, STEPHEN. Born Feb. 26, 1935 in NYC. Graduate Dartmouth Col. Bdwy bow 1964 in "Barefoot in the Park," followed by "La Strada," OB in "Threepenny Opera," "Time of the Key," "Pimpernel," "In White America," "Viet Rock," "Chocolates," "Bloomers," "Richie," "Isn't It Romantic," "Bloodletters."

PEARSON, ELIZABETH. Born Jan. 4 in Cincinnati, OH. Graduate NYU, CalStateU. Debut 1985 OB in "Comedy of Errors."

PEARSON, SCOTT. Born Dec. 13, 1941 in Milwaukee, WI. Attended Valparaiso U, UWisc. Bdwy debut 1966 in "A Joyful Noise," followed by "Promises, Promises," "A Chorus Line."

PELIKAN, LISA. Born July 12 in Paris, Fr. Attended Juilliard. Debut 1975 OB in "Spring's Awakening," followed by "An Elephant in the House," "The American Clock," "The Diviners," "The Midnight Visitor," "Love's Labour's Lost," Bdwy in "Romeo and Juliet" (1977).

PEN, POLLY. Born Mar. 11, 1954 in Chicago, IL. Graduate Ithaca Col. Debut 1978 OB in "The Taming of the Shrew," followed by "The Guilded Cage," "Charlotte Sweet," "A . . . My Name is Alice," "Once on a Summer's Day," Bdwy in "The Utter Glory of Morrissey Hall."

PENDLETON, AUSTIN. Born Mar. 27, 1940 in Warren, OH. Attended Yale U. Debut 1962 OB in "Oh, Dad, Poor Dad. . .," followed by "The Last Sweet Days of Isaac," "The Three Sisters," "Say Goodnight, Gracie," "The Office Murders," "Up from Paradise," "The Overcoat," "Two Character Play," Bdwy in "Fiddler on the Roof," "Hail Scrawdyke," "The Little Foxes," "American Millionaire," "The Runner Stumbles," "Doubles."

PENDLETON, DAVID. Born Nov. 5, 1937 in Pittsburgh, PA. Graduate Lincoln U, CCNY. Bdwy debut 1971 in "No Place to Be Somebody," OB in "Screens," "Don't Bother Me, I Can't Cope," "Blueberry Mountain," "Julius Caesar," "Jack and Jill."

PENDLETON, WYMAN. Born Apr. 18, 1916 in Providence, RI. Graduate Brown U. Bdwy in "Tiny Alice" (1964), "Malcolm," "Quotations from Chairman Mao Tse-Tung," "Happy Days," "Henry V," "Othello," "There's One in Every Marriage," "Cat on a Hot Tin Roof," "Scenes and Revelations," OB in "Gallows Humor," "American Dream," "Zoo Story," "Corruption in the Palace of Justice," "Giant's Dance," "Child Buyer," "Happy Days," "Butter and Egg Man," "Othello," "Albee Directs Albee," "Dance for Me, Simeon," "Mary Stuart," "The Collyer Brothers at Home," "Period Piece," "A Bold Stroke for a Wife," "Hitch-hikers."

PENNINGTON, GAIL. Born Oct. 2, 1957 in Kansas City, MO. Graduate SMU. Bdwy debut 1980 in "The Music Man," followed by "Can-Can," "America," "Little Me" (1982), "42nd Street," OB in "The Baker's Wife."

PENNINGTON, MARK. Born Dec. 12, 1956 in St. Joseph, MO. Attended KanStateU. Debut 1984 OB in "Anonymous," followed by "Manhattan Serenade."

PEREZ, LAZARO. Born Dec. 17, 1945 in Havana, Cuba. Bdwy debut 1969 in "Does a Tiger Wear a Necktie?," followed by "Animals," OB in "Romeo and Juliet," "12 Angry Men," "Wonderful Years," "Alive," "G. R. Point," "Primary English Class," "The Man and the Fly," "The Last Latin Lover," "Cabal of Hypocrites," "Balm in Gilead."

PERKINS, DON. Born Oct. 23, 1928 in Boston, MA. Graduate Emerson Col. OB in "Drums under the Window," "Henry VI," "Richard III," "The Dubliners," "The Rehearsal," "Fallen Angels," "Our Lord of Lynchville," "A Touch of the Poet," "Crossing the Bar," Bdwy in "Borstal Boy" (1970).

PERKINS, ELIZABETH. Born Nov. 18, 1960 in Queens, NYC. Attended Goodman Theatre. Bdwy debut 1984 in "Brighton Beach Memoirs," OB in "The Arbor," "Life and Limb."

PERRI, PAUL. Born Nov. 6, 1953 in New Haven, CT. Attended Elmira Col., UMe., Juilliard. Debut 1979 OB in "Say Goodnight, Gracie," followed by "Henry VI," "Agamemnon," "Julius Caesar," "Waiting for Godot," "Home," Bdwy in "Bacchae," "Macbeth," "A View from the Bridge."

PERRY, ELIZABETH. Born Oct. 18, 1937 in Pawtuxet, RI. Attended RISU, AmThWing. Bdwy debut 1956 in "Inherit the Wind," followed by "The Women," with APA in "The Misanthrope," "Hamlet," "Exit the King," "Beckett" and "Macbeth," OB in "Royal Gambit," "Here Be Dragons," "Lady from the Sea," "Heartbreak House," "him," "All the Way Home," "The Frequency," "Fefu and Her Friends," "Out of the Broomcloset," "Ruby Ruby Sam Sam," "Did You See the Elephant?," "Last Stop Blue Jay Lane," "A Difficult Borning," "Presque Isle," "Isn't It Romantic."

PERRY, JAIME. Born June 1, 1958 in Brooklyn, NYC. Attended Manhattan Col. Debut 1978 OB in "Runaways," followed by "The Hooch," "The Mugger," Bdwy in "Runaways" (1978).

PERRY, KEITH. Born Oct. 28, 1931 in Des Moines, IA. Graduate Rice U. Bdwy debut 1965 in "Pickwick," followed by "I'm Solomon," "Copperfield," OB in "Epicene, the Silent Woman," "Hope with Feathers," "Ten Little Indians."

PESATURO, GEORGE. Born July 29, 1949 in Winthrop, MA. Graduate Manhattan Col. Bdwy debut 1976 in "A Chorus Line," OB in "The Music Man" (JB).

PETERS, BERNADETTE. Born Feb. 28, 1948 in Jamaica, NY. Bdwy debut in "Girl in the Freudian Slip," followed by "Johnny No-Trump," "George M!" for which she received a Theatre World Award, "La Strada," "On the Town," "Mack and Mabel," "Sunday in the Park with George," OB in "Curley McDimple," "Penny Friend," "Most Happy Fella," "Dames at Sea," "Nevertheless They Laugh," "Sally and Marsha."

PETERSEN, ERIKA. Born Mar. 24, 1949 in NYC. Attended NYU. Debut 1963 OB in "One Is a Lonely Number," followed by "I Dreamt I Dwelt in Bloomingdale's," "F. Jasmine Addams," "The Dubliners," "P.S. Your Cat Is Dead," "The Possessed," "Murder in the Cathedral," "The Further Inquiry," "State of the Union."

PETERSON, CHRIS. Born Nov. 19, 1962 in Malden, MA. Bdwy debut 1983 in "On Your Toes."

PETERSON, LENKA. Born Oct. 16, 1925 in Omaha, NE. Attended UIowa. Bdwy debut 1946 in "Bathsheba," followed by "Harvest of Years," "Sundown Beach," "Young and Fair," "The Grass Harp," "The Girls of Summer," "The Time of Your Life," "Look Homeward, Angel," "All the Way Home," "Nuts," OB in "Mrs. Minter," "American Night Cry," "Leaving Home," "The Brass Ring," "Father Dreams," "El Bravo," "Levitations," "Cliffhanger," "Quilters."

PETTY, ROSS. Born Aug. 29, 1946 in Winnipeg, Can. Graduate UManitoba. Debut 1975 OB in "Happy Time," followed by "Maggie Flynn," "Carnival," "Little Eyolf," "It's Wilde!," "Romance Is," "A Little Night Music," Bdwy in "Wings."

PEYTON, CAROLINE. Born Oct. 8, 1951 in Brookshaven, MS. Attended Northwestern, UInd. Debut 1983 OB in "Non Pasquale," followed by "The Human Comedy" (also on Bdwy), "La Boheme."

PHELAN, DEBORAH. Born Apr. 15 in New Haven, CT. Graduate Point Park Col. Bdwy debut in "Pippin" (1973), followed by "King of Hearts," "A Chorus Line," "Dancin'," "Encore," "La Cage aux Folles."

PIDDOCK, JIM. Born Apr. 8, 1956 in Rochester Eng. Graduate London U. Bdwy debut in "Present Laughter" (1982), followed by "Noises Off," OB in "The Boy's Own Story," "The Knack."

PIERCE, DAVID. Born Apr. 3, 1959 in Albany, NY. Graduate Yale U. Debut 1982 on Bdwy in "Beyond Therapy," followed by OB in "Summer," "That's It, Folks!," "The Three Sebs," "Donuts."

PIERSON, GEOFFREY. Born June 16, 1949 in Chicago, IL. Graduate Fordham U, Yale U. Debut 1978 OB in "Wings," followed by "Playing with Fire," "Crossing Delancey," Bdwy in "Tricks of the Trade" (1980).

PIETROPINTO, ANGELA. Born Feb. 5, in NYC. Graduate NYU. OB credits include "Henry IV," "Alice in Wonderland," "Endgame," "Our Late Night," "The Sea Gull," "Jinx Bridge," "The Mandrake," "Marie and Bruce," "Green Card Blues," "3 by Pirandello," "The Broken Pitcher," "A Midsummer Night's Dream," "The Rivals," "Cap and Bells," "Thrombo," Bdwy in "The Suicide" (1980).

PITONIAK, ANNE. Born Mar. 30, 1922 in Westfield, MA. Attended UNC Women's Col. Debut 1982 OB in "Talking With," followed by Bdwy in "'night, Mother" (1983) for which she received a Theatre World Award, "The Octette Bridge Club."

PLANK, SCOTT. Born Nov. 11, 1958 in Washington, DC. Attended NCSch of Arts. Bdwy debut 1981 in "Dreamgirls," followed by "A Chorus Line."

PLAYTEN, ALICE. Born Aug. 28, 1947 in NYC. Attended NYU. Bdwy debut 1960 in "Gypsy" followed by "Oliver," "Hello, Dolly!," "Henry Sweet Henry," for which she received a Theatre World Award, "George M!," OB in "Promenade," "The Last Sweet Days of Isaac," "National Lampoon's Lemmings," "Valentine's Day," "Pirates of Penzance," "Up from Paradise," "A Visit," "Sister Mary Ignatius Explains It All," "An Actor's Nightmare," "That's It, Folks."

PLUMLEY, DON. Born Feb. 11, 1934 in Los Angeles, CA. Graduate Pepperdine Col. Debut 1961 OB in "The Cage," followed by "A Midsummer Night's Dream," "Richard II," "Cymbeline," "Much Ado about Nothing," "Henry V," "Saving Grace," "A Whistle in the Dark," "Operation Sidewinder," "An Enemy of the People," "Back Bog Beast Bait," "The Kid," "Salt Lake City Skyline," "True to Life," Bdwy in "Equus" (1975).

PLUMMER, AMANDA. Born Mar. 23, 1957 in NYC. Attended Middlebury Col., Neighborhood Playhouse. Debut 1978 OB in "Artichoke," followed by "A Month in the Country," "A Taste of Honey" for which she received a Theatre World Award, "Alice in Concert," "A Stitch in Time," "Life under Water," Bdwy in "A Taste of Honey," "Agnes of God," "The Glass Menagerie."

POLITO, JON. Born Dec. 29, 1950 in Philadelphia, PA. Graduate Villanova U. Debut 1976 OB in "The Transfiguration of Benno Blimpie," followed by "Gemini," "New Jerusalem," "Emigres," "A Winter's Tale," "Johnny on a Spot," "Barbarians," "The Wedding," "Digby," Bdwy in "American Buffalo" (1977), "Curse of an Aching Heart," "Death of a Salesman" (1984).

POLLACK, DANIEL. Born July 25, 1927 in NYC. Graduate CCNY, Adelphi U., NYU. Debut 1949 OB in "An American Tragedy," followed by "Goodnight, Grandpa," "Victory Bonds," "Imaginary Invalid," Bdwy in "The Price" (1979).

POLTRACK, BEVERLY. Born Apr. 1, 1956 in Greenwich, CT. Graduate Boston Consv. Debut 1983 OB in "Skyline," followed by "Eugene," "Stardust," "The Mikado," "Very Warm for May."

POTTS, CHARLES. Born May 21, 1943 in Washington, IN. Graduate Trinity U. Debut 1984 OB in "She Loves Me," followed by "Dreams of the Son."

POWELL, ANTHONY. Born Dec. 13, 1958 in San Mateo, CA. Graduate UCLA, Temple U. Debut 1984 OB in "Pieces of Eight," followed by "A New Way to Pay Old Debts," "As You Like It," "The Skin of Our Teeth."

PREECE, K. K. Born Nov. 14, 1949 in Anna, IL. Graduate Brenau Col. Debut 1976 OB in "Panama Hattie," followed by "Scrambled Feet," "Bells Are Ringing," Bdwy in "Canterbury Tales" (1980).

PRESCOTT, KEN. Born Dec. 28, 1945 in Omaha, NE. Attended Omaha U. UUtah, Bdwy debut 1971 in "No, No, Nanette," followed by "That's Entertainment," "Follies," "Lorelei," "42nd Street," "The Tap Dance Kid."

PRESTON, WILLIAM. Born Aug. 26, 1921 in Columbia, PA. Graduate PennStateU. Debut 1972 OB in "We Bombed in New Haven," followed by "Hedda Gabler," "Whisper into My Good Ear," "A Nestless Bird," "Friends of Mine," "Iphigenia in Aulis," "Midsummer," "The Fantasticks," "Frozen Assets," "The Golem."

PRICE, LONNY. Born Mar. 9, 1959 in NYC. Attended Juilliard. Debut 1979 OB in "Class Enemy" for which he received a Theatre World Award, followed by "Up from Paradise," "Rommel's Garden," Bdwy 1980 in "The Survivor," followed by "Merrily We Roll Along," "Master Harold and the boys."

PROVAL, DAVID. Born May 20, 1942 in Brooklyn, NYC. Debut 1978 OB in "Momma's Little Angels," followed by Bdwy in "Requiem for a Heavyweight" (1985).

PROVENZA, SAL. Born Sept. 21, 1946 in Brooklyn, NY. Debut 1980 OB in "The Fantasticks," Bdwy in "Oh, Brother!" (1981), "The King and I" (1984).

PRUNEAU, PHILLIP. Born July 10 in Chicago, IL. Attended New School. Bdwy debut 1949 in "The Cellar and the Well" which he wrote, followed by "Sabrina Fair," "The Winner," "The Bad Seed," "There Was A Little Girl," "Sophie" (which he wrote), OB in "The Last Analysis," "The Madwoman of Chaillot," "Clarence," "Vivat! Vivat Regina!," "A Little Bit Less Than Normal," "Legendary Star Dust Boys."

PRYCE, JONATHAN. Born June 1, 1947 in Wales, UK. Attended RADA. Bdwy debut 1976 in "Comedians" for which he received a Theatre World Award, followed by "Accidental Death of an Anarchist" (1984).

PUDENZ, STEVE. Born Sept. 25, 1947 in Carroll, IA. Graduate UIa. Debut 1980 OB in "Dona Rosita," followed by "Dick Deterred," "Lifelines."

PUGH, RICHARD WARREN. Born Oct. 20, 1950 in NYC. Graduate Tarkio Col. Bdwy debut 1979 in "Sweeney Todd," followed by "The Music Man," "The Five O'Clock Girl," "Copperfield," "Zorba" (1983), OB in "Chase a Rainbow."

PURDHAM, DAVID. Born June 3, 1951 in San Antonio, TX. Graduate UMd., UWa. Debut 1980 OB in "Journey's End," followed by "Souvenirs," "Once on a Summer's Day," "Twelfth Night," "Maneuvers," Bdwy in "Piaf" (1981).

QUINLAN, MICHAEL. Born Oct. 9, 1953 in NYC. Graduate Fairfield U. Debut 1984 on Bdwy in "Death of A Salesman."

QUINN, AIDAN. Born March 8, 1959 in Chicago, IL. Debut 1984 OB in "Fool for Love."

QUINN, ANTHONY. Born Apr. 21, 1915 in Chihuahua, Mex. Bdwy debut 1947 in "The Gentleman from Athens," followed by "Borned in Texas," "A Streetcar Named Desire," "Becket," "Chin Chin," "Born Yesterday," "Zorba" (1983).

QUINN, PATRICK. Born Feb. 12, 1950 in Philadelphia, PA. Graduate Temple U. Bdwy debut 1976 in "Fiddler on the Roof," followed by "A Day in Hollywood/A Night in the Ukraine," OB in "It's Better with a Band," "By Strouse," "Forbidden Broadway," "A Little Night Music."

RACKLEFF, OWEN S. Born July 16, 1934 in NYC. Graduate Columbia U, London U. Bdwy debut 1977 in "Piaf," OB in "The Lesson" (1978), "Catsplay," "Arms and the Man," "Escoffier: King of Chefs," "New Way to Pay Old Debts," "Samson Agonistes," "Enter Laughing."

RAGNO, JOSEPH. Born Mar. 11, 1936 in Brooklyn, NYC. Attended Allegheny Col. Debut 1960 OB in "Worm in the Horseradish," followed by "Elizabeth the Queen," "A Country Scandal," "The Shrike," "Cymbeline," "Love Me, Love My Children," "Interrogation of Havana," "The Birds," "Armenians," "Feedlot," "Every Place Is Newark," "Modern Romance," Bdwy in "Indians," "The Iceman Cometh."

RAIDER-WEXLER, VICTOR. Born Dec. 31, 1943 in Toledo, OH. Attended UToledo. Debut 1976 OB in "The Prince of Homburg," followed by "The Passion of Dracula," "Ivanov," "Brandy Before Breakfast," "The Country Girl," Bdwy in "Best Friend" (1976).

RAIKEN, LAWRENCE. Born Feb. 5, 1949 on Long Island, NY. Graduate Wm. & Mary Col., UNC. Debut 1979 OB in "Wake Up, It's Time to Go to Bed," "Rise of David Levinsky," "Bells Are Ringing," Bdwy in "Woman of the Year" (1981).

RAINES, ROGER. Born Nov. 25, 1965 in New York City; Attended NYU. Bdwy debut 1983 in "Brighton Beach Memoirs."

RAMSAY, REMAK. Born Feb. 2, 1937 in Baltimore, MD. Graduate Princeton U. Debut 1964 OB in "Hang Down Your Head and Die," followed by "The Real Inspector Hound," "Landscape of the Body," "All's Well That Ends Well," "Rear Column," "The Winslow Boy," "The Dining Room," "Pygmalion in Concert," Bdwy in "Half a Sixpence," "Sheep on the Runway," "Lovely Ladies, Kind Gentlemen," "On the Town," "Jumpers," "Private Lives," "Dirty Linen," "Every Good Boy Deserves Favor," "Save Grand Central," "Quartermaine's Terms."

RAMSEY, MARION. Born May 10 in Philadelphia, PA. Bdwy debut 1969 in "Hello, Dolly!," followed by "The Me Nobody Knows," "Rachel Lily Rosenbloom," "Eubie!," "Rock 'n' Roll," "Grind," OB in "Soon," "Do It Again," "Wedding of Iphigenia," "2008½."

RANCK, CHRISTINE. Born Dec. 8, 1951 in Columbus, OH. Graduate URochester, Eastman School. Debut 1978 OB in "Company," followed by "A Night at Texas Guinan's," "Trading Places."

RANDEL, MELISSA. Born June 16, 1955 in Portland, ME. Graduate UCal/Irvine. Bdwy debut 1980 in "A Chorus Line."

RANDELL, RON. Born Oct. 8. 1920 in Sydney, Aust. Attended St. Mary's Col. Bdwy debut 1949 in "The Browning Version," followed by "Harlequinade," "Candida," "World of Suzie Wong," "Sherlock Holmes," "Mrs. Warren's Profession," "Measure for Measure," "Bent," OB in "Holy Places," "After You've Gone," "Patrick Pearse Motel," "Maneuvers."

RASHOVICH, GORDANA. Born Sept. 18 in Chicago IL. Graduate Roosevelt U, RADA. Debut 1977 OB in "Fefu and Her Friends" for which she received a Theatre World Award, followed by "Selma," "Couple of the Year."

RAVELO, HENRY. Born Aug. 14, 1958 in Manila, Phil. Attended UWis. Debut 1984 OB in "Pacific Overtures."

RAY, LESLIE ANN. Born May 27, 1946 in NYC. Graduate Hofstra U., AADA. Debut 1969 OB in "Trumpets and Drums," followed by "Godspell," "Anna K.," "Hamlet," "Bonus Army," "Taboo in Revue," Bdwy in "Angel" (1978).

REAGAN, JUDITH. Born Jan. 28 in Newark, NJ. Graduate Notre Dame Col., Catholic U. Debut 1984 OB in "Outtakes," followed by "The Rabinowitz Gambit," "Taming of the Shrew."

REAMS, LEE ROY. Born Aug. 23, 1942 in Covington, KY. Graduate U. Cinn. Cons. Bdwy debut 1966 in "Sweet Charity," followed by "Oklahoma!" (LC), "Applause," "Lorelei" "Show Boat" (JB), "Hello, Dolly!" (1978), "42nd Street," OB in "Sterling Silver," "Potholes," "The Firefly in Concert."

REAVES-PHILLIPS, SANDRA. Born Dec. 23 in Mullins, SC. Bdwy debut 1973 in "Raisin," OB in "Li'l Bit," "Ragtime Blues," "Blues in the Night," "Basin Street," "Karma," "Sparrow in Flight," "Take Care," "American Dreams," "Late Great Ladies," "Oh! Oh! Obesity!.

REBHORN, JAMES. Born Sept. 1, 1948 in Philadelphia, PA. Graduate Wittenberg U, Columbia U. Debut 1972 OB in "Blue Boys," "Are You Now Or Have You Ever Been," "Trouble with Europe," "Othello," "Hunchback of Notre Dame," "Period of Adjustment," "The Freak," "Half a Lifetime," "Touch Black," "To Gillian on Her 37th Birthday," "Rain," "The Hasty Heart," "Husbandry," "Isn't It Romantic."

REDFIELD, ADAM. Born Nov. 4, 1959 in NYC. Attended NYU. Debut 1977 OB in "Hamlet," followed by "Androcles and the Lion," "Twelfth Night," "Reflected Glory," "Movin' Up," "The Unicorn," Bdwy 1980 in "A Life" for which he received a Theatre World Award, followed by "Beethoven's Tenth."

REDFIELD, MARILYN. Born May 2, 1940 in Chicago IL. Graduate Vassar, Harvard. Debut 1973 OB in "The Rainmaker," followed by "Monologia," "Mod Madonna," "King of the U.S.," "Too Much Johnson," "Digby," Bdwy in "Chapter Two" (1979).

REDGRAVE, LYNN. Born Mar. 8, 1943 in London, Eng. Attended Central Sch. of Speech. Bdwy debut 1967 in "Black Comedy," followed by "My Fat Friend," "Mrs. Warren's Profession," "Knock, Knock," "St. Joan," "Aren't We All?," OB in "Sister Mary Ignatius . . ."

REED, ALAINA. Born Nov. 10, 1946 in Springfield, OH. Attended Kent State U. Bdwy debut in "Hair" (1967/1977), followed by "Eubie!," OB in "Sgt. Pepper's Lonely Hearts Club Band," "In Trousers," "A . . . My Name is Alice."

REED, MAGGI-MEG. Born in Columbus, OH. Graduate Harvard U. Debut 1984 OB in "She Stoops to Conquer," followed by "Playboy of the Western World."

REED, PAMELA. Born Apr. 2, 1949 in Tacoma, WA. Graduate UWa. Bdwy debut 1978 in "November People," OB in "The Curse of the Starving Class," "All's Well That Ends Well," "Seduced," "Getting Out," "The Sorrows of Stephen," Standing on My Knees," "Criminal Minds," "Fen."

REGION, DANIEL. Born Nov. 11, 1948 in Sandwich, IL. Debut 1981 OB in "Cowboy Mouth," followed by "Widows and Children First," "A Midsummer Night's Dream," "Beyond Therapy," "Taming of the Shrew," Bdwy in "Torch Song Trilogy" (1982).

REID, CRISTINE. Born Sept. 4, 1950 in Chicago, IL. Graduate SUNY/Fredonia, FlaStateU. Debut 1982 OB in "Send Her to the Beast," followed by "The Tamer Tamed."

REID, KATE. Born Nov. 4, 1930 in London, Eng. Attended Toronto U. Bdwy debut 1962 in "Who's Afraid of Virginia Woolf?," followed by "Dylan," "Slapstick Tragedy," "The Price," "Freedom of the City," "Cat on a Hot Tin Roof," "Bosoms and Neglect," "Morning's at 7," "Death of a Salesman."

REINKING, ANN. Born Nov. 10, 1949 in Seattle, WA. Attended Joffrey School, HB Studio. Bdwy debut 1969 in "Cabaret," followed by "Coco," "Pippin," "Over Here" for which she received a Theatre World Award, "Goodtime Charley," "A Chorus Line," "Chicago," "Dancin'," OB in "One More Song/One More Dance," "Music Moves Me."

REIT, SALLY FAYE. Born Mar. 14, 1957 in Ithaca, NY. Graduate UVer., UIowa. Debut 1982 OB in "Talking With," followed by "Isn't It Romantic."

REMAR, JAMES. Born Dec. 31, 1953 in Boston, MA. Attended Neighborhood Playhouse. Debut 1977 OB in "Yo-Yo," followed by "Early Dark," "California Dog Fight," Bdwy 1980 in "Bent."

REYNOLDS, BRAD J. Born Dec. 3, 1961 in Berea, OH. Graduate UCincinnati Consv. Debut 1985 OB in "Manhattan Serenade."

RHODES, JENNIFER. Born June 27 in Rosiclare, IL. Attended S. Ill. U. Debut 1984 OB in "Lester Sims Retires Tomorrow," followed by "Donogoo," "The Crucible," "Madwoman of Chaillot."

RICE, SARAH. Born Mar. 5, 1955 in Okinawa. Attended AzStateU. Debut 1974 OB in "The Fantasticks," followed by "The Enchantress," "The Music Man," Bdwy 1979 in "Sweeney Todd" for which she received a Theatre World Award.

RICHARDS, CAROL. Born Dec. 26 in Aurora, IL. Graduate Northwestern U, Columbia U. Bdwy debut 1965 in "Half a Sixpence," followed by "Mame," "Last of the Red Hot Lovers," "Company," "Cats."

RICHARDS, JESS. Born Jan. 23, 1943 in Seattle, WA. Attended UWash. Bdwy debut 1966 in "Walking Happy," followed by "South Pacific" (LC) "Two by Two," "On the Town" for which he received a Theatre World Award, "Mack and Mabel," "Musical Chairs," "A Reel American Hero," "Barnum," OB in "One for the Money," "Lovesong," "A Musical Evening with Josh Logan," "The Lullaby of Broadway," "All Night Strut!,""Station Joy."

RICHARDS, PAUL-DAVID. Born Aug. 31, 1935 in Bedford, IN. Graduate IndU. Bdwy debut 1959 in "Once Upon a Mattress," followed by "Camelot," "It's Superman!," "A Joyful Noise," "1776," "Devour the Snow," "My One and Only," OB in "Black Picture Show," "Devour the Snow," "Elizabeth and Essex."

RICHARDSON, PATRICIA. Born Feb. 23 in Bethesda, MD. Graduate SMU. Bdwy debut 1974 in "Gypsy," followed by "Loose Ends," "The Wake of Jamey Foster," OB in "Coroner's Plot," "Vanities," "Hooters," "The Frequency," "Fables for Friends," "The Miss Firecracker Contest."

RICHERT, WANDA. Born Apr. 18, 1958 in Chicago, IL. Bdwy debut 1980 in "42nd Street" for which she received a Theatre World Award, followed by "Nine," "A Chorus Line."

RICHWOOD, PATRICK. Born Nov. 6, 1962 in Burbank, CA. Debut 1983 OB in "The Robber Bridegroom," followed by "What's a Nice Country Like You Still Doing in a State Like This?"

RIDDLE, GEORGE. Born May 21, 1937 in Auburn, IN. OB in "Eddie Fay," "The Prodigal," "The Fantasticks," "Huui, Huui," "The Glorious Age," "The Trial of Dr. Beck," "Downriver."

RIGAN, MICHELE. Born May 15, 1975 in Bridgeport, CT. Bdwy debut 1984 in "Sunday in the Park with George."

RILEY, LARRY. Born June 21, 1952 in Memphis, TN. Graduate Memphis State U. Bdwy debut 1978 in "A Broadway Musical," followed by "I Love My Wife," "Night and Day," "Shakespeare's Cabaret," OB in "Street Songs," "Amerika," "Plane Down," "Sidewalkin'," "Frimbo," "A Soldier's Play," "Maybe I'm Doing It Wrong," "Diamonds."

RITCHIE, MARGARET. Born May 31 in Madison, WI. Graduate UWis., NYU. Debut 1981 OB in "Last Summer at Bluefish Cove," followed by "Who's There," "Telling Tales," "All Soul's Day."

RIVERA, CHITA. Born Jan. 23, 1933 in Washington, DC. Bdwy debut 1950 in "Guys and Dolls," followed by "Call Me Madam," "Can-Can," "Seventh Heaven," "Mr. Wonderful," "West Side Story," "Bye Bye Birdie," "Bajour," "Chicago," "Bring Back Birdie," "Merlin," "The Rink," OB in "Shoestring Revue."

ROBBINS, JANA. Born Apr. 18, 1947 in Johnstown, PA. Graduate Stephens Col. Bdwy debut 1974 in "Good News," followed by "I Love My Wife," "Crimes of the Heart," OB in "Tickles by Tucholsky," "Tip-Toes," "All Night Strut," "Colette Collage," "Circus Gothic."

ROBERTS, GRACE. Born Nov. 9, 1935 in NYC. Debut 1956 OB in "Out of This World," followed by "Affairs of Anatol," "Beethoven/Karl," "Friends Too Numerous to Mention," "Applesauce," "A . . . My Name is Alice," "Briss."

ROBERTS, TONY. Born Oct. 22, 1939 in NYC. Graduate Northwestern U. Bdwy debut 1962 in "Something about a Soldier," followed by "Take Her, She's Mine," "Last Analysis," "Never Too Late," "Barefoot in the Park," "Don't Drink the Water," "How Now, Dow Jones," "Play It Again, Sam," "Promises Promises," "Sugar," "Absurd Person Singular," "Murder at the Howard Johnson's," "They're Playing Our Song," "Doubles," OB in "The Cradle Will Rock," "Losing Time," "The Good Parts," "Time Framed."

ROBERTSON, DEBORAH (formerly Bauers). Born July 19, 1953 in Nashville, TN. Graduate UCol., Smith Col. Bdwy debut 1982 in "Oh! Calcutta!"

ROBERTSON, SCOTT. Born Jan. 4, 1954 in Stamford, CT. Bdwy debut 1976 in "Grease," followed OB by "Scrambled Feet," "Applause," "A Lady Needs a Change," "A Backer's Audition," "She Loves Me," "Secrets of a Lava Lamp."

ROBINS, LAILA. Born Mar. 14, 1959 in St. Paul MN. Graduate UWisc., Yale. Bdwy debut 1984 in "The Real Thing."

ROBINSON, HAL. Born in Bedford, IN. Graduate IndU. Debut 1971 OB in "Memphis Store-Bought Teeth," followed by "From Berlin to Broadway," "The Fantasticks," "Promenade," "The Baker's Wife."

ROBINSON, MARTIN P. Born Mar. 9, 1954 in Dearborn, MI. Graduate WiStateU, AADA. Debut 1980 OB in "The Haggadah," followed by "Yellow Wallpaper," "The Lady's Not for Burning," "Little Shop of Horrors."

ROCHE, TUDI. Born July 19, 1955 in Lubbock, TX. Attended TxChristianU. Bdwy debut 1980 in "A Day in Hollywood/A Night in the Ukraine," followed by "Harrigan 'n Hart," OB in "Preppies" (1983), "Man Enough."

ROCKAFELLOW, MARILYN. Born Jan. 22, 1939 in Middletown, NJ. Graduate Rutgers U. Debut 1976 OB in "La Ronde," followed by "The Art of Dining," "One Act Play Festival," "Open Admissions," "Bathroom Plays," Bdwy in "Clothes for A Summer Hotel" (1980), "Open Admissions," "Play Memory."

ROCKMAN, WENDY. Born June 22, 1973 in NYC. Debut 1982 OB in "Grownups," followed by Young Playwrights Festival.

ROCK-SAVAGE, STEVEN. Born Dec. 14, 1958 in Melville, LA. Attended LaStateU, New School. Debut 1985 OB in "Inherit the Wind."

ROE, PATRICIA. Born Sept. 18, 1932 in NYC. Attended Columbia U., Actors Studio. Bdwy debut 1951 in "Romeo and Juliet," followed by "Cat on a Hot Tin Roof," "Compulsion," "By the Beautiful Sea," "Night Circus," "A Distant Bell," "Look after Lulu," "Night of the Iguana," "A Texas Trilogy," "Horowitz and Mrs. Washington," OB in "The Collection," "After the Fall," "But For Whom Charlie," "The Homecoming," "Bananas," "Transfers," "Milk of Paradise," "A Step Out of Line."

ROGAN, PETER. Born May 11, 1939 in County Leitrim, Ire. Bdwy debut 1966 in "Philadelphia, Here I Come," OB in "The Kitchen," "Nobody Hears a Broken Drum," "Picture of Dorian Gray," "Macbeth," "Sjt. Musgrave's Dance," "Stephen D," "People Are Living There," "The Plough and the Stars," "Look Back in Anger," "Sea Anchor," "The Arbor," "All the Nice People," "The Ballad of Soapy Smith."

ROGERS, ANNE. Born July 29, 1933 in Liverpool, Eng. Attended St. John's Col. Bdwy debut 1957 in "My Fair Lady," followed by "Zenda," "Half a Sixpence," "42nd Street."

RONSTADT, LINDA. Born July 15, 1946 in Tucson, AZ. Debut OB 1980 in "Pirates of Penzance" (that moved to Broadway), followed by "La Boheme."

ROOS, CASPER. Born Mar. 21, 1925 in The Bronx, NY. Attended Manhattan School of Music. Bdwy debut 1959 in "First Impressions," followed by "How to Succeed in Business . . . ," "Mame," "Brigadoon," "Shenandoah," "My One and Only," OB in "Street Scene."

ROSE, CRISTINE. Born Jan. 31, 1951 in Lynwood, CA. Graduate Stanford U. Debut 1979 OB in "The Miracle Worker," followed by "Don Juan Comes Back from the War," "Hunting Scenes from Bavaria," "Three Acts of Recognition," "Winterplay," "Isn't It Romantic."

ROSE, GEORGE. Born Feb. 19, 1920 in Bicester, Eng. Bdwy debut with Old Vic 1946 in "Henry IV," followed by "Much Ado About Nothing," "A Man for All Seasons," "Hamlet," "Royal Hunt of the Sun," "Walking Happy," "Loot," "My Fair Lady," (CC'68), "Canterbury Tales," "Coco," "Wise Child," "Sleuth," "My Fat Friend," "My Fair Lady" (1976), "She Loves Me," "Peter Pan," BAM's "The Play's the Thing," "The Devil's Disciple," and "Julius Caesar," "The Kingfisher," "Pirates of Penzance," "Dance a Little Closer," "You Can't Take It with You," "Beethoven's Tenth," "Aren't We All?"

ROSEN, ABIGAIL. Born Sept. 18, 1946 in Basel, Switz. Graduate Bard Col. OB in "The Living Premise," "International Playgirls," "Home Movies," "Cinderella," "Beclch," "A Small Disturbance," "Dayzed," Bdwy in "Where's Daddy?," "Sign in Sidney Brustein's Window."

ROSENBAUM, DAVID. Born in NYC. Debut OB 1968 in "America Hurrah," followed by "The Cave Dwellers," "Evenings with Chekhov," "Out of the Death Cart," "After Miriam," "The Indian Wants the Bronx," "Allergy," "Family Business," "Beagleman and Brackett," Bdwy in "Oh! Calcutta!"

ROSS, BERTRAM. Born Nov. 14, 1920 in Brooklyn, NY. Attended Oberlin Col. With Martha Graham Company before debut 1983 OB in "The Tempest," followed by "An Evening with Bertram Ross."

ROSS, JAMIE. Born May 4, 1939 in Markinch, Scot. Attended RADA. Bdwy debut 1962 in "Little Moon of Alban," followed by "Moon Beseiged," "Ari," "Different Times," "Woman of the Year," "La Cage aux Folles," OB in "Penny Friend," "Oh, Coward!"

ROSS, JUSTIN. Born Dec. 15, 1954 in Brooklyn, NY. Debut 1974 OB in "More Than You Deserve," followed by "Fourtune," "Ready for More?," "Weekend," Bdwy in "Pippin" (1975), "A Chorus Line," "Got To Go Disco."

ROSSETTER, KATHY. Born July 31 in Abington, PA. Graduate Gettsburg Col. debut 1982 OB in "After the Fall," followed by "The Incredibly Famous Willy Rivers," "A Midsummer Night's Dream," Bdwy in "Death of a Salesman" (1984).

ROTHMAN, NANCY. Born Oct. 13, 1950 in Boston, MA. Graduate Emerson Col. Debut 1983 OB in "Small Help," followed by "Action," "Haunted Lives."

ROWE, HANSFORD. Born May 12, 1924 in Richmond, VA. Graduate URichmond. Bdwy debut 1968 in "We Bombed in New Haven," followed by "Porgy and Bess," "Nuts," OB in "Curley McDimple," "The Fantasticks," "Last Analysis," "God Says There Is No Peter Ott," "Mourning Becomes Electra," "Bus Stop," "Secret Service," "Boy Meets Girl," "Getting Out," "The Unicorn," "The Incredibly Famous Willy Rivers."

ROWE, STEPHEN. Born June 3, 1948 in Johnstown, PA. Graduate Emerson Col., Yale. Debut 1979 OB in "Jungle Coup," followed by "A Private View," "Cinders," "Coming of Age in SoHo."

ROZSA, J. DAVID. Born May 20, 1973 in Montreal, Can. Debut 1985 OB in "Life and Limb."

RUBIN, STAN. Born Jan. 7, 1938 in The Bronx, NYC. Attended Fashion Inst. Debut 1974 OB in "You Can't Take It With You," followed by "The Sign in Sidney Brustein's Window," "A Slight Case of Murder," "Witness for the Prosecution," "Damn Yankees," "Kiss Me Kate," "Gingerbread Lady," "Pearls."

RUBINSTEIN, JOHN. Born Dec. 8, 1946 in Los Angeles, CA. Attended UCLA. Bdwy debut 1972 in "Pippin" for which he received a Theatre World Award, followed by "Children of a Lesser God," "Fools," "The Soldier's Tale," "The Caine Mutiny Court-Martial," "Hurlyburly."

RUCKER, BO. Born Aug. 17, 1948 in Tampa, FL. Debut 1978 OB in "Native Son" for which he received a Theatre World Award, followed by "Blues for Mr. Charlie," "Streamers," "Forty Deuce," "Dustoff."

RUSSELL, CATHY. Born Aug. 6, 1955 in New Canaan, CT. Graduate Cornell U. Debut 1980 OB in "City Sugar," followed by "Miss Schuman's Quartet," "A Resounding Tinkle," "Right to Life," "Collective Choices," "The Lunch Girls."

RUSSELL, CHERYL. Born June 13, 1960 in St. Louis, MO. Attended UMo. Bdwy debut in "Brigadoon" (1980), followed by "Oliver" (1984).

RUSSOM, LEON. Born Dec. 6, 1941 in Little Rock, AR. Attended Southwestern U. Debut 1968 OB in "Futz," followed by "Cyrano de Bergerac," "Boys in the Band," "Oh! Calcutta!," "Trial of the Catonsville 9," "Henry VI," "Richard III," "Shadow of a Gunman," "The New York Idea," "Three Sisters," "Old Flames," "Loving Reno," "Ruffian on the Stair," "Royal Bob," "Our Lord of Lynchville," "Laughing Stock," "State of the Union."

RYAN, MICHAEL M. Born Mar. 19, 1929 in Wichita, KS. Attended St. Benedict's Col., Georgetown U. Bdwy debut 1960 in "Advise and Consent," followed by "The Complaisant Lover," "Best Friend," OB in "Richard III," "King Lear," "Hedda Gabler," "Barroom Monks," "Portrait of the Artist as a Young Man," "Autumn Garden," "Naomi Court," "Caveat Emptor," "Devil's Fable," "The Price," "Arms and the Man."

RYAN, STEVEN. Born June 19, 1947 in NYC. Graduate Boston U., UMn. Debut 1978 OB in "Winning Isn't Everything," followed by "The Beethoven," "September in the Rain," "Romance Language."

SABELLICO, RICHARD. Born June 29, 1951 in NYC. Attended C. W. Post Col. Bdwy debut 1974 in "Gypsy," followed by "Annie," "The Magic Show," OB in "Gay Divorce," "La Ronde," "Manhattan Breakdown," "From Brooks with Love," "Dames at Sea."

SADLER, WILLIAM (BILL). Born Apr. 13, 1950 in Buffalo, NY. Graduate SUNY/Genesco, Cornell U. Debut 1975 OB in "Ivanov," followed by "Limbo Tales," "Chinese Viewing Pavilion," "Lennon," "Necessary Ends," "Hannah," Bdwy in "Biloxi Blues" (1985).

SAFFRAN, CHRISTINA. Born Oct. 21, 1958 in Quincy, IL. Attended Webster Col. Bdwy debut 1978 in "A Chorus Line," followed by "A New York Summer," OB in "Music Moves Me."

SALATA, GREGORY. Born July 21, 1949 in NYC. Graduate Queens Col. Bdwy debut 1975 in "Dance with Me," followed by "Equus," "Bent," OB in "Piaf: A Remembrance," "Sacraments."

SALINGER, MATT. Born in 1961 in New Hampshire. Attended Princeton, Columbia U. Bdwy debut 1985 in "Dancing in the End Zone."

SALISBURY, FRAN. Born Feb. 9, 1945 in NYC. Graduate Shaw U., Columbia U. Bdwy debut 1972 in "Purlie," followed by "The Royal Family," "Reggae," OB in "Prodigal Sister," "The Lion and the Jewel," "Sparrow in Flight," "Helen," "Broadway Soul," "As to the Meaning of Words," "The Scarecrow," "Celebration."

SAMUEL, PETER. Born Aug. 15, 1958 in Pana, IL. Graduate East Ill.U. Bdwy debut 1981 in "The First," followed by "The Three Musketeers," OB in "Little Eyolf," "The Road to Hollywood," "Elizabeth and Essex."

SANCHEZ, JAIME. Born Dec. 19, 1938 in Rincon, PR. Attended Actors Studio. Bdwy debut 1957 in "West Side Story," followed by "Oh, Dad, Poor Dad . . .," "A Midsummer Night's Dream," "Richard III," OB in "The Toilet" (1964) and "Conerico Was Here to Stay" for which he received a Theatre World Award, "The Ox Cart," "The Tempest," "Merry Wives of Windsor," "Julius Caesar," "Coriolanus," "He Who Gets Slapped," "State without Grace."

SANDERS, FRED. Born Feb. 24, 1955 in Philadelphia, PA. Yale graduate. Debut 1981 OB in "Coming Attractions," followed by "The Tempest," "Responsible Parties," "An Evening with Lenny Bruce," "Green Fields," "Incident at Vichy."

SANDERS, JAY O. Born Apr. 16, 1953 in Austin, TX. Graduate SUNY/Purchase. Debut 1976 OB in "Henry V," followed by "Measure for Measure," "Scooping," "Buried Child," "Fables for Friends," "In Trousers," "Girls Girls Girls," "Twelfth Night," "Geniuses," "The Incredibly Famous Willy Rivers," "Rommel's Garden," Bdwy in "Loose Ends' (1979), "The Caine Mutiny Court Martial."

SANTELL, MARIE. Born July 8 in Brooklyn, NY. Bdwy debut 1957 in "Music Man," followed by "A Funny Thing Happened on the Way . . . ," "Flora, the Red Menace," "Pajama Game," "Mack and Mabel," "La Cage aux Folles," OB in "Hi, Paisano!," "Boys from Syracuse," "Peace," "Promenade," "The Drunkard," "Sensations," "The Castaways," "Fathers and Sons."

SANTORO, MICHAEL. Born Nov. 23, 1957 in Brooklyn, NYC. Attended Lee Strasberg Inst. Debut 1985 OB in "The Normal Heart."

SAPUTO, PETER J. Born Feb. 2, 1939 in Detroit, MI. Graduate EMiU, Purdue U. Debut 1977 OB in "King Oedipus," followed by "Twelfth Night," "Bon Voyage," "Happy Haven," "Sleepwalkers," "Humulus the Mute," "The Freak," "Promises, Promises," "The Last of Hitler," "A Touch of the Poet," "Theatre Olympics," "Rude Time," Bdwy in "Once in a Lifetime."

SARANDON, CHRIS. Born July 24, 1942 in Beckley, WVa. Graduate UWVa, Catholic U. Bdwy debut 1970 in "The Rothschilds," followed by "Two Gentlemen of Verona," "Censored Scenes from King Kong," OB in "Marco Polo Sings a Solo," "The Devil's Disciple," "The Woods," "Voice of the Turtle."

SARBER, SUSAN. Born June 22 in Charleston, WVa. Graduate WVaU. Debut 1984 OB in "Bells Are Ringing."

SAVAGE, JACK. Born Dec. 5, 1953 in Kinnelon, NJ. Graduate Manhattan School of Music, FlaStateU. Debut 1984 OB in "Kuni Leml."

SAVELLA, MARCIA. Born Nov. 6, 1947 in Cranston, RI. Graduate UCt. Bdwy debut 1973 in "The Iceman Cometh," OB in "Circus," "Cowpokes," "Eleanor and Franklin," "A Night Out," "Happy Birthday, Wanda June," "Sacraments."

SAVIN, RON LEE. Born July 20, 1947 in Norfolk, VA. Graduate Wm. & Mary Col. Debut 1981 OB in "Francis," followed by "Greater Tuna," "Road to Hollywood," "Streetheat."

SAVIOLA, CAMILLE. Born July 16, 1950 in The Bronx, NY. Debut 1970 OB in "Touch," followed by "Rainbow," "Godspell," "Starmites," "Battle of the Giants," "Dementos," "Spookhouse," "A Vaudeville," "Road to Hollywood," "Hollywood Opera," "Secrets of the Lava Lamp," Bdwy in "Nine" (1982).

SAXTON, WARD. Born Aug. 15, 1970 in Binghamton, NY. Bdwy debut 1982 in "Evita," followed by OB in "Richard III," "Coming of Age in SoHo."

SCALISE, THOMAS DAVID. Born Mar. 12, 1953 in Conneaut, OH. Attended Kent State U. Bdwy debut 1981 in "Fiddler on the Roof," followed by "Zorba" (1983).

SCANLON, BARBARA. Born Jan. 17, 1956 in Detroit, MI. Graduate MiStateU. Debut 1984 OB in "Elizabeth and Essex," followed by "A Little Night Music."

SCARDINO, DON. Born in Feb. 1949 in NYC. Attended CCNY. Bdwy in "Loves of Cass McGuire" (1966), "Johnny No-Trump," "My Daughter, Your Son," "Godspell," "Angel," "King of Hearts," OB in "Shout from the Rooftops," "Rimers of Eldritch," "The Unknown Soldier and His Wife," "Godspell," "Moonchildren," "Kid Champion," "Comedy of Errors," "Secret Service," "Boy Meets Girl," "Scribes," "I'm Getting My Act Together. . .," "As You Like It," "Holeville," "Sorrows of Stephen," "A Midsummer Night's Dream," "The Recruiting Officer," "Jungle of Cities," "Double Feature," "How I Got That Story," "Hang on to the Good Times."

SCARPELLI, GLENN. Born July 6, 1966 in NYC. Bdwy debut 1977 in "Golda," followed by "Richard III," OB in "Streetheat."

SCHAEFFER, IRENE. Born Dec. 15, 1946 in Breslau, Ger. Graduate UMd. Debut 1968 OB in "Istanbul," followed by "The Death of Joe Cino," "Stop, You're Killing Me," "Chamber Music," "Innocent Pleasures," "Camille," "Trespasses."

SCHAFFERT, GREG. Born Apr. 26, 1955 in Aurora, NE. Attended UNeb., AmConTh. Debut 1985 OB in "A Sleep of Prisoners."

SCHAUT, ANN LOUISE. Born Nov. 21, 1956 in Minneapolis, MN. Attended UMn. Bdwy debut 1981 in "A Chorus Line."

SHEINE, RAYNOR. Born Nov. 10 in Emporia, VA. Graduate VaCommonwealthU. Debut 1978 OB in "Curse of the Starving Class," followed by "Blues for Mr. Charlie," "Salt Lake City Skyline," "Mother Courage," "The Lady or the Tiger," "Bathroom Plays," "Wild Life," "Re-Po," "Almos' a Man."

SCHENK, ERNIE. Born Nov. 4, 1940 in Newark, NJ. Graduate Bloomfield Col., NYU. Debut 1969 OB in "Makbeth," followed by "Goose and Tom," "Under Milk Wood," "Glory in the Flower," "Episode 26," Bdwy in "Shenandoah" (1978).

SCHERER, JOHN. Born May 16, 1961 in Buffalo, NY. Graduate Carnegie-Melon U. Debut 1983 OB in "Preppies," followed by "Jass," "Downriver," "Ladies and Gentlemen, Jerome Kern."

SCHIFF, ERIC. Born Aug. 10, 1958 in Huntington, WVa. Attended Amherst Col. Debut 1980 OB in "Details of the 16th Frame," followed by "Levitation," "Love's Labour's Lost."

SCHLAMME, MARTHA. Born Sept. 25 in Vienna, Aust. Debut 1963 OB in "The World of Kurt Weill," followed by "A Month of Sundays," "Mata Hari," "Beethoven and Karl," "Aspirations," "God of Vengeance," "Twilight Cantata," "Mrs. Warren's Profession," Bdwy in "Fiddler on the Roof," "Threepenny Opera," "Solitaire/Double Solitaire," "A Kurt Weill Cabaret."

SCHLARTH, SHARON. Born Jan. 19 in Buffalo, NY. Graduate SUNY/Fredonia. Debut 1983 OB in "Full Hookup," followed by "Fool for Love," "Love's Labour's Lost."

SCHMIDT, JACK. Born Sept. 19, 1927 in San Francisco, CA. Attended UCLA, MexCityCol. Bdwy debut 1976 in "Something's Afoot," OB in "The Fantasticks," "Little Shop of Horrors," "Episode 26."

SCHMIDTKE, NED. Born June 19, 1942 in St. Louis, MO. Graduate Beloit Col., Carnegie-Mellon U. Bdwy debut 1985 in "Aren't We All?"

SCHNEIDER, JAY. Born May 8, 1951 in Brooklyn, NY. Graduate Brandeis U. Debut 1979 OB in "On a Clear Day You Can See Forever," followed by "Pal Joey," "Very Warm for May."

SCHNETZER, STEPHEN. Born June 11, 1948 in Boston, MA. Graduate UMa. Bdwy debut 1971 in "The Incomparable Max," followed by "Filumena," "A Talent for Murder," OB in "Timon of Athens," "Antony and Cleopatra," "Julius Caesar," "Fallen Angels," "Miss Julie," "Lisbon Traviata."

SCHOPPERT, BILL. Born Apr. 25, 1948 in Iowa. Graduate UMin. Debut 1983 OB in "Basement Tapes," followed by "Ground Zero Club."

SCHREINER, WARNER. Born Sept. 24, 1923 in Washington, DC. Graduate Geo.Wash.U. Debut 1960 OB in "Paths of Glory," followed by "Hooray for Paul," "Crawling Arnold," "Daydreams," "The Education of One Miss February," Bdwy in "The Skin of Our Teeth" (1961), "Can Can" (CC'62).

SCOTT, PIPPA. Born Nov. 10, 1935 in Los Angeles, CA. Attended Radliffe, UCLA, RADA. Bdwy debut 1956 in "Child of Fortune" for which she received a Theatre World Award, followed by "Miss Lonelyhearts," "Look Back in Anger," OB in "Isn't It Romantic."

SCOTT, SUSAN ELIZABETH. Born Aug. 9 in Detroit, MI. Graduate UDenver. Debut 1971 OB in "The Drunkard," followed by "Mother," Bdwy in "Music Is" (1976), "On the 20th Century," "Fearless Frank," "1940's Radio Hour," "Dames at Sea."

SEALE, DOUGLAS. Born Oct. 28, 1913 in London, Eng. Graduate Washington Col., RADA. Bdwy debut 1974 in "Emperor Henry IV," followed by "Frankenstein," "The Dresser," "Noises Off."

SEAMON, EDWARD. Born Apr. 15, 1937 in San Diego, CA. Attended San Diego State Col. Debut 1971 OB in "The Life and Times of J. Walter Smintheous," followed by "The Contractor," "The Family," "Fishing," "Feedlot," "Cabin 12," "Rear Column," "Devour the Snow," "Buried Child," "Friends," "Extenuating Circumstances," "Confluence," "Richard II," "Great Grandson of Jedediah Kohler," "Marvelous Gray," "Rime Framed," "The Master Builder," "Full Hookup," "Fool for Love," "The Harvesting," "A Country for Old Men," "Love's Labour's Lost," Bdwy in "The Trip Back Down," "Devour the Snow," "The American Clock."

SEASONGOOD, EDA. Born Oct. 30 in Long Branch, NJ. Attended AADA. Bdwy debut 1975 in "The Skin of Our Teeth," followed by OB in "Entertaining Mr. Sloane," "Quilters," "Surf City."

SEATON, JOHNNY. Born Mar. 19, 1959 in Cheveriv, MD. Debut 1984 OB in "Elvismania."

SEDERHOLM, KAREN. Born July 18, 1954 in Pittsburgh, PA. Graduate PaStateU. Debut 1980 OB in "The Diviners," followed by "Last Summer at Bluefish Cove," "Young Playwrights Festival," "Time and the Conways," "Balm in Gilead," "Cherokee Country."

SEGAL, KATHRIN KING. Born Dec. 8, 1947 in Washington, DC. Attended HB Studio. Debut 1969 OB in "Oh! Calcutta!," followed by "The Drunkard," "Alice in Wonderland," "Pirates of Penzance," "Portfolio Revue," "Philomen," "Butter and Egg Man," "Art of Self-Defense."

SERRA, RAYMOND. Born Aug. 13, 1937 in NYC. Attended Rutgers U., Wagner Col. Debut 1975 OB in "The Shark," followed by "Mamma's Little Angels," "Manny," Bdwy in "The Wheelbarrow Closers," "Marlowe," "Accidental Death of an Anarchist."

SERRANO, NESTOR. Born Nov. 5, 1955 in The Bronx, NYC. Attended Queens Col. Debut 1983 OB in "Union City Thanksgiving," followed by "Diamonds."

SERRECCHIA, MICHAEL. Born Mar. 26, 1951 in Brooklyn, NY. Attended Brockport State U. Teachers Col. Bdwy debut 1972 in "The Selling of the President," followed by "Heathen!," "Seesaw," "A Chorus Line," OB in "Lady Audley's Secret."

SESMA, THOM. Born June 1, 1955 in Sasebo, Japan. Graduate UCal. Bdwy debut 1983 in "La Cage aux Folles."

SETRAKIAN, ED. Born Oct. 1, 1928 in Jenkintown, WVa. Graduate Concord Col. NYU. Debut 1966 OB in "Drums in the Night," followed by "Othello," "Coriolanus," "Macbeth," "Hamlet," "Baal," "Old Glory," "Futz," "Hey Rube," "Seduced," "Shout Across the River," "American Days," "Sheepskin," "Inserts," "Crossing the Bar," Bdwy in "Days in the Trees," "St. Joan," "The Best Little Whorehouse in Texas."

Frank
Nastasi

Mary Ann
Niles

Don
Nute

Jenny
O'Hara

Michael
O'Keefe

Evelyn
Orbach

Giulia
Pagano

Corey
Parker

Elizabeth
Pearson

David
Pendleton

Deborah
Phelan

Jaime
Perry

Daniel
Pollack

Beverly
Poltrack

Aidan
Quinn

Christine
Ranck

Henry
Ravelo

Cristine
Reid

Sally Faye
Reit

Paul David
Richards

Grace
Roberts

Scott
Robertson

Cristine
Rose

Bo
Rucker

Steven
Ryan

Christina
Saffran

Peter
Samuel

Barbara
Scanlon

Ernie
Schenk

Karen
Sederholm

221

SEVRA, ROBERT. Born Apr. 15, 1945 in Kansas City, MO. Graduate Stanford U., UMi. Debut 1972 OB in "Servant of Two Masters," followed by "Lovers," Bdwy in "Charlie and Algernon" (1980), "Torch Song Trilogy."

SEYMOUR, JAMES. Born Dec. 5, 1948 in Short Hills, NJ. Graduate BostonU. Debut 1969 OB in "Next Voyage of the Pequod," followed by "Approaching Simone," "Small Craft Warnings," "Moonchildren," "The Zykovs," "Hazard County Wonder."

SHACKELFORD, SANDI. Born Nov. 5, 1950 in Ft. Bragg, NC. Graduate SMU, USCal. Debut 1984 OB in "Henry V."

SHAFFER, LOUISE. Born July 5 in New Haven, CT. Attended Yale. Bdwy debut 1966 in "First One Asleep Whistle," followed by "We Have Always Lived in a Castle," "The Women," OB in "The Butter and Egg Man," "Bat Masterson's Last Regular Job."

SHARKEY, SUSAN. Born Dec. 12 in NYC. Graduate UAz. Debut 1968 OB in "Guns of Carrar," followed by "Cuba Si," "Playboy of the Western World," "Good Woman of Setzuan," "Enemy of the People," "People Are Living There," "Narrow Road to the Deep North," "Enemies," "The Plough and the Stars," "The Sea," "The Sykovs," "Catsplay," "Ice," "Cubistique," "Frugal Repast," "Summit Conference," "The Maids," Bdwy in "The American Clock" (1980).

SHAPIRO, DEBBIE. Born Sept. 29, 1954 in Los Angeles, CA. Graduate LACC. Bdwy debut 1979 in "They're Playing Our Song," followed by "Perfectly Frank," "Blues in the Night," "Zorba" (1983), OB in "They Say It's Wonderful," "New Moon in Concert."

SHAW, CLARE BYAM. Born Sept. 21, 1957 in London, Eng. Attended LAMBDA. Bdwy debut 1984 with Royal Shakespeare Co. in "Much Ado about Nothing" and "Cyrano de Bergerac" in repertory.

SHAW, MARCIE. Born June 19, 1954 in Franklin Square, NY. Attended UIl. Bdwy debut 1980 in "Pirates of Penzance," OB in "A Midsummer Night's Dream," "Non Pasquale," "Promenade," "La Boheme."

SHAWHAN, APRIL. Born Apr. 10, 1940 in Chicago, IL. Debut 1964 OB in "Jo," followed by "Hamlet," "Oklahoma!," "Mod Donna," "Journey to Gdansk," "Almost in Vegas," Bdwy in "Race of Hairy Men," "3 Bags Full" (1966) for which she received a Theatre World Award, "Dinner at 8," "Cop-Out," "Much Ado about Nothing," "Over Here," "Rex," "A History of the American Film."

SHEETS, J. C. Born May 4, 1953 in Wheeling, WVa. Attended West Liberty Col. Debut 1985 OB in "Jacques Brel Is Alive and Well. . . ."

SHELLEY, CAROLE. Born Aug. 16, 1939 in London, Eng. Bdwy debut 1965 in "The Odd Couple," followed by "The Astrakhan Coat," "Loot," "Noel Coward's Sweet Potato," "Hay Fever," "Absurd Person Singular," "The Norman Conquests," "The Elephant Man," "The Misanthrope," "Noises Off," OB in "Little Murders," "The Devil's Disciple," "The Play's the Thing," "Double Feature," "Twelve Dreams," "Pygmalion in Concert."

SHEPARD, JOHN. Born Dec. 9, 1952 in Huntington Park, CA. Graduate UCal/Irvine. Debut 1982 OB in "Scenes from La Vie de Boheme," "Crimes of Vautrin," "Dr. Faustus," Bdwy in "A View From the Bridge" (1983), followed by "American Buffalo."

SHERMAN, COURTNEY. Born June 23, 1946 in Louisville, KY. Graduate IndU. Debut 1985 OB in "Man Enough."

SHERWOOD, MADELEINE. Born Nov. 13, 1926 in Montreal, Can. Attended Yale U. OB in "Brecht on Brecht," "Medea," "Hey, You, Light Man," "Friends and Relations," "Older People," "O Glorious Tintinnabulation," "Getting Out," "Secret Thighs of New England Women," "Rain," "Ghosts," "Paradise Lost," "Madwoman of Chaillot," Bdwy in "The Chase" (1952), "The Crucible," "Cat on a Hot Tin Roof," "Invitation to a March," "Camelot," "Arturo Ui," "Do I Hear a Waltz?," "Inadmissible Evidence," "All Over!"

SHORT, JOHN. Born July 3, 1956 in Christopher, IL. Graduate Hanover Col. Debut 1981 OB in "Unfettered Letters," followed by "Sister Mary Ignatius . . .", Bdwy in "Big River" (1985).

SHORT, SYLVIA. Born Oct. 22, 1927 in Concord, MA. Attended Smith Col., Old Vic. Debut 1954 OB in "The Clandestine Marriage," followed by "The Golden Apple," "Passion of Gross," "Desire Caught by the Tail," "City Love Story," "Family Reunion," "Beaux Stratagem," "Just a Little Bit Less Than Normal," "Nasty Rumors," "Says I, Says He," "Milk of Paradise," "The Broken Pitcher," "After You've Gone," "Chopin in Space," Bdwy in "King Lear" (1956), "Hide and Seek."

SHROPSHIRE, NOBLE. Born Mar. 2, 1946 in Cartersville, GA. Graduate LaGrange Col., RADA. Debut 1976 OB in "Hound of the Baskervilles," followed by "The Misanthrope," "The Guardsman," "Oedipus Cycle," "Gilles de Rais," "Leonce and Lena," "King Lear," "Danton's Death," "Tartuffe," "The Maids," "Midsummer Night's Dream," "Henry IV," "Richard II," "Marquis of Keith," "Wozzeck," "Peter Gynt," "The Cherry Orchard," "Ghost Sonata," "Faust," "Hamlet," "Big and Little," "Chopin in Space."

SHUE, LARRY. Born July 23, 1946 in New Orleans, LA. Graduate IllWesleyanU. Debut 1984 in "The Foreigner" which he wrote, followed by "The Mystery of Edwin Drood."

SHULL, RICHARD B. Born Feb. 24, 1929 in Evanston, IL. Graduate StateUIowa. Debut 1953 OB in "Coriolanus," followed by "Purple Dust," "Journey to the Day," "American Hamburger League," "Frimbo," "Fade the Game," "Desire under the Elms," "The Marriage of Bette and Boo," Bdwy in "Black-Eyed Susan" (1954), "Wake Up, Darling," "Red Roses for Me," "I Knock at the Door," "Pictures in the Hallway," "Have I Got a Girl for You," "Minnie's Boys," "Goodtime Charley," "Fools," "Oh, Brother!"

SIEGLER, BEN. Born Apr. 9, 1958 in Queens, NY. Attended HB Studio. Debut 1980 OB in "Innocent Thoughts, Harmless Intentions," followed by "Threads," "Many Happy Returns," "Snow Orchid," "The Diviners," "What I Did Last Summer," "Time Framed," "Gifted Children," "Levitations," "Elm Circle," "Romance Language," Bdwy 1981 in "5th of July."

SILLIMAN, MAUREEN. Born Dec. 3 in NYC. Attended Hofstra U. Bdwy debut 1975 in "Shenandoah," followed by "I Remember Mama," "Is There Life after High School?," OB in "Umbrellas of Cherbourg," "Two Rooms," "Macbeth," "Blue Window."

SILVER, JOE. Born Sept. 28, 1922 in Chicago, IL. Attended UIl., AmThWing. Bdwy bow 1942 in "Tobacco Road," followed by "Doughgirls," "Heads or Tails," "Nature's Way," "Gypsy," "Heroine," "Zulu and the Zayda," "You Know I Can't Hear You . . . ," "Lenny," "The Roast," "World of Sholom Aleichem," OB in "Blood Wedding," "Lamp at Midnight," "Joseph and His Brethern," "Victors," "Shrinking Bride," "Family Pieces," "Cakes with Wine," "The Homecoming," "Cold Storage."

SILVER, RON. Born July 2, 1946 in NYC. Graduate SUNY, St. John's U. Debut OB in "El Grande de Coca Cola," followed by "Lotta," "Kaspar," "More Than You Deserve," "Emperor of Late Night Radio," "Friends," Bdwy in "Hurlyburly" (1984).

SILVERMAN, JONATHAN. Born Aug. 5, 1966 in Los Angeles, CA. Attended USCal. Bdwy debut 1983 in "Brighton Beach Memoirs."

SIMMS, GEORGE. Born Nov. 24, 1952 in Philadelphia, PA. Graduate CaseWesternCol. Debut 1981 OB in "King of Hearts," followed by "Bruce Lee Is Dead and I'm Not Feeling Too Good Either," "Mirrors."

SIMONS, LESLIE A. Born Aug. 8, 1957 in Hatboro, PA. Graduate Beaver Col. Bdwy debut 1983 in "La Cage aux Folles."

SINGER, MARLA. Born Aug. 2, 1957 in Oklahoma City, OK. Graduate OkCityU. Debut 1981 OB in "Seesaw," followed by Bdwy's "42nd Street" (1985).

SKINNER, KATE. Born Aug. 10, 1953 in Chicago, IL. Graduate CalStateU, UCLA. Debut 1985 OB in "Outside Waco."

SMALL, LARRY. Born Oct. 6, 1947 in Kansas City, MO. Attended Manhattan School of Music. Bdwy debut 1971 in "1776," followed by "La Strada," "Wild and Wonderful," "A Doll's Life," OB in "Plain and Fancy," "Forbidden Broadway."

SMIAR, BRIAN. Born Aug. 27, 1937 in Cleveland, OH. Graduate KentStateU, Emerson Col. Debut 1982 OB in "Edmond," followed by "3 × 3," "True to Life," Young Playwrights Festival.

SMITH, JENNIFER. Born Mar. 9, 1956 in Lubbock, TX. Graduate TxTechU. Debut 1981 OB in "Seesaw," followed by "Suffragette," Bdwy in "La Cage aux Folles" (1983).

SMITH, LOIS. Born Nov. 3, 1930 in Topeka, KS. Attended UWVa. Bdwy debut 1952 in "Time Out for Ginger," followed by "The Young and the Beautiful," "Wisteria Trees," "The Glass Menagerie," "Orpheus Descending," "Stages," OB in "Sunday Dinner," "Present Tense," "The Iceman Cometh," "Harry Outside," "Hillbilly Women," "Touching Bottom," "Tennessee," "The Articulated Man," "Hannah," "Cabal of Hypocrites," "Marathon '84," "Vienna Notes."

SMITH, SHEILA. Born Apr. 3, 1933 in Coneaut, OH. Attended Kent State U., Cleveland Play House. Bdwy debut 1963 in "Hot Spot," followed by "Mame" for which she received a Theatre World Award, "Follies," "Company," "Sugar," "Five O'Clock Girl," "42nd Street," OB in "Taboo Revue," "Anything Goes," "Best Foot Forward," "Sweet Miami," "Florello," "Taking My Turn," "Jack and Jill."

SMITH, YEARDLEY. Born July 3, 1965 in Paris, France. Bdwy debut 1984 in "The Real Thing."

SMITH-CAMERON, J. Born Sept. 7 in Louisville, KY. Attended FlaStateU. Bdwy debut 1982 in "Crimes of the Heart," OB in "Asian Shade," followed by "The Knack," "Second Prize: 2 Weeks in Leningrad," "The Great Divide," "The Voice of the Turtle."

SMITS, JIMMY. Born July 9, 1955 in NYC. Graduate Brooklyn, Col, Cornell U. Debut 1982 OB in "Hamlet," followed by "Little Victories," "Buck," "Ariano," "The Ballad of Soapy Smith."

SNOVELL, WILLIAM. Born June 2, 1956 in Baltimore, MD. Graduate Catholic U. Debut 1982 OB in "Black Angel," followed by "Ernie and Arnie," "Roundheads and Pointheads," Bdwy in "Passion" (1983).

SNOW, NORMAN. Born Mar. 29, 1950 in Little Rock, AR. Juilliard graduate. Debut 1972 OB in "School for Scandal," followed by "Lower Depths," "Hostage," "Timon of Athens," "Cymbeline," "U.S.A.," "Women Beware Women," "One Crack Out," "A Winter's Tale," "The Wedding," "Johnny on a Spot," "She Stoops to Conquer," "Fantod," "A Midsummer Night's Dream," Bdwy in "Three Sisters" (1973), "Measure for Measure," "Beggar's Opera," "Next Time I'll Sing to You," "Macbeth," "Scenes and Revelations."

SOOK, DENNIS. Born Apr. 29, 1945 in Marshall, MN. Graduate MankatoStateU, S.Ill.U. Debut 1971 OB in "The Debate," followed by "The Fantasticks," "White, Brown, Black," "Stud Silo."

SPACEY, KEVIN. Born July 26, 1959 in South Orange, NJ. Attended LACC, Juilliard. Debut 1981 OB in "Henry IV Part I," followed by "Barbarians," "Uncle Vanya," "The Robbers," "Life and Limb," Bdwy in "Ghosts" (1982), "Hurlyburly."

SPACKMAN, TOM. Born Oct. 4, 1950 in Binghamton, NY. Graduate WayneStateU. Debut 1981 OB in "Peer Gynt," followed by "King Lear," "Ghost Sonata," "Faust," "Wild Oats," "I Am a Camera," "Dance of Death," "Flirtations," "Memories of an Immortal Spirit."

SPAISMAN, ZIPORA. Born Jan. 2, 1920 in Lublin, Poland. Debut 1955 OB in "Lonesome Ship," followed by "In My Father's Court," "Thousand and One Nights," "Eleventh Inheritor," "Enchanting Melody," "Fifth Commandment," "Bronx Express," "The Melody Lingers On," "Yoshke Muzikant," "Stempenyu," "Generations of Green Fields," "Shop," "A Play for the Devil."

SPANO, VINCENT. Born Oct. 18, 1962 in Brooklyn, NYC. Bdwy debut 1977 in "The Shadow Box," followed with OB's "Balm in Gilead" (1984).

SPARER, KATHRYN C. Born Jan. 5, 1956 in NYC. Graduate UChicago. Debut 1982 OB in "Beside the Seaside," followed by "About Iris Berman," "The Rise of Daniel Rocket," "Ladies in Retirement."

SPENCER, ALEXANDER. Born July 31, 1946 in Cambus, Scot. Graduate Manchester U. Bdwy debut 1980 in "Dogg's Hamlet," followed by "Noises Off," OB in "American Days."

SPENCER, VERNON. Born Dec. 1, 1955 in Brooklyn, NY. Attended Queens Col. Debut 1976 OB in "Panama Hattie," followed by "Happy with the Blues," "Street Jesus," "Amahl and the Night Visitors," "Dreams of the Son," Bdwy in "The Human Comedy" (1984).

SPINELLA, STEPHEN. Born Oct. 11, 1956 in Naples, Italy. Graduate NYU. Debut 1982 OB in "The Age of Assassins," followed by Dance for Me, Rosetta," "Bremen Coffee," "The Taming of the Shrew."

SPIVAK, ALICE. Born Aug. 11, 1935 in Brooklyn, NYC. Attended HB Studio. Debut 1954 OB in "Early Primrose," followed by "Of Mice and Men," "Secret Concubine," "Port Royal," "Time for Bed, Take Me to Bed," "House of Blue Leaves," "Deep Six the Briefcase," "Selma," "Ferry Tales."

SQUIRE, PAT. Born Oct. 12, 1941 in The Bronx, NYC. Attended Brooklyn Col, Lehman Col. Debut 1983 OB in "Water Music," followed by "Romeo and Juliet," "Natural Causes," "An Occasion of Sin."

STADLEN, LEWIS J. Born Mar. 7, 1947 in Brooklyn, NY. Attended Stella Adler Studio. Bdwy debut 1970 in "Minnie's Boys" for which he received a Theatre World Award, followed by "The Sunshine Boys," "Candide," "The Odd Couple," OB in "The Happiness Cage," "Heaven on Earth," "Barb-A-Que," "Don Juan and Non Don Juan."

STANLEY, FLORENCE. Born July 1 in Chicago, IL. Graduate Northwestern U. Debut 1960 OB in "Machinal," followed by "Electra," "What's Wrong with This Picture?," Bdwy in "The Glass Menagerie" (1965), "Fiddler on the Roof," "A Safe Place," "Prisoner of Second Avenue," "Secret Affairs of Mildred Wild."

STEEL, AMY. Born May 3 in San Francisco, CA. Debut 1985 OB in "Walk the Dog, Willie."

STEELE, BILL. Born Nov. 25 in Springfield, MA. Yale Graduate. Bdwy debut 1955 in "Tonight in Samarkand," OB in "Noah" (1954), "What Every Woman Knows," "Proposals and Propositions," "The Crucible," "Open 24 Hours," "Satisfaction Guaranteed," "Treasure Island," "Ten Little Indians."

STEHLIN, JACK. Born July 21, 1956 in Allentown, PA. Juilliard graduate. Debut 1984 OB in "Henry V."

STEIN, JUNE. Born June 13, 1950 in NYC. Debut 1979 OB in "The Runner Stumbles," followed by "Confluence," "Am I Blue," "Balm in Gilead," "Danny and the Deep Blue Sea," "The Miss Firecracker Contest."

STELLOS, JAMES. Born Dec. 25, 1957 in Pittsburgh, PA. Graduate Carnegie-Mellon U., UCLA. Debut 1985 OB in "Very Warm for May."

STENBORG, HELEN. Born Jan. 24, 1925 in Minneapolis, MN. Attended Unter Col. OB in "A Doll's House," "A Month in the Country," "Say Nothing," "Rosmersholm," "Rimers of Eldritch," "Trial of the Catonsville 9," "The Hot l Baltimore," "Pericles," "Elephant in the House," "A Tribute to Lili Lamont," "Museum," "5th of July," "In the Recovery Lounge," "The Chisolm Trail," "Time Framed," "Levitations," "Enter a Free Man," Bdwy in "Sheep on the Runway" (1970), "Da," "A Life."

STERNHAGEN, FRANCES. Born Jan. 13, 1932 in Washington, DC. Vassar graduate. OB in "Admirable Bashful," "Thieves' Carnival," "Country Wife," "Ulysses in Nighttown," "Saintliness of Margery Kemp," "The Room," "A Slight Ache," "Displaced Person," "Playboy of the Western World," "The Prevalence of Mrs. Seal," "Summer," "Laughing Stock," "The Return of Herbert Bracewell," Bdwy in "Great Day in the Morning," "Right Honorable Gentleman," with APA in "Cocktail Party," and "Cock-a-Doodle Dandy," "The Sign in Sidney Brustein's Window," "Enemies," (LC), "The Good Doctor," "Equus," "Angel," "On Golden Pond," "The Father," "Grown-ups," "You Can't Take It with You."

STEVENS, FISHER. Born Nov. 27, 1963 in Chicago, IL. Attended NYU. Bdwy debut 1982 in "Torch Song Trilogy," followed by "Brighton Beach Memoirs," OB in "Out of Gas on Lover's Leap."

STEVENS, WESLEY. Born Apr. 6, 1948 in Evansville, IN. Graduate UVa, OhStateU. Debut 1978 in "Othello," followed by "The Importance of Being Earnest," "Candida," "Platonov," "King Lear," "Comedy of Errors."

STILLER, JERRY. Born June 8, 1931 in NYC. Graduate USyracuse. Debut 1953 in "Coriolanus," followed by "The Power and the Glory," "Golden Apple," "Measure for Measure," "Taming of the Shrew," "Carefree Tree," "Diary of a Scoundrel," "Romeo and Juliet," "As You Like It," "Two Gentlemen of Verona," "Passione," "Hurlyburly," Bdwy in "The Ritz," "Unexpected Guests," "Passione."

STOLARSKY, PAUL. Born Feb. 18, 1933 in Detroit, MI. Graduate WayneStateU, UMich. Debut 1972 OB in "Bluebird," followed by "Let Yourself Go," "Rocket to the Moon," "D.," "My Mother, My Father and Me," "Me and Molly," "Shlemiel the First," "The Rachel Plays," Bdwy in "Nuts" (1980).

STOLER, SHIRLEY. Born Mar. 30, 1929 in Brooklyn, NYC. Debut 1955 OB in "Young Disciple," followed by "No Corner in Heaven," "The Breaking Wall," "Can You See a Prince," "Sunset," "Crossing Delancey."

STOVALL, COUNT. Born Jan. 15, 1946 in Los Angeles, CA. Graduate UCal. Debut 1973 OB in "He's Got a Jones," followed by "In White America," "Rashomon," "Sidnee Poet Heroical," "A Photo," "Julius Caesar," "Coriolanus," "Spell #7," "The Jail Diary of Albie Sachs," "To Make a Poet Black," "Transcendental Blues," "Edward II," "Children of the Sun," "Shades of Brown," "American Dreams," "Pantomime," "Stovall," Bdwy in "Inacent Black" (1981), "The Philadelphia Story."

STRIKER, DANIELLE R. Born Feb. 22, 1961 in Queens, NY. Debut 1983 OB in "Skyline," Bdwy in "Zorba" (1983).

STRUTHERS, SALLY. Born July 28, 1948 in Portland, OR. Attended Pasadena Playhouse. Bdwy debut 1981 in "Wally's Cafe," followed by "The Odd Couple" (1985).

STRYKER, CHRISTOPHER. Born Jan. 3, 1963 in NYC. Attended Actors Inst. Bdwy debut in "Torch Song Trilogy" (1982).

STUART, IAN. Born May 25, 1940 in London, Eng. Attended St. Ignatius Col. Debut 1971 OB in "Misalliance," followed by "Count Dracula," "Jack the Ripper Review," "The Accrington Pals," "The Foreigner," Bdwy in "Caesar and Cleopatra" (1977).

SULLIVAN, BRAD. Born Nov. 18, 1931 in Chicago, IL. Graduate UMe, AmThWing. Debut 1961 OB in "Red Roses for Me," followed by "South Pacific," "Hot-House," "Leavin' Cheyenne," "The Ballad of Soapy Smith," Bdwy in "Basic Training of Pavlo Hummel" (1977), "Working," "The Wake of Jamie Foster," "The Caine Mutiny Court-Martial."

SULLIVAN, JEREMIAH. Born Sept. 22, 1937 in NYC. Graduate Harvard. Bdwy debut 1957 in "Compulsion," followed by "The Astrakhan Coat," "Philadelphia, Here I Come!," "A Lion in Winter," "Hamlet," OB in "Ardele," "A Scent of Flowers," "House of Blue Leaves," "Gogol," "The Master and Margarita," "Breakfast Conversations in Miami," "Life Is a Dream."

SUNG, ELIZABETH. Born Oct. 14, 1954 in Hong Kong. Graduate Juilliard. Debut 1982 OB in "Station J," followed by "A Midsummer Night's Dream," "Sound and Beauty," "Eat a Bowl of Tea."

SUTHERLAND, STEVEN. Born May 18 in London, Eng. Attended Bristol Old Vic. Bdwy debut 1977 in "Otherwise Engaged," followed by "Aren't We All?" (1985).

SWADOS, ROBIN. Born May 10, 1953 in NYC. Graduate UMa. Debut 1977 OB in "Hello and Goodbye," followed by "The Would-Be Fiance," "Oblomov."

SWANSEN, LARRY. Born Nov. 10, 1930 in Roosevelt, OK. Graduate UOk. Bdwy debut 1966 in "Those That Play the Clowns," followed by "The Great White Hope," "The King and I," OB in "Dr. Faustus Lights the Lights," "Thistle in My Bed," "A Darker Flower," "Vincent," "MacBird," "Unknown Soldier and His Wife," "Sound of Music," "Conditioning of Charlie One," "Ice Age," "Prince of Homburg," "Who's There."

SWARBRICK, CAROL. Born Mar. 20, 1948 in Inglewood CA. Graduate UCLA, NYU. Debut 1971 OB in "Drat!," followed by "The Glorious Age," Bdwy in "Side by Side by Sondheim," "Whoopee!," "42nd Street."

SWIFT, ALLEN. Born Jan. 16, 1924 in NYC. Debut 1961 OB in "Portrait of the Artist," followed by "A Month of Sundays," "Where Memories Are Magic," "My Old Friends," "Divine Fire," "Royal Bob," "The New Yorkers," Bdwy in "The Student Gypsy" (1963), "Checking Out."

SWIFT, CHERYL. Born Sept. 18, 1959 in Milwaukee, WS. Attended UWisc. Debut 1985 OB in "Very Warm for May."

SYMONDS, ROBERT. Born Dec. 1, 1926 in Bristow, AK. Attended TexU, UMo. With LCRep in "Danton's Death," "Country Wife," "Alchemist," "Galileo," "St. Joan," "Tiger at the Gates," "Cyrano," "Cry of Players," "Inner Journey," "The Miser," "The Time of Your Life," "Camino Real," "Disintegration of James Cherry," "Silence," "Scenes from American Life," "Play Strindberg," "Mary Stuart," "Narrow Road to the Deep North," "Enemies," "The Plough and the Stars," "Merchant of Venice," "A Streetcar Named Desire," "In Celebration," Bdwy 1976 in "The Poison Tree."

SZARABAJKA, KEITH. Born Dec. 2, 1952 in Oak Park, IL. Attended Trinity U, UChicago. Bdwy debut 1973 in "Warp!," followed by "Doonesbury," OB in "Bleacher Bums," "Class Enemy," "Digby."

SZLOSBERG, DIANA. Born Aug. 18, 1957 in NYC. Graduate FlaStateU. Debut 1981 OB in "Seesaw," followed by "Loose Joints," "What's a Nice Country Like You Still Doing in a State Like This?"

TACKABERRY, CELIA. Born in St. Louis, MO. Graduate Southwest MoStateU. Bdwy debut 1980 in "A Day in Hollywood/A Night in the Ukraine," OB in "The Desk Set" (1984).

TALMAN, ANN. Born Sept. 13, 1957 in Welch, WVa. Graduate PaStateU. Debut 1980 OB in "What's So Beautiful about a Sunset over Prairie Avenue?," followed by "Louisiana Summer," "Winterplay," "Prairie Avenue," "Broken Eggs," "Octoberfest," "We're Home," Bdwy in "The Little Foxes" (1981).

TANDY, JESSICA. Born June 7, 1909 in London, Eng. Attended Greet Acad. Bdwy debut 1930 in "The Matriarch," followed by "Last Enemy," "Time and the Conways," "White Steed," "Geneva," "Jupiter Laughs," "Anne of England," "Yesterday's Magic," "A Streetcar Named Desire," "Hilda Crane," "The Fourposter," "The Honeys," "A Day by the Sea," "Man in the Dog Suit," "Triple Play," "Five Finger Exercise," "The Physicists," "A Delicate Balance," "Home," "All Over," "Camino Real," "Not I," "Happy Days," "Noel Coward in Two Keys," "The Gin Game," "Rose," "Foxfire," "The Glass Menagerie," "Salonika."

TARADASH, LAURI. Born June 4, 1959 in NYC. Graduate NYU. Debut 1984 OB in "The Emperor of My Baby's Heart," followed by "Harvest of Strangers."

TARANTINA, BRIAN. Born Mar. 27, 1959 in NYC. Debut 1980 OB in "Innocent Thoughts and Harmless Intentions," followed by "Time Framed," "Fables for Friends," "Balm in Gilead," Bdwy in "Angels Fall" (1983), for which he received a Theatre World Award, "Biloxi Blues."

TARBUCK, BARBARA. Born Jan. 15, 1942 in Detroit, MI. Graduate UMich, LAMDA. Debut 1970 OB in "Landscape"/"Silence," followed by "Amphitryon," "Birthday Party," "The Crucible," "The Carpenters," "The Great American Refrigerator," "An Evening with Sylvia Plath," "Biography for a Woman," "Hot-House," "The Water Engine," Bdwy in "Brighton Beach Memoirs" (1984).

TARDI, PAUL J. Born May 28, 1951 in Detroit, MI. Graduate Eastern MichU. Debut 1984 OB in "Bells Are Ringing."

TARLETON, DIANE. Born Oct. 25, in Baltimore, MD. Graduate UMd. Bdwy debut 1965 in "Anya," followed by "A Joyful Noise," "Elmer Gantry," "Yentl," "Torch Song Trilogy," OB in "A Time for the Gentle People," "Spoon River Anthology," "International Stud," "Too Much Johnson," "To Bury a Cousin," "A Dream Play."

TATUM, MARIANNE. Born Feb. 18, 1951 in Houston, TX. Attended Manhattan School of Music. Debut 1971 OB in "Ruddigore," followed by "The Sound of Music," "The Gilded Cage," Bdwy in "Barnum" (1980), for which she received a Theatre World Award, "The Three Musketeers."

TAYLOR, GEORGE. Born Sept. 18, 1930 in London, Eng. Attended AADA. Debut 1972 OB in "Hamlet," followed by "Enemies," "The Contractor," "Scribes," "Says I, Says He," "Teeth 'n Smiles," "Viaduct," "Translations," "Last of the Knucklemen," "The Accrington Pals," Bdwy in "Emperor Henry IV," "The National Health."

TAYLOR-MORRIS, MAXINE. Born June 26 in NYC. Graduate NYU. Debut 1977 OB in "Counsellor-at-Law," followed by "Manny," "The Devil's Disciple," "Fallen Angels," "Billy Liar," "Uncle Vanya," "What the Butler Saw," "The Subject Was Roses," "Goodnight, Grandpa," "Comedy of Errors."

TEETER, LARA. Born in 1955 in Tulsa, OK. Graduate OkCityU. Bdwy debut in "The Best Little Whorehouse in Texas," followed by "Pirates of Penzance," "7 Brides for 7 Brothers," "On Your Toes," OB in "Jack and Jill."

TEPER, WALTER. Born Apr. 23, 1949 in Brooklyn, NYC. Graduate NYInst. of Tech. Debut 1985 OB in "The Mugger," followed by "Scrapers in the Sky."

THACKER, RUSS. Born June 23, 1946 in Washington, DC. Attended Montgomery Col. Bdwy debut 1967 in "Life with Father" followed by "Music! Music!," "The Grass Harp," "Heathen," "Home Sweet Homer," "Me Jack, You Jill," "Do Black Patent Leather Shoes Really Reflect Up?," OB in "Your Own Thing" for which he received a Theatre World Award, "Dear Oscar," "Once I Saw a Boy Laughing," "Tip-Toes," "Oh, Coward!," "New Moon in Concert," "The Firefly in Concert," "Rosalie in Concert," "Some Enchanted Evening," "Roberta in Concert," "Olio."

THOLE, CYNTHIA. Born Sept. 21, 1957 in Silver Spring, MD. Graduate Butler U. Debut 1982 OB in "Nymph Errant," followed by Bdwy in "42nd Street" (1985).

THOMAS, JAY. Born July 12, 1948 in Kermit, TX. Graduate Jacksonville U. Debut 1983 OB in "The Transfiguration of Benno Blimpie," followed by "Cold Storage," "Isn't It Romantic."

THOMAS, WILLIAM, JR. Born Nov. 8 in Columbus, OH. Graduate OhStateU. Debut 1972 OB in "Touch," followed by "Natural," "Godspell," "Poor Little Lambs," "Loose Joints," "Not-So-New Faces of '81," Bdwy in "Your Arms Too Short to Box with God" (1976), "La Cage aux Folles."

THOME, DAVID. Born July 24, 1951 in Salt Lake City, UT. Bdwy debut 1971 in "No, No, Nanette," followed by "Different Times," "Good News," "Rodgers and Hart," "A Chorus Line," "Dancin'," "Dreamgirls."

THOMPSON, EVAN. Born Sept. 3, 1931 in NYC. Graduate UCal. Bdwy bow 1969 in "Jimmy," followed by "1776," OB in "Mahagonny," "Treasure Island," "Knitters in the Sun," "Half-Life," "Fasnacht Dau," "Importance of Being Earnest," "Under the Gaslight," "Henry V," "The Fantasticks," "Walk the Dog, Willie."

THOMPSON, WEYMAN. Born Dec. 11, 1950 in Detroit, MI. Graduate Wayne State U, UDetroit. Bdwy debut 1980 in "Clothes for a Summer Hotel," followed by "Dreamgirls."

THORNE, RAYMOND. Born Nov. 27, 1934 in Lackawanna, NY. Graduate UCt. Debut 1966 OB in "Man with a Load of Mischief," followed by "Rose," "Dames at Sea," "Love Course," "Blue Boys," "Jack and Jill," Bdwy in "Annie" (1977).

THORSON, LINDA. Born June 18, 1947 in Toronto, Can. Graduate RADA. Bdwy debut 1982 in "Steaming" for which she received a Theatre World Award, followed by "Noises Off."

TIGHE, KEVIN. Born Aug. 13, 1944 in Los Angeles, CA. Graduate USCal. Bdwy debut 1983 in "Open Admissions," followed by OB's "The Ballad of Soapy Smith."

TILLMAN, JUDITH. Born Apr. 25, 1934 in Cleveland, OH. Graduate Case Western Reserve U. Debut 1963 OB in "The Darker Flower," followed by "Do I Hear a Waltz?" "Ten Little Indians," "Patrick Pearse Motel," "Deathtrap."

TIPPIT, WAYNE. Born Dec. 19, 1932 in Lubbock, TX. Graduate UIowa. Bdwy debut 1959 in "Tall Story," followed by "Only in America," "Gantry," OB in "Dr. Faustus," "Under the Sycamore Tree," "Misalliance," "The Alchemist," "MacBird," "Trainor, Dean Liepolt & Co.," "Young Master Dante," "Boys in the Band," "Wayside Motor Inn," "For Sale."

TIRRELL, BARBARA. Born Nov. 24, 1953 in Nahant, MA. Graduate Temple U., Webber-Douglas Acad. Debut 1977 OB in "Six Characters in Search of an Author," followed by "Cyrano," "Romeo and Juliet," "Louis Quinze," "A Day out of Time," "King Lear."

TOLAN, MICHAEL. Born Nov. 27, 1925 in Detroit, MI. Graduate Wayne U. Bdwy debut 1955 in "Will Success Spoil Rock Hunter?," followed by "A Hatful of Rain," "The Genius and the Goddess," "Romanoff and Juliet," "A Majority of One," "A Far Country," "Unlikely Heroes," OB in "Coriolanus," "Journey of the Fifth Horse," "Close Relations," "Faces of Love/Portrait of America," "A Step Out of Line."

TOM, LAUREN. Born Aug. 4, 1959 in Highland Park, IL. Graduate NYU. Debut 1980 OB in "The Music Lesson," followed by "Family Devotions," "Non Pasquale," "Dream of Kitamura," Bdwy in "A Chorus Line (1980), "Doonesbury," "Hurlyburly."

TOMEI, CONCETTA. Born Dec. 30, 1945 in Kenosha, WI. Graduate UWisc, Goodman School. Debut 1979 OB in "Little Eyolf," followed by "Cloud 9," "Lumiere," "Richard III," "A Private View," "Fen," "The Normal Heart," Bdwy in "The Elephant Man" (1979), "Noises Off."

TOMLINSON, ROBERT MICHAEL. Born Aug. 29, 1953 in Brooklyn, NYC. Graduate Temple U. Debut 1984 OB in "Delirious."

TONER, THOMAS D. Born May 25, 1928 in Homestead, PA. Graduate UCLA. Bdwy debut in "Tricks" (1973), followed by "The Good Doctor," "The Elephant Man," "California Suite," "All Over Town," "A Texas Trilogy," "The Inspector General," OB in "Pericles," "Merry Wives of Windsor," "A Midsummer Night's Dream," "Richard III," "My Early Years," "Life and Limb."

TORREN, FRANK. Born Jan. 5, 1939 in Tampa, FL. Attended UTampa, AADA. Debut 1964 OB in "Jo," followed by "No Corner in Heaven," "Treasure Island," "Open Season for Butterflies," "The Brownstone Urge," "The Meehans," "Where's Charley?," "Ladies and Gentlemen, Jerome Kern."

TORRES, ROBERT. Born Apr. 4, 1960 in Camden, NJ. Debut 1985 OB in "Manhattan Serenade."

TOWLER, LAURINE. Born Oct. 19, 1952 in Oberlin, OH. Graduate Stanford U., UCal. Debut 1981 OB in "Godspell," followed by "The Tempest," "Something Old, Something New."

TOY, CHRISTINE. Born Dec. 26, 1959 in Scarsdale, NY. Graduate Sarah Lawrence Col. Debut 1982 OB in "Oh, Johnny!," followed by "Pacific Overtures."

TREVISANI, PAMELA. Born Nov. 3, 1960 in NYC. Graduate Syracuse U. Bdwy debut 1983 in "Zorba."

TREXLER, JEREMY. Born Sept. 12, 1938 in Allentown, PA. Graduate Muhlenberg Col, NYU. Debut 1984 OB in "The Desk Set."

TRIANA, PATRICIA. Born July 28. Graduate George Washington U., RADA. OB in "Blood Wedding," "Graciela," "Miss Julie," "The Public Good," "Mirandolina."

TRIGGER, IAN. Born Sept. 30, 1942 in England. Graduate RADA. Debut 1973 OB in "The Taming of the Shrew," followed by "Scapino," "True History of Squire Jonathan," "Slab Boys," "Cloud 9," "Terra Nova," "The Foreigner," Bdwy in "Scapino," "Habeas Corpus," "13 Rue de l'Amour."

TRONTO, MARILISE. Born Nov. 8, 1953 in Mineola, NY. Graduate SUNY/Genesco, Northwestern U. Debut 1984 OB in "The Hollow," followed by "Twelfth Night."

TROOBNICK, GENE. Born Aug. 23, 1926 in Boston, MA. Attended Ithaca Col., Columbia U. Bdwy debut 1960 in "Second City," followed by "The Odd Couple," "Before You Go," "The Time of Your Life," "Requiem for a Heavyweight," OB in "Dynamite Tonight," "A Gun Play," "Tales of the Hasidim," "Wings," "Sganarelle," "Damien," "The Workroom."

TROY, LOUISE. Born Nov. 9 in NYC. Attended AADA. Debut 1955 OB in "The Infernal Machine," followed by "Merchant of Venice," "Conversation Piece," "Salad Days," "O, Oysters!," "A Doll's House," "Last Analysis," "Judy and Jane," "Heartbreak House," "Rich Girls," Bdwy in "Pipe Dream" (1955), "A Shot in the Dark," "Tovarich," "High Spirits," "Walking Happy," "Equus," "Woman of the Year," "Design for Living."

TSOUTSOUVAS, SAM. Born Aug. 20, 1948 in Santa Barbara, CA. Attended UCal., Juilliard. Debut 1969 OB in "Peer Gynt," followed by "Twelfth Night," "Timon of Athens," "Cymbeline," "School for Scandal," "The Hostage," "Women Beware Women," "Lower Depths," "Emigres," "Hello Dali," Bdwy in "The Three Sisters," "Measure for Measure," "Beggar's Opera," "Scapin," "Dracula."

TUCCI, MARIA. Born June 19, 1941 in Florence, IT. Attended Actors Studio. Bdwy debut 1963 in "The Milk Train Doesn't Stop Here Anymore," followed by "The Rose Tattoo," "The Little Foxes," "The Cuban Thing," "The Great White Hope," "School for Wives," "Lesson from Aloes," "Kingdoms," "Requiem for a Heavyweight," OB in "Corruption in the Palace of Justice," "Five Evenings," "Trojan Women," "White Devil," "Horseman Pass By," "Yerma," "Shepherd of Avenue B," "The Gathering."

TULL, PATRICK. Born July 28, 1941 in Sussex, Eng. Attended LAMDA. Bdwy debut 1967 in "The Astrakhan Coat," OB in "Ten Little Indians," "The Tamer Tamed."

TUNE, TOMMY. Born Feb. 28, 1939 in Wichita Falls, TX. Graduate UTX. Bdwy debut 1965 in "Baker Street," followed by "A Joyful Noise," "How Now Dow Jones," "Seesaw," "My One and Only," OB in "Ichabod."

TURLEY, MYRA. Born Apr. 25, 1947 in NYC. Graduate New Rochelle Col., Columbia U. Debut 1973 OB in "El Grande de Coca Cola," followed by "For the Use of the Hall," "Dreamtime."

TURNER, GLENN. Born Sept. 21, 1957 in Atlanta, GA. Bdwy debut 1984 in "My One and Only."

TURNER, PATRICK. Born Dec. 2, 1952 in Seattle, WA. Attended UWash., AmConsTheatre. Debut 1984 OB in "The Merchant of Venice," followed by "Double Inconstancy," "The Taming of the Shrew."

TURTURRO, JOHN. Born Feb. 28, 1957 in Brooklyn, NYC. Graduate SUNY/New Paltz, Yale U. Debut 1984 OB in "Danny and the Deep Blue Sea" for which he received a Theatre World Award, followed by "Men without Dates," "Chaos and Hard Times," "Steel on Steel," "Tooth of Crime," "Of Mice and Men," "Jamie's Gang," Bdwy in "Death of a Salesman" (1984).

TYZACK, MARGARET. Born Sept. 9, 1931 in London, Eng. Attended RADA. Debut 1975 OB in "Summerfolk," followed by "Tom and Viv," Bdwy in "All's Well that Ends Well" (1983).

UBARRY, HECHTER. Born Sept. 5, 1946 in NYC. Bdwy debut 1965 in "Royal Hunt of the Sun," followed by "Man of La Mancha" (1970/'72/'77), OB in "Romance Language."

ULLRICK, SHARON. Born Mar. 19, 1947 in Dallas, TX. Graduate SMU. Debut 1980 OB in "Vanities," followed by "Jump, I'll Catch You!," Bdwy in "Crimes of the Heart" (1981).

UMILE, MARC. Born Jan. 14, 1959 in Philadelphia, PA. Attended PhilComCol., LaSalleCol. Debut 1984 OB in "The Country Girl."

VALDES, ANA. Born Sept. 7, 1960 in Manila, PI. Graduate Juilliard. Debut 1984 OB in "Pieces of Eight," followed by "As You Like It," "The Skin of Our Teeth," "A New Way to Pay Old Debts."

VALE, MICHAEL. Born June 28, 1922 in Brooklyn, NY. Attended New School. Bdwy debut 1961 in "The Egg" followed by "Cafe Crown," "Last Analysis," "The Impossible Years," "Saturday Sunday Monday," "Unexpected Guests," "California Suite," OB in "Autograph Hound," "Moths," "Now There's the Three of Us," "Tall and Rex," "Kaddish," "42 Seconds from Broadway," "Sunset," "Little Shop of Horrors."

VALLELY, TANNIS. Born Dec. 28, 1975 in NYC. Debut 1984 OB in "Linda Her and the Fairy Garden."

VAN HUNTER, WILLIAM. Born Feb. 1, 1947 in Worcester, MA. Graduate Nassau Col., Syracuse U. Debut 1975 OB in "The Three Musketeers," followed by "Lenz," "Couple of the Year."

VARRONE, GENE. Born Oct. 30, 1929 in Brooklyn, NY. Graduate LIU. Bdwy in "Damn Yankees," "Take Me Along," "Ziegfeld Follies," "Goldilocks," "Wildcat," "Tovarich," "Subways Are for Sleeping," "Bravo Giovanni," "Drat! The Cat," "Fade Out-Fade In," "Don't Drink the Water," "Dear World," "Coco," "A Little Night Music," "So Long 174th St.," "Knickerbocker Holiday," "The Grand Tour," "The Most Happy Fella" (1979), OB in "Promenade," "Kuni Leml."

VENNEMA, JOHN C. Born Aug. 24, 1948 in Houston, TX. Graduate Princeton U, LAMDA. Bdwy debut 1976 in "The Royal Family," followed by "The Elephant Man," "Otherwise Engaged," OB in "Loot" (1973), "Statements after an Arrest. . .," "The Biko Inquest," "No End of Blame," "In Celebration."

VENORA, DIANE. Born in 1952 in Hartford, CT. Graduate Juilliard. Debut 1981 OB in "Penguin Touquet," followed by "A Midsummer Night's Dream," "Hamlet," "Uncle Vanya," "Messiah."

VENTRISS, JENNIE. Born Aug. 7, 1935 in Chicago, IL. Graduate DePaul U. Debut 1964 OB in "Ludlow Fair," followed by "I Can't Keep Running in Place," "Lautrec," Bdwy in "Luv" (1966), "Prisoner of Second Avenue," "Gemini."

VEREEN, BEN. Born Oct. 10, 1946 in Miami, FL. Debut 1965 OB in "Prodigal Son," followed by Bdwy's "Sweet Charity," "Golden Boy," "Hair," "Jesus Christ Superstar" for which he received a Theatre World Award, "Pippin," "Grind."

VIDNOVIC, MARTIN. Born Jan. 4, 1948 in Falls Church, VA. Attended Cincinnati Consv. Debut 1972 OB in "The Fantasticks," followed by "Some Enchanted Evening," "Lies and Legends," Bdwy in "Home Sweet Homer," "The King and I" (1977), "Oklahoma!" (1979), "Brigadoon" (1980), "Baby."

VINOVICH, STEVE. Born Jan. 22, 1945 in Peoria, IL. Graduate UIl, UCLA, Juilliard. Debut 1974 OB in "The Robber Bridegroom," follwed by "King John," "Father Uxbridge Wants to Marry," "Hard Sell," "Ross," "Double Feature," "Tender Places," "A Private View," "Love," "Poker Session," Bdwy in "Robber Bridegroom" (1976), "The Magic Show," "The Grand Tour," "Loose Ends," "A Midsummer Night's Dream."

VIPOND, NEIL. Born Dec. 24, 1929 in Toronto, Can. Bdwy debut 1956 in "Tamburlaine the Great," followed by "Macbeth," OB in "Three Friends," "Sunday Runners," "Hamlet," "Routed," "Mr. Joyce is Leaving Paris."

VOET, DOUG. Born Mar. 1, 1951 in Los Angeles, CA. Graduate BYU. Bdwy debut in "Joseph and the Amazing Technicolor Dreamcoat" (1982), OB in "Forbidden Broadway."

VOIGTS, RICHARD. Born Nov. 25, 1934 in Streator, IL. Graduate InU, Columbia U. Debut 1979 OB in "The Constant Wife," followed by "Company," "The Investigation," "Dune Road," "The Collection," "Miracle Man," "As Time Goes By," "Silence," "Station J," "Frozen Assets," "Happy Birthday, Wanda June," "My Three Angels," "Child's Play."

VOSBURGH, DAVID. Born Mar. 14, 1938 in Coventry, RI. Attended Boston U. Bdwy debut 1968 in "Maggie Flynn," followed by "1776," "A Little Night Music," "Evita," "A Doll's House," "Take Me Along," OB in "Smith."

WAGNER, CHUCK. Born June 20, 1958 in Nashville, TN. Graduate USCal. Bdwy debut 1985 in "The Three Musketeers."

WALDHORN, GARY. Born July 3, 1943 in London, Eng. Attended Yale. Bdwy debut 1982 in "Good," followed by "Joe Egg."

WALDREN, PETER. Born Sept. 7, 1933 in Manila, PI. Graduate Colgate U. Debut 1962 OB in "Bell, Book and Candle," followed by "When the War Was Over," "Napoleon's Dinner," "Open Meeting," "Cabin Fever," "Zin Boogie," "Father Uxbridge Wants to Marry," "Outward Bound."

WALDRON, MICHAEL. Born Nov. 19, 1949 in West Orange, NJ. Graduate Columbia U. Debut 1979 OB in "Mary," followed by "Dulcy," "Romance Is," "New Faces of '52," "What Comes after Ohio?," Bdwy in "Baby" (1983).

WALDROP, MARK. Born July 30, 1954 in Washington, DC. Graduate Cincinnati Consv. Debut 1977 OB in "Movie Buff," Bdwy in "Hello, Dolly!" (1978), "The Grand Tour," "Evita," "La Cage aux Folles."

WALKEN, CHRISTOPHER. Born Mar. 31, 1943 in Astoria, NY. Attended Hofstra U. Bdwy debut 1958 in "J.B.," followed by "High Spirits," "Baker Street," "The Lion in Winter," "Measure for Measure," "The Rose Tattoo" for which he received a Theatre World Award, "The Unknown Soldier and His Wife," "Rosencrantz and Guildenstern Are Dead," "Scenes from American Life," "Cymbeline," "Enemies," "The Plough and the Stars," "Merchant of Venice," "The Tempest," "Troilus and Cressida," "Macbeth," "Sweet Bird of Youth," OB in "Best Foot Forward" (1963), "Iphigenia in Aulis," "Lemon Sky," "Kid Champion," "The Seagull," "Cinders," "Hurlyburly."

WALKER, DANA. Born Apr. 28, 1962 in Lock Haven, PA. Graduate Point Park Col. Debut 1985 OB in "Very Warm for May."

WALL, BRUCE. Born July 14, 1956 in Bath, Eng. Graduate UToronto, RADA. Debut 1979 OB in "Class Enemy," followed by "The Browning Version," "Candida in Concert," "Major Barbara in Concert," "Pygmalion in Concert."

WALLACE, LEE. Born July 15, 1930 in NYC. Attended NYU. Debut 1966 OB in "Journey of the Fifth Horse," followed by "Saturday Night," "An Evening with Garcia Lorca," "Macbeth," "Booth Is Back in Town," "Awake and Sing," "Shepherd of Avenue B," "Basic Training of Pavlo Hummel," "Curtains," "Elephants," "Goodnight, Grandpa," "Jesse's Land," Bdwy in "Secret Affairs of Mildred Wild," "Molly," "Zalmen, or the Madness of God," "Some of My Best Friends," "Grind."

WALSH, TENNEY. Born Oct. 18, 1963 in New Haven, CT. Attended Yale. Debut 1981 OB in "The Wild Duck," followed by "A Think Piece," "Joe Egg," "Even in Laughter," Bdwy in "Joe Egg" (1985).

WALTER, JESSICA. Born Jan. 31, 1944 in NYC. Attended Neighborhood Playhouse. Bdwy debut 1961 in "Advise and Consent," followed by "A Severed Head," "Night Life," "Photo-Finish," OB in "The Murder of Me," "Fighting International Fat."

WALTERS, FREDERICK. Born July 19, 1930 in Schenectady, NY. Graduate Centenary Col., Rutgers U. Debut 1979 OB in "Biography: A Game," followed by "A Midsummer Night's Dream," "Not Now, Darling," "Desire under the Elms," "Man for All Seasons," "Bless Me, Father," "Strictly Dishonorable."

WALTERS, KELLY. Born May 28, 1950 in Amarillo, TX. Graduate UWash. Debut 1973 OB in "Look, We've Come Through," Bdwy in "Candide" (1975), "Canterbury Tales," "Barnum," "Grind."

WARD, DOUGLAS TURNER. Born May 5, 1930 in Burnside, LA. Attended UMi. Bdwy debut 1959 in "A Raisin in the Sun," followed by "One Flew over the Cuckoo's Nest," "Last Breeze of Summer," OB in "The Iceman Cometh," "The Blacks," "Pullman Car Hiawatha," "Bloodknot," "Happy Ending," "Day of Absence," "Kongi's Harvest," "Ceremonies in Dark Old Men," "The Harangues," "The Reckoning," "Frederick Douglass through His Own Words," "River Niger," "Brownsville Raid," "The Offering," "Old Phantoms," "The Michigan," "About Heaven and Earth."

WARING, TODD. Born Apr. 28, 1955 in Saratoga Springs, NY. Graduate Skidmore Col. Debut 1980 OB in "Journey's End," followed by "Mary Stuart," "Henry IV Part II," "Paradise Lost," Bdwy in "The Real Thing" (1984).

WARNER, AMY. Born June 29, 1951 in Minneapolis, MN. Graduate Principia Col. Debut 1982 OB in "Faust," followed by "Ghost Sonata," "Wild Oats," "Big Little/Scenes," "Hamlet," "George Dandin," "The Underpants."

WARREN, JENNIFER LEIGH. Born Aug. 29 in Dallas TX. Graduate Dartmouth Col. Debut 1982 OB in "Little Shop of Horrors," Bdwy in "Big River" (1985).

WARREN, JOSEPH. Born June 5, 1916 in Boston, MA. Graduate UDenver. Bdwy debut 1951 in "Barefoot in Athens," followed by "One Bright Day," "Love of Four Colonels," "Hidden River," "The Advocate," "Philadelphia, Here I Come," "Borstal Boy," "Lincoln Mask," OB in "Brecht on Brecht," "Jonah," "Little Black Sheep," "Black Tuesday," "The Show-Off," "Big Apple Messenger," "The Ballad of Soapy Smith."

WARRILOW, DAVID. Born Dec. 28, 1934 in Stone, Eng. Graduate UReading. Debut 1970 OB in "The Red Horse Animation," followed by "Penguin Touquet," "A Piece of Monologue," "Three Plays by Samuel Beckett," "Messiah."

WASHINGTON, DENZEL. Born Dec. 28, 1954 in Mt. Vernon, NY. Graduate Fordham U. Debut 1975 OB in "The Emperor Jones," followed by "Othello," "Coriolanus," "Mighty Gents," "Becket," "Spell #7," "Ceremonies in Dark Old Men," "One Tiger To a Hill," "A Soldier's Play," "Every Goodbye Ain't Gone."

WASHINGTON, MELVIN. Born Dec. 19 in Brooklyn, NY. Attended CCNY, HB Studio. Debut 1980 OB in "Streamers," followed by "Something to Live For," Bdwy in "My One and Only" (1983).

WASSERMAN, ALLAN. Born May 16, 1952 in The Bronx, NYC. Graduate Boston U. Bdwy debut 1977 in "The Basic Training of Pavlo Hummel," OB in "Coming Attractions," "Saigon Rose," "Cappella," "Saturday Night at the War," "A Perfect Diamond."

WASSON, CRAIG. Born Mar. 15, 1954 in Ontario, OR. Attended LaneComCol., UOre. Bdwy debut 1975 in "All God's Chillun Got Wings," OB in "The Ballad of Soapy Smith" (1984), followed by "For Sale."

WEARY, A. C. Born June 7, 1951 in Chicago, IL. Graduate Ohio U. Debut 1978 OB in "Moliere in spite of Himself," followed by "Tooth of Crime," "A Christmas Carol," "Red, Hot and Blue," "Episode 26."

WEAVER, SIGOURNEY. Born in 1949 in NYC. Attended Yale, Stanford U. Debut 1976 OB in "Titanic," followed by "Das Lusitania Songspiel," "Beyond Therapy," "Hurlyburly."

WEEKS, JAMES RAY. Born Mar 21, 1942 in Seattle, WA. Graduate UOre., AADA. Debut 1972 in LCR's "Enemies," "Merchant of Venice," and "A Streetcar Named Desire," followed by OB's "49 West 87th," "Feedlot," "The Runner Stumbles," "Glorious Morning," "Just the Immediate Family," "The Deserter," "Life and/or Death," "Devour the Snow," "Innocent Thoughts, Harmless Intentions," "The Diviners," "A Tale Told," "Confluence," "Richard II," "Great Grandson of Jedediah Kohler," "Black Angel," "Serenading Louie," "The Harvesting," "Dysan," "California Dog Fight," Bdwy in "My Fat Friend," "We Interrupt This Program," "Devour the Snow."

WEIL, ROBERT E. Born Nov. 18, 1914 in NYC. Attended NYU. Bdwy bow in "New Faces of 1941," followed by "Burlesque," "Becket," "Once upon a Mattress," "Blood, Sweat and Stanley Poole," "Night Life," "Arturo Ui," "Beggar on Horseback," "Lenny," "Happy End," OB in "Love Your Crooked Neighbor," "Felix," "My Old Friends," "Linda Her and the Fairy Garden" "The Golem," "My Old Friends."

WEINER, JOHN. Born Dec. 17, 1954 in Newark, NJ. Graduate Wm. & Mary Col. Bdwy debut 1983 in "La Cage aux Folles."

WELBY, DONNAH. Born May 4, 1952 in Scranton, PA. Graduate Catholic U. Debut 1981 OB in "Between Friends," followed by "Double Inconstancy," "Taming of the Shrew."

WELCH, PATRICIA. Born Sept. 20, 1956 in Steubenville, OH. Attended WVaU. Bdwy debut 1985 in "The King and I."

WELLS, CHRISTOPHER. Born June 18, 1955 in Norwalk, CT. Graduate Amherst Col. Debut 1981 OB in "Big Apple Country," followed by "Broadway Jukebox," "Savage Amusement," "Overruled," "Heart of Darkness," Bdwy in "Harrigan 'n Hart" (1985).

WEST, CARYN. Born June 23, 1954 in Washington, DC. Graduate Stanford U, Temple U. Bdwy debut in "Crimes of the Heart" (1982), followed by OB's "As You Like It," "Burkie," "Art of Self-Defense."

WEST, MATT. Born Oct. 2, 1958 in Downey, CA. Attended Pfiffer-Smith School. Bdwy debut in "A Chorus Line" (1980).

WESTENBERG, ROBERT W. Born Oct. 26, 1953 in Miami Beach, FL. Graduate UCal/Fresno. Debut 1981 OB in "Henry IV Part I," followed by "Hamlet," "The Death of von Richthofen," Bdwy in "Zorba" (1983) for which he received a Theatre World Award, "Sunday in the Park with George."

WESTON, JACK. Born in 1924 in Cleveland, OH. Attended Cleveland Play House, AmThWing. Bdwy debut 1950 in "Season in the Sun," followed by "South Pacific," "Bells Are Ringing," "California Suite," "The Ritz," "Cheaters," "The Floating Light Bulb," OB in "The Baker's Wife."

WESTPHAL, ROBIN. Born Nov. 24, 1953 in Salt Lake City, UT. Graduate UUtah. Debut 1983 OB in "June Moon," followed by "Taming of the Shrew," "Merchant of Venice," "Somewheres Better."

WHEELER, LOIS. Born July 12, 1922 in Stockton, CA. Attended Pasadena and Neighborhood Plahouses. Bdwy debut 1943 in "The Innocent Voyage," followed by "Pick-Up Girl," "Trio," "All My Sons," "The Young and Fair," "Dinosaur Wharf," "The Fifth Season," OB in "The Cost of Living."

WHITE, ALICE. Born Jan. 6, 1945 in Washington, DC. Graduate Oberlin Col. Debut 1977 OB in "The Passion of Dracula," followed by "La Belle au Bois," "Zoology," "Snow Leopards."

WHITE, AMELIA. Born Sept. 14, 1954 in Nottingham, Eng. Attended London's Central School of Speech & Drama. Debut 1984 OB in "The Accrington Pals" for which she received a Theatre World Award.

WHITE, JANE. Born Oct. 30, 1922 in NYC. Attended Smith Col. Bdwy debut 1942 in "Strange Fruit," followed by "The Climate of Eden," "Take a Giant Step," "Jane Eyre," "Once upon a Mattress," "The Cuban Thing," OB in "Razzle Dazzle," "Insect Comedy," "The Power and the Glory," "Hop, Signor," "Trojan Women," "Iphigenia in Aulis," "Cymbeline," "Burnt Flowerbed," "Rosmersholm," "Jane White Who?," "Ah, Men," "Lola," "Madwoman of Chaillot," "Vivat! Vivat Regina!"

WHITE, KATHLEEN D. Born Feb. 19, 1960 in Boston, MA. Graduate San Mateo Col. Bdwy debut 1984 in "The World of Magic."

WHITEHEAD, PAXTON. Born in Kent, Eng. Attended Webber-Douglas Acad. Bdwy debut 1962 in "The Affair," followed by "Beyond the Fringe," "Candida," "Habeas Corpus," "Crucifer of Blood," "Camelot" (1980), "Noises Off," OB in "Gallow's Humor," "One Way Pendulum," "A Doll's House," "Rondelay."

WHYTE, ELLEN. Born July 14, 1950 in Newark, NJ. Attended UMiami, Emerson Col. Debut 1978 OB in "The Ghost of Spring Street," followed by "Grace," "Cherokee County."

WIEST, DIANE. Born Mar. 28, 1948 in Kansas City, MO. Attended UMd. Debut 1976 OB in "Ashes," followed by "Leave It to Beaver Is Dead," "The Art of Dining" for which she received a Theatre World Award, "Bonjour La Bonjour," "Three Sisters," "Serenading Louie," "Other Places," Bdwy in "Frankenstein," "After the Fall," (1980), "Othello," "Beyond Therapy."

WILCOX, PATRICK N. Born Mar. 4, 1971 in Poughkeepsie, NY. Bdwy debut 1982 in "Nine," followed by "Strange Interlude" (1985).

WILDER, CARRIE. Born May 25, 1954 in NYC. Graduate BostonConsv. Bdwy debut 1980 in "Onward Victoria," followed by "Show Boat" (1983), "Oliver" (1984), OB in "Manhattan Serenade."

WILKINSON, KATE. Born Oct. 25 in San Francisco, CA. Attended San Jose State Col. Bdwy debut 1967 in "Little Murders," followed by "Johnny No-Trump," "Watercolor," "Postcards," "Ring Round the Bathtub," "The Last of Mrs. Lincoln," "Man and Superman," "Frankenstein," "The Man Who Came to Dinner," OB in "La Madre," "Ernest in Love," "Story of Mary Surratt," "Bring Me a Warm Body," "Child Buyer," "Rimers of Eldritch," "A Doll's House," "Hedda Gabler," "The Real Inspector Hound," "The Contractor," "When the Old Man Died," "The Overcoat," "Villager," "Good Help Is Hard to Find," "Lumiere," "Rude Times."

WILKOF, LEE. Born June 25, 1951 in Canton, OH. Graduate UCincinnati. Debut 1977 OB in "Present Tense," followed by "Little Shop of Horrors," "Holding Patterns."

WILLIAMS, CURT. Born Nov. 17, 1935 in Mt. Holly, NJ. Graduate Oberlin Col. UMiami. Debut 1964 OB in "The Fantasticks," followed by "Pinafore," "Mikado," "Night Must Fall," "The Hostage," "Macbeth," "Ice Age," "Colored People's Time," "About Heaven and Earth," "Appointment with Death," "Something Old, Something New," "Enter a Free Man," Bdwy in "Purlie" (1970), "Play Memory."

WILLIAMS, ELLIS SKEETER. Born June 28, 1951 in Brunswick, GA. Graduate Boston U. Debut 1977 OB in "Intimation," followed by "Spell #7," "Mother Courage," "Ties That Bind," "Kid Purple," Bdwy in "The Basic Training of Pavlo Hummel," "Pirates of Penzance," "Solomon's Child," "Trio," "Requiem for a Heavyweight."

WILLIAMS, KEITH. Born Oct. 2, 1954 in Scranton, PA. Graduate Mansfield Col., Catholic U. Debut 1983 OB in "Lady Windermere's Fan," followed by "Verdict," "My Three Angels," "Something Old, Something New."

WILLIAMS, RICHARD. Born Aug. 29, 1951 in Memphis, TN. Graduate UTn. Debut 1984 OB in "Inacent Black and the Brothers."

WILLIAMSON, NICOL. Born Sept. 14, 1938 in Hamilton, Scot. Bdwy debut 1965 in "Inadmissible Evidence," followed by "Plaza Suite," "Hamlet," "Uncle Vanya," "Macbeth," "The Real Thing," OB in "Nicol Williamson's Late Show," "Inadmissible Evidence," "The Entertainer."

WILLOUGHBY, RONALD. Born June 3, 1937 in Boss, MS. Graduate Millsaps Col., Northwestern U. Debut 1963 OB in "Walk in Darkness," followed by "Little Eyolf," "Anthony and Cleopatra," "Balm in Gilead," "Dracula: Sabbat," "The Faggot," "King of the U.S.," "Twelfth Night," "Black People's Party," "Mrs. Warren's Profession," "Why Marry?"

WILNER, LORI. Born July 17, 1959 in NYC. Graduate SUNY/Binghamton. OB in "I Never Sang for My Father," "Hair," "School Daze," "Poor Murderer," "Cricket on the Hearth," "Hannah Senesh."

WILSON, ELIZABETH. Born Apr. 4, 1925 in Grand Rapids, MI. Attended Neighborhood Playhouse. Bdwy debut 1953 in "Picnic," followed by "The Desk Set," "Tunnel of Love," "Big Fish, Little Fish," "Sheep on the Runway," "Sticks and Bones," "Secret Affairs of Mildred Wild," "The Importance of Being Earnest," "Morning's at 7," "You Can't Take It with You," OB in "Plaza 9," "Eh?," "Little Murders," "Good Woman of Setzuan," "Uncle Vanya," "Threepenny Opera," "All's Well That Ends Well," "Taken in Marriage," "Salonika."

WILSON, MARY LOUISE. Born Nov. 12, 1936 in New Haven, CT. Graduate Northwestern U. Bdwy debut 1963 in "Hot Spot," followed by "Flora the Red Menace," "Criss-Crossing," "Promises, Promises," "The Women," "The Gypsy," "The Royal Family," "Importance of Being Earnest," "Philadelphia Story," "Fools," "Alice in Wonderland," "The Odd Couple," OB in "Our Town," "Upstairs at the Downstairs," "Threepenny Opera," "A Great Career," "Whispers on the Wind," "Beggar's Opera," "Buried Child," "Sister Mary Ignatius Explains It All," "Actor's Nightmare," "Baby with the Bathwater."

WINSTON, HATTIE. Born Mar. 3, 1945 in Greenville, MS. Attended Howard U. OB in "Prodigal Son," "Day of Absence," "Pins and Needles," "Weary Blues," "Man Better Man," "Billy Noname," "Sambo," "The Great MacDaddy," "A Photo," "Oklahoma!," "The Michigan," "Mother Courage," "God Is a (Guess What?)," "Kongi's Harvest," "Summer of the 17th Doll," "Song of the Lusitanian Bogey," "Long Time Since Yesterday," Bdwy in "The Me Nobody Knows," "Two Gentlemen of Verona," "Does a Tiger Wear a Necktie?," "Hair," "Scapino," "I Love My Wife," "The Tap Dance Kid."

WINTERS, TIME. Born Feb. 3, 1956 in Lebanon, OR. Graduate Lane Com. Col., Stephens Col. Debut 1981 OB in "Nathan the Wise," followed by "Round and Round the Garden," "Fanshen," "Henry V," "Taming of the Shrew," Bdwy in "Amadeus" (1983).

WINTERS, WARRINGTON. Born July 28, 1909 in Bigstone Country, MN. Graduate UMinn. Debut 1975 OB in "Another Language," followed by "A Night at the Black Pig," "Uncle Vanya," "Richard III," "Livin' at the Raccoon Lodge," "The White Crow."

WINTERSTELLER, LYNNE. Born Sept. 18, 1955 in Sandusky, OH. Graduate UMd. Bdwy debut 1982 in "Annie," OB in "Gifts of the Magi" (1984).

WIRTH, DANIEL. Born Oct. 3, 1955 in Bay City, MI. Graduate Central MiU, UCal. Debut 1982 OB in "Twelfth Night," followed by "The Country Wife," "Dubliners," "Hamlet," "Beckett Plays," "Dr. Korczak and Children," "Episode 26."

WISEMAN, JOSEPH. Born May 15, 1919 in Montreal, Can. Attended CCNY. Bdwy in "Journey to Jerusalem," "Abe Lincoln in Illinois," "Candle in the Wind," "Three Sisters," "Storm Operation," "Joan of Lorraine," "Antony and Cleopatra," "Detective Story," "That Lady," "King Lear," "Golden Boy," "The Lark," "Zalmen, or the Madness of God," OB in "Marco Millions," "Incident at Vichy," "In the Matter of J. Robert Oppenheimer," "Enemies," "Duchess of Malfi," "The Last Analysis," "The Lesson," "The Golem."

WITHAM, JOHN. Born Apr. 3, 1947 in Plainfield, NJ. Graduate AMDA. Debut 1972 OB in "Two If By Sea," followed by "Comedy," Bdwy in "1600 Pennsylvania Avenue" (1976), "Take Me Along" (1985).

WOHL, DAVID. Born Sept. 22, 1953 in Brooklyn, NYC. Debut 1981 OB in "The Buddy System," followed by "Awake and Sing," "Portrait of Jenny," "Basement Tapes," "Isn't It Romantic."

WOLPE, LENNY. Born Mar. 25, 1951 in Newburgh, NY. Graduate Geo. Wash. U, UMn. Debut 1978 OB in "Company," followed by "Brownstone," "Mayor," Bdwy in "Onward Victoria" (1980), "Copperfield."

WOODALL, OLIVER. Born Aug. 28, 1953 n Clarksdale, MS. Attended NCSchool of Arts. Bdwy debut 1983 in "The Tap Dance Kid," followed by "Harrigan 'n Hart."

WOODARD, CHARLAINE. Born Dec. 29 in Albany, NY. Graduate Goodman Sch., SUNY. Debut 1975 OB in "Don't Bother Me, I Can't Cope," followed by "Dementos," "Under Fire," "A . . . My Name Is Alice," "Twelfth Night," "Hang on to the Good Times," Bdwy in "Hair" (1977), "Ain't Misbehavin'."

WOODRUFF, KELLY. Born Aug. 12, 1957 in Johnson City, TN. Attended FlaStateU. Debut 1984 OB in "Bells Are Ringing."

WOODS, CAROL. Born Nov. 13, 1943 in Jamaica, NYC. Debut 1980 OB in "One Mo' Time," Bdwy in "Grind" (1985).

WOODS, RICHARD. Born May 9, 1923 in Buffalo, NY. Graduate Ithaca Col. Bdwy in "Beg, Borrow or Steal," "Capt. Brassbound's Conversion," "Sail Away," "Coco," "Last of Mrs. Lincoln," "Gigi," "Sherlock Holmes," "Murder among Friends," "The Royal Family," "Deathtrap," "Man and Superman," "The Man Who Came to Dinner," "The Father," "Present Laughter," "Alice in Wonderland," "You Can't Take It with You," "Design for Living," OB in "The Crucible," "Summer and Smoke," "American Gothic," "Four-in-one," "My Heart's in the Highlands," "Eastward in Eden," "The Long Gallery," "The Year Boston Won the Pennant," "In the Matter of J. Robert Oppenheimer" (LC), with APA in "You Can't Take It with You," "War and Peace," "School for Scandal," "Right You Are," "The Wild Duck," "Pantagleize," "Exit the King," "The Cherry Orchard," "Cock-a-doodle Dandy," and "Hamlet," "Crimes and Dreams," "Marathon 84."

WOODS, RON. Born Apr. 28, 1953 in Hickory, NC. Attended NCSchool of Arts. Debut 1985 OB in "Man Enough."

WRIGHT, AMY. Born Apr. 15, 1950 in Chicago, IL. Graduate Beloit Col. Debut 1977 OB in "The Stronger," followed by "Nightshift," "Hamlet," "Miss Julie," "Slacks and Tops," "Terrible Jim Fitch," "Village Wooing," "The Stronger," "Time Framed," Bdwy in "5th of July" (1980), "Noises Off."

WRIGHT, GARY LANDON. Born Feb. 23, 1962 in Orlando, FL. Attended UCincinnatiConsv. Bdwy debut 1985 in "Take Me Along."

WRIGHT, MARY CATHERINE. Born Mar. 19, 1948 in San Francisco, CA. Attended CCSF, SFState Col. Bdwy debut 1970 in "Othello," followed by "A History of the American Film," "Tintypes," OB in "East Lynne," "Mimi Lights the Candle," "Marvin's Gardens," "The Tempest," "The Doctor in Spite of Himself," "Love's Labour's Lost," "Pushcart Peddlers," "Sister Mary Ignatius Explains It All," "Actor's Nightmare," "Marathon 84," "The Dining Room," "Rimes of Passion."

WRIGHT, MAX. Born Aug. 2, 1943 in Detroit, MI. Attended Wayne State U. Bdwy debut 1968 in "The Great White Hope," followed by "The Cherry Orchard," "Basic Training of Pavlo Hummel," "Stages," "Once in a Lifetime" for which he received a Theatre World Award, "The Inspector General," "Richard III," "Lunch Hour," "Henry IV Part 1 & 2," OB in "Childhood."

WRIGHT, RHNEA. Born Mar. 25, 1958 in Greenville, TX. Graduate TxChristianU. Debut 1982 OB in "Patience," followed by "Broadway Calling."

WYATT, MONA. Born Jan. 31 in Ft. Monmouth, NJ. Attended Shenadoah Consv. Debut 1984 in Radio City Christmas Spectacular, followed by OB's "Manhattan Serenade."

WYMAN, NICHOLAS. Born May 18, 1950 in Portland, ME. Graduate Harvard U. Bdwy debut 1975 in "Very Good Eddie," followed by "Grease," "The Magic Show," "On the 20th Century," "Whoopee!," "My Fair Lady" (1981), "Doubles," OB in "Paris Lights," "When We Dead Awaken," "Charlotte, Sweet," "Kennedy at Colonus," "Once on a Summer's Day."

XIFO, RAY. Born Sept. 3, 1942 in Newark, NJ. Graduate Don Bosco Col. Debut OB 1974 in "The Tempest," followed by "Frogs," "My Uncle Sam," "Shlemiel the First."

YAMAMOTO, RONALD. Born Mar. 13, 1953 in Seattle, WA. Graduate Queens Col. Debut 1983 OB in "A Song for a Nisei Fisherman," followed by "Pacific Overtures."

YANCEY, KIM. Born Sept. 25, 1959 in NYC. Graduate CCNY. Debut 1978 OB in "Why Lillie Won't Spin," followed by "Escape to Freedom," "Dacha," "Blues for Mr. Charlie," "American Dreams," "Ties That Bind."

YEOMAN, JOANN. Born Mar. 19, 1948 in Phoenix, AZ. Graduate AzStateU, Purdue U. Debut 1974 OB in "The Boy Friend," followed by "Texas Starlight," "Ba Ta Clan," "A Christmas Carol."

YORKE, SALLY. Born Dec. 8, 1953 in Williamsport, PA. Graduate PennStateU. Debut 1982 OB in "Oh, Johnny!," followed by "Class Act," "Elizabeth and Essex," "Manhattan Serenade."

ZAGNIT, STUART. Born Mar. 28, 1952 in New Brunswick, NJ. Graduate Montclair State Col. Debut 1978 OB in "The Wager," followed by "Manhattan Transference," "Women in Tune," "Enter Laughing," "Kuni Leml."

ZAKKAI, JAMIL. Born in Bagdad. Graduate Hofstra U. Debut 1960 OB in "The Connection," followed by "The Dybbuk," "In the Jungle of Cities," "Tonight We Improvise," "Agamemnon," "The Golem."

ZALABAK, MARISA. Born Mar. 1, 1958 in Elmhurst, IL. Graduate AADA. Debut 1984 OB in "The Ballad of Soapy Smith."

ZALOOM, PAUL. Born Dec. 14, 1951 in Brooklyn, NYC. Graduate Goddard Col. Debut 1979 OB in "Fruit of Zaloom," followed by "Zalooming Along," "Zaloominations!," "Crazy as Zaloom," "Return of the Creature from Blue Zaloom."

ZANARINI, TOM. Born Oct. 16, 1956 in Peru, IL. Graduate IllStateU. Debut 1984 OB in "Balm in Gilead."

ZAPP, PETER. Born Oct. 2, 1951 in Cleveland, OH. Graduate Baldwin Wallace Col. Debut 1983 OB in "Half a Lifetime," followed by "Strange Behavior," "Plainsong," "Brass Bell Superette," "State of the Union," "Hitch-Hikers," Bdwy in "End of the World . . ." (1984).

ZARISH, JANET. Born Apr. 21, 1954 in Chicago, IL. Graduate Juilliard. Debut 1981 OB in "Villager," followed by "Playing with Fire," "Royal Bob," "An Enemy of the People," "A Midsummer Night's Dream"

ZEISLER, MARK. Born Mar. 23, 1960 in NYC. Graduate SUNY/Purchase. Debut 1984 OB in "Crime and Punishment."

ZELLER, MARK. Born Apr. 20, 1932 in NYC. Attended NYU. Bdwy debut 1956 in "Shangri-La," followed by "Happy Hunting," "Wonderful Town" (CC), "Saratoga," "Ari," OB in "Candle in the Wind," "Margaret's Bed," "Freud," "Kuni Leml."

ZIEMBA, KAREN. Born Nov. 12, 1957 in St. Joseph, MO. Graduate UAkron. Debut 1981 OB in "Seesaw," Bdwy in "A Chorus Line" (1982), "42nd Street."

ZIEN, CHIP. Born in 1947 in Milwaukee, WI. Attended UPa. OB in "You're a Good Man, Charlie Brown," followed by "Kadish," "How to Succeed . . . ," "Dear Mr. G," "Tuscaloosa's Calling," "Hot 1 Baltimore," "El Grande de Coca Cola," "Split," "Real Life Funnies," "March of the Falsettos," "Isn't It Romantic," "Diamonds," Bdwy in "All Over Town" (1974), "The Suicide."

ZOBEL, RICHARD. Born June 5, 1952 in West Chester, PA. Attended Temple U. Debut 1979 OB in "The Taming of the Shrew," followed by "All's Well That Ends Well," "Big Apple Messenger," "The Country Girl," Bdwy in "Nuts" (1980).

ZORICH, LOUIS. Born Feb. 12, 1924 in Chicago, IL. Attended Roosevelt U. OB in "Six Characters in Search of an Author," "Crimes and Crimes," "Henry V," "Thracian Horses," "All Women Are One," "Good Soldier Schweik," "Shadow of Heroes," "To Clothe the Naked," "Sunset," "A Memory of Two Mondays," "They Knew What They Wanted," "The Gathering," "True West," "The Tempest," "Come Dog, Come Night," Bdwy in "Becket," "Moby Dick," "The Odd Couple," "Hadrian VII," "Moonchildren," "Fun City," "Goodtime Charley," "Herzl," "Death of a Salesman" (1984), "Arms and the Man."

ZULLY, STEWART J. Born Aug. 23, 1955 in NYC. Graduate Lehman Col., AADA. Debut 1981 OB in "Extenuating Circumstances," followed by "The Mugger."

ZURICH, TOM. Born Oct. 28, 1959 in Freeport, NY. Graduate Dartmouth Col. Debut 1982 OB in "Going Steady," followed by "Little Birds Fly."

Robert
Sevra

Sandi
Shackelford

Larry
Small

J.
Smith-Cameron

Vernon
Spencer

Pat
Squire

Florence
Stanley

Wesley
Stevens

Elizabeth
Sung

Keith
Szarabajka

Celia
Tackaberry

David
Thome

Evan
Thompson

Judith
Tillman

Patrick
Turner

Sharon
Ullrick

Marc
Umile

Ana
Valdes

Dana
Walker

Lee
Wallace

Jessica
Walter

A. C.
Weary

Alice
White

Curt
Williams

Keith
Williams

Hattie
Winston

Ronald
Yamamoto

Jo Ann
Yeoman

Stuart
Zagnit

Karen
Ziemba

Luther Adler   **Edward Andrews**   **Jay Barney**   **Richard Basehart**   **Vincent Beck**   **Sudie Bond**

OBITUARIES

JUDITH ABBOTT, age not reported, Rochester-born actress, producer, director, casting director, and daughter of George Abbott, died in NYC on July 31, 1984 after a long illness. As an actress, she had appeared in "Jason," "Alice in Arms" and "Take Her She's Mine." She was married and divorced three times. Surviving are her father, two daughters and a son.

LUTHER ADLER, 81, NYC-born stage, film and tv actor, died Dec. 8, 1984 after a long illness in his home in Kutztown, Pa. His father was founder of the Yiddish theatre in America and first introduced his son to an audience at age 5. He established himself as a Bdwy star with the Group Theatre productions of Odets' plays. His many stage credits include "Night over Taos," "Success Story," "Alien Corn," "Men in White," "Gold Eagle Guy," "Awake and Sing," "Paradise Lost," "Johnny Johnson," "Golden Boy," "Rocket to the Moon," "The Russian People," "Two on an Island," "Common Ground," "Beggars Are Coming to Town," "Dunnigan's Daughter," "A Flag Is Born," "Merchant of Venice," "A Month in the Country," "A Very Special Baby," "Passion of Josef D.," "The Three Sisters," and "Fiddler on the Roof." His marriage to actress Sylvia Sidney ended in divorce. He is survived by his widow, a son, and two sisters, Julia and the actress-teacher Stella.

EDWARD ANDREWS, 70, Georgia-born stage, screen and tv actor, died Mar. 8, 1985 of a heart attack in his home in Pacific Palisades, Ca. He made his first stage appearance at the age of 8 in "The Shannons of Broadway," subsequently appearing in "How Beautiful with Shoes," "Of Mice and Men," "The Time of Your Life," "The Glass Menagerie," "I Am a Camera," "Three by Thurber," "A Visit to a Small Planet," "They Knew What They Wanted," "The Gazebo," He is survived by his widow, two daughters and a son.

JAY BARNEY, 72, (Chicago-born John B. Kleinschmidt), stage, film, radio and tv actor, died of cancer May 19, 1985 in Allentown, Pa. He had been a member of Equity's Council from 1973. His theatre credits include "Hope's the Thing with Feathers," "The Respectful Prostitute," "Detective Story," "The Number," "The Grass Harp," "Richard III," "Stockade," "The Immoralist," "The Trial," "The Young and Beautiful," "Eugenia," "Fig Leaves Are Falling," "All the Girls Came Out to Play," "Harold and Maude." No reported survivors.

RICHARD BASEHART, 70, Ohio-born stage, screen and tv actor, died Sept. 17, 1984 after a series of strokes in Los Angeles, CA. He made his Bdwy debut in 1943 in "Counterattack," followed by "Land of Fame," "Othello," "Take It as It Comes," "Hickory Stick," "The Hasty Heart," "The Day the Money Stopped," "Cyrano de Bergerac." He was probably best known for his tv series "Voyage to the Bottom of the Sea." He is survived by his third wife, a son and two daughters.

VINCENT BECK, 56, actor-singer, and union official, died of cancer July 24, 1984 in his NYC home. His credits include "A Flag Is Born," "Peter Pan," "The World of Sholom Aleichem," "The Merchant of Venice," "Oliver," "Irma La Douce," "Gypsy," and "Bells Are Ringing." He has been serving as president of Screen Actors Guild, and as a vice president of Actors Equity Association. A sister survives.

SUDIE BOND, 56, Kentucky-born character actress on stage, screen and tv, died of a respiratory ailment on Nov. 10, 1984 in her Manhattan apartment. She was appearing in the Off Broadway production of "The Foreigner." Her NY debut was in 1952 in "Summer and Smoke" and she subsequently appeared in "Tovarich," "American Dream," "Sandbox," "Endgame," "Waltz of the Toreadors," "Auntie Mame," "The Egg," "Harold," "My Mother, My Father and Me," "The Impossible Years," "Keep It in the Family," "Forty Carats," "Hay Fever," "Grease," "Come Back to the 5 & Dime, Jimmy Dean." She had received three "Obies" for Off-Broadway performances. She is survived by a son.

STIANO BRAGGIOTTI, 80, Italian-born actor, died July 29, 1984 in York Harbor, Me. His credits include "Ten Minute Alibi," "The Closed Room," "L'Aiglon," "Retreat from Folly," "At the Theatre," "Merely Murder," "Empress of Destiny," "My Dear Children," "Kind Lady," "Candle in the Wind," "The Lady Comes Across," "The Two Mrs. Carrolls," "For Heaven's Sake, Mother," "Idiot's Delight," "Dishonored Lady," "Her Amazing Career," "The Time of the Cuckoo." Surviving is a daughter.

FREDERICK BRISSON, 71, Copenhagen-born theatre and film producer, died after a stroke on Oct. 8, 1984 in NYC. His Broadway successes include "The Pajama Game," "Damn Yankees," "New Girl in Town," "The Pleasure of His Company," "The Gazebo," "First Love," "Coco" and "Twigs." For 35 years he was married to the late Rosalind Russell. Surviving are his son, Lance, and his second wife from whom he was separated.

JOSEPH BULOFF, 85, Lithuania-born stage and screen actor, died Feb. 27, 1985 after a long illness at his Manhattan home. He was brought to the U.S. as a star for Maurice Schwartz's Yiddish Art Theatre. He had appeared in over 200 plays, including "Don't Look Now," "Call Me Ziggy," "To Quito and Back," "The Man from Cairo," "Morning Star," "Spring Again," "Oklahoma!," "The Whole World Over," "The Fifth Season," "Once More, with Feeling," "Moonbirds," "The Wall," "A Chekhov Sketchbook," "The Price," "Yoshke Musikant," "Hard to Be a Jew." His widow and a daughter survive.

GEORGE BUNT, 41, dancer, director-choreographer, died Feb. 9, 1985 of heart failure in his NYC home. He had appeared in "It's a Bird . . . It's a Plane . . . It's Superman!," "My Fair Lady" and "Minnie's Boys." He had directed and/or choreographed many productions throughout the States, and had also staged many tv shows. He is survived by his parents and a brother.

JAMES BURGE, 41, Miami-born actor on stage, film and tv, died June 1, 1985 of respiratory failure in his Manhattan home. He was scheduled to receive a Ph.D. from NYCity Univ. that week. After his Bdwy debut in "Grin and Bare It," he appeared in "Happy Hunter," and the revival of "The Royal Family." He had appeared for 3 years on the tv series "Love Is a Many-Splendored Thing," and had portrayed Peter Lawford in the "Kennedy" mini-series. Surviving are his parents and a sister.

ABE BURROWS, 74, (born Abram Solman Borowitz) Librettist, director, author, and Pulitzer Prize winner, died of pneumonia and Alzheimer's disease. He collaborated on "Guys and Dolls," "Can-Can," "How to Succeed in Business without Really Trying" which won a Pulitzer Prize, "Three Wishes for Jamie," and "First Impressions." He wrote and directed "Forty Carats." He is survived by his second wife, a son and a daughter.

RICHARD BURTON, 58, one of the most celebrated actors on stage and screen, died of a cerebral hemorrhage Aug. 5, 1984 in Geneva, Switzerland. He was in residence in his villa near the city. He was the most nominated actor who never won an "Oscar" and the most famous British actor who was never knighted. Born Richard Jenkins in South Wales, he was tutored by Philip Burton, whose name he adopted when he made his London stage debut at 18. In 1950 he made his Bdwy debut in "The Lady's Not for Burning" for which he received a Theatre World Award, followed by "Legend of Lovers," "Time Remembered," "Camelot (1960 & 1980), "Hamlet," "Equus" and "Private Lives." He had appeared in over 40 films, and on tv. Surviving are his fourth wife, and three daughters, including actress Kate Burton. Burial was in Switzerland.

EDWARD BUZZELL, 89, film director who had been a Broadway star, died Jan. 11, 1985 in Los Angeles, CA. His credits on stage (billed as "Eddie" Buzzell) include "The Gingham Girl," "No Other Girl," "Sweetheart Time," "The Desert Song," "Good Boy," and "Lady Fingers" which he wrote. He is survived by his wife, brother, a stepson and stepdaughter.

TRUMAN CAPOTE, 59, christened Truman Streckfus Persons after his birth in New Orleans, La., died in his sleep on Aug. 25, 1984 in Bel-Air, Ca. After dropping out of high school, he became a very successful writer. He adapted his second novel "The Grass Harp" for Broadway, and with Harold Arlen wrote the musical "House of Flowers." He also adapted several of his stories for television. An aunt and several cousins survive.

DAVID CAREY, 41, Massachusetts-born actor-producer, died Mar. 10, 1985 in NYC after a brief illness. His credits include "Oh, What a Wedding," "Let's Sing Yiddish," "Dad Get Married," "Light, Lively and Yiddish," "Wedding Shtetl," "Big Winna," "Rebecca the Rabbi's Daughter," "Wish Me Masel-Tov," "Roumanian Wedding," "The Showgirl," "Glickl Hameln," "Mirele Efros." In 1978 he was a co-founder with Raymond Ariel of the Shalom Yiddish Musical Theatre whose productions are presented annually in Town Hall. Surviving are his mother and a brother.

LYNNE CARTER, 60, female impersonator, died Jan. 11, 1985 in NYC. He had appeared in "The Jewel Box Revue," "Fun City," "Hooray for Hollywood," and many clubs and cabarets throughout the States. He also appeared in Carnegie Hall. There were no survivors.

MILBOURNE CHRISTOPHER, 70, magician and author, died June 17, 1984 of complications following surgery in a NYC hospital. Stage credits include "Now You See It" and "Christopher's Wonders." He had performed on numerous television shows, and had written 24 books, including a biography of Harry Houdini. He is survived by his widow.

INA CLAIRE, 92, one of the most celebrated actresses of high comedy on film and stage, died Feb. 21, 1985 from the effects of a stroke in her San Francisco home. At 13 after the death of her father, her mother took her out of school in Washington, DC, to appear in vaudeville, and eventually musicals, revues and farces. Her Bdwy credits include "The Quaker Girl," "Honeymoon Express," "Ziegfeld Follies of 1915 and 1916," "Polly with a Past," "Gold Diggers," "Bluebeard's Eighth Wife," "Grounds for Divorce," "The Last of Mrs. Cheyney," "Biography," "Ode to Liberty," "Barchester Towers," "End of Summer," "Once Is Enough," "Ninotchka," "The Talley Method," "The Fatal Weakness," and "The Confidential Clerk" (her final play in 1954). Her third husband died in 1976. Her first husband briefly was actor John Gilbert. No relatives survive.

JACKIE CURTIS, 38, playwright, actor and director, died May 15, 1985 of a drug overdose. He was born John Holder, Jr., but adopted the new name in the 1960's. He wrote, and usually played the leading female role, in such Off-Broadway plays as "Glamour, Glory and Gold," "Lucky Wonderful," "Heaven Grand in Another Orbit," "Vain Victory," "Flop," "I Died Yesterday" and "Champagne." His father survives.

DORIS DALTON, 82, Massachusetts-born actress, died July 30, 1984 of cardiac arrest in Prout's Neck, Maine. After graduation from Wellesley, she taught before beginning her successful Bdwy career. Her credits include "Electra," "Petticoat Fever," "The Country Wife," "Life's Too Short," "Sweet, Aloes," "Green Waters," "Blow Ye Winds," "The Fabulous Invalid," "I Killed the Count," "Another Love Story," "The Ryan Girl," "Present Laughter," "The Men We Marry," "Pal Joey," "The Fundamental George," "Seventeen," "The Man Who Came to Dinner," and "Take Me Along" (1960). She had also performed on radio and tv. A sister survives.

FRANK J. DALY, 73, stage and tv actor, died July 30, 1984 in NYC. His debut was in 1937's Federal Theatre production of "Pygmalion," followed by "Diff'rent," "Captain Jinks of the Horse Marines," "No More Peace," "Coriolanus," "King Lear," "The Sudden End of Anne Cinquefoil," "In the Penal Colony," and "The Physicists" in 1964. A sister survives.

PEMBROKE DAVENPORT, 74, Dallas-born conductor, composer and musical director for many Broadway musicals, died Jan. 27, 1985 of pneumonia in Henderson, Nev. His Bdwy debut was with "The Seven Lively Arts," followed by "Carib Song," "Look, Ma, I'm Dancin'," "Kiss Me, Kate," "Out of This World," "Hazel Flagg," "Arabian Nights," "The King and I" (1960), "Hit the Deck," "13 Daughters," "Paradise Island," "Kean," "Pal Joey," "I Had a Ball," "Oklahoma!," (1965), "Where's Charley?" (1966). Surviving are a son and a daughter.

CURT DAWSON, 43, Kansas-born stage and tv actor, died of cancer Jan. 13, 1985 in NYC. His credits include "Futz," "Boys in the Band," "Not Now Darling," "White Nights," "Enter a Free Man," "You Never Can Tell," "Donna Rosita," "The Penultimate Problem of Sherlock Holmes," "Ah, Men," "Absurd Person Singular," "Alice in Wonderland" (1982). He also appeared on several daytime television. He is survived by his mother and three brothers.

STEPHEN DRAPER, 79, theatrical agent, died June 5, 1985 of a heart attack while in his NYC office. Before becoming a talent representative he had been an actor in such productions as "Bare Facts of 1926," "Rapid Transit," and "Sun-Up." He leaves two sisters.

RAOUL PENE DU BOIS, 72, Staten Island-born set and costumes designer, died following a stroke on Jan. 1, 1985 in NYC. He designed his first Broadway show, an edition of "Garrick Gaieties," at the age of 16, and his last was "Sugar Babies" in 1979. His credits include "One for the Money," "Life Begins at 8:40," "Two for the Show," "Carmen Jones," "Too Many Girls," "Firebrand of Florence," "The Music Man," "Gypsy," "Call Me Madam," and he received "Tony" Awards for "Wonderful Town" and "No, No, Nanette," Two cousins survive.

JUNE DUPREZ, 66, film and stage actress, died Oct. 30, 1984 in her native London, Eng., after a long illness. In 1946 she came to NYC and appeared with the American Repertory Theatre in "Henry VIII," "What Every Woman Knows" and "Androcles and the Lion." Two daughters survive.

CHARLES FRIEDMAN, 81, Poland-born director on Broadway and tv, died of pneumonia July 18, 1984 in a Manhattan hospital. His credits include "Rutherford and Son," "Jamboree," "Bitter Stream," "Pins and Needles," "Sing Out the News," "John Henry," "Carmen Jones," "Street Scene," and "My Darlin' Aida." He was the producer-director of the tv series "The Colgate Comedy Hour." His widow survives.

NED GLASS, 78, Poland-born character actor on stage, screen and tv, died June 15, 1984 after a lengthy illness in Encino, CA. Among his many stage credits are "Counsellor-at-Law," "Between Two Worlds," "The Hot Corner." He was a regular on the tv series "Julia," and "Bridget Loves Bernie." A brother survives.

PAUL GODKIN, 70, Texas-born dancer, choreographer and director of theatre, film and tv died of a heart attack June 7, 1985 in Los Angeles. His Bdwy credits include "Stars in Your Eyes," "High Button Shoes," "Ballet Ballads," and "Maggie." A nephew survives.

SCOTT GORDON, 33, Syracuse born actor-singer-dancer, died of cancer Apr. 22, 1985 in Philadelphia, Pa. After his 1971 debut in "Stepping High," he appeared in "Big Foot," "Ulysses in Nighttown," "The Fantasticks," "Bells Are Ringing," "Threepenny Opera," and "Oliver!" He is survived by his parents, two brothers and two sisters.

LLOYD GOUGH, 77, Manhattan-born stage, film and tv actor died of an aortic aneurism July 23, 1984 in Sherman Oaks, CA. His Bdwy debut (1934) in "Yellow Jack," was followed by "Laburnum Grove," "With All My Heart," "Alice Takat," "The Laughing Woman," "Aged 26," "Point of Honor," "Red Harvest," "Ghost of Yankee Doodle," "Shadow and Substance," "My Dear Children," "Young Couple Wanted," "The Weak Link," "Love's Old Sweet Song," "No for an Answer," "Tanyard Street," "Golden Wings," "Heart of a City," "The Cat Screams," "Deep Are the Roots," "The Victim," "Ondine," "The Bad Seed," "Compulsion," "Cue for Passion," "Roman Candle," "The Banker's Daughter." He had appeared in over 100 tv shows, and films. He leaves his widow, two brothers and a stepson.

ADAM GRAMMIS, 37, Pennsylvania-born dancer-choreographer, died in his NYC home Jan. 24, 1985 after a lengthy illness. He had danced in "A Chorus Line," "Wild and Wonderful," "Shirley MacLaine Show," "Dance Continuum" and "Joseph and the Amazing Technicolor Dreamcoat." He had choreographed several industrial shows, the Miss America pageant, and Radio City Music Hall's 50th anniversary production "Encore!" His mother survives.

MARGARET HAMILTON, 82, character actress on stage, screen and tv, died from a heart attack May 16, 1985 in a Salisbury, Ct., nursing home, where she had lived for the past year. She had been a kindergarten teacher before her Bdwy debut (1932) in "Another Language." She subsequently had roles in "Dark Tower," "The Farmer Takes a Wife," "Outrageous Fortune," "The Men We Marry," "Fancy Meeting You Again," "Annie Get Your Gun," "Goldilocks," "UTBU," "Show Boat," "Oklahoma!," "Come Summer," "Our Town," "The New York Idea," "Three Sisters," "A Little Night Music" (on tour) and "The Devil's Disciple." She had appeared in over 70 films, and in the tv series "The Egg and I," and "Ethel and Albert." Her son survives.

NANCY HAMILTON, 76, one of the first successful female lyricists, died after a long illness on Feb. 18, 1985 in her NYC home. She wrote sketches and lyrics for several successful Bdwy revues, including "One for the Money," "Two for the Show," "Three to Make Ready," and "New Faces of 1934" the latter in which she also appeared. She is survived by a sister.

NEIL HAMILTON, 85, Massachusetts-born stage, screen and tv actor, died of complications from asthma on Sept. 24, 1984 in his home in Escondido, CA. After a successful career in films (over 80), he appeared on Bdwy in "Many Happy Returns," "The Deep Mrs. Sykes," "State of the Union," "The Men We Marry," "Late Love," "The Solid Gold Cadillac." His greatest popularity came from the tv series "Batman." He is survived by his widow whom he married in 1919.

LILLIAN HELLMAN, 79, New Orleans-born author, playwright and film scenarist, died of cardiac arrest June 30, 1984 at Martha's Vineyard, Ma. Her plays include "The Children's Hour," "Days to Come," "The Little Foxes," "Watch on the Rhine," "The Searching Wind," "Another Part of the Forest," "Montserrat," "The Autumn Garden," "The Lark," the book for the musical version of "Candide," "Toys in the Attic," "My Mother, My Father and Me." She left no survivors.

DAVID HUFFMAN, 40, Illinois-born stage and film actor was stabbed to death Feb. 27, 1985 in San Diego's Balboa Park where he was appearing in "Of Mice and Men" at the Globe Theatre. In New York he had appeared in "Butterflies Are Free," "Small Craft Warnings" and "Entertaining Mr. Sloane." He is survived by his widow and two sons.

DEL HUGHES, 75, Detroit-born production stage manager, tv director, and former actor, died May 18, 1985 in NYC. He made his acting debut in "Tobacco Road" (1934) and also served as stage manager, as he did for "The Children's Hour," "Death of a Salesman," "Command Decision," "The Crucible," "Montserrat," "The Man," "The Autumn Garden," "A Taste of Honey," "The Price." He was director for the tv serials "The Brighter Day" and "All My Children." A daughter survives.

WALTER WOOLF KING, 88, former singer, stage and film actor, died of a heart attack Oct. 24, 1984 in Beverly Hills, CA. As Walter Woolf, he appeared in NY in "The Passing Show of 1921," "Florodora Girl," "The Last Waltz," "Lady in Ermine," "Countess Maritza," "The Red Rogue," "Dream Girl," "Melody," and "May Wine." For films he added King to his name and appeared in many pictures. He is survived by a daughter and a son.

NAOE KONDO, 79, Atlantic City-born actress, died Oct. 3, 1984 in NYC. She had appeared in "Mary, Mary Quite Contrary," "Houses of Sand," "Arabesque," "Petticoat Fever," "If This Be Treason," "First Lady," "Teahouse of the August Moon" for its entire run. She had also appeared on television. No reported survivors.

NORMAN KRASNA, 74, NYC-born playwright and screenwriter, died of a heart attack Nov. 1, 1984 in Los Angeles, CA. After the success of his first play, "Louder, Please" (1931), he wrote "Small Miracle," "The Man with Blonde Hair," "Dear Ruth," "John Loves Mary," "Time for Elizabeth," "Kind Sir," "Who Was That Lady I Saw You With?," "Sunday in New York," "Love in E Flat," and "Lady Harry." He leaves his second wife and six children.

HAL LeROY, 71, tap dancer and actor on stage and screen, died May 2, 1985 of complications following cardiac surgery in Hackensack, NJ. Born John LeRoy Schotte in Cincinnati, he began dancing as a child, and at 16 he was in "Ziegfeld Follies of 1931." Other credits include "Strike Me Pink," "Count Me In," "The Gang's All Here," "Thumbs Up" and "Too Many Girls." He played the title role in the series of Harold Teen movies. He remained active in supper clubs, tv and summer stock until a year prior to his death. There are no survivors.

EARLE MacVEIGH, 74, Connecticut-born actor-singer-dancer, died of cancer Apr. 13, 1985 in Los Angeles, CA. He had appeared in "May Wine," "On Your Toes," "The Would-Be Gentleman," "Up in Central Park," "The Mikado," "H.M.S. Pinafore," "Trial by Jury," "Kismet," and "Man of LaMancha." His widow survives.

RICHARD MARR, 56, stage, film and tv actor, died suddenly Dec. 18, 1984 in his NYC home. His credits include "The Passion of Gross," "Sappho," "Pilgrim's Progress," "Pimpernel," "How to Succeed in Business without . . .," "Witness," "Make Me Disappear," "Coco," "On the Town," "Goodbye 174th Street," "Baker Street," "The Boy Friend" and "King of Hearts." No immediate survivors.

JAMES MASON, 75, British-born stage, screen and tv actor, died after a heart attack July 27, 1984 in Lausanne, Switz. He had appeared on Bdwy in "Bathsheba" (1947) followed by "The Faith Healer" (1978). Surviving are his second wife, Australian actress Clarissa Kay, a son and a daughter.

GENE MASONER, 41, Kansas-born actor-choreographer-painter, died Mar. 15, 1985 in NYC. Among his credits are "Your Own Thing," "White Devil," "Cherry," "Three Drag Queens from Daytona," "Shenandoah," "Angel" and "Something's Afoot." No reported survivors.

MURRAY MATHESON, 73, Australia-born actor on stage, film and tv, died of heart failure Apr. 25, 1985 in Woodland Hills, CA. He had performed on stage in Australia, Canada and England. In New York he appeared in "The Relapse," "Escapade," "The Third Person" and "Oh, Kay!" A sister survives.

GEORGE MATHEWS, 73, Brooklyn-born actor on stage, film and tv, died of a heart disease Nov. 7, 1984 in Caesar's Head, SC, where he had retired. After his 1937 Bdwy debut in "Professional," he appeared in "Life of Reilly," "Cuckoos on the Hearth," "Eve of St. Mark," "Kiss Them for Me," "Antigone," "Temper the Wind," "Silver Whistle," "A Streetcar Named Desire," "Barefoot in Athens," "Desperate Hours," "Holiday for Lovers," "Shadow of a Gunman," "Triple Play," "Luther," "Catch Me if You Can," "A Time for Singing," "A Joyful Noise," "The Great White Hope," "Do Re Mi," "Abe Lincoln in Illinois" and "Candida." His widow survives.

WAYNE MATTSON, 32, Minnesota-born singer-dancer, died Nov. 5, 1984 in NYC. After his 1974 Bdwy debut in "Lorelei," he appeared in "Music Is," "They're Playing Our Song," "Joseph and the Amazing Technicolor Dreamcoat," "5-6-7-8 Dance." His father and a brother survive.

RICHARD McMURRAY, 68, stage, screen and tv actor, died of lung cancer, Dec. 11, 1984 in Burbank, CA. His career began as a member of the Humphrey-Weidman Dance Group. His stage credits include "Volpone," "The Wedding," "On the Harmfulness of Tobacco," "A Tragedian in spite of Himself," "The Bear," "A Story for Strangers," "Hilda Crane," "The Passion of Gross," "Night Circus," "Send Me No Flowers," "A Case of Libel" for which he received the Clarence Derwent Award, and "One by One." Surviving are his wife, actress Lesley Woods, and son, actor Sam McMurray.

BROOKS MORTON, 51, Kentucky-born actor, composer, lyricist, died July 31, 1984 in NYC after a lengthy illness. After his 1962 debut in "Riverwind," he appeared in "Sunday Dinner," "West Side Story," "Say Darling," "Marathon '33," "Beyond the Fringe," "Three Sisters," "Ivanov," "The Prime of Miss Jean Brodie," "Her First Roman," "Penny Wars," "Company," "Bad Habits," "Sly Fox," and "42nd Street." A son survives.

WILLIAM MOUNT-BURKE, 48, founder, conductor and director of the Light Opera of Manhattan, died after a long illness on July 8, 1984 in NYC. In 1968 he launched LOOM with a performance of Gilbert and Sullivan's "Pirates of Penzance" in his living room with an audience of 12. Today it is the only full time, professional light opera company in America. He is survived by his mother.

DOUGLAS NORWICK, 42, actor-dancer, director-choreographer, died Nov. 7, 1984 in his native NYC. He had appeared in "Rosencrantz and Guildenstern Are Dead," "Purlie" and "Broadway Scandals of 1928."

EDMOND O'BRIEN, 69, Brooklyn-born stage and screen actor, died of Alzheimer's disease May 8, 1985 in Englewood, CA. After studying at Neighborhood Playhouse, he joined the Mercury Players for whom he appeared in "Daughters of Atreus," "Hamlet," "Julius Caesar," "The Star-Wagon," "Henry IV Part I," "Leave Her to Heaven," "Romeo and Juliet," "Winged Victory," "I've Got Sixpence." He received a 1955 "Oscar" for Best Supporting Actor in "The Barefoot Contessa." He is survived by two daughters and a son.

J. PAT O'MALLEY, 80, British-born stage, film and tv character actor, died of a heart condition Feb. 27, 1985 in San Juan Capistrano, CA. He had appeared on Bdwy in "But Not Goodbye" (1944), "Ten Little Indians," "Portrait in Black," "Of Thee I Sing," "Seagulls over Sorrento," "Dial 'M' for Murder," and "Home Is the Hero." He had been a regular character on the tv series "Wendy and Me" and "Touch of Grace." His widow, a son and a daughter survive.

JOHN O'SHAUGHNESSY, 77, director and former actor, died in his Los Angeles home on May 3, 1985. As an actor he appeared in "Six Miracle Plays," "Parade," "Let Freedom Ring," "Bury the Dead," "200 Were Chosen," "Excursion," "Washington Jitters," "The Boys from Syracuse," "Railroads on Parade" (narrator), "The Hostage," "Galileo," "Moon for the Misbegotten," and "Medea." He had directed "One-Man Show," "Paths of Glory," "Command Decision," "The Last Dance," "Church Street," "Afternoon Storm," "Sleepy Hollow," "A Phoenix Too Frequent," "Freight," "Red Roses for Me," "Asmodee," "Cut of the Axe," and "Figure in the Night." A sister survives.

WOODROW PARFREY, 61, NYC-born character actor on stage, screen and tv, died of a heart attack July 29, 1984 in his Los Angeles home. He had Broadway roles in "All the King's Men," "The Millionairess," "The Rehearsal," "Room Service," "Moby Dick," "Cradle Song," "All That Fall," "Winesburg, Ohio," "The Rivalry," "Advise and Consent," "Giants, Sons of Giants" and "The Tiger and the Typist." He moved to California in 1962 where he appeared in many films and over 100 tv shows. Surviving are his wife of 34 years, two sons and two daughters.

JAN PEERCE, 80, operatic tenor, died after a long illness on Dec. 15, 1984 in his native NYC. Born Jacob Pincus Perelmuth, he had been a violinist before concentrating on singing. He began his vocal career at Radio City Music Hall, made his Metropolitan Opera debut in 1941 and performed there for 17 years. He had appeared in "Fiddler on the Roof," on tv, film and in concert. He is survived by his wife of 54 years, a son and two daughters.

ALFORD PERRYMAN, 39, dancer-choreographer-teacher, died of pneumonia Jan. 19, 1985 in his home in Brooklyn, NYC. He had danced with the Olatunji, Pomare, Faison dance companies, and appeared on Bdwy in "Purlie," "Two Gentlemen of Verona," "Raisin," "1600 Pennsylvania Avenue," "The Wiz," and choreographed "Amen Corner." He was artistic director of the Brooklyn Dance Theatre. He leaves his mother, two brothers and two sisters.

MARGARET PHILLIPS, 61, Wales-born stage and tv actress, died of cancer Sept. 9, 1984 in NYC. After her Bdwy debut (1942) in "Proof through the Night," she had roles in "The Late George Apley" for which she received a Theatre World Award, "Another Part of the Forest" for which she won a Derwent Award, "Summer and Smoke," "The Heiress," "The Cocktail Party," "Second Threshold," "The Merchant of Venice," "Dial 'M' for Murder," "Fallen Angels," "The Lady's Not for Burning," "Under the Sycamore Tree," "The Ginger Man." Her last stage appearance was in 1982 in the Hartford Stage Co. production of "The Greeks." No reported survivors.

WALTER PIDGEON, 87, Canada-born stage, screen and tv actor, died after a series of strokes on Sept. 25, 1984 in Santa Monica, CA. After WWI, he moved to NYC and made his acting debut in "You Never Can Tell," followed by "Puzzles of 1925," "No More Ladies," "Something Gay," "There's Wisdom in Women," "Night of January 16," "The Happiest Millionaire," "Take Me Along" and "Dinner at 8." He appeared in over 100 films. His second wife and a daughter survive.

JOHN BOYNTON PRIESTLEY, 89, British novelist, essayist and playwright, died Aug. 14, 1984 at his home in Stratford-on-Avon. He exerted his independence by refusing a knighthood and a peerage. His plays include "The Good Companions," "Dangerous Corner," "Laburnum Grove," "Eden End," "Cornelius," "Duet in Floodlight," "Bees on the Boatdeck," "Springtide" (using the pen name of Peter Goldsmith), "Time and the Conways," "I Have Been Here Before," "People at Sea," "When We Are Married," "Johnson over Jordan," "Music at Night," "Goodnight Children," "They Came to a City," "Desert Highway," "How Are They at Home?," "The Long Mirror," "An Inspector Calls," "Ever Since Paradise," "The Linden Tree," "Home Is Tomorrow," "Summer Day's Dream," "Bright Shadow," "Treasure on Pelican," "Dragon's Mouth," "The White Countess," "Mr. Kettle and Mrs. Moon," "The 31st of June," "The Glass Cage," "A Severed Head." He is survived by his third wife, archeologist Jacquetta Hawkes, a son and four daughters.

ROBERT READICK, 59, stage, film and tv actor, died May 27, 1985 in Trenton, NJ, as a result of injuries in a car accident. His career began as a child actor on radio, and his later Bdwy credits include "George Washington Slept Here," "All in Favor," "Biggest Thief in Town," "In the Penal Colony," "Sweet Bird of Youth." His widow and two sons survive.

SIR MICHAEL REDGRAVE, 77, one of England's most celebrated stage and screen actors, died Mar. 21, 1985 of Parkinson's disease. He made his Bdwy debut 1948 in the title role of "Macbeth," and subsequently appeared in "Tiger at the Gates," "The Merchant of Venice," "The Sleeping Prince," "The Complaisant Lover," "The Hollow Crown" and "Pleasure and Repentance." He is survived by his widow, actress Rachel Kempson, two actress daughters, Vanessa and Lynn, and a son, actor Corin.

ORRIN REILEY, 38, California-born stage and tv actor, died Sept. 24, 1984 in NYC. His credits include "Dear World," "Man of La Mancha," "Applause," "On the Town," "Seesaw," "Knickerbocker Holiday," "They're Playing Our Song," "Do Black Patent Leather Shoes Really Reflect Up?," and the 1983 revival of "You Can't Take It with You." He was married to actress Laura Kenyon.

HOWARD RICHARDSON, 67, South Carolina-born playwright, died Dec. 30, 1984 in NYC. With his cousin and frequent collaborator, William Berney, he wrote his most successful play, "Dark of the Moon." Other plays include "Catch on the Wing," "Sodom, Tennessee," "Design for a Stained Glass Window," "The Cat in the Cage," "Widow's Walk," "Mountain Fire," "Protective Custody," "Giselle," "Birds of Prey," "The Laundry." He wrote for many tv productions, and was a popular lecturer throughout the States. No reported survivors.

HARRY RIGBY, 59, Pittsburgh-born producer, died of natural causes in his Manhattan apartment on Jan. 17, 1985. He co-produced "Make a Wish," "John Murray Anderson's Almanac," "Half a Sixpence," "Hallelujah, Baby," the revival of "Good News," "Knock Knock," "I Love My Wife," "Gorey Stories" and "Sugar Babies." A sister survives.

DAME FLORA ROBSON, 82, one of England's leading stage and film actresses, died in her sleep July 7, 1984 in Brighton, Eng., where she had lived for several years. Her Bdwy debut was 1940 in "Ladies in Retirement," followed by appearances in "Anne of England," "The Damask Cheek," "Macbeth," and "Black Chiffon." She had roles in over 60 films. In 1960 Queen Elizabeth II made her a Dame Commander of the British Empire. No reported survivors.

| Joseph Buloff | James C. Burge | Richard Burton | David Carey | Ina Claire | Curt Dawson |

| June Duprez | Ned Glass | Scott Gordon | Lloyd Gough | Adam Grammis | Margaret Hamilton |

| Neil Hamilton | David Huffman | Walter Woolf King | Richard Marr | James Mason | Gene Masoner |

| Murray Matheson | Brooks Morton | Douglas Norwick | Edmond O'Brien | Woodrow Parfrey | Jan Peerce |

| Margaret Phillips | Walter Pidgeon | Michael Redgrave | Orrin Reiley | Flora Robson | Robert Salvio |

BEN ROSENBERG, 73, Bdwy manager and producer, died of a heart attack Mar. 3, 1985 in Ft. Lauderdale, FL. He was general or company manager of over 20 productions and was co-producer of "Special Occasions," "Same Time, Next Year," "Tribute," and "Romantic Comedy." He is survived by his wife and son.

EDMON RYAN, 79, Kentucky-born stage-film-tv actor, died of a heart attack Aug. 4, 1984 in Louisville, KY. After his Bdwy debut in "Post Road" (1934), he appeared in "Whatever Goes Up," "Dream Girl," "Command Decision," "Legend of Sarah," "A Date with April," "Nature's Way," "The Marriage-Go-Round," "Lord Pengo," "In the Matter of J. Robert Oppenheimer," "The Male Animal," "Hope for the Best." A daughter survives.

ROBERT SALVIO, 42, stage, film and tv actor, died Sept. 23, 1984 in his native NYC. He had appeared in "The Awakening of Spring," "Night of the Dunce," "Hamp" for which he received a Theatre World Award, "Awake and Sing," "Cabaret" and "Billy." He is survived by his mother, a sister and a brother.

FAY SAPPINGTON, 78, Texas-born character actress on stage, screen and tv, died after a long illness on Dec. 7, 1984 in NYC. After her Bdwy debut in "Southern Exposure" (1950), her NYC theatre credits include "The Cellar and the Well," "Glad Tidings," "J. B.," "The Yearling," "The Golden Rainbow," "Pippin," "The Campbells of Boston," "In Case of Accident." Surviving are her husband, actor John Armstrong, and a son.

RUTH SAVILLE, 92, stage, film, radio and tv actress, died Mar. 31, 1985 in Los Angeles, CA. After her professional debut in 1905 with Maude Adams in "Peter Pan," her stage credits include "Quality Street," "L'Aiglon," "The Shanghai Gesture," "The Last Warning," "The Royal Family," "Live Life Again," "I Gotta Get Out," "Hold It," "Jenny Kissed Me," "The House of Bernarda Alba," "The Children's Hour," "State of the Union" and "Night Must Fall." She had been active in the formation of Actors' Equity and was a gold-star life member. There are no survivors.

ZVEE SCOOLER, 85, stage, and film actor, died Mar. 25, 1985 in NYC. He was born in the Ukraine and came to the U.S. in 1912. He became an original member of Maurice Schwartz's Yiddish Ar Theatre, and made his debut in 1921 in "Dybbuk," and performed with the company for 25 years. He spent 50 years as a Yiddish commentator on WEVD radio, and appeared in the entire seven-year Broadway run of "Fiddler on the Roof" as Mordcha the innkeeper. Other stage credits include "Haggadah," "Memoirs of Pontius Pilate," "We Americans," "Command Performance," "God's Thieves," "Town Lunatics," "Little Giants," "Two Hearts," "Brothers Ashkenazi," "Highway Robbery" and "Theater of Peretz." His widow and a daughter survive.

ALEXANDER SCOURBY, 71, Brooklyn-born actor and narrator for the blind, died suddenly Feb. 22, 1985 in Boston, MA. After his 1932 debut in "Hamlet," his credits include "Henry IV Part I," "Richard II," "A Flag Is Born," "Crime and Punishment," "Detective Story," "Darkness at Noon," "St. Joan," "Tonight in Samarkand," "A Month in the Country," "Tovarich" and "Vivat! Vivat Regina!" He had recorded over 250 books for the blind over a period of 40 years. He also narrated many tv documentaries. Surviving are his wife and a daughter. He was cremated.

ARTHUR SCHWARTZ, 83, Brooklyn-born composer, died after suffering a stroke Sept. 3, 1984 in his home in Kintnersville, PA. He is probably best known for the songs he wrote with lyricist Howard Dietz. In 1926 he contributed to "Grand Street Follies," followed by "The Little Show," "Three's a Crowd," "The Band Wagon," "Flying Colors," "At Home Abroad," "Revenge with Music," "Between the Devil," "Virginia," "Stars in Your Eyes," "Park Avenue," "Inside U.S.A." "A Tree Grows in Brooklyn," "By the Beautiful Sea," "The Gay Life" and "Jennie." For 25 years he was director of the American Society of Composers, Authors and Publishers. He is survived by his wife and two sons.

KENT SMITH, 78, NYC-born stage, film and tv actor, died of a heart disease Apr. 23, 1985 in Woodland Hills, CA. He made his Bdwy debut in 1932 in "Men Must Fight," followed by "Heat Lightning," "Spring in Autumn," "Drums Begin," "Dodsworth," "Saint Joan," "Seen but Not Heard," "Wingless Victory," "Candida," "The Star-Wagon," "How to Get Tough about It," "A Doll's House," "Jeremiah," "Christmas Eve," "International Incident," "Old Acquaintance," "The Story of Mary Surratt," "Antony and Cleopatra," "Burning Bright," "Richard II," "The Wisteria Trees," "The Autumn Garden," "Charley's Aunt," "What Every Woman Knows," "Bus Stop." Surviving are his widow and a daughter.

LEONARD SPIGELGASS, 76, Brooklyn-born writer for Broadway and Hollywood, died Feb. 14, 1985 at his home in Los Angeles, CA. His plays for Broadway include "A Majority of One," "Dear Me, the Sky Is Falling," "Wrong Way Light Bulb," "Look to the Lilies." He wrote over 75 film scripts.

JULIE STEVENS, 67, St. Louis-born actress on radio, stage and tv, died of cancer Aug. 26, 1984 at her home in Wellfleet, MA. Her Bdwy credits include "Snookie, "Brooklyn U.S.A." "Proof through the Night," "The World's Full of Girls," "Sleep, My Pretty One," and "The male Animal." From 1944–1960 she played Helen Trent on the radio serial "The Romance of Helen Trent." Two daughters and a sister survive.

HARRY STOCKWELL, 82, Kansas City-born actor-singer, died of heart failure July 19, 1984 in NYC. His Bdwy credits include "Broadway Nights," "As Thousands Cheer," "Earl Carroll's Vanities," "George White's Scandals," "Oklahoma!," "Marinka," "The Desert Song" and "Can-Can." He was the voice of Prince Charming in Disney's "Snow White" film. He retired in 1965. Surviving are two sons, actors Dean and Guy Stockwell.

DOLPH SWEET, 64, NYC-born stage, film and tv actor, died of cancer May 8, 1985 in Los Angeles, CA. After his Bdwy debut (1960) in "Rhinoceros," he had roles in "Romulus," "The Advocate," "The Sign in Sidney Brustein's Window," "The Great Indoors," "Natural Look," "Billy," "Penny Wars," "Too Much Johnson," "Ceremony of Innocence," "Bread," "Streamers." He appeared in 30 feature films, but is best known for his Police Chief Carl Kanisky on the tv series "Gimme a Break." He leaves his widow and a son.

BERTRAM TANSWELL, 78, British-born actor and theatre director, died of cancer June 15, 1984 in Los Angeles, CA. His Broadway credits include "Bachelor Born," "As You Like It," "Jeannie," "Heart of a City," "I Killed the Count," "Harlequinade," "Billy Budd," "Othello," "The Browning Version" and "Teahouse of the August Moon." He was one of the founders of the Old Globe Theatre in San Diego, and for 7 years was an actor/director at the Cleveland Play House. A sister survives.

JOHN-MICHAEL TEBELAK, 36, playwright and director, died of a heart attack Apr. 2, 1985 in his Manhattan home. He wrote the hit rock musical "Godspell" with Stephen Schwartz. He had directed it and "Elizabeth I," "The Glorious One," and "Ka-Boom." He was dramaturg for the Cathedral Church of St. John the Divine in NYC. His parents and a sister survive.

MADGE WEST, 93, NYC-born actress on stage, screen and tv, died of complications from a fall on May 29, 1985 at her home in Memphis, TN. She began her career at 5 in the original stage production of "Ben Hur," and continued to work for many years for director David Belasco. Among her later credits are "The Dreaming Dust," "Age and Grace," "You Never Can Tell," "Lysistrata," "The Living Room." She appeared in many tv shows and commercials. Surviving are a son and a daughter.

JOHN WEXLEY, 77, NYC-born playwright, screenwriter and former actor, died of a heart attack Feb. 4, 1985 in his home in Doylestown, PA. He wrote "The Last Mile," one of the most famous prison dramas, and subsequently "They Shall Not Die." He wrote a number of screenplays, and the book "The Judgment of Julius and Ethel Rosenberg." His widow and a daughter survive.

ESTELLE WINWOOD, 101, England-born actress on stage, screen and tv, died of a heart attack June 20, 1984 at Woodland Hills, CA. After success in England, she came to NYC in 1916 to make her debut in "Hush." She remained in the States and was constantly on stage through 1951, when she began her film career. Among her many credits on Bdwy are "A Successful Calamity," "Too Many Husbands," "The Circle," "Trelawny of the Wells," "Fallen Angels," "The Distaff Side," "The Importance of Being Earnest," "Ladies in Retirement," "Ten Little Indians," "Lady Windermere's Fan," "Madwoman of Chaillot," "The Cocktail Party," "Sabrina Fair," "Mr. Pickwick," "Mrs. Patterson," "Speaking of Murder," "Crazy October," "Nathan Weinstein, Mystic Connecticut," "Merchant of Venice," "Blithe Spirit," "Mrs. Warren's Profession." She is survived by her fourth husband, English director-teacher, Robert Henderson, and a brother.

Fay Sappington

Alexander Scourby

Kent Smith

Harry Stockwell

Dolph Sweet

Estelle Winwood

INDEX

234

237

239

240

241

242

244

246

247

248

251